W9-BNU-578

Mom & Dad,
Thanks for
giving us the
love for & tradition
of summer in August!
in Saratoga

love
Maggie & Joey
Steph & Laura

Mom & Dad —
May you enjoy this book as
much as I have. I know you
enjoy Saratoga as much as I do!

Merry Christmas
1996

Travers Day
1996

They're Off!

To Bob and Liz!

Edward Horatio

They're Off!
Horse Racing at Saratoga

SYRACUSE UNIVERSITY PRESS

Copyright © 1995 by Edward Clinton Hotaling
All Rights Reserved
First Edition 1995
95 96 97 98 99 00 6 5 4 3 2 1

Front page spread: The 1875 Travers. D'Artagnan beating
Milner and Aristedes, the first Kentucky Derby winner, in
the twelfth Travers. Drawn for *Frank Leslie's Illustrated
Newspaper* by Albert Berghaus. *Courtesy of the author.*

The author's preface appeared in a slightly different form
as an article in the *New York Times*.

Quote on page 250 reprinted with permission of Scribner, an imprint
of Simon and Schuster, Inc. from *Champion: Joe Louis, Black Hero in
White America* by Chris Mead. Copyright © 1985 Chris Mead.

Excerpts from *Little Man: Meyer Lansky and the Gangster Life*
by Robert Lacey, copyright © 1991 by Robert Lacey, are
reprinted by permission of Little, Brown and Company.

This book is published with the assistance of a grant from the
John Ben Snow Foundation.

The paper used in this publication meets the minimum requirements
of American National Standard for Information Sciences—Permanence of Paper for Printed Library Materials, ANSI Z39.48-1984. ∞

Library of Congress Cataloging-in-Publication Data

Hotaling, Edward.
    They're off! : horse racing at Saratoga / Edward Hotaling.
        p.   cm.
    Includes bibliographical references (p.   ) and index.
    ISBN 0-8156-0350-9
        1. Horse racing—New York (State)—Saratoga Springs—History.
2. Saratoga Racecourse (Saratoga Springs, N.Y.)—History.
3. Saratoga Springs (N.Y.)—History. I. Title.
SF335.U6N692   1995
798.4'009747'48—dc20   95-7703

Manufactured in the United States of America

A MARTHE

Edward Hotaling is a television writer and producer for NBC's WRC-TV in Washington, D.C. He is a frequent contributor to the *New York Times* and other national publications. He has also been a radio broadcaster for NBC.

CONTENTS

Illustrations *ix*

Preface *xi*

Acknowledgments *xiii*

1. The First Tourist *1*

2. America's First National Resort *6*

3. A Preview of Modern Sports *14*

4. The Old Gray Mare *25*

5. America's First (Two-Legged) Sports Hero *30*

6. The Birth of American Sports *41*

7. You Are Here *51*

8. The Yankees Celebrate *63*

9. Siring the Belmont and Pimlico *76*

10. Longfellow vs. Harry Bassett *88*

11. The Derby and College Sports *101*

12. Isaac Murphy and the Californians *124*

13. Racing Through the Gay Nineties *139*

14. The Women's Betting Ring *151*

15. Saratoga Revived *165*

16. Sysonby and Colin *182*

17. From Regret to the Triple Crown *198*

18. Man o' War *205*

19. Rothstein and the Roaring Twenties *216*

20. Gallant Fox *228*

21. War Admiral, Seabiscuit, Whirlaway *242*

22. Citation, Native Dancer, Tom Fool *258*

23. The Greatest Travers?   270

24. Secretariat, Ruffian, Affirmed vs. Alydar   279

25. John Henry, Go for Wand, Holy Bull   292

    Notes   311

    Bibliography   329

    Index   337

ILLUSTRATIONS

The 1875 Travers   *frontispiece*

First picture of Saratoga   3

French view of the Spa   8

Congress Spring   19

Solomon Northup   22

Lady Suffolk, "The Old
   Gray Mare"   26

John Morrissey   32

Moon's Lake House   38

Commodore Vanderbilt   39

Advertisement for races   43

William R. Travers   49

Union Hall   52

Hurdle race   54

Matthew Brady's Saratoga   55

Kentucky   57

An 1865 finish   67

Winslow Homer's Saratoga   69

The diagonal chute   77

Excelsior Spring   78

An 1868 race card   81

Thomas Nast's Morrissey   85

Morrissey's Club House   89

The Grand Union Hotel   91

Longfellow and John Harper   92

Longfellow racing Harry Bassett   96

Bird's-eye view of Saratoga   104

The United States Hotel   105

"The Intercollegiate Boat-Races"   109

The twelfth Travers   113

Dead heat in the Kenner   114

Ed Brown   120

Duke of Magenta   125

Isaac Murphy   126

Jimmy McLaughlin   127

Grant at Mount McGregor   131

W. H. Vanderbilt   132

Edward "Snapper" Garrison   141

Salvator beating Tenny   142

Alonzo Clayton and James "Soup"
   Perkins   143

Willie Simms and Matthew Earley   144

America's oldest sports stand   148

The King of India at the track   149

Nellie Bly's target   153

The Women's Betting Ring   155

James "Tod" Sloan   163

W. C. Whitney   166

John Cavanagh   167

Whitney's track   170

John "Bet-a-Million" Gates   173

Lil Russell   176

Sysonby   *185*

James B. "Diamond Jim" Brady   *186*

Colin, Marshall Lilly up   *189*

James Lee   *190*

Regret, Rowe, and H. P. Whitney   *200*

Roamer at Saratoga   *202*

Man o' War   *207*

A start: horses behind barrier   *208*

A start: starter springs barrier   *209*

Upset beating Man o' War   *210*

Johnny Loftus and Clarence
    Kummer   *211*

Infield lake   *213*

Man o' War's revenge   *214*

The Brook   *217*

Sporting Blood   *218*

The new clubhouse, 1928   *225*

Gallant Fox   *229*

FDR and Eleanor at the track   *231*

Swans and canoe   *232*

It's Jim Dandy!   *233*

George Smoot   *235*

The starting gate   *239*

Whirlaway   *252*

Saranac Handicap photo finish   *254*

Stymie at Saratoga   *259*

Native Dancer   *263*

Tom Fool   *267*

Jaipur vs. Ridan   *271*

Kelso at Saratoga   *272*

Arts and Letters   *277*

Secretariat at two   *280*

Morning with Secretariat   *281*

Secretariat losing the Whitney   *282*

Sandy Hawley   *283*

Ruffian and Foolish Pleasure   *284*

Alydar and John Veitch   *288*

Steve Cauthen, Boy Wonder   *289*

Cordero and Velasquez   *290*

Affirmed and Alydar   *291*

A day at the races   *296*

Marylou Whitney   *297*

Go for Wand   *299*

Julie Krone   *303*

Tabasco Cat   *305*

Holy Bull   *306*

Illustrations

PREFACE

I WAS FOALED AT Saratoga Hospital. Ruined my first sports coat, a red corduroy that ran like a champion in the rain, selling tip cards at Saratoga Raceway (trotters). Got scared of the dark peddling the Pink Sheet, with its nationwide race results, outside Saratoga Lake's gambling hells. Met my first rich people covering Saratoga Race Course (thoroughbreds) for the daily *Saratogian*. Then I got out of school—and out of Saratoga—and Saratoga got out of me.

So I thought. Turned out I had a Saratoga disease, a frequent ringing in the ears followed by thunder and lasting—well, sometimes it lasts 2:01⅗ and sounds like this:

August 18, 1962: "They're off!" Ridan has half a length into the turn, a head at the half-mile. They're destroying the course, welded together. Flying to the quarter pole, Jaipur edges in front. Ridan sets off more rockets. My father will remember two heads bobbing at the wire, one up, one down. It's Jaipur by a nose hair.

Every summer New York racing shifts to Saratoga, providing a sort of working vacation from the debate over the future, if any, of racetracks. For regulars, it's a return to the scenes of races playing as reruns in our brains. For first-timers, it can mean learning about the greatest or quirkiest Saratoga moments from the small talk on the front porches, or around the paddock where they sold the yearling Man o' War for $5,000.

August 13, 1919. "They're off!" Well, most of them. Man o' War is pointed the wrong way as the starter releases the barrier. But now he shows the stride that ate Saratoga—"responding gamely to punishment," the chart-writer will note, not being a horse. Wipes out daylight 100 feet from home. He's a half-length out. A head. The wire whizzes by. You know the winner's name: Upset. Man o' War's record: 20–1.

Saratoga was once under attack. Crowds were sparse while the New York City tracks were mobbed, so the intelligentsia on the tabloids wanted the midsummer meeting moved downstate. Then something happened. Even the lady who spat her mineral water on your shoes knows what it was: offtrack betting. But what kept it from killing Saratoga? Could it be a new respect for tradition? The sort of appreciation that has raised the profile of the Senior PGA Tour? That had the designers of Cleveland's new ball park repeating the best of Baltimore's, which had preserved the best of Memorial Stadium, Bawlmer's old backyard? Not a mere nod to nostalgia, but a recognition of the past's achievements, singly and in sum, its continuing validity. The way they talk about it very late at the Adelphi Hotel, where the Saratoga track's founder, John Morrissey, died in 1878, even the worst of times gone by don't sound that bad.

August 16, 1930. "They're off!" Millions are out of work. The only one in the country who knows what he's doing is a horse. Governor Roosevelt is here, and the magnificent Gallant Fox is showing him how to win. But after the far turn, the cheering stops. An animal from—where?—California is in front. It's the 100-to-1 Jim Dandy by eight lengths. Thousands will explain why the grocery money went to a Triple Crown laureate.

Those creating our special events should undergo a forced march to Saratoga. They would learn that they don't set the standards. The past does. How to measure greatness if not by the Triple Crown winners who still pound through tales told at Saratoga?

August 19, 1978. "They're off!" in the tightest continuing duel in modern racing. Then, into the turn, "it" happens. Affirmed cuts to the rail. Alydar pulls up, a shaken Jorge Velasquez standing in his irons. "He broke down!" scream voices in the crowd. Affirmed wraps up the Travers, but with a "D" by his name. Disqualified. Alydar wins.

If Wimbledon had been in America, it would have been torn down long ago, but today many would trade Flushing Meadow's airplanes for Wimbledon's humming-bird. Granted, Steffi Graf may have wanted to backhand the bird, but in general some of us have developed new priorities. And the old temples commend to us something more. Character.

July 16, 1872. "They're off!" for the two and a quarter miles of the Saratoga Cup. Longfel-low instantly hits his near forefoot, twisting the plate. He and his great rival Harry Bassett fight it out. At two miles, the horseshoe is doubled over and embedded. Down the stretch blaze America's two greatest. Longfellow wobbles, fights, and loses by a length. "Photo" by Currier and Ives. Ten thousand roar. Then silence. Longfellow is leaving three hoofprints. He'll never race again.

Across the street, Saratoga's National Museum of Racing displays the Currier and Ives. You can almost hear them running.

Edward Hotaling

Washington, D.C.
February 1995

ACKNOWLEDGMENTS

*T*HIS IS A STORY that has never been told, which has made it all the more delightful to research, but which also makes me the more grateful for the help I have had. It is the first history of our oldest, and one of our most beloved, major sports facilities and its colorful, unpredictable impact on American life. Our oldest sports venue, it turns out, was also the cradle of our first national sport, horse racing on a continental scale, with competitors from across the land and a vast audience. It was logical to launch this uniquely American phenomenon at Saratoga, since the Springs was our first and for decades only national resort—indeed, its first typical tourist was George Washington himself. As soon as the horses took off, the place attracted such artists as Winslow Homer, Currier and Ives, Matthew Brady, and Thomas Nast, all of whom make happy contributions to this work. But in researching it, I have found that Saratoga has yet another unknown national distinction: an extraordinary community of devoted and often highly specialized historians. Your average metropolis should be so lucky.

Tom Gilcoyne must know more about the turf than anybody in the country. As volunteer research historian at the National Museum of Racing and Hall of Fame, he fields queries from across the land and beyond. The other day, it was the Royal Canadian Mounted Police on the phone, asking for background on a racer who wound up with them. When the Mounties need help, they turn to Gilcoyne. Besides providing important information and guidance, Tom read much of the manuscript, though any blame belongs with the author.

Among many other helpful nurturers of the Saratoga flame, resident or commuting, were Marylou Whitney, community leader and stable owner; Field Horne, curator of collections at the National Museum of Racing; Robert Joki, historian and owner of an extraordinary collection of nineteenth-century photographs; John Mangona, track superintendent; William Leggett, Michael Veitch, Donna Ross, and Landon Manning, turf writers; and Bill Dunson, former city and racing official who was there with Elaine when we needed them. I am grateful to rare book dealers John De Marco, Frances Steloff, and her successor, Andreas Brown, of the Gotham Book Mart in Manhattan; Professors James Kettlewell and Jane Rehl of Skidmore College; Myra Armstead of Bard College; Martin Berger at Yale; local historians Martha Stonequist, Karen Campola, Lorraine Westcott, Sophie Goldstein, Maria Bucciferro, and Charlotte Helprin; photographers Barbara Livingston, Michael Noonan, and Eric Hotaling; three terrific editors, Fred Eaton, Barbara Lombardo, and Dennis Redmon;

public librarians Jean Stamm, Ellen deLalla, and Doris Armstrong; Mary K. O'Donnell at Skidmore; and historic preservationists Julie Stokes, Mary B. Hotaling, Norm Fox, John Derby, Susan Brome, Holly Hallanan, and Marvin Olick.

The New York Racing Association came through with both information and photographs. Thanks to Steven Crist, Glen Mathes, Dan Leary, John Lee, Bob Coglianese, and also Steve Schwartz of Monmouth Park. Happily, the research soon had me riding through the wonderful rolling horse country due south. In Maryland, the Bowie Public Library and its turf specialist Susan Stephenson revealed the rich secrets of their little-known Selima Room, a treasury of the sport's lore. August Belmont IV chatted from his eastern shore retreat. Across the Potomac in Virginia, I learned much from Mrs. F. Ambrose Clark, whose husband was a turf leader for decades; Peter Winants, director of the National Sporting Library; and librarians Barbara McMillan and Shirley Krein at Mount Vernon.

Bluegrass heaven is the deep armchairs, burnished tables, and tempting volumes of the Keeneland Association library, nestled by the track and sales ring. I studied the glass negatives of the Cook Collection with the invaluable assistance of Cathy Schenck, Phyllis Rogers, Doris Jean Waren, and the staff. I am also indebted to Tony Terry at Churchill Downs; to the Jockey Club and researcher Sam Kanchuger; to Gail Hatton, widow of the famous turf writer Charlie Hatton, who invented the term Triple Crown; and to Angela Price of *The Blood-Horse* magazine, and Laura Tucker of the *Thoroughbred Times*.

It has been an honor to run in the bright orange silks of the Syracuse University Press, under equestrian director Robert Mandel and everybody else in that fine stable, as well as former director Charles Backus. It has been equally pleasurable to run in the peacock colors of NBC, with stablemates Robert Finley, Philip Jacobs, Charlotte Kohrs, Alan Rice, David Rubin, Norman White, and Wayne Wood. Thanks to all the starters and the rabbits at the far turn—John Ashbery, James Baldwin (the first to say write about Saratoga), Edith and Carl Bernard, Ed Bradley, Charles Collingwood, Reid Collins, Walter Cronkite, B. J. Cutler, Carol Cutler, Ted Feurey, Stephen Lee Grover, Peter Jennings, Ruth Johnson, James Jones (write longer), Irving R. Levine, Charles Osgood, Jeff Paley, Dan Rather, Margaret Roohan, Eric Rowinsky, Hughes Rudd, Sue Simmons (though I still can't do the "Taxi!" whistle), Lydie and Iannis Stefanopoulis, and Murray Zinoman.

And down the homestretch. But then Marthe and Greg and Luc already know.

They're Off!

1

THE FIRST TOURIST

GEORGE WASHINGTON'S cocked hat might have been at a slight tilt as he nudged his horse westward. Apparently he had been drinking. An Italian count in the group said that since they couldn't see beyond ten steps, they had resorted to the local custom of taking "antidotes against the ill effects of fog," drinks the Americans jokingly dubbed "antifogmatics."[1] Depending on its density, said the count, a fog might call for up to seven drafts of whiskey, rum, brandy, or other medicine. "Almost everyone in America conforms to this practice with happy results." The count's journal, the only eyewitness account of this liquid adventure, would lay buried at his Milan estate for 186 years, then surface only in an obscure translation, so the story is virtually unknown.

"After lunch (and proper antidote which upon due consideration we unanimously decided should be of the fifth grade), we arrived at the mineral springs." It was July 27, 1783. The six-foot Washington stared at the water gurgling from a hole on the top of a discolored rock three feet high. One of three springs in a marshy little depression, it tasted cold and salty and smelled of sulfur. It was said to cure gout, dropsy, and asthma, and this same July a gentleman had brought his daughter here for "the king's evil," syphilis.[2]

For their illustrious visitor, the few inhabitants of the area decided to bake springwater bread. Not only did they not add salt, but they used no yeast, yet the dough rose in "less than two minutes—to be exact in 1 minute, 40 seconds, and 52 thirds," declared Count Francesco Dal Verme. "Thirds" were sixtieths of a second, which the man with the watch told them he calculated in his head. It was the first Saratoga clocking. As for the bread, Dal Verme pronounced it excellent, and he was Italian. He did not say how much of it the great man consumed, nor how much of the water.

That Sunday George Washington became Saratoga's, perhaps America's, first modern tourist, even to the point of packing a hidden agenda. Long before the Revolution, though, the spot had been a resort of Mohawk and other Indians, who valued the waters as a medicine as much as the first colonists would. One was Chief Loran Tarbel, a contemporary of Washington's, who visited the spring as a boy prior to 1759, before his family moved to Canada.[3] He and his father had to dip the water out of the hole with a cup. According to Indian tradition, he said later, the Great Spirit had angrily stopped the spring from overflowing because women had been using it as a douche, a natural contraceptive that would go unnoticed in medical literature.

To find out how often Mohawk sightseers on the Kayaderosseras Trail had been stopping by lately, Washington would have had to look up somebody like Indian Joe, as the colonists called him.[4] Part European, Joe had lived among Mohawk families occupying sixteen cabins at the springs before the Revolution. They hunted and fished, and some of them, like so many of the colonists, got drunk a lot, their antifogmatics supplied by one of the tavern-keepers who kept going out of business at the spot. Joe himself was thought to have made the first serious clearing in the vicinity, on the South Broadway hill where later a series of hotels would culminate in the Inn at Saratoga. Nobody today knows what Joe's plans were.

Legend had it that the first colonist to stop at the springs was Sir William Johnson, the superintendent of Indian Affairs. He lived thirty miles west at Johnson Hall (still open to visitors), and Mohawks supposedly carried him here to treat an old thigh wound from the French and Indian War. In fact, Chief Tarbel said he was one of the litter-bearers. The consensus is that Sir William may have visited in 1771, but nobody has been able to prove it.[5]

Washington had just ridden over from the country home of the area's other famous resident. Maj. Gen. Philip Schuyler's place was twelve miles east on the Hudson, in the settlement of Saratoga, to be renamed, unfortunately, Schuylerville. The Schuylers had taken house guests to the springs before the Revolution. Some of the African Americans who worked for them, many as slaves, may have come, too. A few desperate patients had made their way in the company of doctors. And American officers posted in the area during the war, as well as enlisted men from Fort Saratoga, had taken time out to see the place they called "the Salt. Springs."[6] But these various visitors were either quartered in the area or feverishly seeking a cure. None was a full-fledged American tourist.

In fact, it was only three years earlier that the word "tourist" had made its debut in the language, designating an odd new race with nothing better to do.[7] Washington fit the bill. He had just resigned his command and was waiting—"with great impatience"—for the confounded Treaty of Paris to arrive and for the British to evacuate Manhattan. At wit's end, he had decided "to wear away a little Time, in performing a Tour to the Northward" from his headquarters at Newburgh on the Hudson.[8] It was the new American version of the "grand tour" that foreign aristocrats like Dal Verme were undertaking in Europe and North America. Like millions to follow, however, this first American tourist at the springs had his agenda: he wanted a piece of the action.

Let Jefferson pursue happiness; as soon as that treaty boat got here, on with the pursuit of property. All Washington got during the war, he complained, was "money paid to me at a depreciated value." Outraged at missing eight years of real estate deals while other Virginians made killings, he was anxious to rebuild his "impaired fortune."[9] Indeed, the evidence now suggests that when he rode away from the springs, his head was spinning. And he did leave that same afternoon: George Washington schlepped here, but he never slept here. He was hardly back at Newburgh before he fired off a letter, widely ignored by historians, to New York Governor George Clinton, who had been with him that foggy day.[10] What, Washington wanted to know, should he do next, "respecting our purchase of the Saratoga Springs."

The first picture of Saratoga Springs. High Rock Spring is in the foregound. *Columbian Magazine, 1787. Courtesy of the author.*

George Washington was actually going to buy the place, and he had just baptized it in print.[11] As an outsider, he quite naturally borrowed the name from the settlement and battlefield to the east and then capitalized its business end: "the Saratoga Springs." The name was a promoter's dream, Washington himself having noted a few weeks earlier that the area had become "famous by being the Theatre of Action in 1777." In fact, the two battles of Saratoga had ended with an entire army, 2,442 British soldiers and 2,198 German mercenaries, laying down their weapons, an astounding development that persuaded France to come to the aid of the Americans. It would be forever famed as the "Turning Point of the Revolution" (it is interpreted to visitors today at the Saratoga National Historical Park). That new species, the tourists, would soon be on the road that Phil Schuyler cut in 1783, the first road to the springs. Washington was in a hurry. "I have money now by me and shall, at any time, be ready to answer your call," he told his partner, the governor.

So the Father of His Country foresaw its first national resort. As he considered the virgin country spread out before him, he found one futuristic project after another crowding his mind. His letters do not spell out this latest dream of his, but he certainly wasn't buying a pasture. He was getting a watering place that was already, as one of his soldiers noted, "a great curiosety" locally.[12] He could also see that for his friends back home, less intense about life and liberty, happiness was a Bath of their own. They had laid out Bath, Virginia, hoping to copy its English namesake with "plated carriages, card games, steaming hot baths and God knows what scandals."[13] There was also great interest in commercial sources of salt for the new country, so these Salt Springs might have a considerable industrial value.

George Washington may have even envisioned the Saratoga racetrack. After all, he was not the stick figure historians have given us but "the best horseman of his age," said Jefferson, and this in America's greatest equestrian era.[14] He had managed a race at Alexandria as early as 1761. He must have thrilled to stories of English champions cheered on by gamblers, royal and otherwise, such as the colt foaled during an eclipse of the sun in 1764. This one inspired the phrase, "Eclipse first—the rest nowhere," and his male line became the most prominent in the breed—indeed, more prominent than possible, for many American owners later named horses "Eclipse" to magnify their talents or price.

Washington joined a racing association, the Williamsburg Jockey Club. "Jockey" then referred not only to professional riders but to gentlemen of all shapes and sizes who often rode their own horses in races, especially on the open road. As for jockey George Washington, he attended the Annapolis and Philadelphia Races and kept a thoroughbred of his own at Mount Vernon. His beloved Magnolia was sired by Lindsey's Arabian, who was imported from England the hard way, via shipwreck off the American coast.

Washington could see racing was bigger still in New York. The colonies' first track had been founded in 1665 at Salisbury Plain (later Hempstead) on Long Island. It was in America, incidentally, that the circular course was developed, supposedly out of a democratic desire to let everybody see the whole race from start to finish.[15] Lately, the British occupiers had taken over a Brooklyn course and rechristened it, with their undefeated sense of humor, Ascot Heath, featuring both male and female jockeys. As for George Washington's own horsemanship, it was legendary among his compatriots. Now, at fifty-one, this easy rider proudly noted he had just logged 750 miles through New York State in nineteen days.[16]

Washington was determined to get his Saratoga Springs. He prescribed them to retired Brig. Gen. Otho Williams, a Baltimore horseman, womanizer ("dear creatures"), and consumptive, who came, drank, and was unconquered. Reporting back, Williams said the spot was now "frequented by the uncivilized people of the back country." But he also told Washington the waters "have certainly a very great quantity of salts. A quart of the water boiled down to a spoonful."[17] Washington refused to fold. He was in Bath two months later, and it was booming. Within a few years, it would be noted, the crowd there "played billiards, they gambled, they had boxing matches, and the ladies rode as though they had all been born on horses."[18] Sixteen months after their visit to the Saratoga marsh, Clinton finally concluded the locals had a lock on it. The great man was uncharacteristically shaken. "I am very sorry we have been disappointed," Washington wrote back as calmly as he could on November 25, 1784, "in our expectation of the Mineral Spring at Saratoga."[19]

Having made his grab for the springs, the first tourist had fathered another Saratoga tradition: being foiled by the natives. There was, actually, a consolation prize. The governor had managed to pick up six thousand acres for Washington in Herkimer, New York—at $9,000 and well before "conflict of interest" got into the dictionary. "Amazingly cheap," said the future president.[20] But he knew he had lost the big one: "I am very sorry we have been disappointed." There is no record of any reply to an ambitious Massachusetts businessman who wrote to Washington in December, requesting a list of all the salt springs in the country, perhaps because it wouldn't have been printable.[21] Still, the Saratoga landowners had made a tremendous contribution to the country. For if Washington had been able to buy the land, would he have accepted the presidency? Maybe not. He would have been busy at his Springs.

2

AMERICA'S FIRST NATIONAL RESORT

GEORGE WASHINGTON'S dream took off. By 1787, it got its first national press coverage: the first picture ever made of "the Saratoga Springs" and an article in the monthly *Columbian Magazine*.[1] Another important story that year was the drafting of a constitution. By that year, too, Phil and Kitty Schuyler had built a two-room frame house near the rock. It has been called America's first summer cottage, rather a fragile claim since Indians undoubtedly maintained summer homes all over the place before that.[2] First modern summer home, maybe.

Indeed, by 1787, enough visitors were arriving for Alexander Bryan to make a go of a tavern and become the first permanent settler. His story would astonish customers at today's Olde Bryan Inn, which his son John built in the 1820s on the bluff where his father had lived, peering down on that valuable spring.[3]

A double agent, Alexander Bryan had been a wartime confidant of both rebels and Tories while keeping an earlier tavern on the river road north of Waterford, thirty miles to the southeast, but he took care to channel the important information to the rebel Committees of Safety. Then the American commander, Gen. Horatio Gates, asked him to accept the most dangerous mission imaginable: to infiltrate the headquarters of the approaching British general, John Burgoyne himself. A slip could mean death. At the same time, the American Tories were asking him to brief Burgoyne. Bryan took both jobs, but let Gates in on it.

The foppish British general interviewed the tavern-keeper and must have liked him, for he gave him a supervisory job in his weapons department. One gray morning, as the British prepared to advance, Bryan hightailed it out of camp at the last minute, losing two horsemen. The next night, on September 16, 1777, he was the first to carry word to the Americans that "Gentleman Johnny" had crossed the Hudson and was heading for Stillwater. This helped the Americans prepare for the first bloody fight at Saratoga on September 19. For more than three decades, Bryan tended his new tavern on the western ridge above the rock, alone with his past and quarreling with his increasingly rich neighbors.

Four years into Washington's presidency, in 1792, another Saratoga spring was discovered by a congressman, Nicholas Gilman of New Hampshire, as he traipsed through the woods south of the rock. Named Congress Spring in his honor, it quickly became the most favored fountain of all, and flows to this day.[4] Five years later, Jedidiah Morse sent Mount Vernon a presentation copy of his *American Gazetteer*. In it the retired president could read that the township "distinguished in history for being the place at which Gen. Burgoyne was obliged to surrender his army" was now "also famous for its medicinal waters, called the *Saratoga Springs*."[5] Washington could hardly be blamed if he mumbled, "Thank you very much."

Forming a crescent, the magic waters gurgled a few miles south, too, in what is now the Saratoga Spa State Park, and also seven miles to the southwest, in "Ball's Town," soon "Ballstown Springs," and finally Ballston Spa, after the great watering place of Spa in Belgium. Actually, Ballston showed the way, putting up ever more elaborate boarding houses and then, in 1804, building the three-story San Souci, the biggest hotel in the country, with more than 100 rooms, a 70-foot ballroom, 162 feet of frontage, and wings reaching 110 feet back."[6]

Copying Ballston, a lumberman named Gideon Putnam assumed the role that escaped George Washington and created modern Saratoga Springs, starting about 1800. He developed its natural fountains, discovered new ones, drew up a far-sighted town plan, and replicated Ballston's transformation from taverns and boarding houses to the modern hotel, a development that would have an enormous impact on American social history.

Even before Putnam started, the little valley was celebrated for other springs besides High Rock and Congress. They included the Flat Rock, behind the site of today's City Hall; the Red, named for its iron content and about fifty-five yards north of High Rock, and the President (later called Iodine, then Star), a block north of High Rock. Concentrating on the south end of the valley, Gideon Putnam tubed Congress Spring in 1804, then three more: the Columbian, a few steps southwest of it; Washington Spring, across Broad Street, where Catholic Central High School now stands; and finally a spring named for Alexander Hamilton, Schuyler's son-in-law, at today's Spring and Putnam streets.

Putnam's plan holds up two centuries later. It boiled down to a north-south line slung across the western ridge above the valley. He honored himself with a narrower, parallel street in the valley bottom. Other street names reflected the national importance he could see the place was assuming: Bath (a little south of today's Spring Street), Congress, Federal, and—after his son as well as the first tourist—Washington. New streets would soon honor Hamilton, Putnam's daughter Phila, and his granddaughter Caroline. But Broad Street was what it was all about. Traversing the ridge, it connected the "Upper Village" developing west of High Rock to the "Lower Village" west of Congress Spring. It was a brazenly optimistic promenade, 120 feet wide and nearly a mile long. It was clear Putnam thought his Broad way would be one of the most celebrated streets in the nation, but could even he have imagined the millions it would accommodate over the next two centuries?[7]

Even sillier, it seemed, was "Putnam's Folly," his boardinghouse and tavern on the west side of Broad, between Washington and Congress. Started in 1802, this three-story wonder with ten windows across the front would grow into Union Hall and then into the Grand Union, a contender for the world's largest hotel. As people kept coming, Putnam sawed, and hammered, and climbed scaffolds as fast as he could too fast. He died in a construction accident while working on a second hotel, Congress Hall, just north of Congress Spring.

A French view. Congress Hall is to the right, opposite Union Hall, and Congress Spring behind the trees at the right. By Jacques Milbert, ca. 1828. *George S. Bolster Collection of the Historical Society of Saratoga Springs.*

These first resorts at Ballston and Saratoga were inventing a new feature of American travel: the hotel not merely as a stopping place for room and board but as the final destination, with its own self-sufficient universe of balls, banquets, and games. Quite naturally, the American hotel became a great trysting place of friends, associates, and strangers with like interests, redefining and expanding social, business, and even political life. It was perfectly natural that it should give birth to that quintessentially democratic institution, the modern convention. In the next century, a glamorous hotel in the Saratoga Spa State Park would be named, in gratitude, the Gideon Putnam. It is the only visible reminder of the man, as few happen by the out-of-the-way cemetery that he designed for the village, and of which he became the first permanent resident. Though he was not the Gideon of the hotel Bible, surely Putnam would merit this epitaph today: "When it comes to American hotels, he wrote the book."

Saratoga needed George Washington's inspiration once again to make a mark on American architecture. The inspiration in question was the piazza, a colonnaded gallery serving as a verandah—a wonderful retreat for rest, reading, recreation, and reunions. And a misnomer. Properly speaking, "piazzas" are Italian city squares, often surrounded on all sides by such galleries. It was the English aristocrats who first copied these galleries, attaching them to residential facades and giving them their erroneous name. Washington introduced the idea to America when he created Mount Vernon's most famous feature. Seen in engravings that circulated all over the thirteen states, the Mount Vernon piazza was copied everywhere and finally would become that beloved institution that allows a person to be inside, outside, and neither: the front porch.

Putnam went Mount Vernon one better, or two, or three.[8] He took Washington's seventy-foot piazza and made it more than two and a half times bigger, raised it above street level, and restored it to a downtown setting. This magnificent production was the 196-foot-long, two-story front porch of his Congress Hall. Another piazza was affixed to Union Hall, and soon Broad Street was lined with these galleries, recreating the Italian idea of a tall, inviting arcade at once private and public. While Mount Vernon's verandah, lined with Windsor chairs, took in a private gulp of the Potomac, Saratoga's long line of piazzas sat in review of the growing parade on Broad Street, helping to create a new American townscape. Later, far more modest versions—flat roofs held up by wooden posts over boardwalks—would add a tiny touch of civility to rural and Western towns. Today the Rip Van Dam Hotel's verandah (1840) and the Adelphi's (1877) survive from the century-and-a-half reign of Saratoga's towering piazzas.

*   *   *   *

But a racetrack, an actual racetrack—which George Washington almost certainly would have attached to his resort by now—well, that was definitely a horse of another color. The Revolution had set back America's favorite sport. Puritan forces, newly empowered like everyone else, found it too English or too sinful and got racing banned in New York State in 1802. Quite accurately defining it as gambling, the law prohibited "all racing and running, pacing or trotting of horses, mares or geldings, for any bet or stakes, in money, goods or chattels, or other valuable thing."[9] With that, the puritans pushed back the birth of modern American sports by more than half a century, for New York, with its advantages of population, location, communications, and—despite the puritans—forward-looking attitudes, was the only place that could have launched racing on anything approaching a national scale. Instead, racing's center of gravity moved south.

Maryland had formed a jockey club in 1783 and soon resumed importing English horses, as racing there shifted from little Annapolis to Otho Williams's growing Baltimore.[10] Next door, the almost empty District of Columbia had a jockey club by 1798, even before it became the nation's capital. The first president to live in the White House, Thomas Jefferson, was also the first to patronize its National Course.

One state became known as the home of the best jockeys, known simply as "Virginia boys." Among them was Altamont, one of George Washington's former slaves. Indeed, Virginia, then the rest of the South, developed a cadre of black jockeys who would earn national glory at Saratoga. The state had three tracks at Richmond in those early days, and was home to America's first great sire, the imported Diomed. The best of the English colts since Eclipse, Diomed had captured ten straight races, including the first Epsom Derby in 1780, then fell into a slump and was retired to stud.

Shipped to Virginia in 1798, this has-been astonished everybody by becoming a foundation sire at age twenty-one. Diomed was the direct ancestor of the champions American Eclipse, Boston, Lexington, and Kentucky, winner of the first Travers.

In Tennessee, future president Andrew Jackson helped found the Clover Bottom track at Nashville, where he bet cash and clothes—"I lost my shirt" has a literal origin—on his Truxton against the speedy Greyhound in 1805.[11] Winning, he declared himself "eased in finances and replenished in my wardrobe," but he didn't have it so easy against Haynie's Maria. This was one of Diomed's last foals, ridden by Monkey Simon, a four-foot-six-inch hunchback said to be an African prince. Jackson tried to beat Haynie's Maria with horse after horse, and once imported the celebrated black jockey Dick from Virginia to do it, all in vain. Asked once if he ever failed at anything, Jackson replied: Beating Haynie's Maria.

When he got to the White House, Jackson actually kept a secret stable in town. Of course, Washington was a sieve even then, and everybody knew it. One day, the popular Southerner had a hell of a time embarrassing his aristocratic Northern vice president, little Martin Van Buren, who had made the mistake of accompanying Jackson to National. Working out before a race, the powerful horse Busiris started getting nervous and "kerlaraping." As they neared the threatening animals, the president shouted, "Get behind me, Mr. Van Buren! They will run over you, Sir!" The newspapers ate it up. Within a few years, American presidents could no longer summon the courage to frequent the racetrack, although English queens would.

Racing was bigger yet in South Carolina, where they had four jockey clubs by 1800 and it was a scandal *not* to race horses. During race week at Charleston, said somebody who was present, "it was *unpopular,* if not *impossible* to be out of spirits and not to mingle with the gay throng." Colonels and belles grew like Spanish moss, and once it was noted: "Charleston, South Carolina, is, we believe, the only place where ladies habitually grace the course with their likeness."[12] As it would turn out, women would be the crucial crowd factor in the launching of modern American sports at Saratoga.

The "western" state of Kentucky had eight race tracks by 1800. More important, it was succeeding Virginia as the chief breeding grounds, for its beautiful stretches of bluegrass were "immediately recognized as the best natural grazing in the world."[13]

The puritans notwithstanding, America's favorite pastime seemed designed for Saratoga. Granted, the earliest pilgrims were often in no mood for it. In 1804, when Sally Nott's ambitious husband was about to become president of Union College in Schenectady, she lay dying in Albany. Sally asked to be removed to the Ballston springs "as the last expedient," although, as she kept telling everybody, "she had no confidence in their efficacy." Her friends were amazed she even survived the overnight trip. Surprisingly, though, "the operation of the waters, of which she drank sparingly, at first appeared favorable." A cure! Three days later, Sally was dead at age twenty-nine. It was not the water. Tears flooded Rev. Eliphalet Nott's cheeks as he eulogized her in his Albany Presbyterian Church, but he did not advertise how a few months before fragile Sally had barely survived the birth of a child, their fourth in six years.[14]

That August, her tuberculosis quite advanced, Rebecca Coxe journeyed the three hundred miles from Philadelphia to Saratoga Springs with her sister and brother-in-law. Overjoyed at the results, the latter wrote back to Tench Coxe, a former assistant treasury secretary, that his wife had not even produced "what the most anxious and timid could denominate a cough." A year later, Rebecca coughed up blood and six months after that died at forty-two.[15] Still they came. The water, or the trip, or the air, or hope—something—worked for many, especially if they were not sick, which increasingly was the case.

George Washington's dream now became reality as Saratoga and Ballston shared the honor of being America's first national resort. While the Virginia springs drew all manner of Southerners and a few others, the accents heard here were from every corner of the land. In 1805, Elkanah Watson found one hundred guests at Ballston's San Souci, many from the South but others from "every part of the Union" and Europe.[16] The Yankee diarist gawked at "males and females intermixed in the true French usage" at table and in the ballroom, where they danced cotillions under blazing chandeliers "in pursuit of health or pleasure, of matrimony or vice." He thought it "the most splendid watering-place in America and scarcely surpassed in Europe," which he had recently toured. (A few years later, in Berkshire County, Massachusetts, Watson would set up the first local agricultural fair, an institution that would help save horse racing from the puritans.)

*   *   *   *

At all this pleasure, the puritans' eyes narrowed on another tradition Washington had encouraged here. By 1808, when Saratoga and Ballston were recommended for "springs of greater celebrity than any in the United States," the "invalids" were drinking much more than minerals, as were a lot of people on the surrounding farms. One rainy night that year, after a round of house calls, a furious Dr. Billy J. Clark burst into a county parsonage and shouted, according to one account, "We shall become a community of drunkards, unless something is speedily done to arrest the progress of intemperance!" That was a mouthful to shout, but within days Billy had established America's first temperance society at the most logical place for it, the Mauney-House Tavern, ten miles northeast of the Springs. So Saratoga invented not only how to have a good time on a national scale, but how not to. As the first temperance society's official historian conceded, however, the Springs went on to be "converted, or rather perverted, into an unsunk Sodom." Indeed, Sodom was such a success that in our time a local history has apologized for Clarks Corners' "notoreity [sic] as the home of the temperance movement."[17]

The puritans were no easy mark in their battle against the "gay and fashionable" for control of Saratoga. One Sunday morning in 1815, as everybody sat down to breakfast in one of the hotels, an insignificant-looking minister from New England began to mumble grace. But as the Reverend Edward Payson's voice slowly gained power, said a witness, the people at the long table were riveted, except for "three gay young men" who "took pains to signify their superiority to such a vulgar custom by clashing the knives and forks, calling upon the waiters, and proceeding to their work"—namely, eating as the others prayed.

That evening, the lodgers assembled for a sermon in the dining hall. Among them were the insolent trio "with a decided Gallio air and manner . . . come to quiz the little parson." He arrived noiselessly and sat to meditate, then rose. Faint at first, his voice again gathered strength—and something else. "He read a familiar hymn, but it seemed new and striking; he read a familiar chapter in the Bible, but it had a depth and meaning not realized before. He took his text, and preached such a sermon as seldom falls from the lips of man. Every heart was thrilled, and even the three young men who came to scoff, remained to pray."[18]

On the fashionable front, Saratoga was emerging as a stylish equestrian center. More typical than the parson were Henry and Edward Williams, lecherous Southerners seeking the prestige of the Northern tour, another precedent set when Washington sent their consumptive father here. The sons having inherited Otho's love of horses, their priorities before this 1815 tour included turning out a filly for "a trial on the turf," trading a pair of bay (reddish-brown) horses for a trotter, and putting a sorrel (a light bright chestnut) out to pasture.[19] Now they would show Baltimore the way to the resorts, boasting, "More style to show forth from this house than any other." And with Baby leading a four-in-hand of chestnuts, the party set out in a Philadelphia-built gig "to go as far east as Boston and to visit Ballston and Saratoga Springs."

There is a gap here in the unpublished Williams letters, but a contemporary guidebook showed that Saratoga, with its "*numerous* houses of entertainment" and surrounding "sources of amusement," had about caught up to Ballston.[20] A few miles east, Saratoga Lake "invites the sportsman to fish on its extensive and limpid waters" or to shoot woodcock. In the piney woods to the east of today's track were the Revolutionary veteran Jacobus Barhyte's fish ponds. He offered anglers a chance to hook "the most delicate and well flavored" trout, but they had to eat them right there at Jacobus's tavern. Barhyte's would be a mecca for decades before it became the Yaddo estate.

★   ★   ★   ★

Already it was clear this was a sporting crowd, and a big crowd at that, one that might support a racetrack. By the summer of 1818, more than forty-two hundred Americans, no doubt from all twenty-one states, were crowding into Saratoga's hotels and boarding houses, and perhaps as many drove over from Ballston or the battlefield just for a look. Saratoga and Ballston were launching a new phenomenon, highly organized tourism on a national scale. Happily, the surviving Williams letters pick up in 1818 as they head north again, inventing modern travel.

Henry and Edward bore both trademarks of future tourists, great organization and careful lack of originality. At Philadelphia, they dutifully took in "West's painting of which you have heard so much," which had to be Benjamin West's huge and disturbing *Death on the Pale Horse*, then on tour.[21] It figured they would like a horse picture. "Certainly worth the ride to it," wrote Edward, also inventing guidebookese. Their local pride was tested; on a Hudson steamer, they were bowled over by "a greater variety of grand and picturesque scenery than any other in the country," including "our Potowmac." An increasingly fearful race, tourists were already banding in groups, but this did not always protect them. A detour to Niagara Falls left the Williams brothers shaken. "Our party were the last to stand on the great cliff of rock extending over the river at the height of 180 feet which fell a few hours after we left it—a fortunate escape." That was the extent of their comment. True tourists, these dull minds were no more or less affected by the earth moving than by anything else on their hectic schedule. There *was* one earth mover who touched them, though. Henry and Edward still had enough spark to lament "the beautiful barmaid we were so unfortunate as to miss" at Waterford in Saratoga County, this landmark having run off to marry.

Whereas Otho died of tuberculosis at forty-six during a pathetic last dash for Sweet Springs, Virginia, his modern sons took a more leisurely approach. It helped that they were not dying. Reaching Ballston's Sans Souci in 1818, they made the same observation as Watson: most of the 190 guests were Southerners, and nine out of ten had come for fun. "Tomorrow we commence with the water drinking," said Edward, making the obligatory show of concern for his health. Nor did one just get a drink. There was a whole routine. The first visit was scheduled before breakfast, followed by others through the day, this regimented lifestyle, and not the water, later being credited for many of the "recoveries." Still inventing resort life, Edward said they would "contrive to introduce ourselves to the folks" at the spring, but proved a chip off Otho's block. "There is nothing very inviting. We are in no danger from beauty."

Henry, on the other hand, was smitten with the Charleston contingent, ever a mixture of brass and belles, including Gen. John Rutledge's "charming daughter Julia." Unfortunately, also included were the Misses Izards, "reported very rich but monstruously ill-favored." True Southerners, Henry and Edward spent as much time looking for a horse to buy for a brother.

Apropos of nothing quite yet, on June 26, 1819, in Ballston, newspaper publisher Ulysses Doubleday's wife bore a son. Ulysses and the Mrs. named him Abner.

3

A PREVIEW OF MODERN SPORTS

A RAUCOUS CROWD from all over caught a preview of modern American sports, the first performance by nationally known athletes before a national audience. It was the opener of the North-South horse races, a series that would show the unifying power of sports. It was a revelation, a glimpse of the real America and its future. An attempt to launch the series the year before in Washington, D.C., had fizzled, but on May 23, 1823, up to twenty thousand Southerners and forty thousand Northerners converged on the Union course in Queen's County, Long Island. It may have been the biggest crowd yet at an American event of any kind, including wars. James Monroe's vice president, the New Yorker Daniel Tompkins, was there, as were General Jackson, Aaron Burr, and the Virginia orator John Randolph.[1] What about the New York State ban? It had been lifted for 1818 and 1819, reimposed, then lifted only for Queen's County in 1821, allowing the new course to open.

The Northern champion, American Eclipse, the first horse worthy of the original's name, faced the best the South could throw at him, Virginia's Henry. The stake was $20,000, with syndicates putting up the money for each side. When it was over, a rider would rush the result to Manhattan, where a white flag over Niblo's Garden café, whose owner was one of the syndicators, would signify a Northern victory, and a mournful black pennant would mean Henry had won, as chauvinism seeped into national sports at the start.

The race consisted of the best two of three heats at four miles each. It was a grueling test already considered cruel in England but to remain popular in America for decades. Over the first four miles, the Long Island–bred champion was horribly navigated, the whip at one point cutting into a testicle, and the Southerner sailed home in a record 7:32½. Because it was common to change riders between heats, the retired gentleman jockey Samuel Purdy had come to the track coyly wearing colors under his long coat. "When he removed the coat, and was announced as the rider of American Eclipse, the Northern crowd went wild."[2] He won the final two heats in 7:49 and 8:49, capturing the most famous race of the century. The *New York Evening Post* broke out the first sports extra in American journalism, and the mellifluous Congressman Randolph soon rose in the House to praise Purdy: "The renown of the performance of that day will go down in the history of civilized society."[3]

All but unnoticed on the program was the first American trotting race on a regulation track. Ridden by jockeys or harnessed to drivers, trotters had competed on the open road since colonial days. In time-conscious America, they were as carefully clocked as George Washington's Saratoga bread. A tamer pastime than the "running races" by thoroughbreds, trotting easily escaped the surveillance of puritan prosecutors. After all, even a minister might get a rush out of a quick step by his own mare, and who knew whether he illegally waged a bit from the collection basket on her? Long natural speedways like New York City's Third Avenue to Harlem made excellent trotting strips for the gentry. Finally, that last Saturday in May 1823 brought three trotters under saddle to an actual racecourse. Topgallant beat Betsey Baker and The Moccasin in two-mile heats for $1,000. Three years later, the first course intended specifically for trotting opened at Centreville, a mile farther east on the Jamaica Turnpike. In racing parlance, a trotting course was not, and is not, a "racetrack," the latter being dedicated to the thoroughbreds. Today, the distinction is preserved in the use of the term "raceway" for trotting tracks. Thus, a half-mile south of the Saratoga racetrack is Saratoga Raceway. In those days, though, tracks built for the runners were sometimes used by trotters, and vice versa.

The Union racetrack had its moments over the next two decades, especially when the North-South contests were revived. But what racing, and American sports, lacked was a program, a regular schedule of events drawing national talent and national audiences.

In the 1820s, Saratoga Springs left the Battlefield and Ballston behind, though the latter was still the nation's second resort. The parade of Saratoga celebrities was led by present and future occupants of the White House, the former being John Quincy Adams and the latter General Jackson and Van Buren, and by two Frenchmen, the touring Lafayette and the late Napoleon's exiled brother Joseph, the former king of Spain. Joseph Bonaparte came five times and tried to buy not only High Rock Spring but Barhyte's place. He offered $20,000 for the property, to which Jacobus replied, "If it's worth that much to you, it's worth that much to me."[4]

The "lions," as the newspapers called them, prowled Saratoga's new brick wonder, the four-and-a-half-story United States Hotel, erected in 1824 at Broad and Division Streets. For the next several decades, it would remain the trend-setting hotel. Beyond the various inviting piazzas, the lions could escape the prying eyes of the newspaper scribblers, if they wanted to, by retiring to the billiard rooms, which were as big an attraction as the ballrooms. They were welcomed to the Springs by the lioness, a scandalous blonde named Madame Eliza Jumel. Mistress of the Jumel Mansion in New York City, she was just back from a residence in Paris and about to build a home near Lake Avenue, the successor of Schuyler's road from the Hudson. Her Greek Revival home, "Les Tuileries," is still there, at 129 Circular Street, not far from a bar that touchingly perpetuates her name.

Not surprisingly, considering the crowd, the idea of a Saratoga racetrack took off at mid-decade. "Sundry inhabitants" sought approval from the state Assembly to build one and won a committee vote of support but got no further.[5] Still, horse racing got underway in Saratoga as early as 1825 without waiting for a track to be built. Indeed, breakneck racing through the streets had gotten so scary that even this horsey town officially banned it that year, not that it really could stop it. The ultimate in road racing was the match race. This was a loudly advertised contest between two horses, or a horse and the clock, originating with a bet by the owners, the crowd, of course, making its own side bets. Match races were illegal under the ban, but who could halt them when the owners were rich tourists? Using whimsical names, the *New York Mirror's* man at Saratoga in 1830 told of a match that may have been based on a real one.[6]

It is one of the earliest recorded Saratoga horse races. A gentleman jockey named Dr. Ganderluch arrived with his crack trotter and won several matches, whereupon a Maine Yankee, Zerubbabel Sykes, rode in on an excellent mare and challenged the doctor to a race under saddle for $50. Dr. Ganderluch won, but the Yankee offered to produce another man's horse and beat him for a larger amount. Having canvassed Saratoga and found no speed like his, the doctor bought the deal and was chuckling away as the Yankee showed up that night. But here was Sykes leading the very same mare, mounted by a friend. What was going on? The crowd—the first race crowd ever reported at the Springs—was baffled.

"That," sputtered the doctor, "is the horse you rode this morning."

"Certain, and it was my property then, but I guess you'll find it is *another man's horse* now." He had "sold" it.

Having plopped that horse patty on its readers, the *Mirror* said the doctor paid rather than be mortified by a mare whose speed obviously would improve with the stakes. Next morning, the rugged man from Maine with the honest American face was nowhere in sight.

By 1830 there were so many gamblers "and other worthies of a similar kind" at Saratoga that the *Mirror's* man was afraid "we republicans" were beginning to ape silly European aristocrats: "We dress, we dance, we gamble, we drive, and race."[7] Rather than going aristocratic, however, Saratoga in the 1830s took a decided turn toward the democratic, and the modern sports crowd developed. It was the future face of America, though again historians would take no notice.

There were the new capitalists, their primacy based not on feudal estates, family, or fame but merely on funds: how much money they had. It was simply success by the numbers, quite a democratic qualification, and as soon as that new creature the "millionaire" was coined (literally and, in 1826, lexicographically), he was off to Saratoga. There he could race, sail, fish, excel at billiards, endure almost nightly balls, drink a lot, perhaps pursue a lecherous affair or two, and wait for the rest of America to catch up. "A new beauty, or a fresh imported *millionaire*," noted a Saratoga correspondent in 1830, "will inevitably supercede the reigning belle of the moment."[8]

Then there was the fake aristocrat, the phony millionaire. The *Mirror* reporter with the fertile mind created the epitome of this character as early as 1830. Arriving a few weeks before the rugged American crook Sykes had come and gone, he was so captivating that a perfect Philadelphian in attendance at the Springs could only wish, said the writer, to make acquaintance with his tailor. It finally came out that he was a foreign noble, "rich and unmated," on the grand tour of the continent. Hardly had he "made his debut" at Congress Hall before he was buried in geranium-scented billets-doux. This figure aroused the attentions of "a Boston mamma" with six daughters at her disposal; a French heiress who was a ringer for Madame Jumel (although Madame was not quite French and Stephen not quite dead) and who "surveyed his high forehead and unrivaled mustachios"; and finally of a certain male "exquisite," nonplussed by the heiress's sudden lack of attention to his own New York self. The next morning, a party was made up for Lake George, and everybody about died when they noticed it was the new personage at the Springs who handed Madame to a seat in his barouche. As he was about to spring to her side, a breathless stranger rode up, shouting:

"Ah, Charley, is that you? How are you, my dear fellow? I left Utica yesterday— your wife and children are well, all well, and send an ocean of love." Saratoga invented *Guys and Dolls* a century before Damon Runyon hit town.

But look who's coming down the street, making their first joint appearance in history. The word "pa" debuted in 1811, to be followed by "ma" in 1829, but here they are together for the first time in 1830: Ma and Pa.[9] The *Mirror* describes them as members of "the most original class" of visitors, "our honest citizens." They put up at a cheap boarding house, perhaps not even one of the nine that made the guidebook, with their hopeful daughter.[10] "Miss may be arrayed in the latest Parisian costume, but the *tournure* is wanting to give effect," noted the reporter, while "pa's bluntness and ma's plainness" stamp the family as "melancholy strangers in a strange land." It was also a century before Grant Wood painted *American Gothic*.

In the sweltering July of 1830, carriages from "every city and village in the Union" seemed to pour into the "rival springs."[11] The greatest resort of them all had already become a microcosm of America, or as the *Mirror* called Saratoga Springs that year, a place where "a microscopic view of mankind can be taken." Six to eight thousand people were collecting here every summer, double that of 1818. The permanent population was two thousand. History leaves out the dust. Yet as other places sprinkled or macadamized their streets, it remained one of this town's most remarkable and obnoxious features. "I got up early, and took a lounge about Saratoga," wrote a famous British actor, Tyrone Power, not to be confused with Hollywood's Tyrone Power of a century later.[12] "The street was a foot deep in light dust, so that every carriage moved in a cloud."

Before you could say "Excuse my dust!" another development further democratized Saratoga. Not surprisingly, the twenty-four states' most fashionable destination was among the first to hook up to the iron horse. Indeed, it contributed significantly to the development of the railroad. The Baltimore and Ohio launched the country's first public service out of Baltimore in 1830. Next, the South Carolina Railroad's *Best Friend of Charleston* provided the first scheduled steam rail service and proof that it was dangerous. The *Best Friend*'s fireman couldn't stand the shrieking whistle so he put his hand over the valve and was blown to smithereens, becoming America's first rail death. Then New York State's first line, the Mohawk and Hudson, ran from Albany to Schenectady in 1831, its locomotive pulling three modified stage coaches hooked to a rail.

The next question was obvious: how to capture the traffic to the Springs? Plans were made for the historic first connection of two railroads, the Mohawk and Hudson with the Saratoga and Schenectady.[13] Way ahead of almost all of America, service to

Saratoga opened on July 12, 1832. Passengers left Albany at six-thirty in the morning, breakfasted at Schenectady, then took the nine o'clock connecting train. The company was in such a hurry it didn't wait for the bridge over the Kayaderosseras to be completed at Ballston, where passengers got into a post coach and took a half-mile detour around the construction site. The train got to Saratoga at eleven-thirty, in time to stroll to the springs, spit out the water, gawk at the crowds, dine at two, and get back on the train at three, arriving in Albany at seven-thirty. Thus was the one-day visit to the Springs created. It was quite amazing. "The two railroads," it was noted, "furnish the citizens of Albany the means of making an excursion of more than seventy miles (without fatigue), of visiting the fashionable watering places and returning to rest, if they choose, at their homes."[14]

The city of Troy was not amused. A group there founded the Rensselaer and Saratoga Railroad and reminded Saratoga-bound tourists that Troy was a crossroads of stage routes from almost everywhere, and that Southerners on the Hudson steamboats could transfer at Albany onto "trim little steamers" to Troy.[15] Switching to open war, it warned that "the inclined plane on the Schenectady road is a terror to many travelers" and claimed that a recent accident on that line "will prevent not a few from hazarding their lives on the strength of a single rope or chain." Besides, "Who wants to climb to high table land and descend to perdition perchance?"

The railroad was the latest climax in America's love affair with speed. A gent returning from Ballston to Troy in 1836 raved about the *fifty-five minutes in which the twenty-five miles were traveled!!*[16] A rider on one of the first trains from Troy to Saratoga said that "while going literally like lightning, one feels as if he was in a vehicle that is constantly running away. . . . If he puts his head out of the car, he must grip his hat very fast, else in a few minutes it will be left miles behind him." It would be three decades before a successful passenger train was operating from New York City as far as Albany, so the steamboat still reigned on the long route. Meantime, one local railroad company after another tried to create links to the resort and cash in on its name: the Saratoga and Schenectady, Rensselaer and Saratoga, Saratoga and Whitehall, Saratoga and Hudson River, Washington and Saratoga, Saratoga and Ogdensburgh.

Water carried the name even farther. Congress Water was one of America's earliest nationally distributed products. By 1822, next to its regular column on doings of the "Congress of the U. States," Washington, D.C.'s daily newspaper, the *National Intelligencer*, was advertising twelve hundred bottles of the other Congress:

Saratoga or Congress Water

We have for sale 100 dozen Saratoga Water, bottled during the drought of July and August, warranted pure and put up in the best manner.

O. M. Linthicum & Co.
Apothecaries and Druggists

"There is scarcely a town in the United States of any magnitude that is not supplied with it," said a guidebook in the 1830s, "nor a vessel destined to any distant port that does not enumerate *Congress water* in the list of her sea stores."[17] It was being exported to Europe six decades before Louis Perrier leased a spring in France, a

Congress Spring. From *Gleason's Pictorial Drawing-Room Companion, 1852. Courtesy of the author.*

century and a half before Perrier was shipped to the United States, its ad writers claiming Perrier was as old as geological time when, in fact, it was not as old as Saratoga water.

This celebrated industry was the monopoly of John Clarke, the most important Saratoga figure since Putnam.[18] Clarke bought Congress Spring in the mid-1820s, and, as Kettlewell has pointed out, he was far ahead of his time in turning the swampy grounds into a public park. Long before New York City got its Central Park, Congress Park became famous as a little gem of a retreat and remains intact as the southern half of today's Congress Park. Clarke decorated it with classical touches, including the famous Danish sculptor Albert Thorwaldsen's 1815 vases, *Night* and *Morning,* which still grace the landscape; a small dome over the nearby Columbian Spring; and an obelisk, which, says Kettlewell, doubled as a tower providing pressure to distribute the Congress water through wooden pipes. The bottling plant was just to the north, behind Congress Hall. Clarke sheltered his valuable Congress fountain with a temple pavilion. Certainly, if Greek Revival architecture was supposed to suggest democracy reborn, America's best known spring more than did its part—not only with its pavilion but with an extraordinary scene that was played out there.

"To this spot, perhaps more than any other on the globe, are seen repairing in the summer mornings, before breakfast, persons of almost every grade and condition, from the most exalted to the most abject," said an 1830 guidebook.[19] "The beautiful and the deformed—the rich and the poor—the devotee of pleasure and the invalid—all congregate here." It was Saratoga as microcosm again. But "the little urchins," the "dipper boys" who served the water, weren't buying it. They liked to keep their microcosm in proper order. The wealthier customers, warned the guidebook, did better by the dipper boys: "An imposing exterior is sure to procure for its possessor their services." They weren't rushing to wait on ma and pa.

Actually, Congress Park was more a microcosm than the writers reported. Frank Johnson's all-black group, the first nationally famous black orchestra, entertained on a bandstand in the park.

What did America's only national resort look like? Off what was soon to be called Broadway, it took on the air of a shining city of ancient Greece. On the eastern bank above his park, Clarke built the 1832 Greek Revival mansion at 46 Circular Street, where it reigned alone. It remains one of Saratoga's surprises that, as the Parthenon presides over the Agora, Clarke's tribute to it dominates his park, a comparison captured by Kettlewell in his lively *Saratoga Springs, An Architectural History*.[20] Saratoga's other leaders rushed to lead the country again by building Greek houses, and more survive than could be expected. Quite extraordinary is the collection of five homes on and off Franklin Square, including Nos. 3 and 4, built by Thomas and James Marvin, who were owners and managers of the United States Hotel. Viewed from Franklin Street, this square transports one to a Greek Revival neighborhood of the 1830s, an experience few cities can match.

But the signature of America's resort was the piazza. More than 200 yards of them fronted the five first-class hotels in 1830. Congress Hall's, nearly 200 feet long, was lined with seventeen columns. Across the street, Union Hall's was 120 feet long and nearly three stories high, with ten columns. The piazzas alternated with more modest structures for half a mile, from the elegant Pavilion, where the City Hall stands today, to the park. They bustled with the 130 to 200 guests at each hotel, a figure that would nearly sextuple in coming decades. The touring British actor wrote of one piazza, probably Congress Hall's, in 1835:

> This was of immense extent, full twenty feet wide, boarded throughout, and covered by the roof of the house, which was supported by lofty pillars of pine. About these columns grew, in the greatest luxuriance, the wild vine of the country, or some other Clematis, covering them from ground to roof, and forming a continuous rich drapery throughout the whole extent of the long piazza. This forms a promenade for the residents of the house and their visitors; and, were it out of reach of the dust, it would be difficult to create one more elegant and agreeable.[21]

The hotels, however, could not hold the whole crowd. Already the tradition of residents renting out rooms was well entrenched. "Every house is an inn . . . every domicil is a tavern, furnishing entertainment for man or beast or both," said a visiting editor from Troy in 1836.[22]

Saratoga invented "the hop" that year. Wrote the Troy editor: "This evening there has been a dance at the United States Hotel; the public invitation termed it a *hop*—a new cognomen for an amusement of this kind." He was disappointed that the hop had not attracted the lions, but a few years after that, this hotel at the corner of Broadway and Division Street—the most fashionable in the country—was a veritable jungle: "At the head table sat President Van Buren. On the right hand of the President was General Scott. On the left hand was Henry Clay. . . . On our right hand General Morgan Lewis was seated, and on our left hand was General Talmadge. Looking up or down the table, the interested observer remarked such gentlemen as Mr. Forsyth, Secretary of State; Mr. Poinsett, Secretary of War." The list goes on; opposite the president, taking all this down, was the founder of the New York *Herald,* James Gordon Bennett. This was "the classic age of Saratoga," he would recall, when "the dignitaries and belles of the North, South, East and West assembled there from almost every capital on the continent . . . and such a thing as a disunited States had never occurred to any one."

"All the world is here," sang another New Yorker, ex-mayor Philip Hone, of that 1839 season, "politicians and dandies, cabinet ministers and ministers of the gospel, officeholders and office seekers . . . anxious mothers and lovely daughters."[23] But he forgot somebody.

*   *   *   *

"While living at the United States Hotel," wrote Solomon Northup, who had a live-in job there in the 1830s, "I frequently met with slaves, who had accompanied their masters from the South." Northup, his wife, Anne, and their three children were among the one hundred or so black residents who formed Saratoga's first cohesive ethnic community. "Almost uniformly," Northup said of the black Southerners brought to Saratoga for the season, "I found they cherished a secret desire for liberty. Some of them expressed the most ardent anxiety to escape."[24] So there was a "disunited States." How could Northup know that he, too, would become a slave? It was a nightmare that would move Harriet Beecher Stowe, who declared that it confirmed her *Uncle Tom's Cabin.*

Northup was strolling down Broadway in March 1841, when two whites approached him near the park. A fiddler of local renown but out of regular work, Northup was conned into joining their road show. Within days they were in Washington, D.C., where Northup was apparently drugged before being thrown into a slave trader's pen with a view of the Capitol. From there, he was shipped south. Almost before he realized it, this recent employee of the Marvins' hotel found himself on a New Orleans auction block, where "customers would feel of our hands and arms and bodies, turn us about, ask us what we could do, make us open our mouths and show our teeth, precisely as a jockey examines a horse which he is about to barter for or purchase." If he dared confront his owner, who looked at him with "the sharp, inquisitive expression of a jockey," and tried to prove his legal status as a "free black," he might be "disposed of as the thief disposes of his stolen horse."

Solomon Northup. Frontispiece to his book *Twelve Years A Slave*, 1853. *Courtesy of Louisiana State University Press.*

This Saratogian wound up being exchanged among three masters in the bayous. He endured sadistic beatings, as did countless thousands of other black Americans, and he had his own memory of the Southland: "The crack of the lash and the shrieking of the slaves can be heard from dark to bedtime." After twelve years, he was able to sneak out a message that, almost miraculously, reached Saratoga Springs attorney Henry Northup, whose ancestors had emancipated Solomon's father. Henry journeyed to the far-off bayous, where he tracked down and rescued his namesake and friend.

So here we are back in Dixie, where, if slavery was an institution, so, by now, was horse racing. Like flies to molasses, the whole South took to "the Races," those fashionable meetings in the crinoline capitals. They seemed an extension of the establishment's favorite fantasy, that life was a chivalric pageant out of medieval England, the obverse of the North's delusional, anti-English puritanism. Maybe it was just that the South was the perfect place for the cult of the horse; its rangy plantations and red-dirt towns were less well-served by its iron substitute. In any event, Southerners loved horse racing.

The sport galloped from the upper South into the Gulf states of Mississippi, Georgia, Alabama, and Louisiana. Louisiana would be slow getting started, then proved unstoppable. Among its lights would be Hark, a slave and trainer at Wellswood Plantation, the largest racing stable in the antebellum South.[25] As Saratoga would discover, there was also Abe Hawkins, who started out as a slave of the Louisiana Jockey Club's president, Duncan Kenner. Just as soon as they were able, African Americans fought for freedom through sports, through prizefighting in a few cases, and horse racing in many more.

The greatest horse of those days was Boston. Sired in 1833, he was named after the card game (he was supposedly the pot), not the city, and was bred in Virginia. This nasty-minded Diomed grandson bit horses that tried to pass him but finally was broken by the African-American jockey Cornelius, a slave. Boston had to campaign through the South to find any takers. He ended up with forty victories, thirty of them at those grueling four-mile heats. No English thoroughbred could have done it then; no American thoroughbred could come close to it today.[26] Boston's even more cele brated son, Lexington, would make it to Saratoga, and Boston's grandson, Kentucky, would win the first Travers Stakes.

The most influential American horse of the period, perhaps of all time, was Glencoe. Imported from England in 1836 to stand in northern Alabama, Glencoe had an incredible 481 children over twenty-one years, including an even more incredible 317 daughters. A century later, a noted turf writer would declare that this unparalleled "filly sire" was the ancestor of every horse in "any great race of any country any year."[27] Glencoe's granddaughters would take Saratoga by storm.

By 1840, the South had no fewer than sixty-three racetracks; Tennessee had ten, and Kentucky seventeen, the most of any state. From the south, racing was making its way westward, into Arkansas, Texas, Missouri, and up into Illinois. Spanish running horses had been running in California since before the Revolution.

The puritan-controlled Northeast had only six racetracks in 1840, four in New Jersey, one in Pennsylvania, and the Union Course on Long Island. Tyrone Power, our British actor, had visited Union a few years earlier, and found black jockeys preeminent, but casual. He noted "appointments of the negro jockeys more pictur-esque than race-like, ill-fitted jackets, trousers dirty, and loose, or stock-net pantaloons ditto, but tight, with Wellingtons over or under, according to the taste of the rider." They had a convenient way to make weight: "shoes without stockings, or stockings without shoes, as weight may be required or rejected." More interesting was the way they rode. Although turf histories say the 1890s jockey Tod Sloan invented the modern riding posture, replacing the erect position with a crouch, a style first called "Monkey-on-a-Stick," that more natural style was actually practiced much earlier. Power noted in 1833 that the jockeys "sit well forward on to the withers; do not seem over steady in their saddles, but cling like monkeys." New York's Dutchess County managed to get approval in 1828 for a track at Poughkeepsie, but it lasted only long enough to launch local boy Gilbert Watson Patrick, to be known simply as "Gilpatrick," the most famous jockey of antebellum America.

The few Northern tracks sometimes drew huge crowds, thanks to the spectacular North-South matches. In 1832, it took so much out of Black Maria to beat Trifle and Lady Relief in five four-mile heats that the black mare lost one hundred pounds. And the little nag Trifle—"nag" not being pejorative in those days—made up for that one by never losing another and scoring nineteen victories in twenty-five races.

Although haphazardly scheduled, the North-South series proved the viability of a national sports schedule if it somehow could be organized. The excitement was there. In 1841, for example, Boston thrilled the racing public by first retiring to stud and covering forty-two mares, then returning to win four starts in a row, all at four-mile heats. Finally, with Gilpatrick up, he faced New Jersey's Fashion in a North-South confrontation at Camden, New Jersey. Exhausted at last, Boston lost. The last North-South match was in 1845, when Tennessee's Peytona beat Fashion at the Union Course before an unprecedented seventy thousand to one hundred thousand spectators.[28] Historians would ignore it, but modern sports, aching to be born, had again produced perhaps the biggest crowd for any event in this country. It was quite an insult to the antiracing forces.

The puritans were still in charge, however, and modern American sports was going to be born over their rigid bodies. As late as 1838, the New York Assembly denied yet another petition for a track, complaining that racing drew not only "numerous gamblers and pick-pockets" but huge crowds of spectators, "to the neglect of their private affairs . . . and the destruction of their morals,"[29] which, of course, was why they loved it. Americans needed to have their affairs neglected, morals destroyed, and pockets picked once in a while.

Saratoga was increasingly glad to oblige. Long a rendezvous for horse lovers, the Springs by 1841 was serving another equestrian function. Hiram Woodruff, the most famous trainer and driver of trotting horses ever, brought a stable of cracks here to rest up for campaigns elsewhere. Horse people have done this ever since, and in recent times, this habit of sending horses to the Springs merely to relax has given rise to the presumptuous compliment that they, too, love Saratoga.

As things turned out, it was a trotter who would inaugurate the first formal race course at Saratoga Springs. Indeed, it was the most beloved trotter—no, the most beloved horse—in all history, for what horse has almost every American sung about since childhood?

4

THE OLD GRAY MARE

O N THE FOURTH OF JULY, 1843, the original Old Gray Mare started down the path to becoming America's first real sports hero. This was Lady Suffolk, immortalized by songwriter Stephen Foster's "The Old Gray Mare, She Ain't What She Used to Be." On that Fourth, she was better. The ten-year-old became the first trotter to break the mystical barrier of two minutes and thirty seconds for a mile on a regulation course. She broke it not once but again and again in the same race, a best-of-five series of mile heats. She and the bay gelding Beppo, who had tied the record of 2:31½, carried jockeys while a third, Independence, pulled a sulky. Lady Suffolk's times: 2:28½, 2:28 (a dead heat with Beppo), 2:29, and 2:32. It was "the most sensational exhibition of speed by trotting horses that had yet been seen," said turf historian John Hervey.[1] A week later, she was at it again with Beppo, who this time was ridden by the best thoroughbred jockey in the land, Gilpatrick. The gray mare won in even more spectacular times: 2:26½, 2:27, 2:27.

The place where it happened, Hoboken's Beacon Course, was itself a slap in the face to New York's antiracing forces. For it was, in effect, a New York City track. Ads claimed ferries could carry ten thousand horseplayers an hour there, and on iffy weather days, they had only to listen for the track cannon to know the races were on. Security was in the hands of 170 goons reporting to James Ambrose, an Englishman who became a bare-knuckle boxing champion under the more profitable name of Yankee Sullivan. Foot races were big at Beacon, too. "Thirty Thousand Persons Present," screamed a *Herald* headline for one of these contests, "America Triumphant." Publisher Bennett was not only inventing sports journalism but was already trying to cash in on its crude offshoot, sports as patriotism.

Next door to Beacon was Manhattan's riverbank playground, a precursor to Central Park known as the Elysian Fields. Here a few gentlemen were birthing another pastime. The New York Base-Ball Club was formed in that same year of 1843. It thrashed a Brooklyn nine at Hoboken on October 21, 1845, and in Brooklyn a few days later, then showed its clout again in a scrimmage that fall.[2] Reference books that give the date of the first modern game as June 19, 1846, are out of date, and many also wrongly identify the first club as the Knickerbockers, formed in 1845. The New York Ball Club, which beat the Knickerbockers in that 1846 game, was two years older. Meantime, Abner Doubleday was nowhere in sight—not yet.

It might be argued that modern American sports was born at Hoboken in the 1840s, but this arena lacked one thing: a national audience. Lady Suffolk, however,

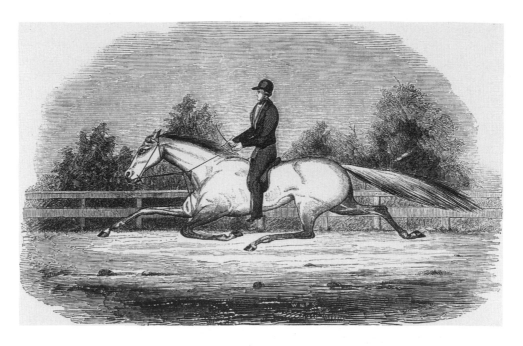

Lady Suffolk. The original "Old Gray Mare" pulled a "wagon" when she won the opener at Saratoga's first race course in 1847. *Courtesy of the author.*

was in the process of proving that such an audience was possible. She kept on winning, breaking the 2:30 record in a sulky. In early August 1847, her owner, the cheap and cruel David Bryan, had her begin a long, hot walk from Long Island to a new track at Saratoga Springs.

By far America's oldest professional sports facility still in use (as a training area), the Saratoga Trotting Course grew from the glimmer of America's first gambling resort. A few short-lived gambling houses had opened in the village in the 1830s. Then Robert Gridley and Ben Scribner founded the first highly successful house in 1841, in an alley off the United States Hotel. It changed the face and the feel of the Springs for good. By 1847, Gridley was also operating thirteen bowling alleys, located opposite the hotel's bar room and backed by its owner, James Marvin. Five of Gridley's alleys were reserved for "private parties of ladies and gentlemen." Indeed, if historians paid more attention to Saratoga women, they would see that the country was far more advanced at that time than they thought. A "great part of the time is occupied by the ladies in bowling, etc.," wrote the *Herald*'s man at the Springs. "This, in fact, is great fun and the best exercise in the world." Gridley's alleys were "the best I ever saw." There were those old favorites, the billiard rooms, and shooting galleries, too. Even ministers followed the fashionable up the river. Bennett's paper feigned indignity at church dignitaries dining alongside Park Row gamblers, a Protestant Episcopal father helping a faro-table keeper to a piece of chicken, a deacon drinking wine with a pimp, and a Methodist parson leering "with a most ungodly expression upon the pretty actress."[3]

Edgar Allan Poe wasn't going to miss this. He came up from Philadelphia in 1842, and was seen driving about with the *New York Mirror* contributor Ann Barhyte. It scandalized Philadelphians at the Springs since Ann was married to Jacobus's son John, who now ran the Tavern and served up the famous trout dinners. One day Poe showed her a poem he was working on, and when he came back the next summer, he boomed it out loud in the garden. The Barhytes' little son James heard the weird visitor in black, and piped up, "Whoever heard of a bird named 'Nevermore'?" Poe, James remembered later, clapped his hands in delight, sat down on his favorite bench nearby, and rewrote: "For we cannot help agreeing / That no living human being." Next door to today's Saratoga Race Course, Edgar Allan Poe was hatching "The Raven."[4]

Who could deny the Old Gray Mare her appearance at the Springs? Besides, the village had a way around the antiracing law. For the first time, it was going to be the site of the New York State Fair, an outgrowth of Elkanah Watson's county fairs and now—at Saratoga—a fine cover for illegal racing. The trotters would merely be giving exhibitions and "trials of speed." This is a service fairs would provide long into the future. Furthermore, for this early use of the ploy, officials claimed the course was beyond their control, as it was just outside the fairgrounds and the village line. It was a mile out East Congress Street extended. Astoundingly, it is still there, across the street from the main track in an area known as Horse Haven. Its wooden rails circle old barns and stables, some of which also date from that era.

The Saratoga Trotting Course was built by local entrepreneurs Alfonso Patten and James M. Cole and apparently backed by Marvin. Cole was trying to make as much as he could from the fair. At his Hamilton Street stables, he charged people twenty-five cents to gawk at a pair of giant oxen. While he was acting like a small-time P. T. Barnum, the real one was quarreling with the village over whether he had to pay twenty-five dollars to exhibit General Tom Thumb at the Fair. Barnum ridiculed the reluctant officials, calling them the general's "fellow dwarfs." Cole and Patten finally opened their Saratoga Trotting Course a month before the fair, pretty much blowing the charade of it being an exhibition.

Opening day drew what looked like America's first dependable sports audience, the sort of well-heeled crowd only Saratoga could guarantee. They paid three dollars for a barouche or hack ride to the unfinished course, two dollars for a one-horse wagon, and twenty-five or twenty-six dollars for an omnibus. The road—today's Union Avenue—was crowded with "pedestrians, equestrians, and carriages of all kinds," said the *Herald,* including "a number of lovely women from the South, whose interest in the event seemed greater than that of the gentlemen."[5] Some "so forgot the name of decency and even common honesty as to climb the fences," but most forked over one dollar for the grandstand and fifty cents for a seat in a lower stand, apparently in the infield.[6] "The straight stretch down the front of the track—a third of a mile—was lined with carriages two deep." Saratoga's first crowd totaled five thousand.

The oblong oval, about sixty-six feet wide, was "said to be one of the finest in America." Actually, with its flat turns and rough surface, it was terrible, a lot of accidents waiting to happen, and a lot short of a mile, though nobody yet seemed to know how much.

The Old Gray Mare was getting lighter as she aged, and she was almost white when she trotted onto the track at about three-thirty in the afternoon of Saturday, August 14, 1847. It was the first day of organized racing at Saratoga, a milestone in sports. She ran "with her head low, and nose thrust out."[7] For the first time in her career, the fourteen-year-old daughter of Engineer II and great-granddaughter of the great Messenger was hitched to a "wagon," also known as a "skeleton wagon." This was not a wagon at all but a four-wheeled sulky held together by wire and with a tiny seat, occupied by owner Bryan. Her opponent was Moscow, a bay gelding with a bald face and white legs. He was pulling a regular two-wheeled sulky and driven by James Whelpley for owner Gen. A. C. Dunham of Troy. Neither horse was in good form; Moscow was said to be sick. The most common odds were $50 to $20 for the mare. They got off at four o'clock in front of the grandstand for the best-of-five one-mile heats and a $150 purse. Moscow broke stride right off, so they started again. Moscow took the lead by a length but broke again and fell back by six lengths. He kept breaking, and the Lady sailed on to win the first heat by six lengths in a horrendous 2:52. In the second heat, it was Lady Suffolk who broke stride, but she recovered and "down the backstretch her speed was perfectly tremendous," said the *Herald*. After the quarter pole, both broke. This was pathetic. Lady Suffolk won in 2:54, which would tie for the slowest time in her career even over a real mile.[8]

Moscow now appeared "extremely distressed," and Dunham asked the judges to withdraw him, so the Lady was announced the winner. This brought on a furious protest. Whelpley said he paid the entrance fee, so Dunham had no right to withdraw, and the judges finally agreed. In the third heat, Moscow rushed in front but broke again, then recovered. "The horses moved at a rate which I have never seen equalled," marveled the *Herald*'s man. A cheer went up for Moscow, but "within 15 rods of the stand, he made a terrible bad break, and consequently the mare beat him by a neck." Time: 2:44.

The Old Gray Mare had won the first formal race at Saratoga. They should give her a corner at the National Museum of Racing in Saratoga, with a Stephen Foster soundtrack.

The remainder of the meeting included a race in double harness—between two pairs of trotters—and a return engagement in which the Old Gray Mare beat Moscow again. It was an ambitious if not very competitive meeting. The records show four more days of racing through August 26.[9] There was more to come once the fair opened.

Who should show up for the September fair but two former presidents, "Little Van" and John Tyler, not to mention future president Millard Fillmore, Daniel Webster, and, of course, Barnum's General Tom Thumb. It is not clear whether any of them went to the races, which were slyly advertised as part of the fair program but no less illegal. Van Buren looked "fat and fine" and wept generously, the tears running down his face, at a eulogy for the governor, Silas Wright, who had just died. Reporters leered at Tyler's attractive wife. The fair was a sprawl of agricultural booths and attractions north of East Congress Street extended and west of the track. The crowd proved rather too much even for Saratoga, as mobs of fairgoers overflowed the Schenectady train and then the United States Hotel.[10]

The first race on the five-day program during the fair was won, as expected, by the star of the meeting, Black Hawk, to whom Lady Suffolk would later be bred. But as turf writer Landon Manning was first to notice, there was a more important event that week, a race for "running horses," overlooked by all but Manning. This first official thoroughbred race at Saratoga happened on Thursday, September 16, 1847. Taking the $100 purse was Lady Digby, a New Jersey product who was sired by Monmouth Eclipse out of an imported mare and owned by a Mr. Mack. She beat Disowned and Hopeful in three straight heats over the truncated mile. Times: 1:58, 1:53, 2:02.

So two mares, Lady Suffolk and Lady Digby, won Saratoga's first trotting and thoroughbred races.

After the last race, the correspondent for the *Spirit of the Times* was startled to see a female driver taking Black Bess around the course for exercise. This was another unknown milestone in sports. As a lark, the reporter offered to bet on the driver, a Mrs. Healy, against any other woman. Perhaps to his surprise, that woman quickly emerged in the person of another horseman's wife, Mrs. Elijah Simmons, driving Elias. The newspaper report delicately referred to the women as "Mrs. H——y" and "Mrs. S——s." Then the correspondent insisted "there might be some danger if the dear creatures were to go by themselves," so it was decided each should be accompanied by "a gentleman."

Mrs. Healy threw that insult back in their faces, objecting to the insinuation "that she could not drive these things without a male accompaniment." But it was already arranged; the race was on. Elias won the first heat in 3:10. Again Mrs. Healy objected. As the supercilious correspondent put it, she charged "it was not fair (although I think Mrs. S——s very fair and beautiful) that a gentleman should be telling her how to drive, when to pull, etc." At that, Mrs. Simmons joined in the protest, saying she didn't want anybody riding with her, either, so the men were thrown out. Black Bess took the second heat. No time was given, and there was no third heat.

Lady Suffolk returned to Saratoga two years later, setting the track's probable trotting record of 2:32 for once around, then pulling up lame with a sprained front ankle. Bryan pigheadedly started her for the second heat, causing her such terrible pain that she had to be withdrawn; in fact, the Old Gray Mare was close to being destroyed at Saratoga. Instead, she recovered to conclude one of racing's most extraordinary careers, for she raced on through age twenty. And in 163 starts in seventeen states, she had an amazing ninety victories and fifty-six second-place finishes and was unplaced in only nine races. On top of that, she may have run an equal number of unofficial races and exhibitions. Of her ninety official wins, forty-four were at distances of two to four miles, an unthinkable feat today.

The Old Gray Mare was America's first truly national sports hero, known across the land even by those who cared little about trotting or horses. The country still lacked a national sports program that might produce other such heros; indeed, it had never yet had a two-legged hero, but it did have a man who would try to fill both of those gaps.

5

AMERICA'S FIRST
(TWO-LEGGED) SPORTS HERO

BABY JOHN came out for the bell in Tipperary in 1831 when Ireland was overrun, to credit all the reports, by famine, typhus, England, and bishops. By his second summer, he was in a tide of Irish babies waving their little fists as they sailed this way. For many of the boys, the ring was a way out.

The emerald flow reached flood stage in the upper Hudson. By 1875, for instance, little Saratoga Springs would list no fewer than 1,441 citizens born in Ireland, and its southwest Third Ward would be dubbed "Dublin."[1] Still later in this American game of musical neighborhoods, the Third Ward would become Italian, yet its Irish moniker would stick, and for decades puzzled visitors would ask as they converged on the glorious pasta houses, "But why do you call it Dublin?"

John Morrissey grew up in Troy, topping out around six feet and landing jobs as an ironworker, whorehouse bouncer, and steamboat hand. On the deck of the *City of Troy,* which plied the Hudson back to New York City, he made two life-changing moves: he took up with the captain's daughter, the intelligent Susie Smith, and he got off the boat.[2] Leaving Susie Smith behind, the seventeen-year-old conquered Gotham the usual way, by racking up mistake after mistake, the first being to inquire about work at the Americus Club, 28 Park Row.

It was 1848. "Nativist" political clubs like the Americus were thriving in the cities and recruiting thugs for direct-action operations such as ballot-stuffing. The nativists were American-born, largely of English stock, and Protestant, while their chosen enemies were the foreign-born, especially the Irish Catholics and Germans. The battle was on full bore in this decade after the Irish potato blight, when immigration was quintupling. The immigrants piled into slums, crime shot up, and competition for jobs increased. The reaction produced angry, full-fledged political parties, such as the Native Americans (who, of course, were blithely unaware of the real Native Americans). The inspired drinking traditions of the "wet" Irish and Germans added another issue in the eyes of "dry" nativists. "It is liquor," huffed a temperance-ridden newspaper, "which fills our prisons with Irish culprits, and makes the gallows hideous with so many Catholic murderers."[3] By all logic, this should have deterred a John Morrissey from knocking at the Americus Club, but he probably figured, in an early application of the Saratoga ethic, a dollar was a dollar.

Unfortunately, the club had gotten wind of him from Susie's father, who had bragged around New York about how tough the boy was. A welcome wagon was rolled out by the club's enforcers, among them a prizefighter, "Butcher Bill" Poole, who was remembered in one account as "the most terrible brawler in New York."[4] They wasted no time beating the hick to death, or a facsimile thereof, with "fists, feet, clubs, pitchers, bottles." That he actually survived impressed them mightily, however, and they took him on as an "immigrant-runner." As threatening as the immigrants were, they could provide one thing: votes. The runners gathered the worried strangers off the boats, "ran" them into certain boarding houses and eventually registered them to vote for anti-immigrant candidates they had never heard of. It was their welcome to America.

In his free time, no thoughts of Susie Smith stopped Morrissey from falling into the arms of voluptuous Kate Ridgely, a famous madam, but he did get burned by it. According to an old Morrissey biography, Kate's previous lover, Tom McCann, decided to confront him at a shooting gallery under the St. James Hotel, where the brawlers knocked over a stove and Morrissey got pinned against the spilled hot coals. He declined to shriek and finally threw off McCann, who wound up unconscious on the floor. Morrissey had won his first public fight.[5]

He moved up again by becoming assistant manager of John Petrie's gaming house on Church Street. Here, at the feet, or fingers, of banker Dad Cunningham, he could master the faro table and roulette, monte and dice. And he may have visited that siren across the Hudson, the Hoboken track, with its hulking timber grandstands that anticipated Saratoga's. Having tasted blood, politics, gambling and both kinds of love, he was a long way from Tipperary, but opportunity knocked again. With Dad, he followed the forty-niners to California, where they found work running a gambling house. The dark young Irishman, a reminder of the Spanish Armada, also hooked up with a sixteen-year-old named Lolita Fernandez.

California improved his resumé. First, he made his debut in bare-knuckle prizefighting against a seasoned Scot, George Thompson. On fight day, August 31, 1852, Morrissey discovered an athlete could have something extra going for him: the crowd. It was a lesson that would pay off. To the screaming Americans and Mexicans, the curlyhead was plainly likeable, and Thompson was cowed from the start. The Scot did draw first blood but was thrown to the ground from a clinch. Under the London Prize Ring Rules they were using, that was legal and ended the round. Back for more, Thompson was knocked down by a blow to the jaw. Like a fall, a knockdown ended a round. Finally, in the eleventh, Thompson was disqualified for grabbing Morrissey by his drawers and slinging him to the ground; that you could not do. Morrissey won $2,000 and a name for himself.

California also introduced him to winning at the track. He pocketed $5,000 by picking the black mare Carmencita over the big bay Alameda in a ten mile match race. Perhaps it was at this rough course on the Santa Barbara plains that he conceived modern Saratoga. For Dad, it merely paid their way to New York; he'd had it with the gold rush.

Back east, life acquired purpose. Morrissey rushed to Susie, who had moved to New York with her father. He organized a gang for the Catholic mayoral candidate, Fernando Wood, and savored revenge as his goons faced down those of the Americus Club. Wood lost, but Morrissey gained a political sponsor. He even went so far as to

John Morrissey. Currier and
Ives portrayed the founder of
Saratoga thoroughbred racing
wearing a Stars-and-Stripes
sash as undefeated boxing
champion, 1860. *Library of
Congress Photo.*

challenge Yankee Sullivan for the championship of America, promising Susie he
would marry her when it was over.

No history of America recounts this New York State title bout of October 12, 1853,
though it was called one of the "bloodiest battles ever fought on the American
continent."[6] They put up the ring a hundred miles north of the city, a quarter-mile
from Boston Corners station on the Harlem Railroad. Morrissey's men hung his
colors on one stake—a scarf bearing the Stars and Stripes. Already he was the bud-
ding promoter. On the opposite stake, Sullivan's men tied a black kerchief, which by
the conventions of the day meant one thing: "victory or death." A few thousand
spectators assembled, many of them probably quite respectable, unlike boxing, which
was illegal in New York State.

Sullivan looked like his opponent's father. He was several years older and reportedly a drinker and thief, but the years had taught him viciousness, and his speed
hadn't deserted him. The kid was three inches taller and twenty pounds heavier. The
London Rules had just been revised, so this was a milestone in American boxing.
They still allowed wrestling, hitting a helpless opponent, and fighting to the finish,

and a round still ended when a man was thrown or knocked down. But the revisions legalized intentional falls and clinches (which persist today) and gave each side an umpire, a species Morrissey had never seen. Maybe he grimaced when he saw the umpire Sullivan had chosen: Bill Poole, he of the Americus Club beating. When would he pay the bastard back?

Round one. As the Englishman's knuckles caught his cheekbone, Morrissey bled right away, and he kept on getting mangled. His face and chest were smeared with blood by round four. But it was Sullivan who was knocked to the grass to end the fifth and then fell again with his own wild swing. Sullivan, knowing something about young men, went after Morrissey's face, turning it into an oozing turnip. By the twenty-first round, the old fox's legendary speed was just that, a legend, and his left eye was closed; in the twenty-third, he got decked by a tremendous right. Still the old man went on, growing bumps on the young one's face. "No modern battle with gloves could produce such punishment," Morrissey biographer Jack Kofoed said.

By the thirty-third round, they were pulp. Morrissey staggered—hemorrhaging, knees shaking, Yankee still pounding—but would not drop. He was too proud. He was ready to spend the rest of his life like this. In the thirty-sixth, he determined to catch the old bandit, and did. He threw his arms around him, lifting him up and against the ropes. The seconds rushed in, and a brawl ensued, until referee Charley Allaire stopped it. A break between rounds lasted thirty seconds. Then the fighters had eight seconds to return to "scratch," a mark in the middle of the ring. Charley told them to come out, but only Morrissey moved. So after thirty-six illegal rounds, he was presented with the belt of the Champion of America. He was twenty-two.

A year later, he made the papers again with a monumental street fight. Revealing the spirit of the time, Horace Greeley's *New York Tribune* that day also carried an elegant piece on the Crimean War by its London stringer, an exile named Karl Marx. The coauthor of the *Communist Manifesto* thought he could rescue the John Morrisseys of the world from ignorant, dirty, exploitative capitalism. It was the police reporters who got to write this story, however, and they applied adjectives like that not to capitalism but to Morrissey. In three separate accounts, the *Tribune* told of the July night when he confronted Bill Poole.[7] Its newsworthiness was enhanced by the fact that Morrissey often packed a pistol and could summon a gang at the drop of an insult. Poole, too, had an army of followers.

The previous night, as one reporter put it, "Poole, Morrissey and others of that ilk, were carousing together at the City Hotel." Morrissey told a man to fork over money from a bet. Poole told him not to. That led to words, and they agreed to fight the next day, at fifty dollars a side. The news must have flashed to every tavern in town: "New York's toughest streetfighter vs. heavyweight champion of America." The *Tribune*:

BRUTAL STREET FIGHT

New York was thoroughly disgraced by an exhibition of this kind yesterday morning by two fighting characters, Poole and Morrissey, at the foot of Amos St.

Poole drove up in a light wagon. Morrissey followed. "Just think of it," said one of Greeley hacks, "two notorious ruffians, whose lives have been nothing but a series of outrages and brutalities . . . accompanied by five hundred thieves, burglars, thimble-riggers, pickpockets and 'gentleman sympathizers.'" Thimble-rigging was the shell game.

The two started to "fight, strike, bite, scratch, kick, gouge and gnaw each other like dogs." Morrissey "led off with a sharp blow upon Poole's right eye." Butcher Bill "chopped and seized Morrissey by the waist, and threw him heavily," then attacked him "with fists and feet, beating him in the most frightful manner, gouging out his right eye, the sight of which, it is thought, he will lose." Poole poured it on, "cutting head, face, ears" and in five minutes "so disfigured him that his identity is said to have departed." Morrissey finally "cried for quarter and was released." But as he got up, he shouted to a friend, "Johnny Ling, give me the pistol!"

Ling reached for it, but one of Poole's thugs knocked him down. "The fight now became general. . . . Morrissey, blind of both eyes, was placed in a wagon and driven home." Poole and pals rowed to Coney Island "to make merry on the stakes," celebrating so hard one of them was killed in a friendly fracas. As for Morrissey's right eye, an ophthalmological view is that pressure probably caused it to bulge, making it look as if it really had popped out.[8] Some time later, he strode into Stanwix Hall, pulled a pistol on Poole and squeezed the trigger. It didn't go off, police broke it up, and John went home to intelligent Susie. But two of his gang returned and fatally shot Poole, who supposedly said, "I die a true American." Many must have found it hard to quibble with that. Morrissey and Poole did have real power in America. The funeral cortege was led by two thousand Poole Association members, followed by four thousand "United Americans" from other cities, a thousand Philadelphians, and thousands of citizens preceding the hearse. After the procession, they were attacked by Morrisseyites armed with stones, bricks, and pistols. The Poole marchers countercharged with bayonets and got the better of it.

Why didn't Morrissey end up like Poole? He always went home to Susie, whom he had, indeed, married. They lived with the captain at 55 Hudson Street. So he had begun to make his own luck. This son of an alcoholic learned to master alcohol. Arrested for pulling a gun, he learned that he had to cash in a political chip to get off. And he moved up a notch politically, backing Wood again for mayor and serving as an adviser, telling him not to grovel for Native American support but to stick with the immigrants. Wood won and launched New York on one of its most corrupt mayoral regimes ever, quite an accomplishment. It set up Morrissey as a minor light in Tammany politics. He began making money as well. Petrie took him in as a partner, and his notoriety boosted business fivefold. He was soon starched, suited, and bediamonded. He would fight one more time, but promised Susie it would be the last.

Morrissey's 1858 defense against John Camel Heenan would be America's most important bout yet. It was also one of the first modern sports news stories. It was one thing for the New York press to cover, as it did, the sixteen New York baseball teams that formed the misnamed "National Association" that season, but it was another for Bennett's *Herald,* the sports-heavy *New York Clipper,* the Philadelphia-based *Spirit of the Times,* and the illustrated *Leslie's Weekly* to dispatch reporters all the way to Canada. The fight was booked at Long Island Point on the other side of Lake Erie, beyond the reach of New York sheriffs. And it had another, surprising distinction: Morrissey was described at the time as "probably the best-trained man that ever entered the American prize-ring."[9]

His training program reveals a thoroughly modern man, and suggests that if sports history had not been buried, Americans might not have had to reinvent the fitness craze. He trained at Lansingburg, New York, now part of Troy. Bennett's reporter found him "in splendid fettle," with "his broad shoulders, tapering waist, massive arms and upper works being supported by the strongest-looking pair of pins we ever saw."[10]

He got up at five, had sherry with beaten eggs in it, and headed out for a five- or six-mile walk. Then it was back to the Abbey Hotel and his makeshift gym, which, in contrast to the grimy histories of the antebellum North, seems like some orderly, futuristic setting. He boxed a sandbag hanging from the ceiling and used three or four sets of dumbbells and pulleys. After a rubdown, he breakfasted on broiled chicken or mutton with no seasoning, a cup of tea, and a slice of toast. Then he took a rest, usually just a chat with his English trainer, two assistants, and friends. At eight-thirty, he went out again for an eight- to ten-mile walk, followed by a half-hour with rope, bells, weights, and bag and another rubdown. Lunch could be beefsteak and currant bread, followed by a glass of sherry. Then he did six or eight more miles, sparred with an assistant, hit the bells, pulleys, rope, and bag, and got a third rubdown. Supper was broiled chicken, a cup of tea without sugar, and a slice of toast, which he soaked in the tea. There could be no spices or seasoning, and little or no water—the reverse of today's regimens—on the belief he would have to work it off. After supper, he rowed or walked four miles and wound it up with a hundred-yard sprint at his top speed, which professional footracers called astonishing. He had a fourth rubdown. Then it was off "to his virtuous pillow, to sleep like a top." Here lay not the shadowy, gambling, fighting political hack of Saratoga legend but perhaps our first modern athlete.

There was one other historic facet to this bout. No other has pitted fighters with such similar backgrounds. Like Morrissey, Heenan was Irish, and his parents were also named Tim and Mary. Like the Morrisseys, the Heenans had their son in Templemore, Tipperary, and named him John. They, too, sailed to New York. They settled in West Troy (Watervliet today). The two Johns worked for the Johnson and Cox iron stove company and fought in the same gang. But one day there was a cock fight, and Tim Morrissey's bird murdered Tim Heenan's.[11] From that moment, the two hated each other's guts. John and John inherited that hatred, yet their similarities multiplied. Young Heenan went west, where he found work as a ship mechanic in Benicia, California. Heenan, who towered even over Morrissey, also became a prize-fighter—"The Benicia Boy." He then returned to New York, where he, like Morrissey, became a dubious celebrity, one of the lovers of the well-hormoned actress Adah Isaacs Menken. So here they were, two huge clones. Round two of the cock fight.

October 20, 1858, brought everybody to Lake Erie, the reporters piling into top-heavy steamboats for the dicey crossing. In another lesson stored for Saratoga, their importance was probably obvious to Morrissey, since he was their favorite victim. Among them was an eighteen-year-old smart-aleck artist Morrissey would never get rid of: Tommy Nast.[12] As he strolled with friends for hours on the beach, Morrissey kept repeating something interesting: he felt like a racehorse. He almost certainly knew of the great English expert Francis Dowling's 1841 boxing manual, and Dowling's advice that "a man put to training is like a colt to be broken in."[13] Dowling even advocated a body or flesh brush, saying: "In training racehorses, indeed, friction is much better understood and more practised than in the training of men." Whether Morrissey brushed his skin is not known, but he was fit, down to 173 pounds, twenty under Heenan. By contrast, the Benicia Boy had been bedridden for a week with an ugly ankle wound. He limped through the sand, his shoe scraping the sore.

Round one. With his usual overconfidence, Morrissey swung left and right to little effect against the man called the fastest of his time, and Heenan cut him under the left eye. Round three saw the clinching hulks crash down, Morrissey on top. After five more rounds, Morrissey's fists rained down on Heenan, who crumpled and was thrown, the champ falling on top again. Round eleven. Morrissey connected, Heenan swung wildly and collapsed in a heap, then struggled to his corner, sitting on his second's knee, his eyes closed—exhausted, and finished. After twenty-one minutes, Morrissey stood there, his attempt to smile "a ghastly thing to see. His eyes were nearly closed, his mouth cut, his lips and tongue swollen, his nose literally battered flat to his face"; he was "a tottering tower of blood but victorious."[14] He retired as undefeated champion of America.

Morrissey watched with extreme interest as Heenan, rather than himself, went on to become America's first (two-legged) national sports hero, for the Lake Erie coverage was nothing next to the front-page blowout for Heenan's next bout. The fight of the century, it would also have been the American sports event of the century except it did not happen in America. On April 17, 1860, Heenan, champion of America by default, fought Tom Sayers, champion of England, for the world title at Farnborough in Hampshire. Morrissey, the most famous American at ringside, created a minor scandal by rejecting sports patriotism and siding with Sayers. He rubbed it in, too, backing Sayers's bets on the fight and appearing with him at the Newmarket races.

Boxing and racing went together hoof and glove in England, and would at Saratoga as well. "Horse-racing and prize-fighting traditionally shared common ground," an English observer has written. "Pugilists performed at the fairs which accompanied race meetings; jockeys and stable lads frequented the ringside. To a large extent, the followings of the two sports were identical."[15] In fact, Sayers, who worked comfortably around stables and was quite "relaxed in the company of dumb beasts," made it a point to train at Newmarket.[16]

Heenan and the Brit bled through forty-two rounds, two hours and twenty minutes—to a draw. And anybody would have come to the same conclusion: Morrissey now had only to fight Heenan again for unending fame and fortune. A letter over Morrissey's name soon appeared in the *Herald*, declaring, "as it seems paradoxical to me and my friends to see a man dubbed champion of the world who has never won a fight in the ring, I will give him the chance he wants." It caused tremendous excitement—for twenty-four hours. Morrissey pronounced it a fake, writing the *Herald*: "I am not training for any fight, but am here for my health, and have business of more importance on hand than preparing for such a contest." "Here" was Saratoga Springs.[17]

"Business of more importance" in Saratoga? For one thing, he had begun creating an empire far beyond the mere sports bars modern athletes covet. He had graduated to owning his Manhattan gambling houses, the most lavish of which was 5 West Twenty-fourth Street, where over eight years he would earn $2,000 a week and become America's best-known gambler. Now he was expanding to Saratoga Springs, where he opened a house on Matilda Street (Woodlawn Avenue today). At the same time, he began cultivating excellence—not excellence, actually, but supremacy, the idea of the best, the crème de la crème, the nonpareil. Nothing else, and nobody else, would do.

Some chemical imperative propelled Morrissey toward people at the top. In early 1861, he met the president-elect, who had run into an icy mob in Democratic New York. Abraham Lincoln "scanned the vast and silent crowd," noted a reporter-poet named Walt Whitman.[18] "There was a sulky silence . . . not a voice, not a sound!" Certainly, the last celebrity expected at the Astor House reception was John Morrissey, the Tammany Democrat who had worked against Lincoln in the election, yet there he was. Lincoln, at six-four, could peer down at the brawler, who was about five-eleven and twenty-two years younger; the lanky westerner discovered a "stout, good-looking Irishman" with glossy black curls and full beard. The latter's 185 pounds were encased in "faultless black broad-cloth," a $5,000 diamond pin blazing from his shirtfront, set off by diamonds on the sleeves. He would have seemed more at home in Barnum's office across the street. But were these two such opposites? A newspaper dared compare them: "[Morrissey] was once a poor man—so was Abe Lincoln, Morrissey was a mechanic—Lincoln was a rail splitter."[19] Morrissey even followed Lincoln to Washington for the inauguration. The crowds outside Willard's Hotel, Lincoln's headquarters, scanned all the tall men as they came out, hoping to get a glimpse of him. But he rarely emerged, and a reporter said they had to settle for Morrissey in a stovepipe hat.[20]

Now the roulette wheel in his brain stopped at one of those ideas so obvious nobody ever thinks of them. First, he may have thought, consider the Springs. The place had fended off all competition to remain the biggest resort in the land. "World renowned Saratoga," as Gleason's magazine had put it in 1852, "stands the first among the watering places of our country."[21] And it was still inventing the America of the future.

- In 1853, a chef at Moon's Lake House invented a new way to fry potatoes. He made them into ultra-crisp slices, later dubbed "Saratoga Chips," then "potato chips," which President Ronald Reagan would find time to declare America's first snack. (Moon's was two miles east of the trotting course, on today's Route 9P, where a latter-day Moon's succeeds it.)[22]

- By 1857, everybody was making fun of the "Saratoga trunk," which had gotten so big one cartoon suggested it would make a good portable dining room but which did not, as widely thought now, have to have a bombé lid.[23]

In 1860, Appleton's Hand-book suggested "Saratoga . . . probably always will be the most famous place of summer resort in the United States."[24]

Next, consider the crowd. Saratoga was not only the longtime refuge of "Commodore" Cornelius Vanderbilt, the steamboat king and contender for richest man in

Moon's Lake House, home of the potato chip. From *Leslie's*, 1862. *Courtesy of the author.*

America, but a favored getaway of another contender, A. T. Stewart, the New York drygoods king and "father of the department store." If there was anything Vanderbilt liked as much as wheeling and dealing, it was speed. Besides steamboats, which he had often raced himself, that meant horses, and he would have his famous trotters join him at the Springs.

More than ever, fast horses were a Saratoga fixation. The most celebrated trotters in America followed the Old Gray Mare to the Saratoga Trotting Course, notably the wildly popular Flora Temple, Stephen Foster's "bob-tailed nag." None of it was legal, but the basis of legalized racing was laid in an 1854 New York law allowing the formation of associations "to improve the breed of horses." Thoroughbreds continued to make occasional appearances at the Springs. The fabled Lexington came up in 1854 to rest up before a Long Island event that never came off. In 1858, the Trotting Course staged hurdle races, among the earliest ever held in America. Around town, the private road teams and turnouts, a reporter from Washington observed, were "among the best in the country." A little jealous, he added that "dashing" had become "the life led by every snob of either sex who habitually comes here."[25]

Commodore Vanderbilt. From *Harper's Weekly*, 1859. *Courtesy of the author.*

So the roulette wheel in John Morrissey's head stopped at this idea: take the biggest resort in the land and add the biggest sport, horse racing. The result? A Saratoga race meeting of the highest order.

Morrissey's races would have to be for thoroughbreds, of course: the real thing. Poor management had driven the "running races" almost to extinction in the Northeast, but they thrived in the antebellum South, where the establishment carried on its chivalric pageant. Meetings were staged at such glamour spots as New Orleans, Savannah, Charleston, Mobile, Memphis, and Gallatin. It all ended one April morn after the meeting at Mobile. At 4:30, Gen. Pierre Gustave T. Beauregard's first shell arched over Charleston Harbor, exploding above Fort Sumter. As it happened, Ballston's Abner Doubleday surfaced here as the Union officer who fired the first shot back, but he still had not made his mark on American sports. In a sort of crinoline daze, Memphis and Gallatin went ahead with their spring racing calendars. And the Southern temple of racing, the great Metairie track at New Orleans, with its state-of-the-art brick and iron grandstand, stayed alive for a December meeting.[26] Then the curtain came down. The pageant was over. Men and horses were needed at the front.

Thoroughbred racing in America, North and South, was dead. It would fall to John Morrissey and a few others to revive it, and invent national spectator sports in America in the middle of a war.

Like Lincoln, he may not have had God on his side, but he had to have Kentucky. The border state was subjected to punishing raids by the rebel John Morgan astride the thoroughbred Glencoe, probably by the fabled sire of that name. But the federal troops there held on, and so did Kentucky's breeders, thanks in good part to the immortal stallion Lexington. "Lexington and his blood," said John Hervey, were the "one great vital force" that survived from antebellum racing. Another turf historian, William H. P. Robertson, called him simply "America's greatest horse." After winning six of seven races, Lexington had begun his spectacular career as a sire and established Woodburn Farm as the country's greatest breeding operation. Kentucky's stables were an international operation as well, replenishing their stock from Britain, and the abbreviation "Imp." would appear before the names of many imported racers throughout the 1860s. Now, however, Kentucky had to look northward for buyers, tracks, and safe havens for their stables. The scene was bleak.

There was just one one-day thoroughbred meeting in the Northeast in 1861, at the Fashion Course, which was principally for trotters, in Newton, Long Island. The next year, however, a group of Kentuckians and Northerners slated twenty-four racing days. They split them among Philadelphia, Jamesburg, New Jersey (near Trenton), the Union Course in Queens, Pawtucket, Rhode Island, and Boston. The year 1863 opened with five racing days in New Jersey, five at Philadelphia, and three at the Centreville trotting track in Queens.[27]

Even as the far-off cannon sounded, something like a modern sports schedule was being created. To the 1863 circuit, it was Morrissey's dream to add not just another stop for horsemen and gamblers but nothing less than the "Bath of America," that microcosm of America on vacation. Here, he gambled, sports would go public, and stay public, war or no war.

6

THE BIRTH OF AMERICAN SPORTS

ON THE FOURTH OF JULY, 1863, twenty-nine thousand hollow-eyed rebels trudged out of the river port of Vicksburg, Mississippi, stacked arms, and surrendered to Maj. Gen. Ulysses S. Grant. With that, the Mississippi was lost to the Yankees and the Confederacy was sliced in two. That same night Gen. Robert E. Lee had been stopped at Gettysburg, where more than seven thousand men were killed in the bloodiest battle of the war.[1] On the thirteenth, Manhattan exploded in the worst riot America had ever seen, leaving 105 people dead. The rioters, at least two-thirds of them Irish, rampaged through the streets for four days against America's first modern draft. Enraged also by Lincoln's Emancipation Proclamation, they lynched several black people. They torched the pro-Republican *New York Tribune* building, chanting, "We'll hang old Horace Greeley to a sour-apple tree!" And they assaulted men who looked well off, screaming, "There goes a $300 man!"—a reference to the official fee for a draft deferment.

They did not chase down slick John Morrissey, who slipped into town from Saratoga on the third day and made his way to Twenty-fourth Street; after all, he had been one of them. If his luck had been different, he might have been plotting an attack at this very moment on the *Times,* where one of its owners, Leonard Jerome, was manning an army machine gun in a north window.[2] Instead, he lunched in his boarded-up salon with Col. Edward Jardine, the commander of an artillery battery against the rioters, and a Saratoga habitué himself. That night, Jardine was shot in the thigh and briefly held by rioters. One version had it that while two soldiers with him were clubbed to death, the colonel was freed because he was a friend of Morrissey's.[3]

It might seem shocking that in the midst of the crisis, Morrissey was about to open a thoroughbred race meeting at the Springs. In fact, he was perfectly in step with the millions who would never appear in the Civil War epics. On July 22, for instance, Manhattanites ferried to the Elysian Fields to watch the Mutual of New York team lose, 10 to 9, to the Eckford nine of Brooklyn, "acknowledged champions of the base-ball world." None of those five thousand wanted to fight or riot, except over a call in the eighth.[4]

Upriver the next day, Josh Ward was outrowing "the Pittsburgh boy," Jim Hamill, in a five-mile battle for the championship of America. The crowds packed Poughkeepsie's hotels and piers. Nobody appeared to mind their absence from the fighting; after all, America's wars had traditionally been fought by volunteers. Indeed, most of those targeted by the new draft avoided it, and it accounted for only two percent of Union forces. The draft dodgers, and the millions of men and women not subject to conscription, made up the forgotten majority.[5]

It is true "a very large crowd" with a clear idea of what was at stake ventured forth on August 1 to watch General Butler fight one of the supreme battles of his career. But this was not Maj. Gen. Benjamin "Beast" Butler, recently relieved as military governor of New Orleans. This was General Butler the black gelding. Naming horses after people was a well-intentioned practice, but somewhat confusing when both were in town. That Saturday, while the human General Butler attended an officer's funeral in Manhattan, the horse assaulted the three-mile record of 7 minutes, 32½ seconds in a trot against time at the Fashion Course on Long Island. The betting was heavy, and in a thrilling finish, the clock won by a second and a half.[6]

An estimated sixteen thousand people repaired to Central Park that day, and the resorts at Newport and in the New Hampshire mountains were booming. But the greatest escape was underway at Saratoga Springs, although the thought that it would plunge the whole country into a new, sports-mad era occurred to nobody, except probably the instigator. Needing no further introduction in the newspapers, he was simply, as the *Times* put it, "John Morrissey, known the country over."

He had inserted an ad for three days of racing in the May editions of the *Spirit of the Times*.[7] The response from stable owners was good enough to extend the meeting to four days, with two races a day. Another ad, in the *Daily Saratogian*, proclaimed: "Running Races! AT SARATOGA." It suggested grand ambitions and even seemed to look beyond the war: "All sections of the North and West, and some portions of the South, will be represented by their best horses, and Canada will also contend for some of the various purses." It was proudly signed: "John Morrissey, Proprietor."[8]

Overnight, America's social mecca became the capital of another subset, the turf crowd, with its own subspecies, such as the New York City gamblers. It was another preview of *Guys and Dolls*. "I think the races will be very fine, sir," said an innocent lady on the Hudson steamer, "for I am informed that all the great betting men of New York are going up on the boat." Even this tough crowd was impressed with the predecessor to the Thomas E. Dewey Thruway known as the Hudson River. One wrote dreamily about "winding in and out among the beautiful hills" and hearing "the rumble of bowls" played by Hendrick Hudson "for the entertainment of honest Rip Van Winkle." He failed to give the odds. The city of Troy brought them back to earth with the railroad and an omen—"a pickpocket, who had relieved a gentleman on the train of his watch and purse."

Two blocks from the Saratoga station, this crowd found a street far more impressive than any strip in Manhattan. Saratoga's Broadway was a canyon flanked by magnificent elms and gargantuan hotels and jammed with men in expensive black broadcloth and women in the latest fashions. The rage in carriage blankets was crimson velvet lined with satin and edged with gold lace. The most stunning driver was a Mrs. Reynolds, who put her servant behind her in the "box" and drove her dashing ponies herself.

One gent in the turf set was amazed to find two thousand people staying at just one hotel, Marvin's United States, still capital of the sports crowd. William H. Vander-

Running Races!
AT SARATOGA.

The Summer Meeting, over the Saratoga Course, will be held on

Monday, Tuesday, Wednesday & Thursday,
AUGUST 3d, 4th, 5th & 6th.
Two Races each Day!

FIRST DAY—*First Race:* Sweepstake for 3 year olds, MILE HEATS, $200 entrance ; $50 forfeit ; $300 added, &c. Closed with 8 entries.
Second Race: Purse $300 ; DASH OF TWO MILES, for all ages.
SECOND DAY—*First Race:* Purse $300 ; MILE HEATS, for all ages.
Second Race: Handicap, DASH OF 2½ MILES ; $40 entrance ; $20 forfeit ; $400 added. Forfeits to go to second horse, if three or more start. Closed with 5 entries.
THIRD DAY—*First Race:* Sweepstake for 3 year olds ; DASH OF TWO MILES ; $200 entrance ; $100 forfeit ; $300 added. Closed with 5 entries.
Second Race: Purse $100, MILE HEATS, BEST THREE IN FIVE, for all ages, &c.
FOURTH DAY—*First Race:* Purse $500 ; TWO MILE HEATS, for all ages, &c.
Second Race: Purse $200, DASH OF 1¼ MILES, for all ages, &c.

☞ Races to commence each day, at 11¼ o'clock.

Cards of Admission, $1,00.

For particulars, see Posters and Bills of each day.
All sections of the North and West, and some portions of the South will be represented by their best horses, and Canada will also contend for some of the various purses. Excellent racing is anticipated.

JOHN MORRISSEY,
Proprietor.

The curtain rises. Advertisement for America's first national thoroughbred race meeting in the *Daily Saratogian, 1863. Courtesy of the author.*

bilt, the eldest son, had checked in on Friday night, July 31. Father had just made his first major railroad killing by cornering the Harlem and Hudson River lines, and W. H. had captured ten thousand Hudson shares himself for a side profit of $270,000.

The States would register no fewer than 3,681 guests over the seventy-five-day "season." Two hotels were bigger. The five-story Union Hall, a block south, was probably the largest in the country, its sixty-seven-yard dining room along Congress Street seating 1,000. It would register 4,813 guests that season. Across the street, Congress Hall would check in 4,236. Four other hotels would welcome more than 1,000 guests each.

New to Broadway was another horsy subset, the Kentuckians, led by none other than John Clay, son of the "Great Compromiser" Henry Clay. They brought "western" color, as did arrivals from Missouri, Wisconsin, Illinois, and Ohio. On discovering Congress Spring, according to one reporter, they were not impressed: "We heard one or two Western gentlemen declare that, for 'steady drinking,' there is nothing at Saratoga equal to the favorite, medicinal beverage of Bourbon County, Kentucky."

Trainers, jockeys, and stable help formed a third subgroup of the traveling turf crowd. Many were African Americans who, of course, faced incredible odds in America.[9] Slavery remained legal even in Unionist Kentucky through this and two more Saratoga racing seasons. Still, they could celebrate the news of the heroic fighting by black troops at Fort Wagner a few days before. Now blacks and whites would be competing together in America's first racially integrated sport; they had been doing it for years in the South, but never in a national spotlight.

The most riveting arrivals, however, were none of the above.

"String after string of the best racers in America have lately wended their way to the Springs," said one reporter. In a stroke of showmanship, they were paraded past the piazzas on Saturday, August 1, each "ridden by a man or boy in racing costume."[10] The standouts among the twenty-seven entered in the races by fourteen stables included:

• Captain Moore, a bay (reddish-brown) colt, owned by James Watson of New Jersey and the best three-year-old of the year;

• Lizzie W., a dark bay by Imp. Scythian. She was purchased in Kentucky by Dr. J. W. Weldon, a Georgia gambler, and trained by the African-American Bill Bird;

• Mamona, a five-year-old bay mare, holder of the American mile record of 1:44½. She was owned by Capt. T. G. Moore of Kentucky (for whom the above colt was named);

• Thunder, a striking four-year-old gray, owned by Dennis Reedy of Canada. Only he could beat Jerome Edgar, who was there, too, under a new name; and

• the former Jerome Edgar, just purchased from Clay for $3,000 by Morrissey, who rechristened him John B. Davidson to honor a backer and maybe to hide his talents. Two days later, this four-year-old bay would be a wreck, shrunken, suffering from a cold, and, according to Clay, worked almost to death.

Organized betting on the races in America was revived in the basement of the United States Hotel that Saturday night. Presiding was Dr. Robert Underwood of Lexington, founding father of modern bookies. A veterinarian, he was also a breeder and seller, offering five colts at the Springs, which makes him a founder of the Saratoga yearling sales as well. Above all, he was the "prince of pool sellers."

The "pool sales" were auctions, and only big spenders could play. The players could not simply buy a ticket on any entry they liked. Dr. Underwood would call for "bids," or bets, on each horse. The top bids on all the horses made up the total to be won (or "bought"), minus three percent for the doctor. A bettor in a race scheduled for Thursday had to bid $435 to get the ticket on Thunder, $425 for John Morgan, or $210 for Sympathy. It made for a total of $1,070 and a pool of $1,038. As the bettors shouted out their bids in the basement of the States, Dr. Underwood "sold" as many pools as he could. But the cost kept many out of it, and there were other drawbacks for the players. For one thing, the odds weren't known until all bets were made. For example, the above pool finally made Sympathy a four-to-one longshot. And the richest bettors could monopolize the logical choices, though it would reduce their winnings.[11]

On Monday morning, August 3, 1863, modern Saratoga Springs was born with the opening of its first thoroughbred racing meeting. Union Hall was racking up a one-day record of 184 checkins. Cornelius Jeremiah Vanderbilt, a gambling addict, joined his older brother at the States. Leonard Jerome, the *Times* stockholder and a partner in the Commodore's railroad deals, registered there, too. By 10:30 A.M., carriage after carriage began depositing some of the wealthiest people in the country at Morrissey's trysting place, which was nothing more than the sixteen-year-old Saratoga Trotting Course. The crowd grew to more than three thousand. They paid one dollar for a "card of admission," so Morrissey immediately recouped his $2,700 in purses and additions to stakes. The women, said the patronizing *Spirit of the Times,* were "graced with every charm of beauty and elegant attire." They had no place to sit, however, and had to watch from their carriages. The track no longer had a grandstand. It was clear that the trotting course had everything wrong with it. There were no good views of the track, for it vanished behind small pines, a barn, stables, and other buildings. The turns were ridiculously sharp, and while mile tracks that only approximated a mile were common, this one was 297 yards short.[12] Still, the purses, the sweepstakes money put up by entrants, and the competition were quite intriguing.

There would be two races a day, starting with a best-of-three one-mile heats, followed by a two-mile dash. It would be misleading to say there were "only" two races daily, as each day's heats and longer dashes equaled a five-race card today. And what the animals went through is hard to imagine today, when a mile and quarter is a major test. A nine-mile race—three heats of three miles each—was still common then. The century's "classic," the four-mile race in multiple heats that often totaled twenty miles, was falling out of fashion.

Saratoga's historic opening race was a winner-take-all sweepstakes for three-year-olds, with $300 added by Morrissey. It cost $200 to get in. Eight owners entered, but six bowed out, each paying a forfeit. The two entry fees totaled $400 and the six forfeits $300, so Captain Moore and Lizzie W. headed into the second great Battle of Saratoga for a purse of $1,000. Nobody seemed to notice it, but Captain Moore's jockey had the same surname as "Gentleman Johnny" Burgoyne, the general defeated at the original battle in that valley visible through the trees to the east. Billy Burgoyne had fractured his leg, so many were surprised to see him there. He and his tack weighed all of ninety pounds, including a five-pound penalty. In tune with the rest of white America, the *Spirit of the Times* brushed off Lizzie W.'s rider as "the one-eyed black boy, Sewell."

11:30 A.M., Monday, August 3, 1863. "The horses went off at the word," said a local reporter, using a cliché that later announcers would reduce to: "They're off!" The word was "Go!"[13]

Captain Moore, on the rail, led to the turn, then it was Lizzie W. She was up two lengths into the backstretch. Going behind the barn at the far turn, they were neck and neck. First to emerge was bird-sized Billy, his canary cap glinting in the swelter-ing sun. At the finish, it was Captain Moore in 1:29½, which the *Spirit* projected to a 1:47½ mile.

The horses cooled off before the crowd for twenty minutes, then were off in the second heat. Lizzie's Sewell had been told to let Captain Moore lead to the home stretch, and the colt had a length going behind the blind side of the barn, but there the one-eyed jockey was king, and it was Lizzie W. by a neck.

In the decisive heat, Sewell was again told to yield, and the captain opened four or five lengths. One more time, he got his education out behind the barn. As the first national report on a race here would reveal, "the filly collared him, and the champion of the year took to the sulks. In the stretch, he would not run a bit, and Lizzie W. beat him."

★   ★   ★   ★

So a Burgoyne was again defeated at Saratoga, and as the years would show, it was another turning point, the beginning of American sports as a national phenome-non. It might also be noted that the first race on a formal course at Saratoga, the first official thoroughbred race, and now the first race of a thoroughbred meeting were all won by mares: Lady Suffolk, Lady Digby, and the not-so-ladylike Lizzie W.

Before the second race, Dr. Underwood's "clear, ringing voice" rose from the crowd. Morrissey's ad had announced "No gambling will be allowed on the Course," but it was hilarious coming from the most notorious gambling operator in the coun-try. What it meant was no gambling other than Dr. Underwood's operation and side bets that could not be stopped. The proprietor's nervousness reflected a loud debate. Betting was part and parcel of almost all sports and threatened to turn baseball games into brawls.[14] Morrissey found it wise to promise in his local ad: "An efficient police . . . will maintain the strictest order." But to come right out and ban betting on the races would ruin them, said the *Spirit of the Times*. "When we see a fire that won't burn anybody, we expect to see first-rate racing without betting," it commented. "The ladies, who would bet if they could"—and, as we shall see, almost certainly did—"and the gentlemen who abstain from betting on principle, know well enough" that a race that does not "fire up the speculative enterprise of betting men is likely to be a very slow and dull affair."

The two-mile dash brought out the famous Gilpatrick. Now forty-five or forty-six, he had replaced Cornelius aboard Boston and piloted his fabulous son Lexington. Here his mount was Morrissey's shriveled John B. Davidson. In a three-way finish, Davidson, Thunder, and Sympathy "rolled by, all in distress and their jockeys whip-ping and spurring. It was a long time in doubt, but the filly won by a neck."

Some five thousand saw five-year-old John Morgan (named for the rebel raider who had just been captured in Ohio) take the mile heats on Tuesday. Then they played the first Saratoga handicap. The track handicapper was a new figure. He was brought in to level the competition by assigning weights to the horses according to their presumed abilities, which in turn attracted entries and increased the betting.

Morrissey's handicapper was Henry Price McGrath, his former gambling partner, who had gone back to Kentucky to become a breeder. McGrath was so good at assigning weights that four horses alternated as the favorite in the pools. As the field of five rounded the hairpin track two and a half times, Burgoyne, his jacket "gleaming like gold in the sunshine," was on Punch. A reporter kissed off "the darkey Sewell" on Seven Oaks—African Americans would get that for more than a century—but he won again. Well, "Gentleman Johnny" had lost twice here, too.

The next day, four thousand spectators did the running. No sooner had Billy broken the Burgoyne hex in a two-mile dash on Aldebaran than everybody dashed for cover. It was the first of countless cloudbursts that enhance the rural thrill of racing at Saratoga and the gamblers' beloved sense of doom.

President Lincoln had set Thursday aside as a day of thanksgiving for victories that suggested "the union of these States will be maintained," a thought he would later refine at Gettysburg. Lincoln called on Americans to assemble in "their customary places of worship."[15] The track was mobbed. On everybody's lips were the two-mile heats pitting Thunder, John Morgan, and Sympathy. The beautiful gray had gone "like blazes" in a morning work-out, but when they put his muzzle back on, a nibbled apple was found in it, the seeds removed and "some substance" inserted. A trainer took a bite. It was hot and bitter. Had Thunder been drugged?

Panic swept the stables. The bell summoned the horses. Thunder's backers wanted him "drawn"—scratched—so they could get their money back. The *Spirit of the Times* worried "he might have swallowed enough to do him great harm while running." The judges finally yanked him, and Sympathy, Gilpatrick up, won in two heats. Her sister Lizzie W., Sewell aboard, then took the mile and a quarter finale to make the meeting symmetrical.

Saratoga nights were born that week. In Broadway bars they had more to shout about than ever:

• the upsets by Lizzie (later sold to Watson to complete an otherwise forgettable career) and her sister;
• the fact that every winner was out of a Glencoe mare, except for Seven Oaks, and she was by Vandal, a Glencoe horse;
• the fact that, as the *Spirit* pointed out, "Bill Bird, the tall, colored trainer . . . started every winner but one from the scratch at the stand." Bird would be back; and
• the brilliance of Sewell, the revenge of Burgoyne. If there had been a jockeys' title, it would have gone to Sewell, with three wins to Burgoyne's two.

*   *   *   *

Often misunderstood because of the poor track conditions, Saratoga's first thoroughbred meeting was, in fact, a huge success. "It was not to be expected," concluded the *Spirit*, "that John Morrissey would go to the expense of purchasing and constructing a new course and erecting suitable buildings thereon. By giving a great deal of money in purses and additions to the stakes, he secured fine sport." He had drawn some fifteen thousand people, for a gate of $15,000 (more than $170,000 today and better than many major tracks do on attendance). He had brought in racing's pros. Charles Wheatly, who managed the track at Lexington as secretary of the Kentucky Association, ran Morrissey's track operation, too. John Hunter of Westchester County, and Bardstown, Kentucky, who owned the leading Northern stud, was a judge.

Prophetically, the *Spirit* added, "the formation of a competent club, and further proceedings, would seem to be a matter of course." They were. For the first time, an American sport would become a regularly scheduled national entertainment, with participants and spectators from the across the country and national press coverage. The meeting's "great success," said the excitable *Spirit,* proved the "feasibility of making Saratoga one of the greatest places on the continent," and the numbers encouraged the bragging. The crowd registered at the hotels and boardinghouses on Thursday alone, the final day of the meet, was 25 percent larger than the best day in 1862.

Saratoga was so irresistible that Maj. Gen. Daniel Sickles arrived the next Tuesday, one month after his leg was shot off at Gettysburg. He held daily levees at the American Hotel (today's Rip Van Dam) and rode past cheering throngs to Congress Spring, where the crowds parted as he hobbled through on crutches to take his glass.[16] By season's end, hotel and boardinghouse visitors totaled more than thirty thousand, up about 45 percent. Open-ended stays were suddenly popular, forcing hotels to turn many away.

The *Spirit* said Morrissey's project "laid the foundation for a great fashionable race meeting at the Springs, like that at Ascot in England." But it was also a declaration of independence from English sports. England had bequeathed America not only racing but boxing, where London still made the rules; rounders, the ancestor of baseball; and cricket, popular with the anglophile editors. The 1863 Saratoga meeting was a radical departure, for it produced a new and powerful institution in an American mold: the country's first national sports organization.

The Commodore and company moved fast. The day after the last race, Vanderbilt backed Morrissey's call for subscriptions to set up a jockey club, the Saratoga Association, and build a new track. In two hours, $10,600 was put up, $3,000 by Vanderbilt.[17] Another $10,000 was quickly subscribed, and an initial ninety-four acres snapped up across the road for the new track, the trotting grounds to be used for training. The Commodore offered to pay for it all, but it was decided to keep membership open.

Vanderbilt stayed behind the scenes, the discreet eight-hundred-pound gorilla, but his influence was all over the project. William R. Travers, a Baltimore-born stockbroker so little known the *Spirit* called him Travis, was named president of the Association. The vice presidents were the lawyer and publisher Leonard Jerome, a partner in Vanderbilt's railroad deals, and John Purdy, wine dealer, gentleman jockey, and son of the Samuel Purdy who triumphed aboard American Eclipse. Purdy had shared the meet's judging duties with stable owner John Hunter. Hunter was named to represent the Association's Executive Committee, but its other members were known for their business connections, not racing experience.

William R. Travers. *George S. Bolster Collection of the Historical Society of Saratoga Springs.*

The *Herald* would describe the committee members as "a guarantee of the thoroughly high-toned character of all the proceedings." Erastus Corning was president of the New York Central Railroad, then just a glimmer in Cornelius Vanderbilt's eye. A Corning grandson and namesake would follow in his footsteps as a long-time mayor of Albany. George A. Osgood was Vanderbilt's son-in-law and loyal rail executive. The now "Hon." James Marvin, the Vanderbilts' favorite hotelier, and a recently elected member of Congress, had been the apparent driving force behind the 1847 course. John Davidson was the Hudson riverboat operator and Morrissey backer, not the Morrissey horse. John H. White, of Saratoga Springs, served as treasurer. They got Wheatly, the sport's top professional, to move up from Lexington to be secretary, at $1,200 a year.

Racing itself was moving back north and getting organized. It was a revolution in American sports. Jockey clubs, or racing associations, had existed since Washington's day, but this one was founded, and soon would be copied, by Northerners who were businessmen first and horsemen second. After using the racing rules of Louisiana's Metairie club in 1863 and 1864, the Saratoga Association would draw up its own and run the operation as a tightly controlled enterprise. The blustery, individualistic tradition of match racing was on the way out. A once semiprivate amusement was becoming mass entertainment, and to manage it, the Saratoga Association introduced modern business management to American sports, long before it was introduced to most businesses.

From all accounts, Morrissey actually provided most of the capital, and he testified to that later, but there was no place on the records for the name of the country's most scandalous gambler, even though he was a hell of a lot of fun in person. As the new powers consigned him to official oblivion, they revealed, indirectly and doubtless unwittingly, what seemed obvious: that the whole idea had been his, and that his drive had pulled it off. "Much credit is due to the lessee," said the quasi-official *Spirit,* "for the energy he displayed in the outset, in originating the plan of operations; but his only connection with the club, and the only one he desires, will be in an executive capacity." In other words, Morrissey, the professional impresario and gambler, would continue running the operation, along with Wheatly, the professional track manager. It did make sense.[18]

Would Morrissey's undefeated heavyweight ego survive his radically reduced profile? He slipped badly, celebrating Christmas night 1863 by getting into a fight with Andy Sheehan, a politician and sport, at Hoyt's bar in Manhattan.[19] Before the fight, Morrissey and pals reportedly had been "making liberal acquaintance" with a couple of long-lost friends, Heidsick and Green Seal. The next night, the fight resumed, and they were both carted off to jail. It was no longer the sort of thing the Saratoga Association was looking for.

Far from the guns, racing's 1864 circuit opened impressively. A seven-day meeting at St. Louis was followed by three days at Paterson, where the Passaic County Agricultural Association put on the first American derby, the Jersey Derby. The circuit was dominated by a trio from the famous stallion Lexington, all three among the horses of the century: Norfolk, Asteroid, and Kentucky. The first two began their undefeated careers at St. Louis, and Norfolk beat a strong field, including Kentucky, in the Jersey Derby. New York followed with brief meetings at Centreville and Watertown, then Saratoga prepared for the grand opening of America's first modern sports facility.

Was there a war on?

7

YOU ARE HERE

ON THE FOURTH OF JULY, 1864, Saratoga exploded, or so it seemed from five urgent dispatches in the *New York Times*, under the headline: "Great Confla gration in Saratoga."[1] Two hundred feet of Broadway between the Clarendon Hotel and Union Hall became "one broad sheet of flame."[2] Touched off by fireworks on the rear piazza of Dr. Bedortha's Water Cure, the fire also attacked John Dinnen's blacksmith shop, John Knickerbocker's Livery, and Union Hall's Washhouse, Soap Factory, and Ice House. Further losses were reported by a branch of Mlle. Demorest's Dress Making Establishment, A. S. Rowe's Hoop Skirt Store, and George Mayer's Lager Beer Saloon. This first in a series of monumental Saratoga fires left a giant gash in Broadway.

On the thirtieth of July, four tons of gunpowder planted by Union troops under the rebel works at Petersburg, Virginia, exploded as planned. An entire rebel regiment was buried, but it was also a disaster for the Union, one of the biggest fiascoes of the war. Apparently confused, the Northerners charged directly into the crater and were mowed down by reb artillery. A black division was cut down, and, as several tried to surrender, they were murdered by the rebels.[3]

On the second of August, a fabulous crowd descended the piazza steps and climbed into hundreds of carriages crammed onto Broadway. They swung into East Congress Street, turning their backs on the ruins of the fire and the news from the distant front. The street had been watered all the way to the track, said the *Times*, "so that the recherche toilets of the ladies should not suffer."[4]

By several measures, this slow-moving traffic jam was America's first modern sports crowd, including as it did "the sporting men from North, South, East and West." Last year's had come from many parts of the country but was not of this size or scope, and many had been only curiosity seekers, watching an experiment at a course that would never open again. But these swells knew exactly what they were going to see: the finest sport the country had to offer and its first ultramodern sports facility, which would never close. Of course, many must have thought they themselves were the attraction.

President Lincoln knew exactly where to find Sen. Edwin D. Morgan, who was running his congressional reelection committee. He wired him at Saratoga, and the senator was on the first train out that morning. The president reached *Times* editor Henry Raymond at the Springs, too, to dispatch him on a diplomatic mission. He could have found House Speaker Schuyler Colfax there as well. But where was his

Union Hall. *Leslie's*, 1864. *Courtesy of the author.*

vagabond son Bob, jokingly called "the Prince of the Rails," who had just graduated from Harvard, dashed off to Long Branch in New Jersey, and then, according to his biographer, disappeared again?

★　　★　　★　　★

At the risk of revealing a state secret, it can be disclosed that Bob had checked into Saratoga, too. Had his father known, he could have wired him yesterday, on his twenty-first birthday. Bob's mother, Mary Todd Lincoln, had made it plain he was too intelligent to be in the war, and he was having his usual good time. He had danced to the music of a twenty-two-piece band Friday night at Union Hall. When somebody asked if he was a relative of the president, he joked, "Distant—about 400 miles." Bob's future father-in-law, Senator James Harlan of Iowa, probably knew more about Bob's doings than his father, since he, too, was at Saratoga.

Among the multimillionaires present was the elderly and dyspeptic William B. Astor, John Jacob's heir, whose estimated $61 million was said to make him the richest man in America (and the world), unless the richest was A. T. Stewart, who reportedly was buying Union Hall, or the Commodore, who was at the United States Hotel.[5] The Vanderbilt heir apparent, William H., was back, too. So was his black sheep gambler of a brother, Cornelius Jeremiah, who signed in at the States as "C. Vanderbilt Jr.," as he so often did, to his father's complete disgust.[6] The Commodore's railroad rival, Daniel Drew, arrived, as did the tobacco king, Pierre Lorillard. Little notice was given the not-yet-famous Delanos, Roosevelts, and Rockefellers. The Commodore of the Spanish fleet in New York led a huge foreign contingent, with some two hundred Cubans at Union Hall alone.

As Lincoln haunted the telegraph office next door to the White House, the railroad chieftains and others tracked their money at the new Western Union offices at Congress and Union Halls. And their rivalries found fierce expression in the ballroom. "Mrs. H——h, of New York, in lilac silk with heavy lace flounces of Honiton lace, decorated with diamonds" was seen doing battle, for example, with the dropdead "Miss A. F——h, of Washington" in "heavy black corded-silk, black velvet point and illusion waist." These ladies never wanted their names in the paper; only the initials so people could figure it out. Sometimes, large hints were given, as in the case of "Mrs. Judge R——t, of New York" in "lavender colored silk, double flounces of black lace, point lace shawl, decorated with diamonds."

On that day in August, the carriage riders turned right into the nation's first modern sports facility, which, astoundingly, survives today as the oldest major sports facility on the continent and one of the oldest in the world. Surrounded by a ten-foot fence, it looked very much in 1864 as it does today if one forgets the current clubhouse and a few other additions. The pedestrians and carriages assembled in an open area of six acres, and there was a six-acre pine grove with a "cooling-ground" for the horses. They were brought over from the old course, where new stables had been built.

The first crowd was estimated at five thousand. "The ladies stepped from the carriages immediately into the grandstand," reported the *Times,* or gathered on the lawn in front of the stand, where the "sporting men" collected. Unless they had bought their tickets at their hotels, the spectators paid fifty cents to get in, one dollar for the grandstand, one dollar to watch from a carriage, or ten dollars for badges admitting them to the grandstand and the quarter stretch for five days. Another day had been added to the schedule.

Two charming, shamrock-shaped windows at either end of the grandstand advertised that this was a house of chance. It was the forefather of today's monumental stadiums. Two hundred feet long by thirty feet wide, it sat about two thousand people under a slate roof and was labeled "a model of elegance," with its back colonnade facing the street and its broad stairways at each end rising to the seating sections. Its views were perfect, free of any barns of oblivion. "Every inch of the track," marveled the local paper, "can be seen at each and every seat." Underneath were "retiring and refreshment rooms, ladies boudoirs and every needful convenience." From the seats, four additional stairways led down to the track. One report said "light fences" had been "appropriately placed upon each side of the track"—the future home of an ornithological subspecies, the American Railbird. On the inside rail, the occupants of the judges' stand testified to the national importance of the affair: Col. Oden Bowie of Maryland, future senator and secretary of state Thomas Bayard of Delaware, and Mr. Colt of New Jersey. On an adjacent stand was H. P. McGrath, back as one of three "timing judges."

But it was the track itself that advertised the new professionalism of sports. It was

Early railbirds watching a hurdle race. From a stereograph, ca. 1868. *Robert Joki Collection, Saratoga Springs.*

designed under the guiding genius of Wheatly, who would be track secretary for decades. In one move, he ended the days of approximate distances and frightful conditions as acceptable for sports venues. His course placed cow pasture and sandlot sports, however beloved, on a lower plane. Precision and statistics would become the new passion. "It is exactly one mile," a local paper proclaimed of Wheatly's dazzling geometry, with "two parallel straight stretches and two half circles or curves."[7] The stretches were "each 37 feet 10 inches over a quarter of a mile" and the turns "each the same amount less than a quarter."

"The width of the front stretch," where the horses fighting for final position would go wide before the screaming crowd, "is 63 feet, the remainder of the course being 43 feet wide."

The *Times* thought it was being nice calling the track "level as a billiard table." But that was the old thinking. For while the front stretch and twenty-five fortieths of the first curve were indeed level, "the remainder (fifteen-fortieths) of the curve ascends at the rate of one tenth foot per rod." As if intoxicated with all this precision, the press release writer, probably Wheatly, went on: "the first half of the back stretch ascends at the rate of one-fiftieth of a foot per rod, and the remainder of it descends at the rate of one-fortieth of a foot per rod."

Just as the generals pursued the unstoppable massacre, the sports planners chased their cold mathematical ideal. "The first fourteen-fortieths of the second curve ascends at the rate of one-twentieth foot per rod, and the remainder descends at the rate of one-tenth foot per rod, thus reaching"—nirvana!—"the level of the front stretch."

The turns suddenly were banked. From the inside to the outside, "there is a gradual ascent to the height of 30 inches." As every spectator would soon understand, this enhanced "the ease and safety of making the turns for horses either under the saddle or in harness" (the track was intended for both). By comparison, the simple dimensions that baseball would adopt were childlike. The unpredictable country surfaces were going out of style, too. The soil here was "a mixture of the sandy surface loam with about two inches of clay, the latter having been drawn upon the track last winter and mellowed by repeated freezing."

At the close of the meeting, Wheatly was rewarded with the opinion of the *Times*

Matthew Brady's Saratoga. Wood engraving from a Brady photograph. *Leslie's,* 1865.
Courtesy of the author.

that Saratoga "will henceforth be regarded as the best race course in the country."
Oddly enough, one hundred thirty years later, some think it still is.

Given the worship of change, it is also extraordinary that the first race of the 1864
season, the Travers Stakes, remains the oldest major feature in American spectator
sports. It is not, however, the oldest featured horse race on the continent. A race for "a
plate to the value of Fifty Guineas" was inaugurated four years earlier at Toronto,
with Queen Victoria's blessing. Don Juan won it, with Charles Littlefield up, and it
has been run every year since 1860. The Travers would be suspended for six seasons
around the turn of the century, but it certainly has been remarkable for its immov-
ability. Whereas the Queen's Plate saw many changes of venue until it was switched
to the old Woodbine course in 1883 and to the new Woodbine in 1956, the Travers
would move for just one three-year period; it was raced at Belmont during World
War II. So sports statisticians who love the picayune, and they all do, may rejoice that
it remains not only America's oldest major feature but the continent's oldest major
race still staged at its original track.

William Riggin Travers was visiting Newport one day when his host showed him
the resort's splendid array of pleasure craft, almost all owned by the rising population
of Wall Street brokers. "Wh-where," asked the sarcastic Travers, in his usual stutter,
"are the c-customers' yachts?"

They would not call him "William R. Travis" again. The Association's president would be celebrated as one of the funniest men in America. He turned his stutter into shtick and became one of the most quoted wits of his time. Wall Streeters like himself were one of his favorite targets. Passing the Union Club in Manhattan, his companion asked if the men in the big chairs at the windows were habitués of the club. "No," said Travers, "some are s-s-sons of habitués."[8]

Under gathering clouds, the bell called the horses to the first Travers. It was a mile and three-quarters (its distance through 1889) for three-year-olds, colts to carry 100 pounds, fillies 97, with a $50 entrance fee. It was "play or pay," which meant the entrance fees were forfeited if a horse were withdrawn. The first race was worth the thirty entry fees it attracted, plus $1,000 added by the Association, or $2,500. The *Herald* listed all thirty candidates as it battled the *Times* to cover the Saratoga story, but the fact was, thoroughbreds were scarce at the height of the war, and racing was on fragile ground.

Five entries were fathered by just one horse, and he was imported. This was another Eclipse, owned by Francis Morris of Westchester County. More amazingly, thirteen entries were sired by Lexington; they included the three fabulous bays, Norfolk, Asteroid, and Kentucky. Only Kentucky, entered by Hunter with Travers and Osgood now buying in as co-owners, would remain in the race, as twenty-five entries were withdrawn. As it happened, Kentucky was lucky to be here at all. John Clay had owned him earlier, and late in the spring, his bluegrass spread had been revisited by disaster in the person of John Morgan, the rebel raider. Morgan had escaped his Ohio jailers, and his men grabbed $25,000 worth of Clay's thoroughbreds, including his famous filly Skedaddle.[9] Kentucky, however, was already in Hunter's hands.

Betting had been hot the night before at Dr. Underwood's pool sales, transferred to White's Hotel on East Congress Street. One bettor had to go to $820 for a ticket on Zeb Ward's Tipperary, the favorite. The same pool had $240 on Morris's unnamed gray colt, $155 on Kentucky, $75 on J. A. Grinstead's chestnut Ringmaster, and $60 on James Watson's filly, Patti. The morning pools and the side betting had them in the same order, with Kentucky attracting only $30 in a pool of $500. He was said to be lame.

The Travers would be another duel between white and black jockeys, though nobody saw it that way then, and this time they were the two most famous riders in the land. Making his Saratoga debut was the veteran Abe Hawkins; this former slave and the president were the only Americans known throughout the country as "Old Abe." Returning was the other veteran, Gilpatrick, considered the greatest jockey of his time. Back, too, was young Billy Burgoyne.

The first Travers got off at 11:30 A.M. on Tuesday, August 2, 1864. After a false start, they were off again at the word "Go!" Tipperary jumped to the lead. At the turn, Gilpatrick moved Kentucky in front, with Morris's colt in a big move to second. The favorite, Tipperary, with Hawkins aboard, was third, then Patti, under Burgoyne, and Ringmaster, that order holding to the half mile. At the home stretch, they bunched up, except for Ringmaster, who was beaten. Kentucky held the lead in front of the crowd, with Tipperary second, the Morris colt and the filly trailing. In the final mile, the leader showed something special. For every burst Tipperary put on,

The first Travers winner. Kentucky, from *Harper's Weekly*, 1867. *Courtesy of the author.*

Kentucky easily shook him, "stalling off Abe's determined efforts," as the *Tribune* put it, as if it were second nature, and sailing home in a four-length victory before the roaring five thousand. Tipperary finished four lengths ahead of the gray, later to be named Throg's Neck, Jr., with Patti a distant fourth and Ringmaster way back.[10]

Time: 3:18¾.

Tuesday's second and final race was riveting: Aldebaran vs. Fleetwing in two-mile heats for $500. Burgoyne rode the underdog Aldebaran "with great tact, creeping inside of the track," and took the first heat by a length. In the second, Fleetwing, with Hawkins up, caught him at the first half mile and stayed there past the frantic crowd. The betting was $100 to $30 on Aldebaran as he pushed ahead by a length again, then was caught once more. Not until the home stretch, with "Abe on Fleetwing plying whip and steel in vain," did Aldebaran pull away, "with plenty of running left in him."[11]

"We may justly quote the now progressing Saratoga meeting as a model institution," declared the *Times*. As for receipts, not counting the $10 season badges, and tickets purchased by members, opening day had brought in a little over $3,000 in admissions. The gate was the tracks' chief source of revenue in this era long before they controlled the betting.

A "glorious rain" on Wednesday brought the first weather cancellation, which would not have happened today, when they run come heat or high water. The Association squeezed the rest of the schedule into three days, as Sunday racing was unthinkable then. Meantime, the wealthier types had a day on the piazzas, watching the showers. The railroad bosses could read about the eight hundred striking Irish Americans, who were driving their fellow immigrants, the German Americans, from their work on the Adirondack Railroad north of Saratoga. The *Times* would soon rhapsodize about how the railroad would turn the Adirondacks into "a suburb of New York" and how "the furnaces of our capitalists will line its valleys and create new fortunes to swell the aggregate of our wealth." In fairness, one should note that it also called for protected Adirondack parks amid the beloved "din and dust of furnaces and foundaries."[12] The piazza generals could play war, as they loved to do, while reading of the 335 dead, 180 of them black soldiers, counted by Greeley's man in the Petersburg crater.

President Lincoln set aside Thursday as "a day of National humiliation and prayer," a fast day, he said, on which to implore God "not to destroy us as a people." The *Tribune* chose this fast day to praise the Association for starting the races at 11:30 A.M., "thus enabling the visitors to return to the hotels for dinner." They paid $3,700 to watch a bay filly named Saratoga win the Saratoga Stakes. It was the feature on the track's first three-race card.

The crowd kept building. Nothing like this had happened before in American sports. The next day the grandstand was "overflowing with elegantly dressed ladies, who then took possession of the steps in front," driving the men onto the lawn. The Association had followed Morrissey's precedent by charging women admission, despite some criticism. Friday receipts topped $4,000. Kentucky repeated in the Sequel Stakes, with Gilpatrick again holding off Hawkins on Tipperary. Even the slow-witted could see that skin color was irrelevant, so Saratoga soared ahead of the rest of the country in sanity, if only during those few minutes around the track.

Friday closed with an incredible marathon called the Congress Spring Purse. Aldebaran, Burgoyne up, beat Fleetwing, under Hawkins, in three three-mile heats. The times: 6:26½, 6:42½, 6:26½. The chestnut four-year-olds went all out for more than nineteen minutes, with breaks of just thirty minutes between heats.

That night the Broadway fashion parade was all the more spectacular because gas lamps had been installed on the principal streets, residents being advised, not too subtly, that they would give a better light if cleaned. The elite were promenading to the ball of the season, "on the tapis" (today it's "on tap") in Union Hall's dining room. This now sat 1,200, quite appropriate for a hotel that had 1,192 guests that night. The committee of arrangements was headed by Daniel Drew, Vanderbilt's wily fellow director on the Harlem Railroad. The Commodore could afford to let Drew have his evening, for in cornering Harlem's stock again that summer, Vanderbilt had not only made another $2 million but had trapped Drew, who once again had sold his company short. Drew was taken for $1 million and finally forced off the Harlem board.

Vanderbilt reportedly took him off the hook by accepting a personal check in lieu of delivering his Harlem stock at the short prices. It may have been then, as Vanderbilt biographer Wheaton Lane guessed, that Drew coined the phrase: "He that sells what isn't his'n. / Must buy it back, or go to prison."[13]

Drew also had to swallow whenever he ran into William H., as he no doubt did that evening, for the Commodore's son had been brought in as chief operating officer of Harlem. With his jowl whiskers that looked like two big bows, W. H. was clearly the heir. Brother George, the third and favorite son, had died earlier that year of tuberculosis, and second son Cornelius Jeremiah was considered of little use. The nine daughters never had a chance. But the old man wasn't going anywhere yet. He had just cornered the Hudson River Railroad as well. So the ball went on, with the twenty-two-piece band, a "supper worthy of the gods . . . a perfect crush of crinoline and a blaze of beauty," the ballroom scene looking from above like "a gorgeous parterre of animated flowers."[14] The cannon and the fighting and the dying forgotten, the biggest party in the country lasted till early morning.

August 6, 1864, was the first great Saturday in American sports, the granddaddy of all those future weekends. Not counting those with $10 season tickets, the 6,345 paid more than $5,000 to get in. Once again the women took over the grandstand, and the *Times* put it bluntly: such a "superb array of beauty and fashion has never previously been seen in America." The five-race card was unprecedented in the North, and it featured the most popular event of the meeting, a Canadian speciality few Americans had ever seen: a hurdle. It was over two miles with gentlemen riders and four hurdles per mile. The crowd was fascinated to see "five horses leap hurdles 3½ feet high, with well-grown men on their backs."[15] On the final jump, Zigzag and Charley Riley fell and rolled over as Garryowen sailed past. Nobody was hurt. Charley Riley's rider remounted "and—game to the backbone—made a desperate charge in with his horse, amid the enthusiastic cheers of the spectators, and was only just beaten."[16]

Patti won the first "selling race." In accordance with the rules, she was immediately auctioned off in front of the judges' stand. Dennis Ready got her for $610, and other owners quickly sold three others. Buying and selling horses was like breathing, which is why it was the most natural thing in the world to excuse oneself by saying, "I have to see a man about a horse." One usually did. Next, Captain Moore took the track's first handicap in a "walk-over," then as now a race that winds up with only one starter, who is required to gallop the distance anyway. The Captain and Aldebaran were the only horses to win on both sides of the road.

It was widely agreed that the meeting was "brilliantly successful."[17] To some, it even suggested a new way of life, but once again they did not get it quite right. A *Herald* editor said it reminded him of "Ascot on a Queen's Cup day, when the sovereign is present."[18] He denounced the "shoddy speculators, contractors and office-holders" living off the war and vacationing at Long Branch, and was relieved to see at Saratoga "the surroundings of rank and fashion rather than the heterogenous assemblages to which we have been too long accustomed." What the editors could not see was that, rather than recreating Ascot, national sports would have the opposite effect. The Saratoga meeting had brought out twenty thousand paying customers, and the message was that sports would soon be affording new expression to those "hetero-genous assemblages." They would have a stabilizing effect on the country, providing unifying spectacles with rituals, rules, and players that everybody knew. They would allow plenty of steam to be blown off, a phenomenon whose value was first suggested by the North-South races. They would not resemble Ascot.

The Association set out to expand again. It would invest $30,000 to $40,000 to enlarge the grounds, improve the buildings, and put up a "ladies' stand" to the west of the grandstand. And what would America's first modern sports arena be without its first modern press box? Because "the next thing to seeing a race is the reading of a report of it," the *Daily Saratogian* pleaded for "a stand for the accommodation of reporters so that they need not be compelled to endure the heat of a broiling sun."[19] So sportswriters, who sometimes feel like interlopers, were in from the start.

The Association hoped to inaugurate a "National Horse Show" after next year's races and to bring in "the finest horses in the country." This was an attempt to formalize the town's long-established role as a horse center, with more than one equestrian activity. It would increase the participants' professional pride while developing a deeper public interest, an old secret that could be adopted by other tracks today.

The meeting lit a fire under the city, too. The *Daily Saratogian* commented proudly, if crudely, that "nearly all other American watering-places have suffered extensively from the great civil commotion which distracts the land" (the "commotion" being the Civil War!). Saratoga, on the other hand, was expanding, under the leadership of Warren W. Leland, manager of Union Hall. The Clarendon Hotel (site today of Central Catholic High School) and Congress Hall had built new wings, the latter's adding a hundred rooms and a hundred parlors. Congress Hall had opened the biggest ballroom in town, 120 by 50 feet. Now it was Leland's turn, and he began signing up investors in a $30,000 opera house with up to fifteen hundred seats, to be tacked onto Union Hall. He found investors to turn East Congress Street into a one-hundred-foot-wide avenue, with a horse railroad alongside. It would extend three and one-half miles from Broadway past the track and out to the lake. This is today's Union Avenue, celebrated for its large Victorian "cottages."

Some parties launched smaller revenue-enriching plans, known affectionately as gouging. Not wanting to appear a foolish victim, *Times* editor Henry Raymond specifically denied he had been charged $500 for a dinner given him by an unnamed party at Saratoga Lake.[20]

John Morrissey had plans of his own, new ways of exploiting his supercharged personality. President Lincoln himself was impressed by him, and joked that one of his generals, who was always asking for advice, was like one of Morrissey's former Tammany flunkies. As Lincoln told it, on hearing that a fellow Tammanyite was getting married, the flunky looked anxious and whispered into the bridegroom's ear, "Have you asked Morrissey yet?" Lincoln added: "This general . . . wouldn't dare order the guard out without asking Morrissey." A reporter noted that Morrissey was in his element at his new track, "with his broad shirt-collar flying loose, and streams of perspiration and dust forming miniature maps of the Mississippi down his cheeks, now betting, now giving instructions to policemen, and continually chewing an unlit segar." If Morrissey was a silent partner, it was only on paper.[21]

He was nobody's victim. His wealth was reckoned at half a million dollars, but it wasn't enough: he had to be on top again. He had made a very dumb play earlier this year, going short on Harlem, as Drew had, and might have become a potential target of Vanderbilt's rage, which was so extreme it could have been mistaken for a weather development. To a group of associates who once tried to grab control of a Vanderbilt property when he was in Europe, the Commodore had written, "Gentlemen, You have undertaken to cheat me. I will not sue, for law takes too long. I will ruin you. Sincerely yours."[22] But Morrissey escaped. With a Gaelic flourish, he presented the Commodore with a beautiful horse and was immediately taken back in his favor, even picking up stock market tips to recoup his losses. The swaggering thirty-three year old became the seventy-year-old's pal, a sort of backdoor protégé.

The two men had a lot in common, actually. Both had been athletes, the older an avid swimmer and famous for physical feats as a young boatman. He had even fought Yankee Sullivan. The Commodore was leading a parade for presidential contender Henry Clay when Sullivan, who had sworn he would stop the procession, grabbed Vanderbilt's reins. Off jumped the latter to thrash Sullivan into a "nearly senseless condition."[23] Both refreshingly crude, Vanderbilt and Morrissey had fought their way to the top and were damn well going to gamble once they got there. In fact, the Commodore never got into racing thoroughbreds—he always preferred trotters— but enjoyed the hell out of betting. Both handsome, too, they were ladies' men and men's men. The old man could find a lot of his bluster in the young one. And Morrissey, itching to get back on top, began a campaign to smooth his way in the resort, clumsily at first.

He bought $20,000 worth of town bonds to finance the hiring of substitutes to fight in the war. It was a common practice but controversial in Saratoga. After all, as a Union soldier's statue in Congress Park testifies, the volunteer "Saratoga Regiment"—the 77th New York Cavalry—had seen some of the worst fighting, including the one real bayonet charge of the war. They suffered five dead and fifty-three wounded in the battle for Marye's Heights behind Fredericksburg, Virginia. The Saratoga area immediately organized a second regiment, which would lose 35 killed in action and 218 dead from sickness and other causes.[24]

Once again, Morrissey's too famous name was left out when the Saratoga Association was incorporated under New York State law, though he apparently owned most of the stock.[25] The club retained the same officers, made Travers, Purdy, Hunter, Davidson, and Marvin directors, and listed Vanderbilt as one of the incorporators. And it lengthened its name with the words "for the Improvement of Horses," the old formula for keeping prosecutors away. It was incorporated on the first day of spring, 1865. Twelve days later, in Virginia, what was meant to be a quick Union rout ended—after nine months.

Petersburg had been the longest siege in American warfare, but at last it was all over. On April 9, Lee surrendered to Grant at Appomattox Courthouse, ending the struggle that had taken some six hundred thousand American lives. Two days later, in a scene recaptured by historian James McPherson, Lincoln addressed a crowd from a White House balcony. He said the South had no organized government, so he would have to treat with various discordant elements. He called on the new government of Louisiana to enfranchise blacks who were literate or veterans, and he would soon announce a broad policy for the South.[26]

A man in the crowd said to a companion, "That means nigger citizenship. Now by God, I'll put him through. This is the last speech he will ever make."[27] His name was John Wilkes Booth, and three nights later, he stepped into the president's box at Ford's Theater.

In the coming days, those in the North who had not lost sons or brothers or fathers planned a "national" celebration, as the victors do after a war. It would be held in the most logical place.

8

THE YANKEES CELEBRATE

O N THE FOURTH OF JULY, Saratoga exploded in the biggest single celebration ending "the great civil commotion." Three months after Lee surrendered to Grant and Lincoln to Booth, the action resumed at "this great battlefield of sport and fashion," said one newspaper, merrily switching fronts. It was the night of the generals in the northern capital of crinolinedom, and the swirl of silk and satin was shot through with Union blue, doubtless literally in some instances. On the honorary arrangements committees for balls on that and subsequent evenings were Majors-General Ben Butler, Frank Blair, Joseph Jackson Bartlett, J. A. Rawlings, and hard-drinking Joe Hooker, who had given his all to the Army of the Potomac and his name to the ladies who followed it. "At 8 o'clock," read a breathless report on the night of the Fourth, "the military and civic guests entered the extensive and prettily decorated *salle a manger* of the largest hotel in the country."[1]

"Imagine," whispered a witness, "1,200 persons seated at dinner at the Union Hotel, a thousand at Congress Hall and a proportionate number at the other hotels." The generals were generalled by a corps that had fought a tougher fight to the top, unless they had played their cards well. Usually, it took both, as in the case of Robert Jackson, second waiter at the Union and later headwaiter at Congress Hall. His grandfather had been Gen. "Light Horse" Harry Lee of Revolutionary renown and his grandmother Mrs. Lee's maid, a slave. His father, free and working for the post office, had chased down a pack of slave-traders heading south with his bride, and with the help of Daniel Webster and John Calhoun, paid to get her back. Ignoring social barriers, Congress Hall guests made it a point to visit the Jacksons at their vine-covered cottage on Washington Street. But that evening, such professionals and their troops were busy running those vast dining halls.[2]

Rising to a toast, Dan Sickles, the political general who had left a leg at Gettysburg, proposed to the devastated South: "Let bygones be bygones." Then they all danced in the Union Hotel opera house, presided over by Lincoln, twelve weeks dead and already a statue. Mary Surratt and three male coconspirators would be hanged in Washington later in the week.

"Who," wondered a reporter, "can estimate the number of bottles of Congress Water drank in Saratoga" during the celebration? Greeley's man could. He said nine thousand glasses of water had been dipped one morning from Congress Spring, and he figured there were "50,000 strangers" in town. A famous war photographer tried to keep up. "Wherever I go in and about Saratoga, Brady's mammoth camera is to be met," noted the *New York World* reporter. "A great many Indians, it is said, have been 'taken alive' by the intrepid artist."

Native Americans sold crafts at the "Indian Camp" on the southern edge of the park and offered, among other things, bow-and-arrow practice. One of them caused a stir by replacing the usual target with live foul, perched about fifteen paces off, which victim was then finished off for the pot. Of course, these merchants had their own jokes to tell on the tourists, such as the Englishwoman who had scoffed at their ancestors' warning that the Great Spirit would sink the canoe of anyone who broke the silence of Saratoga Lake. Halfway across, she let out a scream, then, safely ashore, berated the Mohawks for their credulity. Came the reply of a politically incorrect Mohawk, passed on to a poet: "Our safety shows that God is merciful to old and young. Well He knows the pale-faced woman cannot hold her tongue!" They had to be particularly amused by the customs and costumes of the various Vanderbilt and wannabe tribes, many of whom peddled not baskets but daughters.[3]

"A buxom belle of about twenty was put upon the market," flashed a sarcastic reporter, "under a pressure of dry goods that provoked for her the sympathy of the entire opposite sex." She wore bright red shoes and gauntlet gloves. "After being marched around the piazzas of the hotels and through Congress Park, she was withdrawn—no bids being offered." Moving to the general economy, the reporter noted, "Red hair is on the increase. It can be bought in any quantities at the perruquiers."

There was so much fresh gossip from their national resort that the Americans eating all this up had no way of knowing what had happened a few weeks before. Flames had shot out of the top-floor servants' quarters and gutted the fabled United States, the turf crowd's headquarters. The flames leapt Division Street to devour the Marvin House hotel and arched back toward the railroad, where Union soldiers on a passing train stood on top of the cars to watch the inferno. Saratoga shrugged it off. The town had lost a quarter of its hotel capacity, but people just stepped around the latest gash as other hotels converted parlors to bedrooms. Boardinghouses welcomed the crush.

Broadway burned on, illuminated by balls and "billiard rooms, bowling alleys, shooting galleries and gambling pandemoniums all ablaze" with gas jets flaring. The gaming houses, said the *Tribune,* closed only "with the blushing dawn." Several women in the Cuban contingent convinced one house "to 'open a game' of faro," and they were reportedly "playing high and winning." The *World* wondered whether there might be a future house "for female gamesters." Yes; within a few years, on Manhattan's West Side, women could be cheated at faro and roulette, as social historian Herbert Asbury has written, by "artists of their own sex."[4]

At Morrissey's on Matilda Street, said a reporter, "ten-thousand-dollar ventures on the turning up of a card, or the stoppage of a little ivory ball, are not at all uncommon." Army officers favored his joint, as did gigolos, "wearing gorgeous raiment and tasty jewelry" and placing bets for unnamed women. "The most distinguished man at the springs," said a scribe, tongue only partly in cheek, "is Mr. John Morrissey." Profiting from Vanderbilt's tips, he was suddenly "the great stock operator and financier . . . quite a power in the stock board. . . . He has acquired a million dollars by operating in Central during the last few months." Smart move; strung together from ten trunk lines linking Albany to Buffalo, the New York Central Railroad was about to be swallowed up by the Commodore, who already controlled the New York to Albany route. Morrissey spent his days in the Congress Hall telegraph office, monitoring his money. Susie Morrissey attracted attention, too, even as she cared for their ten-year-old son. Joseph Smith, who picked up hotel guests at the station, said they always wanted to see two celebrities: William H. Vanderbilt and Mrs. John Morrissey, "a beautiful woman with great sparkling black eyes, a queenly form, and a dashing manner."[5]

*　　*　　*　　*

SARATOGA
BRILLIANT OPENING OF THE RACING SEASON

The *World* headline fluttered as high as its nameplate. The races, biggest draw of the season-long celebration, moved to page one, topping even the play given the Heenan-Sayers fight before the war. As a running story in New York City, they beat everything else, including the latest attempt to lay the Atlantic Cable. Editors, too, it seemed, were exhausted by war and happy to help people escape, if only vicariously, to the "Spa," as they were now delighted to call it.

UNPRECEDENTED CONGREGATION OF PLEASURE-SEEKERS AT THE SPA
IMMENSE GATHERING OF BEAUTY AND FASHION[6]

With Morrissey towering over the proceedings—he was thus America's first major sports impresario—the Association unveiled a surprise. It would present a double bill: a great "trotting carnival" and then the third thoroughbred meeting, bringing back the unbeatable Kentucky. As our first sports spectacular, it was great-granddaddy to the World Series and great-great granddaddy to the Super Bowl the first sports event as American apotheosis. For days, the news was shouted from the front pages of the *New York Times, Tribune, Herald,* and *World.* Managed single-handedly by Morrissey, the trotting carnival opened on July 12 with such famous names as owner-trainer-driver Hiram Woodruff, grand old man of the sport, and the trotters Mount Vernon, Dexter, Harry Clay, and Young Morrill. The program was riddled with snafus, but nobody seemed to care, and the six days of running races would be even bigger, the celebration's final explosion.

As the meeting approached, two of the three contenders for the title of richest American, Vanderbilt and Stewart, surfaced on an arrangements committee for one of the balls. Would there be an Astor sighting? And why, actually, did the rich prefer Saratoga to Newport? Editors stretched to create a rivalry between the two watering places, which *Godey's Lady's Book,* noting the shocking quantities of mascara at both, labeled "the Sodom and Gomorrah of our Union." Henry James soon would write reams about "democratic, vulgar Saratoga" versus "substantial and civilised" Newport, the difference, he sniffed, being that "between a group of undiscriminating hotels and a series of organized homes," while a simpler poet would boil it down to, "At one you go into the water; / At t'other it goes into you."[7]

But as plain as the nose on everybody's face was this: Saratoga was more fun. America's robber barons and their spouses could have only a certain amount of fun stuck in a Newport mansion with their families spying on them from behind every grand stairway. At Saratoga, thank God, you were supposed to go out.

On the last Thursday in July, a train brought the most celebrated figure in the land, his fame only enhanced by the murder of Lincoln, his glory greater than it was after Vicksburg, when a local paper had front-paged twenty-nine suggestions for what the "U.S." signified, among them:

Unconditional Surrender Grant
Uncle Sam Grant
Union Saver Grant
Unshackle Slave Grant
Unadulterated Saltpetre Grant

Not since Saratoga's first tourist had won his war had a general been so popular, nor would one be again until Eisenhower. Whereas Washington found only a cluster of springs, the Idol of the Nation put up in cavernous Congress Hall, his schedule requiring the drive to the lake and appearances at the hotels. The *Daily Saratogian* gushed: "At the head table sat Gen. Grant, the greatest captain of the age, and opposite to him, William B. Astor, reported the richest of living men." For the dance that night, Julia Dent Grant had got herself up in "dove-colored mauve antique, hair arranged with natural flowers," while her rough "Ulys" may have been the most uncomfortable person in the room. An observer was reminded of a compliment paid to Washington after the latter had stammered an acknowledgment of thanks; namely, that his "modesty was only equaled by his valor." Yet even this visit did not get the press that heralded the running races and completed the birth of national sports.

When the meeting opened on August 7, many knew it was making history. "Nothing that has been previously attempted in this country," said the *Herald,* could compare. The *Tribune* noted, "The running horses are about to be introduced in this country with almost European prestige. By and by we shall have our Ascots, and Derbys, and Leger days, and Saratoga will be the grand annual meeting." In the end, Americans would indeed be shaped by grand annual sports meetings. After the first four days, the *World* would call the betting "unparalleled in the history of American sporting," and *Harper's Weekly* would declare the races "the most splendid ever witnessed on this continent."

The course—"unreservedly the best race-track in the country"—had yielded a bright stubble of wheat in the infield, where a lone pine stood sentinel. Lengthened by more than half to some 320 feet, the grandstand—"the most beautiful in the country"—had cushioned seats for the two thousand spectators under the roof, and now there was room for another two thousand in an uncovered stand to the west. The seating was whites only at that meeting. The *Tribune* correspondent found this ironic, even as he revealed his own limits:

I should mention as a symptom of this era when the capacity of the human races are [*sic*] to be demurred that half of the jockeys are the blackest Africans, and I have yet to

An 1865 finish. From a Brady photograph. *Leslie's, 1865. Courtesy of the author.*

learn that their color interferes with their fitness for this . . . business. One of them, who passes by the sobriquet of Old Abe, is highly spoken of as a judicious jockey. The same democracy of feeling does not extend to the spectator's galleries, for an addendum to the Programme says: "Colored persons not admitted to the stand."[8]

"Champagne on draft" was passed around freely for the ladies, with ice creams, sodas, and lemonade available below the stands, as they still are. Again the turnout of women was called unprecedented and must have included several hundred, at least. Although Greeley's man tried to explain that there was "a vein of sympathy extending from women to horseflesh," many came to bet. At the trotting carnival, they had wagered fans, cigar cases, "and not a few kid gloves," and some appeared to be in deeper. They gathered on the piazzas, "ladies who know tomorrow's programme like English sportsmen. . . . This feature of the races has increased daily."

The undefeated champion came out of retirement to keep some of the men in line, the ancient role of boxers at the tracks. When some stood and blocked people's view, an equally ancient infraction, "Mr. Morrissey ordered everybody a second and third time to take their seats, but several obstreperous parties refused to obey, whereupon Morrissey seized one of the party, shook him as a big dog might a little puppy, [and] the obnoxious individual agreed to obey orders rather than be ejected from the stand."[9]

Then as now, no serious player sat glued to the seats anyway, nor would many of the women had convention not required it. In an enclosed betting ring in front, four to five hundred sports found a purpose for their paper shirtcuffs, where they scribbled numbers. They bet not only with Dr. Underwood, but with other pool sellers, who kept constant watch on one another. From Saturday night at White's Hotel to opening Monday, the doctor alone sold forty pools totaling $70,000. Most of the betting

The Yankees Celebrate

was blind, though a few sought advice from the experts, many of them black: trainers, assistants, and grooms. And somewhere in this milling mass, Billy Travers might have been telling one of his stories.

A friend complained of rats. "Get a cat." It didn't work. "Get a dog." They put the dog in a pit against six rats, and it killed all but one. This one grabbed him by the lip and held on, the dog yelping madly. "B-b-buy the rat!"[10]

Saratoga catapulted America's athletes onto page one for good. The turf crowd knew that four of the seven jockeys in the Travers were among the best—the veterans Gilpatrick and Hawkins, the young lightweights Sewell and Burgoyne—but tomorrow thousands more would discover them in the papers. As it happened, four were white and three black. Again, this was nothing new, for contrary to today's widespread belief, it was not Jackie Robinson who "integrated" sports. American jockeys had been competing for decades without regard for color, and here again, over the mile and three-quarters of the Travers, the only colors that counted were on their backs: dress blue and yellow, dress scarlet and scarlet, all the clashing colors of the owners' racing silks. They shone all the more when the jockeys sat straight up, English style, the surviving prints suggesting it must have been quite a trick, the rider leaning back to stay upright as the animal lunged forward. The natural crouch that Sir Tyrone had seen on Long Island three decades earlier waited to be approved.

Finally, before five thousand war-weary Americans, it was the one-eyed Sewell, in dress blue and blue, who took the opening honors, as he had in 1863. His mount, Capt. T. G. Moore's Maiden, was the first of seven fillies to win the Travers in its first century and a quarter.[11]

The big draw was the next day's inaugural Saratoga Cup, which would become more popular than the Travers and often measure the greatest horse of the day. It would be contested seventy-five times through 1963. That Tuesday, Hunter was offering $10,000 on his Kentucky, not only in the Cup but against anything else in the country, and the crowd swelled to nearly ten thousand. They watched Gilpatrick, in blazing dress orange and crimson, outride Billy, another fireball in orange and orange, as the first Travers winner did defeat Captain Moore and take the first Cup as well.

On the third day, when Baltimore swept by to win with Hawkins aboard in bright red and white, the women "stood upon the seats, they screamed, they danced, they threw gloves and handkerchiefs in each other's faces, they laughed and cried hysterically." And they were not alone. Many knew little about what was going on, including the local "sporting editor," who had to ask Morrissey to point out the "backstretch," the straightaway on the far side of the track. Yet this naïve crowd had gambled an unprecedented $220,000 on that one $1,750 race.

The *World* reporter could not get over the women, maybe the first female sports crowd he had seen and well beyond the talents of "my poor pen or portraiture on canvas by an artist." He forgot Winslow Homer. Homer's portrait for *Harper's Weekly* showed these wealthy women not as hysterical spectators but as the leaders many were—brilliant, riveted, modern. He gloried not only in the artistry of their sumptuous textiles, but even more in them. They hinted at the future, just as the hundred-

Winslow Homer's Saratoga. *Harper's Weekly, 1865. Courtesy of the author.*

yard-plus grandstand did. Hardly noticeable in Homer's picture was a passé figure (based on his brother Charles) with mustache and pince nez, and even easier to miss was a Union soldier, his face in shadow. Such fighters as Generals Blair and Bartlett were at the track, reminders that the war was hardly over, yet the roar of this first national sports crowd after Appomattox was drowning the echoes of cannon.

Least prominent in Homer's picture were the horses prancing through the bottom right corner. The crowd was still the story. Not even Kentucky had achieved the status won by the Old Gray Mare, nor had any two-legged athlete matched the brief glory of Heenan. They were on the verge, though. When Fleetwing set the track's first national record on Thursday, running three miles in 5:31¾, it made the top of page one in the *Times*. And as Gilpatrick and Hawkins conducted one of their patented duels throughout the meeting, the former with five wins, the latter four, they hastened the day when writers would precede "jockey" with the adjective "star," which later would graduate to nounhood.[12]

By 5 P.M. on Saturday, August 12, 1865, the track was silent. "We are now on the receding wave," said the *Daily Saratogian*. The resort's new subset, those who came only for the races, was already the biggest. They had left behind a record—forty to fifty thousand paying customers over the six days—and opened an era of explosive growth for sports. Not that there weren't dissenters; like everybody else, Greeley's *Tribune* was just learning about organized sport on this scale. That didn't stop it from taking positions. After all, Greeley would be running for president in seven years. From Saratoga, the *Tribune* declared:

The taste for horse-racing, as it now exists, is more acquired than natural. . . . The turf values horses for their speculative and financial worth rather than their aesthetic or enduring qualities. Horse-racing is universally attended with betting. It is another and a huger form of gambling. . . . Men shout and grow frantic in their frenzy as the horses whirl round the track, and as they close upon the goal the spasm becomes stifling, ecstatic and bewildering.

Further, it charged, there was the problem of fraud. "The owners combine in rings to bet upon a certain horse, and his jockey contrives to narrowly lose the race." It did not explain how this might work. "Sometimes the jockeys play tricks upon each other for the choice of inside track. Some of them have been known to catch their rival rider by the foot to throw him from his horses while running at full speed in order to win a race." The fact that turf club rules called for throwing owners and jockeys off the course for "collusion" or misconduct was probably unknown to Greeley's paper, as its rush to criticize was exceeded only by its unfamiliarity with the sport. It saw fraud rather than naïveté where the bettors had not bothered to learn about the handicapper's assignment of weights. Many Americans since have shared the *Tribune*'s cynicism about the supposed high-minded goal of racing.

"Anybody who supposes that this species of amusement has anything to do with the improvement in the breed of horses is capable of believing that prizefighting has for its object the improvement of the breed of man." In what seemed a dig at Morrissey, a *Tribune* target since his brawling days on the docks, it added, "The Ring and the Turf have many features and faces in common, though the latter is eminently the least disreputable." The paper saved its strongest criticism for the treatment of the horses. "One cannot but reflect on the cruelty of spurring these beautiful animals into a foaming and exhausting speed as a matter of sport." Perhaps, it suggested, this is necessary to develop experienced racers, "but one cannot but grieve that experience is attended with so much cruelty." On the other hand, on the day it printed this, the *Tribune* turned over nearly half its front page to news of the Saratoga races. As Ralph Waldo Emerson (then age sixty-two) had put it, "Things are in the saddle / And ride mankind."[13]

The following Monday, America witnessed its biggest "Base Ball" game yet. Atlantic of Brooklyn battled Mutual of New York for "the championship of American ball players." By the *Tribune*'s count, almost twenty thousand people had watched the Atlantics take their earlier game that month, 13 to 12, in five, rain-halted innings. Now a second crowd ferried across the East River—there was no Brooklyn Bridge—and crammed into Brooklyn's Capitoline Ball Ground. "A larger and more orderly assembly never congregated on any ball ground." The home team Atlantics won again, 40 to 28. With that, the *Tribune* decided the cricket vs. baseball issue was resolved, declaring: "Base Ball is decidedly the National game of America." Well, it was and it wasn't.

The New York "National Association" rules were studied religiously in small towns, including Saratoga Springs, and the schedules of urban teams stretched far across state lines. With Americans looking to the west, a vast desert ballpark that could be conquered with a bat, baseball was taking off. But the *Spirit of the Times* had to teach Americans how to make a proper field. "The location of the pitcher's point and the home base are indicated by means of iron quoits, painted white." And even Atlantic vs. Mutual was buried under a tiny headline—"The Field"—in the middle of page eight. Not a single team nor rivalry, and no player, attracted a national following, or anything close to the coverage of "The Saratoga Races" in the summer of '65.

On Tuesday, a richer subset fled south in what the *Herald* called "the Stampede at Saratoga." Edward Ketchum, the son in the Manhattan securities house of Ketchum, Son and Company, had defrauded the company and banks of millions of dollars and was rumored to be catching a steamer to Europe. Panic hit the piazzas. "Half crinolinedom joined in lamentations, and the fair urged the brave to repair instantly to New York. . . . The afternoon train carried away a large portion of Wall street." The *Herald* correspondent was among those who waited a day and drove to the lake to drink milk punches and eat Moon's unique "fried potatoes" (not yet dubbed potato chips), then danced at the evening's hop before grabbing the 7:30 A.M. train. Once aboard, he and others cursed the clerk who hadn't warned that the train would pull in at 3:45 P.M., too late to visit their money. As for Ketchum, they found him in a Manhattan boardinghouse with an assumed name, $49,000 in U.S. legal notes, and sixty-seven forged gold certificates. The season was over.

The town was summed up this way in 1866: "Pure air, fresh breezes, crisp fried potatoes, a great deal of very weak human nature, some exceedingly disagreeable water, and the New York morning papers are here."[14] But it took a hell of a lot of work to create that scene. The women in the Congress Hall linen room were ironing into the night for the 1866 opening when flames broke out and burned down the dream that Gideon Putnam died building. So Broadway's recent gashes now included the ashes of Congress Hall, the charred half block south of the Union Hotel, the burned United States Hotel site, and the cinders of Terwilliger's hardware store and McGee's shirt and collar store at Broadway and Phila Street. To punish the Spa again, an August fire wiped out the Columbian Hotel and other Broadway buildings south of Lake Avenue. The place looked like something out of Sherman's Atlanta, but the visitors kept coming (including Sherman) and the Springs kept building, although it finally understood brick.

The planned "grand turnpike" to the track and the lake was updated in 1866. It was about time. A voyager that summer sarcastically described the current road, East Congress Street extended, this way: "I jumped into the carriage and enjoyed the dust, which couldn't have been more than a foot and a half deep till we reached the Lake House." Organized under state law and headed by the Lelands of the Union Hotel, the builders at one point dreamed up a road that "would hardly have its equal in America," a seven-mile toll pike turning south at Moon's and doubling back around little Lake Lonely, just west of Saratoga Lake. But they returned to the original idea of a three-mile stretch from the park, which would still require expropriating farmland on the south to make it one hundred feet wide.[15]

After less than a half mile, the grand approach to the track would divide into a sixty-foot road with twenty-foot pathways on either side. One pathway, laid with marble, would accommodate strollers, the other equestrians, with rows of trees creating "a delightful shade for the tired nag or the weary pedestrian." The avenue would be the first in town to be macadamized and beveled, though the dust-choked would have to see that. It would be called "the Union." Today Union Avenue still provides a spectacular approach to the track, lined with graceful, turn-of-the-century "cottages." Visitors unaware of its once famous dust and foolish dreams are startled by its out-of-place grandeur. How did this extraordinarily broad boulevard ever get here? How much luck does one little town deserve? Union Avenue replies simply by dividing into two shady roadways and two broad sidewalks, a variation on the original plan, just before it deposits everybody at the races.

America's first modern sports organization came into its own. Initially the Saratoga Association had used the rules of the venerated Metairie track in New Orleans. Now it drew up its own, twelve pages of them, copyrighted in 1866 along with those of eight other clubs and the racing associations of California (which was far ahead of its time in issuing statewide, albeit voluntary, rules). Several trotting associations were included as well. The published volume was a revelation of how far American sports had come.

Although none of the other tracks had anything like the national status of Saratoga, and none would survive, the *Rules and Regulations for the Government of Racing, Trotting, and Betting as Adopted by the Principal Turf Associations Throughout the United States and Canada* confirmed that racing had become a highly organized sport—the country's only organized national sport.[16]

With the zeal for organization and conformity that "wild" sports enthusiasts don't know they harbor, the rules covered everything imaginable. At Saratoga, "the horses shall be summoned for each heat by the bugle-call or by the bell on the Judges' stand." A variation on that survives today at Saratoga in the ringing of a bell (seven times) seven minutes before the bugle trill—the military air "First Call"—is sounded, ten minutes before post time. The starter, who was Wheatly himself, would no longer shout, "Go!" Instead, "the horses shall be started by the tap of the drum," with this important exception: "In races where the horses do not start from the Judges' stand, the horses shall be started by flag."[17]

Riders had to wear "jockey costume, the cap and jacket to be of silk, satin or velvet, the breeches of white cords, corduroy, or drilling, with white-topped boots. Gentlemen who first record their colors with the Secretary shall be entitled to them, and no one else shall be permitted to ride in them." The reference to gentlemen was the only discriminatory wording in the Saratoga rules, although a few tracks, such as Woodlawn at Louisville (but not Metairie in New Orleans), specifically barred African Americans from entering horses.[18]

Following British example, Saratoga adopted the modern birthday rule, by which horses foaled in the current year would be considered one year old—yearlings—on the following January 1. Most regional tracks did the same, but Metairie clung to the May 1 date favored in the Old South.[19]

Betting rules, widely assumed to have been a private affair until the mid-twentieth-century, were prescribed in exquisite detail, with emphasis on when bets were on, or off. If a bet was "play or pay" and the horse did not start, or the race was postponed, the bet was still on—and lost. All single bets on two events, forerunners of the daily double, were play or pay. A single bet on the finishes of several horses (there is nothing very original about today's exotic combinations) had to be carefully spelled out. If a bet was made between heats and all the horses didn't start the next heat, that bet was off. So betting was not only sanctioned but organized by the management. It could only encourage gamblers to presume they had a rightful role in other sports, a presumption that has been fought over ever since.

The Spa lengthened its card to three races a day. As it became increasingly professional, Morrissey's role as impresario and general facilitator faded somewhat, while Wheatly's as secretary and clerk expanded. Wheatly even broadened the resort's role as an equestrian center by designing a professionally graded half-mile trotting track for the county Agricultural Society. It was the best of several such tracks that sprang up around town. In operation beginning with the 1865 county fair, it was between Crescent and Gridley streets, a few blocks from its descendant, today's Saratoga Raceway. Wheatly's name actually began to change, too. He made the newspapers frequently, and as the papers themselves expanded and began to standardize, he saw it more often in its modern version: Wheatley.[20]

As for the athletes, to nobody's surprise, Kentucky repeated in the 1866 Saratoga Cup, with Charles Littlefield up. The bay was on his way to a startling lifetime record of 22–1, the defeat delivered by his half-brother Norfolk. The latter wound up 5–0 and Asteroid, the other great brother from that same Lexington crop, 12–0.[21]

Abe Hawkins bested Gilpatrick to win the third Travers on Merrill in 1866. He remained the most prominent of the many African Americans on the tracks, many of them, like Abe, listed only by first names. Dick rode at Saratoga for Robert A. Alexander, the leading breeder as lord of Kentucky's Woodburn Stud, home of Lexington. Albert was three months old when he and his mother were "purchased," in the terminology used to justify the crime, for $150 by Col. David McDaniel. He grew up on McDaniel's Virginia farm, where sports provided his escape. Everybody could see why McDaniel, as one writer put it, "fairly worships the boy," for at fourteen Albert was winning at Saratoga, beating Littlefield in 1866 and Gilpatrick the following year.

As the sport went national, Gilpatrick and Hawkins and their white and black colleagues offered the whole country a lesson in decency and the logic of freedom. Once they even helped show that thoroughbred racing, with its strong Southern influence, was far freer in a certain respect than trotting, the Northern amateur's passion. "Has a Negro a right to drive?" a reader asked the *Spirit of the Times*, the accepted authority in 1866. He added: "I have bet that a negro could not have won the race which took place at Hamilton (Ontario) this day, if he drove. There never has been an instance in the West where they permitted one to drive; and when he got into the wagon or sulky, the public hooted him down. Now, in all gambling transactions, custom makes the rule."

"You have lost your bet," the *Spirit* answered. "Custom has nothing to do with it. A man has as much right to employ a negro to drive a trotter as to ride a racehorse, and if a negro did drive and win, the owner of the horse would have just as good a right to the money as he would if Hiram Woodruff had driven. Does any man with a pennyweight of brains think the less of Charles Littlefield or Gilpatrick because they ride against Abe or Albert or Alexander's Dick."[22]

The Saratoga experiment in national sports began reproducing itself. The Association's first vice president, the former stock market king Leonard Jerome, had to have a track of his own. It has been suggested that this elegant Anglophile couldn't stand Morrissey, especially after the latter's Irish brethren forced him to man a gun during the draft riots. In fact, like Vanderbilt, Jerome got a kick out of Morrissey and also used his clout among the Tammany-controlled Democrats in his own railroad deals. Still, he had to have his track. In fact, he had to have several tracks, and he started by triumphantly founding the American Jockey Club in Manhattan to run the first one.

Jerome Park was built on its creator's country estate in Fordham, New York, then in Westchester County and now in the Bronx (near Knightsbridge Road and Jerome Avenue), where its name is preserved by the Jerome Park Reservoir. This track, Francis Morris's farm to the southeast at Throgs Neck, and John Hunter's spread a few miles north of that at Pelham, formed a triangle of magnificent horse country in today's east Bronx. Its jewel, Jerome Park, boasted not only racing but dining and dancing, skating and sleighing, trap shooting and the all-but-lost art of that century, coaching.[23]

Jerome drove an exquisite four-in-hand himself, the tall, bony, mustachioed sportsman commanding immediate attention in what a writer judged the best "turn-out" at Newport—until Jerome's friend, the short, genial August Belmont, came along in probably the finest vehicle in the United States.

A fastidious, German-born banker, Belmont had come to America as the representative of the Rothschild banking interests and was now chairman of the Democratic Party. His barouche was drawn by four thoroughbreds, with postilions on the left horse of each pair. The two riders, trained in Europe, wore black silk and velvet jackets and caps ornamented with gold lace, buckskin breeches, and high-top boots. The carriage was lined with satin damask trimmed with heavy gilt. At the rear, two footmen in "extreme livery" were suspended from a high seat called the "ramble" (later the rumble seat on cars). The writer estimated the cost of the horses at $25,000 and observed that when August Belmont appeared on the avenue in Newport, "all other vehicles instinctively give way." It was noted that his "democratic majesty" had a stable of some forty horses worth $1,000 to $8,000 each. It was this future power in Saratoga racing whom Jerome wisely installed as president of his American Jockey Club.[24]

America's second modern sports venue opened on September 25, 1866. A celebrity crowd collected at the eight-thousand-seat clubhouse on a bluff above the course, which was oddly shaped, like an old eyeglass case, with the clubhouse in the indentation. An Englishman noted the elderly pool seller in an elevated box, but was surprised by the eerie absence of shouting bookmakers and by the stubborn American style of one of the black riders. "He has got his saddle forward on the horse's withers, and his feet are apparently kicking at his horse's mouth. . . . It would be difficult to say which ride the worst, the white or black boys, so bad are both." He came to a strange conclusion. "The extraordinary part . . . is that such great speed should be attained with such wretched jockeyship." A preliminary event, a mile and a quarter for three-year-olds, was won by Alexander's Bayswater, Hawkins up.[25]

The Inaugural Stake, two of three four-mile heats, was rich indeed, worth $7,300 plus a $1,500 silver cup, and as expected, Kentucky swept it in two heats. Entered by Hunter, Travers, and Osgood, the five-year-old was quickly snapped up by Jerome for $40,000. In front of the cheering stand, he lifted his twelve-year-old daughter, Jennie with the big brown eyes, and plopped her on Kentucky's back. Horses were Jennie's passion, and she would never forget that moment, just as a lot of people would never forget Jennie.[26]

Clara Jerome, however, was not amused. She had borne it as well as she could when she learned that her husband had suggested his daughter's name in memory of a woman with whom he had a passing but apparently passionate relationship. The Swedish Nightingale Jenny Lind would judge Jerome the best-looking of her admirers, and he said of her: "Her voice is indescribable, like the dawn. Who wants more?" Clara had also suffered through his public competition with Belmont for the attentions of a Boston divorcée, Mrs. Fanny Ronalds.[27]

"Do you remember Fanny's celebrated ball?" Jerome would ask Belmont.

"I ought to, I paid for it," said Belmont.

"Why, how very strange, so did I."[28]

Clara had watched while Jerome helped oversee and finance the career of Jenny Lind's teenage successor, Adalina Patti. And she must have heard the stories about the "sporting men." There was the night Leonard and his brother Larry dropped off Travers after a night of carousing, only to hear Mrs. Travers' wide-awake voice. "Is that you, Bill?"

"Why, yes. Wh-who did you expect?"[29]

Adalina and Fanny even appeared at the Jerome Park opening. The next year Clara would leave for Paris and take Jennie and her two sisters with her, permanently. When she left Jerome Park early that opening day, however, her excuse was merely that she felt faint. Few could have noticed, what with their eyes on the two front-runners, Kentucky and Grant, who was about to be swept aloft in the first presidential election since the assassination. William "Boss" Tweed, who, as grand sachem of Tammany Hall, controlled New York Democrats, was there, too, and the New York Democrat John Morrissey. After paying fifteen years' dues in street and Tammany politics, he had something higher in mind.

9

SIRING THE BELMONT AND PIMLICO

HE SAT AMID THE primary colors of the midcentury—incendiary reds and luminescent blues set off by golds and gilding. From his desk in the next to last row on the eastern side, he faced a pile of white marble slabs, the Speaker's platform. Behind it were standing portraits of Washington and Lafayette. High above hung a rare delight, a cast-iron and stained-glass skylight painted with the seals of all thirty-seven states, reunited at last. Ohio's, for example, drew attention to the desk of James A. Garfield, future president. The Empire State's shone on an immigrant from Ireland, who had floated to the top again on cards, colts, Vanderbilt tips, and Manhattan votes. It was 1867, and the most famous gambling-house operator in America had been elected to Congress.[1]

Dismayed, Congress back then listed his occupation as "banker," and today on Capitol Hill people are still embarrassed to learn about him, yet he was more than the first and last gambling king in Congress. He was the first and last undefeated boxing champion, the first national champion of any sport, to serve. The crowds at the track suggested he might have been more in tune with what was going on than were the others in the House.

He was three months in office when his experiment in national sports reproduced itself again. Just as Saratoga had christened the Travers after its president, Jerome Park inaugurated "the Belmont" for three-year-olds in June 1867, and today it remains the second oldest feature in American spectator sports.

Francis Morris had dropped a hint of things to come back in 1863 at Saratoga, where he brought out a colt named Dangerous. His imported Eclipse then sired five fillies, and Morris gave them even more menacing names: Merciless, Relentless, Regardless, Remorseless, and— deadliest of them all—Ruthless. Their mother, after all, was Barbarity. It was Ruthless who now conquered the inaugural Belmont and the Travers, the first such "double" in major sports titles that survive, and then won the Sequel Stake at Saratoga, all with Gilpatrick up. By the end of that year, she had racked up a record eleven wins and four seconds in fifteen starts but then she injured herself and was retired. One day a hunter went wandering through Morris's farm near today's Throgs Neck Bridge. There was something in the distance. The hunter shot it. It fell. It was the great Ruthless in her paddock, possibly the only famous thoroughbred killed as game.[2]

Ruthless and the new schedule—Jerome Park for three days in May, Saratoga for six in August, Jerome Park again for five in October—showed that organized sports

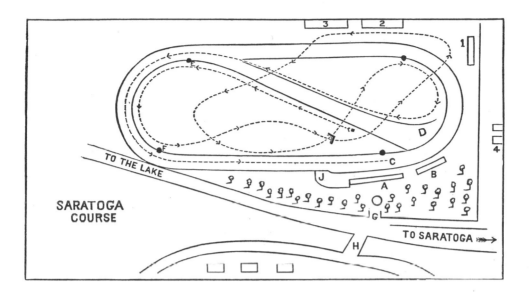

The diagonal chute. It is seen in an early diagram, which also shows: A. Grandstand; B. Public stand; C. Judges' and timers' stands; D, E, F. Alternative starting points; G. Main entrance; H. Entance to training track; J. Betting ring. 1. Pierre Lorillard's stable; 2. August Belmont's stable; 3. T. W. Doswell's stable; 4. David McDaniel's stable. The diagram is from *Krik's Guide to the Turf*, 1878. *Courtesy of the National Museum of Racing and Hall of Fame, Saratoga Springs.*

could mount a serial spectacle from spring through fall. More Americans saw what stardom was going to be like when six-year-old Kentucky challenged the four-mile record of his father, Lexington, in Jerome Park's October meeting. The son fell twelve seconds short, but *Harper's Weekly* splashed his portrait across its cover. And the sport took off. There was racing now throughout the Northeast and Midwest. It had never stopped in California, where San Francisco's Ocean House course ran in December, with other meetings at Sacramento, Stockton, San Joachim, San Jose, Laporte, Marysville, and Petaluma. Down South, it was rising again at the Metairie course in New Orleans, and in Alabama, Tennessee, and Kentucky.

Saratoga even tinkered with the democratic oval. In 1868, borrowing from the English, who built tracks of every shape except regular and with lots of sharp angles, it opened a stretch of track that cut its oval diagonally. It sliced across the infield from the first turn (right of the grandstand) to near the end of the backstretch. It was called, variously, the "cut across," the "sectional," the "three-quarter track," and a "shoot," a misspelling of what came to be its name, a "chute." It gave the public and judges a closer view of both the starts and the finishes of more races.[3]

Races at three-quarters of a mile, for example, could be started in the chute, the horses turning left onto the main track, then racing down the home stretch and past the grandstand to finish. For the mile and three-quarters Travers, they would then circle the main track one time. The term "furlong" (220 yards or an eighth of a mile) had entered American racing, and Saratoga would also start races of five furlongs

Excelsior Spring. This pavilion was moved to the racetrack for a spring drilled in 1966 and named Big Red Spring, after Man o' War. Ca. 1869. *Robert Joki Collection, Saratoga Springs.*

from the chute. Today's chutes at American courses do not usually cut across the infield but are short extensions of the main track's straightaways.

Saratoga Springs grew, too, in every direction: up, as Phila and Spring streets rose from the valley of springs and were opened into Broadway—and down. In early 1868, a mason working on H. H. Hathorn's new Congress Hall—specifically, on the foundation of its separate ballroom across Spring Street—did what came naturally and discovered a spring. Hathorn No. 1 would become more popular than the fabled Congress.[4]

The hotel opened later that year, in brick, and the *Spirit of the Times* correspondent declared, "It is by far the finest hotel on the continent." Its five stories were topped with landmark thirty-foot towers at each end and in the center. Its front piazza was set off by nineteen fluted columns with Corinthian caps and extended 240 feet along the hotel's 460-foot Broadway facade. That piazza wrapped around the north wing, which reached 235 feet back to Putnam Street, while piazzas in the rear looked out on the hotel's gardens. The twelve hundred guests found themselves negotiating a mile and a half of hallways and seven acres of carpeting. In their rooms, they found "bell wires" connecting to an "annunciator" in the office. An elevator, said to be the finest in the country, rose to a rooftop promenade. Saratoga's new Congress Hall and the even bigger Union Hotel formed a canyon of elegance unlike anything in Manhattan.[5]

Morrissey was also puffing himself up. It is true he said nothing on the floor of the Fortieth Congress, and it is true, too, that when the roll was called, he was often absent. When on February 24, 1868, the House took a step unique in its history, the Manhattan Democrat was among those listed as "not voting" on the resolution to impeach the president. He was hardly shy on paper, however. Once he sent an imperious telegram about government jobs to a White House aide: "Don't send any more names for my district until I see you."[6]

THEY'RE OFF!

He got brasher after his colleagues impeached—indicted—Andrew Johnson for "high crimes and misdemeanors," specifically for firing Secretary of War Edwin Stanton without Senate approval. Tried by the Senate, Johnson escaped conviction by just one vote, adding a jewel to Grant's coronation by the Republicans a few days later in Chicago. Morrissey pounced on the wounded Johnson for more patronage. He wired him directly to complain that the appointments of two Manhattan tax inspectors "have not been made in accordance with your directions," to which the White House dutifully responded, "Dispatch of yesterday at once attended to." Another time he fired off a letter to the president. He wanted a mutual friend appointed Surveyor of the Port of New York, and he bluntly reminded Johnson that the current one "certainly has no claims upon you." Here, too, was the Irishman's old levitation. The friend was Chester A. Arthur, future president.

Morrissey got in yet another shot as Johnson prepared his Fourth of July amnesty for the Southern rebels. As they were not going to be prosecuted anyway, the amnesty was viewed as a sop to Southern delegates and their sympathizers, including Tammanyites like Morrissey, then gathering for the Democrats' convention at the new Tammany Hall. "Make no exceptions," Morrissey warned the president in a telegram, "everything hangs on it." Exactly what hung on a meaningless amnesty by a hopeless president wasn't clear to everyone, but long before he went to Congress, Morrissey had favored national reconciliation, notably at his racetrack. Now came a development historians would miss: the Old South renascent, way up north.[7]

A month and a day after the amnesty, the three-year-old Lost Cause flew down the new chute across the infield, showing the way to a Jeff Davis filly and seven others. The Southern forces on hand were led by Maj. T. G. Bacon of South Carolina, owner of Lost Cause; Col. McDaniel of Virginia, owner of the Jeff Davis daughter; Gen. P. C. Hebert, president of Metairie; and William Cottrill, of Alabama. The Yankees were officered by Dan Sickles, of Gettysburg fame; Maj. Gen. John Schofield, commander of the Army of the Ohio; and Brig. Gen. John Cochrane. The rebels would not capture the fifth Travers, but neither would the North. If Lost Cause heard a deathly sound behind her, it was The Banshee, the third filly to take the event in five years, in a record 3:10 ¾. Entered by John Clay, she was owned now by J. O'Fallon, a St. Louis millionaire. In the next race, the gray form of Stonewall Jackson swept the two-mile heats.[8]

Not all Saratoga Southerners were rising again. Sam Duncan used to come up from his Mississippi plantation at Skipwith Landing. He had dumped so much money in Moon's Lake House they named the dining room after him. One summer after the war, a shabby figure entered the bar and ordered a drink. Cary Moon thought he recognized him.[9]

"Hello, Sam, is that you?" Moon told the story to a journalist.

"I didn't think you would know me."

"I should think I'd be a darned fool to forget a man who has spent as many thousand dollars with me as you have."

"Don't mention it." The visitor looked out the window.

"Sam, won't you dine today in Duncan Hall?"

"No, no, Moon." He brushed away a tear. "I'm too poor now. I've lost everything. I'm stopping at a quiet boarding-house in Ballston."

The dapper little Moon ordered him "the best dinner the boys could get up . . . woodcock, trout, and champagne and Santa Cruz rum." (Moon's champagne had a remarkable zing, impregnated as it was with orange peel according to an old Memphis tradition.) Moon did not say whether he served Duncan his famous "flaky fried potatoes," not yet called potato chips, or Saratoga chips, or even chips.

The bigger story was that everybody was back, "from Canada to the West Indies," as one paper put it. Just how important Saratoga was can be judged from the fact that O'Fallon shipped his horses from Missouri on trains with "no proper boxes for the horses, no shelter while they were kept waiting, and no water to give them. At one place, the horses had to stand under the thin shade of some trees for . . . above an hour with the thermometer between ninety and one hundred." There was no other way.[10]

It was a transitional crowd, one of the last with so many from 1863: Dr. Weldon, Clay, Price McGrath, T. G. Moore, John Purdy, John Hunter, Francis Morris, James Watson, and P. C. Bush. The *Spirit of the Times* was moved to remember their entries: "Taken together, a better lot of horses hardly ever faced the flag than when Jerome Edgar, Thunder, Captain Moore, Lizzie W., Mammona, Sympathy, John Morgan, etc. contended on the little track where the stables and exercise grounds still are."

Those six days in 1868 hinted at the future big business of sports. Admissions to the newly painted grandstand reached $22,000 after three days, topping all previous meetings. More than fifty of America's best thoroughbreds had shown up, and no fewer than seventy one-year-olds were being nominated for the Travers two years hence. As for the card, it was unusually rich, offering not only the sweepstakes, in which the winners took home the combined entry fees, but also some $11,000 in purses with no fees attached. The press called this "a liberality the American Jockey Club might imitate" at Jerome Park, where entrants paid five percent of the purse.

Mass entertainment became a bigger factor, too. "Saratoga has always been famous for the excellence of its races over the timbers," the *Spirit* declared, and now it scheduled two hurdle events because of their popularity, "especially for the ladies." The big 1864 spill had brought protests, as had one at Jerome Park in 1867, when an inexperienced rider was killed. But good riders knew how to tumble, the *Spirit* insisted, as it recalled the old woman's comment on the drowning of sailors: "I pities the landsmen, but them other fellers is used to it."

Besides the rising powers of America's national sport, among them Cottrill, McDaniel, and Milton H. Sanford, of New Jersey and Kentucky, there was a more distant glimpse ahead in the listing of a corporate owner for several entries, the Jerome Park Stable. Travers, too, had entered a couple of horses as Annieswood Stable, which he had formed in partnership with Hunter, but they did not start, and Annieswood would never amount to much. It would be years before the names of stables would overshadow those of the rugged individuals on the charts.

Most dramatic of all, Saratoga gave birth again. Sanford threw a dinner party that season, perhaps to celebrate his victory with Lancaster and the sensational English

Programme, Sixth Day.

TUESDAY, AUGUST 11th, 1868.

FIRST RACE—HURDLE RACE,

For all ages, two miles, over 8 hurdles, 3½ feet high; handicap for horses only that started in the second day's hurdle race; $500 to the winner; $100 to the second horse, if three or more start.

ENTRIES:

1. D. Buckley enters ch h Eagle, aged, by Vandal, dam by imp Sovereign. 153 lbs. **Dress Orange with Blue Sash.**
2. Thos. Lawler enters b h Starlight, 6 yrs, by Star Davis, dam Brown Kitty. 153 lbs. **Dress Claret and Gold.**
3. J. M. Brown enters ch h Tycoon, aged, by Omera, dam Nota Price. 146 lbs. **Dress Orange and Blue.**
4. M. H. Cryer enters br m Lobelia, 5 yrs, by imp Bonnie Scotland, dam Capitola. 155 lbs.— **Dress Blue and Black.**

SECOND RACE—PURSE $1,000,

Dash of four miles, for all ages.

ENTRIES:

1. Jno. H. Davis enters ch c Plantagenet, 4 yrs, by Planet, dam Rosa Bonheur, by imp Glencoe. **Dress Green and Orange.**
2. Jno. H. Davis enters b c Pat Molloy, 3 yrs, by Lexington, dam Gloriana, by Eclipse. **Dress Green and Orange.**
3. I. W. Pennock enters ch c J. A. Connelly, 4 yrs, by Vandal, dam by imp Margrave. **Dress Scarlet and White.**

THIRD RACE—PURSE $600,

Dash of one and a half miles; handicap for horses only that have run during the meeting; weights to be announced immediately after the last race on the day previous, and to be accepted at the usual time of closing entries; entrance, 5 per cent., added.

ENTRIES:

1. J. Eckerson enters b f Sleety, 4 yrs, by Rogers, dam Angeline, by Albion. 85 lbs. **Dress Scarlet and White Stripes.**
2. Bowie & Hall enter b c Viley, 3 yrs, by Uncle Vic, dam imp Silver Star, by Kingston. 87 lbs.— **Dress White and Red.**
3. D. McDaniel enters b f Albuera, 3 yrs, by Jeff Davis, dam Ninette, by Revenue. 80 lbs.— **Dress Blue and Red.**
4. D. McDaniel enters ch f Lizzie Rogers, 3 yrs, by Brother to Frank Allen, dam Jenny Rose, by Glencoe. 82 lbs. **Dress Blue and Red.**
5. J. Pincus enters ch f Clara Clarita, 4 yrs, by imp Lapidist, dam Madonna. 83 lbs. **Dress—**

FOURTH RACE—SWEEPSTAKES,

$50 each, catch weights; half a mile.

ENTRIES.

Thos. G. Bacon names gr h, 5 years, by Lightning, dam Minnow by Voucher. **Dress Blue and Yellow.**
J. W. Weldon names b g Jubal, 4 years, by imp Balrownie, dam Julia by imp Glencoe. **Dress Maroon and Red.**

J. J. Bevins names bl f Annie Workman, 4 years, by Wagram, dam Lady Franklin. **Dress—**

The "Daily Saratogian" contains a full account of the Races every morning.

An 1868 race card. They were, literally, cards. *National Museum of Racing and Hall of Fame, Saratoga Springs.*

jockey Billy Hayward in the Saratoga Cup. In the mellowness of it all, a proposal was made: that a "Dinner Party Stakes" be inaugurated. People have always thought up grandiose projects here—it must be the water—but the odd thing is that they often happen, and this time Oden Bowie, soon to be governor of Maryland, took it seriously. He offered a staggering $15,000 as the purse. The Maryland Jockey Club immediately set about building a track for the event near Baltimore, at an obscure place called Pimlico.[11]

The Springs was growing at an alarming rate. At the Union Hotel, the Lelands looked across Broadway at Congress Hall, where Hathorn was brilliantly assisted by James Breslin, and panicked. What was probably the biggest hotel in the country was not big enough. The Lelands tore down their front, and with it any reminders of Putnam's boardinghouse, and threw up a five-story brick facade, covering it with a three-story, three hundred-foot-long iron balcony, the American piazza to end all piazzas. They added a mansard roof to match Hathorn's, opened a two hundred-foot dining room, installed their own "vertical railway," and put "communicators" in the rooms. They now had 824 rooms for 1,700 guests, who could see out 1,890 windows, peep into new courtyard cottages, graze over nine acres of carpets, and run the entire Travers through the halls. Where once they entertained Lt. Gen. U. S. Grant, they would welcome a more important guest in 1869, President U. S. Grant. Vanderbilt, nothing if not stubborn, stuck with Congress Hall, and waited for Marvin to rebuild the United States Hotel.[12]

No names were more important in that 1868 track crowd than the Commodore and Billy, as he still called W. H. Only Morrissey was as important in the early history of the track and the middle history of the town. True, when it came to horses, Vanderbilt still preferred his trotters, stabled behind his house at 10 Washington Place in Manhattan. On better days, he had raced them himself on Harlem Lane, from Central Park to 162nd Street and Jerome Avenue, and one of his best, Mountain Boy, turned in a half mile of 1:06. In late June, Mountain Boy had taken to one of Saratoga's trotting tracks and thrilled the old man by winning a $3,000 purse, probably the biggest yet in trotting at the Spa. But if Vanderbilt chose not to breed or race thoroughbreds, he still went all out backing the running races, not only with his money but with his visibility. The image of the country's most famous millionaire playing whist and euchre on the piazzas all summer long, while dispatching commissioners to place his bets and mulling over the fate of the nation's railroads, confirmed that this was, indeed, America's resort.[13]

It was a painful year for the Commodore. By June, he had suffered his first and only major business defeat, failing in a bid to grab the Erie from Jay Gould and Jim Fisk and thus extend his railroads to Chicago. Six days after the races, his wife, Sophia, died of apoplexy at age seventy-three. "Dignifying her passing," as biographer Wayne Andrews put it, Vanderbilt commanded a private train from Saratoga and reached New York in six hours. He had never been extremely close to anyone since his son George died, not even his other children, and he had ignored Sophia of late, but now he found himself alone.[14]

Morrissey, with "his wind a little thick" and his wheezing, wasn't what he used to be, either, certainly not what he was the year before when he had won a race at Jerome Park. But this was Morrissey the horse, McDaniel's four-year-old bay. Morrissey the Irishman was still a fine figure of a congressman, "in his white flannel suit, huge diamond rings, and pin containing brilliants of the first water," as a contemporary described him at Saratoga. As for the many who thought his election a fluke, he proved them wrong in 1868 by running and winning again.[15]

In 1869, Vanderbilt bounced back with new maneuvers to get to Chicago. He would try to take over a series of trunk lines known collectively as the Lake Shore Railroad. At one point, he summoned another private train, this one from Saratoga to Buffalo and Cleveland (he could order up trains the way others called carriages) to oversee the talks. As the card-playing Commodore wheeled and dealed, the history of the nation's greatest industry seemed oddly interwoven with that of Saratoga Springs and its racetrack.

August Belmont, the banker and Democratic Party chairman, made his first major appearance outside Jerome Park that season, winning the 1869 Travers with his sensational import, Glenelg. The "boy" was the white Charley Miller, the records pointing out that the "C. Miller who rode Corsican was a colored boy." "Boy" wasn't always pejorative at the track; it meant jockey, without regard to age or color. Jerome Park and Saratoga also tried something new in 1869, or rather, something old: a "Match Day" before the regular meeting. A throwback to antebellum days, it featured one-on-one events and a few contests with bigger fields, such as one for "gentleman riders" at Jerome Park and a "private sweepstakes" at Saratoga.

At the Spa, Match Day was remarkable only for W. R. Babcock's spectacular Helmbold, who was going places. This time, for some reason, Babcock passed up a chance for Helmbold to dance with Glenelg in the $3,000 Travers, settling instead for a $500 purse on Match Day. Dead last, by the way, was a trio from the summer of '63: Dr. Weldon's nine-year-old Aldebaran, Gilpatrick up.

Neither Weldon, Aldebaran, nor Gilpatrick himself would be remembered much longer. The Poughkeepsie boy had piloted not only Boston but his son Lexington and his grandson Kentucky. He had won the first Travers, the first Saratoga Cup, the first Belmont, and the fourth Travers. Gilpatrick would quite accurately describe those decades as a remarkable era of American racing, "all of which I saw and a great part of which I was."

Also to be forgotten was Abe Hawkins. Aboard Lecomte, he had delivered Lexington his only loss. He had won America's second and third Derbies (at Paterson) on Richmond and Merrill, then the third Travers, again on Merrill, and the opener at Jerome Park; but he would be cited in modern records only by his former slave name, as some mysterious, unknown "Abe." As for the one-eyed Sewell, who defeated Burgoyne in the battle of Saratoga and captured the second Travers, his given name would never surface; nor would Billy do a fraction as well by history as Gentleman Johnny, though he won more. The 1860s were the lost years.[16]

The publication of annual turf records had been halted by the war, so, officially speaking, the sixties had never happened. Tales might be told about Lizzie W. and Kentucky, about the dueling Gilpatrick and Hawkins, but it was hard to prove. Not until 1901 would a turf statistician, H. G. Crickmore, retrieve and publish the records. Even then, his three statistical volumes were all but unknown outside racing. They became so rare that seventy years later a distinguished history of horse racing would refer to Gilpatrick's ride on Lexington in 1855, when he set the four-mile record, as probably his last.[17]

In recent times, a New York writer, looking for solutions to the decline of racing, commented that the sport had put Saratoga on the map. His remark did not bode well for his search, since the truth was just the opposite. It was Saratoga that had put racing on the map, transforming it from a then predominantly Southern pastime. From Saratoga on Cup Day in 1901, historian W. S. Vosburgh looked back: "the Civil War ended all racing in that section of the country south of the Potomac, which had long been its chief theatre, and a few years later saw its transfer to the North. The inauguration of Saratoga as a racing centre in 1863 was followed by Jerome Park in 1866, and racing, which had fallen in popularity in the North some twenty years previously, began a career which has rendered it the National sport of the country."[18]

In the sun of the decade's final summer, the Commodore met a thirty-year-old. She was Frank Crawford, daughter of a Mobile, Alabama, family ruined by the war. Two weeks after T. G. Moore won the Cup for the old guard with Bayonet, seventy-five-year-old "Cornele" eloped with Frank from Saratoga and got hitched in London, Ontario. Two days later, they were ensconced in Congress Hall.[19] Almost immediately the railroad king was back in action. Again he went after the Chicago route. He started by dumping New York Central's own Lake Shore stocks, sending the price plummeting. Then a historic disaster: on Friday, September 24, an attempt by Gould and Fisk to corner the gold market collapsed and sent stocks plunging.[20]

It was Black Friday, the worst one-day earthquake yet in American financial history, and its aftershocks would be known as the Panic of '69. "Over the pallid faces of some men stole a deadly hue," said the *Herald*. "Others rushed like wildfire through the streets, hatless and caring little about stumbling against their fellows." Congressman Morrissey was one of many who were dangerously long on stocks. In the middle of the crisis, the Commodore decided to go downtown himself, taking offices in the Bank of New York. He bolstered morale on the Street by supporting his own stocks, and a hopeful Morrissey quickly put out the word that Vanderbilt was buying. When the smoke cleared, seventy thousand shares of Lake Shore and control of that railroad were in Vanderbilt's hands. The congressman, however, had not escaped. He was said to have lost $600,000; on the other hand, he knew how to deal.

The representative's house ran better than the House of Representatives. As an antigambling tract sadly conceded, Matilda Street attracted "judges, senators, bankers, millionaires" and launched him into an era of explosive growth. Copying Baden-Baden in Germany and other Continental casinos, a few of the gaming joints at American watering places were gussying themselves up and declaring themselves "club houses," which doubtless helped calm the authorities. Johnny Chamberlin's at Long Branch was famous for lavish dining, enhanced by Partagas cigars and rare wines. In 1870 John Morrissey opened his own club house, a three-story brick casino on East Congress Street across from the park. Though today it stands unappreciated

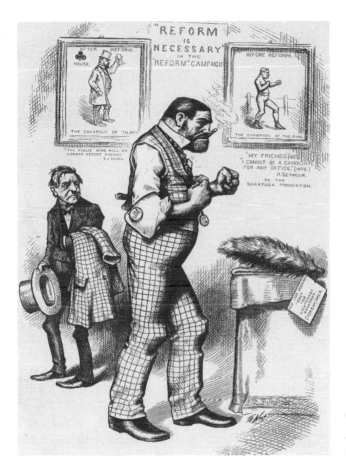

Thomas Nast's Morrissey,
*Harper's Weekly, 1876. Cour-
tesy of the author.*

in the enlarged park, it is a congressional achievement no other member, before or since, could match. The Manhattan representative strengthened his position by breaking with Tweed and cofounding a reform movement, the Young Democracy, in 1870, a year before the Boss had his great fall. He recouped a good chunk of what he lost in the Panic, supposedly earning $500,000 from the Saratoga casino's first two summers on an investment of half that. And he achieved international status. His closest world rival, François Blanc, had abandoned Baden-Baden and was developing Monaco, but it would be another decade before the first section of its Monte Carlo casino would open.

The congressman's establishment really was a club house, a rendezvous of the turf set. Belmont, Travers, and other members of the American Jockey Club reputedly invested in it, and the Commodore was a regular. Though not permitted to play, at least not openly, women patronized Morrissey's dining room from the start, and it became popular for receptions. All were greeted by a tiered fountain outside the Italianate palace, which is now a civic museum and home of the historical society.[21]

One visitor that summer wasn't buying it, particularly when he thought of

Siring the Belmont and Pimlico

Blanc's location. The young Henry James was getting more and more peeved as he heard the local attractions touted as "the finest in the world. One of these is Mr. John Morrissey's casino. I bowed my head submissively to this statement, but privately I thought of the blue Mediterranean, and the little white promontory of Monaco, and the silver-gray verdure of olives, and the view across the outer sea toward the bosky cliffs of Italy." As he dreamed in 1870, the big money behind America's national sport met at Morrissey's.[22]

The successes of the Spa and Jerome Park had proved so irresistible that a third major track had opened, with some of the advantages of both. This was Monmouth Park, near Long Branch, the Jersey watering place, and only a ferry and train ride from Manhattan. It was Belmont's Glenelg, the Travers victor of the year before, who opened Monmouth Park, finally confronting the great Helmbold—and defeat. Unbowed, Belmont unwrapped a new purchase at Saratoga, Daniel Swigert's Kingfisher, who had won the Belmont and made Charley Miller the first rider to take two Travers in a row. Then Kingfisher, too, was upstaged by the hero of Monmouth Park.[23]

A Saratoga lady seemed transfixed by Helmbold. Naturally, the one who spotted her was Henry James, who did not share Winslow Homer's admiration for Saratoga ladies but rather thought them airheads (scant use they would have had for him as well). This one was the ultimate, a beauty "with whom it appears to be an inexorable fate that she shall be nothing more than dressed." She sat "in gorgeous relief against the dusty clapboards of the hotel, with her beautiful hands folded in her silken lap, her head drooping slightly beneath the weight of her *chignon,* her lips parted in a vague contemplative gaze at Mr. Helmbold's well-known advertisement on the opposite fence, her husband beside her reading the New York *Herald.*" Cuckolded by Babcock's chestnut? Actually, the advertiser was H. T. Helmbold, after whom the horse was named, a New York purveyor of exotic pharmaceuticals. Maybe the joke was on James. As Homer knew, she could have been a sports fan.

Horsemen, clotheshorses, horses—all knew Saratoga better than the American intellectual. Those writing about the country, and writing endlessly, and those creating it, and writing nothing, collided at the Springs. Many of the former, however, just didn't get America. They were looking for Europe. An escapee from dry Boston, Henry James did like Moon's, "where you may sit upon a broad piazza and partake of fried potatoes and 'drinks.'" It wasn't the potatoes he was interested in, but they could have taught him a lot about America. They were still not called chips but were already being consumed as fast food, although they certainly weren't called that, either. In one of the earliest descriptions of Americans snacking, a huge wedding party of several brides was spotted on Moon's verandah, "each with a plate of flaky fried potatoes in her hand, while Hubby stood near with a couple of glasses of that detestable water." One day Moon divulged his recipe to a working reporter who, unlike James, was interested in such silly things.[24]

"We slice them as thin as paper, put them in ice-water overnight, wipe them dry with a towel, then fry them quick."

"What else do you do?"

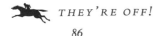

Moon gave the reporter a profound look. "Well, there is one thing that I fool them all on. Do you see this big dark oven?"

"Yes."

"Well, I put them in there, after drying them with the towel, where it is perfectly hot and dark, and dry them to a crisp before they are fried; that makes them light-colored. That's a secret."

It was the drinks, however, that sent the Boston refugee into Jamesian flight, providing, he allowed, "the felicity sighed for by that wanton Italian lady of the anecdote, when, one summer evening, to the sound of music, she wished that to eat an ice were a sin." He would have been mortified to learn he had just eaten America's first snack.

James did think he understood the "democratic, vulgar Saratoga" of 1870, especially its Union Hotel and the piazza, which, "I have been repeatedly informed, is the largest 'in the world.'" Here, he admitted, "they come from the uttermost ends of the Union—from San Francisco, from New Orleans, from Alaska. As they sit with their white hats tilted forward and their chairs tilted back, and their feet tilted up, and their cigars and toothpicks forming various angles . . . I seem to see in their faces a tacit reference to the affairs of a continent."

James was particularly offended by the doings under the ballroom along Washington Street. "A noisy auctioneer, in his shirt and trousers, black in the face with heat and vociferation, was selling 'pools' of the races to a dense crowd of frowsy betting-men." Somehow James lacked the mob's appreciation of Helmbold's smashing victory over Hamburg and Glenelg in the sixth Saratoga Cup. Yet at that moment, countless thousands of Americans were following not Henry James's travels but King-fisher and Helmbold as they headed for a crash with another athlete pounding across the nation's midsection. First, however, the Spa would foal a fourth major sports venue.

Saratoga. Jerome Park. Monmouth Park. Now Pimlico opened, on October 25, 1870. Two days later it staged the race dreamed up at M. H. Sanford's Saratoga party. Sanford himself entered a Lexington colt—he was so ungainly they labeled him a cart horse—and won that improbable Dinner Party Stakes. Three years hence, Pimlico's first hero would become immortal by lending his name to another race there, the Preakness. They must have been hungry at that inaugural meeting, for they also had a Breakfast Stakes, won by Glenelg, and a Supper Stakes, taken by an even more imposing figure of the future, Harry Bassett.[25]

Pimlico promised further thrills at Saratoga, but racing thrived at countless regional courses as well. It was these that were now launching the most celebrated American athlete since the Old Gray Mare and John Heenan—the first of those who much later would be dubbed "superstars."

 *10*

LONGFELLOW VS. HARRY BASSETT

HE WAS KNOWN as the largest racehorse in the land. He stood just under seventeen hands high, and his stride, driven by an "immense propelling power," was said to be about twenty-six feet. He was an ungainly animal, sired either by a committee or imported Leamington out of Nantura. His head was "homely and clumsily put on," said a reporter, and had a broad white band running down his face. He looked like something funny was about to happen.

"He starts off like a camel charged with electricity," the reporter said, "but by and by, when the electricity is going, he settles into a steady, rolling gait. Then his strides become monstrous, and without apparent effort, he shoots by everything on the track." American racing had largely discarded the practice of naming horses after other horses, but naming them for people was in its heyday. So this was Longfellow, after the living poet. He was writing an epic of his own.[1]

Longfellow's backers said he was sick when beaten by Enquirer in his debut at three. After that, he passed everything on the road from Memphis to Lexington to Cincinnati, and by 1871 he looked invincible. He polished off Helmbold and Preakness to capture the second Monmouth Cup and a week later was in Saratoga for a showdown with Belmont's Fisher.

The turf set found Morrissey in full flower. Kicked out of Tammany for espousing reform, he had foregone a third run and left Congress in March at the end of his second term. This gave him time for some important business, the opening of an annex to his summer casino. The new salon on the east was smaller than the original but more elegant still, with tall windows and a French Renaissance interior.

"The finest hell on earth" is what the *New York Times* called Morrissey's Saratoga place. Welcomed into a dark vestibule by an African-American doorman, reporters peeked into Morrissey's office and plush little parlors on the left, a gaming room to the right, the all-important dining room across the rear. A sign reading "Saratoga Club" announced a twenty-five dollar entrance fee and the prices of drinks. A few steps more, and one reporter was blown away. Assigned by his antigambling editors to condemn hell, he found it "almost impossible . . . to repress an exclamation of surprise and pleasure" at the "clink and clatter of the supper room . . . the soft swirl and rustle which accompany the ball in its course around the 'deadly wheel,'" and the soft tapestries, silk upholstered chairs, massive mantels, and black walnut woodwork. Most of the players, he scribbled, getting back to his assignment, were "fast young men" losing with "a strange, unvarying regularity."[2]

Morrissey's Club House. Carriages passing it on the way to the track. *Leslie's, 1873. Courtesy of the author.*

Among the dealers was the "very Satan of coolness," bald and with a dyed black mustache, chatting at the faro table with "Morrissey's hunchback," a "powerful, dangerous-looking man." At roulette, a fat German babbled in Teutonic English alongside "a wretched little specimen of a youth, with light, yellowish hair, gold eyeglasses and pink eyes, like a ferret's." A graybeard ran "the awful dice boxes," and at the second roulette table lived the creepiest croupier of all. When the ball found its niche, this bony face with the air of a deacon would announce, in a dreadful monotone, "twenty-three, black," or "fourteen, red," as if preaching "upon the vanity of human life." When his lone customer drifted off, he sat smoking a cigar, at intervals humming "a mournful psalm."

Actually, Morrissey had terrific dealers. One was Ben Scribner, who had opened one of Saratoga's earliest formal gambling houses two decades earlier. He even got Hamilton Baker, king of faro in Virginia City, Nevada, capital of the Comstock lode. Several American houses wanted him, but Morrissey could pay $4,500 a month. The faro king's reign ended when a railroad accident paralyzed his right side, a tragedy, for that was his dealing side. Baker died as the crusaders would have wished, in poverty.[3]

At rouge-et-noir sat "Mr. Morrissey himself, the gambler, the prize-fighter, Congressman of New York—the fullest type and sign of the political and social degredation of the Great Metropolis of America." With tight curly hair and then-fashionable short beard, he had a broken nose, hoarse voice, and, the crusader could not help adding, "a frank, free and rather kindly and pleasant manner."

Kindly or not, Morrissey barred not only those short of the entrance fee but all local residents. This, it has been said, spared him the suicides that had been so irritating at Baden. It also stood him in good stead with town fathers and mothers, whose approval he continued to purchase. Sometimes he squirreled away racing proceeds for the town, which in 1867 had bought a new No. 7 school, or shared gambling profits

Longfellow vs. Harry Bassett

with churches whose pastors would not inspect a gift horse. In 1871 he subscribed $500 toward sprinkling Lake Avenue, so the dust would not choke people taking the roundabout route to donate money at his track.[4]

Saratoga looked liked something out of Currier and Ives, possibly because it *was* something out of Currier and Ives, who decorated it in their prints with elegant carriages. Reclusive A. T. Stewart lurked behind a pair of stunning Kentucky thoroughbreds. Publisher John Appleton was pulled by a pair of long-tailed bays hitched to a clarence; Charles Wall of Park Avenue, grays to a barouche; Robert Squires, president of the Third Avenue Railroad, blacks to a landau; Frank H. Lord, a span of bays to an English drag; S. W. Coe of East Forty-second Street, ponies to a phaeton filled with children. The sociable Col. J. A. Bridgeland, of Indiana, drove Cadmus bays hitched to a Brewster phaeton big enough to hold the presidents of the Wabash Railroad and First National Bank of Memphis, not to mention Morrissey's old political patron, the ex-Tammany mayor of New York, Fernando Wood. Closing their eyes, today's tourists can bring them back alive.[5]

By 1871, the hotels, too, bulged to the bursting point. The Lelands renamed their giant the *Grand* Union Hotel and promptly went bankrupt. Enter A. T. Stewart, the New York merchant prince. Reputed earlier to have had a piece of perhaps the world's biggest caravansery, he would soon buy it outright, and then, of course, expand. Breslin would cross the street, but he would have to go some to get the turf crowd to follow.[6]

The New York reporter crawled out of his Congress Hall bed at four of a Tuesday morning, July 11, to watch Kingfisher and Longfellow work out for "the grandest race which has ever or will ever take place on this continent." As he drove to the track, he might have reflected, as so many have since, that this was another world. He had only to consider his fellow passenger, Abe Buford, a Confederate cavalry general who had ridden with the maniacal Nathan Bedford Forrest but was now relaxing about as deep in Yankee territory as he could get.[7]

The reporter found the great Belmont at the track but decided to eavesdrop on Longfellow's owner, half-hidden behind a post in the soft dawn light. The New York set loved to make fun of this white-haired Kentuckian, with his accent thick as flies. Three things about him will do for now. His name was John Harper, his father had run Harper's Ferry, and this was the first he had seen of Belmont's Kingfisher.

"How do you like him, old man?" asked John Hunter, who had owned America's previous greatest horse, Kentucky. The journalist, Melville Landon of the *New York Commercial Advertiser,* listened in.

"Full of muscle, Hunter, and he branches off like he had hell in him, sure, but I guess old Longfellow will have his run." After Kingfisher's mile, Harper looked at his old blacksilver watch, which read 1:50. "I reckon he kin do 1:41." Harper played the reporter like a fiddle. Asked if the Fisher would win, he shook his head regretfully and sidestepped. "I was offered $60,000 for old Long at the Branch, and if he wins I can take $100,000 for him; but if he loses, I will sell him for $25,000. So you see I have $75,000 at stake on the race."

"And Belmont is betting even?"

Grand Union Hotel. *Leslie's, 1872. Courtesy of the author.*

"Yes, he offered to take any number of bets, $500 to $500, or $5,000 to $5,000, coming up on the cars."

"Who have you got training this $60,000 worth of horse?"

Harper wasn't about to give his African-American help any credit. He said the stable help could "take care of him." Even the *Spirit of the Times* would admit, "We do not know the name of the intelligent colored man who has trained Longfellow, but he deserves mention." The name would come out later, by accident; the Old South held on at Saratoga. "I bought old Jake there for $1,500 from Dr. Shelby in Kentucky," Harper commented, "but I think as much of him as I do of Longfellow."

"Belmont and Harper have been figuring for the star jockeys," noted the reporter, unwittingly applying the adjective of the future.

Harper's hire turned out to be Bob Swim, who was looking like another Gilpatrick. The story was that Dr. Weldon spotted Swim driving cattle through St. Louis. By 1867, he was winning at the Spa, and he captured the second Belmont on General Duke. "Bob is the smartest jockey in the States," Landon reported. "Light, muscular, and as tricky as Mayor Hall, he is sure to cut across, or through, or over, and win every race." Swim himself warned that with his boss betting $80,000 on the Cup, he would win if it was the last race he rode.

Landon asked the Democratic Party chairman who would ride Kingfisher.

Longfellow and John Harper. *Keeneland Library.*

"Why, Jake." This was another Jake—Jake Palmer. "Jake is an Island boy. I got him pardoned out of the House of Correction. . . . He has the best whip, the best spurs, and is sure to steal the best place on the track."

On the Friday of the race, the owners seemed reflected by their jockeys. As Harper walked around in a slouch hat and homespun suit, Swim sat grimly on Longfellow; and while Belmont, in the grandstand, enlarged himself with a white hat and silver feather, Jake "bobbed around proudly on the back of Kingfisher." Ten thousand spectators knew the suspense.

The white flag dropped, and they were off! It was a terrible start, with Longfellow twisted around, facing the wrong way. They weren't called back, and Longfellow eased into his regular strides, his head out like a camel's. Kingfisher moved nervously on the inside, taking six strides to the camel's five. Longfellow edged forward until, like an arrow, Swim wrenched him straight across the Fisher's path. Harper told Landon to watch his horse gain on the inside, and he did, doing the second mile in 1:40, the fastest mile yet registered on American turf. The compact Belmont rose and inflated again, "surveying the field as a General would survey a battlefield." The old man remained deadpan, "his sharp gray eyes only twinkling, as Bob shot in to the victory," taking the two and a quarter miles of the seventh Saratoga Cup in 4:02¾. The crowd "shreiked and waved their handkerchiefs like a great sea of humanity covered with fluttering sails," and Harper "took his eighty thousand dollars as quietly as you would buy a morning newspaper."[8]

Longfellow had not convinced everybody. This was especially true after he failed to enter a three-mile race won by Kingfisher a few days later. Harper wanted to save him for his debut at four miles, a contest he had been suckered into entering. Saratoga by 1871 was putting on two meetings, and the four-miler was a return engagement in August against Helmbold. Unaccountably, Harper had Long run around the track twice beforehand—to loosen him up, he said. But the distance proved brutal. Racing neck and neck after the third mile, Longfellow began to throw out his tail, the signal that he was beaten, then dropped his head. Helmbold spurted to the lead and kept it.

"How is he, Uncle John?"

"The tendons in his fore legs are shattered and broken. He's ruined—will never run again." That was just Uncle John, as the papers called Harper, carrying on. Longfellow had not yet had his famous day and year.

Two weeks later, on September 11, Morrissey staged an event that would lead in the mid-seventies to the biggest sports story yet. As Josh Ward had shown in the middle of the war, rowing was enormously popular in the Northeast. Professional sculling had come to Saratoga Lake as early as 1865, and now Morrissey brought in Josh and his three brothers to compete in an "International Boat Race" recognized in rowing history as an early world championship. They would face an English club, Poughkeepsie and Pittsburgh crews, and the famous Biglin brothers, the New Yorkers immortalized in a series of rowing paintings by Thomas Eakins.[9]

Another celebrated artist, Thomas Nast, took a break from his attacks on Boss Tweed to sketch the race for *Harper's Weekly*. Nast's crowd, in stovepipe hats and parasols, watched from the hillside south of Moon's, where Morrissey had put up a rudimentary grandstand. It was four miles with one turn. The Wards set a 24:40 record and walked off with a $2,000 cash prize. Twenty-four-year-old Ellis Ward went on to coach at Penn for many years.

In 1872, Monmouth Park and Saratoga opened the era of sports as quite something else; namely, mass entertainment. The hurdles had anticipated this, but now the tracks introduced the first national sports heroes since the Old Gray Mare and the Benicia Boy. Stars, or, since the term still had not achieved nounhood, star performers were born, as the light chestnut Harry Bassett and tragicomic Longfellow headed for a crash at a higher level. In the bargain it would pit the son of the top imported stallion of his day against that of the greatest native sire of any day.[10]

Fathered by Lexington, Harry Bassett stood 16½ hands. A star on his forehead sent a thin blaze flying down his face and over his right nostril. His clean head was held by a strong neck, which ran into powerful shoulders. He was compact yet had "plenty of body and long reach," as the *Times* said. His rear feet were white to the hocks. He had displayed his brilliance early, foreshadowing Man o' War by falling in the 1870 Saratoga Stakes yet flying to a third-place finish. He had won three races as a two-year-old and the fifth Belmont, eighth Travers, and seven other contests at three. Harry Bassett opened 1872 with three more triumphs.

This machine was owned by Colonel McDaniel, who, as one historian said, "cared not for creating an image of himself as a big sport." Not a problem; steeped in the crime of slavery, he remained severely unreconstructed, and as if to remind everybody the war was not over, he named a filly Black Slave. But if less magnificent than his horses, the Virginian was exceedingly successful as a judge of human and equine talent, and his stable would soon dominate Saratoga and American racing. Just as he had seen it in Albert, he spotted potential in a ten-year-old white boy working at a Richmond newsstand and exercising horses for the Exchange Hotel's livery stable. This was Jimmy Rowe, now fifteen and about to mount Harry Bassett.

With his 15–1 record, McDaniel's chestnut was assigned to capture the Monmouth Cup. The same mission went to Harper's dark brown charge, who was 9–2. Uncle John, hardly as backward as he liked people to think, put his giant on a railroad car with a sign that said: "Longfellow on his way to Long Branch to meet his friend Harry Bassett." They brought out the crowd of the next century, up to forty thousand, more than half arriving by steamer and train from New York City, others by carriage from northern New Jersey or special cars from Philadelphia and the South. It was reminiscent of the greatest antebellum match races but with a new quality, permanence.

On that day in Brooklyn, only three hundred people watched the New York Mutuals beat the Atlantics, 11 to 10. The year before, the Mutuals had helped set up the first professional league, the nine-city National Association of Professional Base Ball Players, but it would fade away over the next few years. "Base Ball" simply had not gotten its act together. Abner Doubleday, incidentally, was preparing to retire from the army in a year, but would remain available if called upon to invent something. Meantime, a bunch of collegians had launched another thing, called "Foot-Ball," with Rutgers vs. Princeton in 1869. It bore even less resemblance to today's game than Base Ball.

But if racing was far ahead, the editors who predicted American sports would be an elegant affair, rather like Ascot, were, of course, wrong again. These Americans at Monmouth Park were not waving a sea of hankies. To be sure, such plutocrats as Jay Gould himself were on hand, but the *Times* was startled to see ordinary people, too. The modern sports fans

> were of all classes . . . the rough, pure and simple . . . his brother with the tawdry trappings of Tammany . . . the sturdy laborer . . . the intelligent mechanic of whom we have heard so much during the present strikes . . . tradesmen, brokers, railway men, oil men. There were clerks, there were newspaper boys, there were tired printers who had worked throughout the night. . . . In fine, there was almost every class and condition waiting by the thousands at Pier No. 28 North River to get on board the Plymouth Rock.[11]

If this was the future, however, Monmouth Park wasn't ready. Logistically, it was a disaster. Some New Yorkers had to set out the night before to get a spot on a boat, and some would not get home until midnight. Boats and trains ran late, and, as there was almost nothing to eat on the way or at the track, some shared bits of food and drank from a brook. It seems unlikely that the latter included John Morrissey, who was busy laying a $25,000 side bet on Harry Bassett.

Even the bettors in England, to whom American racing had looked for leadership, looked now to America as London bookmakers got in on it, heavily favoring Harry Bassett. Londoners were said to have invented bookmaking around 1840. A

Philadelphia bookmaking firm began specializing in cricket, regattas, and trotting shortly after the Civil War, and then a New Yorker, James Kelley, opened a book on the 1871 Belmont captured by Harry Bassett. "Public interest in racing led to a demand for a method whereby the small investor could participate," wrote one historian, "and the bookmakers moved in."[12] Rather than getting players to bid up the cost of their tickets, as the pool sellers did, the bookmakers offered a cheaper product— bets to accommodate almost anybody's pocketbook and at fixed odds. Within a few years, they would be shouting their wares alongside the pool sellers in front of the grandstands. Monmouth Park and Saratoga would try something else first, however.

Time out for a quick trip to Paris. Pierre Oller had a perfume shop. Unhappy with the odds he got from bookmakers, he invented a new way to let the public set the odds. He sold tickets in his *parfumerie* at a fixed price for any horse in the race, one price no matter which horse. It was unheard of. The winning ticket holders would split all the money in the pool, minus 5 percent for Monsieur. And the total divided by the amount bet on each horse would reveal the approximate odds.

The French called it the "pari mutuel," literally "mutual bet" but more accurately "betting pool." Rather than the *parfumeries*, the *cafés-tabacs*—cafés that also sold cigarettes—eventually became the official outlets for the PMU (Pari Mutuel-Urbain), the intown betting monopoly. France's PMU outlets are thus the ancestors of America's offtrack betting parlors. The French racetracks quickly adopted Oller's idea and set up pari-mutuel wagering on their own grounds, where it drove out the bookmakers. Simple machines, the early Totalisators, were used to add up the pools, revealing the odds. Soon, borrowing from the French for once, Pierre Lorillard and Leonard Jerome promoted the pari-mutuel system in America, where it was introduced before the bookmakers could really get started. Today, few racing buffs are aware of this early—and ill-fated—appearance of pari-mutuel betting.

"A great feature of the day," the *Spirit of the Times* said of that Monmouth Park meeting in 1872, "were the Paris Mutuel Pools, which did a rushing business, a stand having been erected for them at the lower end of the enclosure." The *Spirit* had confused "pari" with Paris, but it did not miss the point, which was that suddenly "the public did more betting than we can ever remember on any former occasion."

The tickets cost five dollars each, which became the standard price in those years. "Hundreds of men who had never laid eyes on a horse race before bought pools and invested in the Paris Mutuels." Most bet on Longfellow. There were all kinds of action that day. In one of the last side bets, Morrissey wagered another $1,800 to Louis Lorillard's $1,000 on Longfellow. And with the horses on the track, a man walked up and showed a $50 note to John Harper's jockey, an African American so far identified only as Sample. "You win," he said, "and you get this." Sample merely smiled.[13]

They were off! It was neck and neck for a mile and a half "amid cheering of the vast multitude." Between the grandstand and clubhouse, Longfellow surged in front. Rowe flailed away, then dug in with his spurs until, suddenly, Bassett's tail flew up. Longfellow coasted home to win by nearly two hundred yards, having covered the two and a half miles in a very fast 4:34. "As Longfellow passed under the string," the New Yorkers, with their well-known sentimentality, "broke into a pell-mell mass . . .

Longfellow vs. Harry Bassett

95

Longfellow racing Harry Bassett, Sample and Rowe up. By Currier and Ives. *George S. Bolster Collection of the Historical Society of Saratoga Springs.*

and poured tumultuously through the narrow gates onto the railroad platform." On a homeward boat, a New Yorker fell overboard and was presumed rescued.

America had its first modern wonder horse. The press greeted "the idol of the day" with an emotional outpouring that only a few would know in sports. "Longfellow is now crowned king of the turf," said the *Times,* but then it warned: "Bassett will again endeavor to wrest that proud title from him when they meet again in the Saratoga Cup." This would be a better test, it said, since the Spa track was "so wonderfully good and fast." In fact, the prominent horse owner, Zeb Ward, said it was "conceded to be the fastest track in America."

No operation in American sports excelled the Saratoga racetrack at this point, and only Jerome Park and Monmouth Park could match it. Beyond the first turn and the backstretch, some of the most prominent owners now kept private stables, including Belmont, McDaniel, Pierre Lorillard, Thomas Doswell, and the partners Hunter and Travers—although most used the stables across Union Avenue, in and around the old trotting course. On the eve of the first 1872 meeting, 160 horses were on the grounds.

The program had changed radically. It had been lengthened to two six-day meetings, the first in July and the second in August, with three events a day on the average. It revealed America's belated transition from heat racing to dashes. These ranged from three-quarters of a mile to four miles, although most of them were under two miles. Not a single race was in heats. And there was a startling new feature.

It was supposed that in olden days English hunters would race over a field of natural obstacles in the direction of some distant object: a steeple. This idea, too, crossed the water, first to Canada, where steeplechasing was avidly embraced by the military. Earlier, the Canadians had brought a simpler jumping event to Saratoga— the hurdles, which were races over a series of three-and-a-half-foot rail fences. Saratoga staged hurdles as early as 1858 and introduced them to a national audience in the 1864 season. Steeplechases followed, at Paterson and Hoboken in 1865 and at Saratoga in 1870. Steeplechasing was a varied adventure over "a fair hunting course," as it was called, of "about" two or three miles. Flags marked the course like a slalom. The jumper was confronted not only with the usual rails, but with brush or thorn hedges, mud walls and ditches, water jumps, sometimes a stone wall, and sometimes—it turned out—the main track's rail fence.

Within a few years, Saratoga was bragging it had the best steeplechase course in the country. It wove around the infield and across the main track to pass by the Belmont and Doswell stables. Many were thrilled out of their britches. "What is a steeplechase?" asked the awed Landon. "Think of three John Gilpins flying like death on a pale horse . . . think of three fire engines bound for a fire . . . Bret Harte's Chiquita running herself 'clean out of her harness.'" Some, though, were horrified by steeplechase's bloody record of accidents in England.

There was a revolution in the betting. Morrissey introduced the "Paris Mutuals" with the help of "an efficient corps of assistants, who transacted the business without a hitch."[14] Behind his casino, facing Putnam Street, which is a mere walk in the park today, he opened a three-story, clapboard house as a "Pool-Room," for betting on the horse-racing pools. It could not have turned Henry James's shouting mass of sweaty gamblers into a garden club, but the *Spirit* called it "a great improvement on the dives where pools used to be sold." Almost nobody in Saratoga today has ever heard of it.

Again, the irrepressible *Spirit* welcomed this first pari-mutuel system as the greatest imaginable contribution to democracy. "It is somewhat astonishing to see how rapidly these pools are increasing in public favor." They proved "that a much larger part of the community is interested in horse racing" and gave those "outside the ring of large speculators a chance of making their investments on favorable terms." But within a few years, the bookmakers would invade the tracks en masse and drive out the new-fangled pari-mutuel pools.

"The Greatest Contest in the American Turf History." That is how a *Times* headline would describe the eighth Saratoga Cup when it was over, forgetting even American Eclipse vs. Henry in 1823. "Never, perhaps, in the racing history of the Saratoga or any other track has such a scene been witnessed."[15]

They were all there, the cofounders of modern American sports, Morrissey, Travers, Jerome, Belmont, Pierre Lorillard, Bowie—even Dr. Underwood was back. His first pool attracted $340 on Longfellow, making him a big favorite, $100 on Harry Bassett—and $20 on Defender. Who? One of the excuses for Bassett's Monmouth loss was that he was too friendly with Longfellow, so it was thought a third horse would guarantee a race. Defender's owner was none other than Morrissey, who was sometimes seen proudly tending to his charger, bucket and blanket in hand.

Longfellow vs. Harry Bassett

"Going to bet on my horse?" former congressman Morrissey yelled to former congressman Marvin one day.

"Yes."

"How?"

"Going to copper him!" (To copper a faro card was to bet it would lose, and Defender came through for Marvin that day.)[16]

Aboard Defender now was the aged Gilbert Watson Patrick of Poughkeepsie. At fifty-four or fifty-five, Gilpatrick was about to see an unusual side of racing for him, other horses' rear ends.

"At last," said the *Times*, "the bugle sounded for the contest between the giants of the racing world." The record to beat over the two and a quarter miles of this Saratoga Cup: Kentucky's inaugural 4:01½, though he had carried only 104 pounds, most of it Gilpatrick. They would start from the three-quarter pole to the left of the grandstand. (It would be designated the quarter pole later, when the measurements were marked off clockwise, to show not how far the horses had gone but how far they still had to go.) They would race a quarter of a mile to the grandstand, then twice around, providing three exciting passes before the screaming crowd. Could sports get much better?

*　　*　　*　　*

July 16, 1872. An ovation rolled across the grounds as the giants cantered to the top of the home stretch, Sample on Longfellow, Rowe on Harry Bassett.

They were off! With a great jump start—and disaster. Longfellow apparently hit his near forefoot, twisting the plate, but few noticed. It was Bassett by a short length in front of the stand to another huge cheer from the crowd. There would never be daylight between them. On the turn, Longfellow pulled up to Bassett's quarter, his dark brown coat turning to black satin in the sun, his backers screaming. They were running "well within themselves," the chestnut up a length at the quarter pole, Longfellow shooting to his girth on the backstretch, as if it were a game. Defender was out of it. Again, Bassett got a length at the half-pole, "again the cheers roll out over the course," and again Longfellow was up to his quarter as they rounded the lower turn and did the first mile in 1:45½.

Down the stretch, Longfellow came on in a rush, and it was neck and neck at the stand. The hard surface, a witness noted, favored Bassett's "beautiful, daisy-cutting stroke" over "the great rake" of Longfellow, yet Bassett strained as Longfellow moved out by a head. "The men are hoarse with shouting, and the ladies shout with them." Racing inside, "Bassett suddenly shows his head to the front" as they rounded the first turn for the final time. Bassett was up a short length again, but Longfellow reached his shoulder at the quarter pole, the timers putting the third half-mile under :50. Then, under Sample, "a sudden falter, like a lurch." Morrissey shouted, "Longfellow's beat!" But Sample "called on him" and reached Bassett's girth at the half-mile pole, then pulled even. They hit the starting place in 3:30 or 3:31, three or four seconds faster than the fastest two-mile race to date, the chestnut pushing his shoulders in front.

Home they came, "at a pace unknown on the Saratoga track," but with Longfellow apparently in pain, his plate doubled over and embedded. Sample applied "the bat" (whip) and the big animal responded, then faltered again, his forelegs spreading. "The scene beggars description," the *Times* writer said. "The policemen endeavor to make the people keep their seats but without avail. White-haired men are young again." Sample stood and flogged away. Again the animal answered, again he closed on Bassett. "The excitement knows no bounds." Down the Saratoga stretch raced the two most famous horses in America. Longfellow wobbled, fought, and forced Jimmy Rowe to extract every ounce from Bassett.

It was a "photo finish," but by Currier and Ives. In the next century, the print would hang in the National Museum of Racing across the street from the track, along with two of Longfellow's actual plates. The result? The poet lost by a short length, Harry Bassett passing "under the string" in a record 3:59. It was two and a half seconds under Kentucky's Cup mark, which Longfellow must have beaten, too.

The joint exploded. "The colored jockeys and trainers," said the patronizing *Times*, "yelled like maniacs, tumbled over one another, and fought to get to the judges' stand. Hats and sticks literally darkened the air. . . . Men shouted and almost embraced one another; ladies, though half alarmed at the torrent of excitement, waved their handkerchiefs and parasols."

Then silence. The crowd saw Longfellow's continuing pain as he limped to the judges' stand on three feet, then to his stall, followed by the *Spirit's* correspondent. "He stood in his box holding the foot on its mangled edge, and as each visitor came, he would turn his large eyes upon him and then drop them to his foot, as if asking sympathy for his misfortune. Old John Harper sat leaning on his stick, with the big tears trickling down his face."

Harper later wrote of Longfellow as "the best racehorse that this or any other country has known" but gave no credit to his Monmouth and Saratoga Cup jockey or to the horse's great trainer. In the endless postmortems, though, the trainer's partial name, Mose, and the rider's full name, John Sample, slipped out—and were as quickly forgotten.[17]

Longfellow would not race again. A shower drenched Saratoga the next day, and a visitor saw the horse lying in his stall, his foot and ankle dreadfully swollen. The *Times* found it appropriate to quote Byron—"Even the elements weep at thy departure"—while taking liberties with Shakespeare—"Oh! what a noble horse is here!" More down to earth was the opinion in Morrissey's Club House and the Broadway barrooms that Harry Bassett was "a winner, not a conqueror." He could by no means claim Longfellow's laurels, nor could Alarm, a Hunter and Travers colt by Morris's Eclipse, although his 1:42¾ that week broke the official mile record, nor Belmont's Woodbine, who that week took a new race for three-year-old fillies. This was the Alabama Stakes, which would have been the Cottrill Stakes except Captain Cottrill of Mobile was (a) so modest he didn't want a race named for him, or (b) such a diehard he wanted to honor secessionist Alabama, depending on which legend is true, if either. In any case, the race has honored Alabama far longer than anyone could have expected. It remains Saratoga's second oldest feature and the nation's most important test for fillies only.

Other horses did claim Longfellow's mantle, including those suggested for the "honor of being the best two-year-old that has shown in public this year," an early version of today's horse-of-the-year awards. One belonged to Morrissey's old gambling partner, H. P. McGrath, who modestly had baptized his Kentucky spread "McGrathiana." "McGrath," said the *Times*, "takes his siesta regularly on the balcony of the Grand Union, guarded by little angels, who whisper higher promises to his willing ear." They were whispering about big Tom Bowling and his victory in the Flash Stakes earlier that week.[18]

It was blatantly obvious, too, why another stable was dubbed "the McDaniel Confederacy." The colonel had not only captured the Belmont and the Travers with Harry Bassett the year before but had just done that double again with Joe Daniels. He nominated Joe for next year's Cup and two-year-old Springbok to meet Tom Bowling in the Travers.

On May 17, 1873, the Saratoga adventure spun off yet another historic contest, at Pimlico. Dr. Underwood, the old auctioneer, competed with the irritatingly systematic "French pools" that day. Several other Spa regulars, such as McGrath, Belmont, and Bowie, entered horses in the new race. The ten-length margin of Johnny Chamberlin's Survivor survives as a record in the Preakness Stakes, which, after the Travers and the Belmont, is the third oldest major event in American spectator sports. As for Preakness the six-year-old, he had not shown much of late, but he, too, would have his day at the Spa.[19]

There were no national stars in "base ball" or any other human sport in America at the moment. But as the *Times* put it, "There are a thousand and one competitors for Longfellow's vacant place." They were on their way to Saratoga. For the humans, however, even for Leonard Jerome, it was turning into a bumpy ride. Until now, the de facto bachelor had his friends to guarantee that one thing his dinner parties would never be was dull. At one, for example, some bore prattled on about the evolution of bivalves, and finally asked Billy if he happened to believe that even oysters had brains.

"Yes," Travers replied, "just enough to k-keep their mouths shut."[20]

At a party Jerome gave early in 1873, he received a wire, which he read and then laid by his dinner plate. "When dinner was over," said a contemporary, "he rose and asked pardon for the impoliteness of reading the telegram."

He then announced, "But gentlemen, it is a message in which you are all interested. The bottom has fallen out of stocks, and I am a ruined man. But your dinner is paid for, and I did not want to disturb you while you were eating it."

There were some questions, "then a sudden scattering, and Mr. Jerome was left alone with his telegram. He has chosen to remain alone ever since." Made a millionaire by selling short in the Panic of '57, he had been unmade in the slide that would lead to the Panic of '73, a free-fall that would be unequaled until 1929. Actually, Jerome was not quite "ruined," but he had lost status and would never climb back to the top of the social heap.[21]

Saratoga, on the other hand, was beginning to hit its most astonishing strides yet. It was about to reinvent America in ways that the historians, hypnotized by government and politics, might never understand.

11

THE DERBY AND COLLEGE SPORTS

*F*RANK WALWORTH, a law student, was living with his mother in the old frame homestead at the north end of Broadway. His grandfather had reigned there as the most distinguished Saratoga Springs resident of all time. Reuben H. Walworth had often presided at home over the state Court of Chancery, where lawyers such as Daniel Webster argued. The chancellor also headed the American Temperance Union, when he wasn't entertaining John Quincy Adams, Andrew Jackson, Martin Van Buren, James Buchanan, Washington Irving, James Fenimore Cooper, or Edgar Allan Poe—or high-jumping over the furniture. Not surprisingly, Reuben's brilliance helped drive his son mad. Mansfield Walworth became a second-rate novelist, drunk, and wife abuser. He was divorced and living in Manhattan.

One day Frank saw some abusive letters from him. Mansfield even threatened to kill his wife and son, the latter, he said, to wipe out the oppressive name forever. Frank went to New York to confront him on June 3, 1873. They quarreled, Mansfield seemed to go for a gun, and Frank pulled his own, splattering them both across the newspapers.

Dodging the rope, Frank was sentenced to life at hard labor in Sing-Sing, of which sentence he would serve only four years. *Walworth v. People* was a milestone, the first conviction under a new and lesser homicide charge, "murder in the second degree." Frank also may have helped give birth to, of all things, the DAR; his mother, Ellen Hardin Walworth, was one of its four founders. Wouldn't a Daughter of the Revolution, after all, expunge a parricide? Frank had accomplished a lot with his four bullets, but it was a strange way to open the season.[1]

They were still talking about the murder when, the story goes, Price McGrath's angry Tom Bowling was brought out attached to a rope about thirty feet long. He was the "most powerful horse this country has produced," with "immense stifles [the hind knee joints just below the thighs] standing out so wide as to have free action beside his body, like the side-wheels of a steamer."

"Now, Tom, are you going to behave yourself and win the Travers Stakes for me?" McGrath asked him in front of a bunch of reporters. "He winks his eye at me, which is his way of saying, 'I'm all right, go out and bet.'"

Tom Bowling looked "fractious and sulky as usual" to a witness but was controlled by "his herculean negro groom," probably Ansel, his trainer. McGrath's little green and orange ribbons danced foolishly in the furious animal's mane. As the horses were lined up for the start, the edgy spectators were told by the police in front of the grandstand to take their seats. Then, as turf writer William Leggett would reconstruct it, Ansel advised the starter just to point him in the right direction.

The starter let them go, Ansel sliced the rope, and the umpteenth son of Lexington took off. He was still wearing Bob Swim and the rope around his neck as he jogged home by ten lengths, a record that would last ninety-four years.

Tenth Travers trivia: There were two false starts, so Tom Bowling had to be brought back twice. And at the head of the stretch, McDaniel's Springbok fell, cutting his left foreleg and badly injuring Jimmy Rowe. McGrath distributed the green and orange ribbons among the ladies. Bill Travers had been dressing up his race since 1870, with $500 in plate presented to the winner. This year the design was a huge silver cup. "McGrath announced that he would this evening keep it filled to the brim at the poolroom, and asked his friends to come and try to empty it."[2]

In September, twenty-year-old Charles Courtney hit Broadway with $15 for three weeks, so when the Grand Union told him board was $3.50 a day, "I nearly dropped." The dining room scared him to death. "If I reached for a fork, I stuck my fingers in the butter, the soup was so hot I burned my tongue, and in reaching for a glass of water I knocked over the celery dish." Charlie went out to Moon's, headquarters for a regatta put on by the Saratoga Rowing Association, a group of business people. Clubs had come from Canada, Washington, D.C., and all over the Northeast. If it looked as though they were trying to upstage the National Association of Amateur Oarsmen, which planned its first event in Philadelphia in October, they were. The local group vowed to make this "the great National Rowing Regatta Ground," and they would.[3]

Charlie ran into Morrissey at Moon's, and as Moon fed him one of his glorious meals—"biscuit, brook trout, black bass, partridge"—Morrissey fed him tales of training, passing the torch to a future champion.

A few days later, Charlie was rowing his heart out in the two-mile event and so far ahead that the crowd was shouting "Whoa!" which confused him and made him row all the harder. A couple in a boat suggested he stop for a moment and have a lemonade. "I won in 14:15, which was one minute faster than Josh Ward's professional time." He got one of the $5,000 worth of Tiffany silver prizes, and Moon handed him half of the $300 he had laid on him. A gentleman who had bet $600 did likewise. Charlie would remember that he kept that $450 squashed in his fist all the way back to Cayuga Lake. "In the next few years I rowed 88 races in all—and never lost."[4]

Others lost everything. The market collapsed on September 19—the second Black Friday—and the Panic of '73 would be "the end of the long-term expansion in the world economy." As usual, however, the world did not include Saratoga. The *Spirit of the Times* alluded to what was coming here: "The historians of the future will have little hesitation, it appears to us, in describing Americans as an athletic people." Preakness also gave a hint of the excitement ahead. He knocked off Harry Bassett at Jerome Park that fall and had a date in the Cup with Tom Bowling and Springbok. But horse racing wasn't everything anymore.

★   ★   ★   ★

In an unprecedented explosion of news coverage, Saratoga Springs introduced America to college sports in 1874. Harvard and Yale had been competing in rowing, the biggest campus sport, since 1852 and at baseball since after the war, but nobody had seen anything like the fourth regatta of the Rowing Association of American Colleges (RAAC). It was the birth of intercollegiate sports on the modern scale—and the country's greatest sports event of any kind so far. A *New York Times* editorial: "We can scarcely remember an event not involving a war, or some vast issue in politics, which has occasioned so much excitement."[5]

The future was obvious to the *Times*. One day millions would watch college teams compete all over the country—on rivers, lakes, canals. There was no mention of that thing "foot-ball," which they could not even agree how to play, Harvard using a round ball against McGill of Montreal that year and switching to an egg-shaped one under McGill's rules. No, it would happen on water. "The college boat-race is destined to occupy as great a space in the public mind here as the Oxford and Cambridge boat-race occupies in England—perhaps even a greater space, for the contending colleges are more numerous here."

It was the combination of Saratoga and the pictorial press that took the regatta national, but its biggest promoter also had his own motives. Frank Leslie had bought the shore south of Moon's and the high bluff above it, where his villa, Interlaken, sat between Saratoga Lake and little Lake Lonely. He could have named it Interwifen, as he was about to marry his live-in fashion editor. In any event, to enhance the investment and the fashion editor, he publicized the hell out of the regatta in *Leslie's Illustrated Newspaper*.

The larger-circulation *Harper's Weekly* was not far behind with a pull-out map showing the nation's resort in one bird's-eye swoop from the lake to the piazzas. Here at last was the United States Hotel, rebuilt with 768 "sleeping rooms with gas, running water, water-closets" and 65 suites with baths. Its 2,000 guests could stroll 2,700 feet of piazza. For the first time, as local historian James Benton would point out, the States, Grand Union, Congress Hall, and the new Grand Hotel across from Congress Park stood together—the world's largest hotel complex. There was no gash on Broadway.

In the news from Saratoga, the whole country was discovering a new species, one allowed to mutate in an isolated environment and reach a state of togetherness and hormonal unpredictability: the American College Student. Strenuous efforts would be made to keep it out of the military. Chameleonlike, it could take on a variety of colors. Princeton's orange and black were first unveiled here on ribbons given to the freshman crew and sold as souvenirs at the Grand Union, which may have helped them win the freshman race on Wednesday, July 15. Indeed, no college color was dyed in the wool yet, various reports qualifying even Harvard's crimson as magenta, Yale's blue as dark, young Cornell's red as carnation or carnelian.[6]

The college authorities had agonized over whether to expose their innocents to Saratoga, despite plenty of evidence that they were as corrupt as they were going to get. After a Harvard-Yale baseball game and dance in 1868, said a report in the *Times*, "they tore down curtains, broke windows and furniture, overturned everything movable in the streets, tore down signs, and defied the police in abusive language." To ensure such exemplars would not be compromised by his Club House, Morrissey generously closed during regatta week, although the lake was encircled by gamblers, professional and not.

A bird's-eye view. From sketches by Theodore R. Davis, *Harper's Weekly, 1874. Courtesy of the author.*

Twenty-five thousand spectators gathered for the "university" race on Thursday (we had not yet adopted the British shorthand, "varsity"). Some filled the three hundred-yard, nine-row grandstand—bleachers, really—on Leslie's beach, some rode in small craft. A very important person occupied a barge near the finish line, and people wondered whether it was the Commodore, A. T. Stewart, or the president of the United States. It turned out Grant was indeed there, on a specially built pavilion. After maddening delays, whitecaps forced a postponement, unleashing a stampede worthy of Monmouth Park, the crowd crushing Leslie's plantings as it fled. The president, for one, would not reappear for the race on Friday, a good thing, because it, too, was postponed.[7]

A crowd of fifteen thousand watched the nine crews race on Saturday from near Snake Hill to a line three miles north, between the grandstand and the bridge. Pools favored the Blue six in what for many boiled down to another bitter Yale-Harvard tilt. As Yale spurted past them, the Crimson veered and hit the Blue shell, knocking off

United States Hotel, reborn. By Albert Berghaus, *Leslie's*, 1874. *Courtesy of the author.*

her rudder and breaking a Harvard oar. Yale had to drop out and later charged that Harvard had deliberately smashed the rudder. Yale also claimed there were too many crews and announced it would withdraw after the next regatta. It didn't help the quitters that Columbia won in a record sixteen minutes, forty-two seconds, stroke Frank Rees fainting as "the whole concourse of spectators rose on tiptoe, and cheer after cheer went up." Then it was Wesleyan, Harvard, Williams, Dartmouth, Cornell, Trinity, Princeton.

The excitement got Americans thinking about the Olympians two decades before the Olympics were revived, although they hadn't nailed the details. Said the *Times*, "The wreath of parsley which was given to the victors in athletic sports in the old Hellenic days may, metaphorically, be said to encircle the brows of our New York boys." A few days later, pursuing Morrissey's concept of a multisports complex, Saratoga birthed still another major college sport.[8]

"The beginning was made toward a new order of things when the first races were held at Saratoga in July 1874," wrote Samuel Crowther, Jr., and Arthur Ruhl on the origin of intercollegiate "athletics," or track and field. Seven of the regatta colleges put on these "College Games" at Glen Mitchell, a driving park out North Broadway extended, with its half-mile track near today's Loughberry Avenue and Route 9 (northwest corner). No bypasser would know that American intercollegiate track was born here on July 20, 1874. About two thousand people collected in the little grandstand and the field, praying against the threat of midafternoon rain. The starter shouted, "Go!"

Cornell's E. Copeland took the mile in 4:58, Yale's A. B. Nevins the 100-yard dash in 10 ½ seconds, Wesleyan's W. H. Downs the three miles in 18:17 ¾, Yale's Maxwell the 120-yard hurdles in :20 ½. The crowd had seventy-one minutes to gawk at J. B. Eustis, "the Captain of the Wesleyan crew [who] attracted great attention by his magnificent physique," in the seven-mile walk. Harvard, Princeton, Columbia and Williams also ran.

The president settled for a housewarming ball at many a tourist's favorite "Saratoga house." Grant's hosts were George Batcheller, a former Civil War officer and his wife, Catharine, a French teacher and linguist. Built the year before by Nichols and Halcott of Albany, the house at 20 Circular Street mixed Germanic, Italianate, and French Renaissance styles with a tower resembling a minaret. This was prophetic, for Grant soon sent Batcheller to the International Court administering Egypt, where he and Catharine spent nine years.[9]

"Start it, gentlemen!" was how Dr. Underwood opened the bidding on July 24, a herald of the surviving "Gentlemen, start your engines!" Wheatly had exiled the pools to the east end of the grandstand so the bettors wouldn't block everybody else's view. Pierre Lorillard's Attila was selling for $1,000 and K. W. Sears's Acrobat for $700. For the first and only time, they were running the Travers all over again after a dead heat. Acrobat got a new jockey, Billy Hayward, and another Englishman, George Barbee, was on Attila, for the colonies were now attracting top Newmarket riders. The runoff was tight, too: Attila and Barbee by three-quarters of a length.

In the Saratoga Stakes, few noticed a little red colt who failed to place. McGrath's two-year-old Aristides would make history next year.

With Tom Bowling sidelined by a leg injury, it was McDaniel's Springbok vs. Sanford's Preakness (and Barbee vs. Hayward) in the long awaited Cup. Springbok and Barbee took it by eight lengths—the third straight Cup for the colonel, now listed as the "McDaniel Co." as the owners increasingly broadened their bases. McDaniel led the first five-day meeting with $11,450 in winnings against Pierre Lorillard's $4,600. Springbok-Preakness wasn't resolved, however; when they reappeared in a three-miler, it was Springbok by only a head, so it reopened the issue.

The next day, Vanderbilt won. Facing a rate war started by the B. & O. (Baltimore and Ohio Railroad), he and some forty others representing his lines and the Erie, Atlantic and Great Western, Pennsylvania, and Michigan Central, among others, had been meeting at the States and Congress Hall. Now they signed the "Saratoga Compact," setting higher rates. It lasted hardly a year and ignited more wars, but it was an important chapter in the distinguished history of price fixing.[10]

At long last, the second 1874 meeting brought the eclipsing of Lexington's four-mile record of 7:19 ¾. After nineteen years, his grandson, Fellowcraft, owned by the gambler Mark Littell, trimmed only a quarter of a second off it but carried 108 pounds, five more than grandpa. The meeting went so well they added two "Match Days" and two benefit days for the Rowing Association and the public schools.

Charlie Courtney rowed to the state championship in the Saratoga regatta, which floated more entries than the nationals a few days later at Troy. Noting this blossoming of sports, the *Spirit* ranked them: "trotting and racing," then boating, baseball, cricket, and "the Scottish games." It concluded, "with the mixed sources from which our people sprang," there was "a wider and more general range of sport than any other nation enjoys."

One sportsman was not faring as well as the phenomenon he helped launch—even though the Spa would save the West through Leonard Jerome. Clara had packed the girls off to England, where Jennie had become engaged to Lord Randolph Churchill, second son of the Duke of Marlborough. The Duke had hated the notion, uncertain as he was of her fortune and of Leonard's reputation as "a sporting, and I should think vulgar kind of man. I hear he drives about six and eight horses in New York (one may take this as a kind of indication of what the man is)." He had chosen not to observe that he, too, was strapped, nor had his son interjected that he, Randolph, loved horses as well, and had been sporting enough to contract syphilis from a prostitute in his student days. The Duke's lawyers had not cared for it, either; their problem was Jerome's insistence that his $10,000 annual dowry go directly to Jennie, a "most unusual" American idea. Finally, the Duke and Duchess had consented, although they rudely declined to attend the ceremony in Paris.

Leonard Jerome, back from the wedding, could review how he had been "ruined" and had warned Jennie, "You are no heiress," but also how she was now the dashing Lady Randolph Churchill. In November, seven and one-half months after the wedding, Jennie had a baby boy. Millions of newborns might look like Winston Churchill, but this one was, and if the racetrack had not launched his grandfather, would the West have had its savior?[11]

*　　*　　*　　*

A pair of Kentucky Churchills, John and Henry, provided the land for Col. M. Lewis Clark's Louisville Jockey Club and Driving Park. To be nicknamed Churchill Downs eleven years later, it opened on May 17, 1875, with ten thousand on hand. It was old home week for such Spa regulars as McGrath, Buford, Cottrill, Clay, and Grinstead, all of whom had entries in the second race, for three-year-olds.[12]

McGrath's "stable entry" of Chesapeake and Aristides led at $105 in a $495 pool (a stable entry of more than one horse was and is bet as a single entry, giving the player two chances to win). Chesapeake was McGrath's intended winner, but the hard track pleased Aristides, "who likes to hear his plates rattle." Near the top of the stretch, McGrath was out there waving his jockey on, and Oliver Lewis let up. Aristides flew home in 2:37¾, the fastest mile and a half yet for a three-year-old. Morrissey's old gambling partner and his henceforth immortal "little red colt," with a star and two white pasterns behind (just above the hooves), had won the first Kentucky Derby.[13]

It was not true, as sometimes claimed, that the Derby was a minor race at the beginning. It was not as important as the Saratoga Cup, Travers, or Belmont, but the Spirit saw that it "created deep interest throughout the country" and held out "prospects of future great events." With the Preakness often a few days away, however, winning what became known as the Triple Crown—the Derby, Preakness, and Belmont—was rarely feasible in those days. But a Derby-Belmont-Travers triple crown was, and Aristides was going for it.

First Derby trivia: Fourteen of the fifteen jockeys, including Lewis, were African Americans, showing their strength in the South. Aristides's $2,850 win and $16,700 for the year would help Leamington top the sires list, displacing Lexington for the first time in a decade and a half.[14]

Lexington died on July 1. He had once "rusticated" at the Saratoga Trotting Course, but an oversight cut short his racing. When a groom left his door unlocked, Lexington entered the feed room and gorged himself. His trainer, unaware, took him out for a four-mile "brush," and it almost killed him. He began losing his sight, yet "the Blind Hero of Woodburn" became the greatest sire ever, fathering Kentucky (who had died in April), Norfolk and Asteroid, Kingfisher and Harry Bassett, Tom Bowling and Preakness, and the recent winner of the Preakness, Tom Ochiltree. Lexington children had won seven of the first twelve Traverses and were not finished winning it and taking him to the top of the sires list. At his death at twenty-five, the *Spirit* said, "The name of Lexington will be forever green in the American turf."

Neither the Derby, nor the Belmont, in which Aristides finished second, nor the Travers was the top sports event of 1875. "The regatta of 1875 was the greatest that has ever been held in this country," Crowther and Ruhl would write thirty years later. Thirteen colleges competed. The first college athletes to become national celebrities, they were changing priorities on the American campus. Indeed, the pictures from Saratoga now revealed a subspecies: the College Athlete. He sprang full blown from the illustrated papers, often in tight sleeveless shirt or with no shirt at all and knee-length shorts. Confused editors labeled them "muscular intellects" while others settled hopefully on "splendid specimens of American youth." The specimens often had something else in mind, and so did the women hellbent on getting to the lake. On a *Daily Graphic* cover, a young lady placed her folded parasol in a strategic position as she and a rower measured off a length of it, while two other young women concentrated on an oar. The caption: "How the Ladies Inspect a Shell." From the day he appeared at Saratoga, the athlete would be a big man on campus.[15]

For three days running, the trains deposited arrivals at the Springs. Hellraisers from nearby Union College had hit town for years, but now students made up half the players at the Club House, which did not close this time. The lake was at its height. Leslie had created a six-mile lake drive that made the original Union Avenue plan something of a reality. On his beach, two hundred feet of the bleachers were draped with an elegant awning, and somebody would soon have to invent Impressionism to portray such scenes. The college flotillas flickered on the water with little colored flags, twenty-three purple pennants twinkling from the Williams boats. A witness said Brown, which couldn't find brown bunting and went with black instead, "looks like an aquatic funeral procession."[16]

At noon on Tuesday, July 13, ten thousand people watched Cornell capture the freshman race. "As the Cornelians with very little on them . . . and that little wet through with perspiration and water, were carried round in triumph . . . such was the enthusiasm of the fair sex that they forgot to be shocked."

The news electrified Manhattan, crowds gathering at newspaper and railroad offices, which posted the results. With the focus shifting to the university match,

"The Intercollegiate Boat-Races." *Harper's Weekly, 1875. Courtesy of the author.*

collegians and alumni replaced the scruffy crowds in three pool rooms at Twenty-eighth Street. Yale led in the auctions, selling for twenty dollars while Cornell went for ten dollars in a typical sixty-seven dollar pool. In the "French mutual pools," Yale went off at a little more than 4 to 1.[17]

Some thirty thousand people gathered at the lake. The press watched from a thirty-foot tower, a boat of its own, and a barge equipped with writing desks. When the boats passed by in the three-miler, "the partisans of the leading crews made the air ring with their cheers." In fact, it was here that a famous college cheer, "Cornell, yell, yell, ell, Cornell!" was born. It was refined to "Cornell, I yell, yell, Cornell." The Harvard yell heard at Saratoga was "Rah-Rah-Rah," shouted quickly, and Brown's ditto, but slowly. C-O-L-U-M-B-I-A roared its letters, seriatim.[18]

When he got the news that Cornell had won the university race too, the president of the six-year-old college high above Cayuga's waters played the first tune on the campus chimes, cannon fired from hilltops, and all the professors in Ithaca wired congratulations to their heroes. Sports had taken over the American campus. Cornell beat Columbia, Harvard, Dartmouth, Wesleyan, Yale, Amherst, Brown, Williams, and Bowdoin in that order. Hamilton, Union, and Princeton had their problems and were not timed.[19]

Embarrassed by its sixth place finish, Yale took its boat and went home as it had threatened, withdrawing from the RAAC. Again it claimed the regatta was too big, but Crowther and Ruhl would write that the real reason was Yale's "dislike of being beaten by smaller colleges." At Yale's request, Harvard agreed to quit, too, after the

1876 regatta. It was a national scandal; the *Spirit* declared that Harvard and Yale, founders of the sport on these shores, "have fallen from their high position. . . . It is the old story of the scholar surpassing the teacher." The defections were "inspired by nothing more than a false spirit of aristocracy."[20]

More harmonious were the baseball tournament and second track meet at Glen Mitchell. More than three thousand spectators filled the grandstand and crowded the field for these "Olympian games," as the *Times* described them. There were ten events, not limited to the regatta colleges, and the red and blue of Pennsylvania was donned at an intercollegiate event for the first time, by one H. Laussat Geyelin.[21]

A pistol this time sent Amherst's C. H. Barber and Cornell's Copeland "bounding along grandly, Copeland adhering to his Indian lope and Barber, with his head thrown back, and his chest torso erect, and his feet beating the earth twice to the second." The crowd rushed onto the track toward the finish, forming a narrow lane for the milers. "'Now, Amherst,' 'Come, Cornell,' shrieked the human walls, while two gentlemen held the string breast high for the racers. A few seconds later, it was torn from their hands by Barber, who leaped into the arms of his friends 4½ seconds ahead of Copeland." Time: 4:44¾.

Amherst, Harvard, and Yale tied in points, with two firsts each, and then the humans got out of the way. Since at least 1873, Glen Mitchell had been staging a trotting meeting on off days during the thoroughbred season. This year, it ran national ads for its eight days of racing with $3,100 in purses.[22]

Within a week of the regatta came the country's most spectacular gathering of wealth. A Philadelphia bankers' meeting the month before had been judged the largest amount of capital ever assembled on the continent. Then a bigger group—350 delegates from thirty-two states and territories—convened in Saratoga to form the first ABA, the American Bankers Association. After the Panic of '73, fifty more banks had failed, and the bankers were discovering solidarity. As Vanderbilt, Astor, Stewart, Gould, and other robber barons plotted against each other on the piazzas, younger businesspeople pulled up chairs to do the opposite (and what they did not want labor to do): organize. As the bankers' invitations to Saratoga promised, the important issues would "be fully and freely discussed," folly that certainly would never have been countenanced by the Commodore.

So the nation's first Las Vegas had become its first major convention resort. It excelled even the metropolises as a convention center. When problems developed at the Republican convention at Chicago, the *Troy Times* patiently explained: "There is only one place in the country in which to hold a national convention and that place is Saratoga Springs." After meeting on the second floor of the 1870 Town Hall (now City Hall), the bankers could find hotel bars, dances, games, and sports all in easy reach. They probably made several deposits when the track opened two days after their convention.[23]

Racing was taking on an altogether new dimension, and partly as a result the Association had turned the track back to John Morrissey as sole lessee and manager. What was new in racing was the tremendous popularity of the pari-mutuel system, and it also brought bitter controversy. Publisher George Wilkes, whose *Spirit of the*

Times had praised Monsieur Oller's brilliant idea as democracy on the turf, now denounced it and demanded its abolition, insisting it could only produce massive cheating and the demise of the national sport. The *Spirit* and the *Herald* reported that the proliferation of pari-mutuel machines on Parisian boulevards had led to embezzlements by clerks, petty robberies, and an increase in suicides. As a result, the French authorities had closed them down after the war of 1870, as had other European governments. They "found their last refuge at the little principality of Monaco," which they turned into "one vast gambling hell . . . a swarm, both male and female, of the most profligate characters in the world." Meantime, however, the machines had taken the New World by storm, pulling in five-dollar bettors at tracks and city pool rooms.[24]

The dangers were clear, said Wilkes. Operators could change the numbers to indicate more tickets sold on a horse, lowering the odds. They could get jockeys to throw races. They could own horses, even control a track. All this had happened at Monmouth Park, controlled by "the rascally cheating American blackguard," the "two-card faro sharper and notorious manipulator of spring roulettes known as Johnny Chamberlin"—Wilkes's personal enemy.

It didn't matter that Chamberlin had won the first Preakness with Survivor and the third with Tom Ochiltree. "Some measure must be taken to prevent professional rogues from owning and running 'favorites,'" and anyone who thought Chamberlin "would not throw a race, or enter a horse like Tom Ochiltree for the purpose of losing, knows but little of human nature." In fact, Wilkes charged, he and McGrath had done just that. It didn't matter, either, that McGrath had won the Derby and much else. He associated with the enemy and thus was another "double-card skin gambler of the uttermost type." While Chamberlin was banqueting "ropers-in" at his Long Branch casino, McGrath was filling reporters with whiskey, "who pull at his bottle as they would at a teat and then go into ecstasies of type and call him Squire." Specifically, the country's leading sports publisher charged that Chamberlin and McGrath had the first Derby winner lose to a Missouri colt named Ozark at Monmouth Park in July. Some $150,000 changed hands, Wilkes said, and the two gamblers cleaned up on the pari-mutuels in New York, Long Branch, and Philadelphia.

"Fellows like Chamberlin and McGrath have but to touch the electric wire with—'Buy the field against Aristides!'—to milk every pool-room from Montreal to New Orleans of its cash balance. An extra pail of water to the favorite horse will then do the business, and all the spurring that can be administered to the poor animal will but gore his sides."

The soon-to-retire Wilkes stated the obvious: he was not against gambling. Any racing association that counts on it for most of its revenue, however, "will be sure to strip the turf of all its claims to character and to drive it rapidly to ruin." Saratoga was the solution, thought Wilkes. Specifically, Morrissey was the solution, representing "the higher class of what are known as 'sporting men,'" who "deal fairly according to the fixed laws of mathematical percentage" and "the just laws of chance." It was hard to know a square dealer from a cheat, but "the strong hard sense of John Morrissey, who charges for *his* banquets and who has no ropers-in, has solved the question. He

The Derby and College Sports

owned race horses for a while but as he aimed at the management of a race track in the interest of gentlemen, he shrewdly disposed of them." In an attack of blind faith, Wilkes added that if three or four other gamblers would do likewise, the racing associations would not have to make stronger rules to control gambling.

Precisely because of the tidal wave of gambling, Morrissey was now completely in charge. He may well have been the most qualified man to run the country's leading sports venue, which he had created in the first place. "The modern appliance of the Paris Mutual," moaned the *Spirit,* had created "a betting exchange in every capital city of United States" and "a new frenzy for betting on races." Who better to control this frenzy?

To better accommodate the Saratoga crowds, the second stand, now known as the "public stand," had acquired a roof, with the same shamrock windows. The grandstand seats were recushioned and rebacked, the velvet lawns and "botannical display" renovated. The steeplechase course glowed with white-painted stone walls, evergreen hedges, and fences. And to finance "a racing programme second to none on the continent," Morrissey offered $25,000 in purses and additions to stakes.[25]

Worth $4,750, the Travers brought out Aristides, the little red colt, cementing the bond between the Bluegrass and the Springs. Kentucky horse people had been coming here since 1863, but from that first Derby year, owners, breeders, trainers, jockeys, stable help, and journalists would worship at both meccas in annual reunions unrivaled in sports. A pilgrim to one can get all the dirt on the other as if they weren't half a country apart.[26]

Illustrator Albert Berghaus captured the start from the chute, Leslie's printers transferred it to wood, and wide-eyed readers everywhere watched the start of the twelfth Travers. Berghaus also came up with a crowded version of the victory by James Grinstead's "gallant gray," D'Artagnan, while the *Spirit* drew a less crowded and more accurate picture: "Few will ever forget the electric burst of speed with which he shot past his horses on entering the last mile"—and finished in a record 3:06½. He paid ninety-five dollars for a five-dollar pari-mutuel ticket. Aristides finished third to establish another tradition, the Derby laureate losing the Travers more often than not.[27]

Probably the only Spa entry owned by a sitting president came out for the Sequel Stakes on August 3. Though Grant owned three-year-old General Harney, it was noted that his breeder and namesake, J. M. Harney of St. Louis, "retains an interest in his racing qualities," meaning it was Harney who raced him. He ran second to Viator. Pierre Lorillard's Parole cantered into history that season, taking two Spa events for two-year-olds, the Saratoga and the Kentucky Stakes. He would be back, to put it mildly.

The Cup was again the grand event—"one of the most exciting ever witnessed on the American turf"—with some half-million dollars changing hands. Eight-year-old Preakness sprang to the lead at a mile and a quarter, and half way up the home stretch "shouts of 'Sanford wins!' broke simultaneously from a thousand throats." Then five-year-old Springbok closed. Preakness held fast. The jockeys laid into them with whip and spur. The crowd sat in stunned silence, as McDaniel's blue jacket with red sash

The twelfth Travers. The start is in the chute, in front of the completed field, or public, stand. The frontispiece shows the finish. By Albert Berghaus, *Leslie's*, 1875. *Courtesy of the author.*

and Sanford's dark blue flew in a blur under the wire, and the shouting "rent the skies, to be renewed again and again when the judges decided the race was 'a dead heat.'"

It was the only dead heat ever in the Cup. And they did the two and a quarter miles in 3:56¼, knocking almost three seconds off Harry Bassett's mark. "The witnessing of such a race," said a nonhistorian who understood sports, "was a memorable event in a man's life." McDaniel told Sanford that Springbok had come up lame, and M. H. sportingly passed on a runoff, so they divided the $2,050 stakes. Thanks to Preakness, McDaniel could only say he had won three and a half Saratoga Cups in a row. Still, that, plus back to back Traverses and three Belmont wins, wasn't bad for five years' work.[28]

The Kenner Stakes produced a tie, too, between Ozark and Milner, owned by John O'Donnell of Saratoga. Dead heats were not so rare back when mere humans called the races, but out in California, the future was on the way. Central Pacific Railroad President Leland Stanford had hired an English-born photographer with a weird moniker, Eadweard Muybridge, to solve an ancient riddle: Does a galloping horse ever go airborne, or is one hoof always on earth? In 1872, Muybridge's twenty-four mahogany cameras went off in succession and caught a trotter with all landing gear up. Soon a wire would trip Muybridge's cameras as the horse flew past a white sheet with vertical lines—the first photo finish, albeit experimental.[29]

The sniveling little gelding Brigand, owned by Thomas Doswell and Addison Cammack, reappeared on August 17, right after Sanford sold him because of his "cowardly disposition." Now he surprised the world by taking a $500 purse "under the influence of the Dutch courage created by the imbibing of a pint of Gaffney's best whiskey."[30]

"A Cincinnati turf speculator was loud in his offer of $100 to $5" on Rutherford as he rounded the first turn in a four-mile dash and was beaten by Wild Idle. Bookmakers had surfaced at the Spa, noisily sharing the scene with the auction pools and pari-mutuels. And that 1875 season reportedly covered expenses for the first time, the *Spirit* crediting "the superior business management" of Morrissey and "the indefatigable secretary," Wheatly.[31]

Dead heat. Ozark and Milner in the Kenner. *Daily Graphic*, 1875. *Courtesy of the author.*

"Saratoga is wild over Courtney," said the *Times* a few days later. In the Rowing Association's third regatta, Charlie "pulled leisurely home" to take the state championship and senior singles, both times beating Jim Riley, who was born hard by Kayaderosseras Creek. A week later, he "left Riley at anchor" in the third nationals at Troy. Some years afterward, somebody would send Charlie a tiger cat, who followed him everywhere. Charlie named it "Jim Riley."[32]

In minor sports news, it was a good year for the Rock City Falls baseball Thankfuls, who included John Morrissey, Jr. Their winning 1875 season must have touched Pa, for Junior was suffering from Bright's disease, an inflammation of the kidneys, which darkened those years for them. Morrissey was maturing politically, finding his level as he ran for state Senate from Manhattan. Of course, this vastly amused the father of American political cartoonists, who as a kid had rooted against Morrissey in the Heenan fight and still was not buying him. Saddled with a bit of bigotry of his own, Nast skewered Morrissey as the Irish prizefighting gambler trying to pawn himself off as a Reform Democrat. Nast lost again. The *Times* would hail Senator Morrissey as "consistently on the side of good Municipal Government and against the Ring rule of Tammany Hall."[33]

The year closed with a couple of news items. An old jockey dropped by the *Spirit* to say he would go to San Francisco if anybody wanted him for a planned four-mile race out there. His name was Gilpatrick. Milton Sanford was sending a stable to England, the first Yank owner to invade the English turf since Richard Ten Broeck tried it two decades earlier. Sanford himself would return in the spring, but Preakness never would; within two years, he would be sold for breeding and become difficult to handle. In a terrible rage, his English owner, the Duke of Hamilton, would shoot and kill the American idol, the inspiration of the Preakness and the winner of the Saratoga Cup in a dead heat.[34]

*   *   *   *

One day in March, a human being on the top floor of a Boston boardinghouse spoke seven words. Miraculously, a human out of earshot in another room heard the words. They were: "Mr. Watson, come here. I want you." The caller would be succeeded by a long line of bookmakers.

On a June day in the centennial year, a Cavalry officer attacked an Indian encampment in the Montana Territory and found their horsemen far outnumbered his. Forced into broken ground, the attackers dismounted, fought, and died in Custer's Last Stand.

Three weeks later, only six colleges and a practically invisible crowd came to the regatta. Still, July 19 was a good day for Cornell, which swamped Harvard, Columbia, Union, Wesleyan, and Princeton in the university race and swept the single sculls and freshman race, too, "the greatest series of victories ever won by a single college." Then, with the withdrawal of Harvard, the RAAC was history. Cornell and the other teams faded for lack of organized events until the RAAC was reorganized several years later as the Intercollegiate Rowing Association. The IRA regattas survive, still without Harvard and Yale, who pursue their more private rivalry. As for Saratoga Lake, surrounded by small colleges, it could mount a revival.[35]

The Spa made official two-legged history that year. The country's first official intercollegiate track meet started at 10:30 A.M. on Thursday, July 20, 1876, at Glen Mitchell. It was the inaugural event of the Athletic Association of American Colleges, considered the first intercollegiate athletic organization. Founded that year at the Springs, it later became the Intercollegiate Association of Amateur Athletes of America (IC4A).[36]

They parked in a triple row of carriages and gathered in the little grandstand, in a supplementary stand and around the sun-scorched field. Ten teams were competing in thirteen events, and were dripping sweat even before the opening three mile walk, which only two of six survived. Princeton's T. A. Noble strolled home in 28:21½. H. W. Stevens of Williams took the deciding hundred-yard heat in eleven seconds, and Princeton's J. M. Mann one of two field events, the sixteen-pound shot put. But an unofficial "one-mile walk for graduates" was described as "a stupid affair," as Wesleyan's Downs and Dartmouth's S. McCall "crawled along" for a third of the distance, at which point McCall sat down as the crowd jeered, and Downs walked home in the "execrable and disgraceful time of 9m45s."

Yale's W. J. Wakeman ran the fastest 120-yard hurdle on record in :18¼. Princeton's R. A. Greene did the half mile in 2:16½, and Pennsylvania's H. Willoughby broad-jumped 18 feet 3½ inches. "After dinner" came the other field event, "Throwing Regulation Base-Ball," which ought to be revived. Shot-putter Mann hurled it 368 feet, 6 inches.[37]

Although Friday was cooler, only a few saw W. M. Watson of the College of the

City of New York walk a mile in 8:02. E. C. Stimson of Dartmouth ran it in 4:58 ½, then did three in 16:21. Downs won the unofficial mile for graduates in 5:38 ½, Columbia's J. W. Prior the high jump at 5 feet 4 inches, and Stevens the quarter mile in :56. Princeton captured the meet with four firsts, Bowdoin and Harvard also competing in what was not only America's first intercollegiate meet but the last one at Saratoga.[38]

In another first, the four-legged runners debuted not with the Travers but with a $400 five-furlong dash entitled "the Introductory Scramble." Belmont's Sultana became the fourth filly and eighth Lexington offspring to capture Bill's event in thirteen years. The Lorillards were having the most fun, though. George had bought Preakness winner Tom Ochiltree from Chamberlin and sent him against Parole, Pierre's flashy three-year-old. First, Parole carried the cherry and black home in Saratoga's mile-and-a-quarter sweepstakes, then Tom Ochiltree took the Cup by a length in George's new colors, blue jacket and orange sleeves. This was just the beginning of their famous brotherly brouhaha.

Vivacious Jennie Jerome saw Saratoga that year, too, with Lord Randolph and a friend of his. "The beauty of the ladies and the gorgeousness astonished the men," wrote Winston Churchill's mother, but the prices were ridiculous. "Having found the hotel . . . absurdly expensive, I asked my father to remonstrate with the proprietor." It was not entirely the proprietor's fault, however. Jennie and Randolph had begun growing apart. Her biographer speculated that as his syphilis reached the virulent second stage, Randolph had developed guilt, then an aversion to women. The hotel manager simply told Jennie's father: "The Lord and his wife *would* have two rooms, hence the expense."[39]

It was a tragic year for Morrissey. His baseball-loving son died of the kidney ailment at twenty-one. The senator was only forty-five himself, and at the peak of his abilities, yet his world seemed to be crashing. In quick succession, death opened the accounts of the three who contended for the title of richest of them all. William B., heir to the John Jacob Astor fortune in land and tenements, was first to go, in November 1875. He left $40 million. Surely A. T. Stewart had more; it was an open joke that all the drygoods king cared about was money. Presiding at a New York Chamber of Commerce meeting once, he took out a gold pencil and rapped for order, at which point Bill Travers yelled, "C-cash! C-cash!" A. T. joined in the laughter. He died in April 1876. His estate was conservatively estimated at $40 million. It was a tie.

For more than a year the bulletins on the Commodore's health had set off shock waves on the market, and his large family had gathered round his Manhattan bedside more than once. As 1876 ended, he knew he was dying. He sat in a rolling chair and had his trotters brought around to the front of 10 Washington Place so he could see them through the window. It may have eased the pain, which was so fierce he would heave hot water bottles at the doctors.

*   *   *   *

Commodore Vanderbilt died on January 4, 1877. His fortune was even more vast than imagined, considerably beyond Astor's and Stewart's combined: $100 million. Sixty percent was in Central and Hudson River Railroad stock. He certainly did not divide it democratically. All save $3.7 million went to William H. and his sons, which guaranteed W. H. control of Central. Of W. H.'s sons, the oldest, Cornelius II, was favored with nearly thirty-two thousand shares of Central and Hudson River and twenty-three thousand of Harlem. W. H.'s other sons, William K., Frederick, and George, got twenty thousand shares of Central and Hudson. The old man's Saratoga bride, Mrs. Frank Vanderbilt, received $500,000 in bonds and two thousand shares of Central, and his eight surviving daughters $250,000 to $500,000 each. The ill-favored epileptic, Cornelius Jeremiah, got $200,000, and that only in trust.[40]

"A railroad dynasty had been created" through the primogeniture of W. H., biographer Wheaton Lane would point out. "Even though dead, the Commodore, as in life, was to exert a commanding influence." The Springs, which he had turned into a Vanderbilt village, remained the dynasty's summer headquarters. On the north piazza of the United States Hotel, when Vanderbilt talked, people still listened.

A. T. Stewart, on the other hand, had not created a dynasty. His estate went to his barely competent wife, except for $1 million left to the son he never had, Henry Hilton. If today no shopper in the world has heard of A. T. Stewart's, the world's first department store, the reason is Henry Hilton. A lawyer, Tammany judge, and parks official, he had been one of Tweed's "respectabilities" and, more important, was A. T.'s only confidant. The will, which happened to be in Judge Hilton's handwriting, called for him to shut down the Stewart enterprises. Instead, on the day after the funeral, in exchange for that $1 million, the widow signed over the entire drygoods business to Hilton and gave him power of attorney over the rest, including the Grand Union Hotel.

Hilton was launched on what the *Times* judged "the rapid dissipation of one of the greatest fortunes ever amassed by trade," and he had more going for him than remarkable business incompetence. On Thursday, June 14, 1877, New York banker Joseph Seligman, whose fortune may have equaled Stewart's, arrived with his family at the Grand Union, as they had for several summers. They were told that Judge Hilton had given orders to exclude Jews, and they had to leave. The Seligmans were welcomed immediately at the Clarendon. The next day Joe marched a block up Broadway and into the Grand Union and demanded to know if Hilton had really banned him. Invited into an office, he was told it was true. Enraged, Joe warned he would force Hilton to let him in and, from the Clarendon, dashed off an incinerating "Dear Judge" letter that made the front page of the *Times*. It poured scorn on Hilton, then warily suggested that "the civilized world is beginning to be more tolerant."

It was America's first major anti-Semitic scandal. Bankers and the preacher Henry Ward Beecher rushed to Seligman's defense. Jewish merchants pulled their accounts from Stewart's. Panicking, Hilton said he did not object to all "Hebrews," only "the Seligman Jew," whom he proceeded to define in the crudest slurs, which inspired Bret Harte to mock Hilton's order:

> You may give to John Morrissey supper and wine,
> And Madame N. N. to your care I resign;
> You will see that those Jenkins from Missouri Flat

Are properly cared for, but recollect that
Never a Jew
Who's not an Ebrew
Shall take up his lodgings
Here at the Grand U.[41]

As Harte mused ("Shall we keep out Disraeli and take Rothschild in?"), Hilton's managers tried to explain that the Grand Union's survival had been threatened by a rumor that it had become a Jewish boardinghouse. As historian Harry Resseguie has written, the hotel under Stewart and Breslin had indeed attracted New York Jewish leaders, but it was now explained that their friends "swarmed in from outside boarding-houses in legions, freely taking possession of the piazzas at the morning and evening concerts." The *Times* splashed it all over the front page.[42]

Hilton was betting he could make anti-Semitism acceptable in America, and to a degree he did. On one hand, other hotels along Saratoga's Broadway would have no part of it, the Clarendon, Congress Hall, and the States, headquarters of the Vanderbilt and sporting crowds, announcing that they welcomed Christian and Jew alike. So did most hotels around the country. On the other hand, anti-Semitism persisted at the nation's most famous hotel, which encouraged it elsewhere. The *Times* found some Long Branch hotel keepers hostile to Jews and "careful not to give them a foothold." Author Stephen Birmingham noted that the New York Bar Association blackballed a Jew a year later, that City College's fraternities then barred them, and that the Long Island Railroad, trying to develop a Coney Island resort, sounded like Hilton when it announced, "We do not like Jews as a class," and discouraged them from patronizing "our road and hotel." Birmingham concluded that the Hilton-Seligman affair "was to have a profound psychological effect on German Jewish life in New York, making it more defensive. . . . It was out in the open and a fact of life: certain areas of America were closed to Jews." The Grand Union would remain closed to them for thirteen years.[43] Long forgotten is the fact that, in 1891, the year after the ban ended, visiting president Benjamin Harrison stood on the piazza of the Grand Union and declared that America "does not tolerate any distinction between men other than merit."

A different crisis paralyzed the turf. The city pool sellers—seven operated in New York alone—had earned so much off President Rutherford B. Hayes's election that the New York legislature banned all pools as of May 15, 1877. It made for a funereal opening day at Jerome Park. "The voice of the auctioneer is no longer heard," a reporter said, noting an "absence of enthusiasm, excitement, and deep interest in the races." Jerome introduced full-scale English bookmaking to replace the pools, and turf writers tried to explain the English system. Its backers argued that the odds in auction pools, which had never taken hold in England, could be subverted by the withdrawal of a horse and that the pari-mutuels were complete adventures, since the odds would not be known until the betting was over. Under the English system, players could buy tickets from the bookmakers in an "Outer Betting Ring" or pay more to get into the elite "Inner Ring"—Tattersall's Ring in England. On that spring day when the bookmakers took over Jerome Park, the small players found them and their odds, and the betting trends, impossible to understand. Once again the *Spirit* reversed itself, saying the abolition of pools would be "most disastrous."

How did Senator Morrissey respond to the ban on his colleagues' activities?

"Too little, gentlemen!" shouted the auctioneer, Robert Cathcart, Jr., who had succeeded Dr. Underwood at Saratoga. He wanted more than $300 on Baden Baden, the Derby winner, in a $790 pool. The equally illegal "mutual" pools were running, too. It seemed that Morrissey had found the perfect solution to the ban: ignore it. He reportedly held that it did not apply to "the grounds of racing associations," but the reporter added what Morrissey knew best, that during race week "public opinion favors loosening rather than tightening the reins of government."

The lessee's new power was probably further enhanced when Travers resigned that year as president, to be succeeded by the local hotelier James Marvin. Feeling his oats, Morrissey scheduled two seven-day meetings, forty-two races and eighteen stakes worth nearly $50,000. Six extra days would be tacked on, and before it was through, the season would stretch over forty-two days, including occasional breathers, which would be a wise innovation today. It was a spectacular sports program, far beyond anything else in the country, a program into which John Morrissey apparently poured everything he had, almost as if it were going to be his last.

The Spa was in its glory. The great hotel complex added the Adelphi, fronted by a raised piazza with pierced spandrel openings and thin three-story columns, along with high Victorian windows, and Renaissance and Italianate motifs.

The wide road to the track had become a track. The bays driven by Capt. John Shaw of California were "probably the fastest big trotting team in the world" and "may be seen almost daily on Union Avenue." A. S. Cameron, of New York, showed off "a pair of black and chestnut mares that he drives to a three-quarter clarence on Union Avenue every fine afternoon." A few blocks from the Old Gray Mare's former haunt, "they spin along with apparent ease at a 2:30 clip," a time that once only she of all the trotters in the world had made. The record was now below 2:15, so maybe there was something to this improvement of the breed business.[44]

Morrissey must have gotten a huge kick out of the Travers. In one of the great early African-American combinations, Will Walker had ridden and Ed Brown had trained Dan Swigert's Baden Baden when he won the third Derby. Then the fast-moving young William Astor snapped him up, just as he had snapped up Vagrant *before* he won the second Derby. So boarding Baden now was none other than Tom Sayers, son of the same Tom Sayers whom Morrissey had backed against the "Benicia Boy." Little Tommy made Baden the first horse to double in the Derby and the Travers. They wired the news to Astor in Europe and stashed his spectacular silver and gold prize, a double-tiered tray from which rose a column surmounted by a female figure holding a prancing steed (they knew how to make trophies then).

In the next race, Vera Cruz won a startling victory over both Tom Ochiltree and Parole in a mile-and-a-quarter sweepstakes, a bookmaker explaining, "The wrong horse won."

Although nobody knew it yet, one of the top few riders of all time also materialized at the Spa that year. Competing for the first time against the star jockeys of

Ed Brown. *Keeneland Library.*

the East, Isaac Murphy, a Kentucky-born African American, rode Vera Cruz to a win over Ochiltree in another race.[45]

Pierre Lorillard's Parole made good on his word, though. Having been beaten by George's Ochiltree in the 1876 Cup, he turned the tables in the '77 Cup, conquering both Ochiltree and Vera Cruz. (Also ran: Athlene, which showed that while Morrissey no longer owned racehorses, Charles Reed, his partner in the gambling houses, did.)[46] Ochiltree would come back once again to reduce Parole at Jerome Park in the fall—twice. With these two, the tobacco heirs were putting on quite a national show. Pierre had set himself up on seven thousand acres of Orange County, New York, converting five thousand of those acres into a hunting and fishing resort, the celebrated Tuxedo Park. His horse farm, Rancocas Stud, was farther south, in Jobstown, New Jersey. An English paper ran a sketch of its highly unusual "circular race-course"; odd, these Yanks. Pierre was also experimenting with aluminum horseshoes, but as they were not yet manufactured, he had to order from Tiffany's. As for George, he lorded over Westbrook Stable in Islip, Long Island. The brothers would now resolve their Ochiltree-Parole matter in a triangular event with Frank Harper's Ten Broeck, a race that disrupted the Congress of the United States.[47]

A son of Leamington out of Maiden, who was the first filly to win the Travers, Parole was thought the least of the three. After all, Tom Ochiltree had conceded nine pounds in beating him in the fall. Neither, however, had met Ten Broeck. By Phaeton out of the Lexington mare Fanny Holton, he was considered the best, despite a wild career. He lost badly to Aristides in the first Derby, then was put in a famous match with Mollie McCarty, who was 13–0 when shipped east by Elias J. "Lucky" Baldwin, who would develop Rancho Santa Anita, ancestor of the modern mecca outside Los Angeles. Ten Broeck took Mollie, only to lose again to Aristides in another one-on-one in 1876. Then the Kentucky horse took off. He won all seven other races in 1876 and eight straight in 1877, and proved amazingly versatile. He reduced the four-mile record to 7:15 ¾ and, as Robertson pointed out, would hold several other records at retirement, including the two miles at 3:27 ½ and the mile at 1:39 ¾. Ten Broeck was the favorite on October 24, 1877.[48]

The House of Representatives adjourned for the race, and the congressmen headed up the road to Baltimore and through Druid Hill Park to Pimlico. The Senate had wound up its own affairs, so required no special action. A reporter noted nearly half of each house of the "National Legislature" among the ten to fifteen thousand people. Yet no purple prose could make the race more than an anticlimax. It ended up Parole by five lengths over Ten Broeck, with Tom Ochiltree twelve lengths back, and history would show that it did settle the matter of who was best.[49]

Another runner, Morrissey, was wheezing and choking his way through another race. This time it was the state senator, although he was sick as a horse in the last weeks of his reelection campaign. Battered by bronchitis, he still hit the trail, reeling about in his carriage in rotten weather to speak six times a night. He got out of bed to talk about the victory, then his doctor sent him south. After several weeks in Savannah, he wintered in Jacksonville with no sign of recovery except a report in the *Tribune* that he was "disgusted . . . with Florida," a good sign for an Irishman.

*　　*　　*　　*

The senator cheered his friends in February 1878 with the news that he had rallied. He and Susie boarded the *Charleston* and steamed to New York in March. "His face had a healthy glow, and he walked down the gangplank with a firm and steady step." After a day in New York, he took the nightboat to Troy and caught a severe cold.

On April 19, he was taken to the Springs and put up in the new Adelphi. Again he recovered some strength and looked forward to getting back to work in Albany. He simply declined to join his era's dead, who had just recruited Boss Tweed. On Monday, April 29, however, his right arm became paralyzed, and he all but lost his speech in an apparent stroke. On Tuesday, he would say, according to the *Tribune*, and he was quite capable of such blarney, "I am running neck and neck with death, and rapidly tiring."[50]

May Day brought quiet. The New York papers arrived a little after three. He asked for his glass and started to read. About five-thirty, "an unfavorable change occurred, and he sank rapidly." Father John McMenomy appeared and administered

Extreme Unction. "Although Mr. Morrissey was failing perceptibly all the time, he appeared conscious until the last. His wife and several employees were present at his death. He died clasping the hand of the priest." He was forty-seven.[51]

In Manhattan, his friends collected at the hotels and told Morrissey stories. In the rarest tribute, play was suspended at 5 West Twenty-fourth St. His partners there, Reed and Albert Spencer, had left for Saratoga. His other friends would follow in the morning, and if they read the papers on the way up, they saw he was the lead in the *Times* under a final Saratoga dateline, his kaleidoscopic life replayed in column after column of the New York papers. For a moment, the bias that had condemned the Irish fighter and gambler was lifted. The *Times* thought his death "a loss to the cause of good government in New York," adding, "no man ever charged John Morrissey with being a venal legislator or a dishonest politician." The *Tribune,* as moralistic as when Greeley ran it, could not make up its mind. Morrissey "no longer made it a business to exchange blows with a half-naked ruffian for the amusement of the mob . . . yet he made his money by nightly violation of the law" and "the metropolis of America was represented in its Senate by the keeper of a gambling hell," but it had to admit that "He had a good deal of the prize-fighter's respect for fair play and the bruiser's brute courage" and the notion "that workingmen—with whom he had nothing whatever in common—ought somehow to get a living out of the public treasury."

Harper's couldn't figure him out, either. "He was a man of strict integrity," yet his public service can not "make us forget the thousands of young men who have been lured to their destruction in his luxurious Saratoga resort."

It was, of course, the leading sports journal that understood him best. Only the *Spirit of the Times* saw that he had "left a deep and peculiar stamp upon his time," that his death would "draw regrets from tens of thousands who never saw him." As a sports manager, he had a talent "something akin to genius." By enforcing a few rules—no disreputables, no smoking in the ladies' sections, no standing in the grandstand during races—he had made the Spa "the most famous racing point in the Union," while rude crowds had overtaken Jerome Park, Monmouth Park, Pimlico, and Louisville. The *Spirit* thought strict management indispensable to the growth of sports. Morrissey's genius was really in his personality, a mix, as the paper observed, of integrity, purpose, endurance, shrewdness, amiability, "generosity almost to a fault when he believed anyone was worthy of it," talent, and experience. Few editors and no historians noticed, but as an athlete, entertainer, businessman, and politician, "bighearted John" was much of what the country would become.

The people knew, and so did the politicians. New York's City Hall lowered the flag to half-staff, the Senate in Albany adjourned, and more than fifteen thousand people gathered in Troy for the funeral in the rain. "No burial ever evoked so many expressions of sorrow from the mass of the people—the hard, rough workingmen and women," reported the *Times.* "They turned out en masse today, in their working clothes and with the grit upon their faces, to watch with tears in their eyes the passage of the funeral procession." They buried him in St. Peter's Cemetery, next to his son.

Almost all memory of him was buried as well. Although Vanderbilt, Travers, Jerome, and the other original giants had a hell of a time with him, and Wheatly even attended the funeral, history would turn up its nose at his kind. He was just too American, and too soon. If forgotten elsewhere, however, he left his mark—the mark of the Tipperary immigrant, the undefeated boxing champion, the most famous gambler of his time, the street politician quoted by Lincoln, the first star athlete in Congress, the first major impresario of American sports—all over Saratoga Springs: at the Adelphi Hotel, where he died, at his casino in the park, at the trotting grounds where he opened his first season, and at the racetrack that he, more than anyone, created.[52]

 *12*

ISAAC MURPHY AND THE CALIFORNIANS

Aᴍᴇʀɪᴄᴀ ʜɪᴛ ᴛʜᴇ 1880s running. English-, African-, Dutch-, Irish- and other hyphenated American athletes piloted new heroes at new racetracks. Two-legged meets multiplied under the leadership of the New York Athletic Club and its new president, Bill Travers. Along the baselines, the National League was off and running, able to support a journeyman outfielder like Pete "Monkey" Hotaling of Mohawk, New York, as long as he kept switching from Cincinnati to Cleveland to Worcester to Boston, then to Brooklyn in the new American Association. In the ring, they ran to get out of the way of John L. Sullivan, who knocked out Paddy Ryan for the bare-knuckle belt. Rowers had new marks to beat, too. The seventh amateur nationals brought club crews from Massachusetts to Texas, Canada to Louisiana, to the biggest regatta yet, at Saratoga Lake in 1879. The Intercollegiate Rowing Association race was one of the tightest so far, a final stroke pulling Pennsylvania past Cornell, again on Saratoga Lake, in 1884. If they wanted to rerow these moments, they could stop by Riley's Lake House, opened by the oarsman who couldn't beat Courtney.[1]

"There is but one Saratoga," said a newspaper. "It is unique. It is special. It reigns absolutely." Even lawyers were buying it. Seventy-five of them, from twenty-one states, met at the Springs. The youngest, Francis Rawle of Philadelphia, located a carpenter's mallet on Broadway for seventeen cents, and with that gavel, on the second floor of Town Hall, they founded the American Bar Association on August 21, 1878. The official ABA history says some must have slipped off to see Volturno beat Pierre Lorillard's Boardman over five furlongs.[2]

Although the track lessee was Charles Reed, it was almost as if the sporting congressman were still king. His racing center was the most dramatic achievement in American sports until that time, and its 1878 program lived up to it: nearly $100,000 in purses and additions to stakes over two seven-day meetings, with related events every day in between. With this season, running from July 20 through August 25, plus a few extra days tacked on, Saratoga established the typical racing schedule of the future.[3]

The Association made two safety moves. It widened its diagonal chute by moving its western rail farther out, so it could accommodate "20 youngsters abreast." And it shortened the steeplechase course by removing the first wall, behind the judges' stand. That wall, "15 or 20 bounds" from the start, had brought down an English jockey named Meany the year before, seriously injuring him. For the owners, one of Saratoga's biggest assets was across Union Avenue—the "pine grove, known as 'the

Duke of Magenta, *Wilkes'*
Spirit of the Times, 1877.
Keeneland Library.

old track,' where," as Krik's guide put it in 1878, "the air is so cool and salubrious that horses recover from and feel the effects of hard work less than at any race track in the eastern division of the country." In another decade, the Association would christen it Horse Haven.[4]

The Lorillards took over from Belmont and McDaniel as the leading owners that year. George's Duke of Magenta became the first to earn something resembling the modern-day Triple Crown by sweeping the Preakness, Belmont, and fifteenth Travers. The ninth and last Lexington offspring to capture the Travers, the Duke put the late Woodburn hero atop the sires list for a sixteenth and final time, still a record. He helped George top the annual owners list with $67,875. Pierre's Parole grabbed his second straight Saratoga Cup, then sailed the ocean to steal three stakes from the English in eight days—the 1879 Newmarket Handicap, City and Suburban Handicap, and Great Metropolitan Handicap. Parole returned to America and won 59 of 127 races over his career, and a record $82,184.[5]

A stock manipulator of English parents and California breeding confronted the Lorillards. James R. Keene and his first horse, Spendthrift, not only snatched the 1879 Belmont from George's Monitor but rudely won the Lorillard Stakes. He was denied the Travers, though, by Falsetto. At the same time, Falsetto's rider was rising above footnote status. Teenager Ike Murphy had swept all four races on the Fourth of July at a Detroit track that season. At the Spa, he was offered enough to purchase a spread in Kentucky if he would just "pull" Falsetto in the Kenner Stakes. Instead, he added that, too. Pulling by then was highly controversial, and after an incident involving Spendthrift that year, a rule calling for a "declaration to win" was established.[6]

Isaac Murphy.
Keeneland Library.

It was not Keene but a couple of unlikely brothers who pushed the Lorillards off the top. Heirs to a Brooklyn butcher shop, the *frères* Dwyer cast a cold eye on horseflesh and created a "betting stable," which in those days of relatively small purses was one way to make money for nontobacco heirs. Phil bought the horses, Mike bet them. They knew human talent, too, hiring Jimmy Rowe as trainer and Jimmy McLaughlin as jockey. Dignified looking with his handlebar mustache, McLaughlin could have been a banker, said one writer, except for his muscles. Dwyer-Rowe-McLaughlin showed their clout with Bramble, who took the Saratoga Cup and fourteen other races in 1879, but even he couldn't compare with the butchers' real champions.[7]

Jimmy McLaughlin thought the best Dwyer brothers entry ever was Luke Blackburn. It was easy to see why. At three, he won twenty-two of twenty-four races in 1880 and did something at Saratoga no other thoroughbred would approach. The Spa crowd saw him seven times inside a month. First, he beat Checkmate and Volturno in the All-Aged Sweepstakes on July 16, then won two more. Next, he captured the Summer Handicap, conceding twenty pounds to second-place Juanita, then the new United States Hotel Stakes. Adding the Grand Union Prize Handicap, muscular Jimmy was so tired trying to hold back the most muscular horse in the country that he could hardly stand when he got off. Finally, Luke Blackburn won the Kenner

Jimmy McLaughlin.
Keeneland Library.

Stakes on August 12, cutting the two mile record to 3:35¼. The Dwyers left the more famous stakes that year to a lesser three-year-old, Grenada, who gave George the triple again—the 1880 Preakness, Belmont, and Travers. In fact, this Lorillard won an unprecedented five Pimlico classics in a row through 1882, though against little competition. George Lorillard would die on a trip to Europe in 1886.

Jimmy Rowe thought the best Dwyer brothers entry ever was Hindoo. Racing at two for Dan Swigert in 1880, Hindoo showed up in Saratoga for the Windsor Hotel Stakes, and who should he meet but poor Crickmore? Hindoo was known then for winning seven straight, Crickmore only for being a fussy eater, and even that proved to be a lie. The latter was named for turf editor H. G. Crickmore, and trained by Bill Bird, who had handled Lizzie W. in Morrissey's opener. Bet Crickmore, Bird told a friend, slipping him $100.

"But your horse is running against Hindoo, and he ain't been beat," the friend was quoted as saying.

"When Crickmore eats four quarts of oats, he can beat any horse. He ate four quarts last night. Bet that hundred."

Crickmore did win, which may have helped the Dwyers snap up Hindoo for $15,000.[8]

In 1881, Hindoo racked up eighteen straight, Derby included. He was too hot to bet that year, as Mike Dwyer could see when he brought him back to the Spa. All three ways of playing them were thriving. Women, many of whom liked the "French pools," used young men stationed in the grandstand as their betting commissioners, their lapel ribbons reading, "Pool tickets bought." Hindoo stood to pay just $5.70 for a $5 pari-mutuel ticket, was 1 to 10 with the bookmakers, and—an extreme rarity—

wasn't even offered in the auction pools. Of course, he won.[9] Then the Dwyers took him to Sheepshead Bay. This track was what happened when its investors figured out Morrissey's rule that resorts, where people were just enjoying themselves, could flout the antipool laws. Eventually it would work at vacation spots all across the country. Jerome organized the Coney Island Jockey Club in 1879—it was nothing more than the American Jockey Club in vacation clothes—and opened this pretty layout along Ocean Avenue off the bay, with shade trees, cool green expanses, and fine restaurants. Guess who Hindoo met by the seashore?

* * * *

Again Bird fed his bulimic charge four quarts of oats the night before. Again he bet $100. Again Crickmore beat the best in the land.

Dwyer brothers trivia: Hindoo retired with thirty-one victories in thirty-six starts. Mike and Phil would annex a second Travers (with Barnes, 1883), a third (Inspector B., 1886), a fourth (Sir Dixon, 1888), and a fifth (Sir John, 1890), another one of those Saratoga-type records. It would take seventy-three years just to tie it. None in the latter quartet, however, could hold a candle to the Dwyers' Miss Woodford. She owned the 1883 Alabama and thirty-six more in forty-eight starts to amass a record $118,200. McLaughlin would go down as the first to ride three, then four Travers winners, a feat unmatched until Eddie Arcaro did it sixty-three years later. Jimmy would top his Travers record with six Belmonts in seven years (1882–1888), another mark matched by Arcaro, but over fourteen years.

Hard to believe, an equal sensation was out there. Isaac Murphy captured the Saratoga Cup aboard Checkmate in 1881, and three years later, he and Bill Bird became the second African-American combination to win the Kentucky Derby, with Buchanan. That year, too, at Chicago's new Washington Park, he added the inaugural American Derby on Ed Corrigan's Modesty, then the second one on Lucky Baldwin's Volante, the third on Baldwin's Silver Cloud, and the fifth on Baldwin's Emperor of Norfolk.

The tracks were enriching tradition. Churchill Downs was serving the beloved track breakfasts by 1883. Young boys who picked the horses themselves sold tip cards there from 1885 and would soon be working the Saratoga piazzas. The tracks also birthed a thousand and one scams, though not all involved racing. One was sprung by an English turfman, Squire Abingdon Baird, who, if weighted down by his $5,000 brown sable coat, could lean on a sample from his $10,000 collection of walking sticks. On occasion, he squired the actress Lillie Langtry, who shocked Saratoga by appearing with no paint on her face but plenty on her red-lacquered heels. He also put on exhibitions by the light English fighter Charley Mitchell. At the Spa in 1883, they got into a minor argument at the track, the squire ending it by slapping the fighter in the face. There was no retaliation, and the news flashed that Charley was a coward, until he finally broke down and explained, "Why shouldn't I let him do it? The Squire likes it, and since he pays me twenty pounds for every blow he lands, I rather enjoy it myself." It doubtless helped them clean up on the exhibitions, too.[10]

No novelty was so timely as one accepted by the nation in 1883. Until then, people had set their watches by town clocks, which varied depending on where they were. Noon—12:00:00—in Albany was 11:58:59 in New York, 12:10:27 in Baltimore. Few cared, with a notable exception: Saratoga Springs. On the way, travelers had to adjust to local time, or they could forget it, but the minute they arrived, time took over again. The millions who succeeded them would also discover that a vacation was not an escape from time but a surrender. The cold fact that it would end ruled.

The regimented American vacation, invented by colonists at the Virginia springs and the first national crowds at Ballston and Saratoga, had changed only slightly. Instead of strolling to the springs in the crisp morn, visitors fattened in their rooms as armies of waiters headed their way through miles of hallways with oversize bottles of Congress water. Then coffee, breakfast, a cigarette (for the men) on the back piazza. Next, the women dispatched maids, children, or husbands to drugstores to collect, as a confused male reporter put it, "various little articles for the toilet." Then it was time to dress, to dine at three, then a drive to the lake—to the track?—or a siesta on the piazza, and supper at nine, followed by the concert, club house, or hop, which lasted nearly to daylight. Timing was all. Captains of business watched their money rise by the minute at the telegraph office while clerks saw theirs fall at a typical "bucket shop," called the Public Stock Exchange, in the Arcade Building. Rail tycoons had a professional interest in time.

What was the track but a clock? It gave workout time, opening time, post time, betting time, starting time, race time, record time. A few blocks away, Charles Dowd presided over Temple Grove Seminary, a fine girls' school on Circular Street, and on the side nursed his solution to the continent's countless time zones. As early as 1869, he had suggested that the railroads divide it into four "time belts." He became fanatic about this, traveling, lecturing, pamphleteering, until at long last—it must have seemed an eon—the railroads bought it. On November 13, 1883, "the day of the two noons," America's clocks switched to Standard Railway Time, and the world eventually adjusted. The railroads would have a final say, though. Crossing the tracks at Broadway, north of the old Walworth homestead, the man who gave the railroads and the rest of us Standard Time would be killed by a train in 1904.[11]

Next, Saratoga spawned two more organizations that would have a vast impact on education and economic planning: the American Historical Association in 1884 and the American Economic Association in 1885. As it had for decades, the town also staged state political conventions, and served as a back room for national politics. "This is to be a summer of President-making," a commentator wrote in 1884. "On the piazzas at Saratoga, on the beach at Long Branch, and in the Casino at Newport, the various candidates are to be talked over and the nominees selected." On the way out was Morrissey's one-time beneficiary, Chester Arthur, who had succeeded Morrissey's former House colleague, the assassinated James Garfield. The next president they made was Grover Cleveland, the New York governor.[12]

Saratoga was about to bury a president. Bankrupt in New York and suffering from throat cancer, Grant had signed a contract to write his memoirs and thus provide for his family. On June 16, 1885, he was moved to banker Joseph Drexel's cottage on Mount McGregor. As a result, newspapers across the land now focused on this new mountain resort, twenty-odd furlongs north of the track where the president's General Harney had run. Mark Twain, Grant's publisher, came to visit. Sherman came. Sheridan came. Drexel's daughter Elizabeth claimed she heard him say of Lee at Appomattox, "It was awful having to humiliate so fine a soldier. . . . I turned out to meet him in my oldest uniform, wearing no sword or gloves. . . . I knew that he would not expect me to look a gentleman, and I took care to live up to his expectations."[13]

He would sit outside in his wicker chair, silently acknowledging the hundreds who climbed the mountain just to gaze upon him, but he would not tarry on the porch. "I must go to my writing," he would tell Julia. "And so he wrote on and on," she said. They took Ulys to the overlook above the distant ancient battlefield to the east. The general wrote of the time he first faced the possibility of defeat. "As we approached the brow of the hill from which it was expected we could see Harris' camp, and possibly find his men formed ready to meet us, my heart kept getting higher and higher until it felt to me as though it was in my throat."

At last, about July 19, he finished it, and then—"to our dismay," said his wife—weakened, and died on July 23. They took him off the mountain, the black-draped funeral train passing through the Springs, where Civil War veterans stood at attention, to Manhattan's Riverside Park. In the New York procession, the cortege was escorted by three presidents, Hayes, Arthur, and Cleveland, by Union and Confederate generals, by 850 carriages, 12,000 troops, 18,000 veterans, and 42,500 civilians on foot. The generals wept.

Historians would make nothing of the national grief, which continued for years. They would assail his administration's corruption, his drinking problems, his other failings, but the people remembered the general. It was as if they really believed the title somebody had thrown at him, "the nation's savior." The unsuccessful turfman's *Personal Memoirs* would earn a stunning $500,000 in eight years, and no military recollections would come close to their literary value. Twain, and in the next century Edmund Wilson, would judge them the best since Caesar's. Historian James McPherson would write that Grant's old battles and this one on Mount McGregor were similar "triumphs of will and determination," the last illuminating the others. He had converted the cottage from a deathplace to the birthplace of his memoirs. Still, it was not the writer but the general who kept them coming. For half a century they would climb the mountain by the unsung thousands to see Grant's Cottage. The federal government would never rescue it from various insults, such as the construction of a state prison around it, but a band of area citizens would furnish and preserve it as a little museum, its dying visions as inspiring as the Eastern Lookout.

November brought another death. For eight years, he was almost certainly the richest American, watching his money from his summer throne, the north piazza of his family's favorite hotel. "One of the waiters of the United States went up to Mr. Vanderbilt yesterday to hand him a card," said a *Times* reporter one day. "I never saw the human form so nearly bent double before. It was an interesting question whether the waiter could ever straight up again." W. H. did not discourage this, declaring, immortally, to a reporter who asked how the public might react to some railroad issue, "The public be damned."[14]

THEY'RE OFF!

Grant at Mount McGregor. *Courtesy of the author.*

His loyalty to Saratoga was still a family thing. His son, William Kissam, honeymooned here with his bride, Alva. A Western Union clerk, Hamilton Twombly, won W. H.'s approval here to wed his daughter Florence, supposedly because he had the cheek to say he would keep her as well as W. H. had his bride. It was a business thing. Here W. H. plotted with his cohorts and pronounced himself on the latest strikes. A word from his lips, said the reporter, "makes or mars millions." One day, it was reported, a small stock player slipped into a chair nearby, buried himself in a newspaper, and listened as W. H. talked. When Vanderbilt advocated a Lake Shore takeover of Canada Southern, the neighbor "shuffled hastily away" to the telegraph office to invest several thousand.

A chip off the old Commodore, W. H. had a weakness for trotters and drove some of the best. His Maude S. lowered the mile record to 2:09 ¼, although this was after he sold her. The family's first heir, he lived somewhat ostentatiously at the end, building a Fifth Avenue palace at Fifty-second Street chiefly to show off his paintings. On the other hand, he did not handle stress well at all. He suffered a stroke and later went into an apoplectic fit during a business discussion in 1885, and fell dead on the floor of his Grecian library. He had survived the Commodore by only eight years and eleven months, but it was found he had doubled the old man's pile, leaving $200 million. He also protected the dynasty, through his own variation on primogeniture.

His oldest son, Cornelius II, inherited a hefty $67 million and was designated Head of the House of Vanderbilt. William Kissam Vanderbilt was left a thick chunk, too, though—$65 million. Neither would continue the family's more or less permanent summer residence on Saratoga's piazzas. Instead, Cornelius II and Willie K.

W. H. Vanderbilt. The Commodore's heir, with side whiskers, presides over "Vanderbilt's Corner" on the United States Hotel piazza. *Leslie's, 1879. Courtesy of the author.*

would build permanent marble palaces at Newport—the Breakers and Marble House, respectively. But they would keep returning to the Springs, and in the middle of the next century, one of W. H.'s great-grandsons, C. V. Whitney, would establish his home here year-round.[15]

Although Saratoga had lost such originals as Morrissey, the Commodore, W. H., and Grant, contenders were in the wings. One was the grandson of a Turkish army officer, James Ben Ali Haggin, of northern California, who made a fortune in the gold rush, then expanded into silver, copper, and real estate. By the mid-1880s, he was building the biggest thoroughbred farm in history, more than a million grazing acres in California, New Mexico, and Arizona. In 1886, he let the East know he was around by winning the Derby with Ben Ali. The East would be hearing more from James Ben Ali Haggin.

Nothing advertised Saratoga's national character more than the Californians who began to appear. A century before New York and Los Angeles would lay claim to the adjective, the Springs had gone bicoastal. Just as it did with Kentucky, the Spa would share good vibrations with California from at least 1865. That was when a town first called McCartysville, then Bank Mills, switched to the "more elegant and euphonious" Saratoga, California, although its historian would provide one of the less appetizing translations of the Native American name—"floating scum upon the water." Within a year, near springs "up the canyon," those pioneers opened a resort,

Pacific Congress Springs, with a hotel patterned after Congress Hall, and Saratoga, California, has retained a certain class ever since.[16]

Nobody reflected the Golden West more than Lucky Baldwin, who came east from his Rancho Santa Anita near Los Angeles. With his brim hat and brush of a mustache, he seemed, as one writer put it, "a small, solemn-faced, rather stingy-looking version of Mark Twain," so he compensated by tossing money, especially at women. He would let no other male in his lavish coach at the Spa, wrote George Waller, "and only the prettiest women who applied. When the spirit moved him, he selected only blondes, or only brunettes, as his passengers, and whirled them off to the race track to watch his horses run and see him win or lose anywhere from $5,000 to $50,000 on a single nose."[17]

The blondes or brunettes saw them run under Ike Murphy. Baldwin was now paying a $10,000 fee for first call on his services, and he seemed unstoppable. He won the 1885 Alabama on Ed Corrigan's Ida Hope and the 1886 Saratoga Cup on Baldwin's Volante. The next year at the Spa, he confronted the tall young Ed "Snapper" Garrison, whose ability to come from behind would lead to the term "Garrison finish." His riding posture was almost as famous. "Despite his long legs," the turf historian Robertson wrote, "he rode with a very short stirrup, and curled over until he resembled a hunchback." Or Ichabod Crane. There was only one way for Murphy, who rode like an Englishman, to respect him: race him. He met him in an event called the California Stakes, another reflection of the Spa's bicoastal awareness. It was hardly a fair match, Murphy's Volante being a 1 to 20 favorite while the gawky teenager bent over a 20 to 1 shot. Seeing a killing, Mike Dwyer laid $40,000 on Volante against $2,000 on Royal Arch. He lost. And the jockeys—one black, one white, though nobody really noticed that—headed for a more historic rendezvous.[18]

A bigger show-off even than Lucky Baldwin was the minor horseman and major clotheshorse Evender Berry Wall. His father, Charles Wall, who got rich in the cordage business, had brought him here in Morrissey's day. Travers had taught him to be witty and gay. Strolling by the park one day, they met a lady coming from Congress Spring, known for its purgative qualities.

"Lovely water," she said, "I've just had four glasses."

"Then, Madame," said Bill, "p-pray do not let us detain you."[19]

Wall's London tailor sent him something quite different. "I wore it first," he would remember, "at a ball given at the Grand Union Hotel. . . . It was a scandal. I was actually ordered off the floor." What it was, he declared, was the first dinner jacket ever worn in America. A moderate rebel at most, the outcast returned that evening to the United States Hotel and changed into the tails worn by every normal human heir. But the short coat resurfaced, he said, at Pierre Lorillard's Tuxedo Park estate, which lent it its name. The notion that this town finally reduced the toga to the tux brought a scandalized response in recent years from the settlement that grew on Lorillard's spread. In their local newspapers, the two New York towns uncorked the world's most fastidious war. The issue: who invented the tux, Tuxedo Park or Saratoga Springs? The former's historian, Albert Winslow, said it was documented that Pierre's son Griswold had unveiled the tux there in 1886. At this writing, it would seem Wall might have worn it at the Spa in 1887 at the earliest, which would give Tuxedo Park and Grizzy the edge, so it may not be necessary to rename the garment the Saratoga. Yet Wall's claim sits there in his autobiography and other tomes, refusing to go out of print.[20]

It was certainly here, however, that Berry Wall proved he was "King of the Dudes," as the papers crowned him. In 1888, Wall announced that he would make forty complete changes of costume the next day. He showed the next morning in black and white, then ducked back into his Grand Union room to don white linen. As Hugh Bradley told it, bets on whether he would pull it off ran into the thousands. That night at dinner, Wall appeared in a fortieth ensemble, highlighted by a sparkling Prince Albert with vest and lawn tie, as his friend John L. Sullivan scooped up the winnings with his bare knuckles.

Wall and others among the less gifted children of the first great capitalists were also inventing the American playboy, although the term was not yet in use. Jimmy Hilton, the hotelier's son, was another of these rich young men with nothing to do. Gossips said he snatched up $20,000 in stones for the actress Della Fox in just one visit to Dreicer's branch jewelry store at the Grand Union.[21]

Amusing as all this was, neither a tux nor a costume change nor a jewelry raid could have been pulled off at the Grand Union by a Jew, at least not by one staying there. In 1878, the year after Hilton's ban, the *Times* quoted the manager of the nation's largest hotel as announcing, "The interdiction against Jews is to be continued. Mr. [Henry] Clair claims that it has been a profitable movement." Thanks to Edison, a giant light on the roof of the Grand Union now bathed Hilton's Windsor Hotel down Broadway—a forerunner of floodlight advertising—but it is not clear to what extent Jews were proscribed there, if at all, or at the St. James Hotel, also controlled by the Judge, or later at the Woodlawn estate he developed out North Broadway, thought to be the biggest private park in the country, where tours were allowed but regulated by guards and carding. Today, in a touch of poetic justice, the site is a center of enlightenment, the campus of Skidmore College.[22]

Berry Wall joked in his memoirs about anti-Semitic banter at Saratoga back then, mistakenly believing that everybody joined in. Some did, though, notably Seneca Ray Stoddard, a guidebook publisher in the 1880s (canonized by museums a century later for his photography). His guidebooks advised tourists that the Grand Union earlier "lost caste somewhat because of the class of guests who rushed in to possess the land. A valiant attempt was made to purify it, by the famous edict expelling all Jews, and under its present excellent management the objectionable features do not appear." They could not know that the joke would wear out in Europe a half-century later. For its part, the *Times* ran a long report that praised Hilton as the financial savior of the town and avoided any mention of his anti-Semitism. After thirteen years, in 1890, it would be able to report, matter-of-factly: "It is evidence that Judge Hilton no longer holds a controlling interest in the . . . Grand Union Hotel, for Hebrews are once more welcomed there. For a dozen years or more, ever since his famous edict, no member of the Semitic race has gained admission to its portals."

America's first major outbreak of anti-Semitism would be widely ignored by scholars, perhaps because it revealed too much. It not only set a precedent for prejudice elsewhere, as mentioned in the previous chapter, but it had specific local effects. Stephen Birmingham thought it went straight up the road, leading to the ban on Jews at Melville Dewey's Lake Placid Club. At the Spa, the medium-sized Hotel Russell on Franklin Square would later advertise its "Gentile Mgt." The Jewish community in Saratoga Springs would remember the Grand Union forever, though not for the same reasons as other natives, and the memory seared the larger Jewish community as well. In the next century, William S. Paley, chairman of CBS, might have followed his idol, John Hay Whitney, to Saratoga and into the turf world, but did not because he wrongly assumed it to be anti-Semitic.[23]

In fact, the town was famous for, even defined by, its loose and open atmosphere, which created exactly the sort of democratic microcosm that the aristocratic Henry James had hated. Its other hotels declined to follow Hilton. Although Joseph Drexel's daughter Elizabeth, Mrs. Harry Lehr, would claim in her memoirs that the Saratoga hotels accepting Jews, socially speaking, "did not exist," that was the opposite of the truth. The United States Hotel was a more fashionable place to stay, the long summer see of the Vanderbilts (who seem conspicuously enlightened in retrospect), and when they came to work on Morrissey's estate, Travers and Jerome, for instance, stopped at the American (today's Rip Van Dam). Meantime, the Spa continued to appeal strongly to Jews. The Clarendon welcomed back Joe Seligman and his wife the season after the ban, and Hilton's prohibition actually strengthened the Jewish hotel tradition at Saratoga. More than twenty of these hotels would be established during the next three-quarters of a century. Nor did the Grand Union ever revert to anti-Semitism, its new era symbolized the year after the ban ended by the appearance of President Benjamin Harrison on its piazza.[24]

African-American tourists and conventioneers also "did"—as people were already saying—"the Springs." Many of these tourists were seasonal workers who had wound up their jobs in the resort, this group dating back even beyond the bugler Frank Johnson. Johnson's Philadelphia band had played three different hotels six nights a week in the 1820s, and so well they were remembered sixty years later. By now, though, almost all the hotel workers were African Americans. In fact, only three hotels had white waiters: Hilton's Windsor, which boasted about its German help, the American (Rip Van Dam), where white women "in crisp calico gowns" changed the plates, and the Adelphi. In 1891, the Grand Union would convert. "A novelty in this hotel will be white male waiters to supplant the colored ones. It remains to be seen if the other hotels will follow the example which the Windsor set."[25]

The African Americans often had their families up, lodging them in hotels west of Franklin Square, one of which catered to them through the 1950s. "They roll out to the lake and through Woodlawn in victorias," said one writer, "they shop in the bazaars and visit in critical comparison all the spring-water parlors." What did he expect? Whatever they did, wherever they went, the coverage in the *Times* and elsewhere was couched in racist slurs and stereotypes, the black jockeys being the only ones who ever seemed to escape this. When a local paper got the story of a light-fingered visitor to the track, for example, it felt obliged to point out, as newspapers would for decades, that the suspect was "colored."[26] It happened after the fifth race. J. R. Rosenthal, standing by the "reporter's gallery" in the grandstand, "felt a hand in his pocket." As he whirled and yelled "Stop, thief!" the man flew over the benches, knocking people down. Police Officer Fryer jumped him at the back exit, and down the stairs they rolled, to "the green," the lawn behind the stand. Rosenthal said he lost $65. They found one dollar on the pickpocket.

Pickpockets were not the only ones with problems. For the first time, the gambling houses were seriously challenged by a series of crusades. Shaving off his walrus mustache to go undercover, Anthony Comstock, agent of the New York Society for the Supression of Vice, investigated them for three days in 1886. As it happened, he could have left the hair on, since gambling was almost wide open and his investigation ended up a joke, producing not one indictment, yet it might have been the ultimate blow for Morrissey's successor out Union Avenue.

Charles Reed was a flashy gambler who had killed a man in New Orleans during the war but got pardoned. Later he teamed with Albert Spencer in New York, and they joined a syndicate organized by Morrissey to finance 5 West Twenty-fourth Street. When Morrissey died, Reed and Spencer took over the track, Reed holding the lease and Spencer running the pools and the club house in the park. Erecting a $50,000 home on Union Avenue (no longer there), with horse etchings in glass above the transoms, Charlie Reed, the lessee of the most fashionable address in sports, struggled to be accepted into the stratosphere of the summer rich, but he never made it. In 1887, snubbed by Saratoga society and harrassed by the crusaders, he sold out to Spencer. Reed then returned to New York, where he continued his dream of climbing in the turf world while keeping his night job, 5 West Twenty-fourth Street.

In many ways, the track's new operator was Reed's opposite. Spencer was a quiet type, running serious businesses. He was not merely the track's lease-holder but served as the treasurer and a director of the Saratoga Association. He would establish a Spencer Handicap, adding $2,000 to its value, which he insisted the Association keep at $5,000 or more. An aesthete as well, he appreciated paintings, was able to make money unloading them at auction, and doubtless loved artistic Saratoga, with its famous park, which Frederick Law Olmsted had helped redesign, and the exact replica of a Pompeian house being built on the edge of the park as a classical art museum (later converted to other uses and much altered, but still standing at 260 Broadway). However, just two years after Albert Spencer assumed sole control of the track and club house, another crusader was on his high horse. This was Spencer Trask, who had a Wall Street brokerage with an office in the ground floor of the Grand Union. Although the resort was long established as the nation's leading summer gambling center and no easy mark, Trask was a formidable force, too, and he expected the town to conform to him. He had bought the onetime Barhyte estate just east of the track, later to become America's leading retreat for writers and artists. "Yaddo," as Spencer and Katrina Trask named it, was different back then.

Many wealthy visitors had begun abandoning the hotels and throwing up summer "cottages," as they were styled with false modesty. Sixty had gone up in one recent year alone. Only a fraction survive today, although enough to give the place probably the biggest inventory of Victorian mansions on the East Coast. One Edward Leech constructed a $100,000 "cottage" at Union Avenue and Circular Street (long gone), the Daniel S. Lathrops of Albany a lovely Queen Anne adjoining Woodlawn (still standing, at 245 Clinton St.), and Frank Hathorn, "whose fortune gushes out of the ground in a clear, cathartic stream," a cozy retreat on North Broadway (still there, at 740). Even Newporters spoke of deserting the ocean to build by the springs, but Trask was one of the very few who did create a baronial, Newport-scale manse (which burned, was rebuilt in 1891, and today houses those writers on retreat). He had his own motive for wiping out gambling: to turn the Springs into a sedate, year-round community for the wealthy, rather along the lines of Newport. The wealthy weren't interested.[27]

Trask tossed a reported $50,000 at trying to break Saratoga's open illegal gambling, hiring pricey New York detectives to gather evidence. A resident remembered that when he asked a local Roman Catholic priest to help clean the place up, the Father fired back, "Why don't you clean house yourself?" But one of Trask's targets suddenly became vulnerable. At the height of the 1890 season, it was announced that Albert Spencer would sell the track in the fall for $375,000, although it was not clear to whom. Reports spoke of a high-powered syndicate that included Pierre Lorillard and Belmont. In any event, the news took a chunk out of Spencer's political clout, for he could no longer threaten to shut down the races if they closed his casino. This may have encouraged Trask to mount the August police raid that snared seven gambling house operators, including Spencer and a popular Broadway merchant named Caleb Mitchell, one of the founders of the old Glen Mitchell property. The police confiscated a cartload of chips, roulette tables, and faro setups.[28]

Trask's crusade was fought by local business people, who thought the town needed gambling, and the seven were soon out of jail and back in business. Spencer reacted in the grand tradition of Morrissey and future gambling house owners everywhere by bribing the local powers, giving money to the Episcopal parish house, and slipping two village commissioners $1,500 each. As for Mitchell, he seemed to thrive on the confrontation. Earlier he had rubbed his popularity in Trask's face by running front-page advertisements in the *Saratoga Daily Union* for "Cale Mitchell's," nearly opposite the United States Hotel. It offered "Official Reports of all Base Ball and other Sporting Events . . . Wines, Liquors and Cigars . . . Elegant Billiard Parlor," the gambling, of course, being understood. Two years after Mitchell's arrest, Saratogians acted out their dreams by electing their Broadway entertainer village president, or mayor (he had also served a term as mayor many years earlier).[29]

In the national press, it was the "reformers" (antigambling) versus the "liberals" (pro, in varying degrees) in the country's most famous, if no longer unrivaled, resort—the latest outbreak in the long war between America's puritans and libertarians, both of whom had chosen the Springs as one of their principal theaters. Although the track was not the reformers' chief target, it would not end until this first national sports venue was shut down. The track came very close to the bottom when Albert Spencer finally managed to unload it in late 1891. The disaster was underlined by the resignation of the Saratoga Association's second president, then eighty-two.

James Marvin had been no W. R. Travers—not a Wall Street gorilla nor a horseman nor even much of a sportsman, all of which had contributed to Saratoga's slippage, but neither had he been a lightweight. From his 1836 Greek Revival home (still standing, at 3 Franklin Square), he had presided over the inauguration of permanent racing here in 1847, backed Morrissey's track and welcomed him to Congress, and reigned at his United States Hotel as host to the captains of capitalism.

At the end, Marvin was overshadowed at the track only by one other figure, who was also resigning. This was the Association's other original member, Charles Wheatly, whose impact on sports had nearly matched Morrissey's and Jerome's. This pioneer Kentucky racing official had designed not only the Saratoga racetrack but Jerome Park, where he also had served as the indispensable secretary, and he had a hand in many other tracks as well. Charles Wheatly was, quite literally, the architect of American racing and of the country's first modern sports arenas.[30]

When they found out who was taking over racing at the Springs as of 1892, the old-guard stable owners just about dropped dead. It was Gottfried "Dutch Fred" Walbaum, operator of the small Guttenberg Race Track in northern New Jersey and about to take Saratoga downhill fast. As one observer pointed out, though, it was not Walbaum alone who brought about the end of Saratoga's role as America's glittering sports capital. It was success. In launching, then leading the expansion of national sports for a quarter of a century after the Civil War, Saratoga had created a demand that it could not fill by itself. Its child—modern racing—had outgrown it. There were too many breeders, too many owners, too many people wanting to see too many horses. *The American Turf,* a history of racing, would declare in 1898: "The demand that Saratoga had made for racers of the first class had rapidly increased the supply beyond its power to care for them unassisted. Other outlets were needed to make racing profitable to breeders and owners, and also to meet the growing interest of the public. Especially was this true of New York City and vicinity."[31]

 *13*

RACING THROUGH THE GAY NINETIES

THERE WAS Jim Brady, the railroad-car builder reported to own twenty-seven thousand diamonds, including those decorating his underwear. And the dirty little coward who shot "Mr. Howard" had not shot Jesse's brother, so Frank James was at Churchill Downs on that Derby day, too, getting the odds on Spokane from a bookmaker: "ten to one, and the sky's the limit." Frank shot back: "There's $5,000 here, and as far as I'm concerned, that's the sky." That bookmaker may have been relieved that Spokane won.[1]

The national sports phenomenon invented at Saratoga was now outrunning it. That 1889 Derby drew a record twenty-five thousand spectators, and it was exactly the sort of glittering American throng that had made its debut at the Spa after the Civil War. Change was in the air, as pari-mutuel tickets dropped to two dollars at Louisville that year, their standard price for the next several decades, and the old auction pools were finally banned, forced out by the bookmakers. Like Saratoga, though, Churchill Downs was about to face hard times, even as other tracks were thriving. The biggest transformation of all was underway around New York City.

Amazingly, the prime mover was again the tall, elegant elder statesman, he of the drooping mustache and aristocratically chiseled face. Leonard Jerome's Coney Island Jockey Club track, Sheepshead Bay, had reintroduced turf racing, the more stately racing on grass, which had begun giving way long before the Civil War in the face of America's love affair with speed, which meant dirt tracks. It had become the site of major yearling sales, which reflected its investment in the sport's future, and it created such classics as the Suburban in 1884 and the Futurity in 1888. The latter really was futuristic, as it called for nominations even before the entries were born. Its pot grew as the owners first paid entry fees on the mares they nominated, then forfeit fees for the many two-year-olds who did not show for the race. The Futurity purses zoomed to interplanetary highs, such as the inaugural $40,900, and the excitement helped give Sheepshead Bay the biggest crowds in the country.[2]

For his next move, after New York City decided to buy Jerome Park and put in a reservoir, its elderly namesake teamed with John A. Morris in 1889 to open Morris Park in Westchester County. The Belmont was transferred there the next year. With that, Leonard Jerome died in 1891, plainly meriting the title that writers had long since bestowed upon him: "Father of the American Turf." He had cofounded the Saratoga Association, created Jerome Park, Sheepshead Bay, and Morris Park, and along the way introduced the Belmont, ontrack bookmaking, and polo. His grandson, Winston Churchill, turned seventeen that year.

The Brooklyn Jockey Club, organized by the Dwyer brothers in 1885, was thriving in Prospect Park, near Gravesend Bay. Known simply as Gravesend, it alternated racing days with Sheepshead Bay. In New Jersey, a group headed by George Lorillard had taken over Monmouth Park in 1882 and expanded it. It was so successful that a new Monmouth Park opened in 1890. It was the biggest racing operation in the country and boasted the longest course, one and three-quarter miles. Not even the charms of Horse Haven could keep some of the bigger stables from transferring their loyalty to Monmouth. Pierre Lorillard's Rancocas stable was followed there by the Westbrooke, Brookdale, and Chesterbrook stables. Although the new Monmouth would be shut down by New Jersey's ban on pari-mutuel wagering after only three years, it had already dealt a tremendous blow to Saratoga.

The money kept expanding in New York. Old August Belmont raked in $67,675 with Potomac in the 1890 Futurity, more than thirteen times what Sir John won for the Dwyers in the Travers that season. When Belmont died later that year, the sale of his Nursery Stud, based at Babylon, Long Island, was the biggest auction of thoroughbreds to date, the 131 horses bringing $639,500.

A bidder set a record, too, raising the auctioneer from $50,000 to $100,000 for the stallion St. Blaise. This was none other than Charlie Reed, still trying to make it in the turf. Nobody had ever paid that much for a horse before, but St. Blaise never paid Reed back. Two years later, he would sail to Argentina to look over the English Triple Crown winner Ormonde, only to be outbid by William Macdonough, who had figured out cablegrams were faster. One consolation: although Macdonough's $150,000 purchase beat Reed's record, Ormonde shot blanks as a stallion. As for the biggest buyer at Belmont's sale, it turned out to be a major new power in the turf: August Belmont II. He was building a second Nursery Stud.

In 1894, the Queens County Jockey Club opened Aqueduct, an extremely modest plant at first, and a year after that, Belmont *fils* and James R. Keene, soaring again on Wall Street, formed the Westchester Racing Association, which took over Morris Park.[3]

It was the newer tracks that saw the most ballyhooed events in the Gay Nineties, and on June 25, 1890, Sheepshead Bay staged the most electrifying contest of them all. J. B. Haggin's Salvator, one of the giants of the age, met millionaire D. T. Pulsifer's Tenny, who somehow had conquered him four times in six meetings. Haggin's chestnut was 14–9 at that point, the bay Tenny 13–7. The mile-and-a-quarter match was for $5,000 a side, with $5,000 added by the Coney Island Jockey Club. For the jockeys, it was another black-white encounter, but Americans still were not noticing that. Ike Murphy's recent laurels had included the 1889 Alabama aboard Princess Bowling and the 1890 Derby on Ed Corrigan's Riley, making him the first to win two Derbies. As usual, like some Englishman, Murphy sat "well down in his saddle and straight as a dart" while Snapper Garrison rode in his high half-crouch.[4]

Salvator poked his white face in front and stayed there. He beat the mile record, then the mile and a furlong record and looked unbeatable until the Snapper, on Tenny, finally put on his patented finish. Murphy was known for cajoling his mounts,

Edward "Snapper" Garrison.
Keeneland Library.

Garrison for beating the hell out of them, which he proceeded to do, spurring and changing whip hands. "The way Tenny came up with his flying rival in the last 100 yards was a miracle, perfectly stupendous," said the *Spirit of the Times*. Poet Ella Wheeler Wilcox: "We are under the string now—the great race is done— / And Salvator, Salvator, Salvator won!"

Had the orange jacket with blue sleeves really nipped the blue and white by less than a head? The crowd saw only a wonderful blur, but the picture was clear. As historian Robertson pointed out, the *Spirit* ran sketches of the finish, based on "instantaneous photographs." It now advocated using photos as "an immutable record of the positions of horses in a close finish." A few weeks later, Salvator added three more at new Monmouth Park, including a mile against time, the current record being 1:39 ¼. Salvator smashed the clock, lowering the standard to 1:35 ½.

Murphy became the first to take back-to-back Kentucky Derbies, winning in 1891 on Kingman, owned and trained by the African-American Dudley Allen. His three Derby wins would not be matched for another thirty-one years, his lifetime statistics—628 victories in 1,412 starts, for a 44 percent winning average—never. Murphy would die of pneumonia in his thirties. This champion who first met the best in the East at Saratoga would return in spirit in the next century to enter the Hall of Fame of the National Museum of Racing.[5]

They were America's first famous black athletes, but they would disappear so

Famous match race. Salvator beating Tenny at Sheepshead Bay, 1890. *Keeneland Library.*

completely, and for so long, that today millions are ignorant of the fact that they were there at all. There are records of about one hundred in the late nineteenth century, a list that is certainly incomplete since jockeys, white and black, were frequently not mentioned in the results, and also because race, happily, was left out of the charts. African Americans were among the winners of virtually every major stakes race. Besides Murphy, some of the greatest were:

• Isaac Lewis, who won the 1887 Kentucky Derby on Montrose and the 1891 Saratoga Cup on Los Angeles;

• Alonzo Clayton, who became the youngest Derby winner at fifteen on Azra in 1892, then won the Travers with Azra, the Alabama on Ignite, and in 1895 the Saratoga Flash Stakes on Onaretto;

• James "Soup" Perkins, who was fourteen when he scored five out of six at the Spa one day in 1894, then became the only other fifteen-year-old Derby winner, on Halma, and the country's leading rider in 1895;

• Willie Simms, who won Saratoga's Spinaway on Promenade in 1891, went two for two in the Derby, on Ben Brush in 1896 and on Plaudit in 1898, and was the first and last black jockey to win the Preakness, on Sly Fox in 1898. Simms was also the first American jockey to win in England, where he introduced them to the short-stirrup crouch.

Other black winners of major stakes at the Spa, with their mounts:

Alonzo Clayton and James "Soup" Perkins. *Keeneland Library.*

• John "Kid" Stoval, Belle of Runnymede, 1882 Alabama, and Miss Woodford, 1882 Spinaway;

• Ed West, Grisette, 1887 Alabama, and Los Angeles, 1887 Spinaway. He died in a fall at Saratoga;

• Shelby "Pike" Barnes, Princess Bowling, 1888 Flash, Long Dance, 1889 Travers, and Sinaloa II, 1890 Alabama;

• George "Spider" Anderson, Sallie McClelland, 1891 Alabama; and

• Roy "Tiny" Williams, Vallera, 1891 Travers. Incidentally, they enlarged the "betting paddock" that year, making it easier to play Williams and Lewis as they swept the Travers and the Cup.

All told, six African Americans won the Travers in its first twenty-nine runnings (Sewell, Hawkins, Murphy, Barnes, Roy Williams, and Clayton), and they weren't quite done yet. As for trainers, the former slave Ed Brown got used to carrying around a $75,000 bankroll long before modern sports organizations thought they invented big money. He and Bill Bird were only two of the prominent trainers. There were Ansel Williams, winner of the 1866 and 1873 Travers with Merrill and Tom Bowling, respectively; Raleigh Colston, who won the 1870 Travers with Kingfisher; Albert Cooper, who handled the great Domino; and Matthew Earley, whose Charade won the Congress Hall, Grand Union, and Metropolitan Handicap. Many were owners, too, including the Derby winner Dud Allen. To group the black talent and money distorts the picture, for there was no ethnic roster; the talent in the stables, paddocks, and winners' circles was white and black.[6]

It was a world of increasing prizes, in which His Highness, snapped up for $3,400 at Belmont's sale, could win $61,675 in the fourth Futurity. This horse became the first

Willie Simms and Matthew Earley. *Keeneland Library.*

in America to top the $100,000 mark in one year, with $106,900. The African-American riders were very much in it at the start. It was Pike Barnes who won the first Futurity on Proctor Knott, and Anthony Hamilton the third on Potomac. By 1893, Lorillard reportedly was paying $12,000 for Simms's services, which, as one paper said, seemed like a lot of money for "a boy like Simms." At the track, "boy" still meant jockey, white or black, and this was indeed a lot of money for a twenty-three-year-old. The white riders were freer to deal. Although none yet made a percentage of the purse, a rider like Fred Taral, "the Dutch demon," could command $12,000 from owners Walcott and Campbell for first call and another $8,000 from Keene and his son Foxhall for second. He could push his celebrity to the outer limits, running around with John L. while folks dubbed them "Big and Little Casino." That hilarious world was not open to black Americans, jockeys included.

The horses began knocking each other from the earnings peak like so many dominoes. Domino, owned by James R. and Foxie Keene, and America's first great sprinter, won the 1893 Futurity and, in a crime of *lese majeste,* succeeded His Highness as the record annual earnings winner, with $170,790. He also had a career record of $193,550. The stakes were raised among bettors, too, as the number of bookmakers multiplied. The two most famous turned out at Brooklyn's Gravesend track for one of the biggest matches of the day, Domino at three versus Henry of Navarre, winner of the Belmont and the Travers.[7]

At the big tracks, as many as sixty bookmakers would show up in their usual spots, often small cages in the betting ring, paying $100 a day for the privilege. They ranged from the daring, such as foulmouthed Virginia Carroll, who, to attract attention, would tear up ten-dollar bills and throw them at his cashier or put them in his mouth and chew away, to the more daring. Riley Grannon would even try to outthink Mike Dwyer's betting "commissioners," who in turn would devote their scientific lives to ruining him.

Professional bettors, those who were not also bookmakers, were still another breed. One of these, George Shannon, could walk around the ring with a cool $2,000 commission from a rich owner with nobody noticing that Shannon was just fifteen years old. Of course, they also operated in town. Once "Honest John Kelly" got a tip from the Whitten Brothers stable that their filly Melanie was hot in the fifth at Saratoga, so he toured the Manhattan "pool rooms" with commissions "for as much as the pencilers would take," and wound up plunging $5,000. The next day he was back on the tour with "an enormous wad of the bookies' pasteboards"—tickets—that called for up to $15,000, not bad for a day's work. As the headline in New York's *Sporting World* put it, "Better Far Than Baseball."[8] (Etymologists will note several news flashes here: "Pool rooms" still usually meant betting parlors, "bookies" had entered in the language, and "baseball" had melded into one word.)

Back at the track, a small-time operator might try "shaving," as a *Herald* profile of these unstudied entrepreneurs explained. He would lay $500 with a colleague advertising equal money on a horse, then slink back to his own stand and offer $500 against the same entry at four to five. So if the horse came in, he would collect $500 from his colleague while dropping $400 at his own stand. It was lossproof. Even if the horse lost, the $500 he forked over to the other bookmaker would be recouped at his own stand.

None of these geniuses could get away with much, though, because the public was well trained, too. The newspapers frequently ran an "index" or chart on the horses, and a specialized press had developed, such as the daily *Sporting World,* which was printed on pink paper. (This tradition survives. In July and August of 1889 at the Spa, a woman published a small newspaper with social items and personals and called it the "pink sheet," which it was. Later the *Daily Saratogian,* would add a "Pink Sheet" section with racing news.) By the Gay Nineties, the public knew that the horses most often finished the way the charts said they would. Long shots were already called long shots, and the *Herald* said that the smart bettor would have nothing to do with them.[9]

On September 15, 1894, at Gravesend, the most respected (among his own kind) bookmaker in the country, George "Pittsburgh Phil" Smith, ran into young Riley Grannon. Robertson recounts that they both moved "from book to book" to place their own money, until Phil said in front of a witness, "Riley, let's quit piking. How much do you want to bet on this race?"

Riley answered, "I've got $100,000 that says Henry of Navarre will win."

Sports had become a huge business. With all that money on them, the Keenes' Domino and Byron McClelland's Henry were to go a mile and an eighth. It was the maximum for Domino, who, as Robertson pointed out, had registered eighteen of his nineteen wins in twenty-five starts at a mile or less. He also had as much as he could take on his back. Domino hated the whipper Fred Taral's guts, and if the rider ever approached him, he would lunge and rear. "The only way you could get Domino quiet long enough for Taral to get into the saddle," said a trainer, "was to hold a rubbing cloth over the horse's eyes." Henry of Navarre probably knew how he felt. He had carried Taral in the Travers.[10]

They were off!—changing leads until Henry led by half a length coming home. "Suddenly Taral was seen to straighten up in the saddle," said one report. "Then the cruel whip descended upon the black's side with a swish that could be heard almost above the yells of the crowd."[11] Domino pulled even, Henry moved up a head, Domino came back. "Whip and spur were applied mercilessly" until "neither horse could gain an inch on the other. Stride for stride they ran to the finish," a dead heat. The Domino win pool and the smaller Henry win pool were merged, and the total divided in half. The favorite's backers actually lost money, getting $3.50 for $5 while Henry's collected $6.50.

Success at new tracks meant crises at old ones, cutbacks, closures, and cancellations. In the year New York City opted to make Jerome Park a reservoir, the Maryland Jockey Club suspended its operations at Pimlico. They moved the Preakness north, where it joined the Belmont at Morris Park in 1890. This was only temporary, however; for the next three years the Preakness would not be run at all, then it would go to Gravesend for fifteen runnings, through 1908. In the midst of all this, Pierre Lorillard tried to bring order to racing by organizing the Board of Control in 1891. Made up of some major track operators and a few owners, it was supposed to oversee racing, but its authority was pretty much limited to the New York City–area tracks.[12]

In view of all this turmoil, Saratoga's predicament was understandable. It might have been solved by a Morrissey, but Fred—they also called him Gus—Walbaum was something else, the outcome of a process that began when the Association replaced Travers with the mere local potentate, Marvin, then responded to the rise of sports and gambling by turning everything over to Morrissey. He was not supposed to die.

A former gambling-house operator in the Bowery, where he was known as Dutch Fred, Walbaum had leased the old Guttenberg racetrack across the Hudson from Manhattan, in those same New Jersey wilds where the Beacon course once flourished and baseball was born. Walbaum was not as dumb as a lot of people thought. In fact, he was startlingly successful as an innovator, converting Guttenberg into a money-maker by instituting winter racing.

"The public had no place to waste its money except in policy-shops, stocks, etc.," said an 1890s contemporary, "and the venture caught on. Guttenberg's winter racing became famous. Jockeys wore gloves and mufflers to protect them from the cold. Spectators shivered and the poor old horses staggered around the course. . . . The newspapers ridiculed winter racing and those who attended, but still the crowd went, paid its admission and bet its money. The bookmakers flourished and the pool-rooms of New York and Jersey City did a big business."[13]

Walbaum branched into bookmaking himself, at one point backing ten bookies who did an average business of $4,000 a day, and he also started his own racing stable.

It was said his horses won only when he played them. He made most of his money from some 320 East Coast pool rooms, which paid him $10 a day for wired overnight entries and daily results. Walbaum had his defenders; the trainer Sam Hildreth, who raced his own stable at Guttenberg, said the operation was on the level, that its reputation was sullied by gambling houses outside the grounds. Others, though, called it "a synonym for all the crookedness . . . in the horse-racing business," and the turf establishment would have nothing to do with it. Still, when the respected operators on the Board of Control outlawed winter racing, "the Guttenbergers laughed and went on making money," as the 1890s writer put it. "It was noticeable that Mr. Walbaum made more money than all the rest."

When it finally got out that Gottfried Walbaum was actually buying the temple of American racing, the old guard almost went into shock. Walbaum was accused of all manner of things, including having used electric prods and narcotics on horses. The *Sporting World* said Saratoga's establishment feared "their peace and perhaps their very lives would be in danger as soon as the horde of outlawed officials and horsemen were prepared for their attack on the village." The attack began by late 1891, by which time Walbaum had replaced the venerable Wheatly with one Samuel Whitehead as secretary. The following spring, Walbaum was in full personal control, opening the 1892 season with himself as president of the once august Saratoga Association.[14]

Lacking a press agent, a species that Morrissey had not only helped invent but personified, Dutch Fred was simply out there, something of a trip to wonderful northern New Jersey. Surprisingly, given his previous career, he was legendary for a certain innocence about betting. In fact, the "Dutch Book" was reportedly named after him. As Hugh Bradley explained, this was a book in which the odds were figured so, well, stupidly, that a player could make a profit just by betting every horse. Walbaum himself also accepted bets after the races started, often from his own employees. This old practice was on the way out, but as Bradley pointed out, it allowed Walbaum's employees to skin him in "one of the oldest of race-track flimflams." One employee would simply station himself where he could see the race and signal the others when a horse took a big lead.

Walbaum's 1892 Spa inaugural was declared a huge success by his backers in the sporting press, which boasted that the ninety winning owners represented not only the Board of Control but the "outlaws," and that the crowd was "unprecedented in the history of track." Walbaum's greatest achievement, it would turn out, was a new grandstand, clubhouse, and betting ring. It would go largely unrecorded—and unrecognized until this writing—as the oldest stand still in use in American professional sports. The honor befits the country's oldest sports facility, which dated from the opening of the Saratoga Trotting Course in 1847. The new grandstand opened on July 25, 1892. It was 418 feet long, with a beautiful slate roof, and sat five thousand. A second floor stairway led to the clubhouse, with its balcony ending in Queen Anne circles and a bright lawn running to the track. At the eastern end was the betting pavilion, paved and with its own sharply sloping roof. Saratoga's new grandstand predated that of Churchill Downs by three years and baseball's Fenway Park in Bos-

America's oldest sports stand, ca. 1892. *Robert Joki Collection, Saratoga Springs.*

ton and Tiger Stadium in Detroit by twenty years, and its multisteepled Victorian roof would be Saratoga's most beloved feature more than a century later.

Yet Walbaum's era was a disaster for the sport. Great races disappeared. Even before he got there, the Saratoga Cup had been suspended from 1887 through 1890. It was revived in 1891, when Lucky Baldwin's Los Angeles won it, but under Walbaum the Cup vanished again for the rest of the century. The Spinaway was cancelled in 1892 and the Alabama would go away in 1893—both of them until 1901, except for an 1897 running of the latter. The great Travers Stakes lost its prestige as its value, already modest, plunged. It dropped by more than $1,000 to the $2,900 earned by Vallera in 1891 and would never return even to that level under Walbaum. Its all-time low was the $1,125 that the filly Liza presented in 1895 to an aging owner who did not need it, Pierre Lorillard.

If that were not trouble enough, the innovative Walbaum got ahead of his times again, moving the starting time of his program from 11:30 A.M. to 2:30 P.M. It makes perfect sense now, but almost everybody hated it then. The hotels and their visitors had made the morning races part of the regimen, their daily social card, with breakfast and a perusal of the racing program followed by the fast whirl to the track in the finest turnouts outside of Newport. After the races came dinner—"the great dining room event of the day"—and later a drive about the lake with a stop at Moon's or Riley's. "King of the Track Walbaum smashed the card," said the *New York World*. Even other bookmakers protested, telling Walbaum their best customers—"your water-drinker"—didn't like it. "Oh, to ——— with the ——— water drinkers," Wal-

PAUL C. GRENING.   C. F. MASSEY,   R. P. FLOWER,   KING KAPURTHALA & WIFE,   GEN. B. F. TRACEY,   A. HIGGINS,
G. WALBAUM.   Lieut. Col.   Governor,   and Suite of India.   Secretary of the Navy.   U. S. Senator.
British Army.   State of New York.   MRS. I. H. DAHLMAN.
MRS. G. WALBAUM.

The King of India at the track, 1893. Gottfried Walbaum is standing at left, behind man in turban and Mrs. Walbaum. *George S. Bolster Collection of the Historical Society of Saratoga Springs.*

baum was quoted as replying. This was before newspapers would swear. "I don't want them out to the track anyhow."

"The fight is still on," said the *World* some time later. "People who love their racing better than dinner or their afternoon drive go to the races, eat sandwiches for luncheon and curse the Walbaum management. The others make firm resolves to shun the races, but in the end give up the dinner and drives. In the meantime, Mr. Walbaum is a nightly figure at the club house, where he gets up from the gambling about 4 o'clock in the morning and then sleeps until noon." Even the street commissioners objected, sarcastically noting that neither villagers nor summer people "believe the principal aim of life is to play faro all night, sleep in the morning, and play the races in the afternoon." The local paper smugly concluded, "It is doubtful if the change will prove as successful as the management anticipates." Walbaum was too far out front again. If he had a certain self-confidence, it could only have been encouraged by such guests at his new clubhouse as the King of India, Kapurthala, and his suite, who came in 1893 with the secretary of the navy, a senator, the governor, and a British Army representative.

As the Panic of '93 was strangling the country, Saratoga Springs acquired an angel. Albert Spencer took a Manhattan gambling-house operator, Richard Albert Canfield, as partner and the next year sold the casino to him for $250,000. Spencer, the frustrated intellectual and art critic, soon sailed away to a country that understood his kind, and before his death in France in 1907, he would will that his ashes be scattered so they could never be returned to America.

Richard A. Canfield, on the other hand, had to love the country. New England–born and in gambling from age eighteen, Canfield was thirty-nine and rising, averaging $100,000 a year at his Madison Square Club at 22 West Twenty-sixth Street. He saw that Saratoga was even more valuable and immediately proved it. He set astronomical house limits and was the first to provide guests with credit, which, of course, increased their investments. Canfield was on his way to succeeding Morrissey as America's most famous gambling figure, his place in the park to become, according to Herbert Asbury, "the greatest gambling asset the United States has ever known."

The Springs cooperated, the piazzas producing their usual glitter: Berry Wall; the music-hall queen Lillian Russell; the Wall Street plunger John "Bet-A-Million" Gates; the railroader George Pullman, in the midst of a major strike; and Frank James (although he was trying to avoid being recognized and asked about Jesse). The five thousand-seat Convention Hall had opened on the edge of the park (it would burn down in 1965), and the town put on the first of its Floral Fetes.

In addition to Canfield's casino, there were at least ten full-scale gambling joints going, including Village President Mitchell's on Broadway. Some of the others were the Chicago Club, the Manhattan Club, and the United States Club, these operations offering poker, faro, roulette, and dice. And saloons had little back rooms where customers could play for a nickel or a dime. The expression everybody was using was "wide open," a phrase that would ring like the bells of a cathedral throughout the history of America's sin cities. Saratoga, it was whispered, was "wide open" in 1894. They had gone about as far as they could go.

Mitchell said they might have even been helped by the latest crusader, America's most famous journalist. Her career-making coup had been her trip around the world in a record seventy-two days, beating Jules Verne's *Around the World in Eighty Days*. Nellie Bly was still going strong, and when she hit Saratoga, her exposé inspired a stack of headlines in the *New York World*: "Wild Vortex of Gambling and Betting by Men, Women and Children" and "Sports, Touts, Criminals and Race-Track Riff-Raff Crazed by the Mania for Gold" and the "Rise of the Racing Czar Walbaum."[15]

 *14*

THE WOMEN'S BETTING RING

NELLIE BLY began: "Saratoga is the wickedest spot in the United States. Crime is holding a convention there and vice is enjoying a festival such as it never dared approach before." At the hotels, "gamblers, horse-owners, jockeys, millionaires and actors mingle together promiscuously," said the celebrated reporter. "A man will leave his wife on the veranda and go in to talk with an actress or a woman of questionable character." In the ballroom, "men of no standing and bad morals" took "pretty girls more than ten and less than fifteen aside to chat with them." At Canfield's, she invaded the restaurant, "a long room, very well lighted, with gorgeous palms to make it look summery and with real French waiters—the only good waiters in Saratoga." The men went into an adjoining room, "from which comes the seductive whirl of the wheel," and where "men are so densely packed that it is impossible to see the tables." Six roulette wheels and three faro layouts were in operation from 10 A.M. to 1 P.M., then business resumed in the evening. White chips were $10 a stack, or fifty cents each, at two tables and $50 a stack at a third. Reds were double.

Bly's dining partners were a group of loudly dressed women, one a "bleached-haired actress" who kept giving money to a man to bet. "She plays the races all the day and plays roulette all evening." Another was surrounded by men who bet their own money for her and gave her half if they won. Bly noted there were "large poker games conducted by women for women in every hotel, and the amounts that change hands are said to be enormous." At the Grand Union, the Saratoga woman of the Gay Nineties had a "bar-room set apart for her exclusive use where she can go for a morning cocktail after a night's dissipation."

Bly decided to confront the most notorious gambler in town, not the still-rising Canfield but the village president himself, Caleb W. Mitchell, whom the *World* called "Saratoga's Boss Gambler." Behind the saloon and also on the second floor of Cale Mitchell's, opposite the United States Hotel, there were gambling rooms offering roulette, faro, craps, English hazard, stud poker, and several other games, especially "The Bookmaker's Wheel," a tacky version of roulette. Decorated with greenbacks and protected by plate glass, it gave Mitchell a little more than 20 percent, making it the worst deal anywhere for bettors, yet the fact that they could play not only silver dollars but even halves and quarters helped make it the most popular game in town. Mitchell's take halfway through that season was said to be $60,000.

"White and black gamble together, poor and rich," said Bly, a little uncomfortable with the fact that Cale's was so democratically integrated. Unlike Canfield's but like the other houses, it admitted Saratogians, which helped make it the chief target of the reformers. "They lay the disgrace of Saratoga being the wickedest spot on earth at his door." She was quite taken with him, though. "I was told that . . . his looks were enough to send chills down one's back if one met him in a lonely spot." But what she found was "a little man . . . holding a Panama hat in his hand," his well-made gray suit set off by a light vest, black and red scarf, and immense amethysts ringed with diamonds, both on his shirt and on a ring. He was clean-shaven, his hair "all there but a little thin," his eyes "blue and clear and keen and sharp, yes, very sharp."

"'Married, I suppose?'" asked Nellie Bly. He was fifty-eight but had scarcely any lines on his face. "'Oh yes, thank God!' He looked at me. His eyes were no longer clear. Tears filled them." Mitchell had lived like Morrissey, had followed the gold rushers west, been a fine rough-and-tumble fighter, and found salvation in his family and also, in his case, the Catholic Church. In the Morrissey tradition, he gave up to $5,000 a year to charities and had donated $300 the day Bly came calling. He was oddly emotional about all this, tears filling his eyes when he spoke as village president at religious and Sunday-school gatherings. When he mentioned his family, he thought of death. "'I have nine children, all living, and three grandchildren. . . . Yes, my home life has been blessed. It has been a most happy one and when the call comes, I'm ready to go.'"

"'What do you mean, that you are tired of life?'" asked Nellie Bly, not one to let that one get away.

"'No, that I have nothing to complain of and that I feel at peace with Heaven.'"

His blue eyes filled with tears again. "I don't know what to make of him," said Bly, stumped and enthralled. "'I'm sorry I've met you. I could have said meaner things about you if I hadn't.'"

"'That is right, little girl,'" Cale Mitchell told Nellie Bly, his hand on her arm. He defended gambling as "no worse than selling ribbon over the cost of production." It was the percentage that gave the bettor the worst of it, and he insisted Saratoga gambling houses were upright. As for the details, on his biggest day he had made $10,000 in twenty-four hours. On his worst a man took him for $17,500 in ten hours.

> "The biggest bet I ever saw made was made by a man named Owen. The game was Spanish monte. Owen bet $50,000 on the turn of a card, lost, and bet it again and won."
>
> "Supposing a woman would come to you and say her husband was losing all his money with you and she was being starved, what would you do?"
>
> "I'd adopt her."
>
> "And her husband?"
>
> "I'd kill him and swear he died in a fit," he vowed so emphatically that I had to laugh.
>
> "Did you ever kill a man?"
>
> "Not that I know of, but I'd rather kill one hundred than let one kill me."

It was a prophetic reply, to be punctuated one day by a bullet.

"Twenty-five cents to the race track!" Two- and three-seated surreys with a fringe on top and tired-looking horses were making the run. Bly was hurrying there, too. The old place had hardly changed. Draped with blankets bearing the initials of

Nellie Bly's target. *National Museum of Racing and Hall of Fame, Saratoga Springs.*

their stables, the magnificent animals crossed the broad avenue from Horse Haven, and the jockeys, in billowing silk shirts and white pants, queued to weigh in. "The horses seemed to enjoy it, too," said Bob Wickham, a high schooler who worked at the track.[1]

Admission was two dollars.

"Although I had expected a crowd," Bly wrote, "I was amazed when I entered the grandstand. There was a perfect mass of people in gala attire." Obviously, Walbaum was not ruining things for everybody. On the inside of the rail, at the finish line, stood the judges' stand, now with a glass-enclosed top. The spectacle of horses working lightly in front of the stand before the races had now culminated in the modern post parade, although Bly wasn't much of a sport about it. "The horses were marched past the grandstand, led by a man in yellow skin-tight trousers and black velvet jacket. He . . . seemed to think the march was for his especial gratification as he made the horse do high-school pranks and took off his hat very frequently, like an organ-grinder's monkey."

Bly spotted a group of "painted faces and pencilled, inviting eyes," clutching programs, betting tickets and paper money, as they still called it. "'Mamma, did that lady get all those rings for Christmas?'" a little girl asked. "'Mamma, do the ladies get all that money from the horse races?'"

"'Yes, darling.'" The mother looked around "to see if her neighbors noticed how clever the child was."

Two boys, about eight and ten, hung their legs over the back of her seat and talked about what horse they would "play." Their three sisters made up pools with their mother of twenty-five cents each. Two young men were supposed to be with them, except they were always leaving to go where even Nellie Bly would not follow. Women were not admitted.

The betting ring, to the east of the grandstand, was roofed, with open sides. It was not just a bunch of bookies with tickets and paper money sticking out of their plaid pockets. Though resembling the farther reaches of a Middle Eastern bazaar, it was also a highly organized mall and not much different from today's ontrack betting operations, except the bookmakers ran it. It was the only place a man could place a bet, unless it was with a friend.

A circle of stalls on stilts housed the bookmakers, their "sheetwriters," and their payoff men. Each stall bore the name of the tenant—Wickham remembered "Carroll, Burton, Schreiber, Gleason, Wolfgang"—and below each name was the crucial blackboard, with the entries for each race and the odds chalked up next to them. Standing on a shelf to watch the other blackboards, each bookmaker bid against the others, stopping to ask his sheetwriter how much he risked by changing the odds. The customers played "straight" (to win), "place" (finish first or second), or "show" (finish first, second, or third).

To keep them from doctoring the tickets, the bookmakers used different colored paper and printing designs for each race. They also printed their business names and a number on the tickets. The sheetwriter would use indelible ink to inscribe the bet on each ticket, as he did for Wickham one Saturday: "Ballarat, 15 to 9 to win." If that steeplechaser came in, the payoff man, who had his own window, would pay twenty-four dollars on the fifteen dollar bet. Ballarat had indeed come in on three earlier Saturdays in a row, Bob and a friend collecting each time, so they put their winnings on his nose. Later, the torn-up tickets littering the ring and first floor of the stand probably included theirs for loser Ballarat. Bob never bet again.

He was one of the "messenger boys." Wearing a long blue coat with brass buttons and a white cap with a number on it, Bob circulated in the stand, offering to take bets for women for a charge of ten cents, plus ten cents to cash in if they won. Occasionally he invested five cents on gum at a booth beneath the stand because it came with a free tipsheet, which intelligence he shared with his bettors. With his ten dollar weekly salary and tips, Bob banked several hundred dollars at the end of the season, bought winter clothes and books, and had something left over.

If Bob was Saratoga's idea of a wholesome boyhood, Nellie Bly wasn't buying it. For one thing, he was not allowed to place the women's bets at the main betting ring but had to take them to a separate bookmakers' operation on the top landing in the rear of the grandstand. The *World* called it "the only race-track betting ring in America for women." Bly decided that, if they must bet, it was better for women to go there themselves.

Up Bly went to the most dramatic of Fred Walbaum's innovations. Trimmed in natural woods and opening into "retiring rooms" for its customers, the women's ring, or "pool-room," had a counter behind a wire screen at one end, where three book-

The Women's Betting Ring. Nellie Bly's illustrator was not above stereotyping. *The World,* 1894. *Courtesy of the author.*

makers operated, with their ticket sellers, cashiers, and a blackboard giving entries and odds. This operation was connected to the main ring by telephone, a man down there monitoring the boards and flashing the odds back upstairs. It was here that Bly uncovered a scandal that historians may now insert in their texts.

"The other day," she revealed, "when a horse won with odds something like 200 to 1, I have forgotten the exact figures, there had been two bets sold in the women's pool-room, and the odds were only 40 to 1." In other words, the women got worse odds. In his touching memoirs, Bob the messenger boy confirmed this. He remembered a horse that was 400 to 1 in the ring but had only one ticket holder, a lady in the stand. She got 40 to 1.

America's most celebrated reporter found her doubts about women's suffrage confirmed at the track. "If one enjoys a democratic crowd then one would love this woman's pool-room," Nellie Bly declared. "If woman's suffrage would produce such a scene, then God prevent suffrage. I claim to be liberal in my views; I believe in liberty and the right to do as one pleases, but I don't think I should like to see such an assemblage again, even at the day of judgment." Much less racist than most of the Northern establishment, she nevertheless chose to justify this condemnation by the example of "a negro woman, with paint upon her yellow cheeks, diamonds as large as peas in her ears, her breast ablaze with costly pins and her gown straight from Paris and never worn before." (Walbaum did not bar African Americans from his grandstand, the way they had been in that 1865 season.) Bly spared hardly anyone; the woman in the Paris gown nodded "familiarly to a big fat white woman in black and gold silk, a woman who entertains every night in the year and is not particular about introductions."

"Dozens of children are in the room. Little girls from six years up, boys in knee-breeches. They are all betting, some silver—for 50-cent bets are taken here—and some have bills." One little girl with two dollars in her hand explained, "'Mamma told me to bet it on Ducat.'" There was "the woman who has a house of her own, carriages galore and who has no rich relatives and still never labored; there is a poor woman hushing a babe in long clothes on her shoulder as she waits to bet the bit of silver she clutches in her hand," and "a fat, jolly-looking creature with a half-dozen gaily dressed girls with her." And, "at the door, handing some bills to an English girl . . . a man who is worth millions and is known the world over. At his side is a man who has taken religious vows, anxiously consulting a racing card, and nearby is a woman who certainly looked as if her sins were as scarlet.

"We walk over to the club-house." Both the gambling houses in town and the place where Bly was headed were called club houses. The latter was simply a more exclusive and better appointed seating area than the grandstand, but it was also a milestone. It had turned the grandstand, which formerly displayed the Vanderbilt crowd, into a second-tier facility and continued the class system in spectator seating. Walbaum's clubhouse, Wickham remembered, had café tables "behind low flower boxes of begonias, nasturtiums, sweet Williams, and petunias," but Bly knew her readers' real interests. "At the tables upon the veranda sit a number of women, actresses and society women but all women whose names appear frequently in print. They are betting and drinking, but with the exception of one woman, who is rapidly and surely becoming intoxicated, they are orderly. If women must bet, I supposed this is the least objectionable way." She was nothing if not a snob.

Walbaum's problems were getting worse. Turf historian Landon Manning pointed out that on one July day in that 1894 season they had to call off the rest of the program after Walbaum's own stable won the first four races and there were no entrants for the fifth and sixth. Walbaum tried everything. In recent years, bookmakers had monopolized the betting, but in 1894, he brought back both the old auction pools, with Harry Banigan succeeding the "mellifluous" Bobby Cathcart, and the mechanical "Pari mutuels," run by a Jack Spencer. Walbaum's best efforts could not keep him out of trouble, however. As Manning pointed out, his relations with the bookmakers soured when Riley Grannon offered to take almost any amount, into the thousands of dollars, on horses he didn't like. This upset a few smaller bookmakers who apparently were partners with Walbaum, so he asked Grannon to stay away. It was another public relations mistake. Grannon won out as most of his colleagues signed a petition in his favor. It prompted the *New York Times* to note that Walbaum was "getting himself generally disliked by his dictatorial acts."[2]

Still, 1894 was one of the breakthrough years in American racing, if not at the Spa. A group of stable owners decided that if the sport's weakness was fragmentation—the turmoil of countless tracks competing madly and slashing purses wherever they could—its strength was an endless pool of talent, equine and human, rich and poor, if somehow it could only be brought under one roof. Like circus people, this talent appeared at one track after another in an exhilarating, nomadic life, as it still does—all except the foundation talent: the breeders back on the farms. They now formed a great industry, still centered in Kentucky. The white-fenced bluegrass was a land of not only beauty but unparalleled tradition. Under R. A. Alexander, Woodburn Farm in Woodford County had harbored Lexington, who produced Kentucky, Kingfisher, Harry Bassett, Preakness, Tom Bowling, and Tom Ochiltree, among many others. Woodburn would boast a record five Derby winners, the last of them, His Eminence, in 1901. Also dripping with history were Nantura Stud, established by old John Harper and embellished by Longfellow; Ashland Stud, the home of Henry Clay and his heirs; Runnymede; and, in Tennessee, Belle Meade.[3]

The sport was discovering what one day would be labeled agribusiness. After Morrissey's old gambling partner died, McGrathiana, at Lexington, was purchased by Milton Young, who expanded it to two thousand acres with more than a hundred broodmares. Its offspring led the 1890 season with 378 wins and $335,150. Young bought Hanover, who had won the United States Hotel Stakes and thirty-one other victories in fifty starts. Young also bred Broomstick, who fathered a record sixty-six stakes winners. Out west, Marcus Daly, the copper king, reigned over Bitter Root Stock Farm in Montana while maintaining others in France and England. The king of kings was James Ben Ali Haggin. He would transfer his stud from California to Kentucky, buying Elmendorf Farm and expanding it to eighty-seven hundred acres. It was vast enough to be split later into a smaller Elmendorf Farm, Greentree Stud, the C. V. Whitney Farm, Normandy Farm, and parts of Spendthrift Farm. And reaching down from Wall Street was James R. Keene, who was expanding Castleton Farm near Lexington.[4]

It was Keene who saw that racing had to organize. After all, baseball's efforts were beginning to pay off. The American Association had folded in 1891, but Charlie Comiskey, manager of the Cincinnati Reds, was talking of setting up another circuit that would become the American League. Other sports were organizing as well. The United States Golf Association was founded in 1894. The National Association of Amateur Oarsmen was still together. It brought its regatta to Saratoga Lake again in 1892 and 1894 and would return in 1895 and 1896. Reorganized, the Intercollegiate Rowing Association would come back to the lake for its 1898 regatta, with Pennsylvania accepting the brand new silver cup that the IRA still awards today.[5] The New York State tennis championships were played at Hilton's Woodlawn Oval in 1893 and 1894. Other sports were getting started. One day in 1891, for instance, James Naismith, a physical education teacher, went to one end of his gymnasium in Springfield, Massachusetts, and hung a peach basket there.

Keene organized racing by getting a group to form the Jockey Club, which in 1894 succeeded Lorillard's Board of Control. This was not to be confused with the late, wistfully named American Jockey Club, set up just to run Jerome Park. The new organization established its authority in and around New York. It was chaired by John Hunter, managed by seven stewards, including Hunter, Keene, and August Belmont II, and limited at first to fifty breeder-owner members. Hunter would be succeeded the following year by Belmont, whose reign lasted until 1924. The Jockey Club's authority would be increasingly recognized as it brought order to racing at last, writing the rules, licensing jockeys and trainers, setting racing dates, publishing the American Stud Book—its only accepted listing of thoroughbreds—and maintaining a "forfeit list" of race entrants who were banned until they paid any fees in arrears.

At the beginning the Jockey Club was not nearly as strong as it wanted people to believe. It was true that any course rejecting its authority would be deemed an "outlaw" track with "outlaw" horses, who would not be allowed on Club-approved tracks until reinstated. A great many tracks were quite willing to risk such opprobrium, however, and so were many owners. Outlaw horses would number more than twelve hundred at one point. Still, the Jockey Club represented racing's greatest hope for survival as a national sport.[6]

The survival of Saratoga Springs as a sporting town, however, was suddenly in doubt, for that wide open year brought an equal and opposite reaction. Yet another reformer appeared in the wake of Comstock, Trask, and Nellie Bly. This was State Sen. Edgar Truman Brackett, who cleverly saw that the people, faced with a choice between his ideas of good and evil, would vote for evil any day. So Brackett got the legislature to pass a law providing for the elected village trustees, instead of the people, to pick the village president. Out there in the open, unable to hide behind the ballot, the trustees had to be conservative and respectable and law abiding. They immediately replaced Cale Mitchell with one Charles Sturges, who ordered all gambling-house operators to close down in 1895. They complied, including the politically astute Canfield, who was ready to give his gold mine time, and even the mercurial Mitchell. Although Brackett had been the latest crusader to ride in, it could easily be argued, given her national impact, that it was Nellie Bly who had shut down Saratoga.[7]

The next year was even worse for the proracing liberals, although it was not always apparent. Diamond Jim Brady showed up in 1896, but not chiefly to gamble. He was there to boost his business by impressing delegates to the Master Car Builders' convention, so he put them up in three cottages, which were staffed by twenty-seven Japanese houseboys and supplied with corned beef and cabbage, caviar and foie gras, and plenty of Havana cigars. One of the cottages was decorated with a gold-plated bicycle and a silver-plated railroad car made by Brady's company. (Although Lil Russell was often with him, the rumors of his many intimate affairs were far-fetched, according to Berry Wall. "He was much too fat for that.") Still, it was the reformers who were in control.

For the first time, after thirty-three years, the Spa racecourse was shut down in 1896, a fact somehow missed by turf and local historians. Although Brackett's campaign was the catalyst, it might be said that Nellie Bly had shut down the racetrack, too. The local backlash, however, proved just as extreme. The following spring, the

New York Times reported, the lines between the liberals and the reformers were clearly drawn. The liberals swept the village election, and the new trustees, all Democrats, picked a politically cautious liberal, A P Knapp, for mayor. He immediately allowed Canfield and five other gambling-house operators to reopen, but not Cale Mitchell, for wide-open gambling was never again going to be allowed on Broadway. Out of office and out of his Broadway palace, Mitchell had paid the price for being wooed by the leading reporter in the country and having both his picture and his caricature splashed across her newspaper, with its circulation of more than four hundred thousand. Suddenly, he was hardly anybody.[8]

The track reopened in 1897, with Walbaum assuming a lower profile. Replacing him and Whitehead as Association president and secretary, respectively, were Edward Kearney and B. A. Chilton. "Twenty days of good racing" were to be followed by a horse show. Sports would top the Springs agenda again, with an Eastern open championship at Saratoga Golf Club west of the village and the League of American Wheelmen's state bicycle championships at Woodlawn Oval. Walbaum's operation, however, was still sick. Neither the Saratoga Cup nor the Spinaway was revived, and it would be the last season in the century for the Travers (won by Rensselaer), the Alabama (Poetess), and the Flash (Hamburg).[9] Once again Walbaum admitted children, which a *Times* reporter, for one, thought delightful. Ranging "from the year-or-two-old baby in a cap to the sixteen-year-old girl," they created "a family atmosphere about the place," but didn't do much for business.[10]

Enter, at last, Williams Collins Whitney. As one writer put it, "no man exercised so profound an influence in so short a time" on the American turf. "Steady as a New England clock," to use one of his own expressions, he was as affable as he was brilliant. The son of a public-spirited Massachusetts family, he went to Yale, started out as a New York City lawyer, and quickly became well-connected by marrying Flora Payne, the sister of a Yale friend, "Ol" Payne. Oliver Hazard Payne, future treasurer of Standard Oil, would become Will and Flora's frequent housemate and benefactor, eventually combining the roles by buying them a Fifth Avenue mansion at 2 West Fifty-seventh Street, opposite the Vanderbilts.

Young Whitney entered city politics as a reform Democrat, operating in lawyerly groups more educated but far less effective than the rowdier reformers like John Morrissey, who was only ten years his senior. A group led by Senator Morrissey and another including Whitney and August Belmont actually found themselves locked in debate at the 1876 state convention, but the two factions merged after Morrissey died. Whitney then became New York City's lawyer, the Corporation Counsel, battling Tweed in the already defeated Boss's final days and reforming the city's Law Department. From that inside position, he watched the frenetic growth of transportation as the metropolis crossed the Harlem River and incorporated the "Annexed District," later the south Bronx, near Jerome Park. The built-up part of Fifth Avenue pushed north to Central Park and the elevated railroads to Sixty-seventh Street, Eighty-third Street, then the Harlem River. There was a fortune to be made in this urban sprawl.

After returning to private practice, Will continued to connect. He soldiered as a lawyer in the battles of the Commodore and W. H. Vanderbilt, Andrew Carnegie, and

The Women's Betting Ring

159

William Rockefeller. He reached up by becoming a stockholder in the Metropolitan Opera, alongside Vanderbilts, John Jacob Astor, J. P. Morgan, J. W. Drexel, and the feudal owner of Yorkville, William Rhinelander. From his base of law and modest wealth, he entered state politics, wheeling and dealing at the Democratic State Committee at Saratoga in 1882 (the Republican state convention was convened there, too, of course) and helping to elect Grover Cleveland governor. Tall, athletically trim, with a pince-nez, neat mustache, properly receding hairline, and Prince Albert coat, Whitney was highly presentable, something Cleveland sought in men, and three years later President Cleveland made him not only secretary of the navy but best man at his White House wedding. Whitney ran Cleveland's 1892 reelection campaign, and they won, but Will declined an offer to become secretary of state.

He had begun to create his empire on wheels. He had become a director of the New York Cable Rail Company, founded by Thomas Fortune Ryan, with whom Whitney formed a permanent partnership. They created the Metropolitan Street Railway Company, which swallowed up one cable and electric railway company after another. They forged alliances with such forces as Peter A. B. Widener, the street railway king of Philadelphia, and battled the likes of Jay Gould, who controlled the elevated railroads. By mid-1900, Ryan and Whitney would control virtually all street railways in Manhattan and the Bronx. Well before then, however, another event, the death of Flora in 1893, had shaken the family even more than they knew.[11]

In the calm before the storm, Will and his children shared memories of a woman at least as brilliant as he and not afraid to let him know it, but everything began to change in 1896. That pressure-filled year brought two political declarations, one Will's and one well remembered today. Cleveland had avoided committing himself to a third term, but Whitney nevertheless took on the job of point man in the Democratic infighting over the biggest issue: "sound money," silver versus gold. Whitney basked in glory at the party's state powwow in Saratoga's shiny Convention Hall on the Broadway hill. When he walked down the aisle to sit with the New York City delegation shortly after noon on June 24, the place went wild. After all, he had won it all for Cleveland four years earlier and was one of the party's most successful capitalists. The roll was called, and again the delegates rose, waved their hats and gave three cheers for Will. They unhesitatingly adopted Whitney's plank, which pronounced the Democrats "opposed to the free and unlimited coinage of silver. . . . We favor the rigid maintenance of the present gold standard." He took it to the national convention two weeks later in Chicago, where he was greeted by Whitney-for-President buttons and prepared the uphill battle for gold. His plank might have a thin chance, unless the opposition arguments were laid out by some William Jennings Bryan.

The lanky form of William Jennings Bryan, with his black hair and big nose, jumped out of his seat and rushed to the speaker's platform to give the speech of his life. He had been preparing it in his mind for years and lately reworking it over and over. "You shall not crucify mankind upon a cross of gold!"

The place exploded. The minority financial plank was voted down, 626 to 303. To put it as mildly as possible, Bryan was a hard act to follow. If historians have forgotten the man who did have to follow him with some sort of reaction, maybe it was because the best thing Will could come up with when reporters chased him down was, "The fight of the gold men here has certainly been without result." Bryan was nominated. William McKinley and the Republicans won the election, suggesting that perhaps Whitney was right, but the silver tongue and populism finally had captured the Democratic Party from the Whitneys, Belmonts, Vanderbilts, and friends.

Will hardly had time to recover before his first son, Harry Payne, showed he had Father's gift for connecting. A month after the convention, Harry married Gertrude, the girl next door, or rather across the street; she also happened to be the daughter of Cornelius Vanderbilt II. It was a hell of a merger and all-American at that. By then, heiresses were looking abroad for men who could put them in castles, and the latter to America for women who could pay for them. Gertrude's cousin, Consuelo Vanderbilt, had just one-upped Jennie Jerome by marrying not merely a brother of, but the actual (ninth) Duke of Marlborough. Gertrude's wedding to Harry Whitney seemed so patriotic that on the bridal morning at the Breakers the orchestra leader couldn't help but break into "The Star-Spangled Banner."

Nor was 1896 over. There was a not well-received coupling toward the end of September. Having survived several major transitions that summer, Will put Flora behind him and wed Edith Randolph, widow of a British army captain and at thirty-seven nearly two decades his junior. The groom seemed in love, but it broke the family in half. Ol Payne was so devoted to his sister's memory that he ended his long friendship with Will, and that was not the end of it, for the bachelor Standard Oil magnate would leave one of the country's great fortunes, far bigger than Whitney's. As his closest kin, Flora's children—Harry, Pauline, William Payne (known simply as Payne), and Dorothy—were his heirs apparent. In his fury, says Will's biographer, Mark Hirsch, the embittered uncle now succeeded in turning Pauline and Payne against their father and virtually disowned Harry and Dorothy for their filial loyalty.

The year 1899 was mixed, too. After three years of marriage, Edith died of injuries suffered in a fall from a horse, and Will was devastated. But Harry and Gertrude gave him a grandson whose name would ring loud at the Springs: Cornelius Vanderbilt Whitney. That same year, Gertrude's father died of multiple strokes. Typically Vanderbilt, he surprised many by the size of his estate, the New York Central chairman having made but a few sentimental investments, such as his small ones in Newport's Casino and Saratoga's United States Hotel. He left nearly $73 million. Half went to his son Alfred Gwynne, new head of the House of Vanderbilt, who also arranged for his wife to secure 1 West Fifty-seventh Street and the Breakers. Among the other children, Gertrude got more than $7 million.

For Will, threatening business challenges loomed. The Metropolitan Street Railway Company may have ruled on the East Side, West Side, all around the town by mid-1900, but unsightly cable railroads were not going to be allowed, so it had to consider electrifying the rest of its network, a huge expense. Unsettling, too, was the prospect that, like cable, electric railways might be a thing of the past. Whitney and his colleagues joined in a Byzantine legal battle against Belmont and others for a chunk of the future: subways.

Through all this, one thing only seemed to offer Will solace, an occasional clean

The Women's Betting Ring

fight, even pleasure: the turf. He long had been vaguely interested in breeding and loved talking horses with Harry, ex-polo champ at Yale. He had become a charter member of the Jockey Club in 1894 and the next year he built a home at Old Westbury, Long Island, partly because his friend Thomas Hitchcock had a residence, stable, and private track nearby. Later he would follow Hitchcock to Aiken, South Carolina, and build a mansion, stable, and mile track there.

In 1897, it was a fair bet that Whitney was mightily impressed by something that moved as fast as he, and damn the weights, Kentucky owner-trainer John Madden's Hamburg. As the two-year-old ate up one handicap event after another, they added poundage. By the time he took the half-mile Saratoga Flash, he was lugging 129. He carried 134 for the Congress Hall Stakes, then 135 for the Great Eastern at Sheepshead Bay, where he conceded 24 pounds to the runner-up. Whitney might have liked the looks of Madden's Plaudit, too, as Willie Simms piloted him to a Derby victory the next year. Here, surely, was his escape.

"Now." That's what Whitney said in 1898. He had asked Sam Hildreth if he would like to train a stable for him, and Hildreth had wondered, "When would you like an answer?"[12]

Whitney turned fifty-seven that year. He began his turf career in earnest under the name and colors of Pauline's brother-in-law, the Englishman Sydney Paget. Buying out Hildreth's stable, he took Hildreth himself as trainer and Madden as consultant, and captured twenty-five races, earning some $38,000. By 1899, he had paid $30,000 for Jean Beraud, who won the Belmont, and $25,000 for Plaudit. That year he had twenty-seven horses and won thirty-two races, earning $61,550.

Whitney began racing under his own name. He leased La Belle Farm at Lexington as his base and constructed a private plant at his Old Westbury estate on Long Island. It included a two-section stable that measured 800 by 75 feet and was surrounded by an exercise track. Whitney moved into the English turf as well.

"Are you fond of your colours?" Sydney Paget's father, Gerald Paget, asked trainer George Lambton one day at York, England.

"No, I hate the sight of them." Lambton's Eton blue with brown cap were continually finishing second. Would he take a hundred pounds for them?

"Give me the money, and they are yours." Lambton then learned he had sold his Eton blue and brown to the American, W. C. Whitney.[13]

It was the 1900 Futurity at Sheepshead Bay that started Whitney toward the top. When his Futurity-bound colt, Ballyhoo Bey, lost his first start, he lost no time dumping Hildreth and making Madden his trainer. When the time for the race came, Whitney was on a ship sailing home from England and had a banquet served at the moment the race was being run. With no way of knowing the result, he asked his guests to raise a glass to Ballyhoo Bey, "winner of the Futurity." It was an amateurish move.[14]

Back at Sheepshead Bay, James R. Keene—the man Whitney had targeted as his arch turf enemy—had the favorites, a stable entry of Olympian, Tommy Atkins, and Cap and Bells. On the other hand, Whitney had Tod Sloan, an Indiana kid and the most flamboyant jockey of that ridiculous age. Tiny Tod's arrogance had grown with

James "Tod" Sloan.
Keeneland Library.

his triumphs, of which he had amassed 166 in 1898 for a .46 winning percentage. The latter included five for five at Gravesend, and the next year, prefiguring Babe Ruth, he had told reporters he would do it again at Ingleside in California. He did.[15]

On the other hand, it took something to be noticed at Saratoga. You had to be somebody like Giulia Morosini, banker's daughter and contributor to the notion that women handle horses better. She did things they didn't do on Broadway. She rode horses, for one thing. Bob Wickham saw her mount in front of the United States and canter down the street in a long-skirted blue riding suit, "a gold-handled riding whip in one gloved hand and the reins in the other." Here was a gentlewoman jockey. She rode many mornings, and reappeared with a trap in late afternoons. Once, in 1899, she was at the white-colored reins of a tandem team of bays, sporting yellow bands with yellow rosettes across their foreheads while, the *Times* observed, "the tiger in the perch behind wears on his coat lapel a huge rosette of similar brilliance." Bob saw her atop a high-seated gig, threading not a pair but a triplet through crowded Broadway—"a graceful exhibition of daring and skillful horsewomanship."[16]

Tod got noticed. A friend of Diamond Jim and Lil Russell, he could be just as pushy, and one account had him demanding the best suite at the Grand Union, only to be informed that the great Keene had reserved it. The jockey moved in anyway, advising the clerk that Keene could find something else when he got there. Sloan himself said that on another occasion, when he took an apartment at the Grand Union, August Belmont II arrived later "and made a little fuss about paying twenty-five dollars a day for his room or rooms, but the manager . . . said, "Oh no, sir, I assure you I am not asking too much, especially to a gentleman of your position, for Mr. Tod Sloan is paying more than twenty-five dollars a day."

The rider went to Saratoga to prep Ballyhoo Bey for several weeks before the Futurity and, according to Hugh Bradley, marched into the United States Hotel this time. "I understand Mr. Belmont is not going to use his suite," he told the clerk, "I'll take it." Then he went to Canfield's and had his friends order anything they wanted at his expense. He called his memoirs *Tod Sloan By HIMSELF.* Tradition awards short-legged Sloan the credit for the "monkey-on-a-stick" posture that finally did replace the English style, even though long-legged Garrison had adopted a high crouch, and six decades earlier Sir Tyrone Power had seen black riders hugging their horses. The jockey also took credit for a piece of advice to Whitney. "He would pay any price for a horse that I said was worth while." On an earlier visit to Saratoga, Sloan claimed, he had talked Whitney into buying a little mare named Martha. As it turned out, Whitney was no fool, either, for Martha foaled Ballyhoo Bey.

With Tod crouching over him, Ballyhoo Bey did beat Keene's trio in the 1900 Futurity, collecting $33,580, just as the ocean-going Whitney had blithely assumed. Several weeks later, Will reminded Tod that he had not been paid, except for a $5,000 advance on expenses. "I'll give you all I have in my pocket." With that, Whitney pulled out a wad totaling $9,000, then took out his watch and gave him that, too, adding, "Now you have all I've got." Whitney won thirty other races that year, with earnings of $92,545.

Something else happened in 1900. For the third straight season, nobody was listed in Goodwin's official turf guide as president of the Saratoga Association, only a C. F. Ruh, Jr., as secretary. On the cover of programs for the races, however, a president was clearly named: G. Walbaum. It was as if he were exacting some final revenge, for the following year his name, too, was gone, and a new president was identified in the programs: W. C. Whitney.

 *15*

SARATOGA REVIVED

"THE PUFFING, grunting automobile, with its careless habits," said a New York reporter looking around Saratoga, "is almost unknown. It is so easy to make speed with a good team over the excellent roads that the need of electric and steam and gasolene steeds has not been felt."[1]

It was 1901. Saratoga was back. Its new angel, W. C. Whitney, was one of the early promoters of the automobile, but he loved horses more, and he was in his glory. He got a young betting commissioner, Johnny Walters, to make a list of all the Whitney guests in town and their servants, maids, and some of their tradesmen—some 120 names. He told Johnny to bet a hundred dollars for each of them on the Whitney entry, Goldsmith, in a new event called the Saratoga Special. It was still Walbaum's plant, but the whole program had begun to change.[2]

The Special was a winner-take-all for twos, worth the kind of prize Fred never offered—$14,500 and a $500 silver cup. Goldsmith, 6 to 1, beat Blue Girl by a short head, and Johnny left everybody's surprises in envelopes marked "W. C. W." They were starting to like the Whitneys at Saratoga. Goldsmith also won the revived Flash and Morningside, and King Hanover the Alabama and new Grand Union Hotel Stakes, respectively. The Travers was back, too, worth $6,750, nearly five times the value of its last running four years earlier, and was won by Charles Fleischmann's Sons' Blues, the first to capture the Travers and the Cup in one season. But the Travers no longer launched the meeting.

The 1901 opener, the $10,000 Saratoga Handicap, saw Green Morris's Watercure and J. B. Haggin's Water Color swamped by Rockton, cheered on by the locals in the field stand. They liked him for one reason: he was bred by Gen. Stephen Sanford, a West Point graduate and Amsterdam, New York, carpet manufacturer. The general had been coming to the Spa for decades and, if he had a horse running, bringing much of Amsterdam with him. An area institution, he gave his three thousand millworkers a day off every year for a racing program at his own Hurricana Farm—a little preview of the Spa season. The Sanfords showed their deep affection for the neighborhood in the names they gave their horses. Among them were Molly Brant (Sir William Johnson's beloved), Mohawk II, who would win the Saratoga Special four years later, and Caughnawaga, who would take the Cup to Amsterdam that same year.[3]

By 1901, the "Cavanagh Special" was running. Named for the New York book-maker John G. Cavanagh, this was the deluxe train of up to eight Pullmans that brought the bookmakers in from New York for the season. Under Whitney and the

J. G. Madden   *W. C. Whitney*   *Denby*

W. C. Whitney, with owner-trainer John Madden and other friends at the track in 1904. *National Museum of Racing and Hall of Fame, Saratoga Springs.*

Association, the hundred or so bookies would no longer call the shots the way they did in Walbaum's day, but with their monopoly on organized betting, and their work force of some four hundred, they would retain a powerful position at the track through 1939.[4] Some of them, like the devout Barney Shreiber, still owned horses and named a number after priests. Another, Bill Cowan, reportedly dumped $250,000 at the New York tracks, won $750,000 at the Spa, then dropped it all at Belmont. As for the bookies' rivals, the big plungers and their betting commissioners, Cowan said he lost more money to Pittsburgh Phil alone than to any twenty others. Riley Grannon was up to his old tricks. Hugh Bradley said Riley kept trying to break the bookmakers with bets of $50,000 or more. The Spa was a bank.

"Saratoga On Verge of Boom," cried the *New York Daily Tribune* that first year of the century. "The famous resort is not going to make any cheap bid for added and more modern fame. No Midway will be built and equipped. The remarkable old hotels are not going to be torn down and replaced with modern skyscrapers." And the male journalists hadn't reformed after forty years: "The prettiest summer girls in the country are to be found at Saratoga."[5]

The place has always mixed tradition with change, which becomes tradition. Now August was established as the racing month for most of the century. Horse sales became more important, Clarence Mackay buying Madden's Heno at the Spa in 1901 and the Messrs. Fleischmann putting their string on the block in the paddock. One of

Cavanagh arrives! The arrival of the "Cavanagh Special" opened the season. Photographer C. C. Cook ("Cookie") was active at American tracks for more than four decades. *National Musuem of Racing and Hall of Fame, Saratoga Springs.*

Saratoga's greatest assets, the training facility across Union Avenue, was enlarged to handle the crowd of thoroughbreds, the *Trib* dubbing Horse Haven "a summer hotel for blooded horses." The increasingly powerful Jockey Club put its seal of approval on the operation, as August Belmont II, Tommy Hitchcock's brother Francis, and the Club's other stewards convened its first formal meeting at the track.

By the time his work was done, Saratoga would be a triumph for Whitney. He had begun this adventure in 1900 by backing the visionary plan of New York banker Richard T. Wilson, Jr., a long-time Spa loyalist who wanted to buy out Walbaum and restore the track's grandeur. Bringing together a Jockey Club group, they did the deal in December for a reported $365,000, electing Whitney president and Andrew Miller secretary and treasurer. The club's new name revived the time-honored formula: the Saratoga Association for the Improvement of the Breed of Horses.[6]

The year 1901 was a watershed for Whitney. He began it with some forty horses in America and England. In January, at the sale of Marcus Daly's Bitter Root Farm, handled by the later celebrated Fasig Tipton Company at the old Madison Square Garden, Whitney outbid Haggin to get the great Hamburg for $60,000. Hamburg was demonstrating the remarkable profiteering possible in horse trading. The Kentucky trainer-owner John Madden had bought him for $1,200, and after he won $39,950 at age two, sold him to Daly for $40,000, nor was Hamburg finished changing hands.[7]

After the 1901 Spa season, Will Whitney was in a mood to buy every good horse he saw—"as beginners usually are," said track handicapper Walter Vosburgh—and he went after the twos. He got Endurance by Right, who Vosburgh said was the best two-year-old filly in twenty-five years and would keep that rank for another twenty-five. She won sixteen in eighteen starts but could not be trained at three and died early.[8] Whitney would add Madden's Blue Girl by the end of the year. He was already half-owner with Madden of Yankee, but after that colt won his first two, both at Saratoga, and the $36,580 Futurity, he bought out Madden's interest. And he edged out Madden to lead the owners in 1901 with $108,440. Although this was less than half James R. and Foxhall Keene's record $279,458 in 1893, it must have been satisfying to top them at last.

*   *   *   *

It was in June that year that Whitney went after the ultimate. The Derby at Epsom Downs was inaugurated in 1780, and the only Yank winner had been Pierre Lorillard with Iroquois in 1881. An Englishman said this victory did more for the United States in British public opinion than anything accomplished in letters, arts, or arms. So there was quite a stir when Whitney did it, Volodyovski accomplishing the mile and a half in a record 2:40 ⅘. He had not really matched Lorillard; for one thing, Iroquois was American-bred, albeit by imported Leamington, whereas Volodyovski was not. Whitney didn't even own him. He leased him—leased "his racing qualities," as the expression went—from Lady Meux. So the *New York Times* carped that this was not an American victory at all but at most a New York City one, adding sarcastically, "Whoever has paid a street car fare in New York since the system went into operation is entitled to some billionths of a share" in the honors. People had begun to ask if public transportation shouldn't be publicly owned.[9]

The Whitneys handled it with their customary class. Beaming with delight, son Harry led in the winner, looking up at the American jockey, Lester Reiff, in his light blue jacket and brown cap, and saying, "Good boy! Good boy!" Will wasn't there, but reporters trapped him at his current home, at Sixty-eighth and Fifth. "I personally am more pleased at Mr. Huggins' success," he said, giving the credit to John Huggins, first American to train an English Derby winner. Asked whether he liked Ballyhoo Bey or Volodyovski better now, Will said he would just like to win the Derby with a horse he had bred himself. Meanwhile, he turned in thirty-nine other English victories with his own American-breds that year, maintaining what one authority called "probably the best-rounded table ever raced in England by an American." He won in France, too, but by then he had decided to concentrate on improving the sport in America.[10]

"Certain gentlemen have devoted most of their time to this work," he said, "and I considered it my duty as one who derives great satisfaction from horses, to second their efforts in every way. It was for this reason that I cooperated with them to revive the Saratoga Association and abandoned a contemplated trip abroad this summer."[11]

He aimed to revive not only Saratoga but racing. In 1901, he published H. G.

Crickmore's *Racing Calendars*, the three volumes of American and Canadian racing charts for the "lost" years of 1861 through 1869. The preface by Vosburgh claimed racing was still "the National sport of the country." Baseball had certainly made that arguable, but the American League was only a year old and that sport would be in chaos again in a few years. The thing in sports was Saratoga.[12]

The 1902 season was the biggest yet, but the "Boss Gambler" wasn't in on it. After Cale Mitchell's Broadway joint had been shut down by the one-two punch of Nellie Bly and Senator Brackett in 1895, he left town. About 1899, as Herbert Asbury told it, he was back and running a pool room—these were still betting operations—near the track with "a Texas sharper named Dan Stuart." The police started getting complaints from customers that Mitchell and Stuart had robbed them, and in 1901, at Whitney's request, they were closed by the village authorities. Mitchell fought back. He blamed it all not on Whitney (Cale was, after all, a politician) but on Richard Canfield and Brackett. He even hired a couple of fancy lawyers, who got warrants for Canfield's arrest from small-town magistrates. A grand jury refused to indict.[13]

In late 1901, Cale went around telling everybody Brackett was trying to ruin him and his family. And Nellie Bly herself had told the world how much he loved his family. It got more pathetic after Brackett protected Canfield by introducing a bill to invalidate arrest warrants in the village if not endorsed locally. Mitchell began to talk to himself in public. On January 29, 1902, as the Senate prepared to debate the bill, he stopped at a hardware store to buy a gun and box of bullets. He said he wanted to kill some wild dogs in his neighborhood, but he seemed impatient. He took the first revolver the clerk showed him, loaded it with six bullets, and left the rest on the counter. He headed for Senator Brackett's office in the Town Hall at the corner of Lake Avenue. Had he not told Nellie Bly he could kill somebody who threatened his family? He knocked on the door. A caretaker told him he did not expect Brackett in that day, then disappeared.

A shot rang out from the hallway. They came running and found Cale had indeed killed somebody. The blood dripped from his temple as he lay on Brackett's doorsill. The senator was catching the train for Albany.

Cale missed a hell of a season, the grand opening of the renovated plant that New York architect Charles Leavitt had begun creating for Whitney and the Association the previous October. Leavitt had built Whitney's private track on Long Island. Much of his creation for the Saratoga Association was finished for 1902, at a cost of at least $1 million, and on opening day, August 4, nine thousand people poured through a new iron gate flanked by two squat brick columns, each marked "SA." They found the admission hiked from two dollars to three dollars, which Whitney explained by saying the crowds would be less than half those at Sheepshead Bay, Gravesend, and Morris Park.[14]

They also found that the track, America's latest sports challenge, had been lengthened from a mile to a mile and an eighth. Two-year-old Irish Lad helped inaugurate the new course, eating up three-quarters of a mile to win the Special, worth $18,000. It was enough to top the horses' and owners' money-winning lists for the meeting—a nice introduction to big winnings for Will's son Harry. He and Herman

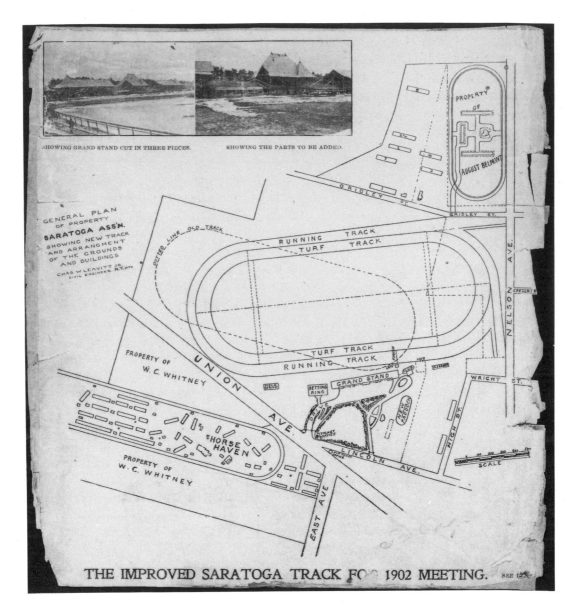

SHOWING GRAND STAND CUT IN THREE PIECES.   SHOWING THE PARTS TO BE ADDED.

GENERAL PLAN
OF PROPERTY
SARATOGA ASS'N.
SHOWING NEW TRACK
AND ARRANGMENT
OF THE GROUNDS
AND BUILDINGS
CHAS W LEAVITT JR
CIVIL ENGINEER N.Y. CITY

THE IMPROVED SARATOGA TRACK FOR 1902 MEETING.

Whitney's track. Insets show Walbaum's grandstand cut in three and preserved. *National Museum of Racing and Hall of Fame, Saratoga Springs.*

Duryea had bought him from Madden for $17,500, and he paid it back in spades by winning the Special and the Great Trial, then the Saratoga Champion and two other stakes at three.

Leavitt's assistant, W. E. Spinner, filled in a reporter. The course offered 1,485-foot stretches, banked turns of the same length, and a 1,135-foot race to the finish, the "home run," as they called it before baseball monopolized the term. It was 100 feet wide, except for the 65-foot second turn. Drained by catch basins every 250 feet, it could be watered from a three-inch pipe around the track, with hydrants every 200 feet and four water cranes as a backup. A driveway circled it.[15]

Inside it was a mile turf course, 70 feet wide on the straightaways, 65 on the turns, with an 1,100-foot home run. Just seeded, it wasn't ready for the season. On the infield, a new steeplechase course presented nine obstacles, including a water jump. After thirty-four years, the three-quarter chute across the infield was gone, and two new ones added, but not across the field. There was a one-mile chute at the western turn and a seven-furlong chute at the southwestern end. These created longer straightaways in the starts for a mile or seven furlongs, somewhat reducing the dangerous bunching up of horses as they rounded the first turn. The track officials were starter C. J. Fitzgerald, judges C. McDowell and Charles Pettingill, handicapper Vosburgh, timer W. H. Barretto, paddock judge J. L. Hall, paddock judge and clerk of scales Algernon Daingerfield.

The crowd? For them, Leavitt moved Walbaum's whole grandstand. It was cut in three, then those sections, the clubhouse, betting ring, and field stand shifted 400 feet to the west, closer to the track, and rotated counterclockwise a bit. Two additions built between the grandstand sections lengthened it by half, from 418 to 556 feet, and increased its capacity from five to six thousand. They sat on new raised seats facing south-southeast, and the late afternoon sun no longer hit them in the face.

The grandstand included a reconstructed ground floor with more air and light, a renovated café, dining room and new kitchen, a telegraph room, secretary's office, and gates to be lowered in bad weather. The lengthened Walbaum roof was the thing for those who would love the place going on a century later. Supported by wooden trusses, this single slate roof was trimmed in dark red stain and bottle-green paint. Walbaum's late Victorian motif was preserved and came to define the racetrack look, with its three pointy towers at the center and one at each end, these steeples each topped by a gilded finial. Because this strong feature has been saved, Professor Kettlewell wrote, "what everyone says may well be true, that the racetrack at Saratoga Springs is the most beautiful in the world."[16] Architectural historian Nancy Stout added, "In terms of design, nearly all the other American Thoroughbred tracks repeat something of Saratoga."[17]

There was the flaw, however. Spotted by a group of women tourists, it revealed what had been lost in the transition of sports from private pleasure to mass entertainment. The women talked to a reporter, who promptly exposed this built-in "blemish," which would be only partially resolved by word-of-mouth, radio, and television: "The finish line is placed at the extreme west end of the grandstand, where it joins the clubhouse, so that but a select few can see the finish." Little did the reporter imagine that one day millions would tune in to secondhand sports, rarely experiencing the real thing. Or go to the tracks and settle for watching it all on little monitors strung about the grounds.[18]

*　　*　　*　　*

Actually, the grandstand view had been improved by raising the clubhouse roof five feet. The barn of a clubhouse had "a handsome ladies' parlor" on the left side of the stairway, a buffet opposite it, and offices and a "culinary department" above. Three dormer windows projected from its steep roof fore and aft. Its trademark was the two-story front porch overlooking the finish line. It extended east and west, Queen Anne style, to form two circular ends, each with a coned, pointy roof of its own. The clubhouse was the kingdom of the association officers and members, the former now including, besides Whitney, Vice President F. R. Hitchcock, Secretary H. K. Knapp, Treasurer Andrew Miller and directors Wilson, Phil Dwyer, Perry Belmont (August's brother), Tommy Hitchcock, and W. W. Worden.

The races started at 2:15 P.M. This was the time poor Freddie Walbaum had thought up in the first place and for which he was roundly criticized. Instead of going to track in late morning and returning to a late afternoon or early evening dinner (with supper even later), Americans were wolfing down an ungodly "noon dinner" at the hotels. The sated procession got underway about 1:15 P.M. The start was also convenient for Albany, Troy, and other nearby people. The new program included six races, as did the New York tracks, instead of five.

The betting ring was enlarged by a twenty-five-foot overhang facing the course, its sides raised four feet to let in more light. A "monitor," or slit in the slanting roof, served the same purpose. The ring was 175 feet long by 90 feet wide and had a brick pavement leading to the elegant trackside lawn. It was not a bad layout for somebody like Pittsburgh Phil, who reportedly won $60,000 on just two horses in that 1902 season, Red Knight at 10 to 1 and Skillful at 8 to 1. Bet-a-Million Gates outdid that. He headed to the ring to drop $50,000 on High Chancellor at 12 to 1, but as he moved from one bookie to another, the odds dropped to even money. He still broke the record for winnings on a single race by doubling his fifty grand. That was nothing, as Gates himself would soon prove. To protect the locals from all this, two fences separated the ring from a field stand to the east, where seats cost just seventy-five cents.[19]

To the rear of the clubhouse, an immense saddling paddock, 240 by 72 feet, harbored twenty-five stalls; near the track entrance was a cottage for jockeys, the clerk of the scales, and other track officials. Two hundred feet west of the clubhouse was another field stand, just for jockeys, since they were not allowed in the grand-stand or the ring on working days. Eight-and-a-half-foot fences surrounded the prop-erty, which had been considerably enlarged to the south, the Association purchasing the land below Gridley Street. Stables for 370 horses were put up on the new property. Within this extension, too, along Nelson Avenue, was the delightful $75,000 private training park of August Belmont.

Belmont seemed to merit this place of honor not only as chairman of the Jockey Club and first among three equals on the state racing commission—the others were E. D. Morgan, Jr., and John Sanford, the General's son—but because it was an exten-sion of August I's historic stables on the south side of the track. Besides, Belmont and Whitney had become business allies in the subway battles. They were also Demo-cratic party cohorts, Belmont the son of a former chairman, Whitney the former campaign manager. Most dramatically, it was Saratoga, as always, that furnished a mellow meeting ground for sometime enemies. Belmont's digs even included quar-ters for Whitney, though Will was staying in a cottage at the States.

John "Bet-a-Million" Gates, at Saratoga with stable owner Charles E. Durnell. *Keeneland-Cook.*

This Belmont park had thirty-six stalls for racehorses, another stable for thirty-six yearlings, and a third for twelve polo ponies, but the most surprising feature was a lighted $10,000 tunnel. It led unsuspecting victors from Nelson Avenue into the infield of a half-mile track, set in a retreat of trees and vines. The track ran around a rustic cottage, the three stables, and a "cookhouse and dining room" for the help. The tunnel (still there) allowed Belmont and his visitors to come and go without disturbing the thoroughbreds as they worked, and the trainers used it to lead them to the main track. All in all, said a writer of the day, it was one of the finest training parks "of this or any other country."[20]

Across Nelson, abutting the later Raceway site, General Sanford began building his own extensive stables in 1902. It would include sheltered walking tracks for bad weather, stable manager and groom accommodations, and dining and kitchen facilities.[21] Saratoga was turning into a model again for a reviving industry, even as the reformers prepared to strike.

Local kids rated the place high, too. One was Frank Sullivan, later a writer in the *New Yorker* magazine stable. "The racetrack was a playground made to order for youngsters," he reminisced. "It lent itself wonderfully to all sorts of games, especially those needing plenty of room. The horse barns provided unlimited hiding places, the steeplechase jumps served admirably as forts, and the harrows stored in the paddock in the off season made fine Roman chariots."[22]

Whitney and the Association planned a much bigger playground, partially inspired by two sales. For guess who was back in town? Morrissey's old partner, Charlie Reed, selling yearlings from his Fairview Stud in Tennessee, including ten by costly St. Blaise. His sale was run by Fasig Tipton, soon to be part of the landscape. Charlie got only $23,500 for twenty-seven head, but that sale and another by Mackay inspired a grand design to establish here "the annual yearling sales of the great breeding establishments of Kentucky, Tennessee and California."

This idea of a national sale went off in Whitney's mind at the Mackay sale, said the *Thoroughbred Record*. The potential clientele was obvious, for the list of sixty owners who had won at least $700 at the 1902 meeting was extremely impressive. They included the Keenes, Haggin, Madden, the Sanfords, Joseph Widener, heir to the Philadelphia meat-supply and street-railway fortune, and the Canadians J. E. Seagram and J. Fleischmann, plus many more besides the Whitneys and the Belmonts. "Everyone who amounted to anything in the horse world, or who ever hoped to, was present" at the Mackay sale, the *Record* observed. They needed something to do. "There is nothing to do here of mornings except to drink water." A further draw was the fact that this was still "the regular meeting place of the Eastern and Western stables, and as such attracts Western horsemen who can not conveniently get to the Sheepshead Bay and Gravesend meetings in the early Spring." To fund the project, the Association expected to have an $80,000 to $100,000 surplus at season's end after paying a 5 percent dividend to stockholders and distributing $231,135 among winning owners, a daily average of $10,506.

The Association planned stables across Union Avenue near Horse Haven to house nine hundred yearlings and a three-quarter-mile straightaway to break them. The stalls would be let to breeding and auction companies, and buyers could use all the Saratoga tracks after the summer meeting to exercise their purchases. Construction would be financed by the gate from the crowds expected at the sales. Whitney quickly paid a reported $40,000 for the land surrounding and including Horse Haven, amounting to 120 acres east of East Avenue. As it turned out, the training track, in use by 1904, became not merely a straightaway but a one-mile course, one of the unsung early morning splendors of Saratoga. This area north of Horse Haven was soon nicknamed "Oklahoma," supposedly because somebody said it was that far from the main track. East of Horse Haven, Whitney planned a big frame building for the recreation of the track's seasonal employees, who now numbered nearly a thousand. It would have the then fashionable "natatorium"—an indoor swimming pool.

★   ★   ★   ★

"America has never had a resort that equalled Saratoga," said the *Tribune*, raving again. "There is no place like it and none can ever replace it." Actually, Hot Springs in Arkansas was rather like it and that same year added its own beautiful racecourse, Oaklawn Park, still thriving, but Whitney's money had indeed restored Saratoga's confidence and class, its stature and excitement. In addition to the track and golf, there was "an improved polo field" and a new "magnificent speedway for the autocratic trotter and his gentleman driver." For the horse was "the thing" here, as another reporter noted, and he was still creating the language of the future.

"Speedway" was the fashionable new term for a drag strip, a tradition that dated to colonial America. Saratoga's, built in 1902 along Fifth Avenue extended, on the northern edge of the training grounds, was tremendously popular. A Judge Griffiths of Troy and James Shevlin of Brooklyn were about to match their "roadsters" (the term being applied to horses first) in a contest that was lathering up their friends. As one reporter was pleased to observe, the Speedway had "driven 'automobiling' to the background." The few automobiles in town were "a nuisance, and gentlemen who drive high-spirited teams dread to meet them." Nevertheless, a local merchant advertised: "Have Your Photograph Taken in Your Own Automobile—No Extra Charge for the Machine." They all stood in line for their chance to don a "mobe" cap, grab the lever, and hold still.[23]

With Victor Herbert and fifty members of the Pittsburgh Symphony playing the Grand Union, and Gartland's Tenth Regiment Band booked with a list of tenors, sopranos, and contraltos at Congress Park, the Springs was also, as a magazine phrased it, "the summer music capital," a performing arts center before they called them that. John Philip Sousa brought his band to the park, Enrico Caruso came, and the singer-actor Chauncey Olcott, who had written the tearjerker "My Wild Irish Rose," not only came but stayed. His home and garden, with a thatched-roof cottage, survives on Clinton Street, opposite Skidmore College. Lillian Russell and Diamond Jim were still seen around town.

All of this happened at a forgotten pace. One of Sullivan's classmates, Monty Woolley, son of the Grand Union's manager and the future movie actor who became "The Man Who Came to Dinner," remembered, "Even the weather was warmer. God, what a lovely time it was to live!"[24]

The throbbing heart of the place was Canfield's Club House.[25] The biggest faro game in history was played in that summer of '02 at Canfield's, "the greatest gambling asset the United States has ever known," to repeat Asbury's assessment of 1938. Before accompanying Bet-a-Million Gates to his game, though, it might be good to catch up on his host.

*   *   *   *

Canfield was pouring everything into the Spa. His Manhattan operation had reached its peak in late 1899, when he opened the Saratoga Club at 5 East Forty-fourth Street, Gotham's biggest gambling house ever. For two years, it was the home away from home of:

• horsemen Phil Dwyer, who lost $90,000 at roulette on one occasion, and John Drake, son of an Iowa governor;
• the sitting senator Edward Wolcott, (R.-Colo.), who sometimes sat gambling for a couple of days and nights nonstop and who would actually die in heaven, Monte Carlo;

Lil Russell, at the Spa with banker Jesse Lewisohn in 1906. Reportedly ordered by his doctor to choose between Lil and his health, he chose his health. *National Museum of Racing and Hall of Fame, Saratoga Springs.*

● State Sen. Patrick McCarren of Brooklyn, who once dropped $100,000 at faro;

● Reggie Vanderbilt, the Commodore's great-grandson, Gertrude's brother, and Gloria's father, who ran up a $300,000 IOU at Canfield's but did not, as unfairly reported, celebrate his twenty-first birthday by losing $70,000 there (he did that at Davy Johnson's); and

● Gates himself, who made his fortune the old-fashioned way, in the market, and would soon control the Louisville and Nashville Railroad before selling out to J. P. Morgan for $1 million.[26]

The only joint approaching Canfield's was the House with the Bronze Door, 33 West Thirty-third Street, run by Freddie Walbaum, who had found his true vocation, and a few friends.

Strangely, the crusader who drove Canfield out of Manhattan and for a time shut down Walbaum and everybody else was descended, spiritually and literally, from three of the greatest sportsmen of their day. This was "the minister's son" in reverse.

"It's a boy, Billy," said Larry Jerome, Leonard's brother, over steak, oysters, and champagne. A waiter had brought the news: Larry's last son had been born that night, April 18, 1859. Of course, the nineteenth-century father did not hover nervously about the delivery room. "Only when the infant achieved a recognizable human shape," wrote this baby's biographer, "did the American male begin to consider it worthy of his attention." Father got the news at Delmonico's.

"What's his name?"

Inspired, Larry looked at his friend and said, "William Travers Jerome."[27]

First as judge, then as district attorney, William Travers Jerome became the first great prosecutor of the century in New York, the nemesis of the gamblers. Canfield, his biggest target, so feared him he closed 5 East Forty-fourth Street on New Year's Eve, 1901, and never reopened. Jerome thought he was operating on the sly and continued to harass him.

Cornered in Manhattan, the country's most famous gambler expanded in Saratoga in 1902. Here, "Canfield still owned the most profitable gambling property in the United States," as Asbury put it, one far more elegant than anything Las Vegas would ever see. He threw an estimated $1 million into improvements. In the public gaming room, the smaller building to the east, he installed the largest seamless carpet yet made, measuring seventy-two by forty-four feet, woven for $10,000 at the Templeton Mills in Glasgow, Scotland, and brought to town on two flatcars. It was set off by massive chandeliers and mirrors, statuettes in armor and marble-topped tables, roulette wheels made of hickory and ivory, and ivory chips, too.

Expanding, he rounded as he aged. Now forty-seven, five feet eight, and about two hundred pounds, he added a corset to his wardrobe as he picked up forty more. Clean shaven, with heavy jowls, he smoked too much and sometimes got drunk on wine, but he never gambled and would not let his employees, either, according to Asbury. He spent his evenings at the Club House, but avoided the gaming rooms and the track; they could come to him.

Canfield's Club House was still for all practical purposes a track annex. When Bet-a-Million Gates lost $375,000 on the horses one day in 1902, he naturally headed there to recoup at faro—and make history. Indeed, if the puritans were right, it would be hard to underestimate faro's importance in history, for they said it was the ruin of thousands. Perhaps it was even a blessing that women were banned from casinos and their faro tables. Where might the country be if Susan B. Anthony, when she attended meetings in Saratoga, had slipped off to "fight the tiger" at faro? Actually, the reason faro spread so fast in the nineteenth century, and was rejected so fast by the houses of the 1930s, was that it offered a better percentage than other games. Bet-a-Million began his struggle in the first-floor public room. It offered two to four faro layouts and eight to ten roulette wheels. Also on the first floor was the office, with Morrissey's six-by-nine-foot, four-combination safe, where Canfield stashed $1 million, for emergencies only since the winners accepted checks. A reader and art connoisseur, considerably more accomplished than Spencer in both domains, Canfield also maintained a library of rare books in his office, soothed by the light of a $10,000 Tiffany window.

How did America play the card game called faro? Gates gazed upon a layout that displayed pictures of the thirteen cards in one suit, usually spades, though only the denomination counted. A deck was shuffled, cut, and placed in the dealing box, faces up. Gates put his chips on the picture of any denomination he thought might come up a winner. He could choose one or more. He could bet against cards, too, placing the proverbial copper disk, or penny, on top of his chips on any denomination he thought would be a loser. Gates, $375,000 in the hole at the track, now began his meeting with fate. The exposed first card didn't count and was turned over. The second always counted as a loser, the third as a winner. That ended the turn, and the house collected any bets on the second card or paid if Gates had coppered it. It also paid if Gates had played the third card but collected if he had coppered it. So it went, turn by turn.

After losing heavily in the first few turns at the house limit of $1,000 per bet, Gates suggested they move upstairs. Here they plunged at a faro box and two roulette wheels. (Apparently the house never offered the game named after Canfield, a form of solitaire.) The limit for Gates was hiked to $5,000. He kept losing. By ten that night, he was out $150,000 on top of his track losses, more than half a million dollars. America had never seen anything like it. He went downstairs to ask Canfield to raise the limit again, to $10,000. Canfield agreed, and supposedly added, sarcastically, "Are you sure that's enough?"

"Betting from five to ten thousand dollars at every turn of the cards," Asbury reported, Gates played through. "Two hours after midnight he had won back the $150,000 lost in the early evening, and at dawn when he quit playing, he had won another $150,000, and so had cut the day's losses to the comparatively modest sum of $225,000."[28]

Richard A. Canfield sucked a half a million dollars out of Saratoga in a month and a half in 1902, which helped him pay for an expansion under the talented hands of New York architect Clarence Luce. Like most gourmets, the host was determined that others should eat well, so he spent some $200,000 on a rear wing for a new dining room—his crowning achievement, as local historian Eugene O'Connor noted. Octagonal stained-glass windows were set like jewels in a vaulted ceiling, twelve studded with signs of the Zodiac. They sparkled above a shining hall flanked by white columns and arches. A glow emanated from somewhere behind the archways and cooled air from the basement, thanks to Luce's very early indirect lighting and air-conditioning.[29]

It was nothing less than the finest restaurant in the country in one writer's estimation—"one of the truly great eating places in the world." Chef Jean Columbin was paid $5,000 for the season, then dispatched to Europe to improve his menu. The fifty waiters were given $1 a day plus rail fare from New York but averaged another $50 in daily tips. The restaurant was so lavish that even though it took in $5,000 a day, it still lost money. On one occasion, Whitney didn't help. He told Canfield he had heard a charming dinner orchestra in Paris and offered to install it here at his own expense. Canfield was flattered but wouldn't hear of such generosity. He sailed to Paris himself and brought them back, spending some $30,000, only to find out they had already been playing at a restaurant on Sixth Avenue for four years. The owner usually came out ahead. Once, George Kessler, a wine supplier, lost $28,000 at Canfield's and at first refused to pay. Canfield stopped taking his wine; Kessler paid.

Saratoga was inventing modern times again. The Club House kitchen supposedly first came up with that very American dinner on the run—meat, condiment, vegetable, salad, bread, *pourquoi pas un fromage*? The Club sandwich. Already having invented the chips on the side.[30]

The gambler bought the adjoining hillside in 1902. This ended the hilltop "Indian Encampment," which had charmed tourists for decades with craft sales and exotic forest games but had become a shantytown. He tore down cottages along Putnam Street behind the Club House. He ordered Luce to convert his ten acres behind Congress Hall, between East Congress and Spring streets, into an Italian garden for his Italianate palace. Luce brought it alive with formal flower beds, a pine grove, winding paths, hidden nooks, classical columns, and statuary imported from Florence. Two seated marble Tritons, nicknamed Spit and Spat, sprayed water at each other in an oblong pool (and survived the vandals, delighting children and grownups ever since). He had promised the most beautiful casino in North America and he delivered.

Canfield's 1902 profits also helped for his vacation the next year in England, where he bought paintings, saw his friend, the American expatriate James Whistler, and sat for his portrait. "Whistler's Mother" would become a symbol of maudlin American sentimentality—Freud on the farm—but now the painter showed this was not his fault by jokingly dubbing his unfinished picture of the gambler "His Reverence." No matter how many books or paintings they amassed, casino operators got no respect. Not only did Jerome continue to believe, mistakenly, that Canfield was operating in Manhattan, but the puritans were closing in again on Saratoga. By 1903, as the local antigambling movement was reawakening, Canfield kept his magnificent gaming rooms open but their magnificent doors closed. Seeing he was in trouble, a group of wealthy investors, including Whitney, Wilson, Belmont, Keene, Sanford, Gates, and Clarence Mackay, reportedly tried, not to help, but to buy a section of Congress Park to build a rival casino. They couldn't get a clear deed.[31]

It was then, in the midst of Saratoga's, and America's, splashiest gambling era that W. C. Whitney became one of the true founders of contemporary sports. The good times did not prevent him from imparting what *Harper's Weekly* called a "classic dignity to sport," while baseball was still trying to get organized. The American and National Leagues staged their first modern World Series in 1903, but then chaos returned, wiping out the series. Albert Spalding, former pitcher, promoter, and president of the "Largest Sporting Goods House in America," that year contested the claim that baseball had evolved from rounders and cricket. He said it was purely American, and he called for a commission to prove it. Headed by National League president A. G. Mills, the commission invited the whole country to send in information. Had anyone seen anyone founding baseball? The opinion of Ballston Spa's Abner Doubleday on all of this was unknown as he remained confined to his ten-year-old grave. In the meantime, the restoration of Saratoga hinted at a "Golden Age" of sports, and Will never stopped working on the foundation, whose building blocks included many new events.[32]

The country's most famous two-year-old test, the Hopeful, made its Saratoga debut in 1903. It was fairly rich, worth $22,275, compared with the $8,150 won by the filly Ada Nay in the Travers that year, and its name nicely captured the state of the owners. It would prove prophetic, counting among its victors Regret, Man o' War, Whirlaway, Native Dancer, Nashua, Jaipur, Buckpasser, Secretariat, Affirmed, Foolish Pleasure, Chief's Crown, and Summer Squall. It was only one of many tests for twos at the time, including Saratoga's Flash, which Remorseless inaugurated in 1869; the Spina-way, begun in 1881; and the Saratoga Special, from 1901. The event's pregnant name is more ancient in this country than modern records indicate, since two-year-old tests called the Hopeful were major events at Jerome Park and Memphis in 1869. One of Frank Morris's unnamed chestnuts by his imported Eclipse beat Tom Bowling in the Monmouth Hopeful in 1872. That was hardly prophetic, but when James R. Keene's Delhi captured the Spa's inaugural three-quarter-mile Hopeful, it was, as will soon be seen, an auspicious occasion.

And who has heard of the Saratoga Derby? America began borrowing the name Derby very early to designate a premier event for three-year-olds. Its first, the Jersey Derby, got off at Paterson at the height of the Civil War with a field greater than the first Kentucky Derby's eleven years later. Norfolk dealt his half-brother Kentucky his only loss in that 1864 event. Not long after the Kentucky classic began in 1875, derbies blossomed, the most celebrated being the American Derby at Chicago. In 1904, the Spa tried on its own, and Keene's Delhi made good on his promise by taking that inaugural, too, plus Saratoga's Great Republic, the Belmont, and three other events in ten starts that year, and the Brooklyn Handicap the next. As for the Saratoga Derby, Sydney Paget's Cairngorm would win the second, and Diamond Jim's Accountant paid off in the third and last in 1906.[33]

*　　*　　*　　*

Whitney's role in the revival of racing reached beyond the Spa. Unlike the Dwyers, who tried to buy proven winners, Whitney actually believed in the Improvement of the Breed of Horses, if not primarily for the horses' sake. Tod Sloan said Whitney "loved the sport for its own sake as much as any man I have ever known." In 1903, he churned out another seminal book—"the most elaborate thoroughbred catalogue ever compiled in the U.S."[34] The *Whitney Stud Book* listed his stallions and mares with seven-cross pedigrees plus racing and produce records back to the eleventh dam. It expounded his breeding theories, notably an extension of Count Lehndorff's argument that top race mares make the best broodmares. Practicing what he preached, Whitney wound up with eighty-one mares at La Belle Farm, including fifty-nine winners, 39 percent of them stakes winners, which historian Dan Bowmar called unparalleled for a stud of that size. Whitney's theory flew in the face of another rule, which said race mares actually made poor broodmares, but he made it work. After Hurley Burley had won nine out of thirteen races for trainer-owner Sam Hildreth, he sold her to Whitney, who mated her with Hamburg, which produced the hippo-like, thirteen hundred-pound Burgomaster, who went on to eat seven stakes.[35]

Whitney now showed how sports brought rivals together, as an outlet, a blood-less metaphor, a very American secret missed by historians. He, August Belmont, Tommy Hitchcock, E. D. Morgan, and J. P. Morgan bought 650 acres on Long Island, where they planned to build America's greatest sports facility yet. To many, Long Island looked like the future. In 1903, for instance, a group called the Metropolitan Jockey Club opened a track at Jamaica, which had a nine thousand-seat grandstand and was known as "the people's track." Robertson pointed out that because of its egg-shaped track, the finish line was on a slant, which made it hard to tell the winner. "Unless a horse won by five lengths or more, the official result invariably was greeted by howls of protest."[36]

Whitney and Belmont had something else in mind. It was they, Bowmar wrote, who insisted on a huge property, and "it was Whitney who suggested that the plant be called Belmont Park, in honor of the first August Belmont." In 1905, after a decade at Morris Park in the Bronx, the Westchester Racing Association, headed by August II and Keene, moved to its spread near Floral Park in Queens. Costing a reported $2.5 million, it had a 650-foot grandstand, a fabulous clubhouse, a one-and-a-half-mile track—still the largest track in the United States—with a seven-furlong straightaway, and a one-mile training track. One writer claimed it was due to Whitney's English bias that they decided to race clockwise, which they did until 1920. In any event, when, on May 4, 1905, they opened Belmont Park, Whitney was there only in spirit.[37]

He had died in New York on February 2, 1904, of complications from appendicitis. He was sixty-two. Harry and Dorothy were there, Harry so distraught he would not leave his room for three days. Payne arrived too late but made the funeral. Pauline was on her way back from England. Whitney's once dear friend, Oliver Payne, did not appear. The loss was deeply felt in government, politics, and business. The navy flew its flags at half staff, and former president Cleveland declared that Whitney had "more calm, forceful efficiency than any man I ever knew." The future secretary of state, Elihu Root, called it "a great misfortune for the Democratic party," and some thought Whitney the one man who could have beaten Teddy Roosevelt that year.[38]

To the public, he was simply a rich man, a transportation millionaire who owned many homes, including his last townhouse, 871 Fifth Avenue at Sixty-eighth, and vast lands, notably a game preserve consisting of seventy thousand acres and fifty-two lakes in the Adirondacks; a rich man who raced horses and was lucky enough to have heard, not long before he died, his own best epitaph. It was read at a party at Sherry's by his friend Finley Peter Dunne.

In Old New York there lives a man
        of very great renown,
Who owns a palace in, and forty
        houses out of town;
He owns the tunnels, owns the cabs,
        and owns the trolleys, too,
And if you get run over, why the only
        man to sue
        is Mr. Whitney!
        "Who was that hit me?
Pick me up and take me down to old
        Bellevue,
        An' Mr. Whitney
        Will come an' get me
For I'm the only man that bet on
        Ballyhoo!"[39]

 *16*

SYSONBY AND COLIN

H̲E̲ ̲W̲A̲S̲N̲'̲T̲ as rich as everybody thought. He had retired early and disposed of many of his transportation holdings. He wasn't nearly as rich as his partner, whose middle name was money. Thomas Fortune Ryan lived up to it, too, with holdings of $125 million. But then W. C. Whitney, as they say, wasn't poor, either. His biographer reported that he left $21 million, including $9 million in American Tobacco Company holdings. The latter were a reminder of a foray by Whitney and Ryan into James Buchanan Duke's empire, although Whitney's profit from it was only $1.5 million. Half of his $21 million went to eldest son Harry, the Yale Phi Beta Kappa and aggressive investor who would triple that inheritance. Three-tenths went to Dorothy, and only one-tenth each to the disaffected Payne and Pauline, who were, after all, Oliver Payne's heirs apparent.[1]

Whitney left America's most cherished racetrack in capable hands. Francis Hitchcock was elected president, Harry Payne Whitney vice president, and Andrew Miller secretary-treasurer. The directors included Wilson, Tommy Hitchcock, Jr., Phil Dwyer, Perry Belmont, Knapp, Mackay, W. W. Worden, J. H. Alexandre, J. A. Bradford, and J. G. Hechscher.

Will's own racing interests totaled $1.5 million. Most of his runners were leased to Herman Duryea for 1904, taking him to the top of the list with $200,107. They included the Hamburg filly Artful, who gave Will posthumous revenge over Keene and his great Sysonby in the Futurity, and her stable partner Tanya, who won both the second Hopeful and the Spinaway. Their success riveted attention on the sale of the Whitney stud, which got underway dramatically in October. Hamburg was led first into the sawdust ring at the Fourth Avenue end of Madison Square Garden.[2]

"'What will you give me, gentlemen?'

"There was a deathlike stillness for a moment," noted a reporter, "and the crowd looked in the direction of Harry Payne Whitney, who sat beside his racing partner, Herman B. Duryea. Mr. Whitney said, '$50,000.'

"'$60,000', cried Milton Young."

"'$70,000', cried Whitney."

This was the last bid. The sales of Will's yearlings, race horses, and breeding stock totaled $618,750, the highest since the dispersal of August Belmont's. They would have topped Belmont's $639,500 if Harry had not privately bought most of his father's 1904 and 1905 yearlings.

The son was headed for an even greater career at the track than that of his father.

Madden said Harry had few if any equals in spotting a future winner. In 1905, the first year he raced under his own name, and in his father's brown and blue, he won $174,447, second only to Keene's $228,724. His winners included Artful, who won all three of her starts in eleven days; Tanya, who won the Belmont; and Hamburg's Burgomaster, one of the yearlings Harry got from his father's estate. Big Burgomaster ate up the Flash and United States Hotel tests at Saratoga and three other stakes at two, then the Belmont at three. Harry finished third in earnings in 1906 with $83,570, then second with $137,694 in 1907, and he was just getting started.

Canfield, on the other hand, was in trouble again. The season after Whitney's death, Jerome pushed through a law under which New York City gambling-house customers could be jailed for refusing to testify. Even though Canfield still was not operating in the city, he was under indictment as a common gambler and very much afraid he could wind up in Sing-Sing because Jerome knew he had been jailed years ago in Rhode Island. Canfield was so scared he shut down his Saratoga casino, including the restaurant, although the racing officials begged him to open. To compensate, they opened the track clubhouse at night for the last several weeks of the season, for whatever sad sport the patrons could dream up. Finally, late in 1904, apparently convinced that Canfield's Manhattan house really had not been operating, Jerome let him off with a $1,000 fine and closed the case.

In 1905, Saratoga's eight main houses, including Canfield's and the new Whist Bridge Club on Phila Street, all opened, but they had to close by 2 A.M. Some of the plungers were scared away by the thought that Jerome's law might be used here, and on top of that there were bomb threats. One crude device, apparently planted by a crank, actually went off outside one of Canfield's private dining rooms. Extra guards were put on for the rest of the season, and Canfield cleared $200,000. In 1906, his place, the Manhattan Club, and the United States Club were allowed to operate, but with the doors to the gaming room closed. Canfield opened on August 6, as allowed. But the next day the governor suddenly ordered the sheriff to shut down every joint in the county.

It was the beginning of the end. "Canfield immediately removed all gaming apparatus from the building," wrote Asbury, "and except for a few days in 1907, when the restaurant was open, and an occasional game was played in a private room upstairs, the whir of the Roulette wheel and the click of the Faro casekeeper were heard no more in the Club House which for forty years had been one of the great gambling establishments of the world."[3] They were not heard in the other houses, either. Gambling equipment was banned in Saratoga Springs, though the wheels would spin again one day at the lake. Canfield sold the Club House to the village for $150,000 in 1910 and auctioned off the furnishings. Its last host died of a skull fracture from a fall in the Fourteenth Street subway station on December 11, 1914. He was 59.

Richard Canfield was "the richest professional gambler in all history" when he closed his Saratoga place, Asbury noted. His $13 million included $8 million in Wall Street profits and $5 million from gambling, about half of it from Saratoga. He got clobbered, however, when the market collapsed in 1907, and he left an estate worth only $841,485. Today the Historical Society of Saratoga Springs maintains the place, which has long been called simply the Casino, in silent splendor. An unhinged little cast-iron gate at a corner of Congress Park displays the monogram RAC. Even if they noticed it, not many would know who he was—a figure on the scale of John Morrissey, Commodore Vanderbilt, W. C. Whitney. Nor was anyone's memory jogged by the gift he left to local friends, according to Eugene O'Connor. It was a parrot. Nobody could figure out why the parrot kept saying, over and over, "Arthur!" Did the parrot know yet another Canfield story?

In the meantime, Whitney's rival was back. J. R. Keene's comet lit up the American sky for thirty years, then disappeared forever. He made his first fortune speculating in mining and railroad stocks in San Francisco, then, as mentioned earlier, came east, bought his first horse, Spendthrift, and set out to break the Lorillards' grip on racing. From various accounts, Keene was as mean as he looked—beady eyes, gaunt face, jutting nose, and goatee—but this was the East, and Jay Gould warned, "Keene came east in a private car—I'll send him back in a box car."[4]

He did, in effect. Keene got trapped in a move to corner the Chicago wheat market in 1884, and Gould destroyed him. Inside six years, though, Keene was back on the street, helping William Havemeyer control the sugar market and on his way to becoming America's most sensational broker, out just for the thrill of the deal. On the side, he spearheaded formation of the Jockey Club, established Castleton Stud in Kentucky, and won the 1893 Futurity with Domino. The colt's $170,790 and Keene's $279,458 that year were both still records when Whitney died.

Off the track, Keene had made himself Whitney's worst enemy. First, he actually joined Whitney and Ryan in a move to grab more of American Tobacco, only to defect and sell out to Oliver Payne, all of people. One of American Tobacco's incorporators said Ryan and Whitney were out to capture "Buck" Duke's company and that Whitney never forgave Keene. With the battle in the open, Keene backed the Third Avenue railway in 1900 to try to keep Metropolitan from getting it. He got caught short-selling the Third, however, with Ryan himself the secret buyer. Ryan pushed up the price again and demanded Keene cover his sales. It was a suddenly soft-hearted Whitney who actually talked him out of ruining Keene. Will got his kicks, though, as Ballyhoo Bey beat the Keene trio in the Futurity that year.[5]

Keene remained a major turf power over the next few years, and with Whitney dead, he was right back on top. He led the owners from 1905 through 1908. His winners and some of their triumphs: Peter Pan (the Flash, Hopeful, and Belmont); Court Dress (Spinaway); Maskette (Spinaway, Futurity); Helmet (Hopeful); and Ballot (Great Republic).

★   ★   ★   ★

James R. Keene presented the twentieth century with its first two all-time champions. There was Sysonby, with an English pedigree. His dam, Optime, was already in foal to Melton when Keene bought her from the late Marcus Daly's English stud in 1901. It was Keene's son Foxhall who named the colt after his own English hunting lodge. Vosburgh, the handicapper, looked at Sysonby, a light bay, and saw a large head, a muscular neck, a massive body, and a huge stride, "with which no horse could

Sysonby winning the Great Republic. Oiseau second, Broomstick third. *Keeneland-Cook.*

contend." In walking, "the average race horse rarely does more than slightly overstep the print of his forefoot. Sysonby cleared it, showing the wonderful leverage of his hind leg, which in galloping must have given him enormous propulsion. . . . Sysonby appeared a superhorse." He was perhaps the first American athlete to earn that designation.[6]

At two, the superhorse was at the Spa. He took the Flash and the Saratoga Special while racking up five wins in six starts for 1904. Foxhall Keene claimed that the single loss, to Artful in the Futurity, came only after Sysonby was doped by a groom. In any event, the colt was such a sensation that year that turf historians would all but forget Belmont's filly Beldame, who won twelve out of fourteen, including the Alabama by four lengths, the Saratoga Cup by six, and four more in a row. All field glasses were on Sysonby. He began his third year by conceding one year and ten pounds to Race King and still ran him to a dead heat. After that, he carried J. R. Keene's white jacket with blue spots to six straight wins. Then came one of the races of the century, and one of those Saratoga starts.

*   *   *   *

August 12, 1905. The $50,000 mile-and-a-quarter Great Republic Stakes would start in front of the betting ring. Foxie Keene was sure the gamblers were out to get Sysonby that day. He had never even been headed, except in the dubious Futurity, and now they saw a killing. "Chief among this cabal," said Foxie, was Diamond Jim Brady, who owned Oiseau, "a colt capable of a tremendous burst of speed. . . . He entered

James B. "Diamond Jim" Brady. A Spa regular. *Keeneland-Cook.*

Oiseau and ordered Redfern, his jockey, to get out ahead at all costs." Brady didn't seem to care who won. As long as Sysonby was beaten, fat, excitable Jim would be jumping up and down as he did when his own horse came through.

Canfield himself was there, an extremely rare event, for it was said that the king of the Club House never appeared at the track. He was rumored to have $30,000 on Oiseau. "Syse" was going off at 2 to 5, Oiseau 3 to 1, and Capt. Sam Brown's Broomstick (the Travers winner), Prince Hamburg, and Dandelion "at any price you wanted." Foxie, his leg in a cast, was on crutches, but now he lost them and wouldn't realize it for fifteen minutes.

A postcard photographer caught the scene as starter Mars Cassidy stood on a platform on the infield side and prepared to spring the barrier net, but the photographer apparently missed the next second or so, when Mars did spring the barrier. Who would want to watch it through a little hole in a camera?

Disaster! Sysonby was turned sideways and left at the post. A groan went up from the crowd of twenty thousand. Dave Nicol swung Sysonby around and "gathered him up," but the rest were one hundred yards ahead as the big colt took off. Said Vosburgh, "He'll never catch them, everybody agreed."

But did Sysonby take off! Foxie said he ran the first three furlongs—660 yards and on a curve—in 32 ⅘ seconds, which would not be matched in three-furlong sprints for years. He caught them there and at the half-mile flew past Oiseau. Vosburgh: "People shook their heads. 'The effort was too great; he'll stop,' they said. But no; he drew away; Oiseau and Broomstick were racing for their very lives, but the great powerful strides of Sysonby kept him in the lead." He was coasting now, Nicol looking back at the victims.

"The cheering of the crowd as he came up the stretch was like roaring winds," and he won it by three lengths. "Never, in all the thousands of races I have attended," Foxie would write, "have I seen anything that even approached the scene as Sysonby came back to the judges' stand. The people were crazy. They almost mobbed him, and even after he had been taken back to his stall, thousands came to have another look him."

Vosburgh: "He won, amid a scene such as has seldom been witnessed at the historic ground where Kentucky, Harry Bassett, Longfellow, Kingfisher, Hindoo, Hanover, and Henry of Navarre had won their great triumphs."

Sysonby won fourteen of fifteen starts, including that dead heat, and $184,438 in two years. He was hailed as "the horse of the century," but in 1906 he died of an infection, in his stall at Sheepshead Bay. He was buried at that track before a crowd of four thousand, and later his bones were exhumed and displayed at the American Museum of Natural History in New York. They are still there now, in the research collection.

Then there was Colin, by Keene's Belmont winner Commando (best product of Domino). He was a brown colt, and Vosburgh, the ultimate expert in horseflesh, said he had a good-looking head, pricked ear, white stripe, and white hind and right fore pasterns.[7]

The trainer for both Colin and Sysonby was none other than Jimmy Rowe, who already had heard a lot of applause. More than thirty years earlier, he had ridden Harry Bassett to victory over Longfellow at Saratoga in one of the great races of all time, and now he was one of the greatest trainers of his day. One historian would declare him "the cement which held racing together during the shaky transitional period" at the turn of the century. Rowe would say he wanted only three words on his tombstone:

HE TRAINED COLIN.[8]

Colin had the century's first great jockey, on a level with Gilpatrick, Hawkins, and Murphy. Walter Miller had an amazing 1,348 mounts in 1906, when he became the first to win more than 300. His 388 included all five on the card on two occasions, at Brighton Beach on Coney Island and at Benning in Washington, D.C., plus the Alabama on the filly Running Water and the Travers aboard Wilson's Gallavant. In 1907, the year he took Colin's reins, he had 334 wins, including another five-race sweep at Oakland, five out of six at Benning, and the Saratoga Cup on Running Water. In those two years, Miller racked up a winning average of 28 percent.

Like Sysonby, Colin ran only fifteen races. At two, with Miller, he won the Futurity and appeared at Saratoga. The Springs was going strong even though another financial panic was around the corner, and they had to sneak in at night at Canfield's, and a rival meet was underway at the upstart Empire City track on the site of today's Yonkers Raceway. Colin was going strong, too. "His fame was so great already," said Vosburgh, "that for the Saratoga Special only Uncle opposed him." Then he added the Grand Union Hotel Stakes, going twelve for twelve that year in races Foxie Keene called "too dull to describe." Among the few who looked vaguely threatening was Belmont's Fair Play, who won the Flash that year.[9]

Colin's 1907 earnings were $130,566, far below Domino's first season but not to be beaten by another two-year-old for twenty-one years. He helped Keene break his own mark as he became the first to exceed $300,000—with no less than $397,342—and he made Commando top sire with $270,345. The latter two records would stand for sixteen years, and Commando's average of $22,529 for twelve offspring that season would not be equaled until purses were inflated in the 1950s.[10]

In 1908, Colin won two straight, then went into the Belmont in a violent thunderstorm, and something strange happened. Despite a bowed tendon, Colin led all the way, and the crowd thought it was over at the usual finish line, where Joe Notter eased up on Colin. But it wasn't; there were fifty yards to the finish below the judges' stand, with Fair Play a desperate contender. Had Notter thought it over, too, or was he confused by the crowd, or by going clockwise? As it was, Colin barely edged Fair Play. Notter denied he was confused and said Colin had slowed because his leg hurt. Indeed, after another win, the leg forced him into retirement, with earnings of $181,610. Fair Play's revenge would be siring a colt as great as Colin—perhaps the greatest of all, Man o' War.

The rider Lucien Lyne would look back in 1947 and declare he had seen "only three colts that I thought were particularly outstanding. They were Sysonby, Colin, and Man o' War."[11]

Baseball was finding its feet. For example, a Charles Ebbets started buying up land in Flatbush in 1909 as a home for a team. And after getting a letter from an alleged boyhood friend and future mental patient, the Mills Commission had let it be known in early 1908 that Abner Doubleday devised the game at Cooperstown back in 1839. There was something appealing about it. The names Abner and Doubleday had charm, as did his Civil War career from Sumter to Gettysburg. For most of the century, children would be taught that he was a folk hero, another Johnny Appleseed, a Paul Bunyan. What American didn't know that Abner Doubleday invented baseball? They could have used it as a test question for German and Japanese spies. Suddenly, the experts no longer believe it. They are not even sure he was in Cooperstown at the time. They have gone back to the rounders-cricket explanation, although modern, organized baseball did have its own beginnings in the mid-1840s around Hoboken and New York City. The National Baseball Hall of Fame at Cooperstown is as appealing as ever, encrusted as it is with all of baseball's glories. Across the street from the National Museum of Racing and Hall of Fame at Saratoga Springs, however, Sysonby and Colin really did appear, although they, too, were hard to believe.[12]

Colin, Marshall Lilly up. *Keeneland-Cook.*

These were high-water years for racing's human athletes as well. After Miller, Notter and Vince Powers topped the "money won" and "wins" columns. In 1908, Notter's mounts took in an astounding $464,322, and Powers chalked up 324 wins. Notter's mark would hold till Earl Sande crashed through it in 1923, but Miller's and Powers's numbers would not be matched until Willie Shoemaker, Bill Hartack, and Tony DeSpirito did it more than four decades later. Other standouts included the Travers winners Willie Shaw (Blues, 1901; Dandelion, 1905) and Tommy Burns (Broomstick, 1904). There was suddenly something very different about the sport's human athletes.

Virtually all of them were white. Where were the African Americans? Just about gone. They were increasingly limited to training (if they were extraordinarily lucky) and exercising. There was Willie Simms, who had invested his winnings and was wealthy when he turned to training in 1902, settling in Asbury Park, N.J. The most famous exercise rider was Marshall Lilly, who wore his trademark derby even while working Colin. The few remaining black riders often found themselves harassed by the other jockeys. Historian Charles Parmer claimed it started in the jockey rooms when black riders got a little too cocky to suit their colleagues. "The white boys retaliated by ganging up against the black riders on the rails. A black boy would be pocketed, thrust back in a race; or his mount would be bumped out of contention on a white boy's stirrup, and toss him out of the saddle. . . . those white fellows would slash out and cut the nearest Negro rider. . . . they literally ran the black boys off the track."[13]

Jimmy Winkfield was one of the last of the all-time greats, never out of the money in four Derby starts. He finished third in 1900, then did an Ike Murphy with back-to-back wins on His Eminence in 1901 and Alan-a-Dale in 1902, this consecutive double matched by only Ron Turcotte and Eddie Delahoussaye in the next ninety

James Lee. *Keeneland-Cook.*

years. Winkfield nearly made it three in a row in 1903 when he moved early on Early, losing his lead to Judge Himes by less than a length. He was the fifteenth black winner in the Derby's first twenty-eight runnings, and the last. In 1904, supposedly after a feud with Madden, he moved to France, where he was a leading jockey for two more decades. He was estimated to have won twenty-three hundred races by the time he retired and then became a successful trainer, sending his mounts throughout the Continent.

People forget James Lee, the twenty-year-old from Raceland, Louisiana, who lit up the bluegrass in 1907 by winning the Clipsetta, Latonia Derby, Latonia Oaks, and Kentucky Oaks. He then made world racing history in June at Churchill Downs. Until then, only the legendary Fred Archer in England and the African-American William "Monk" Overton had gone six for six in one day, Archer in 1877 and again in 1882, and Overton at Washington Park in 1891. But on June 5, 1907, Jimmy Lee had an even better day, declining no races and winning his six on a six-race card: six for six for six. Albert Whittaker would top that by sweeping a seven-event card in New Zealand three years later, but the only American to match Lee's perfection would be H. Phillips at Reno in 1916.[14]

"The Black Demon," as they sometimes called Jimmy Lee, captured six more stakes in 1908, among them the forty-first Travers on Dorante, saddled by the black trainer Raleigh Colston. But no African-American jockey followed him to glory. They all but vanished after Jess Conley finished third in the 1911 Kentucky Derby aboard Colston, named after his trainer. In contrast to the first Derby, which had only one white, Conley was the only black rider in that year's Derby and the last for more than eight decades.

"The black rider was finished as far as big money was concerned," one later writer said, "and only a few hardy steeplechase jockeys remained through the 1940s."

*　　*　　*　　*

Big money was indeed a huge factor, as we have seen, starting in the 1890s. But it was not only at the tracks that African-Americans' destinies were shifting. The breakup of the Old South and the growth of the cities were producing a mass migration to urban areas, especially in the North. By 1910, most African Americans were living in or near cities, where they were rarely exposed to the rarefied world of horse racing. Turf writer Philip Von Borries even argued that the black rider was really not pushed out. "He simply moved away from the farms where he could learn his craft, into the urban areas where the main sports were baseball, football and basketball that required far less space." There was more to it than that. He did not just move away. The migration was hastened by the hopeless prospects of anyone left behind, by the headlines reporting countless lynchings in rural areas, and by stories of the night riders of the Klan.[15]

Even those already working at the tracks had no chance of becoming riders. "By 1910, racial discrimination had firmly set in, and the only jobs most blacks could obtain in racing were as exercise boys or grooms," wrote still another observer. "Some jockeys tried without success to become rider-owners while a few found employment as trainers and others went to Europe." The biggest owners might have been able to change it early on, but, like most others of all colors, they lacked that sort of tolerance or courage. Keene's racist attitudes would be cited casually years later by his son, with no apology. The tennis champion and brilliant sports historian Arthur Ashe, Jr., would sum it up in 1988: "The sport of horse racing is the only instance where the participation of blacks stopped almost completely while the sport itself continued—a sad commentary on American life. . . . Isaac Murphy, so highly admired during his time for his skills and character, would have been ashamed of his sport."[16]

Actually, a black rider was about to burst on the scene at the Spa. He was a steeplechaser, to be sure, but one of the greats.

Meantime, the victims of racism coped, and some made the best of it. A man at the Saratoga clubhouse took care of the field glasses that were left overnight. They knew him only by the name "Beaut," as if the place were a surviving plantation, but he developed an ingenious method of surviving. If a horse had an unbeatable lead as they raced down the stretch, he would slip into a room off the clubhouse porch, where he stored his personal collection of racing colors. Soon he reappeared, all smiles and draped in the winning hues to show the owner he had backed him all along. Everybody was in on it, obviously, but it got him big tips.[17]

Two final blows destroyed whatever hopes African Americans might have nursed to become regulation jockeys. Ironically, the first was delivered by an African American, and it left Tommy Burns on his rear end. Prizefighter Jack Johnson's rise to the top heightened racist tension across the country, with help from the headline writers. He beat Burns for the disputed world crown in Sydney in 1908 (*Chicago Record-Herald:* "Negro Floors White Man in Early Periods and Is Clever at Boxing

Game"), then made it unofficial by clobbering former champ Jim Jeffries at Reno on the Fourth of July, 1910 (Portland's *Sunday Oregonian*: "Crushing Defeat of White Giant, Black Proclaimed Champion, Race Riots Break Out After Fight"). Arthur Ashe tracked down a chilling record of those riots in the July 5 *New York Times*:

THREE KILLED IN VIDALIA [Georgia] . . . OMAHA NEGRO KILLED . . . TWO NEGROES SLAIN . . . BLACKS SHOOT UP TOWN . . . HOUSTON MAN KILLS NEGRO . . . NEGRO SHOOTS WHITE MAN . . . NEGRO HURT IN PHILADELPHIA . . . OUTBREAKS IN NEW ORLEANS . . . POLICE CLUB RIOTING NEGROES . . . MOB BEATS NEGROES IN MACON . . . 70 ARRESTED IN BALTIMORE . . . ALMOST LYNCH NEGRO

While Johnson wore his crown, the headlines continued. When he beat Frank Moran in 1914, the *Chicago Herald* blared, "Johnson is Victor over White Hope," and the *Oregonian*, "Great Ladies See Battle, Black's White Wife Gay.") To put it mildly, it was not a hospitable time for African Americans in sports. "The backlash against Johnson," according to one sports historian, "most assuredly affected the fate of the black jockey and all other black athletes."[18]

The other blow was the worst of all for everybody in racing. The reformers were back and targeting gambling at the tracks, which to those in the sport was the same as attacking racing itself. By 1908, the number of tracks already had fallen from 314 to 25, the reformers having shut down most of the major courses in every state but New York, Maryland, and Kentucky. New York was next, they warned. The fact that Governor Charles Evans Hughes was born just up the road in Glens Falls did not stop this future secretary of state and chief justice from zeroing in on Saratoga's leading amusement. He backed a draconian bill that would make it illegal for anybody to quote odds openly, solicit bets, or record bets in a fixed place. If that wouldn't kill New York racing, the heart of the industry, what would? The turf's biggest owner issued a counterwarning. "I shall retire from racing if this bill passes," threatened James R. Keene.[19]

It became law on June 11, 1908, and was an immediate disaster for the New York City tracks. The seasons of 1908, 1909, and 1910 were terrible failures, confirming for any doubters that New Yorkers had not been going out to Brooklyn and Long Island to look at beautiful animals, while at the same time business at the tracks in Maryland, Kentucky, and Canada improved.

Saratoga was different. Just as it had when street racing was banned in the 1820s, when trotters were posed as fair exhibits, and when Morrissey ignored the ban on pools in 1877, it got away with more. It was just an innocent vacation spot. As Hugh Bradley pointed out, "bookies and big bettors, living for a month in the same hotels, found it fairly convenient to bet in advance and collect at leisure." Besides, "people continued to come to the spa for vacations and, while there, continued to go out to see the horses run." In the bargain, Saratoga had other attractions that big-city tracks, lost in their urban or suburban wastelands, could not offer. It would teach the big city the lesson again eight decades later. Most reassuring of all, the country's most celebrated racetrack remained in good hands.[20]

By 1910, Richard T. Wilson had moved up to the presidency of the Association, with Harry Payne Whitney still vice president and Miller secretary-treasurer. Wilson was heir to an old Georgia fortune built on keeping the Confederate Army in cotton blankets and other supplies, and he had married an Astor. Wearing the casual-elegant racetrack uniform of the day, a stiff collar and beribboned straw boater, he proved a comforting and enduring presence in these difficult days and an able administrator. Francis Hitchcock stayed on as a director, and J. R. Keene himself joined the board, a touching final commitment.

As Keene confronted his shrinking world and prepared to exit, an unlikely champion rose. Not that Keene was done; among his best, Maskette had taken the Alabama, Hilarious the Travers, and Sweep the Futurity in 1909, that event's last year at Sheepshead Bay. Sweep (by Kentucky Derby winner Ben Brush) would win the 1910 Belmont, and Iron Mask the Grand Union Stakes. Now Sam Hildreth replaced Keene as top owner and stole the show from such social luminaries as Whitney, the Phi Beta Kappa polo player. If anyone had mentioned Phi Beta Kappa to Hildreth, he might have replied, "If you bet a couple of what?"

Hildreth's career soared over America's racetracks like a rock thrown by some kid, landing in a pile of manure, then burnishing slowly to gold. Born in Missouri, this son of a small-time horse trader and owner grew up on tracks across the country, finally becoming a respected trainer-owner. He lived and breathed racing, for better and for worse, and he called his memoirs *The Spell of the Turf*.

"If you have felt the spell of the race track and know what it means to hear the song of the bugle and to see the field go parading to the post, in single file past the judges' stand, with the smell of the stable and the fragrance of the flowers tingling in your vein . . . then you understand."[21]

Hildreth plunged on his horses, but when he brought his string to Walbaum's Guttenberg in 1889 and ran up a string of wins, it backfired. The bookies started giving him rotten odds. Then he met a sheepish-looking, soft-spoken man who could have been a bank teller but was a sheet writer for one of the books. This man offered himself to Hildreth as a betting agent. He was Jesse's brother. Frank James taught Sam Hildreth a lot about life, such as: don't take it. He said that when he was young, Civil War outlaws attacked his family, and he and Jess vowed then and there to get even with the world. And: never give up your gun. Frank repeated to Sam what he told the governor of Missouri when he finally came out of hiding. "I surrender. I surrender, and there's my gun. From the day I got it there's never a man except me had a hand on that gun before. It's the first time I haven't had it right where I could get it in a hurry when need be. If Jesse hadn't been so careless with his gun he'd be here today."

Also: keep your bets secret. The trick was to let Frank do the betting. None of the bookies would suspect it, and the odds would hold. Just before the horses went to the post, Frank would sidle by with his left hand in his overcoat pocket, or a handkerchief sticking out, to show Sam how much he was betting. The bookies were stumped. Why wasn't Sam betting? At night Frank would sneak down country roads and around trees and bushes to Sam's house, and they would total their accounts. He even brought the tickets for proof, since his friends the other sheet writers let him have them. It wasn't bank robbery, but it was probably the best work Frank could get.

Sam Hildreth was strolling through Saratoga in 1892 with the trainer Fred Burlew and a couple of pals when he ran into "the greatest prize that has ever come to me." It seemed to happen all the time at the Spa. After the time-honored whirlwind court-ship, Mary Cook was his. Stable owner Frank Farrell, who later also would own the New York Yankees, whisked them down to the city on the Albany boat, and they got hitched before a small and horsey crowd at the Church of the Holy Cross. Mary's guidance doubtless helped Sam climb steadily, until at last he succeeded Keene. He earned more than $150,000 in 1909 and again in 1910. It helped that he had the top jockeys for those years, Eddie Dugan and Carroll Shilling, respectively. Some thought hot-tempered Cal Shilling the best ever. Hildreth defined his perfection:

> an almost uncanny ability to break two-year-olds away from the post, judgement of pace that made you think he must have a stop watch ticking before your eyes, a seat so light that he was like a feather on a horse's back, and a knack for getting every ounce out of his mount, whether at the barrier, the half post or the finish. He was a master mechanic astride a horse, with natural riding instincts that his boyhood on the cattle ranches of Texas had brought to the utmost.

They watched that perfection on Dalmatian as he won the 1910 Travers (worth only $4,825, which was still twelve times more than the $400 Hildreth paid Perry Belmont for the colt.)

The performer Hildreth remembered best was two-year-old Novelty, who ar-rived at the Springs that season after four wins, two seconds, and a third in seven starts. Then Wilson's Naushon beat him in the United States Hotel Stakes and stood to do it again in the Saratoga Special. It was Saturday, August 13. In his clubhouse hideaway, Beaut prepared to slip into Wilson's yellow silks with green chevrons. If Naushon didn't win, though, the white with blue spots carried by Keene's Iron Mask certainly would. They had forgotten to tell all this to Novelty. Hildreth was on the clubhouse porch as his colt cruised home first, and he looked through a window to see Beaut frantically tearing off Wilson's colors and replacing them with the Hildreth black with white sash and blue sleeves. Hildreth and the others confronted him, but Beaut quickly explained that all the talk about Naushon had confused him. In the general hilarity, he got a bigger tip than usual.[22]

Novelty wasn't finished at the Spa, however. They were still putting on match races—the shoot-outs of the old days—and Novelty knocked off Tom Monahan's Textile at $5,000 a side, plus a silver cup offered by the association. He then won the third Hopeful, the Rensselaer, and the $25,360 Futurity, which had been moved up to Saratoga for the first time. Novelty led the country for the year with $72,630.

As for his rider, Shilling would register 969 wins in 3,838 starts for a brilliant .25 winning percentage. His career would have been much longer if hotheaded Cal had not slugged it out in a fist fight with another jockey as they dueled head to head in the stretch at the Havre de Grace, Maryland, track one day in 1912. He was sus-pended indefinitely, a suspension made permanent when his public battle with the turf establishment ended up in a riot at Pimlico in 1920. Ruled off for life, he hit the bottle and finally, in January 1950, one of the great athletes of his day was found dead of exposure under a van outside Belmont Park. No one who saw him ride ever forgot him.[23]

New York State racing, with Sam Hildreth at its summit, drew to a close in 1911. When the city tracks shut down that year, it was permanent for historic Sheepshead Bay, Gravesend, and Brighton Beach. It was obvious that Saratoga could not operate without the rest of the circuit so it, too, shut down, for the second time in its forty-eight-year history. This would turn out to be a less permanent change than several others at the Springs, many of them for the better.

Senator Brackett pushed through legislation in 1910 and 1911 to finance a Spa Reservation, the spectacular state park south of town, originally dedicated to "the Geysers" and their promise as America's greatest spa.

Lucy Skidmore Scribner, in 1911, began converting her Young Women's Industrial Club, opened in 1903, into the Skidmore School of Arts, the future Skidmore College. It was housed in the 86 Circular Street building of 1856 (still standing), in which Temple Grove principal Charles Dowd had spent so much time worrying about how to streamline America's countless time zones. The building would get a plaque if anyone ever put together a list of all the extraordinary American women educated in that structure.

The village acquired Congress Hall and tore it down in 1911, leaving only its former ballroom across Spring Street (still standing). This property, with the "Canfield Casino," as it came to be called, and the gambler's gardens, would double the size of Congress Park.

Spencer Trask was killed in a train accident in 1909. His widow, Katrina, commissioned Daniel Chester French to create a memorial. The result was the *Spirit of Life*, a bronze female figure standing in a setting by architect Henry Bacon on the Congress Hall site. French and Bacon would then create the Lincoln Memorial in Washington, but the sculptor would remember the *Spirit's* head as "the best thing of the kind I ever made."[24]

If the Springs survived the racing ban, forty thousand track employees in the state did not. They were thrown out of work, and the owners exited as best they could. Hildreth went to Canada to race one more year, which put him on top for the third straight time with a measly $47,473. Then he sold out to Charles Kohler, a piano manufacturer who ran the Ramapo Farm. Hildreth hired on as Kohler's trainer and took the stable to France. There, Novelty was made a jumper because American-bred runners could not race in France, and his dam, Curiosity, wound up in the French cavalry in World War I just as Kentucky thoroughbreds had carried Confederate officers.

*   *   *   *

As American racing died, many other owners dumped their horses. Milton Young had sold his McGrathiana Stud for only $80,360 in 1908. Ed Corrigan sold 92 horses for $22,995, including McGee for $1,300, the latter becoming the sire of Exterminator. J. B. Haggin sold 119 for $85,000 in Argentina and 34 for $17,747 in Germany. Horses were shipped to South America, England, and France, glutting markets and getting extremely low prices, Foxhall Keene said. "In this country you could hardly give them away. My father and I had two million dollars' worth of race horses and nowhere for them to go." So one day in 1910 the Keene saga reached the end.

*   *   *   *

Few in the Spa crowd could have suspected it, but on August 23, when Helmet, the Hopeful winner two years earlier, came through in a handicap, he became the last Keene victor in a third of a century on the turf. Disgusted and ailing, J. R. sold Castleton Farm in 1911 and his horses over the next two years. There were bargains galore. Charles W. Moore paid $17,500 for Sweep, leading sire of 1918 and 1925, and A. B. Hancock, founder of Claiborne Farm in Kentucky, spent $20,000 on Celt, leading sire of 1921. Price McKinney, of Cleveland, got Colin for $30,000. But Harry Whitney did best. Top price was $38,000 for Peter Pan, who went to Jimmy Rowe, who bought him for Payne Whitney, who turned him over to Harry. Along with Peter Pan, Harry got his son Pennant, who cost $1,700 and would win the $15,060 Futurity in 1913 and sire Equipoise. As Dan Bowmar pointed out, another bargain was Delhi's Dominant. Rowe paid $2,200 for him, and in 1915, racing for Whitney, he would take the Hopeful, Saratoga Special, and United States Hotel stakes. So the Whitneys not only gave, but got.

The sale helped out the only Vanderbilt who had yet ventured onto the turf. Gertrude's uncle, William Kissam Vanderbilt, had registered his colors, white with a black hoop on the sleeve and black cap, and after a mediocre tryout in the States switched to the French turf, where recently he had been cleaning up. Willie K. took Keene's Saratoga veteran Maskette and several other mares to France.

Stripped of his empire, the inconquerable Keene died on January 3, 1913, after a stomach operation. As for his son, he had established his own reputation as a star athlete. He was captain of the American polo team in its first match against England at Newport in 1886 and again in 1902. He was a top steeplechase rider with a record 79 wins in 101 races one year. He had shot a 73 in golf and made the third U.S. Open in 1897. Most of all, Foxie hunted the hounds whenever he could and lived, as the title of his memoirs announced, "Full Tilt." This man on a horse had no business head and no wife, either, so when his father died, the Keene name vanished from the turf, except in the stud books, where their stallions' blood would run strong for generations. It was one of racing's gifts.[25]

W. C. Whitney's first son busied himself on both sides of the water. He, too, was a superb athlete. He, too, captained the American polo team. It was not such a coincidence, for horse racing was polo's midwife and landlord, as it still is to some extent at Saratoga. It has always been an expensive, therefore elite, sport but is no less dangerous for that, involving rare skills—fast stops, quick turns, powerful hitting—and rough, often dirty tactics. Mere playboys couldn't play, nor could many horses. Perhaps Persian in origin, it was imported from India by England and by 1877 was introduced to America by publisher James Gordon Bennett, Jr., a New York City riding academy, and Leonard Jerome at his racetrack. An early city field was the Polo Grounds at 156th Street. With such turf figures as August Belmont II, Tommy Hitchcock, Sr., and Foxhall Keene among the strong early players, it was only natural that the new Saratoga should include polo stables and grounds.

Harry Payne Whitney was more than merely strong. As he led the American four to their first victory against the English in 1909, they not only destroyed them but changed the sport forever with their fast, powerful, wide-open game, then beat the British again in the next two meetings, in 1911 and 1913.

At the same time, Harry kept shopping for thoroughbreds, getting two smart buys from Captain Brown's estate. The first, purchased second-hand from the trainer A. J. (Jack) Joyner for $2,500, was Whisk Broom II—by Broomstick, by Ben Brush, by Bramble—who for a start would perform very profitably in England. The second was Broomstick himself, who cost $7,250 but would pay it back, to put it mildly, leading the sires list in 1913, 1914, and 1915.

As Keene did with Will gone, Harry Payne was reaching new heights with Keene gone, even during the blackout. Unlike his father, who based his breeding operation in Kentucky, Harry set up headquarters at Brookdale Farm, near Red Bank, New Jersey. He sent runners and broodmares to his English stud at Newmarket and also shipped mares to French stallions. During New York's second dark year, 1912, Whitney won thirty races in England with Whisk Broom II and others.

Actually, it was August Belmont II who did much of the work to restore racing. A leader of the unsuccessful Albany fight, he injected money into the New York City tracks even as they died off, and, along with two other stockholders, paid off Belmont Park's $120,000 debt so it could reopen in 1913. Meantime, he, too, had expanded abroad, the Nursery becoming somewhat depleted as he sent about a third of its mares to his French stud. As the history of the turf would never forget, Belmont also had Fair Play. A son of Hastings, who was a Belmont winner and twice leading sire, winner himself of several major stakes, and near conqueror of Colin, Fair Play was given an unsuccessful sabbatical in England, then was retired to the Nursery in 1909. There on Long Island he would father a colt to be cheered by millions who knew nothing of the Belmonts, Keenes, or Whitneys.

But first came a filly and a few others.

 *17*

FROM REGRET TO THE TRIPLE CROWN

REGRET, the filly of the century, made her debut at Saratoga. It was in 1914, the year after Harry Whitney and a few friends had led racing out of the dark.

Harry had found ten thousand people waiting outside Belmont Park on that Decoration Day the year before, ready to raise the sport from its grave. He told the Pinkertons to let them all in—he would pick up the tab. It wasn't all that generous, since he got it back fast. Whisk Broom II, whisked from his English career, won the Metropolitan on that May 30, then the Brooklyn Handicap, and the Suburban, under no less than 139 pounds, the most ever lugged in a great American handicap. With that, he received "such an ovation as no winner has ever received in the history of the race."[1]

Now it was the Spa's turn. Sam Hildreth, whom Belmont had just talked back from France to be his trainer, caught the mood as he and his Saratoga bride rediscovered the place in 1913. "It was a beautiful summer day, the day of our return, and the fragrance of the flowers and the soft beauty of the green shrubbery lining the walks of the Saratoga course, and the flags flying and the band up there in the grandstand thumping out a lively tune, while the old crowds moved around the broad lawns in the same old carefree way, all of it gave me the thrill that comes once in a lifetime." Like a lot of others, Sam was as racist as ever, noting that he ran around shaking hands with everybody, and it did not matter whether they were Jockey Club members "or one of the little darkies in the stables."[2]

Whisk Broom II contributed a page to the track's quirky history by striking himself, thus concluding one of racing's winningest bicontinental resumés. He had helped Whitney and Jimmy Rowe lead the money columns, the owner's skimpy $55,056 revealing that racing was far from recovered. The runner who brought home the most ($19,057) was the first in a series of remarkable geldings. H. C. Applegate's Old Rosebud deflowered the Flash, U.S. Hotel Stakes, and four others—they raced the hell out of two-year-olds—and at three would become the first of a record six Derby winners bred by John Madden.[3]

The Springs also unveiled an event that in six years would produce the most controversial race of all time, the Sanford Memorial Stakes, the Amsterdam carpetmaker having died in February. The Futurity, the country's most famous test for youngsters, was run twice more at the Spa, too, its value slashed 40 percent as the sport struggled. Harry Whitney's Pennant carried the Futurity flag in 1913, then it was 20-to-1 Trojan, slogging through the trenches of 1914. In that same muddy month, as World War I was getting underway, Regret appeared on the betting slips.

The law against soliciting or recording bets in a fixed place had not been repealed, but it had been circumvented by a system of "oral betting." This seemed even more chaotic than the ring's previous system, especially since Churchill Downs and Maryland already had moved ahead, replacing bookies with the efficient pari-mutuel machines. In any event, a New York bookie could not solicit but could quote odds to anybody who asked, and the inquirer could then write his bet on a slip of paper, hand it over, and pay or collect the next day. "Few reform waves have left such a prize example of hypocrisy," wrote Hugh Bradley. The bookies "wandered about the tracks much as they pleased. Many of them went into business on shoestring capital and were quickly unable to pay. Bettors welched for an estimated $250,000 a year. Police attributed various gangland killings to the system of betting."[4]

Regret and the boys soared above it. They had that edge over other athletes: they were not human, and they seemed to get better as the Golden Age approached. The filly was already there. A chestnut rubbed shiny, and a charmer at that, she had a funny broad blaze down her face that drew attention to large, laughing eyes. This Broomstick daughter out of a Hamburg mare, Jersey Lightning, was managed by the same man who had ridden Harry Bassett in 1872 and trained Sysonby and Colin. Jimmy Rowe worked Regret a lot, and at two she was more than ready to challenge the colts at the Spa, in great numbers.

First, Harry sent her against Pebbles, a richly symbolic opponent. He was owned by a New York City grocery magnate, James Butler, who had no fear of what he called the Long Island "silk hat crowd," the Belmont and Whitney types. Butler owned Empire City at Yonkers, and after daring to run simultaneously with Saratoga in 1907, he had forced Jockey Club chairman Belmont to assign it its own dates in the circuit. Silk-hat Harry and jockey Joe Notter won the first skirmish. Under 119 pounds, the debutante defeated Pebbles, 122, and six others in a hard-fought Saratoga Special.[5]

She carried eight more pounds in the first renewal of the Sanford, again triumphant against seven others. In a third outing, she faced ten in the Hopeful—and took it by a head, once more under 127, with Andrew M., 110, second, and Pebbles, 130, third. That was it at two. Her Spa triumphs piled up $17,390, which led the country. They pointed her toward Louisville.

In 1915—on May Day, oddly enough—one of Harry's brothers-in-law declared, "The Germans would not dare attack this ship," as he set sail on the *Lusitania*. The Germans had warned in a newspaper ad that morning against boarding the Cunard liner, which they suspected of harboring munitions as well as rich people. Harry's trotting, coaching, yachting, and motor-car enthusiast of a brother-in-law responded with an insult worthy of the head of the House of Vanderbilt: "How can Germany, after what she has done, ever think of being classed as a country of sportsmen and men of honor on a par with America, England and France?"[6]

He was going to offer his services to the British Red Cross. At 2:12 P.M., on the day before the Derby, two unsportsmanlike torpedoes struck amidships. Alfred Gwynne Vanderbilt, by several accounts, had responded heroically. He told his valet, "Find all the kiddies you can, boy," gave his lifebelt to a lady, and joined hands with four other men as they lurched bottomward. He stood there, said a survivor, "the personifica-

Regret, Jimmy Rowe, and H. P. Whitney in the winner's circle. *National Museum of Racing and Hall of Fame, Saratoga Springs.*

tion of sportsmanlike coolness. In my eyes, he was the figure of a gentleman waiting for a train."

The Irish coast was far away, much farther than the maps show, and the Kentucky Derby went on. Whitney did consider pulling Regret, but instead chose another gesture of respect for his brother-in-law. He turned over his entire stable for the rest of the year to L. S. Thompson, owner of Brookdale Farm, which Whitney leased. Regret and fifteen colts, the event's biggest field yet, paraded to the post. They were about to create the modern Kentucky Derby—to make it what its originators actually intended, the most glamorous race in the country.

Forty thousand turned out, but Matt Winn was ready. General manager since 1904, he was in the process of reviving the Downs, which had fallen on hard times after 1890. When bookies were banned locally in 1908, he dredged up some old French pari-mutuel machines and reintroduced the two-dollar bet. He had the first American machines built in 1912 and the next year learned the value of publicity as Derby winner Donerail paid the highest price yet for $2—$184.90—and set a track mark for the mile and a quarter, 2:04 ⅘. The next year Old Rosebud bettered that in 2:03 ⅖, which would stand for seventeen years. "This was regarded as a sensational performance by a three-year-old so early in the season," Winn noted, "and Old Rosebud created even more headlines for our Derby than had Donerail."[7]

The eighth of May was indeed early to ship a colt, and more so a filly, over the chilly mountains. No filly had won the Derby in its forty years. Still, they mobbed Matt's machines with two bucks on the girl who had conquered Saratoga. Butler had brought Pebbles, who had five wins in ten starts. "Other Eastern-owned horses were nominated," said Winn, "and the Derby, for the first time since we took over, had truly national representation." It was worth $11,450.

Regret got off fast, grabbed the lead from the boys, held it through the homestretch, and won easing up, Pebbles driving two lengths back. 2:05 ⅖. "I do not care if she never wins another race or if she never starts in another race," said Harry. "She has won the greatest race in America, and I am satisfied."

To hear Matt Winn tell it, the Derby was all about publicity. The Derby "needed only a victory by Regret to create for us some coast-to-coast publicity, and Regret did not fail us. . . . The Derby was thus 'made' as an American institution." Matt added what could be the Derby motto: "I am a devout believer in the mighty value of publicity and advertising." It would be sixty-five years before another filly, Genuine Risk, would don the roses. But the trip had told. Regret had caught a cold, and it affected her wind. She raced once more at three, dismissing Trial by Jury in the Spa's Saranac Handicap. She kept to the Spa in 1916, too, but lost badly to Belmont's Stromboli in the Saratoga Handicap, then took a mile event. At five, she won three out of four for a career nine victories in eleven starts. No filly ever beat her.

By coincidence, a filly won the Travers in 1915, too, the last one to do so for eight decades. Lady Rotha, owned by Association secretary-treasurer Andy Miller, beat the colt called Saratoga. That season's Spa standout was one of Whitney's bargains from the Keene sales. Dominant dominated the Special, U.S. Hotel, and Hopeful, and led the two-year-olds with $18,945. Meantime, Whitney's Borrow won the handicap division with $20,195, his whole herd allowing Thompson to pace the owners with $104,106. Whitney also began gradually to shift his operations to Kentucky, where he bought 614 acres from the James Ben Ali Haggin estate. Meanwhile, under managing director E. J. Tranter, the Fasig Tipton Co. had finally created the great national sale of Will Whitney's dreams in Saratoga.

One of the top riders, believe it or not, was an African American. The turf had not suddenly discovered tolerance, for Charlie Smoot was a steeplechaser. He literally launched his fifteen-year string of triumphs over the jumps, winning the Shillelah, Beverwyck, and North American at Saratoga in 1916, then the latter, the Saratoga Steeplechase, and the Belmont Corinthian the next year, and on and on, sailing merrily over fences, ditches, and rock-hard racism.

It was a gelding who succeeded Regret as national star of the stables. A year older than she, and by Knight Errant out of the blind Rose Tree II, he was appropriately

Roamer at Saratoga, Andy Schuttinger up. *Keeneland Library.*

dubbed Roamer. He found his way to thirty-nine wins in ninety-eight starts under Miller's "cardinal, white sash, black cap." Over seven years, he amassed more than $98,000, much of it at Saratoga. As the historian Robertson said, he was "one of the original 'horses for courses.' . . . He kept the old spa bubbling." He also swelled the secretary-treasurer's chest, and wallet, with the Special in 1913, the Travers in 1914, the Cup in 1915, and the Saratoga Handicap in 1915, 1917, and 1918.

It was on August 21, 1918, at the Spa that little Roamer ran his celebrated mile. Miller's, and trainer Jack Goldsborough's, target was Salvator's record 1:35½ against the clock twenty-eight years earlier. If he could do it, Roamer's would be the last mile record against time, as subsequent marks had to be against competition. The track was fast, to put it mildly. As Landon Manning pointed out, it had been so well resurfaced by superintendent Billy Myers that six track records fell in the first four days and nineteen during the meeting, including three world marks. Willis Sharpe Kilmer's Sun Briar, that year's Travers champion, had already smashed the standard for a mile against competition on Myers's surface with a 1:36⅕.[8]

A crowd of two thousand watched Roamer against the clock. Even Salvator's aging trainer, Matt Byrnes, made the trip up, and must have noted that Roamer was bearing 110 pounds, just as his champ had. Andy Schuttinger was up, and they had a stablemate, Lightning, start, too, so Roamer would not think it was a workout. "Mars

Cassidy sent them both away flying." Roamer put Lightning out fast and covered the first quarter in :23 ⅗, the second in a blistering :22 ⅖. The next fraction was :24 ⅕.

"When Roamer came tearing down the homestretch, he was greeted with applause such as has seldom been heard on a race track in this century," said an old *Saratogian* clipping that Landon dug up. The new mark: 1:34 ⅘. After failing to win a fourth straight Saratoga Handicap, Roamer limped into history, and after breaking his leg, he was destroyed on January 1, 1920, two days after Andy Miller died.

Only a Roamer could have overshadowed his unsexed rival by Fair Play. Stromboli erupted in thirty of sixty-four races through age six, leaving them in lava in the Saranac and the Saratoga Handicap, and he exploded occasionally after that, too, with two more in 1918. Hildreth bought the dormant "Stromey," doted on him and got him to cough up two more wins in 1921 at age ten.

Among other favorites was Spurt, whom Jim Butler raced no fewer than twenty-one times at three, when he won the 1916 Travers and seven others. And there was Wilson's two-year-old Campfire that year. He did a Regret in the Special, Sanford, and Hopeful, carrying twenty pounds more than Omar Khayyam in the latter, and won the Futurity at Belmont. As for Omar Khayyam, he was a gorgeous golden chestnut with a stripe on his face—"a picture horse," Walter Vosburgh said. He delivered the 1917 Derby, Travers, Saratoga Cup, and six others to owners C. K. G. Billings and Fred Johnson.[9]

"He doesn't measure more around than a polo pony." "More like a lean mule than a thoroughbred horse." Under the trees in the paddock, Vosburgh was listening to them gossip about Billy Kelly, owned by a Montrealer, Cmdr. J. K. L. Ross, as they saddled him for the Flash. Pony, mule, or whatever he was, he won that, the Sanford, and twelve others in seventeen starts in 1918, then fourteen more in his next thirty-one outings.

Then came the greatest gelding of them all, the skinny giant Exterminator, which is what he did. Lexington horseman Cal Milam picked him up for $1,500 at the same 1916 Saratoga yearling sale at which Kilmer got Sun Briar. Two years later, trainer Henry McDaniel, son of the unforgettable Col. David McDaniel, caught Exterminator working at Lexington. He purchased him for $10,000 for Kilmer, as a pacemaker to ready Sun Briar for the Derby. As it turned out, Sun Briar didn't make it, but Exterminator did—and won it. The next year he began his multi-year assault on the Saratoga Cup's grueling mile and three-quarters. It was almost as if he had swallowed some of owner Kilmer's Swamp Root, the cure-all that coughed up a fortune for the Binghamton, New York, publisher and turfman, for he exterminated the rest in his first Cup in a record 2:58.

But Exterminator was not the most famous horse charging into the twenties, nor the second most famous. The latter was Sir Barton. A dud at first, he ran unplaced in the Tremont at Aqueduct and in the Flash, U.S. Hotel, and Sanford, so John Madden unloaded him for $10,000 to Commander Ross in the 1918 Saratoga sales. After being unplaced in the Hopeful, he managed second in the Futurity. But none of this would matter a hoot, for there was one simple reason why Sir Barton would be a knight forever: he was the first to win what future publicists would call the "Triple Crown."

They didn't call it that then. In fact, there had been times when scheduling made it impossible to shoot for a Derby-Preakness-Belmont triple, nor was it all that compelling. As noted, early May was early to race a colt, and for those not already on bluegrass, a daunting voyage. Under Matt Winn's stewardship, the Derby pot had grown to $20,825 for the winner in 1919, Maryland's Preakness had more than doubled to $24,500, and the Belmont in still-struggling New York had been hiked by $2,000 to $11,950. It all helped Ross look down at the owners for a second straight year, with $209,303.

Who could be more famous than the Triple Crown laureate?

 *18*

MAN O' WAR

H̲E WAS FOALED on March 29, 1917, at the second Nursery Stud in Kentucky. His father was Fair Play, his mother the exotic Mahubah.[1] He was the product of two debatable Belmont theories: that whatever Count Lehndorff, W. C. Whitney, or anybody else had said, lightly raced mares—Mahubah ran only five times, winning once—made the best broodmares, and that fabulous offspring could result from "nicks," the joining of two powerful lines. The colt's sire had nearly stolen the Belmont Stakes from Colin, and his paternal grandfather, Hastings, had won it. So had Hastings's father, Spendthrift. As for Mahubah, she was by imported Rock Sand, the English Derby winner. The colt was a bright, reddish chestnut with a diamond on his forehead.

"Man o' War." It was August II's wife, the actress Eleanor Robson Belmont, who insisted on christening the Nursery foals. After all, she knew marquee value. "Mahubah" was a pretty Arabic greeting she had heard in Tunis ("Marhabah" would have been a little more accurate). The colt's name was suggested by the news as the country finally got into World War I that April. It was a compliment to her husband, too. At sixty-five, August II was offering his services to the army. It commissioned him a major and dispatched him to Europe.

Another remarkable woman, Elizabeth Kane, was the Nursery Stud's managing director. She raised the colt and watched him grow bigger, taller, faster than the others, so when Major Belmont offered his yearling crop in a private sale after being ordered abroad, he decided to hold this one back.

Samuel D. Riddle was a textile industrialist from Pennsylvania who was not trying to get into the army. What he and his wife were trying to do in 1917 was recruit a top-flight racing stable, just as their niece and her husband, Mr. and Mrs. Walter Jeffords, were doing. Riddle deployed trainers Louis Feustel and Mike Daly to Lexington to check out Belmont's yearlings, but they found them undersized, so the major cabled orders from Paris to ship them to the Saratoga sales—except that red one. At the last minute, though, he figured it would look as though he were just dumping his weaker stock, so he shot off another cable from Paris: Send Man o' War.

The twenty-one yearlings arrived at the Spa several days before the August 17, 1918, sale. The Riddles were ensconced in their large frame home at 215 (now 125) Union Avenue (still there), a block from the track, and Sam, Louie, and Mike went up for another gander at Belmont's shipment. Sam agreed they were nothing special— until they reached the last stall. A big chestnut hovered in the shadows.

"Lead him out where I can see him," Sam said, and he remembered later, "He simply bowled me over. . . . So I turned to Louie and Mikey and asked, 'What's the matter with this colt?'" They said the Nursery hadn't shown them that one.

When the yearling Man o' War came to town, Fasig Tipton's paddock and sales ring along East Avenue were one year old. But other horse auctions were still conducted under the trees in the track paddock, "the most picturesque in America," noted Hervey. As the auctioneer sang his song, Mrs. Jeffords went to $15,600, the high price of the sales, for Golden Broom, a gorgeous chestnut with white markings.

It was over in the track paddock that the Powers-Hunter Co. was handling Belmont's offerings, which topped out at $14,000 and averaged $2,474. Riddle figured he could get his colt for about that average, but "two well-known ladies who in some way got wind of the fancy I had taken to him" told their husbands, and the red one went all the way to $5,000. It would be judged the horse bargain of all time. Man o' War and many of the others were kept at the Spa to be broken and trained. "He fought like a tiger, he screamed with rage," Riddle said. "It took several days before he could be handled with safety." But they stayed gentle with him, and because he was so brainy, he saw that he couldn't win and eventually gave up, but he never forgot. "I don't think we saddled him once during his races . . . that he didn't show by his actions that he remembered his breaking."

The first track he ever met was the Spa's, and former jockey Harry Vititoe was first on board. "When it came to galloping," said Vosburgh, the Jockey Club and Saratoga handicapper, "they soon found he had a tremendous burst of speed." Come the end of September, he went to Glen Riddle Farm on Maryland's eastern shore to winter with Golden Broom and the other Jeffords colts.

Man o' War opened fire in June 1919. He bore Riddle's black and yellow silks to the fore in five straight—a $500 purse and the Keene Memorial at Belmont, the Youthful at Jamaica, the Hudson and Tremont at Aqueduct—daylight behind him in each. He grew quickly, too, weighing close to 1,000 pounds (few three-year-olds topped 1,050, according to Hervey). Track regulars started calling him Big Red, a name he would share with his rival for the century's honors, Secretariat.[2]

He had the best jockey of the day. As one writer noted before they invented the term "Triple Crown," John Loftus pulled off a "four-cornered feat"—the Derby-Preakness-Withers-Belmont on Sir Barton—in addition to Big Red's first five. Then Man o' War headed back to Saratoga.[3]

The Riddles couldn't get enough of the place. Their columned home on Union Avenue overflowed with flowers, thoroughbred prints, and American antiques, Hervey said, and it was open house for the turf society, a source of tea and cakes and "perhaps something more exhilarating" after every day's races. Man o' War got to Horse Haven in July, and he apparently loved the Spa. "The Adirondack air, the fair days and cool, bracing nights, the sylvan surroundings, luxuriant grass and sparkling water, did not fail . . . to work their accustomed wonders." Refreshed, on August 2 the colt collected the $10,000 guaranteed for the U.S. Hotel Stakes, his richest yet. He wore 130 pounds and gave Harry Whitney's Upset 15, but the bumblebee colors still buzzed home ahead of "Eton blue, brown cap" by two lengths.

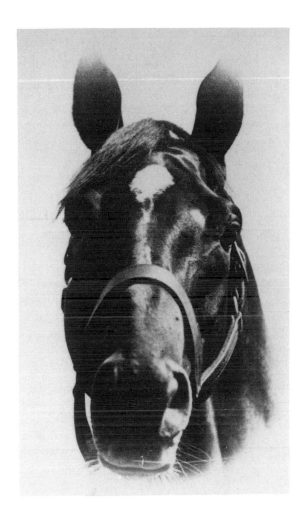

Man o' War. *National Museum of Racing and Hall of Fame, Saratoga Springs.*

Eleven days later came the seventh Sanford Stakes. It would be the most talked-about race of all time. The talk started early, for a few days before the race, the owners of Man o' War and Golden Broom "tried" them—as horse people put it—over three furlongs. An excited crowd of insiders saw Fair Play's son take his neighbor by three lengths in :33 flat, a half-second faster than the record. Mrs. Jeffords's colt looked good, and on August 9 he looked even better as he won the Special. The morning of the Sanford, anybody with a *Times* could find out what insiders knew, that the "stars"—the term had graduated to a noun—were the red and golden chestnuts. To honor them, John Sanford added a cup to the winner's $3,925. They were further "honored" with 130 pounds each and odds of 1 to 2 on Big Red, 2 to 1 on Broom. Third pick was Upset, 115 pounds and 7 to 1, but 2 to 5 to show. John Madden entered Capt. Alcock, and the other starters were Armistice, Donnacona, and the Swimmer.[4]

August 13, 1919. Ty Cobb was headed for .384, Knute Rockne for his first sensational season, Man o' War—in sixth position, next to the outside, a good spot—for his seventh straight before some two thousand spectators. The Golden Age was here at

A start at Saratoga: assistant starters line them up behind a narrow net barrier. *Keeneland-Cook.*

last, and in more ways than one, unfortunately, for aging Charlie Pettingill. Starter Mars Cassidy was laid up sick at White Sulfur Springs, Virginia, and Charlie, the former starter and presiding judge, was filling in—badly.

Bad starts had been a bone of contention forever. Assistants would push in the outside horse and the inside horse, and the starter, on his little platform, would spring the elastic barrier at the moment they seemed aligned. Charlie already had been blamed for the worst start ever; it took him an hour and a half to launch the 1893 American Derby in Chicago. There were twenty-five breaks through the barrier, and according to one estimate, the horses did six miles before the real start. This was not a good day, either. Upset tried to break through the tape, and Golden Broom actually did, three times. "Pettingill spent several minutes trying to get the horses lined up," said the *Times,* "and then sent them away with only those near the rail ready for the start." Fair Play's son was pointed the wrong way.[5]

By the time Big Red got set and took off, next to last, Golden Broom, on the rail with Eddy Ambrose up, was nearly two lengths ahead of Upset, under Bill Knapp. Donnacona was third. Man o' War was four lengths back. As Golden Broom swept the clubhouse turn, "Man o' War was beginning to show what a really great horse he was," said the *Times* witness. "Off almost last, he gained his speed in a few strides, and then started to pass horses all along the back stretch. Armistice and the Swimmer were soon disposed of, and making the turn the Glen Riddle Farm's racer drew up to fourth."

Man o' War "got into close quarters" at the stretch turn, the official chart would note, while third-place Donnacona "was carried wide . . . and tired."

Into the homestretch, Man o' War was two lengths behind Upset, who had not gained on the leader. "Golden Broom suddenly gave up," the *Times* reporter said, "and Upset raced past him." So did Big Red. As the chart would put it, Man o' War

A start at Saratoga: starter springs the barrier. *Keeneland-Cook.*

"came to the outside in the final eighth and, responding gamely to punishment, was gaining in the closing strides."

The *Times:* "It became a question whether Upset could last to win. Man o' War received a fine ride from Loftus, who gave the colt every assistance within his power. Steadily Man o' War drew up on Upset. A hundred feet from the wire he was three-fourths of a length away. At the wire he was a scant neck out of the first position, and in another twenty feet he would have passed the Whitney horse."

The chart made Upset's margin half a length. Time: 1:11⅕. The Riddle colt's record was suddenly 6–1.

Upset, he of the providential monicker, was saddled by the man who had ridden Harry Bassett and trained Colin and Regret, and Jimmy Rowe's accomplishments now included the defeat of Man o' War, but almost everybody thought Man o' War was the true winner. There was scarcely a witness who did not believe Man o' War "would have walked home," said the *Times,* "with anything like a fair chance."

The fingers pointed at Charlie. There is no way to recapture the buzz in the bars that night, but the next morning the *Times* baldly opined, "The start was responsible for the defeat of Man o' War." Fingers would point elsewhere, too, especially after the pointers noted his two more gate-boosting victories at the Spa and his now obvious value to the struggling sport. Sportswriters began to wax historic and, along with the establishment, to seek a scapegoat for the Sanford. "Man o' War has now been quite favorably compared with the great Colin," the *Times* declared, "and it is regretted by many horsemen that the son of Fair Play was permitted to be beaten when he so clearly outclasses his field. . . . In the records, it will lie as a mark against him."

Suddenly the *Times,* which had blamed Pettingill the morning after, decided, "It was the fault of Loftus and not Man o' War that caused the colt to be left at the post in

Upset beating Man o' War. His landing gear up, Man o' War narrowly loses the 1919 Sanford. Golden Broom third. *Keeneland-Cook.*

the Sanford Memorial." The same paper, which had praised Loftus's "fine ride" and had never mentioned the colt's getting boxed at the stretch turn, added, "Even then he would have won, but for a bungling ride in which Loftus found every pocket on the track."[6]

It looked as though Loftus was going to take the hit. Hervey, writing later but listening closely to Riddle and others, agreed it was the jockey's fault. He said that at the start, "Loftus, after showing great anxiety to get off, was finally caught napping, and his colt was turned almost the wrong way." On top of that, he said several of the starters were maidens, new to the game, so once Man o' War got straight, "he ran into and almost over a couple of them, and had to be pulled up and squared away a second time, losing many lengths."

As Man o' War "began devouring the space which separated him from the others," according to Hervey, "it seemed to onlookers that Loftus, then our premier rider, had lost his head completely. . . . Into the upper turn of the track, Loftus drove him in next the rail where he was again shut off. There was nothing left but to take him back and come around them."

There was still time for Man o' War to win, for he was outrunning them, "but for the third time, his judgment apparently forsaking him altogether, Loftus shot Man o' War toward the rail and endeavored to come through there. For the third time, it proved impossible—there was no room. He pulled him out again." Finally, "Man o' War got to Upset, lapped him"—lapped, in this case, meaning he had caught up and was alongside him—"and was passing him when the post was reached and the race was over."

Strangely, except for the colt's getting into close quarters at the stretch turn, none of this was noted by the chart writer when the race was run.

Johnny Loftus and Clarence Kummer with colleagues. *From left:* Tommy Davies, Loftus, T. McTaggart, unidentified, Kummer, and Andy Ferguson. *National Museum of Racing and Hall of Fame, Saratoga Springs.*

For the moment, Loftus was still on Big Red. Their next appearance, in the Grand Union Stakes on August 23, broke all known attendance records for the Spa. More than thirty-five thousand people created a traffic jam that reminded one New Yorker of Fifth Avenue at rush hour. Under his usual 130 pounds, Red gave Upset, 7 to 1, five pounds and beat him by a length.

Buckets of rain drenched the Hopeful field as it lined up on August 30, and they were off—in the colt's first rain and mud test, for $24,600. The crowd could hardly see anything through the heavy storm, and as they headed home, Riddle said, "something jumped out in front of the others and ran away from them." It was his soaking colt, by four lengths.

The press poured it on some more after he conquered the Belmont Futurity by two and a half lengths over Whitney's John P. Grier. Upset was fifth. The *Times* promoted Big Red to "horse of a decade . . . one of the truly great racers of all time . . . the Ty Cobb of the turf." He led the twos for the year with $83,325. Loftus led the jockeys with $252,707. His 65 wins on 177 mounts produced a brilliant .37 winning percentage, but the pilot of Sir Barton and Man o' War never rode again after 1919. Loftus and Bill Knapp, Upset's rider, were denied their 1920 jockey's licenses. They were not told why, which was standard practice, but everybody pointed to the Sanford. Historian Robertson would write that "Knapp obviously had fulfilled perfectly his primary obligation of trying to win" while quoting him as saying he could have passed Golden Broom earlier but waited until the sixteenth pole so Man o' War wouldn't have time to catch him. Loftus became "the guy who lost that race on Man o' War."[7]

At three, in April 1920, this Man o' War displaced 1,100 pounds and stood 16.2 hands. There were not many capable of judging him with a cool head. One was

Vosburgh, who handicapped him. "Man o' War is a red chestnut with a star and an indistinct short gray stripe in his forehead," he wrote. He was "rather broad across the chest—more so than we like to see. His back was rather longer than the average. . . . He had the size and power of a sprinter, with the conformation of a stayer." He girthed 72 inches.

He did not make the trip from the eastern shore to the May 8 Derby. Nobody found this unusual, although it meant the century's most famous race could not claim its most famous horse. It was Paul Jones who won at Churchill Downs, heading the driving Upset. Riddle was aiming at Pimlico, but on May 1 he sent Big Red to work at Belmont because it had better facilities, and Long Island was actually quieter. A few weeks later, he was back for the Preakness, and Jimmy Rowe was waiting for him.

Rowe was one of the few in the country who thought Big Red could be brought down, and should be. Hervey said Rowe was embittered by the defeats that a single colt and an upstart stable had handed the country's greatest living trainer and the unparalleled Whitney enterprise. But once again, in the classic Preakness, Upset belied his name, by a length and a half.

It started getting tough to find opponents. Back at Belmont Park, in the Withers, the star of Glen Riddle faced only Rowe's Wildair and W. R. Coe's David Harum. Neither stopped him from lowering the American record for a mile against competition to 1:35⅘. Two weeks later it was the Belmont, which his granddad and great-granddad had won. Here only the candy king G. W. Loft's Donnacona met him, and Red restored his family's honor, leaving the other twenty lengths up the course and dropping the world standard for 1⅜ miles to 2:14⅕.

Crossing Queens, he found only Yellow Hand, owned by Saratoga president R. T. Wilson, in the Stuyvesant Handicap at Jamaica. He was quoted at 1 to 100 at the post, reportedly the shortest odds ever against an American horse. At least it was a colorful finish: the black cap and vest with yellow sash and striped sleeves, then the yellow silks with green chevrons flapping prettily eight lengths back.

By then Jimmy Rowe actually hated Man o' War. Or, in Hervey's words, he had a "burning determination" to "topple from his pedestal the colt which he had come to hate with an unremitting intensity." He sent out John B. Grier, who gave Red the greatest fight of his career in the mile-and-an-eighth Dwyer Stakes at Aqueduct. Even Vosburgh got carried away. "The two champions appeared, walking slowly to the post together, like the kings, Richard of England and Philip of France, going to the Crusades." Richard the red had eighteen pounds more. Mars Cassidy saw them off on their crusade, and they did the first six furlongs of it together in 1:09⅗, faster than the track record for the distance. For the only time ever, Man o' War was incontestably headed, at the three-sixteenths pole. "He's got hi——!" cried Clem McCarthy, the writer and future NBC Radio announcer, but for once Clem never got to finish the sentence. Man o' War's new jockey, Clarence Kummer, replied with the whip, and Big Red pulled it out by a length and a half. It was another world record, 1:49⅕. Harry Whitney leaped over the boxes to congratulate Sam Riddle. Hervey said Rowe had a new watchword: "Wait till Saratoga."

Man o' War returned to a Saratoga-in-progess. After Miller's death, George H.

An infield lake appears, not that the horses stopped to look. *Keeneland-Cook.*

Bull had been elected secretary-treasurer and launched a beautification program, planting more trees, shrubs, and flowers. Earlier, a hole had been dug in the infield to produce dirt for resurfacing the track, and had been made into a lake; Bull added four fountains. In what later would be something of a contradiction in terms, it was noted that "a beautiful park has been laid out for the parking of the motor cars." [8]

Big Red had been joined in town by Sir Barton and Exterminator, and the atmosphere was electric. On opening day, August 2, Sir Barton won the Saratoga Handicap in an American record mile-and-a-quarter, 2:01⅘, beating Exterminator. They started talking about a Man o' War–Sir Barton match. The next day Red tried nine furlongs—the length of the course—before a riveted gallery. He blasted it in 1:49⅕, same as his fresh world mark.

On August 7, he entered the Miller Stakes, formerly the Kenner, Andy's widow adding a massive silver trophy to the prize of about $5,000. Donnacona and a Prince Albert were entered. Even for this no-brainer, extra police controlled the crowds and made saddling and walking space for Red. It inspired the *Daily Racing Form* to declare Man o' War "the greatest drawing card" ever in American racing. The jockey who would become the era's most famous now got on its most famous horse, Kummer having fractured his shoulder in a fall at Aqueduct. Earl Sande made Red 15 and 1.

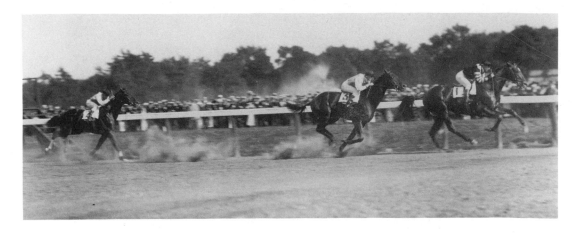

Man o' War's revenge. Often mistakenly described as the finish, this is the first time around in the 1920 Travers, with Man o' War leading John Grier, then Upset, who would move to second. *Keeneland-Cook.*

Jimmy Rowe could almost taste revenge. He had the only others in the August 21 Travers. John P. Grier would carry Man o' War for a mile, then Upset would take over for the final quarter mile. "This was the only time I was ever nervous, really nervous, about the outcome of a race that Man o' War went into," said Riddle. "I knew of the boasts that [Rowe] had made that the day of the downfall of Man o' War was at hand." What made him worry most was that people warned "something was going to happen and for me to look out for it." He expected nothing unsportsmanlike from Whitney or Rowe, but because of the threat he had Red watched day and night before the Travers.

For the first time, they opened the infield, and five thousand people rushed in. Altogether, some thirty-five thousand turned out. Riddle, meantime, had resolved another problem. Kummer had come back, and Sande had left for Canada a few days earlier. Then Kummer, still lame, was grounded by doctors. They discovered the availability of Andy Schuttinger, the passenger on Roamer's mile and reputedly a great judge of pace. So Andy sat there for the $9,275 Travers, as Riddle warned him about Grier.

"Go away from the rise of the barrier. Run away from him."

Schuttinger did. The huge crowd sounded off as they flew by the grandstand for the first time. "I let him go into the lead to get the rail," Andy said later, "but after that he was under restraint all the way." Grier never had it, and fell behind Upset, who finished two and a half lengths out. The 2:01⅗ equaled the track record that Sir Barton had set opening day, and would not be bettered in the Travers until Jaipur forty-two years later. The Travers was Upset's sixth and final loss to Man o' War, his fifth since the Sanford.

Records kept falling. At Belmont in the fall, Riddle's pride set his third and last world mark, accomplishing the Lawrence Realization, a mile and five-eighths, in 2:40⅘. Historians might find it embarrassing to mention his margin over the other horse,

Hoodwink. It was a hundred lengths. Before the track was raked, it occurred to somebody to repair an oversight. They had never measured Red's stride. So now they did. It was twenty-five feet from the leaping start, a foot short of Longfellow's, and twenty-four feet, eight inches on the run.

Next came Red's second and final American record as he collected the Jockey Club Stakes, a mile and a half, in 2:28 ⅖. Then home country and Havre de Grace, Maryland, for what Riddle considered Red's finest hour. Under 138 pounds, the biggest burden ever given a three-year-old, he conceded 30 pounds to Rowe's last challenge, Wildair, and deflated him by a length and a half.

After that, what a career finale!—or so everybody thought. Man o' War was confronting Sir Barton for the turf's greatest purse yet, $75,000 plus a $5,000 Tiffany gold cup, at Kenilworth Park, Canada. Commander Ross's horse, a year older, had not only beaten Exterminator in the Saratoga Handicap but had won the Spa's Merchants and Citizens Handicap under 133 pounds. So they gave him 126 pounds to Red's 120. As Vosburgh neatly summed it up, it was a farce, albeit one of the first ever filmed. Millions in both countries saw Man o' War run the sore knight into the ground over a mile and a quarter. His last margin: seven lengths; his lifetime record: 20–1.

He never won by less than a length. He bankrolled $249,465, which beat Domino's twenty-seven-year-old lifetime mark of $193,550. "We do not know to this day how fast he was, as we were afraid to let him down," Riddle said after his retirement. "We feared he might injure himself." Today visitors to Saratoga would not be dreaming pipe dreams if they imagined Man o' War being broken before their eyes, or flying through nearly a third of his races. This is where it happened.[9]

 *19*

ROTHSTEIN AND THE ROARING TWENTIES

ARNOLD ROTHSTEIN was said to have made his debut as a Saratoga gambler when he was just twenty-one, arriving with the bookies on Cavanagh's Special in 1904. Five years later, like Commodore Vanderbilt, Sam Hildreth, and so many others before him, he found himself in love at the Spa. He married beautiful Caroline Greene, a showgirl, during the 1909 racing season. On their wedding night, he borrowed her jewelry as collateral for his bets. Over the next few years Rothstein graduated from floating crap games in Manhattan to a reputation as one of New York's most flamboyant plungers, operating out of a hotel suite and sometimes on ocean liners.[1] He also operated as a clubhouse bookie and made some $40,000 on one Saratoga race.

Rothstein returned to the Spa and created the Brook, the nightclub that launched Saratoga's revival as America's gambling capital. It was west of town on Church Street extended, at Locust Grove Road. Rothstein reportedly split 56 percent of the profits with a partner, Nat Evans. Others, including bookmaker Henry Tobin, had pieces of it, with 16 percent held out for local political campaign funds, according to Toney Betts, a historian of the turf and gambling. Rothstein was also said to have been a silent partner in the Chicago Club, which restored gambling in the heart of town, at Division Street and Woodlawn Avenue, the back-of-Broadway neighborhood where it had a history older than most local churches.

The Brook catered to the superrich with chemin de fer, roulette, and hazard, and at the beginning it was no frills: no small-time dice games, no entertainment, no food. Betts said Rothstein was briefly run out of town as a common gambler, and legend made him the top gambler behind the Chicago "Black Sox" dive in the World Series, although it was never proven. He was said to be a powerful force in the underworld, masterminding financial frauds and narcotics rings.[2]

Suddenly racketeers across the country got a windfall, the puritans' unwitting gift of 1920: Prohibition. As the FBI put it, "the rackets spawned by enactment of the Prohibition Amendment—illegal brewing, distilling and distribution of beer and liquor—were viewed as 'growth industries.'" Rothstein developed an aggressive bootlegging operation, distributing to "restaurants, nightclubs, and gambling clubs in which he already had a financial interest," author Robert Lacey has written. He put in the time-honored local fix and used protégés as subcontractors in the restaurant, bar, and gaming operations, Lacey said. His protégés in bootlegging and gambling at the Brook, where he quickly reestablished himself, were a couple of childhood friends from the Lower East Side.

Arnold Rothstein's place. A horse joins the fun at the Brook. *National Museum of Racing and Hall of Fame.*

"It was through running franchises inside Rothstein's Saratoga casinos," Lacey wrote, "that Meyer Lansky and (Charles) Lucky Luciano graduated from crap games to greater things." Among other things, the suave Saratoga gambler taught Charlie Luciana, as he was still known then, how to dress and how to act. Rothstein, Lansky said later, was amused when Charlie wanted to know "how to behave when I meet classy broads." Others mentioned as Rothstein pupils at the Spa were Frank Costello, Dutch Schultz (Arthur Flegenheim), Waxey Gordon (Irving Wexler), and Jack "Legs" Diamond.[3]

Although he would later be viewed as a godfather of modern crime, Rothstein's operations were not fully known at the time. To many he was merely the latest Manhattan and Saratoga impresario, a spiritual successor to Morrissey and Canfield. Soon the country was gushing again with gossip from the Springs—about oil-company founder and turfman Harry Sinclair dropping $48,000 at the Brook and adding a tip of $2,000 anyway, or Charles Stoneham, owner of baseball's New York Giants and a Havana casino, calling from his rented house on Nelson Avenue to ask Rothstein where the wheel had stopped. "On the black," was the answer.

"Then bet me a thousand dollars on the red." Red won. One night Sam Rosoff, the subway builder, was running $400,000 ahead at the Brook. Worried, Rothstein phoned his pal Stoneham to rush him $300,000 (he had it in a safe) in case the house kept losing. It didn't, and Sam finished the night out $100,000. Everybody seemed to be calling everybody. Once, said Betts, when gambler Sidney Staeger was desperately short in Saratoga, he called his associate Rothstein at Lindy's in Manhattan. "I can't hear you! I can't hear you!" Rothstein kept shouting. Finally, the sympathetic operator helpfully cut in. "He says won't you please send him $500?"

"If you heard him," said A. R., "you send him the money."[4]

Rothstein wins the Travers. Sporting Blood beating Prudery. *Keeneland-Cook.*

A. R. even ran a string of horses. He made a huge killing on the Fourth of July, 1921, at Aqueduct, when he had someone else enter Sidereal. The horse had been working fast, but nobody outside Rothstein's circle knew it. He kept the workouts secret, and Sidereal was out of the money in three races before the holiday. On the Fourth he opened at 30 to 1. Using three betting commissioners, and borrowing from wealthy friends, Rothstein piled money on him. And when Sidereal won, he came away with $800,000, the biggest payoff in American turf history.[5]

His Redstone Stable (Roth = red, stein = stone) harbored a fine Fair Play colt with a great name, Sporting Blood, and he was entered in the 1921 Travers. His only opponent was a certain favorite: Harry Whitney's filly, Prudery, winner of the Alabama. Rothstein had heard Prudery was in poor condition, and saw a killing. Then something stranger happened; on the very morning of the Travers, Hildreth entered the great Rancocas colt Grey Lag, who had beaten Sporting Blood in the Belmont by three lengths.[6]

The betting focused on Grey Lag and Prudery, and Sporting Blood's odds got a little longer. As Hugh Bradley told it, Rothstein wired agents around the country to lay $150,000 on his colt with "handbooks," individual street bookmakers who took bets on the spot. They got around 3 to 1. Since Sporting Blood had no chance, the handbooks held this sucker's money for themselves rather than wiring it back to the track to bet with bookies there. As a result, Rothstein's money did not affect the odds.

Then it happened; at the last minute Hildreth pulled Grey Lag with no clear explanation. Prudery's odds shortened to 2 to 7, but the troubled filly fell apart after a mile, and Redstone's Sporting Blood romped home by two lengths. The venerated Travers brought the reputed godfather of modern crime $10,275—plus $450,000 from the handbooks.

Toney Betts said there was plenty of crookedness in New York racing but did not single out any tracks as better or worse. "Many stables, including those of millionaires, stimulated horses with narcotics and other drugs, and bookmakers paid spongers to insert a sponge in a favorite's nose to hamper his breathing." There were bookmakers who had interests in stables and sometimes controlled jockeys. Sometimes they had assistant starters hold a favorite at the post, while trainers would have them send them off fast.[7]

As for Sporting Blood, it was almost poetic justice that as he raced on, it was under the colors of H. C. "Bud" Fisher, creator of the comic strip "Mutt and Jeff." Rather in the same silly vein, there was the Tin Pan Alley writer Walter Donaldson. A heavy bettor, he once wrote out a bet of $10,000 to $500 on a two-year-old that came in at the Spa, but forgot to give the slip to his bookie. So he got drunk and wound up at jockey Johnny Callahan's cottage, banging on the piano and shouting, "Callahan, Callahan, we don't give a good goddam, he's our man!" He segued into something like "There she goes, on her toes, all dressed up in her Sunday clothes," and it became the 1925 hit "My Best Girl."[8]

As for the Brook, Rothstein sold his interest in it by 1925, but it thrived and added frills to the thrills, including a worthy kitchen. The clientele dressed, and the menus bore nothing so tacky as prices. It was perhaps the country's most exclusive nightspot. As the National Turf Digest explained, the proper routine was to watch the thoroughbreds work in the morning, observe the yearlings at the sales paddocks, take in the races, and after dinner stop by Fasig Tipton's, or "drop into the United States or the Grand Union Hotel to exchange pleasantries with one's acquaintances and then perchance take a drive to the Brook, to while away an hour or two. . . . After a month of this kind of living one returns to the city absolutely unconscious of nerves." The club's creator, on the other hand, died of lead poisoning. A. R. was gunned down by unknown killers outside the service entrance of Manhattan's Park Central Hotel in 1928.[9]

After Man o' War, who else was there? Exterminator, for one. Old Bones repeated in the Saratoga Cup in 1920, breaking his own record in 2:56⅘. Kentucky had doubled in the Cup in 1866, and so had Springbok, and Parole, but none had won it a third time, as Exterminator did in a walkover in 1921. Then he beat Mad Hatter for a fourth straight Cup. Eight years brought him fifty victories in one hundred starts (five in fourteen at the Spa). He was out of the money only sixteen times.

There was Zev. He was from the powerhouse formed when Sam Hildreth linked up with Harry Sinclair to revive Pierre Lorillard's Rancocas stable in New Jersey. Starting in 1921, Rancocas led the money chart for three years, concluding the streak spectacularly as Zev turned into a cash register. His nine straight wins in 1923, including the Derby, deposited $272,008, crushing Domino's one-year record of $170,790. All the money marks collapsed under Zev's 1923 juggernaut. Sinclair beat Keene's record and became the first owner to exceed $400,000, with $438,849. Others Zev put on top that season: breeder Madden, $623,630; sire The Finn, passing Commando with $285,759; trainer Hildreth, $392,124; and rider Sande, with $569,394, a mark that lasted twenty years. Zev raced another year, his lifetime earnings soaring above Man o' War's, to $313,639.

Master Charlie was pretty terrific, too, but almost nobody knew it, at least not the wandering "oral" bookmakers, who had him at 50 to 1 in the 1924 Hopeful. This despite the fact that the English-born colt, owned by William Daniel of Chicago, had taken the Tijuana Futurity and was on his way to the two-year-old championship. They were smarter in an informal ring outside the gates on Union Avenue. There his odds fell fast, yet one New York bookie held out, offering 30 to 1 and putting all his customers' money on the favorite for himself. Long shot Master Charlie won, the smart aleck disappeared, and that pretty much ended the raucous ring out on Union Avenue.[10]

There was Fair Play's Display. He was known as the Iron Horse for his 103 starts in six years, including 23 firsts and 75 in the money, but he was also a bad actor. Starter Mars Cassidy's son George, who was an assistant starter, said it was horses like Display that often made it almost impossible to get them off. He remembered one time at the Spa. "There were four horses in the race and, do you know, we were at post 30 minutes. We couldn't get them near the tape. Display was one, and he was a demon. He'd lunge and pitch as soon as he saw the tape. I handled him, and I'm not kidding, when I was finished, I was dripping, absolutely dripping."[11]

The plant improved every year under secretary Bull. On opening day in 1926, visitors "emanated gasps of surprise" at the infield, where the artificial lake had sprouted a lovely environment of shrubs and foliage, a small flotilla of swans, and "two brightly colored canoes." Records of the latter would fade away, but they were the ancestors of a later Travers canoe tradition. The lawn in front of the clubhouse and grandstand not only survived but became an institution. Since the betting ring, that "fixed place," was still illegal, the wandering bookies tended to operate, often rather furtively, on the lawn. So their headquarters, such as it was, became known simply as the Lawn.

Just east of the track, Yaddo found its vocation in 1926. The estate was turned into an artists' retreat, soon to be celebrated nationally and developed according to the plans of the late Katrina Trask, widow of Spencer. At the same time Yaddo remained the homestead of her second husband, George Foster Peabody, the multimillionaire banker and philanthropist (for whom broadcasting's Peabody Awards are named). At the other great estate, Woodlawn, out North Broadway, Judge Hilton's buildings began their long decline. George W. Loft, the candy millionaire who had twice let Man o' War run over his Donnacona, reportedly had purchased part of Woodlawn, after which it fell into the hands of Charles Morse, a shipbuilder and Wall Street plunger, who would soon leave it at the mercy of vandals and fires.[12]

Because it was isolated on the west side of town, the Brook had more in common with the earlier Morrissey-Canfield tradition of a single self-sufficient casino than with America's future gambling centers. Along the western shore of Saratoga Lake rose the latest prototype for Las Vegas, a true strip. A player driving his Hispano-Suiza or Dusie hit the Lido Venice, built in the mid-twenties on the north side of Union Avenue about a mile past the track. Up the lake hill sat the Arrowhead Inn in some woods, then Jim Riley's old sports bar, hard by Lake Lonely and the only one of the casinos still standing today, sort of. Next was Newman's Lake House, perched right on the road.[13]

Food, sports, and gambling had been the lake houses' claim to national fame since Moon's. Now they approached a flashier age with a melange of high-quality cuisine, service, much of it provided by black help, and chic entertainment. The Arrowhead Inn, for instance, would feature Paul Whiteman's Orchestra and his new group, the Rhythm Boys, with a guy who, very oddly—unlike, say, Eddie Cantor—didn't shout. It was a whole new approach. His name was Bing Crosby.

But the secret of the clubs' success was to keep the illegal gambling in a separate room. This allowed them to put on the lid whenever necessary. It also let them double as dining and dancing spots for social and community affairs, the perfect cover. At high season, of course, it was all very worldly, the jeweled side of the Jazz Age. That age may have been just a rumor for millions of hard-working Americans, but as they could tell from their newspapers, it was actually happening at Saratoga Springs. There was a flip side to these flappers, though, not that anyone saw it at the time. Rothstein's pupils, led by Lansky and Luciano, were learning fast, and they would be entrenched at the lake by the thirties.

"Hello, Fred: Dempsey has his training camp here. We go over to see him training every day. . . . Edna."[14]

As Edna revealed on her postcard, Man o' War wasn't the only superathlete who made Saratoga a dateline of the Golden Age. Sports reporter and historian Joseph Durso would sum up the era: "Babe Ruth . . . hitting the ball out of sight . . . Bill Tilden dominating the men's singles championships . . . the Four Horsemen of Notre Dame winning ten straight . . . And Man o' War finishing first in twenty of the twenty-one races that he ran. But the performer who captured the public's fancy in the most basic way was Jack Dempsey."

Dempsey had mauled Jess Willard for the heavyweight title in 1919. Now, four years later, the Manassa Mauler was about to fight the Wild Bull of the Pampas, Luis Angel Firpo. "My training quarters were at Uncle Tom Luther's small place on Saratoga Lake," he remembered. This was the White Sulphur Spring Hotel, which by 1916 had been running a nationally known training camp for boxers on the northern shore. Dempsey sipped the sparkly with Luther at the springhouse and remembered him unkindly as "quite a character, always walking around wringing his hands, crying about this and that. He was both a walking crying towel and a nervous wreck." What might have kept Tom in a state was that Edna was only one of some three thousand who would show up when Dempsey sparred at the ring near the bathhouse—sometimes with brazen outsiders.

There was J. Paul Getty, for instance, "a good-looking guy," said Dempsey, "about my height but slimmer, who messed around with oil. One September morning, he walked briskly into Luther's camp and asked to get in the ring with me. . . . Incredibly, he gave me a good, speedy workout. He was a fast and dangerous fighter, light on his feet, and he could pedal both forward and backward. Then overconfidence took over."

"'Hit me a little harder, Jack, go ahead, I can take it,'" said Getty. Jack did, and Getty crumpled in a heap.

Firpo, on the other hand, sent Dempsey flying head first through the ropes, though the champ finally caught him with a left to the jaw. In 1926, Dempsey's business manager "suggested I hole up in Saratoga" again while they dickered over a fight with Gene Tunney. When the fight was announced at the Spa, all hell broke out. "The writers rushed to the Saratoga Western Union office where there were seven or eight outlets to New York and only one operator."

"Honey, I forgot to duck," he told Estelle Taylor after losing the decision and the crown. The next year, he was back prepping for Jack Sharkey. It was not a good time for him. Since he sometimes trained in secret, Dempsey said, "thousands of people were turned away from the camp. Balding Tom Luther cried over how much it was costing him per day and complained about the headache the sports writers were giving him." Tom usually got fifty cents per person for the sparring matches.

Reconditioned at Saratoga, Dempsey floored Sharkey in July. Two months later, however, he forgot something else; to go to a neutral corner when Tunney was down in the seventh round. When he finally did, the Long Count started again at one. Tunney was up at nine, and still champ.

So was Harry Whitney, who led the owners in 1920, 1924, 1926, 1927, and 1929. He again replaced Madden as top breeder, with a record $825,374 in 1929. Meantime, the family's other branch had appeared on the turf. When Oliver Hazard Payne died in 1917, he left nephew Payne approximately $75 million, nephew Harry a painting, and niece Dorothy nothing. The preferred niece, Pauline, had died the previous November. Nephew Payne increased his pile through investments, and in 1924 only Henry Ford and John D. Rockefeller, Jr., paid more taxes.[15]

Women and horses; it was a powerful combination. It was not Payne but his wife Helen Hay Whitney who led that branch's turf empire as she formed Greentree Stable, Payne becoming an active partner only in the mid-1920s. In 1923, Greentree was second on the earnings list, though it would not approach Harry's stable in those years. Payne's fortune was quite another matter. When he died in 1928, he left what was termed the largest estate that ever went to probate in America, one conservative estimate putting it at $178 million. It was to be held in trust for son John Hay (Jock) and daughter Joan.[16]

The decade saw the fading of the Belmonts' half-century on the turf. August II's Westchester Racing Association had found itself in deep trouble after financing the return of New York racing. It had to rebuild after much of Belmont Park was destroyed in 1917 by fires, believed set by German sympathizers after reports it was to be used for prisoners of war. Finally, after spending most of 1918 in France and Spain, August II unloaded most of his racehorses.

Confronted with the death of August III of a ruptured appendix at age thirty-six and with his mounting business problems, Belmont sold most of his 1919 yearlings and the 1920 crop as well. He returned for a few final years of racing, and died in December 1924. His 115 head of breeding and racing stock and yearlings sold the next year for an estimated $1.1 million, nearly double August I's previous record dispersal of 1890–91. August II had bred the winners of six Belmont Stakes, five Jockey Club Gold Cups, and four Saratoga Cups. And Man o' War.[17]

His death and the spectacular sell-off of his Nursery Stud raised the profile of a new family. When his brother George went down with the *Titanic*, Joseph Widener became the principal heir of Peter A. B. Widener's Philadelphia street railway fortune. He moved to France during the New York racing blackout and became an ardent francophile, which would show as he encouraged saliva tests for horses and pari-mutuel betting. Upon his return he set up at Elmendorf Farm in Kentucky, on a piece of James Ben Ali Haggin's original Elmendorf Stud. Then, in the Belmont sell-off, he bought the yearlings and breeding stock, redispersing much of the latter the same year. The racing stock was acquired by young railroad heir W. Averell Harriman for Log Cabin Stable, which he had formed with banker G. Herbert Walker.[18]

Widener followed August II as president of Belmont Park, modernized that huge plant, then looked south. He would soon get together a group to buy Hialeah, completing a triangular Kentucky–New York–Florida empire. His protégés on the turf would be his son Peter A. B. II, and especially his nephew, George, Jr. The latter had bought the old Pennsylvania stud farm called Erdenheim in 1916. At the 1922 Saratoga sales, George purchased St. James, who came right back the next year and won the U.S. Hotel Stakes and the Special, then the Belmont Futurity and the two-year-old championship. As historian Bernard Livingston pointed out, it threw George into the front ranks of racing, where he remained for nearly half a century.[19]

Frank K. Sturgis succeeded Belmont as chairman of the New York–dominated Jockey Club. By then, it had lost much of its power over the turf. Maryland and Kentucky had shown the way as their state racing commissions asserted their independence, banning bookmakers and restoring the old pari-mutuel system. Prestigious New York was still the apple of racing's eye, however. Some time before 1921, this was summed up in a term invented by turf people and institutionalized by a Saratoga Springs–born writer in his *Morning Telegraph* column, "Around the Big Apple with John J. FitzGerald." It meant not the city as a whole, but its racetracks. The Big Apple, of course, always adjourned for its annual haj.[20]

"All roads are leading to Saratoga," the *Times-Union* reported from Albany in 1928, a season that typified the boom years before the Crash. "Thousands of persons are pouring into the city from every state in the Union—by boat, automobile, train, trolley and"—a relatively new passenger conveyance—"airplane." The Spa's Chamber of Commerce had opened a small airport, with flights provided by "Earl C. Woodington, formerly an aviator in the service of the United States."[21]

"Henry Ford starts work on 6,000,000 acres for rubber growing in Brazil," an unrelated article noted, while "Ford's friend, Firestone, is making a big rubber experiment in Africa." Judging from the rush to the Springs, they would need it. "More than 2,000 passengers and 125 automobiles arrived from New York this morning by boat." On one route north, Menands Road, Police Chief George Gay led six agents to a house, where they said the occupant unwittingly welcomed them with six bottles of liquor in his arms. The agents allegedly found a vault containing "champagne, rye, Scotch, Canadian ale and cordials," supposedly worth $12,000 and destined for Saratoga. An adjacent article had New York City mayor Jimmy Walker vacationing in Canada, the source of much of the finest bootleg liquor. And a *Times-Union* cartoon proclaimed, "I believe in stopping licker. I stop all that comes my way."

"The lid was ordered closed on gambling at Saratoga. All gambling places at

Albany also are reported to have been closed." That item was hard to believe, and in fact, a few days later, charging that gambling was on again at the Spa, reform lawyer Carl McMahon threatened to turn over the names of four joints to Governor Al Smith. The D.A. and sheriff declined to comment. For "thousands" now, the *Times-Union* advised, the prevailing offtrack betting method was illegal "gambling rooms," soon better known as "horse rooms." On the nightclub circuit, the Lido Venice opened the Saturday before the races to a proper crowd of the Albany and Saratoga bourgeoisie.

The aristocracy was about to take over. Mrs. Graham Fair Vanderbilt, Willie K. II's first wife and one of the great turfwomen of the day, was ensconced in the Lawn, Blanche Nolan's 1870s home at 24 Circular Street (still there, with its spectacular Japanese sunflower cast-iron fence). The Averell Harrimans were renting out North Broadway again at Broadview Lodge, the charming Tudor country estate later called the Surrey (today part of Skidmore College). The William O. duPonts had taken 39 Fifth Avenue. The gambler and Mrs. Tom Pendergast represented Kansas City. The Hotel Russell on Franklin Square ran an ad in the *New York Morning Telegraph* and put up signs announcing "Gentile Management."

C. V. B. Cushman (Eastland Farms) went up to the Fasig Tipton sales, which had long since moved to East Avenue, and bid the most anybody ever had there, or would for years: $75,000 for the Whisk Broom II yearling New Broom. The sales had been setting long-lasting records at a fast clip—an average price of $3,825 in 1925, total sales of $1,901,525 in 1926.

When the crowd of more than fifteen thousand got to the track on opening Monday, they discovered its contribution to the sport's nationwide expansion. In the Chicago area, Washington Park, Lincoln Fields, and Arlington Park had all opened in the past two years. Now President Richard Wilson welcomed Mr. and Mrs. Kermit Roosevelt, future secretary of the treasury Ogden Mills, and Jimmy Walker's wife to a new clubhouse.

It looked to an admiring reporter like "one huge hanging garden." Ornery James Rowe said some colt being led onto the track would probably crash through the hedge and into the chairs and tables. Meant for three thousand humans, the clubhouse had twelve hundred box seats. At the moment, they displayed the American woman's new insistence on sportswear, if she could afford it, especially "sports suits, pure white, brilliant blues and yellows predominating. Sheer frocks of crepe de chine, fashioned with deep circular collars, and having a wide sash at the waist of contrasting colors were also popular." Cloche hats were all over the place. The men had "some weird and awful clothes combinations." A man named Jesse had Beaut's job in the clubhouse in the mid-twenties.

Here the races "take on a polish and glamor," the *Times-Union* said. "The patrol judge rides out in a snappy black and red coupe of expensive make, the kind you see abroad, and the starter and his crew make the trip to the barrier in a big red bus."

The thirty-day meeting offered more than $500,000 in stakes and purses. Nationwide, the total had boomed to $13.9 million the year before, a height not to be matched for a decade. Saratoga's richest, the Hopeful, was worth more than $50,000 for the second straight year. Its 1928 lineup featured a new weight-for-age test for threes and

The new clubhouse, 1928. *Keeneland-Cook.*

over, the mile-and-a quarter Whitney, named for the late Payne Whitney. Black Maria won it, Laverne Fator up.

Earl Sande was still the great jockey of the moment. When he won with Chance Shot on opening day, he got an ovation, for he had demonstrated enormous courage in recent years. He had fallen at the Spa in 1924, James Butler's Spurt rolling over on him and breaking his legs, an arm and six ribs, his life in the balance as doctors applied silver plates to make him more or less whole. In 1927, his wife had died, and the Maryland Racing Commission had revoked his license for using the filly Bateau to ram Reigh Count into the rail in the Pimlico Futurity. Now, the license restored and his winning percentage at .27 in some thirty-five hundred races, Sande was still, as the *Times-Union* put it, "the white-haired boy with the crowd." He soon retired and went into training, but he would be back yet again, big-time.[22]

Fator was probably the second best, although he once lost a Saratoga race by watching a horse on the outside while another got by the rail, inspiring James Rowe's advice, "Remember, Laverne, every horse has two sides." He brought both sides of Prudery home in the 1921 Alabama and took the Hopeful on Pompey in 1925, and back-to-back Cups on Mad Play and Espino in 1925 and 1926. He doubled in the Travers, first on Little Chief in 1922 and again on Brown Bud in 1927, when it was officially renamed the Travers Midsummer Derby.

In booming 1928, Americans depressed by the French musketeers' defeat of Tilden and the American Davis Cuppers could thrill to the strongest Travers field since the days of darkness. There were:

• Petee-Wrack. His dam, Marguerite, has been purchased at the Saratoga year-ling sales (by William Woodward), and so had he (by John Macomber, of Boston). At two, he almost always had been a real factor, though never more;

• Harry Whitney's Victorian, winner of the Preakness and Withers;

• the good three-year-old Sun Edwin; and

• the great Reigh Count. Like so many other stars, he had changed hands at the Spa. After losing six straight, he had broken his maiden and produced a payoff for bettor John D. Hertz, founder of the Yellow Cab company and the car-rental empire. With that, Hertz bought him from W. S. Kilmer for $12,500 and added him to his wife's stable. A year later, Reigh Count took the Kentucky Derby from twenty-one others, the biggest field yet. Then he came to the Springs and easily added the Miller. He was a shade under Victorian in the betting on the Midsummer Derby.

As it turned out, however, the above list was also the order of finish in the midsummer mud, except there were four other horses between Sun Edwin and the great Reigh Count. It was the latest of Saratoga's eternal surprises. Actually, it was no surprise to the old betting commissioner, Johnny Walters, who took wagers of $50,000 each on Victorian and Reigh Count but had his own money on Petee-Wrack. After the Travers, the Hertz colt tried harder and captured the Huron and then the Saratoga Cup in a record 2:55.[23]

Another new building was the recreation center across Union Avenue from the eastern end of the track. Like the clubhouse, it was designed by Samuel Adams Clark and financed by subscriptions from racing people. Built for the jockeys and back-stretch help ("backstretch" now meaning any stable and training areas), it was also used as the "Racetrack YMCA." They called it the Jockey Y. It had two wings, one for whites, one for blacks—an outpost of formal "segregation" that evoked memories of the ancient Southern colony at Saratoga. Long afterwards local kids going to day camp here would discover a wall dividing the pool, one side for whites, the other for blacks. The fact that there was no above-water divider somehow made it seem even more absurd. In any event, black riders did not have much use for the pool, since there were virtually none—with a notable exception.

Charlie Smoot went into that 1928 season as the national steeplechase riding champion. The fact that he was surrounded by virulent racism makes it seem all the more dramatic in retrospect. The *Times-Union,* for example, ran cartoons with ugly racist stereotypes, unconcerned with what black or intelligent white readers might think. Reporting on his five-day suspension for interference in the Shillelah, its writer called Smoot "the dusky rider of Pink Star" and three times spelled his name "Smooth."

Yet his courage and talent told. The same *Times-Union* writer had to admit he was, "as a matter of fact, a clean rider." As the story went on, the two-mile Shillelah got more and more interesting. The favorite, Eider, carried the crack Englishman George Duller, said to be the first steeplechase rider to adopt a forward seat. But the horse took "a silly spill on the next to last obstacle. There appeared to be no reason for the tumble, and it came with Eider leading and apparently an easy winner." The spill created a jam, with another horse falling, Smoot bumping Sanford's Thorndale, and 30-to-1 shot Thracian going on to win. Why did Eider fall? Whatever the answer, one rider took the heat. "One feature of the jam," said the *Times-Union,* "was Smooth's willingness to take the blame and admit his offense."

Misspelled or ignored then, this national champion's name remains unknown today. Courageous, too, were those who hired him despite the exclusion of black jockeys. He rode Pink Star for the Cooperstown stables of Mrs. F. Ambrose Clark, another great woman of the turf. As for the rec center, it long since has been "desegregated," with one of the wings turned to administration purposes. The pool itself survives, and so does the wall, a reminder.[24]

The Eider case is a reminder of a long day at the track for Giuseppi "Joe the Boss" Masseria, reputed leader of the New York bootleggers and racketeers. In deep, he finally bet a bundle when told a jump rider was going to take a fall on the favorite, but the horse led all the way. "When da jock on da fave, he's a gonna fall?" screamed Masseria, according to Toney Betts, né Anthony Zito, who had a nice ear for accents. At the last hedge, he fell.

So would the Boss, when a hit team allegedly organized by Lansky and abetted by Luciano murdered him in a Coney Island restaurant a few years later. It would make Luciano the new boss of the New York rackets. On another occasion, Betts said the Brooklyn operator Anthony "Little Augie Pisano" Carfano put a friend, the gambler Harry Segal, under house arrest at the United States Hotel and also had trainer Henry Goldberg held captive in a lake cottage until a little known sure thing, My Son, reached the track. He was helping them keep their mouths shut. My Son won in the mud.[25]

If the racketeers never got control of horse racing, it was not entirely for lack of trying. It was one of the items on the agenda of the first major crime bosses' summit in Atlantic City in 1929. Present were the well-known Chicago racing fan Al Capone, and a New York contingent that included Luciano and Lansky. The idea was to find a way to hook up to the racing wire of publisher Moses Annenberg and his *Morning Telegraph*. At one point, when mobsters backed a competing sheet and copied the *Morning Telegraph*'s charts, Annenberg sprang a trap for them by running a wrong result, which the mob sheet copied. He would wind up in complete control of the wire himself, forming the Nation Wide News Service, which served wire offices and horse rooms, but the government in turn would go after him for income-tax evasion.[26]

The Roaring Twenties ended for Saratoga with the deaths of several giants of the turf. On August 2, 1929, James Rowe died at Saratoga, and President Richard Wilson ordered the flags flown at half staff, the first time that had ever been done for a trainer. Rowe had ridden Harry Bassett to victory over Longfellow in the Saratoga Cup of 1872 and went on to train the winners of three Travers, six Futurities, and seven Belmonts. James Rowe, Jr., succeeded him. A month later, Sam Hildreth died. He had trained for Lucky Baldwin, Will Whitney, August Belmont II, and Harry Sinclair and led the trainers list six times, three times with his own horses. In October, Mars Cassidy died. He had been the first to use any sort of barrier regularly. Son George followed him as New York State's chief starter, and sons Marshall and Wendell also became racing officials. In November, it was John Madden, who had bred five Kentucky Derby winners and helped lead the Whitneys into racing.

The year closed with the death of Richard T. Wilson. He was the visionary who convinced W. C. Whitney to revive the Spa, then led it through its worst crises. He was succeeded by Secretary George Bull. The new secretary was John A. Morris, who contributed a sense of continuity. His great-grandfather, Francis, had raced Dangerous here in 1863 and imported his Eclipse, who produced the deadly sisters led by Ruthless.

 *20*

GALLANT FOX

R IGHT FROM THE START, and with every stride, he pointed to a New Deal. His dam, Marguerite, had been purchased the usual way, for $4,700 at the Saratoga sales, but his sire, imported Sir Gallahad III, had been acquired in one of America's first stallion syndicates, organized by A. B. Hancock, founder of Claiborne Stud in Kentucky.[1]

Gallant Fox was the first in a series of new champions with unforgettable names that promised glamour in the midst of terrible times—Twenty Grand, War Admiral, Seabiscuit, Whirlaway, Count Fleet. His trainer was the future, too. Born on the land that became the Sheepshead Bay course, James Fitzsimmons had ridden, then trained, at the old city tracks in the shadow of the three giants—Rowe, Hildreth, and their surviving pal, Jack Joyner. But "Sunny Jim" was to become a giant himself.

The colt's owner was a fast-rising power as well. He was syndicate member William Woodward, heir to the pre-Revolutionary Belair Stud. Today, on a patch of what used to be Belair, the Bowie, Maryland, Public Library harbors a little known treasure: the Selima Room, an archive of the turf, including the fantastic flights of the Fox.[2]

He wasn't so hot at the start. A contemporary, John Hervey, said the colt was so curious he couldn't concentrate. At two he took Saratoga's Flash and only one other in seven tries. Still, he was more impressive than, say, Los Angeles millionaire Chaffee Earl's Jim Dandy, who was unplaced in sixteen of nineteen outings, though this one did win the Grand Union in the mud at 50 to 1.

It was when Gallant Fox turned three, six months after the Crash of 1929, that he showed Americans how to succeed in business, unveiling the New Deal along the way. After scoring in the Wood Memorial at Jamaica, he burst out of something called a starting gate in the Preakness, the first American classic in which that device was used. Primitive gates—as well as simpler barriers and tapes—had begun to appear on the tracks in the 1890s, and there was much experimenting again in the twenties. By 1930, George Bull had put in a stationary stall gate for Spa races from the chute. It would be another year before New York tracks would see regular use of the huge gates on wheels with twelve or fourteen stalls welded together and extra horses lined up outside them. Saratoga would not resort to the portable gate until three years after that.[3]

Eight days after his Preakness, the Fox added the Derby. The Preakness, *then* the Derby? It was one of the eleven times that happened. It was also the third Derby win for Earl Sande, the first jockey to pull that off since Ike Murphy in 1891. Forgetting his retirement, he was back in the saddle on the Fox and sopping up a returning hero's welcome from the crowds.

Gallant Fox, Sande up.
Keeneland-Cook.

With the Belmont, the colt became the second Triple Crown winner and the first actually called that. Turf writer Charles Hatton dreamed up the term that year—his wife said "it fell out of his typewriter"—though it would be many more years before publicity departments would milk it.

His flight proceeded with the Dwyer at Aqueduct and the Classic at Arlington Park in Illinois, where his appearance again disclosed the future, for the governor was among the fifty thousand spectators. He had performed for governors in the Preakness and Derby, but it was something new elsewhere. Suddenly the states were finding the sport respectable. Many more began to create racing commissions, which licensed tracks and personnel, allotted dates, and heard grievances, while recognizing the Jockey Club's preeminence in writing the rules. What they found most respectable was money. Following the examples of Canada, Kentucky, Maryland, and Illinois, states began replacing bookmakers at the tracks with pari-mutuel machines and early tote boards showing the number of tickets sold on each entry, the "straight," place and show pools, and thus the odds. Again, it would be several years before the pari-mutuels would return to bookie-rich New York.

The Depression victims found the track a great escape. Of course, Saratoga always had been. At the moment Congress Theater at Broadway and Spring (still there) had two world premieres: *Whoopee,* with Eddie Cantor, and *The King of Jazz,* introducing Bing Crosby. Those who missed the latter could catch its stars—Bing, the Rhythm Boys, and the Whiteman Orchestra— out at the Arrowhead.

Some escaped expensively. With the Fox giving an edge to everything, the yearling sales brought out Mrs. Vincent Astor, in a fawn-colored, fur-trimmed evening wrap over a pale green chiffon gown, and Mrs. Graham Fair Vanderbilt, consulting one of the catalogues, which for the first time ran out. "It is not often," said a New York paper, "that Saratoga . . . is treated to the sight of a Vanderbilt and an Astor all in the same evening." Actually, it was old hat, the Commodore and William B. Astor having appeared in 1865, with A. T. Stewart thrown in. But the sales had indeed become a huge event. More than six hundred head were offered, among them some fourteen or fifteen each by Sir Gallahad III and John P. Grier, and others by Upset and Sun Briar.

The star slipped into town four weeks early, and looked the part. A bay who had black points, a blaze that widened over the muzzle, and "unusual heart room," he had "an air of intense, almost flaming vitality," said witness Hervey. "His action was high, rapid and flying."

Again he brought out the relevant governor. It had been nineteen years since Charles Evans Hughes had backed legislation closing New York's tracks. But this one was a real governor, at least for the turf, and happy days were here again. The people were happy, too, especially George Bull, who welcomed Franklin and Eleanor to the track. The balding Association president usually affected a dapper look, wore pink silk pajamas, and would present sumptuous entertainments at his 1 Fifth Avenue digs a few blocks away.

Nobody, however, could have been happier than chain-smoking little Louis Howe, Roosevelt's chief of staff. He grew up a few steps away at 131 Phila Street (still there) and would wind up living in the Lincoln Room. FDR's gang was having a hell of a time in hell.[4] "You see, racing is all right here, but betting is illegal," Eleanor's secretary explained to five young ladies on Howe's staff. "So steer clear of those 'betting boys' who go through the crowd. You are in the Governor's box, and everybody will be watching you." They found her ban irresistible. "We 'made book' . . . and laid bets among ourselves," one wrote, "keeping a wary eye on Mrs. Graham Fair Vanderbilt in the next box."

Damon Runyon, the best reporter to hit the track since Nellie Bly, put it this way: "It is against the law, of course, to make book on horse races in New York State, so gentlemanly gentlemen stand around in convenient spots and permit you to hand them slips of paper on which you might note your theory of a race. You pay off, or collect, as the case may be, the next day."[5]

The customers frequently welshed. "I've got $3,000 in cash," one bookmaker had moaned at the end of a season, "and $100,000 in paper." Runyon would use this assignment as the basis for a short story about one Frankie Buzzsaw, who was in

Franklin and Eleanor. George Bull welcoming them on one of their visits to the track. *George S. Bolster Collection of the Historical Society of Saratoga Springs.*

deep. A bookie had threatened to break his legs if he didn't ante up, so Frankie sat in the United States Hotel, contemplating the antique rope fire escape attached to a hook, its length determined by how many floors down it was. He tied it around his neck and jumped, but the rope split, and he landed right on the leg-breaker. "The bookie chased Frankie plumb to Mechanicsville." Still, he had the favorite in the next day's Travers Midsummer Derby with Gallant Fox.[6]

The biggest crowd in years came out, the estimates ranging up to fifty thousand (*New York Herald-Tribune*). They abandoned motor cars two miles away. Because most were from out of town, Runyon figured it cost them an average of $100 per head to make the trip, including the $3.85 at the gate and another $4.95 for the clubhouse. Gene Tunney was walking through the throng, greeting everybody who had come to see what Runyon called "the equine Jack Dempsey." From the press box, "high up in the quaint old fashioned grandstand," Runyon admired the infield with its sparkling little lake and big white swans. "There is no doubt about it," he concluded, "Saratoga is the most beautiful race course in the United States, because it has age behind it. They can't grow spreading trees and gorgeous hedges overnight."

For the first time at Saratoga, Harry M. Stevens ran out of clam chowder, and

The swans and the canoe. Photographed by C. C. Cook. *Keeneland-Cook.*

there were so many requests for tables he had to serve lunch on the top deck of the clubhouse. From a box at the edge of the terrace, near the grandstand, FDR looked east to where they would break, midway down the stretch. He would have loved to have the Fox's numbers, 1 to 2.[7]

"The bugle brought the horses out on the track at 5:20," Runyon reported. "The red-hooded Gallant Fox was first, right behind 'Red Coat' Murray on his lead pony. . . . The crowd began applauding, and the Fox peered around knowingly." George Cassidy was in the starter's pulpit, ready to give them the word. They were hardly lined up, Runyon said, when Cassidy sent them off with "Come on!"

It was August 16, 1930. Bread lines had formed, four million were out of work, and the only one in the country who knew what he was doing was a horse. They were off!—and one hundred thousand eyes fixed on a lurching mass of horseflesh struggling to separate. Gallant Fox had won it all—six straight classics—but Harry Payne Whitney's Whichone got clear first. He had just won the Saranac, Whitney, and Miller, and the bookies had him at 7 to 5. Grab the lead, Ray Workman had been told, and keep it.

At the clubhouse turn, Whichone, on the rail, and Gallant Fox were neck and neck. Whichone picked up half a length round the bend. Into the backstretch, the Fox pulled even, and nudged ahead. Then Whichone closed, and nosed in front. "It was a horse race fit for the Gods of Sports," said the *Herald-Tribune*. The Fox fought back from outside. They were head and head again. Sonny Workman was trying to keep the Fox on the outside so "Handy Sande" couldn't pull his old trick of locking legs if he got inside.

The going? Track superintendent Tom Clare had done what he could, but it was the worst mud of the meeting. "It rained intermittently just before the race," Runyon said. "It rained at times while the sun was shining." The others? Kilmer's Sun Falcon was 12 to 1, Jim Dandy 100 to 1. Into the far turn, Whichone finally began to weaken, and Workman went wide, taking the Fox with him—until the Whitney colt collapsed.

The Fox raced on at last. But the cheering stopped. There was something like

It's Jim Dandy! *Keeneland-Cook.*

silence. Said Runyon: "The experts in the press stand with their glasses leveled on the lunging horses began murmuring the name of Jim Dandy. The crowd could see it, too. They could see that chestnut, with little Frankie Baker kicking his sleek sides, moving up inch by inch."

Staid John Hervey would be moved to an exclamation point. Jim Dandy "had dashed up from the rear, passed on through next the inner rail and assumed the lead! It was like a transformation scene in a stage spectacle and left the entire assemblage . . . gasping in amazement. . . . The rank outsider came romping through the mud to win as he liked."

The Fox finished eight lengths behind, exhausted by his furious struggle with Whichone, who was eleven lengths farther back and broken down, never to race again. The *New York American:*

By Damon Runyon

Saratoga Springs, N.Y., Aug. 16.—You only dream the thing that happened here this afternoon.

Sande walked to the jockey room, visibly upset. "Was beaten by a natural mud runner," he told the reporters. "I am sorry, more than you can imagine, for it hurts to lose on such a great horse."

The $27,050 Travers would be Jim Dandy's only win in twenty starts that year. The *Times* said it was Reigh Count in the mud versus Whitney's Victorian versus unheralded Petee-Wrack all over again. What it was, was Saratoga.

*   *   *   *

Nobody recorded how many Depression victims cashed in at 100 to 1. One person who did was subway builder Sam Rosoff, who reportedly bet $500 and picked up $50,000. After the races, the fat gambler would stand on the porch of his brick mansion across from the track (where the National Museum of Racing is today) and holler to his gambling friends, who would stop and have a drink. He would hand out fives, tens, twenties, and more to some of them, and some promised to pay him back.

"I should live so long," he would answer.

"Nobody really went stone broke in those days," wrote Toney Betts, a witness to the times. "There was a community feeling of good fellowship, and a gambler in a winning streak wouldn't shirk the responsibility of being his brother's keeper." Years later a Jersey horse room near the George Washington Bridge would still have a sign above the cashier's window reading: "PLEASE DO NOT ASK FOR CARFARE."

Before FDR hit town, a former policeman had sent him a list of eighteen gambling joints and fourteen other questionable places at the Spa. This forced him to order the lid closed before he got there, and apparently it was, more or less. The Brook put on its nicest face. George Bull gave a dinner dance there for Mrs. Vanderbilt, Mrs. Riddle, the Chauncey Olcotts, and such. Near the lake, the Piping Rock was behaving, too. The former Lido Venice, it was a low-slung affair in exotic desert stucco that gave the distinct impression that Rudolf Valentino was not dead. Its new name was taken from the Long Island set's little Piping Rock racetrack, polo field, and hunting course at Locust Valley. It was the perfect symbol of Thirties glamour, a mix of money that people could only dream of, show business, and gambling. On this weekend, though, it was hosting highly respectable high-society parties.

The *New York American* said Saratoga's sudden reform wave "reached flood tide when Governor Roosevelt was in town yesterday," then receded. The town had stayed good "until almost a whole minute after the Governor drove away." By Monday, it reported, it was "wide open again," and "the boys who spin the alluring wheel and rake in the prettily colored chips . . . who excel at what is commonly called 'rolling the bones'. . . who sit in their shirt sleeves behind the green-topped card tables" returned to "fishing for 'suckers' down at the lake resorts." FDR won in a landslide, the first Democratic governor to carry upstate.

Two weeks after the Travers, Gallant Fox was back, capturing the Saratoga Cup and ending up with nine out of ten for 1930. It made him the first horse in the world to earn $300,000 in a year, with $308,275, and gave him a record lifetime $328,165. He pushed his sire to an unprecedented $422,200 for the year. Fitzsimmons led the trainers list with a record $397,355. Woodward succeeded Frank Sturgis as chairman of the Jockey Club in November.

Sande would soon turn to training again, but not for good. Steeplechase rider Charlie Smoot was still winning, taking the Broad Hollow at Belmont and later repeating in the Shillelah at Saratoga. His brother George was almost as good, winning the Saratoga in 1931 and several others over the next few years. A third brother, Tom, also jumped. High society was represented over the hedges, and brilliantly, by George (Pete) Bostwick and Rigan McKinney.

Absent the Fox, Equipoise would be better remembered. Another name might have helped, though Hervey measured him and concluded that his physique—clean, closely knit, nothing overemphasized—made Equipoise "one of the most perfectly named of champions." Because of his lustrous coat, he did have a nickname, the Chocolate Soldier, and at two he fought a pair of battles few witnesses could forget. They pitted the branches of the turf's leading family, Harry Whitney and Payne's widow.[8]

George Smoot. Winner of several steeplechases in the 1920s and 1930s. Here he's on Chuckle, winner of the 1925 Stillwater Handicap. *Courtesy of James Kettlewell and Jane Rehl.*

The first battle, the Kentucky Jockey Club Stakes on October 16, 1930, some called the greatest juvenile race this country had ever seen. Head and head down the stretch, Equipoise and Twenty Grand did the mile in a Louisville record of 1:36. Officials thought the winner was Twenty Grand's nostril. That set up the rematch.

Ten days later, Harry Payne Whitney—"the first sportsman of his time," said the *American Racing Manual*—died of pneumonia at his home, 871 Fifth Avenue. He had tripled his inheritance and recently created the firm that became Hudson Bay Mining and Smelting Co., one of the biggest copper producers on the continent. On the turf, operating from the Whitney Stud in Kentucky and his Brookdale training farm in New Jersey, he won close to $4 million, twice as much as anybody else, and bred more winners than anyone, including 140 stakes champions. With him were his wife, Gertrude, sculptor and founder of the Whitney Museum of Art; their daughters, Flora and Barbara; and their son, Cornelius Vanderbilt Whitney, who had married Marie Norton in 1923. Harry Payne Whitney left $71 million to his children. Sonny would later proudly point out that he paid for the turf empire.[9]

Thirty-one-year-old Sonny had grown up in the luxury of Fifth Avenue, the Long Island estate, Newport, and the eighty-five thousand-acre Whitney Park in the Adirondacks. Before he was twenty, however, he had trained as one of America's earliest fighter pilots, and before he was thirty he had cofounded Pan American Airways. He would run the Hudson Bay firm and create Marineland in Florida. He hardly had time for horses, and could not remember seeing a horse race until 1927. Of course, it was the Kentucky Derby, and it was won by his father, with Whiskery, by Whisk Broom II, out of Prudery. Four years later, Sonny took over the greatest turf empire America had ever seen. His father had left orders before his death that even this event should not interfere with something more important at that moment: running Equipoise, the greatest horse he ever bred, against the hero of Greentree.

So Sonny dispatched Equipoise to face Twenty Grand again in Pimlico's version of the Futurity. Turned sideways when they started from the stall gate, which he hated, the Chocolate Soldier lost both front plates as he ran but he marched through the mud to beat Twenty Grand by half a length. Sonny jumped for joy, looking a little strange in his mourning suit, but it would be his name, after all, at the top of the owners chart in 1930.

In fact, Equipoise won just half his sixteen races at two, and looked no better on paper than George D. Widener's Jamestown, who headed him in the Futurity and swept the Flash, U.S. Hotel, Saratoga Special, and Grand Union Hotel Stakes. Nor was Equipoise able to prove much the next year. After winning one and losing one, he pulled up in the Preakness with azoturia, a urinary and muscular ailment. The field was open to his great rival.

★   ★   ★   ★

Twenty Grand cashed in on eight of ten races in 1931. Fifty years—minus a day—after James Rowe, Sr., saddled his first Derby winner, Hindoo, James Jr. saddled his, Twenty Grand. And fifty years after Hindoo took the Travers, Twenty Grand won it, then added the Saratoga Cup. With fourteen wins in twenty-five outings, he was his trainer's greatest reward. Jimmy Jr. died later that year, two seasons after his father.

It was a filly who deposited the most in 1931, $219,000, keeping Sonny Whitney on top of the list. She was Top Flight, evoking memories of Regret by embarrassing the colts in the Saratoga Special, the fillies in the Spinaway, and the colts again in the Futurity, winning all her seven starts. She would add the Alabama and four others at three.

A Saratoga incident shook the turf in 1931. Ladana, the Rancocas entry in the Burnt Hills Handicap, was scratched after she showed swollen, drooling lips. She had been given chloral hydrate, a sleep inducer, according to Betts. "The fixers planned to book against her and bet on the favorite, Harry Scott, who won at odds-on." It harkened back to 1863 and the apple that did in Thunder. This time a stableboy reportedly confessed, but the green and white silks were barred for the rest of the meeting. Betts suspected that the Jockey Club really wanted to drive Rancocas owner Harry Sinclair out of racing, and that's exactly what happened. The oilman had done six months for contempt as a result of the Teapot Dome scandal in 1929. He played the horses from his cell, and just as soon as he got out he visited his own at Rancocas. By comparison this Saratoga scandal seemed a tempest in a teapot, and he was fed up. He sold his racers and yearlings later that year and most of his breeding stock the next. As Robertson pointed out, the case established the principle that owners, even if not guilty of misdeeds, were expected to protect the public from them.[10]

Another 1931 milestone was the renovation of Hialeah Park, northwest of Miami Beach. It was in part another Spa spinoff, for its creator was Joe Widener, who had witnessed Will Whitney's renovation of the Spa and now had a design based partly on Saratoga, except he went further. By his second Florida season, Hialeah had pari-mutuel betting and a modernized Australian Totalisator, a tote board first used for Australian elections. Though Saratoga-influenced, the Spa had met its match or more in beauty, for the francophile's course looked like a slice of the Riviera, a tropical park. Actually, there was a Tropical Park. It opened at the same time and split Florida's winter season with Hialeah, as the state raked in the revenues. California brought back big-time racing, too, as did nine other states.

Meantime, Equipoise was back. He won seven straight in 1932, lowering the mile mark to 1:34⅖ at Arlington Park. He did have to share the Spa spotlight with War Hero, a Man o' War colt who became the first to conquer the Travers (the last one called the Midsummer Derby), the Huron Handicap, and the Cup. As Hervey noted, many had tried that hat trick but had never pulled it off. As for Equipoise, his ten wins in fourteen starts included the Whitney and the mile Wilson Stakes, founded in 1930.

Equipoise exploded again in 1933, opening with five straight. After repeating in the Wilson, Sonny was offered a crack at Gallant Sir over a mile and a quarter at Hawthorne Race Track outside Chicago. It was near Al Capone's old neighborhood, but Scarface himself was safely behind bars until 1939. The lure was $17,250 and a gold cup, an unusually healthy prize, for the Depression had caught up with racing. Admission at top tracks had fallen to $1, the national average price for a yearling to $569, purse money to $8.5 million, the first time it was below $10 million in a decade. The Wilson had just paid Sonny a pathetic $2,350. Saratoga's richest event, the Hopeful, had plunged to $35,550. "Even the skies were depressed," wrote Betts of 1933 at the Spa, "and wept every day of the meeting." Equipoise made the side trip to Hawthorne, and pulled away in the stretch to win. Nine days later, trainer Tom Healey saddled him under the trees again to win the Saratoga Cup.[11]

Equipoise's career twenty-nine wins in fifty-one starts helped keep Sonny at the head of the owners through 1933. His father had led the list six times and his grandfather twice, giving the stable a so far unequaled twelve years at the top. Harry and Will's horses were also out front during the two years in which they were leased. The Eton blue and brown would not be back on top for another quarter of a century, but the Whitneys remained endlessly intriguing. Sonny, who had married Gwladys Crosby Hopkins in 1931 (his first wife, Marie Norton, wed Averell Harriman next), was a spearhead of the Old Westbury polo team, which won the U.S. championship. His mother, the sculptor Gertrude Vanderbilt Whitney, founded the Whitney Museum of American Art. *Her* mother, Alice Gwynne Vanderbilt, died in 1934, leaving Gertrude the proceeds from the sale of 1 West Fifty-seventh Street, which had been sold years earlier for $7,100,000. That's not all Sonny's mother got in 1934. She also got her niece, who lived with her at 871 Fifth Avenue.[12]

Gertrude won custody of ten-year-old Gloria after an ugly court fight with her sister-in-law, the girl's mother. It was still hard to tell the Vanderbilts without a program, but the mother was Gloria Morgan Vanderbilt, widow of Reginald, the gambler and heavy drinker. *Her* mother, Mrs. Henry Hayes Morgan, was not at all helpful. She was quoted as saying her daughter lived in Europe after Gloria was born and "never wrote or inquired as to the baby's condition." The case also produced one of the great newspaper headlines, about the comings and goings of the child: "Sick Gloria in Transit Monday."[13]

Back at the track, Helen Hay Whitney had built Greentree into a formidable operation, but the first woman to head the owners list was Isabel Dodge Sloane. Her Brookmeade Stable was one of several studs that had revived the horse country of Virginia, and she succeeded Sonny at the top in 1934. She stayed at Broadview Lodge that season and eventually bought a home on Myrtle Street, overlooking the ancient golf course, where she was sometimes spotted when not at its lawn tennis courts. With Inlander, she had won the Travers the year before and had been able to top the three-year-olds with a mere $57,430, but she had a better breadwinner this season, Cavalcade. Snapped up by trainer Bob Smith at the Spa yearling sales for only $1,500, he took Mrs. Sloane's white silks with blue cross sashes home in the Derby and five other races in 1934. Moved, she named her Saratoga stable area Cavalcade Park (Horse Haven's alleys bore such older famous names as Springbok, Hanover, and Kingston).

Many women were among the leaders in the twenties and thirties, far more than today. The Wheatley Stable belonged to Mrs. Henry Carnegie Phipps and her brother, Ogden Mills, Hoover's last secretary of the treasury. They shared Sunny Jim's training talents with Belair, and they had Dark Secret, who won eight at age three and nine at five. Among the latter was an unprecedented 1934 triple in the marathons: the mile and three-quarters Saratoga Cup, the mile and a half Manhattan Handicap, and the two-mile Jockey Club Gold Cup in the mud. In the last sixteenth of the Gold Cup, Charlie Kurtsinger felt his mount sort of drop out from under him, but he raced on, and won by a head. It was only then that the horse nearly collapsed, and displayed a dark secret, a leg broken so badly he had to be destroyed then and there.

The biggest news by far in 1934 was the end of the Oral Days. New York's 1908 antigambling law was finally repealed. The bill that accomplished this made formal bookmaking—open, cash-in-hand, recorded betting—perfectly possible again, if not completely legal. It carried a $1,000 fine and a possible year and a day in prison, except where another penalty was available. And it was, everywhere: the bookie could be sued and forced to compensate the customer for losses. It rarely happened, but when it did, the bookmakers would readily settle. So the bookies ended their diaspora across the Lawn and beyond, and went home to their fixed address east of the grandstand, Will Whitney's old betting ring, renovated and slightly enlarged. Another ring was opened for the field stand up the stretch.

The legislators happily counted some $9,000 a day from state levies on the bookies, who handled anywhere from $300,000 to $700,000 in daily bets. It was a great change after twenty years in the wilderness. One bookie said he lost $4 million to welshers one year.[14]

The new age, 1934 through 1939, would be remembered as the Days of the Slates. Short, powerful John Cavanagh was still the boss of the bookies at age seventy-eight, and their arrival on the Cavanagh Special still heralded the season. Some one

The starting gate. Inaugurated in 1934, the Spa's first portable starting gate was pulled by horses, seen on the infield behind the starter's platform. *Keeneland-Cook.*

hundred showed up for their 1934 rehabilitation. By now, each required at least eight employees: the "block man," usually the bookie himself who handled the slate and decided the odds; the sheet writer, who recorded the bets; the money taker; and the cashier, who paid. Then there were runners, who picked up tips; morning clockers; and a representative or two in the clubhouse. At times, major bookmakers were based in the clubhouse. They all paid a daily fee to Cavanagh, who turned it over to the track.

Some of them, in their suits and ties and fedoras, could have passed for Wall Streeters, but a newcomer could never quite know with whom he was dealing. Betts remembered that one gangster, the reputed ruthless killer Albert Anastasia, worked openly as a bookmaker at the tracks, "with the name of the firm on the slate, 'Albert A.'" At Saratoga, he almost went belly up but turned down an offer by gambler Tommy Francis to bail him out.[15]

Quiet, conservatively dressed six-foot-three Tom Shaw—"notable throughout his world for his swift and paperless mathematics"—was the foremost bookmaker of the moment. "Other bookies check on his prices through field glasses." Second was a curly-headed big mouth, Tim Mara. Then there were Bob Shannon, Max (Kid Rags) Kalik, and Maurice "the Dancer" Hyams, who used to be in show business. No Wall Streeter, the Dancer would show off in front of the Grand Union in the morning, hoofing it, delivering one-liners and offering the earliest odds of anyone. At the track, he "has been known to gallop the whole length of the homestretch, rooting for the horse he wants to win."[16]

The official "morning line," the list of opening odds with the bookmakers, was set by Gene Austin. He got tips from small-time bookies serving the backstretch, and his odds were so accurate they even frustrated ancient John Sanford. The king of Amsterdam would hold his money when his two-year-olds were not up to snuff, thus building their odds. When they were ready, the old man bet wads, only to find the morning line had plunged, sending him into a rage. What he did not realize was that Austin's backstretch buddies also knew.[17]

Just as Nellie Bly had found, women were still barred from the ring. It was the same old story. "They had to sit in the grandstand or clubhouse," said Betts, "and take 15 to 1 on 100 to 1 shots from small operators."

One who didn't take to playing the ponies at all was Frances Steloff, who at the turn of the century had been a flower child in Saratoga's Broadway pageants. She settled in Manhattan, opened the famous Gotham Book Mart, and dealt with the likes of Theodore Dreiser, John Dos Passos, and Eugene O'Neill. Her brother was also into books. In fact, Betts said Ike Steloff was the master "builder" of those days. A builder was a gambler who operated at small pari-mutuel tracks where there wasn't much action. He would buy a bunch of tickets on one or more horses, lowering their price and building the odds on the horse he really liked, which he played heavily with offtrack bookmakers. Steloff once operated at Charles Town in West Virginia. "He was known on the wire as 'Newark Ike,'" and his only flaw was that he "got a bigger kick out of winning $10,000 on a builder than making $100,000 as a bookmaker."[18]

Not all the money was real. Some excellent $100 bills made their debut at Saratoga nightclubs in 1933, and in two years examples totaling $165,000 were passed at New York tracks. They had a flaw in Ben Franklin's eye shadow, but few noticed him winking. They were the chefs-d'oeuvre of William Watts and his partner, an international confidence man named "Count" Victor Lustig. The feds broke the case when Sam Rosoff innocently distributed some to showgirls at the Spa. The bills were traced to the clubhouse and Long Tom Shaw, who unknowingly had taken $1,200 worth. Watts and Lustig were arrested soon afterward.[19]

The track was still rustic. Sans pari-mutuels, there was no need for a tote board, and the infield was pastoral. The swans by this time had been removed, reportedly because it was feared they would attack somebody. In their place were some ducks, "with a few little ones which looked like fluffy brown balls," said Joe Palmer. The ducks preferred the water jump, which led to another of those unusual Saratoga jobs, "duck-shooer." The latter specialist, Palmer said, "would put a plank across the water and moved it steadily to one end, herding the ducks in front it. When it came to a choice of getting out or becoming pressed duck, the little rascals got out and waddled into the tall grass beside the course."[20]

There was a fountain of geysers inside the clubhouse turn, a small officials' stand, and three tall poles topped by gold-painted balls—"change poles" with signs that were run up to indicate jockey changes, scratches, and other earth-shaking developments (the original set of change poles is nearly opposite the clubhouse today). On this side of the picture, crumpled betting slips littered the lawn. The place was as quirky as ever. In the last race on the last day of the 1934 meeting, the first three horses were all disqualified. For months an army of bettors chased the bookies with the ancient refrain: they had the winner but had thrown out their tickets.[21]

The return of the ring was a boon to business. The full brunt of the Depression had come late to the big tracks, and now it left early and they were on the rise again. National receipts, including gate, concessions, and bookmakers' fees, doubled to $2.8 million in 1934. Saratoga's climbed to $509,400, with the new legislation giving the state 15 percent of the gate, the federal government 10 percent. Its paid admissions rose to 191,200, for a daily average of 6,373. The Days of the Slates also brought a brilliant racing commission, appointed by Governor Herbert H. Lehman. "Never before or since has a politician run an entry of State Racing Commissioners who knew so much about horse racing as those three," Betts said of Chairman Herbert Bayard Swope, John Hay Whitney, and John Sloan.[22]

Busy, too, was Paddy Barrie, the last of the great artists. Whereas some did landscapes, some portraits, Barrie painted horses. He had studied in England, at least until Scotland Yard caught up with him. As a stableboy, he had conned Lady Mary Cameron into selling him a dappled gray mare for $85, dyed her reddish-brown and resold the bay to the Lady for $1,500. By the 1920s, he was in America, perfecting his art with a dye supposedly made of heroin, cola nut extract, glycerin, and strychnine. In 1931, the 52-to-1 shot Shem surprised at Havre de Grace in Maryland by beating Greentree's Byzantine, but it turned out Shem was a sham. It was really Barrie's fleet Aknahthon, for whom he had paid $4,300, then colored a dark sorrel. Criminal elements linked to Barrie picked up an estimated $1 million on that "ringer," a term for a horse entered under another name, usually a superior horse running for a weak one.

In 1934, the painter was at the Spa. So were the "Pinkertons," panting for him. The Pinkerton detective agency had grown into a national operation as both the railroads and interstate crime outstripped the development of local police following the Civil War. The police themselves frequently had turned to "The Eye That Never Sleeps." Founder Allan Pinkerton was succeeded by sons Robert and William (Billy moonlighted as an offtrack betting commissioner for Sam Hildreth while Frank James handled his ontrack business, making quite a pair). With the creation of the FBI, the Eye's role narrowed. It included union-busting in the thirties, which all but ruined its reputation, and more traditional services, especially racetrack security.

At the Spa, the Eye focused on a snazzy, beautiful woman—just the kind chubby Paddy liked. In fact, as recounted by Fred J. Cook, a historian of the Pinkertons, she looked like a woman involved in one of Barrie's earlier ringings. Under the track's shady boughs, the Pinkertons tailed her. "She led them to Barrie, sitting behind the wheel of a horse van, about to drive a nag away." The last of the great artists was deported to Scotland and died six months later. The case led to more controls at the tracks, including the tattooing of an identification number on the horse's upper lip. Earlier, the agency had introduced the photographing of a horse's unique "nighteyes" or "chestnuts," calluses on the inner side of each leg, and files of detailed horse descriptions.[23]

 *21*

WAR ADMIRAL, SEABISCUIT, WHIRLAWAY

*B*OOZE WAS BACK, not that it had left. They had even tippled at the track. Betts remembered the turf-sheet publisher E. Phocian Howard entertaining him at the field-glasses stand, "where one got off-the-record miniature bottles of whiskey during Prohibition."

The Noble Experiment was repealed in December 1933, and FDR asked that Americans practice moderation and that the states avoid a return of the saloon. So, said *Fortune*'s report on its 1934 visit, after the races "you float along . . . up into town where, first thing, everyone has a drink, and then nearly everyone has another, and a good many have a third." In a matter of minutes, every bar, restaurant, and hot dog stand had standing room only. They were doing more drinking here than George Washington had.[1]

The classiest oasis was the Worden Hotel bar, across Division Street from the United States Hotel. It was half a floor below Broadway, so customers could watch the passing scene on their way to hell. Owner Edward C. Sweeney revived there all the earlier Spa charm captured in his beloved Currier and Ives collection. Here was the home of the literati, and they had a way of making the best of the place and the times. During the dryness they had sung "sob ballads" composed by former mayor Clarence Knapp. And Saratogian Frank Sullivan, the *New Yorker* writer, held forth here, explaining to Betts why he never wintered in Miami. "I get enough of summer in the summer-time." Who couldn't have drunk to that?

Others burst in to wreck the afternoon quiet at the Grand Union and the States. In spite of the latter's decline, Colonel Bradley and Warren Wright, the Whitneys, the Wideners, and the Vanderbilts stopped at the ancient sportsmen's hangout. "They'd come boiling in when the races were over," old employees would remember, "to leave again after dinner, in evening dress, for the horse auctions, gambling casinos and night clubs." *Fortune*'s man, on the other hand, didn't get out much. "Now Broadway is abloom, full-blown, with prostitutes," he said cleverly. Prostitution "is rarely more noticeable in the U.S. than at Saratoga in season. The girls come in all shades and from many places"—the Deep South, "the railroad streets of Troy," Albany's corridors, New Orleans, Manhattan. A few whorehouses were clustered around Congress Street in the darkness behind the Grand Union.[2]

That same year, 1934, the Little Club in Saratoga presented Jack Mason's Playboy Revue, with sixteen female impersonators. It was "America's dizziest season in America's daftest town."

Most of all they gambled. A sports writer found all the Spa's "resorts" crowded, "from those which display slot machines to the dinner-establishments out near the lake. . . . You can bring your wife, anybody else's wife, your mother, the girl who winked at you on the corner, or your baby daughter. Many do." There were horse rooms and small clubs all around town, one of the former located in the angular building still standing at Caroline and Putnam streets. The biggest in-town deal was the Chicago Club on Woodlawn Avenue, across Division Street from the States. Open from 1 P.M. until past dawn, it employed sixty-five people. Visitors were greeted by a horse room, then all sorts of games. "Men in wet shirts, open at the necks, push one another aside with frantic elbows." Moneylenders stood by, asking a mere 10 percent interest in some cases. Upstairs, amid summery wicker furniture and suave croupiers, fancy patrons plunged at old-fashioned faro and roulette. In the mid-thirties, the club grossed an estimated $2 million in August, for a profit of $200,000.[3]

The Chicago Club was now controlled by Lucky Luciano, who, after allegedly setting up Joe the Boss Masseria for murder, succeeded him as New York's biggest racketeer. Although a silent partner in the club, he was often present in August. Reputed multiple killer Legs Diamond was seen there, but not after mid-December 1931. That's when two gunmen came upon "the beer baron of the Catskills" sleeping in Albany, and kept him that way.[4]

*   *   *   *

Dutch Schultz, who moved from bootlegging to the numbers racket, patronized the Adelphi Hotel, but not after late October 1935, when two gunmen fatally shot him in the washroom of the Palace Chophouse in Newark. Mostly the Saratoga gamblers were gamblers, engaged in a trade later taken over by governors. They had been part of the scene for a century. A reporter in 1934 spotted Nick the Greek, who, it was wildly claimed, "controls most of the chemin-de-fer games operated north of Yonkers," strolling by "on his way to drink Vichy water in the store down the street."

That year brought the reopening of the West, too. Again the Saratoga regulars turned out, as they always had at new tracks going back to Jerome Park and that old Churchill place in Kentucky. This time it was Lucky Baldwin's estate at Los Angeles. The first official course there had opened in 1908, but after two years the legislators shut it down. On December 25, 1934, Santa Anita reopened. Among its original stockholders was Bing Crosby, who had sung for his supper at Saratoga Lake. As for the owner who looked under his tree and found the first Christmas Handicap victory, it was none other than Sonny Whitney, with his filly High Glee. Two months later Sonny's Equipoise, Aunt Helen's Twenty Grand, and Mrs. Sloane's Cavalcade all came west for the turf's richest purse yet, the $100,000-added Santa Anita Handicap. Azucar won it.

As befit a track run by movie producer Hal Roach, Santa Anita featured a slow-motion camera that provided pictures of the finish in three minutes. Two seasons later, there would be photo finishes at Saratoga. The New York Racing Commission added eye tests for judges, just to be sure.

Back east, Cavalcade had run like a motorcade over Discovery, defeating him in the 1934 Kentucky, American, and Detroit Derbies, the Preakness, and the Arlington Classic. Then, with Cavalcade finally out of action, Discovery discovered himself at Saratoga. He calmly "paraded" home, as Hervey put it, in the Kenner (this was the Miller, which had been changed back to its original name), and he won cantering in the Whitney. Discovery had eight straight in 1935. He won the Wilson, then transported a load of 139 pounds in Saratoga's Merchants and Citizens Handicap, the first time that much had been lugged in winning a major American handicap since Whisk Broom II's 1913 Suburban. In fact, Hervey thought Discovery the greatest American weight carrier ever. A repeat in the Whitney was among his other eleven victories in nineteen events that year, which brought his young owner to the top of the list. He was Alfred Gwynne Vanderbilt II, whose father had sailed on the *Lusitania*. Of course, this was not spreading the money around much, since he was Sonny's first cousin, but he was very popular around the barns and played softball with the jockeys at Saratoga.

At five, Discovery returned to startle the Spa in five appearances. With Johnny Bejshak up, he romped by six lengths under the most weight yet toted in the Saratoga Handicap, 132 pounds. He repeated in the Wilson, and then was asked to carry an unthinkable 143 pounds in the Merchants and Citizens. Only one horse in the world had ever won with that much, Carbine under 145 in the 1890 Melbourne Cup. That load and a slow track left Discovery far behind in fifth, but he gleamed again in his unprecedented third straight Whitney, which set up one of the races of the year, the 1936 Saratoga Cup. As he passed the three-eighths pole for the second time, Discovery lost a shoe, and Granville was the winner.

Another golden chestnut was Omaha. He followed his 1935 Derby with the Preakness and Belmont, making Gallant Fox the only Triple Crown winner to sire another. Fitzsimmons became the only trainer to saddle two. Omaha did come to the Springs, but as the turf world waited to watch him in the Travers and Saratoga Cup, he turned up lame in his work. Omaha never raced again in America, but at four ran brilliantly in England.[5]

What about luck? A fire broke out in a horse car on its way to the Springs in 1935. Two horses died, but a groom held a two-year-old's head out the window to give him air. This was Bold Venture. He won three that year but threw his jockey in one race, ran seventh in another, and showed zero in the Hopeful. So when owner Morton L. Schwartz sold his thoroughbreds, nobody wanted Bold Venture, and Schwartz bought him back for $7,100. In 1936, on the last turn in a race, jockey Charlie Kurtsinger was about to drive He Did down the stretch when a spectator on the inner rail reached out and grabbed the whip out of his left hand. He Did didn't, finishing seventh. It was unwanted Bold Venture who won. The race was the Kentucky Derby.[6]

Two weeks later, the fire survivor took the Preakness and was headed for a Triple Crown. But as luck would then have it, he bowed his tendon and had to retire. Three years after that, Robert Kleberg bought him from Schwartz for $40,000 to stand at the King Ranch in Texas. He produced the 1946 Triple Crown winner, Assault.

Luck had an ever more glittering background at the Spa. As quiet as any town of 13,700 for eleven months, in August it was "such a city of 45,000 as you will not find the like of anywhere else on earth." The state-owned "Saratoga Spa"—"the first true spa in the European sense of the word ever developed in America"—opened in 1935. Some ten state-owned springs were the foci of this new park, developed under a commission appointed by Roosevelt as governor and headed by Bernard Baruch. Sprawled across the southern edge of town, it cost $8.5 million. Even before it opened, the bathhouses had become quite successful. A bath or treatment cost $1.50 to $3.50 at the Washington Bath House, which had private rooms, and less at the Lincoln Bath House, which had a "semiprivate" bathing area. A drinking cup cost a penny. The springs were still said to be good for arthritis and some heart afflictions, as a psychological boost, and as a laxative. Said *Fortune*: "They come in three strengths: digestive aid, mild cathartic, and action-within-fifteen-minutes."

In 1934, six thousand people had taken fifty thousand baths in July and August alone. George Bull took the baths. So did Isabel Dodge Sloane. For years they enjoyed a large Jewish clientele. *Fortune* added that throughout the warm months, except for August, all conversation in Saratoga "is narrowed to two topics: how am I doing and how is he doing." It said the state could count on three developments: the fact that Americans spent up to $150 million at European spas, "that even the wealthy brackets of the Jewish trade are cut away from the greatest spas, which are in Germany, and . . . that trouble boils ever more ominously toward the lid of the European coffeepot."

Among nine buildings completed by 1935 were two new bathhouses, increasing capacity to five thousand baths a day, a research lab, and the Gideon Putnam Hotel, named after the town's first developer. Soon to open was the Hall of Springs, a spectacle for spectacle's sake, featuring "huge bulbs in the central hall into which the several strengths and sorts of water will continually wash" and "a balconied symphony orchestra." For puritan America, it was a thrilling concept but one Saratoga had known forever—a temple of aesthetic pleasure in a place for the sick. There was also a "therapeutic" golf course ("flat, for weak hearts, but tricky"). In sum, it was "a place where recreation, living conditions and entertainment are such that the patient is made to forget he is ill." This extraordinary statement of New Deal idealism survives, its cement cracked here and there, but its dream inspiring against a backdrop of Northern pines, springs, bathhouses, lawns, Georgian colonnades, picnic tables, golf links, pools, and a hotel that knows what leisure used to be. It awaits a Roosevelt or Baruch to make it an updated spa in the age of fitness.

There was also more boxing in 1935—a professional program every week at Convention Hall, matches at Luther's on the Lake, where Dempsey now owned a cottage, and amateur bouts at the Jockey Y.

Saratoga was a happy town. "We had five cat houses, no stick-ups, no muggings, no dope, no rapes," one Saratogian would reminisce to a reporter. A favorite area was the Italian but formerly Irish neighborhood, still called Dublin, around Beekman Street. Along with duPonts, Vanderbilts, Gene Tunney, and the rest of the racing and summer crowds, the underworld kings made a beeline to Dublin's Italian restaurants. The hit man Joe Adonis would be remembered locally as "nice looking," which would have pleased him since he thought so, too, which was one reason why he changed his name from Giuseppe Doto. Luciano was "pleasant, nice, low key"—but not after the summer of 1936, for another crusader had appeared in Manhattan, special prosecutor Thomas E. Dewey, and he got Luciano on charges of running a multimillion-dollar prostitution ring in the city. Sentenced to thirty to fifty years, he was sent up to Dannemora, near the Canadian border.[7]

The hottest neighborhood was "Saratoga's imported Harlem," as *Fortune* called Congress Street west of Broadway, noting that Jack's, the Hi-de-Ho, Harlem Club, and Green Cave "have been warming it up since around midnight." Years later "urban renewal" would wipe out all trace of them. The most important clubs were the casinos just out of town. The Brook had taken a step down by 1934, no longer requiring formal dress and membership in what *Fortune* called "the human stud-book." It was a moot point since the place burned to the ground at the end of the year. That left the casinos at the lake. Every evening, the rich would motor to these prototypical nightclubs, or they would send a carriage. Their floor shows, as a reporter put it, ran "less to the hot than to potted-palm styles of entertainment," such as bandmasters Ben Bernie and Whiteman. The real attractions were the games. *Fortune* listed "the wheels (for the sophisticates) and the crap tables (for the vulgar)" and "bird cages (one kind of crap device; highest odds against you of any sucker game; the ladies love it; you can buy it in New York at Abercrombie's)."

First and foremost now was the Piping Rock. Among its headliners were Luciano's favorite, the singer Helen Morgan, and Sophie Tucker. Very few at the time knew it was controlled by Luciano's associate in crime, Meyer Lansky. Thus, two of the most powerful figures in the New York rackets controlled the top two joints in Saratoga. Lansky hardly looked like it. One of his first arrests had been for beating up New York pushcart vendors who didn't pay for protection, but after that he didn't grow much. He was about five-three, insignificant-looking, and stayed in the background. "You didn't even know he was there," a former craps dealer told Lansky's biographer, Robert Lacey, "and when he was there, he looked like nothing." Local ownership fronted Lansky's interest, and even behind the scenes it was in the name of his brother Jake.[8]

Lansky learned. "It was in the course of his Saratoga summers that he discovered he was made to run casinos," wrote Lacey. "Everyone who came into my casino," Lansky said later of his various operations, "knew that if he lost his money, it wouldn't be because he was cheated." He would have two principal partners in the Piping Rock. Frank Costello, a Luciano lieutenant, supplied the managers and materiel. Joe Adonis brought his New Jersey croupiers and many of his customers. Lansky and Adonis both reportedly had interests in the Arrowhead Inn as well.

By 1936, the Piping Rock's elegant twin had opened across the road. This was the Meadow Brook, also named after one of Long Island's horsy clubs. It soon became just the Brook, not to be confused with the burned-down Brook.

The lake casinos had started something that would later reappear like a fabulous mirage in the western desert, gangsters and all, but as the astute Lacey pointed out, another institution would come first: the carpet joint. "Modeled on the Saratoga lake house," he wrote, it was "an upgrading of the more venerable and familiar sawdust joint with its rough-and-ready crap game in the back of a saloon or pool parlor." The carpet was proof of its superior tone. It could add a restaurant, nightclub, doorman, maître d', and games as good as the local fix would allow.

Carpet joints sprang up all over America. As Lacey pointed out, they copied Saratoga Lake's by keeping the gaming separate from the restaurant and the whole joint separate from the town. Lansky opened several at Hallandale, Florida, in 1936, importing some of his best Saratoga people. He applied his Piping Rock and Arrowhead lessons to Batista's Havana and Council Bluffs, Iowa, of all places. Still, he remained family man enough to rent a cottage on the Jersey shore, where his son Buddy could play with the Adonis kids and the Siegel girls. There would be visits from "Uncle" Ben Siegel, who was in California running crap games for movie producers and making book at Santa Anita. In the meantime, his friend Lansky kept returning in August to his first and greatest carpet joint, the Piping Rock.

The most exclusive Saratoga gatherings were something else. Something very, very plain. They were the stable breakfasts, said to have been invented in the 1870s by Southern horsemen. Since pricy horseflesh required careful security, only owners, trainers, guests, and help could watch the morning workouts up close. Even for those peeking through fences, though, they were and are worth getting up for. Fortune's man remembered looking across "the great dim swash of dewy, coleus-embossed grass" to see "the loveliest running, as pure unadorned running, as you'll ever see."

The insiders broke fast in the kitchens on the same fare as the help, black and white, who slept in the low, white-washed dormitories alongside the stables. These were extremely hearty breakfasts, as anyone knows who has woken up in the South. Later, when ladies were welcomed, more correct food appeared on tables outside. By the thirties, the fare had reached vast proportions. It included, for example, the famous Saratoga melons, fried chicken or steak, creamed potatoes, cornbread, and homemade preserves. The Kentucky colonel Edward R. Bradley was said to lay out the very finest breakfast at Horse Haven.[9]

It was an evening event that was the season's social high: the action on George Street, surrounded by paddocks with five hundred stalls. The records of the twenties were not equaled, but this was still the greatest horse sale in the world. Even in 1933, when the rest of the country sold 389 yearlings for $90,000, Saratoga sold 388 for $429,000. The average price, depressed everywhere, was $151 in Virginia, $157 in Maryland, and $259 in Kentucky—but $1,105 at Saratoga. The glowing youngsters were paraded before the leaders of the turf, their glorious motorcars crowded round the ring, the night carrying the singsong of E. J. Tranter.

"There is no scene in America, or elsewhere" said Hugh Bradley, "just like sales night."

"Looking around the ringside, you'd get snow-blind with starched facades," said Fortune, "Klieg-eyed for the diamonds." One woman was throwing great amounts at the yearlings, but then it was her candy store. Ethel V. Mars was the sweetest owner in town since G. W. Loft, and she was busy buying for her Milky Way Farm in Tennessee. She unwrapped more than $100,000 of her late husband's candy fortune at the 1935 sales and more the next year, when her efforts paid off: she became the second woman to lead the owners.

The Spa helped spin off another course in 1936. Keeneland Race Course at Lexington was the dream of John Oliver Keene, no kin to J. R. of earlier days. It was meant to be a nonprofit horse center, a retreat for stabling, training, and racing in the bluegrass, mixing tradition and professionalism. Hal Price Headley, Maj. Louie Beard, the Whitneys, and others joined to realize Keene's dream in the Keeneland Association. It was called the "Saratoga of the South." Nobody seemed to mind that the Fair Grounds at New Orleans already had used that title in its ads.

Sonny and Jock made another dream come true in 1936. They had formed a movie company, and now they paid something under $50,000 for a script their office employee called "a love story between a strong man and a strong girl." But they had to fight the Hayes censorship office, which wanted one of the lines changed to "Frankly, my dear, I don't give a darn." Gallant Fox's Granville was gone with the wind in 1936, too, bringing home the Belmont, Travers, Kenner, and Saratoga Cup.

The next opening day brought the biggest Saratoga betting coup since Pittsburgh Phil and Bet-a-Million Gates. The gambler was Art Rooney, owner of the football Pittsburgh Steelers. Betts, who was there, said Rooney moved from one bookie to another and didn't bet "until it was too late for any bookmaker to rush a 'No Go' message to a jockey." In his loud green suit, Rooney collected $12,000 in louder green on the first race, then $10,000 on a steeplechase. He was up $84,000 going into the Flash, which set him back $10,000 as Maetall took it with the coming English-born jockey, Johnny Longden. The mudder John Jay put him $88,000 ahead after the fifth, and the clubhouse bookies were now very shy of him. He managed to get $3,000 down on the winner of the sixth and $9,000 on the seventh to go home $124,000 ahead.[10]

Nine days later, Greentree's Gillie, a mean character, was leading the way when Thorson moved on the inside. Gillie turned and tried to bite Thorson's throat. He went on to win but was disqualified for the attack, one of the ultra-rare occasions when a horse's behavior brought a disqualification.[11]

Another horse taught a lesson to a high school student in Steubenville, Ohio. Jimmy Snyder, born Demetrios Synodinos, was dealing cards at Steubenville's Half Moon casino, feeling big after picking a string of winners from the *Daily Racing Form* and squeezing $700 from his boss. The boss goaded him into risking it on a Wheatley filly, Merrie Lassie, running in the seventh at Saratoga the next day. Merrie Lassie was a Spinaway winner. The next day he was in the Academy Pool Room, listening to the call, with Merrie Lassie leading, only to hear, "There is a photo in the seventh. . . . The winner is Clodian." It "was one of many instances that led me to give up horse racing as a serious betting proposition," said Jimmy the Greek decades later, when he was a regular at the Spa only for the sheer pleasure of it.[12]

For high drama in 1937, it would be hard to find a more distinguished sire for a Triple Crown winner than another one, the only such progenitor being Gallant Fox. War Admiral's sire, however, was even better: Man o' War. The Admiral had come to Saratoga at two, finishing second in the Sanford and unplaced in the U.S. Hotel and Special. He had his great year at three, when Sam Riddle finally consented to enter that earlybird classic, the Derby. War Admiral carried Kurtsinger to personal revenge at Louisville on his way to the Triple Crown and eight for eight. It was nine of eleven in 1938; he opened that campaign with an eight-length romp through the mud in the Wilson, rested three days and won the Saratoga Handicap, then the Whitney and Saratoga Cup. After collecting the Jockey Club Gold Cup at Belmont, he headed for one of the most famous match races of the century, at Pimlico.

It was a family affair: War Admiral against a Man o' War grandson, Seabiscuit. Saratoga had seen Seabiscuit run for Wheatley four times, as he came in sixth and ninth in two purses at two and took the Mohawk Claiming Stakes and Johren Handicap at three. Nobody picked him up after that claiming race, but later the Californian Charles Howard bought him for a reported $7,500, and he was a changed horse. He won eleven in 1937 and added five in 1938 before taking on War Admiral. They were head and head at six furlongs, then the Biscuit pulled it out halfway down the stretch and beat the Admiral by four lengths. Seabiscuit had thirty-three wins, fifteen seconds, and thirteen thirds in an amazing eighty-nine starts, and was the first to gross more than $400,000, with $437,730. War Admiral won twenty-one of twenty-six.[13]

The most famous horse of the day was neither Man o' War's son nor his grandson. It was Man o' War. His birthday was celebrated that year with a cake and candles and a national broadcast from Riddle's Faraway Farm in Kentucky. Each year thousands came to see him. Eventually his groom, Will Harbut, became famous, too, reciting his exploits in a monologue that proclaimed him "the mostest horse that ever was." If anyone didn't believe it, Sam was happy to prove it with the Man o' War movies he showed at his place on Union Avenue.[14]

New heroes kept emerging, especially in the Travers. Its value had not recovered from the mid-thirties dip, though. Thanksgiving put only $14,400 on Mrs. Parker Corning's plate in the 1938 Travers, but she had to be thankful for two remarkable talents that day. One was Mary Hirsch, the first woman to saddle a Travers winner. The daughter of the great trainer Max Hirsch, she had become the first licensed woman trainer two years earlier. The other talent was Thanksgiving's rider, Kentucky-born Eddie Arcaro. He was moving up fast. In the 1935 Saratoga Special, he had guided Coldstream in a dead heat with Red Rain. This year, he had won his first Derby on Lawrin. Before he was through, he would be considered by many the greatest American jockey ever. Meantime, a black rider was finding prominence in the jumps. A. Scott captured the Harbor Hill at Aqueduct in 1933, 1935, and 1941, the International at Belmont in 1937 and 1940, and the North American at Saratoga in 1939. Another black rider, C. Brooks, would emerge to capture several jumping events in 1941.

Eight-Thirty's 1939 Travers introduced a record five-time repeater, George D. Widener. In a renewal of the Travers cup tradition of the 1870s, his prize was the classic's first "Man o' War Cup." This was the sleek gold vessel by Tiffany that Big Red had won in his Canadian finale. The Travers winner could retain it for a year, and also got a silver replica, which he could keep. Eight-Thirty made it quite a season for the dark and light blue, as he was also on time in the Wilson, Whitney, and Saratoga Handicap.

The world was changing. Everybody knew the ontrack bookmaking era was

War Admiral, Seabiscuit, Whirlaway

seeing its last summer, and in a sort of final tribute many gathered around the Dancer down by the Grand Union. Toney Betts listened to them reminisce. Abe "Sparky" Nussbaum remembered leaving Empire City one year and checking five bags of money with the armored car service as he headed to Saratoga. "Couldn't happen to a nicer guy," said the guard, not knowing that four of the bags were for a gambling-house syndicate—"bankroll money for the big dice game," Betts said. "When Sparky returned to the armored car with only one bag, the guard screamed, 'What happened, Sparky?'"

Betts also remembered soldiers from Plattsburgh marching in the streets of Saratoga that August of 1939. On September 1, Nazi Germany invaded Poland to open World War II. But isolated America was still more interested in such matters as Joe Louis's latest battle. After five knockouts, a TKO, and a decision, he faced Bob Pastor, who became a local hero when he moved to Saratoga. A product of the Bronx and New York University football, Pastor rose through the Golden Gloves, as Louis had. He fought Louis first before a sellout crowd at Madison Square Garden in 1937, when Louis, already a major draw, was looking for a shot at Braddock. The Garden's promoter, Jimmy Johnston, managed Pastor, and told him to run away from Louis. Pastor did, for ten rounds, after which, thinking he had won, he ran to his corner, jumped up, and waved his arms. The decision went to Louis, whose biographer, Chris Mead, said the crowd booed for thirty minutes to show its disgust, not with Pastor but with Louis for failing to catch him, and with the nonfight. Nearly half a century later, Pastor still thought he had won, and he said the judges knew it.

"But they didn't know what to do, because [manager Mike] Jacobs had Louis, and Johnston had me," Pastor told Mead. "Jacobs had all the dough, and he had Louis, so he was paying 'em. I know what happened."[15]

Although Pastor would be dubbed "Bicycle Bob," the criticism of Louis for failing to nail him was harsher, and much of it was racist. Now, in his hometown of Detroit, Louis faced him again. Sportswriter Shirley Povich said it was Pastor—not Billy Conn, as widely believed—who inspired the famous Louis threat: "He can run but he can't hide." This time Pastor was determined to prove he could fight. He weighed only 183 pounds to Louis's 200 but showed incredible guts. He went down three times in the first and, as he later said, was out on his feet for the first six rounds. He then fought back to win the seventh, eighth, ninth, and tenth rounds. "I was five-four-one going into the eleventh round. And then that punch came again, boy. I went down. I got up, moved around trying to hold, but he hit me again, down I went again. I got up, and the referee stopped it. Which was nice, 'cause he saved my life, probably saved my life. I couldn't see out of one eye, and he was hitting me pretty well. He was a terrific puncher." Later he was also kayoed by Conn as the latter moved up to challenge Louis—and got knocked out himself.

It was a KO for the track bookmakers, too. The 1940 season brought the pari-mutuel machines back to New York (twenty-three other states already had them). Their ancestors had made their Saratoga debut under Morrissey and survived nearly two decades before the bookies drove them out. Now it was the taxpayers who restored them, New York voters in 1939 overwhelmingly approving a constitutional amendment permitting pari-mutuel wagering. It would be taxed 10 percent, to be split by the state and the tracks. The next spring, State Senator John Dunnigan sponsored implementing legislation outlawing bookmaking.[16]

Wary Saratogians and almost everybody else adjusted as the machines arrived and tote boards blossomed in Morrissey's infield. The Association spent $220,000 to install the machines in 307 windows, 72 of them on the floor of the grandstand. They were operated by 450 men. The clubhouse was remodeled and enlarged by Albany architects Marcus T. Reynolds and Associates. And the money poured in. Opening day brought a crowd of 7,228 and a handle of $262,526. The number of women betting shot way up, for they no longer had to send male runners to the bookies.

Whirlaway whirled in, too. Among his seven victories were the Saratoga Special and the Hopeful in the pouring rain, both under Longden. There was the usual daffiness. They had a highly unusual two-horse walkover in the Cup, featuring Belair's Travers winner, Fenelon, and stablemate Isolater, who had won the Cup the year before. And there was Sickle T. Turf writer Joe Palmer said a bettor once noticed that Sickle T. was listed in the program as a gelding, but that the animal in the stall called Sickle T. certainly was not. "Ringer!" he thought, and bet him and won, and did the same on another day. It turned out it was the program that was wrong. Sickle T. was not a gelding. He was as much horse as any other—and better than most. On that day, though, he even paid off as a gelding. Sickle T.'s wins included the Saratoga Handicap.[17]

A few blocks away, Fasig Tipton's was still a ring of dreams. Chicago lawyer Albert Sabath paid $700 for Thomas Piatt's modest Alsab. He won fifteen at two, the most ever for a juvenile, beat Whirlaway in two out of three encounters, and banked $350,015.

At the end of New York's first modern pari-mutuel season, Commission Chairman Swope reported that the public had bet $103 million. Attendance was up about 30 percent, including a record 281,377 at the Spa. The state was now a bigger gambling operator than Morrissey, Canfield, Rothstein, and Lansky combined. Some thought it was ruining the sport. "It was the beginning of racing as a tax-grabbing gambling racket," Betts was still fuming years later, "the end of racing as a sport." His friend, E. Phocian Howard, agreed. "In the mutuel machines, a monkey gets the same price as a man."[18]

It was the culmination of a decade that transformed the experience of America's first national sport. There was the huge, ugly gate, which for the first time blocked the public's view of the start; the photo finish, which basically told them to shut up; the scratchy, far-away sound of the radio broadcast, which added that they could stay home if they wanted to; and now there were the tote board and the betting machines at the windows, all but silencing any intercourse people might wish to have with those they were betting with. Certainly they wouldn't want to bother the anonymous ticket sellers with names, such as Whirlaway, when numbers would do. "When what had always been regarded as a sport is transformed into what is really Big Business," John Hervey worried, "what will the sequel be? Has the sport . . . bartered its birthright for something which, at long last, will be its nemesis?"[19]

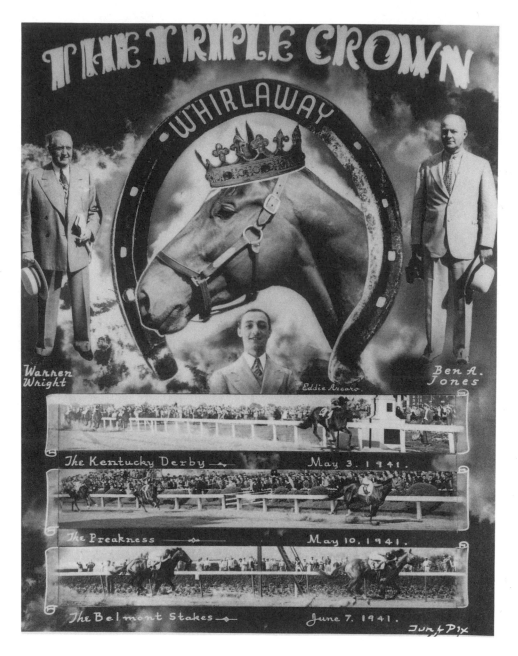

A Whirlaway poster. He then added the Travers. *National Museum of Racing and Hall of Fame, Saratoga Springs.*

The sport certainly was getting bigger. Several more tracks had opened, among them Delaware Park and Del Mar in California in 1937, Hollywood Park the next year. From the Crash, when there were thirty-four, to the beginning of World War II, twenty-four more were created, according to Robertson. Purse distribution climbed to $15.9 million in 1940, and for the first time, California passed New York. The classics picked up cash. The Derby was worth $60,150, a new high, to Milky Way's Gallahadion, and Whirlaway banked $37,850 from his Hopeful.[20]

What war in Europe? The boom continued in 1941, as it had when the Depression first hit. More records were set, the number of foals registered approaching seven thousand, the number of horses racing, fourteen thousand, total purses just under $18 million. New York State introduced the Daily Double, and women loved it. Whirlaway got even better, with thirteen victories in twenty starts. He gave Arcaro the second of his five Derbies, the first of his six Preaknesses, the first of his six Belmonts. Then Alfred Robertson climbed aboard the triple laureate for the Spa's Saranac Handicap, and the picture wasn't quite so clear. Whirlaway was declared the Saranac winner, but the print seemed to favor Man o' War's War Relic. It was one of the first big controversies over the photo finish, causing "a near riot," encouraged by Sam Riddle. With a turf sheet in one hand and his cane in the other, Sam stood in the clubhouse entrance—which Joe Palmer said fit him "about the way the Panama Canal fits the U.S.S. *Missouri*"—proclaiming victory. On closer examination of the picture, however, what seemed to be a hoofprint in the soil turned out to be the tip of Whirlaway's nose, which is why the judges gave it to him "by a nostril."

Noses did count. In 1937, to end arguments over outstretched feet, New York had followed other states in making the "n" the official winning part of a horse in a photo finish. The "nk"—neck—was already in use as the next closest margin of victory. This was one of the few times the photo cleared things up. For many years, it did just the opposite. Earlier, noted one turf writer, the judges had decided the order of finish by "shutting one eye, sighting from a perpendicular rod on the stand to another on the winning post, and making up their minds in the instant the leaders dashed by." Usually one or the other seemed ahead by a hair, the way Twenty Grand beat Equipoise that day. With the photo, that race might have been a dead heat. "Now the judges simply look at an enlarged picture, which occasionally gives neither horse the slightest advantage." The writer noted that only 25 dead heats had been recorded in 1935, but the next year, when a few big tracks installed the cameras, there were 115 and finally, by 1941, 318. The problem seemed most common at smaller tracks.[21]

On August 16, 1941, Whirlaway followed his Triple Crown with the Travers (in a small field and mud) to become the first to achieve what might be called racing's gram slam or Quadruple Crown. At least as significant, though, was his owner, Calumet Farm. The devil's red, with blue bars on the sleeves and blue collar, led the money-winning list for the first time, its $475,091 breaking Sinclair's 1923 mark. It was, as they say, just the beginning. Calumet had been founded as a farm for trotters by Ohioan William Wright, a baking powder manufacturer. His heir, Warren Wright, turned it into a thoroughbred operation in 1931. Five years later, he bought the future great sire Bull Lea and joined syndicator A. B. Hancock in importing Blenheim II, sire

War Admiral, Seabiscuit, Whirlaway

It's Whirlaway! No, it's War Relic! The Saranac Handicap photo finish. Whirlaway is nearest the camera. *NYRA Photo.*

of Whirlaway. The devil's red was about to become the greatest power on the turf since the Eton blue and brown.

An auspicious local event in 1941 was the founding of Saratoga Raceway, with its half-mile track off Nelson Avenue, just south of the flat track. It restored the ancient Saratoga trotting tradition that had begun with the Old Gray Mare and company.

Pearl Harbor was the wake-up call. Among those killed in the war were jockeys

Herbert Chinn, Warren Hawley, and George King, trainer Edward Haughton, Jr., owner C. J. Amendola, former racing commissioner Pearson Jones, and Tommy Hitchcock, Jr., widely rated as the greatest American polo player of all time and son of one of the Saratoga track's founding fathers. Many of the sport's leaders quit the turf as soon as war was declared. Col. John Hay Whitney was captured by the Germans but escaped when the train taking the prisoners from France to Germany was attacked by the Americans. C. V. Whitney enlisted in the army air corps, serving in North Africa and the Pacific. Alfred Vanderbilt quit the presidencies of both Belmont Park and Pimlico to join the navy.

In 1942, the navy asked Meyer Lansky to help infiltrate the New York waterfront to stop supplies from getting to U-boats. He was to work through Luciano in prison. That August, on one of his many trips to see Luciano, he picked up a Piping Rock group headed by Frank Costello, who about that time owned 30 percent of the casino. In an extraordinary scene, the two racketeers, Luciano and Costello, conferred in Italian in a Dannemora interrogation room.

Racing thrived at first during the war with the blessing of the states, except California. The military asked that Santa Anita be closed, and the track suffered the ignominy of being used as a "Japanese Assembly Camp," an internment camp for Japanese Americans, then was converted into an Army Ordnance Training Center. Later the other California tracks closed. Oaklawn in Arkansas suspended racing. Fasig Tipton had a terrible year at Saratoga, the average falling below $1,000. This prompted the new Thoroughbred Racing Associations to recommend that breeders share in the winnings by giving them 3 percent of the added money in stakes. Only New York went for it. Otherwise, the sport was booming.

*　　*　　*　　*

There were about eighteen thousand races in 1942. Unprecedented throngs mobbed the tracks, Belmont registering a record of 51,903 on Memorial Day. They bet $2.1 million, also a record, and there were a number of million-dollar handles. The state now got more, having upped its pari-mutuel cut to 6 percent. Racing finally returned to New Jersey, where it had been banned for half a century, with the opening of the Garden State track at Camden. Whirlaway came back to thrill a crowd in the Massachusetts Handicap at Suffolk Downs and smashed the half-million barrier, with a lifetime $561,161. Helen Hay Whitney's pink and black (chosen long before in memory of a well-loved gown) finally put Greentree at the head of the owners, thanks largely to Equipoise's Shut Out (Mrs. Whitney was a great baseball fan and a great namer). He shut out fourteen others in the Derby and took the Belmont and Travers, the latter by five lengths. It was the second Travers for Arcaro.[22]

In 1943, the Empire City meeting at Yonkers was switched to Jamaica, Hialeah was taken over by the Air Force, and Delaware Park was closed. On a few Saturdays, though, they couldn't hear the war for the crowds, for there was another Triple Crown champ. He was Count Fleet, sired by Reigh Count and owned by Mrs. Hertz, whose husband counted his fortune in taxi fleets. Having put ten wins on the meter in sixteen juvenile rides, he went six for six at three, all easily. But the last of these, the

Belmont, also ended his career, for as he romped home by twenty-five lengths, he struck himself. His resumé mentioned sixteen wins in twenty-one contests and pushed Johnny Longden to unheard of one-year winnings of $573,276. Just as they had said of Man o' War, Longden said of Count Fleet, "We never asked him for all the speed he could give us. But how were we to know?"[23]

Count Fleet would not have made it to the foothills of the Adirondacks anyway. They weren't running. In its first disruption in thirty seasons, the meeting was transferred to Belmont for three years. It was not clear why, Governor Dewey declaring that the government wanted to save on gasoline and tires but the government saying it did not object to keeping Saratoga open as long as no special arrangements were made for shipping horses. Writer Landon Manning thought poor attendance at Saratoga, in contrast to Belmont, was the real reason. Saratoga-at-Belmont set a national record with a daily average handle of $3.1 million.

There was also a major development in the sales world in 1943: the birth of the Keeneland yearling sales. With no meeting at the Spa and breeders desperate, Hancock and others financed an auction in Kentucky. Staged by Fasig Tipton in the Keeneland paddock, it was an encouraging success, with the prices averaging $3,538. This was more than three times the low Saratoga had hit in 1942, when no yearling brought more than $9,000. Keeneland's high was $66,000. Things were looking up in the North, too. Sales at Meadow Brook on Long Island did even better, averaging $4,614.

The end of a Saratoga era coincided with a change in command. On George Bull's death, F. Skiddy Von Stade, the vice president, became president of the Saratoga Association for the Improvement of the Breed of Horses, as they stubbornly called it, although it was still operating out of town. In 1944, for the first time, a filly, Calumet's Twilight Tear, led the threes for the year, although Vienna beat her in the Alabama at Belmont. Pavot won the Hopeful, Saratoga Special, U.S. Hotel, and Grand Union stakes and his four other starts.

What about the Springs? They still came for the waters. "There are about five thousand of them in town the year round," the New Yorker magazine reported,

> and though they don't have the dash of the race-track crowds, it's likely that they are at least as profitable to the town. . . . Bars are crowded, and restaurant prices are high; the town is prosperous. The one really dead spot on its main thoroughfare is the sidewalk in front of the States. The old building stands there, hump-backed and dreary, with its porch yawning cavernously, and it seemed to be that the people who passed there walked a little faster and talked louder, as a person will when he passes a cemetery late at night.

The former headquarters of the turf crowd, with its three-story wooden piazza, still ran along Broadway, around "Vanderbilt's Corner," and back up Division Street, an unbelievable monster replicated by another one on the garden. There were 926 empty guest rooms and thirty or so empty suites. The States, its bricks painted dusty yellow and trimmed in brown, had been dying off room by room. Its season had been cut from five months to three to one. The trains still ran out back, as they did that day when Civil War soldiers gawked from the tops of the cars to see the flames devouring the first States. This second one's employees would tell how comedian Joe E. Lewis called the front desk after an engine let off steam under his window. "What time does this room leave for Chicago?"[24]

Edna Ferber and playwright George S. Kaufman visited one weekend to consider confecting a Saratoga play. Instead it became the 1941 Ferber novel *Saratoga Trunk*, a story of New Orleans and Saratoga in the 1880s, and then the 1945 Ingrid Bergman–Gary Cooper movie, preserving the glories of the States, albeit on mere celluloid. The hotel finally failed in 1942, and the city claimed it for back taxes in 1943. When the furnishings were auctioned off the next year, American Locomotive, the war-booming plant, bought six hundred wardrobe closets. The auctioneer figured, "Maybe they couldn't get any more steel lockers for the men at the plant and thought they'd use these." Indeed, the livelihoods of Saratogians now lay elsewhere as they found work in the war industries—at General Electric and ALCO in Schenectady and at railroad shops in Mechanicville. In the future this would blunt the reaction of many to the passing of Saratoga landmarks.[25]

The first lady of the turf, Helen Hay Whitney, died that September. Jock and Joan (Mrs. Charles Shipman Payson) announced that Greentree would continue. Just before Christmas, the office of War Mobilization asked that all racetracks suspend operations, claiming a need for the manpower, railroads, and gasoline required to keep them in business. The tracks agreed, but in May 1945, the request was lifted. They were back in business, big time.

Germany surrendered on May 7. On Memorial Day, May 30, Jamaica set a New York record with 64,537 fans. The $3.5 million-plus handle was a world record. Arcaro matched Sande's and Murphy's record with his third Derby, on Hoop, Jr. The Spa meeting continued at Belmont, and Longden rode four-year-old Stymie to victory in the 1945 Cup. King Ranch of Texas captured the Hopeful with Bold Venture's Assault.

The bombs were dropped in August. They celebrated again in September with another world record handle, more than $5 million at Belmont. It was the way we also were.

War Admiral, Seabiscuit, Whirlaway

 *22*

CITATION, NATIVE DANCER, TOM FOOL

THE WAR ECHOED in the names of new champions. Assault seized the Derby one Saturday, the Preakness the next, the Belmont three weeks later. Like the close of the Civil War, the long prayed-for peace set off an explosion in sports. The Triple Crown and other stakes rose to added values of $100,000, which helped the King Ranch colt earn $424,195 in 1946, topping Gallant Fox's record. More horses (17,601) ran more races (23,940) for more money (average purse $2,058) than ever before.[1]

Though Assault had captured the Flash at Belmont, he never attacked the Springs itself. Instead, when racing returned to the Spa, old Stymie was the star. They called him "the people's horse," in part because trainer-owner Hirsch Jacobs was from Brooklyn, but also because Stymie worked like a horse. He had won only seven at ages two and three but had been out there trying fifty-seven times. At four it was nine for nineteen, including the Saratoga Cup at Belmont. He might be flying Mrs. Jacobs's pink and bright green, but Stymie was a blue-collar champion.

This working stiff fit in at New York tracks after the war, for they weren't basking in the turf's national expansion. New York City and Saratoga Springs had slapped extra 5 percent municipal taxes on wagering, which hurt business. New Jersey's Monmouth Park had risen from the dead after more than a half a century, which did not help New York. The Spa handle was less than half what it had been at Belmont the year before. In this setting, Stymie got a bonus with a walkover in the Saratoga Cup and added the Whitney. It transformed his trainer's career. For an unheard-of eleven years since the thirties, Jacobs had led the trainers in number of winners, but now he headed that more important list, his chargers bringing home $560,077.[2]

The first million-dollar mark was posted that year, too. The Canadian-born, serious-minded "Professor," Ted Atkinson, went to the head of the class with $1,036,825, including the $24,750 he and Natchez earned for Mrs. Jeffords in the Travers. Several more million-dollar barriers were smashed in 1947, thanks to Warren Wright and his Calumet Farm. Wright was the leading owner with $1.4 million and the leading breeder with $1.8 million. Calumet's Bull Lea had sired the winners of $1.2 million and would lead the list for four more years. Jealous competitors well might have noted that Bull Lea had been purchased at Saratoga in 1936 for $14,000. Finally, Calumet's Jimmy Jones, son of Ben, was the top trainer, with earnings of $1.3 million.

The best three-year-old wore C. V. Whitney's blue and brown. Phalanx placed in the Travers behind Young Peter and lost the Derby to Jet Pilot by a head, the closest

The working stiff. Stymie at Saratoga, Basil James up, in 1946. *Keeneland-Morgan.*

Sonny ever came to that honor, although Whitney outranked the Pilot by taking an appointment as first assistant secretary of the U.S. Air Force. Phalanx won plenty else for Sonny and trainer Syl Veitch, notably the Wood, Dwyer, and Jockey Club Gold Cup, and $269,250. So far, though, no single horse had grossed a million—not in a year, not in a lifetime. One was about to, and he would be compared with the hero of the century, then dining on the last of his bluegrass.

The author of the *Black Stallion* series for boys and girls, Walter Farley, was a boy himself when he went to see "the flame-colored stallion," as his dad called him—"the greatest horse that ever lived." As they stood waiting, groom Will Harbut was about to begin his famous monologue about "de mostest hoss" who's got "everything a hoss ought to have, and he's got it where a hoss ought to have it," when Walt felt his father's hand tighten on his arm.[3]

> Man o' War stood in the doorway, statuesque and magnificent. There was a lordly lift to his head and his sharp eyes were bright. He didn't look *at* us, but far out over our heads. If his red coat and mane and tail had faded with time, as my father said later, I was not aware of it. . . . I was aware only of one thing, that for the first time and perhaps the only time in my life I was standing in the presence of a horse which was *truly* great.

Man o' War died in 1947 at thirty. That year, Calumet introduced his first rival in the century's annals. Bull Lea's Citation overshadowed such juveniles as My Request (victor in the U.S. Hotel and Grand Union), Better Self (Special), Star Bout (Flash),

Relic (Hopeful), Bellesoeur (Spinaway), and Spat (Schuylerville), most of whom prevailed because Citation was elsewhere. With race cards expanding, celebrated events were no longer assured of attracting all or even most of the best. So Calumet sent Citation to Washington Park instead of Saratoga, only to see him suffer his first loss there, to the filly Bewitch.[4]

Citation compiled the best three-year-old's resumé ever seen. It included the sixth Triple Crown in thirteen years, the last for a quarter of a century. Thanks to him, Arcaro broke the Murphy-Sande record of three Derbies and, having ridden Whirlaway, became the only jock to win the Triple Crown twice. But the turf had dropped into a brief recession, and purses again were shrinking, so Cy again headed for Illinois and the $38,000 Stars and Stripes Handicap and $66,450 American Derby, instead of the Travers, which would have netted him only $19,650. For the record, he did beat the Travers champ, Ace Admiral, while winning 19 for 20 that year. His 27 for 29 to date compared with Man o' War's 20 for 21.

In Cy's favor, noted Robertson as he compared him with Big Red, the latter raced only in Maryland and New York and once in Canada, whereas the dark bay performed in seven states. Although Red starred among 4,032 horses racing, Cy stood out among 20,254. On the other hand, Man o' War ran in steel shoes over slower tracks while Citation wore aluminum. Red broke more records and lugged much more weight at two and three. Cy's final two seasons, in California, yielded just five wins in sixteen starts. Still, his lifetime 32 for 45 made him the first millionaire, with $1,085,670. Toting it up, Robertson concluded: "It is axiomatic that such comparisons are futile."[5]

Again the best made them forget the good, which at Saratoga meant Maine Chance Farm. Its owner was the latest of the Spa denizens with household names: Pullman, Seagram, Fleischmann, Sinclair, duPont, Loft, Mars, Hertz—and Elizabeth Arden Graham. Some trainers complained that she used Elizabeth Arden on her horses; it worked, too, for in 1948 they included such sweet-smellers as Ace Admiral and the best juvenile filly, twelve-length Spinaway winner Myrtle Charm.

The sales made a lot of people happy. Although the snack-food industry never paid Saratoga back for inventing it, the place again helped it out. Starting with a couple of yearlings he bought at the 1948 sales, Harry Husman, founder of the Potato Products Company of Cincinnati, set up Potato Chip Farm, which raced as far afield as Hialeah. Then there was the one snatched for $4,500 in 1949; Battlefield would present Eric Guerin with the first of his record three Hopefuls in a row. The colt would take the Special, too, on the way to ringing up $198,677 at two. At three, his in-the-money streak reached twenty-five and gave George Widener his third Travers. It was also Arcaro's fourth and final Travers, equaling Jimmy McLaughlin's record. Eddie would remember Battlefield as a problem horse: "he would only stay in front for so long. Also he was content to win by half-a-length or so."[6]

The Pinkertons were cleaning up. In seersucker suit and crew cut, blue-eyed Jerry O'Grady, head of their racetrack division, led his men through the clubhouses, booting out bookies and other undesirables, such as Joe Adonis himself in 1947, reportedly after Adonis had fed thousands to Saratoga's mutuel machines. O'Grady had a drink with Adonis on the lake that night. "I'd like you to carry a message to them,"

Adonis told the Pink, speaking bitterly about the track owners, who, he suggested, preyed on the poor. "Please tell them that the poverty-stricken people I see in their joints are barred from gambling houses I've been interested in."[7]

The hells were going through a nervous era. They had come on strong after the war. "Downstreet," as Saratogians still called it, seemed as busy as ever, with horse rooms on Phila, Carolina, and Putnam Streets. "Money was flowing very freely," one employee remembered, "Probably the best season ever was in 1946." The Chicago Club was still operating. From his backyard, a kid gaped at planes pulling letters-in-the-sky that spelled out "HILDEGARDE," and he wondered which was sexier, she or the plane. She was at the Piping Rock in those years, and so was Gypsy Rose Lee. Piping Rock nights there ticked away to the clicks of twelve roulette wheels, five craps tables, two bird cages, and two card tables, with slightly more modest layouts at the Arrowhead; Smith's Interlaken, near the ruins of Mrs. Leslie's Interlaken; Riley's; and Newman's. Riley's was sometimes known as Delmonico's, as was the Piping Rock.[8]

Saratoga had the best little church bazaar in the world, only the boy wondering about Hildegarde didn't know it. He thought every church bazaar was like this one, booking this guy with a Spanish accent and hilarious soft fists with faces painted on them. It was the ventriloquist Señor Wences before the rest of the country discovered him. The game booths sparkled in this outdoor casino for Christ, and taught the boy that when the wheel repeatedly stopped at nine, and he repeatedly collected prizes, that could be his lucky number for life. But how did Saratoga get the best little church bazaar in the world? Simple; in the Morrissey tradition, the lake houses wanted to ensure "that the local charities received their fair share," as Lansky biographer Lacey explained it. "The Redemptorist Fathers of St. Clement's Church ran their fund-raising bazaar every year in the month of August," he noted. "The food was catered by the lake houses' gourmet chefs, and the bingo stall was operated by gentlemen whose mastery of the numbers patter was polished with most evident expertise. The highlight . . . was entertainment by one or more of the acts currently appearing beside the lake—Sophie Tucker, Hildegarde, the comedy duo Cross and Dunn. The good fathers could not believe their luck."[9] Across town, while the celebrant at St. Peter's joked that the attendance was not what it should be, his smile revealed his pleasure at the handle.

As for the mob, it was never clear who was backing which joint, but Lansky's relationships were simplified in 1947. One pal, Lucky Luciano, was deported to Genoa. Another, Bugsy Siegel, was wiped out in California, apparently because he had overspent trying to recreate Saratoga in Las Vegas. Suspicion would focus on Lansky, for as Siegel himself was supposed to have said, "We only kill each other." It was the latest reformer who was really making them nervous in 1948, however.

Governor Dewey, the mustachioed "man on the wedding cake," was running for president and hoping Truman would be linked with the Kansas City machine founded by his fellow horse-racing fan and ex-Spa visitor, Tom Pendergast. The word came from Albany: no gambling in his own backyard. At 3:10 P.M. on opening Monday of the racing season, local detectives raided nine horse rooms simultaneously. The lake houses were outside city limits, but it was a warning to them, too, and they got it. There wasn't a light on that night in the Arrowhead, where Lansky's and, reportedly, Adonis's interests were concentrated. "The moaning was terrific," said the *New York Daily News*. "Piping Rock, for instance, has booked a show that will cost the management $25,000 a week—with attractions like Joe E. Lewis and Kay Thompson and the Williams Brothers—and you can't meet that on the income from food and liquor—even at Saratoga prices."[10]

The casinos were back in 1949, when a Saratogian remembered working as a "ladder man" at Smith's, watching for cheaters at craps from a walkway above the game. The separate rooms for gambling proved wise. For instance, the kid who got his lucky number at church was peddling the Pink Sheet with its race results at the gambling hells but was actually scared to go beyond the kitchen at the Piping Rock and Newman's. So was a city detective, who said he couldn't look farther than the dining room or he would lose his job. Some cops reportedly got ten dollars a night to escort cash from the casinos to the bank. Even the racetrack was not untouched. In 1950, the *New York Daily Mirror* reported, ten bookies had concessions "in the bushes" behind the course, where a motorcycle cop picked up his daily "winning ticket."

To destroy all this evil gambling, a final crusader burst through the Adirondack woods, his trademark the coonskin cap he wore on the stump in Tennessee. Estes Kefauver was building a reputation for crime busting, which would make him a candidate for the Democratic presidential nomination. His Senate Special Committee to Investigate Crime in Interstate Commerce held hearings in fourteen cities, winding up in New York City and on nationwide television in 1951. When a lawyer objected to showing onetime Piping Rock partner Frank Costello on TV, the cameras focused instead on his manicured hands, which made it all the more riveting.

Like Nellie Bly, the Tennessean did shut down the place (except for the track), and this time for good. After Kefauver had exposed its criminal element, it was all over for "wide open" Saratoga after more than a century, most of it as America's leading hell. Dewey got into the act by ordering a state commission to pursue its own investigation. "Saratoga is terrorized and paralyzed," reported the *Mirror*. "Almost everybody, including bartenders and waiters, is under subpoena." The Piping Rock, Smith's, and Riley's were closed, and Newman's, Toto's, and the Brook shared a terrible complaint: they had nothing but food and drink. A county grand jury dealt the final blow in early 1953, scoring more than convictions on gambling and related charges.

If Saratoga launched Lansky into the big time, it compensated by being the first jurisdiction to imprison the Brain of the Mob. Meyer Lansky began his three-month sentence in the county jail at Ballston Spa in May. "Everybody knew there was gambling up there," he would say later. "The place was full of casinos. I had investments in the Arrowhead Inn and in the Piping Rock, too. I'm sure the reason why the cops in Saratoga suddenly took action was that Governor Dewey ordered an investigation because of the Kefauver Report. It was just bad timing."[11]

Lansky toughened his small, muscular frame by fast-walking the cellblock and doing calesthenics, and showed off his mental skills to a fellow prisoner. "Meyer would challenge him to write down a block of figures, seven or eight digits across, with as many figures down," Lacey wrote. "Meyer would then start in the top right-

Native Dancer. *National Museum of Racing and Hall of Fame, Saratoga Springs.*

hand corner, and would run his finger rapidly up and down the column as if he were a calculating machine, reeling off the totals in a matter of seconds." He had lunch and dinner brought in from nearby restaurants at his and his neighbor's expense, and called his son Buddy in New York a few times a week to check on stock prices. His younger son, Paul, who had honored the family by getting into West Point on his own, would come up on the train to see him.

Lansky asked the guards to bring him a dictionary and a Bible. "I thought I might as well use the time to improve my mind and study the holy book. A few days later I was astonished to see in the newspapers that I'd turned religious and was going to become a Christian." Lansky decided the problem was that he had also been visited by a priest. He had asked for a rabbi but nobody had come until the priest happened by, "maybe because he thought I was lonely. Finally, on the last day of my imprisonment, a rabbi turned up. I said to him, 'Rabbi, they've tried to make a Christian out of me. By the time you decided to come to my rescue, I could have been thrown to the lions several times over.'"

The last of the big-time Saratoga operators, from John Morrissey to Richard Canfield to Arnold Rothstein, got out for good behavior after two months and left the area forever, moving his main residence from New York to Florida. After shadow-boxing with the police for another three decades, including a failed attempt to win citizenship in Israel, Meyer Lansky died in Florida in 1983.

The latest champion waltzed around the Spa again and again. By Polynesian out of Geisha, exotic Native Dancer was the turf's first TV star: the Gray Ghost. Leading it into the fifties, he hulaed through the Flash, Special, Grand Union, Hopeful, and nine for nine. He kept it up for two more years, seizing everything in sight except one event, which happened to be the 1953 Kentucky Derby. Dark horse Dark Star led from the get-go, the Ghost closing to lose by a head. Native Dancer returned to a Saratoga encrusted with a few more traditions.

The swans were back (the ducks gone), and a mysterious canoe floated on the lake, a spiritual descendant of the pair in the twenties but painted blue. Nobody knew when it first appeared—or why. Joe Palmer marveled again at the place's summer jobs, such as bailing rainwater out of the canoe, shutting off the fountains before races, drawing the winner's circle in chalk at the finish line before it was scuffed up, to be redrawn again. The latter was perhaps unique, being a real circle and actually drawn in the dirt, instead of the marked-off rectangular spaces called winning circles at other tracks. A Saratoga circle was an honest circle. The Pink Sheet boy had switched to peddling a tip sheet at the Raceway. One rainy night his red corduroy coat ran faster than the trotters in his "Rube's Selections." It almost didn't matter how fast they ran, since Rube picked so many it was easy the next night to impress the crowd by shouting out all the winners he had.[12]

Like so many of the Commodore's descendants, Native Dancer's owner, Alfred Gwynne Vanderbilt, had a great sense of fun. He hung out around the Vanderbilt barn with chauffeur Mike McGrath, exercisers Jimmy Varner and Milton Woodward, trainer Lee McCoy, stable agent Bill Reedy, the groom Specs, and blacksmith Duke Montura. The writer Frank Graham was visiting one day when Alfred poured coffee from some big old cups and talked horses with them. Alfred was worried about one of those terrible dilemmas that trouble the very rich: whether to go to the sale of his yearlings. "If you don't go, they say you are not interested, and if you do and your horses don't bring any money, your friends are embarrassed and think they ought to bid." At the end of the day, a bunch of them jumped into Alfred's car. "Get in back," he told Mike the chauffeur. "I can drive as well as you can."

"I know it."

"That's the old oil," Alfred said.

"That's the old, old oil," said Mike. Alfred wheeled them over to the clubhouse. Harry Stevens had breakfast ready.

Native Dancer danced home in the 1953 Travers by five and a half lengths, and never lost again. In his farewell at four, more or less a victory lap in the Spa's seven-furlong Oneonta, the dramatic gray won by nine lengths under a huge load of 137 pounds. He won twenty-one of his twenty-two races.

It was champions like the Dancer and his owner who saved Saratoga from a developing crisis as elsewhere the turf emerged from its recession and threatened to leave behind the little upstate oval, which seemed increasingly irrelevant to the New York City bean counters. Help came, too, from a few writers, notably Palmer. Joe had not been easy to please. He couldn't stand "the damn public address system," for example, and it was certainly true no change had been so startling (still is, to new-comers). It drowned out the ancient human cries—Morrissey screaming, "Long-fellow's beat!"—and the first horse to hear it as it blared its account of the race, if that was what it was rasping about, must have wondered, "What the hell is that?" The P.A. system took the crowd out of the competition and had no use for the colors, either, for there was no time for description in the tinny amplifier's account. Yet under the trees you could still almost recapture America's past. "One of the soft charms of Saratoga," Palmer said, "is that you remember things you had forgotten, and that the memories come back with gentle pleasure." His valediction was entitled, "Saratoga, or the Horse at Home."[13]

> Any time you want to know whether racing in New York can still consider itself a sport or whether it is a highly elaborate pin-ball machine, just look to see if Saratoga has dates. After five months of concrete and asphalt and gravel . . . Saratoga applies an anesthetic, of tranquil shaded lawns, of big white quiet houses, of a leafy and mellowed antiquity, and morning after morning of golden serenity. . . . For the casual racegoer, Saratoga is about the only place in the East where he can see racing. Elsewhere he merely sees races, which isn't the same thing at all. . . . A man who would change it would stir champagne.

It was the "gathering of the clan. Nowhere, not even in Lexington, Ky., is there such a concentration of owners, trainers, jockeys, touts, officials and racetrack presidents." They started gathering at the Saratoga Trotting Course after 1847 and still had no plans to leave. On the contrary, they had created a permanent temple here, the National Museum of Racing, housed temporarily in Morrissey's casino in the park as of 1950. With C. V. Whitney as its first president, it displayed the silks and souvenirs of America's first major sport in the town that launched it as a national pastime. But the place's value was more than sentimental. "If it ever comes to the point that there will be no Saratoga again," Palmer warned, "I think there will be some important dispersal sales in the fall."

If the old track seemed threatened, so did the town. There was the pile on Broadway. "There probably isn't a hotel porch like the Grand Union's left in America, and Saratoga citizens would be very shortsighted to let this one perish," Palmer warned again. The only one like it, the States, had survived the war years, but not by much. The kid and his brothers had raced down the States's elephantine boardwalk with its towering roof on their way to church at St. Peter's—only to find another vast wooden runway, so they kept going! across the Grand Union's even more spectacular piazza—piazza without end. The States finally came down in 1946, the race named after it to last another decade. The Grand Union followed in 1952, its race to survive through 1959.

Professor Kettlewell described the fifties as a time of general "collapse" for the town. As the casinos closed and the track barely hung on, the grand "cottages" along Union Avenue were fast becoming rooming houses or Skidmore dorms, although in the season of 1951 the great patron of the turf, William Woodward, still took his mansion on that avenue. Sam Rosoff's mansion had become a high-class boarding-house, however, and somebody was trying to turn it into a bottle club. The *Mirror* noted: "Cottages which were rented far in advance at $750 and up for the month are available at half that price now. 'For Rent' signs punctuate the best streets."[14]

Citation, Native Dancer, Tom Fool

Other landmarks were threatened by "remodeling." At times this was confined to the drawing board, such as a plan that would have placed a "modern" facade over the giant columns that fronted Morrissey's last hangout, the Adelphi. At times it was actually perpetrated, as when Louis Howe's Victorian homestead was married to the one next door, later to be luckily divorced. The remodelers had not yet confronted the preservationists. When the two sides did meet later, it often resembled a scene in a TV comedy, in which the cheerful Flying Nun and airborne Mary Poppins crashed head-on, both plunging straight to the ground. Much of the resort had built-in protection. The conversions saved many old cottages and the look of the nineteenth-century East Side. Skidmore would save the landscape a second time, creating a new campus on Judge Hilton's development-threatened hilltop to the north and northwest. Although few Americans believed in mineral water anymore, the state Spa protected the southern flank while its Gideon Putnam Hotel put up the rich in style.

East of the track, too, where Poe had practiced the Raven with that little boy, the developers were verboten. Here Yaddo pursued its mission as America's leading literary retreat, with an eye for winners any bookie would have admired. A 1946 guest was a puffy blond boy who liked to curl up amidst the Trasks' neogothic decor. Truman Capote. Other Yaddo alums: James Farrell, Aaron Copland, Henri Cartier-Bresson, Carson McCullers, Katherine Anne Porter, Eudora Welty, Langston Hughes, James Baldwin, Saul Bellow, Dorothy Parker, Leonard Bernstein, Philip Roth. Sometimes these giggling geniuses would jump in a station wagon to go rollicking down to the movies at the Community Theater on Broadway, where the lady at the candy counter would take one look and wonder what the hell they would think up next.[15]

The next local hero was Tom Fool, trained by John Gaver and usually ridden by Ted Atkinson. Over his three racing seasons, Tom Fool appeared at the Springs nine times. He made his 1951 racing debut by stealing a modest Spa purse by four lengths, then added the Sanford and Grand Union. At three, his worst year, he owned the Wilson by four and a half lengths, but lost the Caughnawaga by a nose and ran a poor third in the Travers, the first time he had gone a mile and a quarter. For Tom Fool, a poor year meant six firsts and five seconds in thirteen sorties.

The next year Greentree's musclebound bay was unstoppable. While Native Dancer was collecting the Wood, Preakness, Belmont, Travers, and American Derby among his nine of ten, Tom Fool was looking even better, at least on paper, for he accomplished the extreme rarity of going undefeated at four. Opening with six handicap triumphs in a row, he took the ultrarare Handicap Triple Crown—the Metropolitan, Suburban, and Brooklyn—and then it was back to the Springs. He grabbed the Wilson again, by eight lengths, and the Whitney by three and a half, on his way to ten straight. Tom Fool won twenty-one in thirty tries.

That 1953 season was singular for jockeys nationwide. With One Count and then Native Dancer, Eric Guerin became the first back-to-back Travers victor since George Barbee in 1874 and 1875. Earl Sande returned at the age of fifty-five to steal a race at Jamaica. Most notable of all, a four-foot-ten-inch Texan who could have lived in a shoe won 485 races, a mark that would last two decades. It was Bill Shoemaker. Bill Hartack won 350 and Tony DeSpirito, who had the previous record of 390, took 311.

Tom Fool, Ted Atkinson aboard. After winning the 1951 Grand Union Hotel Stakes. *Keeneland-Morgan.*

Shoemaker and Hartack towered over their era. Before he was through, Shoe would lead the money list ten times. Hartack topped it twice, in 1956 when he broke the $2 million barrier and in 1957, when he turned around and topped the $3 million level.

It might be advisable to sit for the story of Nashua, the new prince of Belair. Like Gallant Fox, the Nasrullah colt was foaled at Claiborne Farm and saddled by Sunny Jim Fitzsimmons. With the death of William Woodward in 1953, William Jr. was heir to the stable, and after two wins and a loss at Garden State, Nashua was pointed toward the Spa. There, as Robertson pointed out, he wore blinkers for the first time and the great Arcaro. He captured the Grand Union by nearly two lengths over Pyrenees, who had a seven-pound pull. In the Hopeful, he met his frequent nemesis, Summer Tan, owned by the latest brand name around town, Mrs. Russell Firestone. It was Nashua by a neck. That autumn Mrs. Woodward thought she heard a prowler on their estate at Oyster Bay, Long Island. So she let go in the night with a shotgun, and her husband, William Woodward, Jr., lay dying. Belair Stud was sold for $2.2 million, including a record $1.2 million for Nashua. He went to a syndication headed by the Kentucky breeder Leslie Combs II. Nashua raced another year, going Tom Fool one better, with twenty-two firsts in thirty starts and a total of $1.2 million, the new record.[16]

The administration of the turf changed radically in the fifties. In 1895 New York had been the first state to assert some control by establishing its racing commission, but in 1951 it became the last to strip the private Jockey Club of its licensing power. It was transferred to the commission. The courts acted on an application for an owner's license from Jules Fink, whom the Jockey Club had turned down. Fink was the leader of the most successful gambling syndicate of the pari-mutuel age, which Runyon dubbed "the Speed Boys." They ignored the favorites, since the public had a habit of losing. They ignored time, except early fractions that might indicate a horse wanted to run. They didn't like bad breakers. They did like a speed horse on the inside, a speed horse in cheap company, a stretch-running speedster. Fink knew a lot, maybe too much. The commission also turned him down.[17]

The Jockey Club retained considerable power by maintaining the *Stud Book,* the registry of thoroughbreds and their names, and by training officials and approving colors in most states. The old guard soon had a friend in the governor's chair. As Betts put it, Dewey "had never visited a race track in twelve years, while racing fans were enriching the state with more than $300,000,000 in revenue," but the former diplomat W. Averell Harriman had owned Log Cabin Stud and summered out North Broadway in the twenties. Now he returned to dedicate the new museum of racing, which had found a better spot—on the lawn where Sam Rosoff had offered booze and bucks to hard-up horseplayers, a touching heritage. As George Waller pointed out, the airy Georgian museum aired the silks of Queen Elizabeth and Sir Winston Churchill and of such royalty as Bing Crosby and Fred Astaire, not to mention a pair of Longfellow's plates, Tod Sloan's cane, the saddle that kept Loftus on Man o' War, and Mr. Fitz's watch. Under its new president, Walter Jeffords, Sr., it also opened racing's Hall of Fame.

If the open-ended Hall of Fame showed that the sport was looking ahead, the message was sent more dramatically in October 1955, when Saratoga and the state's other big racing associations disappeared. The turf club born in August of 1863 had survived ninety-two years. Now the Jockey Club, reorganized as the Greater New York Association, bought out the Big Four—Saratoga, Belmont, Aqueduct, and Jamaica—for $30 million. The new organization, which soon would rename itself the New York Racing Association, got a franchise to operate tracks in the state for twenty-five years on a nonprofit basis. In return, the state temporarily would divert 1 percent of the pari-mutuel handle from the tax coffers to NYRA for track improvements.[18]

The local club tradition was preserved in one critical way: exclusive dates. In 1957, Harriman signed a bill guaranteeing the Spa twenty-four exclusive racing days. Although the place had staged many meetings of more than thirty days—and more than forty in the nineteenth century—this was a fabulous gift in the current climate. It preserved Saratoga's place in the sun on the national calendar. Two years later, in another NYRA stretch for money, the daily card was lengthened to nine races. It complicated the latest job held by the boy who had pushed the Pink Sheet. Now he edited it, and its deadline was typical Saratoga low-tech. Hot with results from across the land, it had to fly from the press into the hands of the latest kids so they could run around to the front of the newspaper plant and hit the homebound losers driving by at a notably morose pace.

The twenty-four-day guarantee convinced NYRA that it could invest in the Spa.

The initial improvements included a new racing surface, new stables, and bunk-houses for the help. In 1961 there would be $400,000 more in improvements, among them a turf course that harkened back to Will Whitney's day, updated dining facilities, and a clubhouse elevator. NYRA's real plans were for New York City, where it created the world's largest racetrack. It was the $33 million new Aqueduct, designed by Arthur Froelich and Associates, of Beverly Hills, and opened on September 14, 1959. Visitors discovered a private subway station, nine elevators, eighteen escalators, 738 pari-mutuel windows, and accommodations for eighty thousand spectators. Its immediate average daily attendance of more than thirty-three thousand was still below Hollywood Park's, but produced more money. For instance, its record $2.69 million average daily handle in the first year boosted revenues to the state by $12.5 million, and it went up from there. Jamaica, once "the people's track," vanished from the racing calendar. Would Saratoga be next?

About the only change up there had been to stop loaning the Man o' War Cup to the winning Travers owner for a year while presenting a silver replica to keep. Instead, Mrs. Sloane got her name inscribed on the Cup and a gold-plated replica to bring back to Virginia. A newcomer, Panamanian Manuel Ycaza, had climbed aboard her Sword Dancer for the Travers, the first of the Latin-American riders—from Panama, Puerto Rico, Mexico, South America—just now entering the sport in force. Little things like that happened. Quiet things.

The Big A was more exciting. Still, Walter Farley, the *Black Stallion* author, thought something was missing. He had a fictional kid visit the fabulous facility, and the young man found himself estranged. "Just a big supermarket. A fellow could bring his girl to Aqueduct now and lose her for a week." He discovered the jockeys' steam room wasn't hot enough, so they had to do road work. "I ain't surprised that they ain't got the steam hot enough for the jocks," he said. "Imagine that, over $30,000,000 for the plushiest racing plant in the country an' they can't get up enough steam!"[19]

 *23*

THE GREATEST TRAVERS?

I T W A S August 18, 1962. Presidents John F. Kennedy and Nikita S. Khrushchev were in a race of their own, to the moon. But the two manned craft about to go into orbit were Jaipur and Ridan.[1]

They were off—and the fair-weather crowd would never see daylight again. Ridan had the rail and half a length into the turn. Jaipur, No. 2, closed it to a head at the half-mile. They were chasing Man o' War's Travers mark of 2:01⅘. Smart money said Jaipur would fire his second rockets anytime. After all, he loved this track, had won the Flash and Hopeful in the slop under Arcaro. Now he carried Shoe, and the bettors liked him back so much it took a rocket scientist to figure his odds, 13 to 20. Ridan was a little more than 5 to 2. The handle would be a record $1.8 million.

Driving slightly in front, Ridan kept his head down. His stride had been measured at twenty-eight feet. He had won the Arlington Classic. He had placed but made Greek Money spend everything in the Preakness, where Jaipur was tenth. Side by side now, they were destroying the old course, and everybody began to realize something incredible was going on, among them Joe Nichols of the *Times*: "one of the most exciting races imaginable."

It got better. Flying to the quarter pole, Jaipur slipped in front by a head. The trainer Syl Veitch, who figured only four inches separated them every step of the way, would call it his biggest thrill ever here, the ultimate compliment since neither horse was his. The other five were out of sight, out of mind.

Shoe just could not shake Ridan. The whole day had been a race for him, for the sport was no longer a leisurely affair, however much Saratoga faked it. Shoe had flown from Chicago that morning, air-taxied to Ballston Spa, and hit the track at 1 P.M. He was still airborne, a head up on blazing Ridan at the top of the stretch. Here is where Mrs. Moody Jolley's Ridan was scheduled to drop out. He was not just up to a mile and a quarter. He had forgotten to read the papers, however, and with Manuel Ycaza aboard, he fired his own reserve rockets in the stretch. A spectator, Charles Hotaling, Sr., would remember only their heads—their two heads bobbing, bobbing, one up, one down. At the finish, one bobbed down: the winner. But which? "For an instant," the *Times* reported, Ridan "seemed to head Jaipur." George Widener agreed, and he owned Jaipur. "I thought I'd lost it by a nose."

Ridan's rider: "I really didn't know who won it. I was busy riding him out."

LeRoy Jolley, Ridan's trainer: "I knew Jaipur beat us. I saw Shoe drop his horse's head at the wire." Shoe knew, too: "I felt I had him right on the wire, but it sure was close."

Jaipur vs. Ridan. The 1962 Travers. George D. Widener's Jaipur is in the center. *NYRA Photo.*

A pug nose. Jaipur, carrying 126, had shaved a fifth off the mark set by Big Red under 129, and had tied the track record. Ridan, also under 126, may have knocked a hair off it, too. In his history of the era, William H. Rudy would call it "an epic of the turf." It was worth $53,722 to Widener, and the next year, with Crewman, he would smash the Dwyer brothers' record of four Travers wins in the 1880s. Four years after that, Bert Mulholland, who trained all five Widener winners, would have a heart attack on the Spa backstretch and miss his induction into the Hall of Fame. It was all the sadder for the fact that his boss had recently become president of the museum, succeeding the late Walter Jeffords.[2]

Informal horse-of-the-year honors dated at least to the nineteenth century. In 1936, formal designations of champions in all categories, and an overall horse of the year, were inaugurated by Triangle Publications and the *Turf and Sports Digest,* based on polls of journalists. In 1950, the Thoroughbred Racing Associations established its own list, decided by its track secretaries, and in 1954 the *Thoroughbred Record* began picking them based on stakes performances. In 1971, all these honors were consolidated and became the Eclipse awards, based on voting by the TRA, National Turf Writers Association, and *Daily Racing Form.* The honors confer tremendous prestige and can enhance a well-bred horse's stud or broodmare career.[3]

The Greatest Travers?

Kelso at Saratoga. *NYRA Photo by Bob Coglianese.*

From 1960 through 1964, something hard to believe happened. The same candidate was Horse of the Year five times in a row. No previous horse had won it more than twice. This phenomenon was Kelso, owned by Allaire duPont's Bohemia Stable and trained by Carl Hanford. By Your Host out of Count Fleet's Maid of Flight, Kelso was a gelding. He won one and placed in two Atlantic City purses at two, and did not reappear at three until after the Triple Crown races. Once he got started, he got started—winning eight of nine, including the Jockey Club Gold Cup at Aqueduct.

For the next half-decade, the Gold Cup would prove Kelso's gleaming grail, going a long way toward making him Horse of the Year every time. The Big A was his track, the vast hippodrome seemingly built for lanky King Kelly, as they called him. Kelso and the Big A led America's first national sport into another tremendous expansion, with the 1960 crowds across the country totaling 37.5 million and betting more than $2.5 billion, $250 million of it going to the states. Memorial Day brought a record crowd of 70,992 to Aqueduct. Taking note of this phenomenon, the IRS started getting the identification of bettors who collected more than $600 for $2.[4]

Like the gelding Exterminator, Kelso would prove one of the greatest stayers of them all. At four, he acquired the Handicap Triple Crown—a rare honor because it kept getting harder as they piled on the weight. Kelso won the Metropolitan, Suburban, and Brooklyn in a cumulative time faster than the only two others to don it, Whisk Broom II and Tom Fool, and he carried more total weight (130, 133, and 136). He also won the Whitney that year, when it was run at Belmont.

His upstate appearances were telling. His Spa debut at five in 1962 was his first trip under Ismael Valenzuela. The new team introduced themselves by beating Call the Witness, who had a seven-pound pull in the mile and one-sixteenth Stowaway Purse, and from then on out, it was Milo Valenzuela who donned Kelso's gray and yellow silks. It signaled a changing of the guard among American jockeys, for Valenzuela was succeeding two older greats, Arcaro and Shoemaker, aboard the champion. Arcaro had retired that spring with two Triple Crowns (Whirlaway and Citation), five Derbies, four Travers, and four Hopefuls among 4,779 victories, leaving Shoe to carry on. The following season another Spa favorite would retire: Mr. Fitz at age eighty-nine, after sixty-three years of training, his own two Triple Crowns (Gallant Fox and Omaha), a record seven Jockey Club Gold Cups, the Travers with Granville and Fenelon, and 140 other stakes wins.

Old Kelso was not retiring, though. He and Milo were back for Saratoga's 1963 centennial, cruising in the Whitney under 130 pounds. He was in his longest streak ever—eight stakes. At seven, he returned for another one-day stand, ripping off the mile and one-eighth Mechanicville in an American record 1:46 ⅗. At eight, it was his third Whitney, by a nose. This, the king's fourth Spa triumph, should have been his last appearance here, for in his only outing at nine, he cracked a foot bone at Hialeah and was retired after thirty-nine wins in sixty-three appearances. He had won a world record $1.9 million.

Mrs. duPont brought Kelso and his sidekicks, the old pony Spray and the dog Charlie Potatoes, back to the farm in Maryland. "A few months later, between races at Saratoga," wrote Lew Koch, "Kelso put on an exhibition of dressage and jumping." The Spa had launched the king on a new career as a jumper. He gave exhibitions at ten and eleven from Saratoga to Madison Square Garden. One National Steeplechase Day found him leaping timber at Saratoga, and it was almost Standing Room Only. Lou De Fichy, then of the National Steeplechase and Hunt Association, remembered the great one bobbling momentarily while skimming a rail. "A huge gasp went over the crowd."[5]

At Monmouth Park, former Olympic rider Mike Plumb let go of Kelso's reins. "I felt him start to go," Plumb said. "I felt that power, but I got him back quickly." Even at the end he would put in a dramatic appearance. In 1983, he and Forego would lead the post parade for the Jockey Club Gold Cup at Belmont, and a little more than twenty-four hours later, Kelso would be dead of a colic attack at age twenty-six.

Sonny Whitney had opened the sixties in style. His third marriage, to Eleanor Searle, had lasted seventeen years, and in 1958 he had wed the woman whose role at the Spa would be as important as his, the actress Marie Louise Schroeder Hosford, to be known in the turf world simply as Marylou. Ever since wrapping up the inaugural Christmas feature at Santa Anita in 1934, Whitney had symbolized the sport's transcontinental profile. His filly Silver Spoon was the toast of the coast in 1958 and 1959, whipping the colts in the Santa Anita Derby and beating her Kentucky Derby conqueror, Tomy Lee, in the Cinema Handicap. His elegant little Tompion was bicoastal, too. He settled the Spa's 1959 free-for-all among two-year-olds by delivering in the Hopeful, still the track's richest feature and now doubled to $73,434 for the winner.

The Eton blue and brown charged into 1960 with the same two front-runners. Citation's Silver Spoon won five stakes in California. Tom Fool's champion Tompion added the second Bernard Baruch Handicap at the Spa and the Travers, now up to a high of $53,165. At year's end, Sonny Whitney was the leading owner again for the first time in twenty-seven years, with $1,039,091. Altogether, then, the Whitney power-house—W. C., Harry P., and C. V.—led the American stables thirteen times since 1900, not counting 1904, when it ran in H. B. Duryea's name, or 1915, when Harry turned his horses over to Thompson, who led the list that year. It was the greatest stable in the annals of the turf by that one measure of years on top. The number might have been higher had Sonny not been away during World War II and on government assignment frequently afterwards. Even that hardly describes the family's impact, for under Aunt Helen and her children Jock and Joan, Greentree was another Whitney powerhouse and led the list twice. Sonny, incidentally, led the breeders as well in 1960, for the first time since 1938.

The giant Calumet topped the owners one year fewer than Whitney. It had been owned since Warren Wright's death in 1950 by his widow, Lucille, who later married movie producer and writer Gene Markey, the Markeys becoming fixtures on the Spa scene. Beau Prince won the Travers to help Calumet collect $759,856 in 1961, its twelfth and final year at the top. By many other measures, of course, the Calumet goliath was the biggest stable ever. It had topped $1 million six times before Sonny became the second owner to do it. It led the breeders' money list fourteen times compared with Harry and Sonny's eleven, and it wasn't finished yet.

Another star of the day was the 1960 juvenile champ Hail to Reason, happily misprinted once as Reason to Hail. Under Bob Ussery, he grabbed the Sanford and breezed in the Hopeful by ten lengths—in a track record 1:16 for the six and a half furlongs. Owned by Hirsch Jacobs's daughter Patrice, Hail retired after shattering a foreleg in a workout at Aqueduct. His nemesis, Carry Back, came back to win the Derby and the 1962 Whitney for Jack and Katherine Price.

It was in those years, too, that Paul Mellon took to the flats. The banking heir was hardly green at racing, having been hunting, point-to-pointing, and steeplechasing since 1933. He finally decided to move to the flat track in England and the U.S. because the money was far better. In the early sixties, like so many others of the American turf, he began building his foundation at the corner of George Street and East Avenue. "I was buying only fillies at the time because it seemed foolish to buy expensive colts when if things didn't work out racing, they would have little value. A well-bred filly, on the other hand, whatever she did on the racetrack, could be a good prospect as a broodmare. I paid the top price of the sale and bought this filly for eighty-three thousand dollars, very little these days, but a record at the time. . . . The filly didn't turn out to be much good."[6]

His Rokeby Stable was now in the game with his young trainer, Elliott Burch, who had succeeded his father, Preston, at nearby Brookmeade Farm. Brookmeade had been dispersed on Mrs. Sloane's death in 1962, and two years later Elliott won the Belmont for Mellon with Quadrangle, the first Rokeby victory in an American classic. Then, one hundred years after the great Kentucky, Gilpatrick up, captured the first

Travers, Quadrangle, Ycaza up, captured the ninety-fifth, launching Mellon on a mighty career in that event. In return, he would play a major role in the restoration of the Spa.

The restoration was just getting underway. NYRA completed a $3.5 million expansion of the track in time for the 1965 season. It proved a prophetic move, but it was not the obvious one. Downstate the Big A's eighty thousand capacity was nearly triple the upstate plant's thirty thousand, and so were the receipts. These were moving numbers to legislators, who would see the state take in $70 million from thoroughbred racing that year. What sense did it make to guarantee twenty-four days of exclusive racing in the Adirondacks and deny it to the millions who could hop the subway to the Big A? The foothills' charms prevailed, however, with the support of Governor Nelson Rockefeller, who naturally understood the old guard.

The changes began in 1963 at some expense to that old charm. The paddock behind the grandstand was converted to a pari-mutuel annex. Here they had sold Man o' War and many others and walked and saddled the horses on rainy days. This commingling of fans, horse people, and horses was almost unique and one of the loveliest traditions in American sports. Happily, in nice weather the walking and saddling around the nearby trees would continue another twenty years after they turned the old paddock into a pari-mutuel shed. Many lining up at the windows today, or handicapping the races from their lawn chairs in front of this "pari-mutuel paddock," have no idea what they have missed. Whether the experience somehow might have been saved is an interesting question.[7]

A five hundred-foot section was added to the east end of the grandstand, increasing capacity to eight thousand. Done by Froelich, with Robert Krause as design architect, it continued the lines and Victorian look of the Whitney creation. It wiped out the sloped-roofed betting ring, ancestral home of the bookies who served Bet-a-Million Gates but twice abandoned—when bookmaking in a "fixed place" was outlawed and when the pari-mutuels arrived for good in 1940. It also eliminated the old field stand to the east. One tradition few if any were sorry to see go was segregation at the rec across from the avenue, the old "Jockey Y." Segregation went, the Y stayed, and one can only hope that little structure will be saved. It's a rare statement about America, sports, and the turf, and about this strange seasonal enclave—not all of it bad, either, for it speaks of the Spa's history and much else: of the sport's intention to provide for its talent, the turf's traveling way of life, the ties between boxing and racing, the story of physical education and the Y's, and recreational architecture. It is a useful space as well.[8]

Suddenly the whole town was emerging from the fifties collapse. On a hill above a limestone boulder bulging with tales of Indian visitors to the waters, amidst the dreamy landscape of FDR's and Baruch's health resort, rose the Saratoga Performing Arts Center, summer home of the Philadelphia Orchestra, New York City Ballet, New York City Opera, and Newport Jazz Festival–Saratoga. Governor Rockefeller broke ground for it, and along with brothers Laurance and John D. III joined the Whitneys and other turf aristocrats in coughing up. Breeders offered their stallions' services, sending the stud fees to SPAC, a seminal contribution to American sports. It opened in 1966. To that same Spa complex Sonny and Marilou then led the way in founding the National Museum of Dance.

The place got its own off-Broadway, too, as Café Lena, a Phila Street coffee house, nurtured such struggling troubadours as the unknown Bob Dylan and many others, helping birth the national folk-singing movement of the sixties, with many of Lena's "students" returning later as stars to keep the place going. It was then, too, that Skidmore College evacuated the grand "cottages" around Union Avenue and moved across town to a $36 million, twelve hundred-acre campus on the old Hilton estate. A few years later, a pioneer historic preservation movement was brought into being, largely by the crusading efforts of Julie Stokes. It won national recognition for infusing the place with an appreciation of its architectural history—including, the *New York Times* once pointed out, the greatest collection of Victorian homes on the East Coast. Business and community leaders Bea Sweeney, Norm Fox, Joe Dalton, Bill Dake, Newman ("Pete") Wait, Jr., Charles Wait, and others played critical roles in protecting the profile of the place, one of the few in America where downtown supporters won significant battles against the hangar-like suburban malls.[9]

SPAC, the new Skidmore, with its own strong public arts and sports programs, the Phila Street happenings, and Yaddo provided a powerful new cultural setting for America's most ancient racetrack. It was reminiscent of the place at the turn of the century and in the early thirties. And into this starry ambience trotted more champions. First to turn heads was Buckpasser, flying the black silks and cherry cap of Odgen Phipps and playing hurt. He had "a quarter crack in the days when there were no patches," rider Braulio Baeza would remember. "With the patches, I'm sure he would have been a Triple Crown champion. He was always in pain. He'd win with just heart and class." The Panamanian star steered Tom Fool's best son home in the Hopeful on the way to the divisional championship. He did the same in the Travers in 1966, when he won thirteen of fourteen and lowered the mile record to 1:32⅗ at Arlington. Buckpasser was also Handicapper and Horse of the Year. Rare as he was, another collected those same honors the next year.[10]

Like a new star in the east, Damascus captured the 1967 Preakness and Belmont, then met Buckpasser in the Woodward and beat him by ten lengths. That was nothing. He won the Travers from Hail to Reason by twenty-two lengths, more than twice the record set by Tom Bowling in 1873. A son of Travers champ Sword Dancer, Damascus gave Shoemaker his third and last win in that event. Most touching of all, he brought Belair's white with red polka dots back to the winner's circle, for the owner was the daughter of William Woodward, Sr., Mrs. Thomas Bancroft.

*   *   *   *

One after the other they came. The Horse of 1968 was Dr. Fager. Named for trainer John Nerud's brain surgeon, he made a house call at the Springs and added the 1968 Whitney. In the Washington Park Handicap he lowered Buckpasser's mile to 1:32 ⅕, a mark that would be standing 26 years later. It had taken 105 years to knock 12 ³⁄₁₀ seconds off the record Mamona owned when she paraded through Saratoga in 1863.

The three-year-old honors were shared by Stage Door Johnny and Forward Pass.

Arts and Letters. The 1969 Travers winner with owner Paul Mellon and the sphinx-like Braulio Baeza, nicknamed "the great stone face." *NYRA Photo.*

It was Johnny who opened the new $30.7 million Belmont Park—racing's latest great hope—by winning the one hundredth running of the Belmont, but it was Forward Pass who scored in the Kentucky, Florida, and American Derbies and in the Preakness. Guess where he was upset? In the Travers, by Tompion's Chompion, Frenchman Jean Cruguet up. Sonny's third Travers tied Calumet for third on the classic's winning list.

The hundredth Travers was staged in 1969. Even though it was inaugurated in 1864, three years earlier than the Belmont, it had missed four renewals during the Walbaum era (1896, 1898–1900). Neither event was moved elsewhere when New York shut down in 1911 and 1912. Not to start something, but if a race were only as old as the times it has been run, then America's oldest stakes would be the Belmont. If on the other hand it is as old as its inaugural, the Travers retains the honor. It was Arts and Letters who paid homage to the artists and literati next door at Yaddo by delivering the centennial edition, and by more than six lengths. "He just overpowered the field," Baeza remembered. It was Travers number two for him and Mellon, three for Burch. Arts and Letters equaled the Buckpasser and Damascus sweeps as Three-year-old, Handicapper, and Horse of the Year.

The decade that saw Jaipur and Ridan in one of the greatest races closed on one of the strangest. As they charged into the final quarter of the 1969 Hopeful, not a length and a half separated the first five. Down the stretch there were six, fighting for the greatness this event was supposed to single out, but looking from the rail like a single mass of hopeful horseflesh. "Photo!" Not for the usual two, or three, or four, or five—but all six—one of the weirdest endings in modern racing. Some twenty-four thousand spectators waited for their prince to come in. Rarely had so few tickets been dashed hopelessly to the ground before the results were announced. The wait was the longer because Syl Veitch instructed jockey Pete Anderson to file an objection, charging Hagley had interfered with Pontifex. It was rejected. NYRA president James Cox Brady presented the trophy to Mrs. Henry Carnegie Phipps. As the chart put it, it was Irish Castle no, Hagley hd, Pontifex hd, Away From Holme hd, Walker's hd, and High Echelon, less than a length behind the winner. It was also Baeza's fourth Hopeful on his way to a record five. As for Irish Castle, he would star at stud, getting Derby and Belmont victor Bold Forbes.[11]

*　　*　　*　　*

Yet Mrs. Phipps had, as Rudy put it, a better one in the barn, the greatest stallion of the century. Before he was through, Bold Ruler's get would top the money list eight times, from 1963 through 1969 and again in 1973. Only sixteen-time leader Lexington exceeded that. Back at the track, though, nobody had seen anything lately as superb as Kelso, not to speak of Citation, or Man o' War. Or, reaching into the mists, Longfellow and Kentucky. They were about to, though. He was a Bold Ruler.

 *24*

SECRETARIAT, RUFFIAN, AFFIRMED VS. ALYDAR

WHAT THE HELL was this? Seven lengths back, red was taking off like a plane. He had come up here unnoticed, after losing one and winning one. He had taken an allowance race, with Ron Turcotte on him for the first time. Then he faced Linda's Chief, who had racked up five straight, and beat him by an impressive three lengths in the Sanford. Now what? Surging out of last after a quarter mile, he ate up the Hopeful's six and a half furlongs in 1:16⅕ and won by five lengths. Here was the two-year-old of 1972. In fact, after adding the Belmont and Laurel Futurities and Garden State, and finishing first (though set back for bumping) in the Champagne, he was Horse of the Year.[1]

Secretariat was by Bold Ruler from Somethingroyal. The stars he beat out for Horse of 1972 included stablemate Riva Ridge, who validated his Flash victory in the Derby and Belmont. Even better was Rokeby's Key to the Mint, who won the Whitney on the Spa's first Saturday, the Travers on the third, and the three-year-old title.

In 1973, Secretariat came out to challenge Man o' War's claim to horse-of-the-century honors. Even before he hit the tracks his future was decided. His owner, Christopher Chenery, a utilities tycoon and Saratoga regular, died in January, never having seen this one race. His daughter, Helen (Penny) Tweedy had been operating the family's Meadow Stable in Doswell, Virginia, and now she took over officially. Reportedly to pay off the taxes on her father's estate, she syndicated the colt in advance. Seth Hancock, whose father had pioneered syndications, organized this one, selling thirty two shares at $190,000 each, for a total of $6,080,000. After this season, Secretariat would stand at Hancock's Claiborne Farm.

Aiming for the Derby, French-Canadian trainer Lucien Laurin sent Secretariat cruising through the Bay Shore and Gotham stakes. Angle Light then upset him in the Wood Memorial, a shocker, but apparently he had developed an abcess on his upper lip, the pain worsening through the pounding of the race. For the Derby, he was back in his glory, beating his frequent challenger, Sigmund Sommer's Sham, by two and a half lengths in a Downs record 1:59⅖ for the mile and a quarter. In the Preakness, he exposed Sham again. If the *Racing Form* clockers were right, he also beat Canonero II's 1:54 record for that mile and three-sixteenths event, but the officials made it 1:54⅖.

America now saw what a superstar could do for a sport. The Belmont was staged on an oppressively muggy day, and it wasn't blacked out on New York area television. Worse, the sport's greatest threat was in full swing. It was offtrack betting, widely

Secretariat at two. In the winner's circle with jockey Ron Turcotte, owner Penny Tweedy, and trainer Lucien Laurin. *NYRA Photo.*

considered a new monster but simply the descendant of nineteenth-century pari-mutuel halls in France and pool rooms in America. It had opened two years earlier with five OTB shops in New York City. Now there were 113.

Secretariat's try for the first Triple Crown in a quarter of a century brought out the second largest crowd in Belmont history, 69,138. The crowd that saw the Mets beat the Dodgers that day totaled 47,800, Shea Stadium's biggest of the year. Racing had become America's biggest spectator sport, with a record 54,813 horses competing in a record 62,272 races. Today they would see the best of the 54,813 and that challenger Sham. NYRA, shaken by OTB, emerged from what the *Times* called its "old days of indifference" and gussied it up. A Dixieland combo played the clubhouse, a Brooklyn steel band blared by the eighth pole, and another band boomed marches as the star came out. He wasn't there long.

One eyewitness, reporter Steve Cady, called it "racing's version of a moonshot" and said the crowd never stopped yelling as Secretariat flew the first mile and a quarter a tick faster than his record Derby. By now he was twenty lengths ahead. This "reincarnation of Pegasus" stretched it to twenty-eight at the eighth pole, for which reason that pole now stands in front of the National Museum of Racing, and took

Morning with Secretariat. Working out at America's oldest sports facility. *NYRA Photo.*

Turcotte all the way home by thirty-one lengths. The rest (a trivia question Secretariat had made extremely tough): Twice a Prince, My Gallant, Pvt. Smiles, and, last, Sham. Secretariat's 2:24 would remain the dirt record for a mile and a half two decades later.[2]

The most memorable finish in modern racing was worth $90,120 to the winner and $2.20 to you and me, though many saved their souvenir tickets. "We can look back and say we were here," bubbled a visitor from Long Branch, New Jersey. Imagine how many visitors Secretariat might have drawn without those 113 OTB parlors. As it was, he also proved what a superhorse could not do. His crowd was still far below the mark of two years earlier, when OTB was just finding its legs and 82,640 turned out to see Canonero II's Belmont.

Oddly, things were looking up for racing upstate and for Secretariat, too. After a nine-length win in an "Arlington Invitational," he returned to the track that "discovered" him. His assignments: win the Whitney, then the Travers. NYRA president Jack Krumpe hadn't slept for weeks. Reservations and ticket requests had been coming in from all over. Could the Spa handle it? What about security? "I just don't know when I'll ever relax." While Krumpe worried, visitors enjoyed one of those rare Spa treats, like the ones Man o' War had served up. This time it was Secretariat working out. For starters he beat the track mile, doing 1:34 in the mud. Some five thousand watched him in another outing on a quiet Wednesday.

A few handicappers noted this was Secretariat's debut against older horses. They made another note that the second favorite came off a two-and-a-half-month rest that week to set a track mark of 1:15 ⅗ over six and a half furlongs, winning by eight lengths. This was a four-year-old gelding owned by Hobeau Farm and baptized Onion, the neatest moniker since Upset. Onion was expected to set the pace for the Whitney's

Losing the Whitney. Onion, in the foreground, with Secretariat, at right, in second place. *NYRA Photo.*

nine furlongs, and the line was: "He'll be dangerous if he gets loose." Onion would go off at 10 to 1 and Secretariat 1 to 10. Each would carry 119.

A record crowd of 30,119 turned out. It should be called a "modern" record, since Gallant Fox and Man o' War and perhaps others drew bigger crowds. But millions more were watching as they saddled them on the turf course in front of the stand. Nobody was much surprised when they took off and Onion set the pace, and kept setting it. Secretariat raced out of fourth to third by the half, then second, closing powerfully to within a head in the stretch. Onion had enough left to peel off and win by a length in racing's most historic upset since Upset's on this same old oval.

Onion brought emotional sobs of joy to trainer Jerkens as he accepted the trophy. He said he told Vasquez not to let Onion loose at all but to slow the pace if he could so he would have something left. Turcotte and Laurin said Secretariat didn't like the track. The first-day excuses piled up. Turcotte said Secretariat hit his head in the gate. Laurin said he should have raced wider. Afterwards, it was found Secretariat had a mild virus, and with that he was pulled from the Travers. Trivialists will note that Annihilate 'Em won it, and that Onion's Jacinto Vasquez also rode Angle Light when

Sandy Hawley. The jockey at his induction into the Hall of Fame, and turf historian Tom Gilcoyne. *Courtesy of Barbara Livingston.*

he beat Secretariat in the Wood. And that Secretariat's stable mate, Riva Ridge, got upset that week, too, by 56-to-1 Wichita Oil.

To get back into the pantheon, Secretariat needed to prove himself at Belmont in the inaugural Marlboro Cup, dreamed up by John Landry, a Saratogian and executive of the Philip Morris Company. Here he faced Riva Ridge, Onion, Annihilate 'Em, and Key to the Mint, among others. He won dramatically, beating Riva Ridge by three and a half lengths in a world record 1:45 ⅖ over the mile and an eighth. The legend was back, only to be dented again with an unexplained loss to Prove Out in the Woodward. After that Secretariat faced his first test on turf. It was against Tentam, who on Saratoga's grass course had matched Secretariat's mile and an eighth dirt record. It was Secretariat by five lengths. Finally, he finished like Man o' War in Canada, by six and a half lengths in the Woodbine International. Secretariat had sixteen wins in twenty-one starts.

Jockey bulletin: in 1973, Sandy Hawley became the first to win more than 500 races, with 515, and Panamanian Lafitte Pincay, Jr., the first to bring in winners of $4 million.

Worried that they would not see a Secretariat every few years, New York officials moved to counter OTB's assault on attendance and handle at the city tracks. As Rudy

Ruffian and Foolish Pleasure. The filly is at the left. *NYRA Photo.*

noted, it was then that New York temporarily cut the "takeout" from 17 to 14 percent at Aqueduct to encourage more betting. It created the three-person Racing and Wagering Board to supervise the tracks and OTB. It introduced "triple" betting, a wager on the first three finishers in the ninth race. It extended the New York season to twelve months and in 1975 it would introduce Sunday racing. NYRA treasurer Thomas Fitzgerald succeeded Krumpe as president. Nicholas Brady, future secretary of the treasury, succeeded Ogden Phipps as chairman of the Jockey Club.

Jockey bulletin: Jimmy Winkfield, the last black rider to win the Kentucky Derby, and who rode for a quarter of a century more in France, died there in 1974. He was ninety-one. There were still virtually no black jockeys in this country.

Astonishingly, the decade did produce a Secretariat every few years. Or almost. One was Ruffian, by Bold Ruler's Reviewer from Native Dancer's Shenanigans. A small star marked her head, and purple tints made her darkish brown coat seem black, as Rudy noted in admiration. "Was she the greatest filly of all time?" he asked. "Or was she more than that—the greatest Thoroughbred?"[3]

He also said that those who knew her saw something scary. "She used so much of herself," said trainer Frank Whiteley. As with Secretariat, it was Saratoga that revealed her. Her arrival followed four wins at Belmont, Aqueduct, and Monmouth by an average of about eight lengths, each in a stakes or track record, yet her debut at the Spa was even better. Rudy ranked it among the most awesome moments in the sport, including Jaipur vs. Ridan. "Why does the remembrance of Ruffian in the Spinaway, rounding the turn into the Saratoga stretch, lengths alone against a not-outstanding field, rank with those moments in excitement? There is no answer. Ruffian set her own standards, set the stage for her own dramas, and in a sense dug her own grave."

Her Spinaway opponent Laughing Bridge was actually no laughing matter, having won the Adirondack by five lengths and the Schuylerville by thirteen. Yet, as Rudy said, Ruffian "led from the start, almost loafed down the backstretch, and when she turned it on around the turn, as Laughing Bridge mildly challenged, Ruffian's beautiful long stride fairly lifted her above the track surface. She seemed to be flying." She won by close to thirteen lengths in 1:08 ⅗. It was, they said, another stakes record. What they did not say until later, as Ruffian biographer Jane Schwartz would point out, was that it was not just the fastest Spinaway. It was the fastest six furlongs ever run at Saratoga by any two-year-old, including Man o' War, Native Dancer, and Secretariat.[4]

When Ruffian's crew led her to the hand-drawn winner's circle, "Ruffian stood still, poised and regal, and gradually the crowd grew quiet," Schwartz wrote. "Then the filly tossed her head and pranced sideways a few steps and the audience screamed its approval. She wanted to get back on the track! She wanted to keep running!" Rudy quoted trainer Laz Barrera as saying the next morning, "If that filly was in the Hopeful today, she would win by 20 lengths." The Hopeful winner was Foolish Pleasure, a $20,000 Saratoga yearling with whom Ruffian would have a tragic date.

The filly returned to competition in 1975 to win two more, followed by the Filly Triple Crown—the Acorn, Mother Goose, and Coaching Club American Oaks. Her breeder-owners, Mr. and Mrs. Stuart Janney, Jr., of Locust Hill Farm, in Maryland, then agreed to a match race at a full mile and a quarter, her first contest with a colt and New York's first match race in twenty eight years. It was Foolish Pleasure, the male of the moment, who had gone to add the Derby and Wood Memorial. The winner would get $225,000. They were off—and Ruffian, second out of the Belmont gate, gained the early lead. She was half a length ahead approaching the half mile, when Vasquez on Ruffian and Baeza on Foolish Pleasure heard a crack. "Ruffian careened across the wide track to the outside rail," said Rudy, "held on her feet only by Vasquez's tight hold and her own will not to go down. . . . Her right front pastern was horribly shattered." Surgeons tried to save her but as she came out of the medication, "she threw us around like little children," Dr. Alex Harhill said. "Ruffian was fighting for her life and it was costing her her life," as Rudy put it. They put her down the next morning, July 7, 1975, and buried her that night by Belmont's infield flagpole.

It was hard to believe, but the decade that produced Secretariat and Ruffian also introduced Forego. By Forli from Lady Golconda—thus "Forego"—the gelding was a big dark bay just under seventeen hands and was owned by another of the many women at the top, though their sports and business achievements never have been noticed by those outside the turf. Mrs. Martha Gerry ran the Lazy F Ranch Stable with her mother, Mrs. Libby Rice Farish. Forego was a year older than Ruffian. On the weekend that was Ruffian's last, five-year-old Forego broke Whisk Broom's and

Kelso's 2:00 Belmont record for a mile and a quarter, doing the Brooklyn Handicap quicker by a tick. Now he faced the Travers winner, Wajima.[5]

Wajima reflected the growing foreign presence in American racing. The Japanese were among the syndicators who had picked up this handsome colt, mainly for stud, for a record $600,000 at the Keeneland auctions, the Saratoga spinoff whose totals now often surpassed the Spa's. They had named him after a Japanese wrestler and raced him under the flag of the global East-West Stable. His ten-length Travers had been his third in a row, and his sun was still rising.

Forego confronted not only Wajima but Foolish Pleasure in the Governor, and they beat him in that order. Ancient Title was third. Fourth-place Forego, on the other hand, carried 134 pounds to Wajima's 115. He was now given five pounds less for the Marlboro, still ten more than Wajima, who beat him again—but by only a head in a wicked 2:00 for that mile and a quarter. Forego finally wrestled Wajima to the ground in the Woodward, leaving him back nearly two lengths, and headed for his second coronation as Horse of the Year.

Marching on, the long runner beat Lord Rebeau and Foolish Pleasure to win his third Brooklyn in 1976. Then it was Honest Pleasure. Like Foolish, Honest was a Spa yearling, Bertram Firestone having snapped him up for $45,000. And like Wajima the year before, Honest had just won the Travers, and in a local record of 2:00 ⅕. Six-year-old Forego gave the three-year-old fourteen pounds, carried 135, and still beat Dance Spell and Honest to win his third Woodward. In the Marlboro, he transported 137 pounds, much of it Bill Shoemaker. This time it was eighteen more than Honest Pleasure's load, but Forego came out of fifth at the top of the Belmont stretch to put on his most sensational finish ever. He passed three in the muddy mist, caught Honest Pleasure and headed him. Shoemaker had not even needed the whip.

Forego was the only performer other than Kelso to be thrice Horse of the Year (and ironically both were geldings). He would be back, and Saratoga, where he had raced once at three and lost, would be waiting.

Hard to believe, but the decade that produced Secretariat, Ruffian, and Forego now gave us a second Triple Crown laureate—the first to win it while unbeaten. For the last jewel of that crown, Seattle Slew drew a crowd any baseball team would have died for, 71,026 at Belmont, the last such megacrowd there, as Rudy pointed out. He had been purchased by the young couples Karen and Mickey Taylor and Jim and Sally Hill for a lousy $17,500. Now on his way to earning $1,208,726 on the track alone, Seattle Slew was ballyhooed with circus-like publicity, and the tracks begged for him. He never made it to Saratoga but his unlikely rival for Horse of 1977 did.

It was old Forego. He opened the year under a frightening sign of the times—a wimpy turnout of 7,514 at Belmont. A strike by mutuel workers had shut down betting, and as they had warned at Saratoga in 1863, first-rate racing without betting would occur "when we see a fire that won't burn anybody." There were several more cold days in hell that summer as the strike dragged on. In August, Forego returned to the Springs for the Whitney. The contrast was telling. Despite sweltering heat after a night rain, the seven-year-old star lured a record first-Saturday crowd to the country oval, 29,102.[6]

They watched Forego finish dead last in the mud, Shoemaker not bothering to force the issue. A horse modestly named Nearly On Time was, and by eighteen lengths. Then Forego returned to his horse-of-the-year form. With Shoe aboard, he captured an unprecedented fourth Woodward. He had won 34 of 57, was second in 9 and third in 7. Still, the horse of 1977 was Seattle Slew, who had a career 14 wins in 17 efforts.

Hard to believe, but the decade that produced Secretariat, Ruffian, Forego, and Seattle Slew next came up with Affirmed and Alydar. They gave us the tightest long-running duel in modern racing, its intensity harkening, for those who could harken, to Longfellow and Harry Bassett, Lexington and Leconte. Their patented stretch battle was revealed to the world—why was this no surprise?—at Saratoga.[7]

They were direct descendants of Native Dancer. Alydar was a grandson, by the Dancer's Raise a Native, out of Sweet Tooth. He was also Calumet's bid to return the devil's red and blue to glory. Affirmed was a great-grandson, by Raise a Native's Exclusive Native, from Won't Tell You. He was owned by Lou Wolfson's Harbor View Farm.

Each was associated with another famous name in racing. In Alydar's case it was Veitch. To some, the story of the turf had been largely that of the wealthy owners who began taking it over in 1863. Less known was the equally strong family tradition among the trainers, a grandparent-to-parent-to-son-or-daughter heritage that has produced many of the best—the Rowes, Burches, Hirsches, Jacobs—the list is endless. The sons of the Ontario-born cross-country rider Silas Veitch went into racing, too. Among them was the great Syl Veitch, and Syl's son John was now taking over as Calumet's trainer. Another of Silas's descendants is Mike Veitch, one of the country's top turf writers.

Affirmed was linked with perhaps the most extraordinary apprentice jockey ever. All of sixteen, he looked thirteen. Steve Cauthen was from Walton, Kentucky, and America took to fresh-faced "Kid Cauthen" as soon as he lost his "bug"—his five-pound apprentice's allowance—in 1977. He rode six winners on a card three times and five winners four times. Before he was through that year, he would win 487 and break both the $5 million and the $6 million barrier for annual earnings by a jockey's mounts. The Associated Press looked over the football, baseball, and basketball stars and voted Cauthen Athlete of the Year.

It was at Saratoga that Cauthen first rode Affirmed, winning the Sanford, though with Alydar elsewhere. Then Affirmed and Alydar met in the Hopeful. Each had beaten the other soundly once before. Affirmed had taken the Youthful, leaving the Calumet colt in fifth (the last time he would be worse than second against Affirmed). Alydar had won the Great American, beating Affirmed by three and a half lengths. But in that Hopeful, the historic breathtaking finishes of Affirmed and Alydar were born on the old Spa stretch. The favored Alydar, Eddie Maple up, ran hard and wide, but Kid Cauthen kept his eye on the prize and won it by half a length. Next it was Affirmed by a nose in the Futurity, Alydar by a length and a quarter in the Champagne, Affirmed by a neck in the Laurel Futurity. For 1977, it was Affirmed 4, Alydar 2.

At three, they headed for separate sunshine states, each winning four, Affirmed in California, Alydar in Florida and at Keeneland. They then squared off at Churchill Downs, Pimlico, and Belmont: the Triple Crown. After a twenty-five-year drought, the seventies had not only provided two Triple Crown winners already (Secretariat

Secretariat, Ruffian, Affirmed vs. Alydar

Alydar and John Veitch.
Jorge Velasquez up.
NYRA Photo.

and Seattle Slew) but now produced them back-to-back for the first time. And it was the only Triple Crown with the same two in front all the way. Affirmed beat Alydar by a combined margin of less than two lengths, the closest ever. The difference had kept narrowing. A length and a half in the Derby, a neck in the Preakness, a head in the Belmont. Which body part was next?

It was Affirmed 7, Alydar 2. Said John Veitch: "I will be looking forward toward the Travers." First, though, each turned in a sensational preliminary act at the Spa. Alydar had stopped off at Arlington Park to win the Classic by thirteen lengths and then took the Whitney by ten. "Alydar was better at Saratoga than he's ever been in his life," Veitch would remember. "His victory in the Whitney was just absolutely super." Affirmed won a stretch duel with Sensitive Prince to take a thrilling Jim Dandy by half a length. It was show time.

To get an idea of where New York racing was going, consider that Affirmed and

Steve Cauthen, Boy Wonder. The 16-year old "bug" rider. *National Museum of Racing and Hall of Fame, Saratoga Springs.*

Alydar had drawn a crowd of 65,417 to Belmont but still set no attendance mark. The city tracks were still slipping. Little Saratoga, rising, was swamped with 50,122, more than a third over its previous modern mark. It would register record ontrack and total handles that day of $3.8 million and $6.5 million.[8]

It was August 19, 1978. Pincay was subbing for Cauthen, who had separated his shoulder in a spill. Jorge Velasquez was on Alydar. Oddly, it was the jockeys who would decide it. They were off! Shake Shake Shake took the lead and kept it through the half, paced by Affirmed. Racing on the outside, Affirmed had two lengths on Alydar.

The Calumet colt had not made his move, but when he did it would be a hell of a surprise. As turf writer Andrew Beyer would point out, he usually made it on the outside. As they approached the far turn, Angel Cordero on Shake Shake Shake was racing off the rail so there was an opening inside, and Alydar took it. Affirmed's trainer, Laz Barrera, had to be furious. He suspected Velasquez knew Cordero would give him the opening.

"Alydar don't got no business on the rail," he would say, "if he don't know Cordero is going to open the inside for him." Veitch called it just smart. "I thought Pincay had a chance a little bit earlier to get to the rail, but it looked to me like he went to sleep." It wasn't over, though.

Shake Shake Shake stopped shaking at six furlongs, and Alydar turned it on. He slipped to within half a length of Affirmed on the inside. Then, into the final turn, it happened: Pincay made a mistake. "I saw Velasquez coming up on the inside of me.

Secretariat, Ruffian, Affirmed vs. Alydar

Angel Cordero, Jr., and Jorge Velasquez. *National Museum of Racing and Hall of Fame, Saratoga Springs.*

However, I did not think there was enough room for him to get through." He cut sharply to the left.

For Alydar it was like hitting a brick wall. He pulled up, Velasquez standing in his irons, and dropped six lengths back. "He broke down!" screamed people in the crowd. Now it was Veitch who was furious, after Velasquez told him he was just an inch from being thrown. "That was bad riding on Pincay's part," Veitch would say. "You might be able to get away with that in California, but not there. The thing that really upsets me about it is that the chance of injury is great enough without something like that happening."

Alydar had fought back out of the turn but could never recover. Affirmed wrapped up the mile and a quarter in 2:02, up a length and three-quarters. He was supposed to pay $3.40. But there was a "D" by his name. Pincay would call the disqualification "borderline," but few others would. It was Alydar who won, paying $4.

★   ★   ★   ★

They would never meet again. It was Affirmed 7, Alydar 3. And over the 10 ⁵⁄₁₆ miles they ran against each other, it was Affirmed by just four and a half lengths. Two

Affirmed beating Alydar to the finish line in the Travers. *NYRA Photo by Bob Coglianese.*

years later, he would enter the Hall of Fame across the street. Eleven years after that, Alydar would canter in.

Affirmed-Alydar—the LP of Jaipur-Ridan—all but erased the final memories of that decade, which is too bad. Less than a month later, Affirmed met Seattle Slew at Belmont in the only confrontation of Triple Crown winners. It was the Slew by three lengths, "confirming the old adage that a good older horse will beat a good three-year-old," said historian Edward Bowen.[9]

Bert Firestone's and Secretariat's United Nations–inspired offspring, General Assembly, would win the Special, the Hopeful, and the muddy 1979 Travers in 2:00 flat, a record that would be alive sixteen years later.

*   *   *   *

More spectacular was Hawksworth Farm's Spectacular Bid, who outran General Assembly in the Derby. He and four-year-old Affirmed became the first to win a million bucks in a single year, 1979. Affirmed got more spectacular still. In his last effort, he proved Ed Bowen's adage to his own advantage, beating Spectacular Bid in the Jockey Club Gold Cup. When all was said and done, Affirmed had won 22 of 29, Spectacular Bid 26 of 30. Each would smash the $2 million lifetime barrier, Affirmed with $2.3 million, then Spectacular Bid—another one of those yearling bargains at $37,000—with $2.7 million.

JOHN HENRY, GO FOR WAND, HOLY BULL

RACING HEADED INTO the twenty-first century with more problems than it could handle, so they threw more money at it. Tradition and sport went out the window, except at a few places, such as Saratoga and Keeneland and Churchill Downs; Oaklawn in Arkansas and Aiken in South Carolina; Del Mar, where the thunder of hooves echoed the crashing of the California surf. Places where sport and a certain decency had a role, too.

"Horses are like people," Virginia Payson told reporter Joe Durso one day. They were just outside the Spa track, at the stable she had set up in 1980, when NYRA had no available stall space. She bought seven lots to create a five-and-a-half-acre park, with a modern barn, paddocks, and pastures. "Each horse is different from every other, at the mental level, at the physical level, at every level. And two-year-old horses are babies." She was against rushing them. "Even their knee bones aren't closed and firm. Horses keep growing until they're six. You know I never push a colt toward the Kentucky Derby. Look at the fields for the last 10 or 15 Derbies. You never hear of half of them again. . . . I prefer to aim a colt for the Travers instead."[1]

"They develop an attitude here," her trainer, Jim Bond, said. "They go to the races. They're like children going to the fair. We don't even train them on the regular track. The training track is softer, better for their legs, much kinder to their wheels."

"We even graze them on the grass here," Payson added. "Horses live in a box for 23 hours a day in their barn. But God made them to run in pastures."

They also ran for money, and the purses had started climbing. When in 1980 Genuine Risk became the first filly to win the Derby since Regret, it was worth a record $250,550. Temperence Hill beat her to a record $176,000 in the Belmont and took the first Travers worth more than $100,000. But such sums could not save a track in trouble. So in 1981 Arlington Park offered the first $1 million purse in thoroughbred history—the "Arlington Million"—with some $600,000 for the winner, a television broadcast to twenty countries and plenty of hype, including some sort of drink called the "Cool Million." It was the opening of the money wars that would roar through the eighties.[2]

As long as they were throwing money, John Henry would go after it. Here was a funny horse. Sold as a yearling for $1,100, he kicked around Louisiana tracks and was resold five more times. Finally, a New York horseplayer and bicycle importer, Sam Rubin, paid $25,000 for him at three and turned him over to Ron McAnally, the miracle worker. At five, John Henry won eight of twelve and was the Eclipse Grass

Horse of 1980, a title he would own four times. At six he and Bill Shoemaker showed up for this Arlington Million thing and charged out of eighth to win in a photo. John Henry pushed his earnings that season past a record $3 million. The only other horse remotely in the running for Horse of 1981 was Derby, Preakness, and Woodward winner Pleasant Colony, but he had lost to Willow Hour in the Travers and retired before the Jockey Club Gold Cup, which John Henry won. So old John was the first unanimously crowned Horse of the Year.

The following year several stars proceeded as usual to the Spa. Preakness winner Aloma's Ruler, Belmont winner Conquistador Cielo, and Derby winner Gato Del Sol all entered the Travers. That's the way those Triple Crowners finished—as bridesmaids behind long shot Runaway Groom. Still Conquistador did go on to become the Horse of 1982. In case anybody doubted the spoiling power of the Travers, though, Play Fellow took the next edition, beating the three-year-old champion, Seattle Slew's Slew o' Gold.

"Like old wine . . ." With that opening, the presenter in Los Angeles brought down the house as he announced that the Horse of 1984 was John Henry, the oldest honoree ever. Kelso had been seven when he took it the fifth time, but John was nine. He had repeated in what was now the Budweiser-Arlington Million and added five others. Once again the loser, in tight balloting, was Slew o' Gold. "It's a joke, a popularity contest," co-owner Mickey Taylor was quoted as complaining. Definitely not a joke were John's 39 wins in 83 starts (37 in 66 after McAnally got him) and record earnings of $6.5 million, nearly twice Slew o' Gold's. His rider wasn't doing half bad, either. Five more years, and Shoe would retire with a record 8,833 victories.[3]

"I bought five more horses," Sam Rubin reminisced when they inducted John Henry into the Hall of Fame. "Two are with the Canadian mounted police. One's directing traffic out on Union Avenue. One is up at Cornell University: they can't figure out if it's male or female. And the last one a friend bought for $5,000 to spare me further embarrassment."

John Henry didn't even go for the $1,350,000 he could have won in the explosion of money that shook up racing in 1984. He was out with a ligament injury. The second salvo of the money wars, it was called the Breeders' Cup, a series of seven races worth millions of dollars—including the richest yet, the $3 million Breeders' Cup Classic. This big gamble by the breeders was supposed to save racing, "a stagnant sport," as columnist George Vecsey put it, "that loses its best performers at an early age to syndication and cannot agree on uniform rules for medication" and was "trying to rebuild its support system with Super Bowl/World Series aspirations."[4]

It actually was a throwback, not that anybody noticed it, to the national racing festival of 1865. That was the beginning of an expansion age, whereas 1984, as Vecsey pointed out, found racing "hemmed in by an expanding entertainment market—the same recreation trend that has threatened pro football's television ratings, off-track betting and state lotteries." He quoted one of the more vocal Breeders' Cup supporters. "We've got to the reach the young people," said trainer John Nerud. "We've always known that young girls love horses and boys love contact sports. Now we've got to make racing fashionable for young people."

John Henry, Go for Wand, Holy Bull

The first Breeders' Cup was a moderate success. It made for four hours of lively TV from Hollywood Park, including a controversy in the Classic, when Wild Again's win was vindicated, Gate Dancer disqualified, and the unlucky Slew o' Gold moved up to second. It established a tradition of influencing the annual championships, locking up the two-year-old title, for instance, for Chief's Crown (who would validate it giving Angel Cordero his first Travers after thirteen tries). The organizers even outdid the Arlington Million with hype, calling it "the Greatest Day in the History of Racing" when what they meant was "the Greatest Day in the History of Money," a much duller matter.

It hardly created a youth movement, since those have never been about money, or any other kind of movement. The crowd of 64,254 on a sunny Saturday was 15,000 fewer than expected. Perhaps the most troubling aspect of it all was the contradiction of what was good in sports, and what was bad. Telegenic "controversy" was suddenly more attractive than talent, a disqualification more interesting than a great finish. "The series got off to an exciting start," said one report, "with two changes of finish following stewards' inquiries."

Something worse than unsportsmanlike waited in the wings. "Maybe the huge jackpot," one hopeful commentator wished, "will develop a tradition of hard riding and intense inquiries." He meant only harder competition and disputed results, a strange goal in any case, but in six years "jackpot" and "hard" and "intense" would have a different ring after the most visible tragedy in the history of the turf.[5]

As the inflationary trends raged through the eighties, nobody brought in more big winners than a former basketball coach from California, D. Wayne Lukas. He succeeded Charlie Whittingham as the top money-winning trainer and stayed there for a record ten years, his horses topping $17 million in 1987 and 1988. Jockeys Chris McCarron, Angel Cordero, Lafitte Pincay, Jr., and José Santos alternated in riding winners of more than $10 million, $12 million, $14 million a year.

Among breeders, E. P. Taylor, operating from home in Ontario, Canada, and from Maryland, continued a Canadian-American tradition begun in 1863 at the Spa. His sires included Northern Dancer, who had the unusual distinction of winning both the Kentucky Derby and North America's oldest stakes, the Queen's Plate, then siring three winners of the Epsom Derby. Taylor far surpassed H. P. Whitney as top breeder of stakes winners with 323, and led the money list nine times.[6]

How was business at Keeneland and at the modern pavilion on George Street, down the street from where Man o' War went for $5,000? Top yearling prices had jumped from the $100,000s in the 1960s to $250,000 for Majestic Prince at Keeneland in 1969, to the millions in the 1980s. To some it made as much sense as the insane market for tulips in ancient Holland. Others were thinking about how Mellon's agent, Mack Miller, picked up Fit to Fight for $175,000 at Saratoga, then saw him become the fourth horse to win the Handicap Triple Crown and earn about $1 million. Even luckier were Henryk de Kwiatkowski and his trainer Woody Stephens, who got Conquistador Cielo for $150,000 at the Spa in 1980 and finally syndicated him for an astounding $36 million.

International forces like the Englishman Robert Sangster, the Japanese, and

Sheikh Maktoum bin Rashid al Maktoum and his three brothers, of Dubai, got into the act. The Sangster group outbid the Maktoums to get Seattle Slew's half-brother, Seattle Dancer, for $13.1 million. By 1985, the Keeneland and Saratoga auctions averaged $416,515 per yearling. It made for an exotic atmosphere on George Street, where the local folks wondered who the hell were these Sangsters and Maktoums and where did they get all that money? The Japanese they knew. They were driving their cars.

Andy Beyer wrote that the town was bursting.

> In the early 1970s the fraternity of handicappers here thought of Saratoga as our little secret. And then, of course, a phenomenon occurred that radically altered this quiet little track: Saratoga was "discovered." Off-track betting had come to upstate New York and exposed the residents to horse racing year-round; suddenly they discovered that America's greatest track—one that had been a playground of out-of-town visitors—was in their own backyard.[7]

Attendance and handle records were set repeatedly for a variety of reasons, such as the lowering of the takeout to 15 percent in 1981 and the closing of Delaware Park in 1983. When NYRA began simulcasting Saratoga to Aqueduct in 1984, the handle jumped to more than $100 million.

Plans were announced to expand Spa capacity by five thousand, to fifty thousand, by developing a recreation area along the site of the old horse path into the grounds. It encroached again on the place's loveliest charm, the "backyard," where people scooted out of the way as the thoroughbreds were led by. The new area had more of everything—picnic grounds, television monitors, betting windows, and concession stands—except charm, but it beat building a bigger grandstand. It also confirmed that, since money long had been the prime concern of NYRA and the only concern of the state, independent vigilance on the part of Saratoga's supporters was more urgent than ever.

A clear setback, for instance, was the blacktopping of the Saratoga Trotting Course (the Horse Haven track). Here—not that the blacktoppers knew any of this—was where the Old Gray Mare ran in 1847, where the first thoroughbreds raced, where the first thoroughbred meeting was held, where ever since, trainers had schooled youngsters not ready for Oklahoma. It was a treasure, still a marvelous working area and a living museum, many of its barns dating from before the Civil War. What it needed was not blacktop but restoration.

The spirit of Will Whitney, the place's first major renovator, was still strong. His grandson, C. V., was as loyal as ever to the place, and the popular Mrs. Whitney's devotion to it put her in a rare historic class with Sonny, Will himself, the Commodore, and Morrissey. When Sonny died in 1992, the *Times* would point out that the couple had lived well indeed. "For three and a half decades, Marylou and Sonny Whitney reigned in high society from the half-dozen homes that they maintained in splendor on two continents: in the Adirondacks, on Fifth Avenue, on the farm in Kentucky, in Palm Beach, Fla., and in Spain, as well as in Saratoga Springs." They had the Commodore's and Will's American zest for travel and sports and adventure. But

John Henry, Go for Wand, Holy Bull

A day at the races. Marthe Vincent and Charles A. Hotaling, Sr. *Courtesy of the author.*

their philanthropies were far-reaching as well, and their attitudes were as democratic as the next guy's.

Beyond their contributions as founders of the National Museum of Racing, National Museum of Dance, and SPAC, and their support of countless local projects, there were frequent rescue missions, sometimes reaching far afield, such as their aid to the financially strapped 1980 Winter Olympics at Lake Placid. Mrs. Whitney has continued the good works. Everybody may know her as Marylou, but nobody underestimates her, and with good reason. Sonny had not wanted her to go into racing, for instance, but she finally did anyway. "He never let me come to the backstretch," Mrs. Whitney told a reporter one day at a backstretch coffeeshop. "He said ladies don't belong on the backstretch." But in the late eighties, she formed her own Blue Goose Stable, originally with Leslie Combs, of Spendthrift Farm, and won her first trophy with Dance King at Gulfstream. She has spoken out for broadening the base of racing. "I may be a lot of things," she told another reporter, "but I'm not a snob. If you really try, you can make it. There shouldn't be any snobbism in racing. It should be for everyone who can afford it."[8]

It was only a matter of seasons before NYRA joined the million-dollar race. In

Marylou Whitney. With her Best Blush, at Saratoga's "Oklahoma" stables, 1993.
Gazette Newspapers Photo by Bruce Squiers.

1987, it upped the Belmont and the Travers to more than $1 million—more than the Run for the Roses—and they started calling the Travers the summertime Derby again. They did not start calling it the Run for the Melons, but maybe the less said the better. The pitch of the place picked up. The first million-dollar Travers brought in Chicago and Kentucky jockey Pat Day, no slouch when it came to hopping planes for big bucks, and he impressed the hell out of Mack Miller. "He can do it all. It's funny that he rides in the Midwest considering how good he is." Day took over the latest Mellon-Miller dynamo, Java Gold, winning the Whitney, then targeting the $1.12 million biggie.[9]

Java Gold's golden father, Key to the Mint, had won it $1 million ago. It was true Java had not won any Triple Crown races but it was for lack of trying. He wasn't in them. Now he faced Derby and Preakness winner Alysheba and Belmont winner Bet Twice. Day knew his horse. "The best horses in America only have a real good run of a quarter of a mile," he said, and what was best for Java Gold was to "let him make his move at the five-sixteenths pole."

John Henry, Go for Wand, Holy Bull

297

It had rained cats and dogs, but Day didn't mind. "This colt would run well over broken bottles." Pat wore three sets of goggles, pulling down a new one whenever the front-runners muddied his vision. "The third pair had a lot of dirt on them, but there was room enough to see where the wire was." He crossed it two lengths in front of Cryptoclearance and Angel Cordero. It was also the year José Santos broke Cordero's eleven-year streak as the meeting's top rider. Cordero regained it the next year and kept it in 1989, winding up with thirteen crowns in fourteen years.

The numbers kept rising until Saratoga, which had launched racing as a national sport in 1863–65, was suddenly the busiest track in America again. Average daily attendance hit 28,407 in 1987. Two years later, when the Big A's collapsed to 10,025 and Belmont's to 12,471, the Spa's was 28,479. True, its season ran only twenty-four days, about 8 percent of the NYRA schedule, but it drew 17 percent of NYRA attendance and raked in a record $85 million, nearly 10 percent of the handle. They were heady days in the oases where jockeys, trainers, owners, fans, everybody but the horses, gathered, among them Siro's next to the track, Lillian's and the Trattoria around Broadway, Bob Lee's Wishing Well north of town, and every spot in between. There was no place like it in America.

No recent name touched the turf with magic the way a filly dubbed Go for Wand did in 1990. The recent contenders had been plentiful. There was Winning Colors, first filly to win the Derby since Genuine Risk, and there were three successive two-year-old champions who became Travers winners, Forty-Niner, Easy Goer, and Rhythm.

The latter two were sent out by a father and a son who represented the survival of the great families of the turf—and more than mere survival. Ogden Phipps broke the $6 million mark as leading breeder and led the owners with a record $5.8 million in 1988. While the son, Ogden Mills Phipps, raced Rhythm, the father fielded the unforgotten Easy Goer. He swept the Belmont, Woodward, and Jockey Club Gold Cup, and like some equine Moses made the seas of people divide of their own will as he walked through the backyard, some human holding on lightly. He won both the Whitney and Travers in 1989. Even an August Belmont had come back, the IVth, to win the 1983 Belmont with Caveat and serve briefly as Jockey Club chairman, to be succeeded by Ogden Mills Phipps. From his home on Maryland's eastern shore, Belmont allowed, however, as how V, VI, and VII did not appear headed for the turf, at least not so far.[10]

There was Criminal Type, who represented one of the greatest stables of the past. This Alydar son had upset both Easy Goer and Sunday Silence just before they retired with leg injuries. Under Wayne Lukas, Criminal Type showed this was no fluke by convincingly winning the 1990 Whitney. There was Housebuster, who at the Spa that summer scored his eighth win in ten events as he headed for the first of two Sprinter-of-the-Year titles, and a few lesser notables, among them Prospector's Gamble, who beat the favored four-year-old, Mr. Nickerson, in the A Phenomenon Stakes.

Yet there was something about Go for Wand, unless it is only in sad retrospect. Owned by Jane duPont Lunger's Christiana Farm and trained by Billy Badgett, she had been the champion two-year-old. At three, she was six for eight and coming off a seven-week rest in the Saratoga Test. As Steve Crist reported, this was supposed to be

Go for Wand. Winning
the Test, Randy Romero
aboard. *NYRA Photo.*

merely her prep for the Alabama, but once again everybody forgot to tell the horse. With Randy Romero up, she zipped the seven furlongs to win by two lengths and tie the Test record of 1:21:09 (NYRA had become the first American track operators to time them in hundredths).[11]

Nobody knew that as they broke, Token Dance hit her head on the side of the gate. It was only after the race that her jockey, Eddie Maple, learned it had torn out three teeth and a piece of her jaw. By then Go for Wand was established as the best filly of this year. In the mile-and-a-quarter Alabama, she took an immediate one-length lead, with Charon, Craig Perret aboard, pressing her past the first mile.

Suddenly Go for Wand took off down the stretch to win the 118-year-old Alabama bigger than anybody ever had, by seven lengths and in a stakes record of 2:00:84. In 126 years only the colts Honest Pleasure and General Assembly had run the mile-and-a-quarter Travers faster. Perret: "My filly ran her heart out, but the other filly is just a

John Henry, Go for Wand, Holy Bull

super horse." Would they pit her against the boys in the Travers? No. Badgett was saving her for the Breeders' Cup. There was no way he would push her into a third race in sixteen days, even for the better part of a million bucks.

So when Belmont finally got the Breeders' Cup that fall, it also got a sensational match in the Distaff. It was Go for Wand, now "one of the greatest three-year-old fillies in the history of the sport," against the West Coast star, the older Bayakoa, headed for her second straight handicap title. This seventh Breeders' series, however, had opened tragically, with the popular Mr. Nickerson suffering a massive pulmonary hemorrhage and collapsing on the backstretch of the Sprint. He was bleeding from the nose and mouth. Shaker Knit had fallen on top of him, landing on his spine, and would have to be destroyed. Mr. Nickerson's rider, Chris Antley, broke his collarbone. Some in the crowd had seen a fatal spill before, perhaps Ruffian's on the same track fifteen years earlier, but many watching on television had never seen such a thing. They had witnessed countless baseball, football, and basketball games that had nothing to do with death. So racing's great day, with its record $10.5 million handle, already had them troubled and confused.[12]

An hour later, Go for Wand and Bayakoa came out. They were off—and in no time they were neck and neck, which meant neither could relax, almost every step a head-to-head duel—until the three-year-old pulled in front by half a length. Go for Wand seemed headed for her most stunning triumph to date as they rocketed into the last hundred yards. Just before the final pole Go for Wand went off stride, shifting her weight to an ankle and crashing to the dirt, shattering her foreleg. She struggled up and limped to the finish line, then fell again, a few feet from the winner's circle that awaited Bayakoa. She was put down with a lethal injection. "Fans crowding the rail forced themselves to watch the fallen filly's final heaves, staring transfixed."[13]

The *New York Times* two days later: "Go for Wand was buried Sunday night near the infield flagpole facing the winner's circle at Saratoga. The gesture was perfect. No filly in 127 years of Saratoga has dominated that meeting the way Go for Wand did." Like Ruffian, she would be the three-year-old filly of the year.

Nobody blamed anybody. In all three cases, it was agreed, the deaths had been accidents. Some explained Go for Wand's by saying what they had said about Ruffian. "They're good because they try so hard," commented Easy Goer's trainer, Shug McGaughey. "Nearly every day at a race track somewhere, a horse breaks down or pulls up lame and is relegated to at best an uncertain future," wrote Crist. "Some can be saved, others cannot. . . . If you pass a life around this game, all you can do is rationalize and harden yourself to it, try not to think about it too much and turn the page to the next race."

But to many nonprofessionals the question had to be, not whether the horses were worth saving, but whether racing was worth saving. For what? For the states, gamblers, and some irresponsible owners to profit from these animals? For 1990 had seen a "litany of misfortune." Sunday Silence, Easy Goer, and Horse of the Year Criminal Type had been retired with leg injuries, and Summer Squall and Housebuster had been taken out early, too. The careers of the colt Eastern Echo and the stakes-winning filly Gorgeous were ended by injury.

The issue was complicated by medication, specifically furosemide, or Lasix. This was a powerful diuretic used on horses at some tracks to control exercise-induced lung or nasal bleeding, but which New York banned. The evidence was mixed. Mr. Nickerson had raced without it and had not bled. Unbridled had won the Derby on Lasix that year, did badly without it in the Belmont, but had come back to win the Breeders' Cup Classic without it. Few seemed to consider the welfare of the horse, as one side argued for medicating him so he could run, the other for making him run without the protection. To many outside racing, the question was whether a horse that could bleed should run at all. There were other questions, including the stress of racing year round in New York and elsewhere.

As if that were not enough, one night down in Kentucky a few weeks later on, Alydar was heard struggling in his stall. He had broken a hind leg and had to be destroyed. Ann Hagedorn Auerbach would report in her book *Wild Ride* that fifteen-year-old Alydar had been under an intense stud regime. Some twenty lifetime breeding rights to him reportedly had been sold for as much as $2.5 million each. In addition, Auerbach said, once-a-season rights had been sold for up to $350,000. If only a few people had any inkling of this, fewer still knew that Calumet, its red-trimmed barns a twinkling Camelot on the rolling hills of Lexington, was, in effect, mortgaged to Alydar's stud fees. The world would know soon enough, as Calumet went bankrupt, to be bought at auction for $17 million by Henryk de Kwiatkowski. The colors, the legendary devil's red and blue, went for $12,000 to a Brazilian horse breeder. The plaque awarded to Alydar on his induction into the Hall of Fame was sold for $2,700.[14]

The series of tragedies—especially the Breeders' Cup accidents—produced a debate over the coming months. John Hoyt, president of the Humane Society, declared that any sport needing drugs was "seriously suspect" and unloaded a barrage of specific criticisms:

- the FDA had approved Lasix only as a diuretic, not as an anti-bleeding drug;
- injured horses were given corticosteroids and phenylbutazone, or "bute," to reduce joint swelling or kill pain, whereas "the only real treatment is time and rest";
- thousands of immature animals were forced into competition each year for money, and before their bones and muscles were fully developed, which was like "putting a twelve-year-old boy in a professional football game"; and
- the Breeders' Cup breakdowns were "an occupational hazard, not an exception. On average a horse breaks down on a track and has to be destroyed once every three days. A similar incidence in baseball would amount to two player deaths a week."
- "For every million-dollar star like Secretariat, there are thousands of worn out, sick, drugged horses that are run into the ground and end up in a slaughterhouse. Surely the 'sport of kings' owes more to its royal competitors than that."

USA Today, which published the debate, left the reply to Thomas Meeker, president of Churchill Downs and of the Thoroughbred Racing Associations.

- Whether raised for racing or sale, he said, a foal was treated "with meticulous attention to its nutrition and health";

- at the track, under the care of a licensed trainer, the horses were given diets "expertly planned to maintain peak physical shape," and customized shoes "to minimize the strain of running." They were monitored closely by vets;

- a state veterinarian checked them before they were led into the starting gate, and stewards closely scrutinized the race; and

- the horses in the more than 80,000 races then run in North America shared the same benefits on the farm and on the track as those in the Derby and "competed under the same strict regulation."

- "In 80,000 races, just as in any other athletic endeavor, there will be accidents and injuries, but not from indifference or cruelty. The vast majority of owners, trainers and grooms in this sport do not ever come close to the riches evident in a race like the Kentucky Derby. They devote their lives not to the sport but to its soul—the thoroughbred."[15]

It was Ruffian's biographer, Jane Schwartz, who made the most appealing case. "At its best, racing is an exercise in devotion to the running horse; each animal is a respected individual cared for and trained to achieve its fullest potential. At its worst, the game is rife with greed and exploitation and mismanagement."

There would be accidents, of course, when 1,000-pound horses were running at up to forty miles per hour on slender legs. "I hope we never get used to it. I hope men and women will always cry when a horse like Go for Wand breaks down, when any horse breaks down. . . ." In the meantime, thoroughbreds filled "a hunger for something grand and noble in our lives," Schwartz wrote.

> Certain horses always battle back, dig in, and somehow find reserves of sheer desire to propel them past the finish. Any trainer will tell you that the best ones know exactly what they're doing: they want to win. . . . These thoroughbreds remind us of the exhilaration that comes from giving everything, from pushing ourselves to the limit. . . . We ride vicariously on their backs, so whether we bet on them or not the outcome matters.[16]

A few more seasons will tell the story. As Belmont and Aqueduct withered, the Spa led the country again with a daily attendance average of 27,556 in 1990, so NYRA expanded the meeting to five weeks in 1991, starting in July. Everyone declared this a historic first, although it often had run in July, even in June, and exceeded thirty days in the nineteenth century.

Despite the expansion, the place managed an average attendance of 24,380 and would jump 1,000 the following year. They kept upgrading the facilities, with the town's preservationists keeping a close watch. There was a row over an attempt to pave the property's old brick sidewalk, which the preservationists appreciated as a pleasant and wonderful relic. A new Carousel dining pavilion behind the grandstand had them inspecting it for any signs of the enemies plastic and fiberglass; they allegedly found a little of the latter. Another battle, for the meeting's riders' championship, went to the last day as Mike Smith beat Julie Krone by one win and Cordero by two.[17]

The biggest historical item didn't quite come off. Lewis Burrell, Sr., and his sons, including Stanley (the rap star M. C. Hammer), were supposed to bring their filly Lite

Julie Krone flashes five after becoming only the third jockey in Saratoga history to win five in one day, August 20, 1993, the fifth aboard Ratings in the Diana Handicap. Cordero did it in 1968, Turcotte in 1972. *NYRA Photo.*

Light to town after winning the Coaching Club American Oaks at Belmont. Instead they went home to California. If they had come, they would not have made as much history as they thought. Hammer noted they were the first African Americans to win a big New York race, his brother Louis thought racing was finally "attracting the type of people it should have attracted a long time ago," and various writers said the sport "has always been overwhelmingly white." The Burrells were certainly a welcome change, but African Americans once had been very prominent on the turf. People had to know Saratoga to know that.[18]

People were reminded of Campfire when Dehere swept the Special, Sanford, and Hopeful in 1993. Everybody said it was the first time anybody had taken all the major juveniles here since he did it in 1916. Again it was not as rare as they thought. There had been other big two-year-old tests that others had swept. Man o' War swallowed up the U.S. Hotel, Grand Union, and Hopeful stakes. Jamestown took four: the Special, Flash, U.S. Hotel, and Grand Union. So did Native Dancer: the Special, Flash, Grand Union, and Hopeful. They had to know the place to know that, or that Pavot swept four at Saratoga-at-Belmont.

The little-known fact that women were riding on "Ascot Heath" before that Brooklyn course left the Empire, or that they were driving at Saratoga before the Civil War, would not have lessened Julie Krone's feats as the most successful female jockey in history. On the day before the 1993 Travers she became the first rider in twenty years and the third in Spa history to win five on a card. Cordero and Turcotte were the other two, Angel having done it eight times in New York. To give Julie's story a Saratoga

John Henry, Go for Wand, Holy Bull

ending, Seattle Way threw her near the top of the stretch on the last day of the season. She suffered multiple fractures of the ankle and was out for the year.

Paul Mellon made history that season, too, and so did his horse. Under Mack Miller, Sea Hero won at Louisville and made Mellon the only owner in the world to have won the most prestigious races of three countries, the Kentucky Derby, the Epsom Derby, and the Prix de l'Arc de Triomphe. It also made him the first to double in the Derby and the midsummer Derby since Shut Out, fifty-one years earlier. And Mellon's fifth tied George Widener for the most Travers victories by an owner. In return, NYRA honored him by designating its main grass oval "the Mellon Turf Course."

Few knew, however, of his behind-the-scenes role at the National Museum of Racing. "It was over the years a static and sleepy gallery," as he commented recently. It featured paintings of horses and mementos of the turf and by the mid-1980s was "on course to languish into oblivion as its traditional patrons died off." Trustee Mellon proposed a complete renovation, and while the board thought it over, he already had targeted a British design team. With the backing of Whitney Tower, who headed the board, the museum was overhauled and updated at a cost of $6 million. A starting gate, "complete with bells," as Mellon happily pointed out, serves as the getaway to a circular tour of lively exhibits and exotic paraphernalia.[19]

Before the far turn, visitors hit the Hall of Fame, where they can punch up television tapes of their favorites. There's also a fifteen-minute movie, *Race America*, which includes a moving sequence of a foaling in the midst of a booming panorama of the sport. It stars none other than Mackenzie "Mack" Miller as narrator, and it's one of the rewards visitors share with Hall of Fame laureates. "I never tire of watching it," says Mellon himself, "and only fear that Hollywood might want Mack for a screen test!"

Amidst the gloom in the Big Apple, the Spa next moved to an unprecedented ten races on sixteen of the thirty racing days. Average attendance still reached 26,176, plus another 7,145 who went out to Aqueduct to watch the Spa proceedings on television. Some $322 million was bet through OTB and on the track. Figuring they should keep this goose going, NYRA added four more days in 1994, which turned out to be a zoo.[20]

The 125th Travers, by now trimmed to $750,000, starred a bull and a cat with stories to tell, a rabbit who showed up at the last minute, and the devil in a cameo. It had started, sort of, when Jimmy Croll, who had been around for seventy-three years and trained for Rachel Carpenter for half of them, took a phone call at Monmouth Park the previous August. Mrs. Carpenter had died, and she had left him her little stable of seven horses, including a gray named Holy Bull. Three hours after that call, the beautiful gray won for the first time. By the time he got to the Travers, he was ten for twelve and gorgeous.[21]

The cat's tale was traumatic. A hot number by Storm Cat, Tabasco Cat was well-named and as edgy as the proverbial cat in a roomful of rocking chairs. This cat was co-owned by William Young, who bred him in Kentucky, and by the town's latest brand name, David Reynolds, of the Reynolds Aluminum Reynolds. The previous December, the two-year-old chestnut had created a tragedy for the Lukas family. He had broken away in their Santa Anita barn and trampled Wayne's thirty-six-year-old

Tabasco Cat at two, after his maiden win, at the Spa in 1993, Richard Migliore up. *NYRA Photo by Bob Coglianese.*

son and deputy trainer, Jeff. Talking about it with Joe Durso out by Barn 83 at Oklahoma, the father said he had struggled to keep the tragedy separate from the horse's career. While Jeff was in a coma, he said, "I could feel the tension around the barn, the undercurrent of animosity toward the horse." He told the grooms and riders and others: "Enough said about this horse."[22]

Lukas went beyond merely protecting Cat from what might have seemed justifiable fury. Rather, he said, "I wanted our people to see the boss taking a personal interest in the horse. I felt he was a special horse who got tougher as the year got longer." Indeed, although he had been knocked off track as the top money-winning trainer, he was back to his winning ways, thanks to Tabasco Cat. Like Holy Bull, Cat had lost badly in a crowded Kentucky Derby—it was Go for Gin who got the mint juleps. He came back to beat Go for Gin in the next two legs of the Triple Crown, which Holy Bull had skipped. At Saratoga, Tabasco Cat had lost to Unaccounted For in the Jim Dandy, but it was not really unaccounted for. Cat had not gone all out.

Holy Bull. He's a neck up on Concern and Jerry Bailey in the 1994 Travers. *NYRA Photo.*

"He and Jeff are now on separate but parallel paths," said the father. "Jeff is ready to saddle horses again. Cat is a visible candidate for Horse of the Year." But just in case, Lukas was also fielding a rabbit, Commanche Trail, in the Travers to pull the bull into early speed—until the cat made his move and ran him down. Jimmy Rowe, the reader may remember, had tried it with John P. Grier in Man o' War's Travers.

It didn't work this time either. If Holy Bull had to be concerned about anybody, it was Concern, but Croll's horse and Mike Smith held off his rally by a neck. Tabasco Cat was seventeen lengths back. Bull then confirmed his supremacy with a smashing five-length win in the Woodward. As if to rub it in, it was Concern who next beat Tabasco Cat in the Breeders' Cup, although Lukas himself was clearly back. He not only had a second place in the Classic but won the Juvenile and Juvenile Fillies. Most impressive of all, though, had been Croll's refusal to put Holy Bull in the Breeders' Cup, even for the money, and even if it had been necessary to guarantee him a shot at the annual honors, which it no longer was. For Croll it was simple. Holy Bull needed a rest. Out at the Saratoga barns, he had explained to Joe Durso, "If I don't think there's another top performance there, I'm not going to run him. He's done enough for me already. It's great to get the Eclipse Award, but I wouldn't sacrifice my horse to do it." As it turned out, Holy Bull charged into 1995 by winning the Donn at Gulfstream Park, strained some ligaments in his next start, and was retired with a memorable thirteen wins in sixteen starts.

As for the devil, he made his cameo five days after the Travers, in the form of more than a dozen IRS agents swooping down on trainer Allen Jerkens's barn. They posted a notice of seizure on the stall and bridle of a five-year-old owned by Edith LiButti. The IRS claimed he was actually owned by her father, Ralph, and that Ralph owed taxes. As so often happened at the launching pad of Upset and Onion, the horse had a perfect name: Devil His Due. As the agents could have told you, he had finished in the money in twenty-one of thirty-four races, winning eleven and $3.4 million. NYRA ruled he could run in the upcoming Whitney, but his earnings would be frozen. They came to $77,000, for second behind Colonial Affair. And then who should run second again in the Woodward? Devil His Due, but by now he had won a respite from a federal judge, who said that the government had a lousy case and had better let that horse run.

The trouble with Saratoga—ask anybody on Broadway—is that it doesn't stop. On the afternoon of the Whitney, for example, the Spa honored an old favorite. He was a nine-year-old gelding named Fourstardave. Dave had raced ninety-four times—shades of Exterminator!—and had won at least one here in each of the past eight years. They had a ceremony for him in front of the grandstand after the fifth, but Dave wasn't even there. He had cracked an ankle running third in a handicap and was recovering from surgery in hopes he could run again. So Dave wasn't there, but here was the grandstand crowd cheering at an empty space. At just the thought of him.[23]

Where else?

NOTES

BIBLIOGRAPHY

INDEX

NOTES

1. The First Tourist

1. Francesco dal Verme, *Seeing America and Its Great Men: The Journal and Letters of Count Francesco dal Verme 1783–1784,* trans. and ed. Elizabeth Cometti (Charlottesville: Univ. Press of Virginia, 1969), 15–16, 108–9.

2. G. Turner, "Description of the Chalybeate Springs, near Saratoga," *The Columbian Magazine,* Mar. 1787, 306–7.

3. Evelyn Barrett Britten, *Chronicles of Saratoga* (Saratoga Springs: Evelyn Barrett Britten, 1959), 145. Britten quotes directly from remarks by Reuben Hyde Walworth, who interviewed the chief.

4. John H Steel, *An Analysis of the Mineral Waters of Saratoga and Ballston,* 2d ed. (Saratoga Springs: G. M. Davison, 1838), 31–32.

5. See discussions in Arthur Pound, *Johnson of the Mohawks* (New York: Macmillan, 1930), 534–35; Edward F. Grose, *Centennial History of the Village of Ballston Spa* (Ballston Spa: The Ballston Journal, 1907), 65–66; and James K. Kettlewell, *Saratoga Springs: An Architectural History* (Saratoga Springs: Lyrical Ballad Book Store, 1991), 4.

6. See Mary Gay Humphreys, *Catherine Schuyler* (New York: Scribner's, 1897), 98, and Robert C. Bray and Paul E. Bushnell, eds., *Diary of a Common Soldier in the American Revolution 1775–1783* (DeKalb: Northern Illinois Univ. Press, 1978), 264–65.

7. *Merriam-Webster's Collegiate Dictionary,* 10th ed., s.v. "tourist."

8. John C Fitzpatrick, ed., *Writings of George Washington* (Washington, D.C.: PO, 1938), 27:60, 70.

9. Ibid, 60. For a discussion of Washington's lust for real estate at the time, see Halsted L. Ritter, *Washington As a Businessman* (New York: Sears Publishing Co., 1931), 141; and Douglas Southall Freeman, *George Washington* (New York: Scribner's, 1952), 5:44–45.

10. Fitzpatrick, *Writings,* 27:99–100.

11. John Booth, a nineteenth-century Ballston historian, quotes Sir William Johnson as calling them "Saratoga Springs" before his death in 1774, but gives no citation. In 1911, many of the Johnson manuscripts were destroyed in a fire at the state capitol in Albany. Booth is quoted in Grose, *Centennial History,* 66.

12. Bray and Bushnell, *Diary,* 265.

13. Perceval Reniers, *The Springs of Virginia* (Chapel Hill: Univ. of North Carolina Press, 1955), 34.

14. The author used two principal sources on the general history of horse racing. One is the Jockey Club's extraordinary six-volume history, whose authors also serve as primary sources, having witnessed many of the events they recorded. The volumes, in chronological order, are John Hervey, *Racing in America 1665–1865* (New York: Scribner Press, 1944); W. S. Vosburgh, *Racing in America 1866–1921* (New York: Scribner Press, 1922); John Hervey, *Racing in America 1922–1936* (New York: Scribner Press, 1937); Robert F. Kelley, *Racing in America 1937–1959* (New York: Scribner Press, 1960); William H. Rudy, *Racing in America 1960–1979* (New York: Scribner Press, 1980); and Edward L. Bowen, *The Jockey Club's Illustrated History of Thoroughbred Racing in America* (Boston: Little, Brown, 1994). The second major source is William H. P. Robertson's excellent treatment, *The History of Thoroughbred Racing* (New York: Bonanza, 1964). Others include Roger Longrigg, *The History of Horse Racing* (New York: Stein and Day, 1972), and Charles B. Parmer, *For Gold and Glory, The Story of Thoroughbred Racing in America* (New York: Carrick and Evans, Inc., 1939). George Washington's man-

agement of an Alexandria race is documented in W. W. Abbot and Dorothy Twohig, eds., *Papers of George Washington, Colonial Series* (Charlottesville: Univ. Press of Virginia, 1982), 7:111n 86.

15. Robertson, *History of Thoroughbred Racing*, 8.

16. Fitzpatrick, *Writings*, 27:82.

17. W. W. Abbot and Dorothy Twohig, eds., *Papers of George Washington, Confederation Series* (Charlottesville: Univ. Press of Virginia, 1992), 1:502–3.

18. Reniers, *Springs of Virginia*, 36.

19. Fitzpatrick, *Writings*, 27:501.

20. Ibid.

21. Abbot and Twohig, *Papers, Confederation Series*, 2:192–93.

2. America's First National Resort

1. Turner, "Description of the Chalybeate Springs."

2. Britten, *Chronicles*, 148–49.

3. Steel, *Analysis of the Mineral Waters*, 2d ed., 33–36.

4. The name was probably also intended to honor his brother John, who had been a member of the Continental Congress. John was with him on the Saratoga trip but not, apparently, at the spring that day. Britten, *Chronicles*, 49–50.

5. The book is still in Mount Vernon's library. The author's copy is Jedidiah Morse, *An Abridgment of the American Gazetteer* (Boston: Thomas and Andrews, 1798). See 312.

6. *In a Pleasant Situation* (Ballston Spa, N.Y.: Saratoga County Historical Society, 1986), 3.

7. One of the better treatments of Putnam, especially in connection with the springs, is Grace Maguire Swanner, *Saratoga Queen of Spas* (Utica, N.Y.: North Country Books, 1988, 109–11. Steel, *Analysis of the Mineral Waters*, 2d ed., 43, says the original width of Broad Street was 140 feet.

8. Kettlewell, *Saratoga Springs*, 2–3, 8, 57. A Mount Vernon–style piazza also graces Ballston's first big boardinghouse, Aldridges, built in 1792 and now part of Brookside, the Saratoga County History Center.

9. Quoted in Landon Manning, *The Noble Animals: Tales of the Saratoga Turf* (Saratoga Springs: Landon Manning, 1973), 8. Manning, the most detailed source on early racing in Sar-

atoga Springs, also has a good discussion of the early battles with antiracing forces.

10. The best state-by-state discussion of early American racing is Longrigg, *History of Horse Racing*, especially 205–48 and 281–86.

11. Robertson, *History of Thoroughbred Racing*, 41–44.

12. Longrigg, *History of Horse Racing*, 208.

13. Ibid, 209.

14. Eliphalet Nott, *A Disclosure Delivered in the Presbyterian Church, in the City of Albany, Before the Ladies' Society for the Relief of Distressed Women and Children, March 18, 1804* (Albany: Webster, 1804), including "Appendix, by a Friend," which is an obituary of Sally Nott, 37–39. The author's copy has a handwritten marginal note describing Nott's tears as he referred to his wife in the Discourse. See also Codman Hislop, *Eliphalet Nott* (Middletown, Conn.: Wesleyan Univ. Press, 1971), 33, 57–59.

15. Jacob E. Cooke, *Tench Coxe and the Early Republic* (Chapel Hill: Univ. of North Carolina Press, 1978), 449–50.

16. Watson's journal is subject to some doubt, since he has himself visiting Congress Hall in 1805, six years before other sources say construction on it began. This may have resulted from his "revision" of the journal in 1821, and perhaps from his son's editing. See Winslow C. Watson, ed., *Men and Times of the Revolution, or Memoirs of Elkanah Watson* (New York: Dana, 1856), iv, 349–50. My copy, with an inscription by Winslow, has notations that appear to be in his hand, but they do not explain his father's prescience.

17. The springs were recommended in Elijah Parish, *A Compendious System of Universal Geography* (Newburyport, Mass.: Thomas and Whipple, 1808), 61. The author's battered copy suggests a tremendous practical interest in the subject among early Americans. On the drinking, see *A History of Temperance in Saratoga County, N.Y.* (Saratoga Springs: G. M. Davison, 1855), 3, 15, 33, and *Saratoga County Communities* (Clifton Park, N.Y.: Saratoga County Planning Board, 1980), 77.

18. S. G. Goodrich, *Recollections of a Lifetime* (New York: Miller, Orton and Mulligan, 1857), 2:75n.

19. The Williams family's unpublished letters are held by the Maryland Historical Society in Baltimore. Otho Holland Williams papers, MS. 908.

20. Steel, *An Analysis of the Mineral Waters of Saratoga and Ballston* (Albany: Hosford, 1817), 20.

21. The painting is still at the Pennsylvania Institute of Fine Arts in Philadelphia. The Institute mortgaged its building to buy it in 1836.

3. A Preview of Modern Sports

1. For accounts of America's first national sports event, see Hervey, *Racing* 1:261–69; Robertson, *History of Thoroughbred Racing*, 52–57; Longrigg, *History of Horse Racing*, 212 13, 237–39.

2. For a good portrait of American Eclipse and rider, see Bowen, *Illustrated History*, 35.

3. Randolph is quoted in Parmer, *For Gold and Glory*, 73. See also Robertson, *History of Thoroughbred Racing*, 52.

4. Swanner, *Saratoga*, 115.

5. The best treatment of these Saratoga Springs developments is Manning, *Noble Horses*, 7–10.

6. H. I., *New York Mirror*, Aug. 14, 1830, 8:44. The present author's 1830–31 volume reveals this "Repository of Polite Literature and the Arts" to be a treasure of social history, with early first printings of Edgar Allan Poe and others, early sallies into American slang, and the Springs in a prominent role.

7. Ibid., 36.

8. Ibid., 44.

9. Ibid., 44.

10. *The Fashionable Tour: A Guide to Travellers Touring the Northern and Middle States*, 4th ed. (Saratoga Springs: G. M. Davison, 1830). The frontispiece in the author's copy shows America's leading resort lined with hotel piazzas on both sides of Broadway, from Congress Spring northward.

11. H. I., *Mirror*, 36.

12. Tyrone Power, *Impressions of America* (Philadelphia: Carey, Lea Blanchard, 1836), 1: 252. The author's copy, badly battered since it escaped Gist Blair's library at what became Blair House in Washington, indicates a heavy reliance on these early foreigners' impressions.

13. Frank Walker Stevens, *Beginnings of the New York Central Railroad* (New York: Putnam, 1926), 63–64.

14. "Saratoga and Schenectady Railroad," *American Railroad Journal*, July 21, 1832, 1. The

author's mint copy shows that the practice of binding fragile journals and newspapers saved these detailed histories from disintegration.

15. "From the American Traveller," *Troy Whig*, July 18, 1836, 2.

16. Observer, *Troy Whig*, July 21, 1836, 2.

17. Steel, *Analysis*, 126.

18. Kettlewell, *Saratoga Springs*, 11–12.

19. *Fashionable Tour*, 158.

20. Kettlewell, *Saratoga Springs*, 11–12.

21. Power, *Impressions*, 252.

22. "Saratoga, Past and Present," *New York Herald*, Aug. 8, 1863, 2. An unsigned reminiscence, but unmistakably the work of the publisher James Gordon Bennett.

23. Bayard Tuckerman, ed., *Diary of Philip Hone* (New York: Dodd, Mead, 1889), 376.

24. Sue Eakin and Joseph Logsdon, eds., *Twelve Years a Slave, by Solomon Northup* (Baton Rouge: Louisiana State Univ. Press, 1968), 10.

25. Robertson, *History of Thoroughbred Racing*, 70.

26. Longrigg, *History of Horse Racing*, 213, 216.

27. Robertson, *History of Thoroughbred Racing*, 45.

28. Ibid., 63–65.

29. Cited by Manning, *Noble Animals*, 10.

4. The Old Gray Mare

1. Hervey, *Lady Suffolk, the Old Grey Mare of Long Island* (New York: Derrydale, 1936), 49.

2. For previously ignored accounts of modern organized baseball at its birth, and James Gordon Bennett's newspaper in the process of creating sports journalism, see files of *New York Herald* for Oct. 21, 22, 24, 25, Nov. 11, 1845. *New York Times*, Oct. 5, 1990, cites *New York Morning News* coverage of Oct. 21, 1845, game.

3. See the heavy coverage of the 1847 Saratoga season in the *New York Herald*, especially on Aug. 5, 7, 17, 19, 23, 24, 27. Also Manning's excellent *Noble Animals*, 15–42.

4. Hervey Allen, *Israfel, The Life and Times of Edgar Allan Poe* (New York: Farrar and Rinehart, 1934), 433, 452; Marjorie Peabody Waite, *Yaddo Yesterday and Today* (Saratoga Springs: Marjorie Peabody Waite, 1933), 16–23.

5. The author has the original newspaper containing the early mention of a racetrack to be built at Saratoga Springs: "Challenge from

Black Hawk," *Spirit of the Times,* May 22, 1847."
The date has been misprinted elsewhere. For
more on the inaugural trotting season, see
"The Watering Places," *New York Herald,*
Aug. 17, 1847, 2.

6. Ibid.

7. According to Hiram Woodruff, who had
driven her, cited in Manning, *Noble Animals,* 23.
Woodruff collected his reminiscences in the
nineteenth-century sports classic, *Trotting
Horse of America,* 18th ed. (Philadelphia: Porter
and Coates, 1876), first published in 1867. The
best later account is Hervey, *Lady Suffolk,* 261–
69.

8. A full account of Saratoga's first race is
"Trotting at Saratoga Springs," *Spirit of the
Times,* Oct. 9, 1847, 386. The *Spirit* was a weekly
newspaper devoted largely to the turf.

9. Gleaned from newspaper accounts.

10. "The State Fair," *Spirit of the Times,* Oct.
2, 1847, 375. See also the running coverage in the
New York Herald in middle and late September.

5. America's First (Two-Legged) Sports Hero

1. Beatrice Sweeney, "Saratoga Springs," in
Saratoga County Heritage, ed. Violet B. Dunn,
Robert S. Hayden, and Clayton H. Brown
(Ballston Spa: Saratoga County, 1974), 547.

2. Morrissey needs a new biography.
Though it is somewhat imaginatively written,
the rough guide used here for Morrissey's background, along with contemporary newspaper
accounts, is Jack Kofoed's biography, *Brandy for
Heroes* (New York: Dutton, 1938).

3. Quoted in James M. McPherson, *Battle Cry
of Freedom* (New York: Ballantine, 1988), 135.

4. Kofoed, *Brandy,* 41.

5. Ibid., 61–68.

6. Ibid., 108.

7. In the author's uncut *New York Daily
Tribune,* July 28, 1854, "Brutal Street Fight,"
"Brutal Fight Between Bill Poole and John
Morrissey," and "Terrible Skylarking Affair—
Results of the Brutal Fight" take up about two
censorious but obviously joyful columns, ver-
sus three for Greeley reporter Karl Marx's sar-
castic "State of Europe."

8. The author's helpful family doctor suggests the frequent reports of gouging also may
have referred to a torn eyelid or other torn tis-

sue, making it appear to reporters that the eye
was hanging out.

9. Quoted in Kofoed, *Brandy,* 164.

10. Ibid., 160–62. Saratoga Springs businessman Norm Fox owns a training device presented to Morrissey, with the fighter's picture
on it.

11. Ibid., 148.

12. Albert Bigelow Paine, *Th. Nast, His Period
and His Pictures* (1904; reprint, Princeton: Pyne,
1974), 24–29.

13. Alan Lloyd, *The Great Prize Fight* (New
York: Coward, McCann and Geoghegan), 29,
79.

14. Paine, *Th. Nast,* 26.

15. Lloyd, *Fight,* 76.

16. Ibid., 79.

17. Quoted in Kofoed, *Brandy,* 204.

18. Ibid., 208.

19. Ibid., 237.

20. Margaret Leach, *Reveille in Washington*
(New York: Harper, 1941), 42.

21. No other national publications disagreed.

22. The exact date of the invention, and the
identity of the first customer to be served
them, occasionally has provoked intense controversy at the Springs. But soon Moon's "fried
potatoes" were hailed as a minor delicacy; e.g.,
in "Moon's Lake House," *Frank Leslie's Illustrated Newspaper,* July 26, 1862, 286.

23. Computers cannot yet call up the seven
cartoons inspired by the Saratoga trunk in the
author's stray *Harper's Weekly,* Aug. 15, 1857, 527.

24. "Saratoga Springs," *Appleton's Illustrated
Hand Book of American Travel* (New York:
Appleton, 1860), 149.

25. "W. D. W——H," in four long letters
from Saratoga Springs, gives a slightly bitter
Southerner's view on the eve of the war. These
appeared in *The Weekly Star,* Aug. 13, 1859, 253–
54. Although by now the six-foot Vanderbilt
was Saratoga's leading horseman, a profile recalled his earlier rugged days as a boatman off
Staten Island, suggesting a particularly American connection between his athleticism and his
energy as a capitalist. See "Commodore Vanderbilt," *Harper's Weekly,* Mar. 5, 1859, 1. The
chief sources here for Vanderbilt history are
Wheaton J. Lane, *Commodore Vanderbilt: An
Epic of the Steam Age* (New York: Knopf, 1942),
and Wayne Andrews, *The Vanderbilt Legend*
(New York: Harcourt, Brace, 1941).

26. For a brief discussion of the rise and fall of Metairie, see Robertson, *History of Thoroughbred Racing*, 70–72, 88.

27. The only complete records of the American and Canadian race meetings from 1861 to 1869 are found in H. G. Crickmore, ed. *Racing Calendars*, 3 vols. (New York: Printed by W. C. Whitney, 1901).

6. The Birth of American Sports

1. Civil War casualty figures vary. These are from William F. Fox, *Regimental Losses in the American Civil War, 1861–1865* (Dayton, Ohio: Morningside Bookshop, 1985); the staff of the Vicksburg National Military Park; and Thomas L. Livermore, *Numbers and Losses in the Civil War in America, 1861–1865* (Boston: Houghton Mifflin, 1901). The sources are recommended by U.S. Army archivists. The Civil War–era background through the next three chapters relies partly on McPherson's brilliant single-volume history, *Battle Cry*.

2. On the draft problems and riots, see Adrian Cook, *Armies of the Streets* (Lexington: Univ. Press of Kentucky), 1974; for Leonard Jerome's involvement, see Meyer Berger, *Story of the* New York Times (New York: Simon and Schuster, 1951), 23–26. For Morrissey's role, see Kofoed, *Brandy*, 217–24.

3. Kofoed, *Brandy*, 222.

4. Thus, baseball fans already were thinking in "world" terms. See "Out-Door Sports," *The World*, Aug. 5, 1863, 8.

5. See Whiteclay Chambers II, *To Raise an Army* (New York: Free Press, 1987). McPherson discusses conscription problems in *Battle Cry*, 308–38, 591–625.

6. "City Items," *New York Daily Tribune*, Aug. 3, 1863, 3.

7. By now publisher George Wilkes advertised himself in the nameplate of *Wilkes' Spirit of the Times*. This bible of the early turf is the source of most of the quotations and details on Saratoga's first meeting cited in this volume. In discrepancies with Crickmore's statistics, the author has followed the *Spirit*, which was on the spot and generally agreed with the daily and weekly *Saratogian* and with Morrissey's ads.

8. These ads ran during the week before the races in the *Daily Saratogian*, July 27–31, 1863, 2.

9. The critical role of African Americans in early racing is a largely unmined field; see, e.g., Robertson, *History of Thoroughbred Racing*, 21–70.

10. *Daily Saratogian*, Aug. 1, 1863, 2.

11. Robertson discusses the auction system in *History of Thoroughbred Racing*, 93–94.

12. A wonderful study of the stable area around the old Trotting Course, which was renamed Horse Haven many years later, is Carol Chandler Smith's "Splendid Survivors: Horse Racing Stable Construction," a 1987 Cornell University master's thesis. A brief sketch of early and later Saratoga racing plants is Landon Manning's "Saratoga Racing History," *Saratoga County Heritage* (Ballston Spa, N.Y.: Saratoga County, 1974), 151–71.

13. Delightfully, "go" would still be an acceptable alternative to a drum tap in "Cassady's (Larkin) By-Laws," *Rules and Regulations of Racing, Trotting and Betting as Adopted by the Principal Turf Associations Throughout the United States and Canada* (New York: Brown, 1866), 220.

14. For example, the hot-tempered, heavily wagered Atlantic of Brooklyn vs. Mutual of New York game in "Out-Door Sports," *World*, Aug. 4, 1863, 8. New York won, 27 to 26.

15. "Our Recent Victories," *New York Daily Tribune*, Aug. 6, 1863, 4.

16. "Our Saratoga Correspondence," *New York Herald*, Aug. 23, 1863, 2.

17. "Great Prospects for Saratoga," *Spirit*, Aug. 22, 1863.

18. Ibid.

19. "Fight Between Morrissey and Sheehan," *New York Times*, Dec. 27, 1863, 8.

7. You Are Here

1. *New York Times*, July 6, 1864, 5.

2. "Destructive Fire," *Daily Saratogian*, July 6, 1864, 2.

3. "The Petersburg Lines," *New York Times*, Aug. 2, 1864, 1. See also McPherson, *Battle Cry*, 758–60.

4. "Turf Record," *New York Times*, Aug. 4, 1864, 3.

5. "Saratoga," *World*, July 10, 1865, 1. Stewart would not become the owner of record until several years later.

6. Lane, *Commodore Vanderbilt*, 82.

7. "Home Matters," *Daily Saratogian*, June 28, 1864, 2.

8. Unfortunately Travers's witticisms have

never been published in a collection, but the author has uncovered a bundle in various accounts of the period, such as those of Melville Landon [Eli Perkins, pseud.] in *Saratoga in 1901* (New York: Sheldon, 1872), 19; Richard O'Connor, *Courtroom Warrior: The Combative Career of William Travers Jerome* (Boston: Little, Brown, 1963), 4, 9, 30; and George Waller in *Saratoga: Saga of an Impious Era* (Englewood Cliffs, N.J.: Prentice-Hall, 1966), 190. One of today's Saratoga leaders, J. E. Aulisi, suggests to the author that the "sons of habitués" line was invented not by Travers but by *Vanity Fair* editor Frank Crowninshield, and that the club was not the Union but the University.

9. "Morgan's Rout Complete," *Daily Saratogian*, June 16, 1864, 2, and untitled item mentioning Skedaddle in *Daily Saratogian*, June 27, 1864, 2.

10. Accounts of the first Travers vary slightly. Compare, for example, "Saratoga Summer Races," *Spirit*, Aug. 13, 1864, 372; "The Saratoga Races," *New York Times*, Aug. 3, 1864, 5; "Turf Record," *New York Times*, Aug. 4, 1864, 3; "The Turf," *New York Herald*, Aug. 3, 1864, 5; "First Day's Races," *Daily Saratogian*, Aug. 3, 1864, 2.

11. Greeley's newspaper also praised Abe Hawkins's "determined efforts." See "The Turf," *New York Daily Tribune*, Aug. 4, 1864, 8.

12. "Adirondack," *New York Times*, Aug. 9, 1864, 4.

13. Lane, *Commodore Vanderbilt*, is still the best treatment of Vanderbilt's rivalry with Drew and other capitalist giants.

14. "The Turf," *New York Herald*, Aug. 10, 1864, 8.

15. "Fourth and Last Day's Races," *Daily Saratogian*, Aug. 8, 1864, 2.

16. "The Turf," *Herald*, Aug. 10, 1864, 8.

17. Ibid.

18. Ibid.; also "Union Leaguers in Council," *New York Herald*, Aug. 1, 1864, 4.

19. "Fourth and Last Day's Races," *Daily Saratogian*, Aug. 8, 1864, 2.

20. *Daily Saratogian*, Aug. 23, 1864, 2.

21. Carl Sandburg, *Abraham Lincoln, The War Years* (New York: Harcourt, Brace, 1941), 3: 332.

22. Matthew Josephson, *The Robber Barons*, (New York: Harcourt, Brace, 1934), 15.

23. Lane, *Commodore Vanderbilt*, 83.

24. "Good Investment," *Daily Saratogian*, Aug. 23, 1864, 2. Also, Britten, *Chronicles*, 258.

25. Ibid., 90.

26. McPherson, *Battle Cry*, 852.

27. Ibid.

8. *The Yankees Celebrate*

1. The portrayal of this national celebration is based largely on newspaper coverage. In the author's collection of New York City newspapers, no fewer than seventeen editions played it above the fold on page one, often as the lead story.

2. "From Saratoga," *New York Daily Tribune*, Aug. 14, 1865, 1. For some detail on Robert Jackson, see Landon, *Saratoga*, 35. Landon's book and its accompanying drawings by Arthur Lumley are full of detail about life at the Springs but are often marred by their racism.

3. "From Saratoga," *New York Daily Tribune*, July 17, 1865, 6; "Cruel Sport," *Daily Saratogian*, July 25, 1865, 2; John Godfrey Saxe, "Lake Saratoga," *Poetical Works of John Godfrey Saxe* (Boston: Houghton Mifflin, 1892), 170; Britten, *Chronicles*, 217–18.

4. "How Is This?" *Daily Saratogian*, July 26, 1865, 2; Herbert Asbury, *Sucker's Progress* (New York: Dodd, Mead, 1939), 358. Asbury's "Informal History of Gambling in America," should be required reading for political historians.

5. Joseph Smith, *Reminiscences of Saratoga* (New York: Knickerbocker, 1897), 63–64. The author's copy of this remarkable work by the head usher at the United States, replete with portraits of its wealthy guests, well merits its gilded edges.

6. "Saratoga," *World*, July 6, 1865, 1; "Saratoga," *World*, July 13, 1865, 1; "From Saratoga," *New York Daily Tribune*, Aug. 14, 1865, 1.

7. *Daily Saratogian*, July 28, 1865, 2.

8. "From Saratoga," *New York Daily Tribune*, Aug. 11, 1865, 1. The physical plant is described by several newspapers and in Manning, *County Heritage*, 158–59.

9. "Sports of the Turf," *New York Times*, Aug. 11, 1865, 1.

10. Landon points out that Travers would insist on telling his stories over and over. Landon, *Saratoga*, 128.

11. The seventh was Lady Rotha in 1915.

12. Landon uses the term "star jockey" in 1871. Landon, *Saratoga*, 12.

13. "From Saratoga," *New York Daily Tribune*, Aug. 11, 1865, 1.

14. "Our Watering Places," *New York Times*, June 25, 1866, 8. The local newspapers also discuss street developments in some detail from 1864 on.

15. Ibid.

16. The long forgotten *Rules and Regulations* discovered by the author and cited in note 13 for chapter 6, was the first rule book for America's first truly national sport. It included the club rules of Saratoga and the other tracks. Compiled by *Wilkes' Spirit of the Times*, it also underlined that publication's position as the leading authority on the turf.

17. *Rules and Regulations*, 28.

18. Hugh Bradley, author of a Saratoga history, wrote, "For some years notices barring Negroes from the grounds were prominently displayed." This ban, he says, was "out of deference to the sensibilities of Southern visitors" but, "of course, was never enforced." Bradley did not name his source, "a contemporary reporter." As he pointed out, African-American talent was actually very prominent at the track. See Hugh Bradley, *Such Was Saratoga* (New York: Doubleday, Doran, 1940), 163. For Woodlawn and Metairie, see *Rules and Regulations*, 81–95, 225–34. For an excellent discussion of racial and other problems at the famous New Orleans track, see Dale A. Somers, *The Rise of Sports in New Orleans* (Baton Rouge: Louisiana State Univ. Press, 1972), 94–107.

19. The birthday issue is discussed briefly in Robertson, *The History of Thoroughbred Racing*, 91.

20. Ads for the track indicated that Wheatly himself preferred it without the second "e."

21. Thomas Gilcoyne, volunteer historian at the National Museum of Racing, compiled the records from *Racing Calendars*. Conversations with Gilcoyne, one of the leading authorities on the history of the turf, were an important source for this work.

22. "The Turfman's Referee," *Rules and Regulations for the Government of Racing, Trotting and Betting* (New York: Brown, 1867), 17. The "Referee," appended to the *Rules and Regulations*, was comprised of "Answers to Correspondents as given to *Wilkes' Spirit of the Times*."

23. For brief discussions of Jerome Park, see Longrigg, *History of Horse Racing*, 222–24, and Robertson, *History of Thoroughbred Racing*, 103–6. On Jerome and Morrissey, see O'Connor, *Courtroom Warrior*, 10, 12–13.

24. The description of Belmont with full equipage at Newport is in "Watering Place Correspondence," *Evening Post*, Aug. 26, 1864, 1.

25. The shocked Englishman is quoted in Longrigg, *History of Horse Racing*, 223–24.

26. Ralph G. Martin, *Jennie: The Life of Lady Randolph Churchill* (Englewood Cliffs, N.J.: New American Library, 1969), 27.

27. Ibid., 18.

28. Ibid., 22.

29. This Travers line played vaudeville for years. It returned in O'Connor, *Courtroom Warrior*, 30, and Martin, *Jennie*, 326.

9. Siring the Belmont and Pimlico

1. Although seating charts for the various sessions of Congress located his desk, which was usually no. 78 (it was switched briefly to no. 76 in 1869), Morrissey left no record of a speech to be preserved in the records.

2. Neil E. Nelson, "Grand in Manner, Grand in History," *The Blood-Horse* 115, no. 16 (Apr. 22, 1989): 2204–6. It is a brief history of the Belmont Stakes and the role of Francis Morris, Ruthless and others.

3. The first Travers start from "the new three-quarter track" is mentioned in "The Turf," *New York Times*, Aug. 6, 1868, 5.

4. Swanner, *Saratoga*, 66.

5. Ibid., 133. Also, "Saratoga Springs," *Spirit*, Oct. 1, 1868, 440.

6. Morrissey's letters to President Johnson and replies from the "Executive Mansion" are contained in the Andrew Johnson Papers, Manuscripts Division, Library of Congress. Photocopies in the author's collection.

7. Southerners' influence on Saratoga, which could be traced back to Washington, the Williamses, and their thing for springs, would extend far into the next century, thanks to an equal passion for horses.

8. The 1968 season was followed in detail in both the *New York Times* and the *Spirit of the Times* (Wilkes's name was dropped from the nameplate as of July 4, 1868).

9. Landon, *Saratoga*, 54.

10. "The Saratoga Meeting," *Spirit*, Aug. 8, 1868, 457.

11. For a next-day account of the party that gave birth to Pimlico, see "The Turf," *New York Times*, Aug. 11, 1868, 1.

12. Swanner, *Saratoga*, 133–35, has a good brief description of the biggest hotels.

13. Manning, *Noble Animals*, 48. Also, Bernard Livingston, *Their Turf: America's Horsey Set & Its Princely Dynasties* (New York: Arbor House, 1973), 165.

14. Lane, *Commodore Vanderbilt*, 308. Andrews, *Vanderbilt Legend*, 144–45.

15. For Morrissey the horse, see "The Saratoga Summer Meeting," *Spirit*, Aug. 8, 1868, 467. For the human, read the scandalized Matthew Hale Smith in *Sunshine and Shadow in New York* (Hartford: Burr, 1869), 398–402.

16. Sewell is often given the first initial W. in records released by the New York Racing Association, but the source for this is not known.

17. "Krik's" statistics are cited in note 27 for chapter 5. They were obviously of special value to those with a major interest in the turf. Volume 3 of the author's copy, stamped "The Property of James Gordon Bennett, *New York Herald* Library," had long since been buried in a Middleburg, Va., bookstore but its beat up condition suggested a long and useful life.

18. W. S. Vosburgh, "Preface," *Racing Calendars*.

19. Lane, *Commodore Vanderbilt*, 308. Andrews, *Vanderbilt Legend*, 145.

20. Lane, *Commodore Vanderbilt*, 267.

21. Although Americans have found irony in a casino used as a civic center, Europeans, who are not frightened by casinos, have long used them for just that.

22. The James article was later included in his *Portraits of Places* (Boston: Houghton Mifflin, 1883), 324–37.

23. Miller's record would soon be matched by George Barbee, but nobody would do it again until Eric Guerin in the 1950s.

24. Landon, *Saratoga*, 56.

25. These and other historical highlights appear in the Maryland track's annual guidebook. See, for example, *Laurel and Pimlico '94 Media Guide* (Baltimore: Maryland Jockey Club, 1994), 7.

10. Longfellow vs. Harry Bassett

1. The description of Longfellow is by eyewitness Landon in *Saratoga*, 8–9. In 1863, Wilkes was editorializing against naming horses after horses, and ran a letter to the editor attacking this "absurd practice of adopting for unknown, untried and frequently worthless animals the names of noted horses . . . the owners of spurious 'Eclipses' and 'Flora Temples' simply bring themselves and their pretentious titles into ridicule." "Nomenclature of Horse Names Claimed," *Spirit*, July 25, 1863, 339.

2. The long attack on Morrissey's Club House appeared in "Saratoga, the American Baden-Baden," *Every Saturday*, Sept. 9, 1871, 257–62.

3. Bradley, *Such Was Saratoga*, 147–48.

4. Ibid., 146.

5. Landon lists the "turnouts" in *Saratoga*, 50–52.

6. Breslin was usually listed as "proprietor," meaning he owned the business. See also Beatrice Sweeney's brochure, *The Grand Union Hotel: A Memorial and a Lament* (Saratoga Springs: Saratoga Springs Historical Society, 1982), with reproductions of paintings by Raymond Calkins.

7. Landon, *Saratoga*, 7–10.

8. Ibid., 14–15.

9. "The Saratoga Boat-Race," *Harper's Weekly*, Sept. 30, 1871, 908–9. Thomas C. Mendenhall, "The Isms of Rowing: Amateur and Professional," *The Oarsman* 7, no. 4 (Sept.–Oct. 1975): 27–28.

10. The newspapers covered the rivalry extensively. For a historical perspective, see Robertson, *History of Thoroughbred Racing*, 107–8; Longrigg, *History of Horse Racing*, 225–6.

11. "The Great Race," *New York Times*, July 3, 1872, 5.

12. Robertson has a good discussion of betting in *History of Thoroughbred Racing*, 93–98. The newspapers filled in many of the details.

13. "The Great Race," *New York Times*, July 3, 1872, 5.

14. "The Saratoga Races," *Spirit*, July 7, 1872, 355–56.

15. "Saratoga: The Greatest Contest in American Turf History," *New York Times*, July 17, 1872.

16. Landon, *Saratoga*, 19.

17. "The Saratoga Cup," *Spirit*, Sept 14, 1872, 65.

18. Formal horse-of-the-year awards would be established in 1936.

19. For a time line on Maryland racing, see *Laurel and Pimlico Media Guide*, 7.

20. O'Connor, *Courtroom Warrior*, 9.

21. Stephen Fiske, *Off-Hand Portraits of Prominent New Yorkers* (1884; reprint, New York: Arno, 1975) 200; Martin, *Jennie*, 75.

11. The Derby and College Sports

1. "The Walworth Murder," *Leslie's*, June 21, 1873, 286. "The Walworth Tragedy," *Harper's Weekly*, June 21, 1873, 526. Britten, 234–35.

2. "The Saratoga Races," *New York Times*, July 25, 1873, 5. Tom Bowling's start is described by turf writer William Leggett in "Midsummer Derby: A Dream Race," *Post Parade*, Aug. 1992, 2–3.

3. Courtney is quoted in C. V. P. Young, *Courtney and Cornell Rowing* (Ithaca, N.Y.: Cornell Publications, 1923), 21–23. Also, Margaret K. Look, *Courtney: Master Oarsman—Champion Coach* (Interlaken, N.Y.: Empire State Books, 1989). For Saratoga's role in early collegiate rowing, see the running newspaper coverage and, notably, Samuel Crowther and Arthur Ruhl, *Rowing and Track Athletics* (New York: Macmillan, 1905) and Manning, *Noble Animals*, 129–39. The author's copy of Crowther is peppered with a passionate fan's statistics on Harvard and Yale.

4. Courtney turned professional in 1877 and later became one of the most famous coaches in Cornell history.

5. "The Unrowed Race," *New York Times*, July 18, 1874, 2.

6. Bradley, *Such Was Saratoga*, 180–81.

7. The newspapers paid far more attention to the stampede than to the president. See also Manning, *Noble Animals*, 134–36.

8. "The Contest Reviewed," *New York Times*, July 19, 1874, 1. "The College Games," *New York Times*, July 22, 1874, 5. "The College Regatta," *Ballston Journal*, July 17, 1875, 3.

9. Crowther and Ruhl, *Rowing*, 268–70. On the Batcheller mansion, see Kettlewell, *Saratoga Springs*, 69–70, and James E. Benton, Sr., in "Springs," *Saratoga County Heritage*, 190.

10. Lane, *Commodore Vanderbilt*, 193.

11. Martin, *Jennie*, 71, 75.

12. One of the best books about the Kentucky Derby is Brownie Leach, *The Kentucky Derby Diamond Jubilee* (New York: Dial, 1949). The first Derby is described on pages 7, 16, and 17. See also the statistics and vignettes in the event's annual media guide; for example, *One Hundred Nineteenth Kentucky Derby* (Louisville: Churchill Downs, 1993).

13. "Review of the Racing Season of 1875," *Spirit*, Nov. 20, 1875, 357.

14. See the records in *One Hundred Nineteenth Kentucky Derby*.

15. The principal illustrated newspapers, which gave heavy coverage to the regattas, were *Harper's Weekly*, *Leslie's*, and the *Daily Graphic*. The *Graphic's* cover was on July 13, 1875.

16. Amidst the college colors reigned the colorful Mrs. Leslie. Her Saratoga interlude is described in Madeleine B. Stern, *Purple Passage: The Life of Mrs. Frank Leslie* (Norman: Univ. of Oklahoma Press, 1953), 75–77.

17. The liveliest coverage of the regatta is in the July editions of the *Spirit of the Times*.

18. The Ithaca forces' cry was also heard as "Cornell, I yell, yell, Cornell." Bradley, *Such Was Saratoga*, 180, suggests this was in 1874, but the *Spirit* quotes the 1875 students as saying they were yelling it for the first time.

19. The results and the Cornell president's elation were reported in "The Intercollegiate Boat-Race," *Harper's Weekly*, July 31, 1875, 618.

20. "American Rowing," *Spirit*, Sept. 4, 1875, 90.

21. Crowther and Ruhl, *Rowing*, 270–71.

22. Ibid. The trots, advertised in the *Spirit of the Times*, and the flat races provided nineteen days of racing.

23. W. Espey Albig, "The Origin of the American Bankers Association," *Banking*, Sept. 1942, 172–76. *Troy Times* is quoted in Sweeney, "Saratoga Springs," *County Heritage*, 549.

24. "The Paris Mutuels," *Spirit*, May 29, 1875, 407. "The Danger to the Turf," *Spirit*, July 31, 1875, 644–45.

25. Although they appear alike in engravings, the "grandstand was better appointed than the "field" or "public" stand to its right.

26. Modern records show the Travers as worth $100 more. The author used the contemporary figure, from the *Spirit of the Times*.

27. Of the twenty Derby winners in the Travers through 1994, eight won both.

28. The account of the dead heat in the Cup and the "memorable event" quotation are from "Saratoga's First Summer Meeting," *Spirit,* Aug. 7, 1875, 661.

29. James L. Sheldon and Jock Reynolds, *Motion and Document—Sequence and Time: Eadweard Muybridge and Contemporary American Photography* (Andover, Mass.: Addison Gallery of American Art, 1991). This exhibition catalogue describes the famous experiments.

30. "Saratoga's Second Summer Meeting," *Spirit,* Aug. 21, 1875, 32.

31. "The Saratoga Second Summer Meeting," *Spirit,* Aug. 28, 1875, 62.

32. Britten, *Chronicles,* 161–63. Look, *Courtney,* 70–71.

33. "Death of John Morrissey," *New York Times,* May 2, 1878, 2.

34. Joe Kelly, ed. "The Horse Gave His Name to a Classic," *114th Preakness* (Baltimore: Maryland Jockey Club, 1989), 10–11.

35. Led by Skidmore College, the crews in recent years have returned to the lake, which doubtless could sustain a lively revival.

36. Harvard University's Department of Athletics has maintained detailed records of these intercollegiate track meets ever since.

37. "Sports at Saratoga," *New York Times,* July 21, 1876, 1. "The Sports at Saratoga," *New York Times,* July 22, 1876, 8.

38. "Athletics," *Spirit,* July 29, 1876, 657.

39. Martin, *Jennie,* 114, 123, 313–19.

40. Lane, *Commodore Vanderbilt,* 318. Andrews, *Vanderbilt Legend,* 179–80.

41. Saratogian Norm Fox provided the poem, which Harte is said to have knocked off in time for a June number of the Washington, D.C., *Capital* and which, in any case, appeared in the *Detroit Post* of July 1, 1877. It was reprinted in full as "That Ebrew Jew," *American Jewish Archives,* June 1954, 148. Actually, Morrissey did not stay at the Grand Union. Another Saratogian, Sophie Goldstein, has been the leading recent authority on the history of Saratoga's Jewish community. Charlotte Helprin has also been prominent in the field.

42. See, for example, "Hotel Discrimination," *New York Times,* June 20, 1877, 1, and "The Hebrew Controversy," *New York Times,* July 19, 1877.

43. The only comprehensive study of Hilton is an unpublished manuscript, Harry E. Res-
seguie's "Merchant Prince: The Life and Times of Alexander Turney Stewart with Something about Henry Hilton," completed in 1963. The Harvard Business School and Skidmore College Library own copies. A good historical perspective can be found in Stephen Birmingham, *Our Crowd: The Great Jewish Families of New York* (New York: Dell, 1967), 169–82. For a still broader history, see Leonard Dinnerstein, *Anti-Semitism in America* (New York: Oxford, 1994). Harrison's speech is covered in "The President's Busy Day," *New York Times,* Aug. 22, 1891, 5.

44. A new avenue would become the racing strip for amateur drivers a quarter of a century later. See chapter 15.

45. The role of Murphy and other top African-American jockeys is discussed in chapter 13.

46. Reed would remain prominent in racing through the 1890s.

47. The old Lorillard spread would enjoy a major revival in the 1920s. See chapter 19.

48. Robertson, *History of Thoroughbred Racing,* has an excellent account of this three-way race, 124–26.

49. Ibid., 125.

50. "Death of John Morrissey," *New York Daily Tribune,* May 2, 1878, 2.

51. Ibid.

52. Bradley, *Such Was Saratoga,* 168–75, is good on Morrissey's last years.

12. Isaac Murphy and the Californians

1. Crowther and Ruhl, *Rowing,* 94–95, 172–74.

2. "Summer Life at Saratoga," *Leslie's,* Aug. 30, 1879, 427. Gerald Carson, *A Good Day at Saratoga* (New York: American Bar Association, 1978), 7–8, 15–16.

3. "Summer Life at Saratoga," *Leslie's,* Aug. 30, 1879, 427.

4. "The Season at Saratoga," *New York Times,* June 17, 1878, 1.

5. Robertson, *History of Thoroughbred Racing,* 127–30.

6. Ibid., 158.

7. Ibid., 130–33; Bradley, *Such Was Saratoga,* 233; Mel Heimer, *Fabulous Bawd: The Story of Saratoga* (New York: Holt, 1952), 100.

8. Leach, *Kentucky Derby,* 29, 35.

9. "The Season at Saratoga," *New York Times,* Aug. 2, 1881, 2.

10. Bradley, *Such Was Saratoga*, 119–20.

11. Charles N. Dowd, M.D., *Charles F. Dowd, A.M., Ph.D.* (New York: Knickerbocker, 1930) is an account of the introduction of Standard Time by the elder Dowd, a Saratogian.

12. Fiske, *Off-Hand Portraits*, 26.

13. Elizabeth Drexel Lehr, *'King Lehr' and the Gilded Age* (Philadelphia: Lippincott, 1935), 249–50. John Y. Simon, ed. *The Personal Memoirs of Julia Dent Grant* (New York: Putnam, 1975), 330–31.

14. "The Guests at Saratoga," *New York Times*, July 14, 1878.

15. Andrews, *Vanderbilt Legend*, 236–37.

16. Florence R. Cunningham, *Saratoga's First Hundred Years* (Fresno, Calif.: Valley, 1967), 51, 52, 71.

17. Waller, *Saratoga*, 207.

18. Bradley, *Such Was Saratoga*, 235.

19. E. Berry Wall, *Neither Pest Nor Puritan* (New York: Dial, 1940), 75.

20. Ibid., 77.

21. Bradley, *Such Was Saratoga*, 192–94.

22. "The Season at Saratoga," *New York Times*, July 17, 1878, 1. "At the Season's Height," *New York Times*, July 22, 1880.

23. Sally Bedell Smith, *In All His Glory: The Life of William S. Paley* (New York: Simon and Schuster), 1990, 333.

24. President Benjamin Harrison stayed at the newly tolerant Grand Union in 1891. His long forgotten appearance seems remarkable today not for its symbolism but for the fact that the symbolism was widely ignored. "The President's Busy Day," *New York Times*, Aug. 22, 1891, 5.

25. "The Saratoga Season," *New York Times*, May 10, 1891.

26. "Another Colored Pickpocket Arrest," *Saratoga Daily Union*, Aug. 5, 1887, 1.

27. "Saratoga's Open Arms," *New York Times*, July 5, 1886, 3.

28. "A Famous Evening Garden Party—Gamblers Arrested," *New York Times*, Aug. 31, 1890.

29. Advertisement in *Saratoga Daily Union*, Aug. 5, 1887, 1. See also Bradley, *Such Was Saratoga*, 228.

30. Manning discusses the transition from the Wheatly era in *Noble Animals*, 83–89.

31. *The American Turf* (New York: The Historical Co., 1898), 462.

13. Racing Through the Gay Nineties

1. Leach, *Kentucky Derby*, 45.

2. Robertson, *History of Thoroughbred Racing*, 138, 148.

3. Ibid., 177–78, 183.

4. Ibid., 138–42. The author's account of this race is based largely on Robertson's, one of the best brief descriptions.

5. Ibid., 166. Leach, *Kentucky Derby*, 48.

6. Tom Gilcoyne provided the author with an invaluable list of black jockeys, compiled by the late Fred Burlew, a turf historian and son of a noted trainer. It named eighty-one of the later African-American jockeys. As discussed, several others competed prior to, during, and just after the Civil War era. Some details are provided in both Leach, *Kentucky Derby*, and in Derby media guides, such as the previously cited *One Hundred Nineteenth Kentucky Derby* (the author's collection of media guides reveals a wealth of statistics and anecdotal information not easily found in libraries).

7. "Jockeys Retained for Next Year," *Sporting World*, Sept. 1, 1892, 1. This was one of the earliest "pink sheets." As the author's fragile copies show, its rarity is explained partly by the cheap woodpulp on which it was printed. See also Robertson, *History of Thoroughbred Racing*, 152, 167, 177.

8. "Better By Far than Baseball," *Sporting World*, Sept. 2, 1892, 4.

9. Robertson, *History of Thoroughbred Racing*, 94, 154.

10. Leach, *Kentucky Derby*, 65.

11. Domino was registered as brown but looked black.

12. The National Museum of Racing has the 1892–94 minutes of the Board of Control. Robertson, *History of Thoroughbred Racing*, 175.

13. Nellie Bly, "Our Wickedest Summer Resort," *The World*, Aug. 19, 1894, 22.

14. "Saratoga's Gala Meeting," *Sporting World*, Sept. 6, 1892, 1. See also Manning, *Noble Animals*, 83–89; Bradley, *Such Was Saratoga*, 209, 238.

15. Bly, "Our Wickedest Summer Resort," 21.

14. The Women's Betting Ring

1. Robert S. Wickham, *A Saratoga Boyhood*

(Syracuse, N.Y.: Orange Publishing Co., 1948), 16–25, 36–46.

2. Quoted in Manning, *Noble Animals*, 88–89.

3. Leach, *Kentucky Derby*, 69. Longrigg, *History of Horse Racing*, is one of the best sources for tracing this sport by geographical region.

4. Leach, *Kentucky Derby*, 57. Bradley, *Such Was Saratoga*, 234. Robertson, *History of Thoroughbred Racing*, 135–58.

5. For more on the rowing developments involving Saratoga, see Crowther and Ruhl, *Rowing*, 86, 89–90, 161–90. Also, the annual program for the IRA regatta generally includes historical vignettes on that group's history.

6. The newspapers followed the lively business of the "outlaw" tracks. See also the memoirs of Sam Hildreth, a trainer who knew them well: Samuel C. Hildreth and James R. Crowell, *The Spell of the Turf* (Philadelphia: Lippincott, 1925), 46–62, 87–97. Also Jimmy Breslin, *Sunny Jim* (Garden City, N.Y.: Doubleday, 1962), 114–26, and Robertson, *History of Thoroughbred Racing*, 174–76.

7. Bradley, *Such Was Saratoga*, 230–31.

8. "The Season at Saratoga," *New York Times*, June 20, 1897. Diamond Jim and Lil Russell live again in Waller, *Saratoga*, 243–44. Bradley is good on the politics of gambling, *Such Was Saratoga*, 231.

9. The best quick source for time lines and statistics on stakes races at Saratoga and elsewhere, including major foreign stakes, is the *American Racing Manual*, published annually by the *Daily Racing Form*.

10. Quoted in Manning, *Noble Animals*, 89.

11. Among the better sources on W. C. Whitney's life are Mark D. Hirsch, *William C. Whitney, Modern Warwick* (1948; reprint, Hamden, Conn.: Archon, 1969) and W. A. Swanberg, *Whitney Father, Whitney Heiress* (New York: Scribner's, 1980), the latter with a section on Saratoga, 205–12. But best on the Whitneys and the turf is Dan M. Bowmar III, *Giants of the Turf* (Lexington, Ky.: The Blood-Horse, 1960), 146–213. See also Livingston, *Their Turf*, 45–92.

12. Hildreth, *Spell of the Turf*, 108–9.

13. Quoted in Bowmar, *Giants*, 173.

14. Robertson tells of Whitney's daring toast in *History of Thoroughbred Racing*, 184.

15. Ibid., 168–71. The jockey's autobiography is *Tod Sloan by HIMSELF* (London: Grant Richards, 1915).

16. "Echoes of Saratoga Life," *New York Times*, Aug. 9, 1899. Wickham, *A Saratoga Boyhood*, 21–22.

15. Saratoga Revived

1. "Saratoga on Verge of A Boom," *New York Daily Tribune*, June 30, 1901, 4. The newsprint is by now so poor that this paper in the author's collection tears at every attempt to turn a page.

2. Bradley, *Such Was Saratoga*, 242–43.

3. "Rockton Wins Big Stake," *New York Times*, Aug. 6, 1901. An excellent study of the turf family founded by the general is Alex M. Robb's *The Sanfords of Amsterdam* (New York: William-Frederick, 1969).

4. Bradley, *Such Was Saratoga*, 282–83.

5. "Saratoga on Verge of A Boom," *New York Daily Tribune*, June 30, 1901, 4.

6. Ibid. Hirsch, *Whitney*, 589–90. Manning, "Saratoga Racing History," 160–61.

7. Vosburgh, *Racing 1866–1921*, 185. Vosburgh was the handicapper at Saratoga and other New York tracks at the time and for many years afterwards.

8. Ibid.

9. "Mr. Whitney's Derby," *New York Times*, June 6, 1901, 2, an editorial.

10. "Whitney Won the Derby," *New York Times*, June 6, 1901. The story ran a full column and a half.

11. Hirsch, *Whitney*, 591. Manning, "Saratoga Racing History," 161.

12. The title page of the previously cited *Racing Calendars* was careful to note that it was "printed, not published" by Whitney.

13. Asbury, *Sucker's Progress*, 464–65. Bradley, *Such Was Saratoga*, 259.

14. Among the better reports on Whitney's plant were "Saratoga Track Is Ready for Racing," *The Thoroughbred Record*, July 26, 1902, 1; "The Transformation of Saratoga—the New Race Course," *Turf, Field and Farm*, July 25, 1902, 713; "The Saratoga Racetrack Has Been Extensively Improved for the Racing Season, Which Opens Tomorrow," *New York Daily Tribune*, Aug. 3, 1902, 7. The latter, with illustrations, takes up more than a full page. Donna M. Ross studies Whitney's operation and later Saratoga developments in "Preservation, Art and the Charm of Old Saratoga," *The Blood-Horse*, Aug. 6, 1983, 5402–6.

15. "Transformation of Saratoga," 713.

16. Nancy Stout, *Great American Thoroughbred Racetracks* (New York: Rizzoli, 1991), 223. Kettlewell, *Saratoga Springs*, 91.

17. Stout, *Great American Thoroughbred Racetracks*, 239.

18. "Transformation of Saratoga," 713.

19. Manning, *Noble Animals*, 122–23.

20. "Transformation of Saratoga," 713.

21. In her remarkable study of the stables, Carol Chandler Smith pays special attention to the Sanford operation. *Splendid Survivors*, 118–29.

22. Waller, *Saratoga*, 275.

23. "Transformation of Saratoga," 713.

24. Woolley is quoted in Waller, *Saratoga*, 382.

25. Swanner, *Saratoga*, 71.

26. The best overview of these gamblers is still Asbury's in *Sucker's Progress*, especially 446, 460.

27. O'Connor, *Courtroom Warrior*, 3.

28. Asbury is good on Gates's historic night, *Sucker's Progress*, 446–48.

29. Eugene O'Connor, *The Casino* (Saratoga Springs, N.Y.: Historical Society of Saratoga Springs, 1979), a good historical brochure with unnumbered pages.

30. Ibid.

31. Britten, *Chronicles*, 70.

32. "Abner's False Rep," *Eastern Review*, Aug. 1983, 48–55. A reprint from *American Heritage Magazine*.

33. Montreal had a "Derby" a year before the Jersey Derby.

34. *Tod Sloan by HIMSELF*, 38–39. Bowmar, *Giants*, 175.

35. Bowmar, *Giants*, 185.

36. Robertson, *History of Thoroughbred Racing*, 183.

37. Ibid., 183. Hirsch, *Whitney*, 591–92.

38. Hirsch, *Whitney*, 594.

39. Ibid, 578–79. Hirsch found the poem in Elmer Ellis's *Mr. Dooley's America* (New York: Knopf, 1941), 185–86.

16. Sysonby and Colin

1. Hirsch, *Whitney*, 548, 598–99.

2. Ibid., 592. Bowmar, *Giants*, 180–83.

3. Asbury, *Sucker's Progress*, 467–69.

4. Alden Hatch and Foxhall Keene, *Full Tilt: The Sporting Memoirs of Foxhall Keene* (New York: Derrydale, 1938), 9.

5. Bowmar, *Giants*, 120–22. Hirsch, *Whitney*, 545.

6. Bowmar, *Giants*, 127–30.

7. Vosburgh, *Racing in America*, 2:202.

8. Quoted in Robertson, *History of Thoroughbred Racing*, 211–12.

9. Bradley, *Such Was Saratoga*, 279–81.

10. See chapter 22.

11. Quoted in Bowmar, *Giants*, 129.

12. For the development of the museum and racing's Hall of Fame, see chapters 22–25.

13. Charles B. Parmer, *For Gold and Glory* (New York: Carrick and Evans, 1939), 150–51.

14. The annual *American Racing Manual* updates these "Remarkable Riding Feats" each year, if necessary.

15. This debate is far from settled among turf historians.

16. Arthur R. Ashe, Jr., *A Hard Road to Glory* (New York: Warner, 1988), 1:53. Part of a brilliant three-volume history of African Americans in sports by the late tennis star.

17. Hildreth, *Spell of the Turf*, 179. Bradley, *Such Was Saratoga*, 303.

18. Art Rust, Jr., "Backlash KO'd Black Jockeys," *New York Daily News*, Jan. 15, 1989.

19. Quoted in Bowmar, *Giants*, 135.

20. Bradley, *Such Was Saratoga*, 297.

21. Hildreth, *Spell of the Turf*, 173.

22. Ibid., 180.

23. Tom Gilcoyne, at the National Museum of Racing, was a helpful source (once again) on the Shilling story. Robertson, *History of Thoroughbred Racing*, 206.

24. Michael Richman, *Daniel Chester French* (New York: Metropolitan Museum of Art, 1977), 139.

25. Foxie recalls his adventures in the previously cited Hatch and Keene, *Full Tilt*. See also Bowmar, *Giants*, 141.

17. From Regret to the Triple Crown

1. Vosburgh, *Racing 1866–1921*, 220.

2. Hildreth, *Spell of the Turf*, 205–6.

3. Madden is listed officially as the breeder of five Derby winners, but he also bred the first Triple Crown winner, Sir Barton, in partnership with Vivian Gooch of England. If the honors are assigned to breeding operations,

the Maddens made it seven when grandson Preston bred Alysheba at the family's Hamburg Place in 1987. Calumet would beat John Madden's record with nine, but four of these were bred after the death of owner Warren Wright. See, for example, *One Hundred Nineteenth Kentucky Derby*, 24.

4. Bradley, *Such Was Saratoga*, 300–301.

5. Butler is quoted in Frank G. Menke, *Down the Stretch: The Story of Colonel Matt Winn, As Told to Frank G. Menke* (New York: Smith and Durrell, 1945), 59.

6. Andrews, *Vanderbilt Legend*, 395–97.

7. *Down the Stretch*, 123.

8. Manning, *Noble Animals*, 96–97.

9. Vosburgh, *Racing 1866–1921*, 216.

18. Man o' War

1. In addition to newspapers, especially the weekly *Thoroughbred Record*, the author's chief source on Man o' War is a little-known biography of the champion by the great turf authority John Hervey. He died before it could be published as a book, but all twenty-four chapters were serialized as "The Turf Career of Man o' War," starting in the magazine *Horse* from Aug. 1959 through Dec. 1960 and continuing in *The Chronicle of the Horse*, through Mar. 3, 1961. The author treasures even his photocopy of this work. See also the fresh recollections of handicapper Vosburgh, writing at the close of Man o' War's career in *Racing*, 232–35. Also Robertson, *History of Thoroughbred Racing*, 238–45; Hildreth, *Spell of the Turf*, 229; and Bowmar, *Giants*, 87–88.

2. See chapter 24.

3. Records put the purse at $500, though Hervey says it was $700. For the origin of the term "Triple Crown," see chapter 20.

4. "Star Youngsters Race Today," *New York Times*, Aug. 13, 1919.

5. "Upset Beats Man o' War," *New York Times*, Aug. 14, 1919. Reprinted in *The Fireside Book of Horse Racing* (New York: Simon and Schuster, 1963), 295–96, which identifies the reporter as Fred Van Ness (The *Times* carried no byline).

6. The Sept. 7, 1919, *Times*, second-guessing itself on Loftus, also told of speed trials between Man o' War, Golden Broom, and Kinnoul on Riddle's Maryland farm.

7. Robertson, *History of Thoroughbred Racing*, 241.

8. Vosburgh, *Racing 1866–1921*, 22.

9. Ibid., 2:234.

19. Rothstein and the Roaring Twenties

1. The most revealing, and engaging, memoir of the "godfather" of American organized crime is the one sympathetic portrait, by his Saratoga bride, no lightweight moll. See Carolyn Rothstein, *Now I'll Tell* (New York: Vanguard, 1934). Also, Robert Lacey, *Little Man: Meyer Lansky and the Gangster Life* (Boston: Little, Brown, 1991), 48–61; Toney Betts, *Across the Board* (New York: Citadel, 1956), 223–38, and Virgil W. Peterson, *The Mob* (Ottawa, Ill.: Green Hill, 1983), 78–84.

2. For glimpses of Rothstein at his Brook, see Betts, *Across the Board*, 227–28; Bradley, *Such Was Saratoga*, 319–20; and Waller, *Saratoga*, 304–5.

3. See the lively series on Saratoga's casino days by Maria Bucciferro in the *Saratogian*, Sept. 14 and 15, 1989. Also Lacey, *Little Man*, 51–52, 82–83.

4. Bradley, *Such Was Saratoga*, 319–20; Waller, *Saratoga*, 305; Betts, *Across the Board*, 237–38.

5. Again, the most interesting account of this record racetrack betting coup is Mrs. Rothstein's in *Now I'll Tell*, 84–89.

6. Bradley, *Such Was Saratoga*, 317–19. Bradley witnessed many of the events he recounted.

7. Betts, *Across the Board*, 92. Betts, too, is a primary source, a reporter at the tracks from the 1920s through the 1950s.

8. Ibid., 192–93.

9. Neil Newman, "Saratoga—Its Fall and Rise," *National Turf Digest*, Sept. 1930, 965.

10. Bradley, *Such Was Saratoga*, 337; Robertson, *History of Thoroughbred Racing*, 259; and Betts, *Across the Board*, 123.

11. Quoted in Janet Barrett, "George Cassidy, Alone at the Start," *Thoroughbred Record*, Nov. 5, 1980, 2182–86. This Cassidy went on to become, like his father Mars, one of the best known starters and launched the famous Seabiscuit–War Admiral match. See chapter 21.

12. Neighborhood kids occasionally climbed to the top of the hilltop wreck after World War II. The author remembers being surprised to

see only the top of Hilton's Grand Union answering it across the skyline.

13. Newman's much later became the headquarters of the prom set.

14. From a postcard in the author's collection. Dempsey's Saratoga adventures are told in Jack Dempsey, with Barbara Piatelli Dempsey, *Dempsey* (New York: Harper and Row, 1977). Introduction by turf writer Joseph Durso.

15. Bowmar, *Giants,* 203.

16. Ibid., 205. Also, Hervey, *Racing 1922–1936,* 166.

17. August III's passing described by August IV in a telephone conversation with the author from Maryland's eastern shore. See also Hervey, *Racing,* 69.

18. Bradley, *Such Was Saratoga,* 311. Robertson, *History of Thoroughbred Racing,* 260, 300. Bowmar, *Giants,* 94.

19. Livingston, *Their Turf,* 112.

20. Skidmore College Library staffer Mary K. O'Donnell unearthed the Big Apple find in an article by Barry Popik, "The Green 'Big Apple,'" *Irish America Magazine,* Jan.–Feb. 1994, 1A.

21. The chief source for details of the 1928 season, including the new clubhouse and recreation center, is the running coverage in the *Albany Times-Union.* See also the full page of stories in the *Morning Telegraph,* New York, July 29, 1928.

22. Bradley, *Such Was Saratoga,* 333–34.

23. Betts, *Across the Board,* 119.

24. A number of Saratogians, including the author, recall swimming alongside that mysterious wall.

25. Betts, *Across the Board,* 190, 216.

26. Ibid., 170–74.

20. Gallant Fox

1. Marguerite was by Celt, champion sire of 1921, and Celt by the great Commando. For Hancock and the beginnings of Claiborne Stud, see Robertson, *History of Thoroughbred Racing,* 279–80.

2. Selima was a Godolphin Arabian daughter brought to Maryland in 1750. This library's unusually accessible turf collection is one of the great secrets of the sport, unknown even to many librarians.

3. Hervey, who knew the horse personally, is best on his career, in *Racing,* 151–57. For details on the gate, see the coverage of the 1934 meeting in the *Saratogian.* Also, Manning, *County Heritage,* 164. Turf writer Charles Hatton was one of the authorities on Gallant Fox, and his widow, Gail, who lives in Lexington, related to the author how this led Charlie to invent the term Triple Crown.

4. Howe aide Lela Stiles told of the FDR gang's trip to Saratoga in *The Man Behind Roosevelt* (Cleveland, Oh.: World Pub. Co., 1954), 163–64. Another good account of Howe's career, including his Saratoga days, is Alfred B. Rollins, Jr., *Roosevelt and Howe* (New York: Knopf, 1962).

5. Damon Runyon, "Jim Dandy, 100–1, Beats Gallant Fox," *New York American,* Aug. 17, 1930, Sports Section, 1.

6. The Runyon short story is quoted in Waller, *Saratoga,* 130.

7. Crowd estimates ranged from Runyon's 25,000 to the *New York Herald Tribune's* 50,000. Reports on the odds varied. Sam Rosoff's killing and his open house were mentioned in many accounts, including Betts, *Across the Board,* 254–55, and Bradley, *Such Was Saratoga,* 313–15.

8. Hervey, *Racing,* 225–26.

9. Sonny Whitney, the independent-minded and highly accomplished businessman, made a point of his having purchased rather than simply inherited his father's turf empire. For more on this transition, see Bowmar, *Giants,* 210.

10. Robertson, *History of Thoroughbred Racing,* 288–89.

11. Sonny got his dates and Capones mixed up in a later tale of the Equipoise-Hawthorne-Capone connection. See C. V. Whitney, *High Peaks* (Lexington, Ky.: Univ. Press of Kentucky, 1977), 33–38. Hervey, *Racing,* 140–42, discusses the Depression at the tracks. Also, Betts, *Across the Board,* 173.

12. Andrews, *Vanderbilt Legend,* 362.

13. Ibid., 382–88. The headline is still tossed about by the few survivors of journalism's good days.

14. A good on-the-spot report, based on a visit the previous season, is "August at Saratoga," *Fortune,* Aug. 1935, 62–69, 96–100, with color reproductions of paintings by Sanford Ross. Curator Field Horne advises that some of

Ross's originals are at the National Museum of Racing. The author's mint copy of the magazine reveals its lavish quality in the midst of hard times, a dichotomy that marked Saratoga as well.

15. Betts, *Across the Board*, 129, 133, 206.

16. "August at Saratoga," *Fortune*, Aug. 1935, 69.

17. Bradley, *Such Was Saratoga*, 335–36.

18. Betts, *Across the Board*, 113–14.

19. Ibid., 254–56.

20. Joe H. Palmer, *This Was Racing*, ed. Red Smith (New York: Barnes, 1953). The high regard in which Palmer was held is symbolized by the author's boxed, leatherbound, limited edition signed by editor Smith and illustrator Willard Mullin.

21. As for the pari-mutuel tickets that blanket the grounds after every race, nobody was better than Elizabeth Hotaling, the author's mother, at reading them cold from a standing position, to see if somebody foolishly had discarded a winner. Track manager John Mangona discussed the poles with the author. For the quirky 1934 finish, see Bradley, *Such Was Saratoga*, 335.

22. Betts, *Across the Board*, 143.

23. "Barrie, Alleged Swindler, Given Hearing in Court," *Saratogian*, Aug. 17, 1934, with a picture of Barrie looking innocent as hell under a fedora, as though his arrest were a case of mistaken identity, like some of his horses. The paper came from a sale under the Rip Van Dam piazza, a typical Saratoga experience. See also Fred J. Cook, *The Pinkertons* (Garden City, N.Y.: Doubleday, 1974), 167–71.

21. War Admiral, Seabiscuit, Whirlaway

1. "August at Saratoga," *Fortune* 12, no. 2 (Aug. 1935): 98.

2. Ibid., 100; Robert M. Coates, "A Reporter At Large," *The New Yorker* 20, no. 35 (Oct. 14, 1944): 50.

3. Bradley, *Such Was Saratoga*, 323–27.

4. Bucciferro, "Mob Feasted in Saratoga," *Saratogian*, Sept. 15, 1989, 1C.

5. Hervey, *Racing*, 233–34.

6. Leach, *Kentucky Derby*, 159.

7. Bucciferro, "Mob Feasted in Saratoga."

8. Lacey, *Little Man*, 83–88.

9. Bradley, *Such Was Saratoga*, 329–30.

10. Betts, *Across the Board*, 197–99.

11. Bradley, *Such Was Saratoga*, 335.

12. Jimmy Snyder, *Jimmy the Greek: By Himself* (Chicago: Playboy Press, 1975), 8, 15–17. The author could locate no record of that race, but the point is well taken, and a horse named Clodion definitely beat Merrie Lassie by a length in the fourth at Jamaica on Apr. 20, 1935.

13. Kelley, *Racing 1937–1959*, 17–18. Robertson, *History of Thoroughbred Racing*, 322–27.

14. Robertson, *History of Thoroughbred Racing*, 244. Regarding Riddle's digs, the street numbering had changed several years earlier, his house switching from 215 to 125.

15. Pastor is quoted in Chris Mead, *Champion, Joe Louis: Black Hero in White America* (New York: Scribner's, 1985), 111–12, 166–67, 171. A boyhood friend of his son Albie, also a terrific athlete, the author remembers admiring the fighter from a distance as a boy.

16. Charles Evan Hughes, who as governor had led the fight to shut down the scandalous tracks, was now safely in a position where he could do no harm—chief justice of the Supreme Court.

17. Palmer, *This Was Racing 1937–1959*, 249.

18. Betts, *Across the Board*, 53, 166.

19. Quoted in Kelley, *Racing 1937–1959*, 55.

20. Ibid., 43–44. Both Robertson, *History of Thoroughbred Racing*, and Bowen, *Illustrated History*, have year-by-year statistical appendixes.

21. "The Race Track," *The New Yorker*, Dec. 6, 1941, 125. As the date suggests, the events of the times, as in 1863, did not shut down racing, at least not yet.

22. Robertson, *History of Thoroughbred Racing*, 269.

23. Kelley, *Racing 1937–1959*, 77–78.

24. Waller, *Saratoga*, 330.

25. Among the many whose livelihoods now turned on Schenectady instead was the author's father, Charles A. Hotaling, Sr., who went to work for General Electric.

22. Citation, Native Dancer, Tom Fool

1. Along with memoirs, and New York City and Saratoga Springs newspapers, the author's chief source on turf developments in the postwar decade is Robertson, *History of Thoroughbred Racing*, 373–488.

2. Ibid., 374.

3. Walter Farley, preface to *Man o' War* (New York: Random House, 1962). A fictional biography based closely on Hervey and the true story.

4. Robertson, *History of Thoroughbred Racing*, 401, 475.

5. Ibid., 412.

6. Edward Arcaro, "Eddie Arcaro's Favorite Travers," *The Travers*, 4, the 1988 official souvenir program.

7. Betts, *Across the Board*, 156.

8. Bucciferro, "Saratoga once crowded with lake houses, horse rooms," *Saratogian*, Sept. 14, 1989, 3C. The backyard was the author's.

9. St. Clement's is a few furlongs northeast of the track, on Lake Avenue.

10. David Charnay, "Saratoga Moans the Blues," *New York Daily News*, Aug. 3, 1948, 2.

11. Quoted in Dennis Eisenberg, Uri Dan and Eli Landau, *Meyer Lansky: Mogul of the Mob* (New York: Paddington, 1979), 288.

12. Palmer, *This Was Racing*, 91–92. The kid was the author.

13. Ibid., 159–73.

14. Jack Lait, "Broadway and Elsewhere," *New York Daily Mirror*, 8.

15. The candy counter critic was Elizabeth Hotaling.

16. Betts, *Across the Board*, 68; Robertson, *History of Thoroughbred Racing*, 482.

17. Betts, *Across the Board*, 79–91.

18. Ibid., 69–70. Robertson, *History of Thoroughbred Racing*, 527.

19. Farley, *Man o' War*, 5.

23. The Greatest Travers?

1. Along with the recollections of witnesses, the main sources for this great race were Joseph C. Nichols, "Saratoga Choice First By Nose," *New York Times*, Aug. 19, 1992, Sports section, 1, and Rudy, *Racing 1960–1979*, 29–30.

2. Dan Mearns, "Bert Mulholland," *Members in the National Museum of Racing Hall of Fame* (Saratoga Springs, N.Y.: National Museum of Racing). Excellent thumbnail sketches by members of the National Turf Writers Association.

3. For students of the former process, Robertson, *History of Thoroughbred Racing*, indexes the choices of all four voting groups, 600–601.

4. Ibid., 549–52. Rudy, *Racing 1960–1979*, 13, 16–17.

5. Lew Koch, "Incredible Kelso," *SPUR*, Sept.–Oct. 1990, 88–94. Also, Lou DeFichy (formerly with National Steeplechase and Hunt Association) to author, Aug. 5, 1990.

6. Paul Mellon, with John Baskett, *Reflections in A Silver Spoon* (New York: Morrow, 1992), 244–69.

7. It would be easy to remove the windows and television monitors and return W. C. Whitney's saddling paddock to its original purpose, but not without resolving how to accommodate today's big crowds.

8. In the face of uncertainty, at best, when it comes to official interest in preservation, the Y is one more argument for aggressive activism by local preservationists.

9. It would be impossible to name them all in what has become perhaps the most historically alert city in America, though there is still a minority that can't see the economic value in history. Waller is good on the 1960s revival in *Saratoga*, 346–47.

10. Braulio Baeza, "Travers Triumphs in Stone," *The Travers*, 42. By the famously stone-faced jockey. Again, from the excellent 1988 program. The author is indebted to Tom Gilcoyne for his copy.

11. Joe Nichols, "Irish Castle Takes Hopeful," *New York Times*, Aug. 24, 1969, Sports section, 1.

24. Secretariat, Ruffian, Affirmed vs. Alydar

1. Again, besides by reminiscences and the daily coverage, the principal source on Secretariat and his contemporaries has been Rudy's brilliant *Racing*, 206–13. See also Bowen, *Illustrated History*, 145–54. Livingston wrote that Secretariat was named after Elizabeth Ham, secretary and financial adviser to his eventual owner, Helen (Penny) Chenery. He also provided insight on her taking over Meadow Stable after her father died. See *Their Turf*, 280–95.

2. See Steve Cady, "Secretariat's Record Romp Electrifies His Fans," and the unbylined "A Carnival Air at Belmont Day," *New York Times*, June 10, 1973, Sports section, 3. Also, Joe Nichols, "Secretariat Sweeps to Triple Crown by 31 Lengths," *New York Times*, June 10, 1973,

Sports section, 1. For Secretariat's Whitney, see Nichols's "Secretariat's Popularity Puts NYRA Chief on a Spot," *New York Times*, Aug. 3, 1973, Sports section; "Secretariat Aims Today for Million-Dollar Mark," *New York Times*, Aug. 4, 1973, Sports section, 15; and "Secretariat Is Beaten by Onion," *New York Times*, Aug. 5, 1973, Sports section, 1.

3. Rudy, *Racing*, 233–38.

4. Jane Schwartz's excellent biography is *Ruffian: Burning from the Start* (New York: Ballantine, 1991).

5. A measure of Forego's endurance is the frequency with which he reappears in any account of the period, such as Rudy, *Racing*, 220–25, 238–44, 249–52, 267–69. For Ruffian and Forego, see also Bowen, 133–34, 142.

6. Ibid., 268.

7. For a terrific first-day report, see Andrew Beyer, "Affirmed Disqualified, Alydar Wins Travers," *Washington Star*, Sports section, E-1, and Rudy, *Racing*, 269–70, 280–83.

8. Saratoga records are updated in *Travers Stakes Press Guide* (New York: New York Racing Association, 1994), 35.

9. Bowen, *Illustrated History*, 146.

25. John Henry, Go for Wand, Holy Bull

1. Quoted in Joseph Durso, "On Horse Racing," *New York Times*, Aug. 23, 1991, Sports section.

2. Steven Crist, "Arlington Million Comes Up Short of Its Billing," *New York Times*, Aug. 30, 1982, Sports section, 10.

3. "John Henry Voted Top Horse By a Nose," *New York Times*, Feb. 10, 1985, Sports section, 6.

4. George Vecsey, "Promising Beginning," *New York Times*, Nov. 12, 1984, Sports setion, 3.

5. Ibid.

6. Bowen, 139.

7. Andrew Beyer, "It's Still Saratoga By a Nose," *Washington Post*, July 30, 1994. Beyer is one of the turf's most thoughtful commentators. He also has authored several books on handicapping and betting, including *The Winning Horseplayer* (Boston: Houghton Mifflin, 1983) and *Beyer on Speed* (Boston: Houghton Mifflin, 1993).

8. Quoted in Edward Fitzpatrick, "As Generations Go By," in the *Daily Gazette*, July 29, 1994, A6.

9. Bill Christine, "Java Gold Is Sparkling in Soggy Travers Stakes," *Los Angeles Times*, Aug. 23, 1987, Sports section, 1, and Steven Crist, "Java Gold's Late Run Captures Travers," *New York Times*, Aug. 23, 1987, Sports section, 1.

10. August IV spoke with author from his eastern shore home in Maryland.

11. Steven Crist, "Go for Wand Captures Test Stakes With Ease," *New York Times*, Aug. 3, 1990, 21.

12. Crist wrote several *Times* pieces on the tragedy. See, for example, "A Day of Champions Turns Into A Day of Tragedy," Oct. 28, 1990, 1; "A Season of Misfortune Raises Many Questions," and Aug. 28, 1990, Sports section, 6.

13. Steven Crist, "Death on the Track Offers Glimpse of a Hard Reality," Oct. 30, 1990, Sports section, 9.

14. Ann Hagedorn Auerbach, *Wild Ride: The Rise and Tragic Fall of Calumet Farm, Inc., America's Premier Racing Dynasty* (New York: Holt, 1994), 9, 14.

15. John A. Hoyt and Thomas H. Meeker, "Face-Off: Run for the Roses," *USA Today*, May 3, 1991.

16. Jane Schwartz, "Views of Sport: In Horses, We Glimpse Our Lost Nobility," *New York Times*, Feb. 3, 1991, Sports section, 7.

17. Edward Hotaling, "What's Doing in Saratoga," *New York Times*, June 16, 1991, Travel section, 10.

18. On African Americans in racing, see, for example, chapters 6, 7, 13, 15, 17, 19.

19. Mellon, *Reflections in a Silver Spoon*, 256–58.

20. Edward Hotaling, "What's Doing in Saratoga," *New York Times*, June 13, 1993, Travel section, 10.

21. Joseph Durso, "A Special Horse, A Special Trainer," *New York Times*, Sept. 15, 1994, Sports section, B17.

22. Joseph Durso, "Tabasco Cat Ready to Stalk the Bull," *New York Times*, B13.

23. Durso reported on Fourstardave's last 1994 performance in "Horse Racing," *New York Times*, Aug. 14, 1994, Sports section, 3.

BIBLIOGRAPHY

Abbot, W. W., and Dorothy Twohig, eds. *Papers of George Washington, Colonial Series.* Charlottesville: Univ. Press of Virginia, 1982.

Abbot, W. W., and Dorothy Twohig, eds. *Papers of George Washington, Confederation Series.* Charlottesville: Univ. Press of Virginia, 1992.

"Abner's False Rep." *Eastern Review,* Aug. 1983. Reprinted from *American Heritage Magazine.*

Albig, W. Espey. "The Origin of the American Heritage Bankers Association." *Banking,* Sept. 1942.

The American Turf. New York: The Historical Co., 1898.

Andrews, Wayne. *The Vanderbilt Legend.* New York: Harcourt, Brace, 1941.

Appleton's Illustrated Hand Book of American Travel. New York: Appleton, 1860.

Arcaro, Edward. "Eddie Arcaro's Favorite Travers." *The Travers,* 1988 official souvenir program.

Asbury, Herbert. *The Gangs of New York.* New York: Capricorn, 1927.

———. *Sucker's Progress.* New York: Dodd, Mead, 1939.

Ashe, Arthur R., Jr. *A Hard Road to Glory.* New York: Warner, 1988.

Auerbach, Ann Hagedorn. *Wild Ride: The Rise and Tragic Fall of Calumet Farm, Inc., America's Premier Racing Dynasty.* New York: Holt, 1994.

"August at Saratoga." *Fortune* 12, no. 2 (Aug. 1935): 62–69, 96–100.

Barrett, Janet. "George Cassidy, Alone at the Start." *Thoroughbred Record,* Nov. 5, 1980.

Benton, James E., Sr. "Springs." In *Saratoga County Heritage,* edited by Violet B. Dunn; Robert S. Hayden; and Clayton H. Brown, 189–207. Ballston Spa, N.Y.: Saratoga County, 1974.

Berger, Meyer. *The Story of the New York Times.* New York: Simon and Schuster, 1951.

Betts, Toney. *Across the Board.* New York: Citadel, 1956.

Beyer, Andrew. *Beyer on Speed.* Boston: Houghton Mifflin, 1993.

———. *The Winning Horseplayer.* Boston: Houghton Mifflin, 1983.

Birmingham, Stephen. *Our Crowd: The Great Jewish Families of New York.* New York: Dell, 1967.

Bly, Nellie. "Our Wickedest Summer Resort." *The World,* Aug. 19, 1894.

Bowen, Edward L., *The Jockey Club's Illustrated History of Thoroughbred Racing in America.* Boston: Little, Brown, 1994.

Bowmar, Dan M., III. *Giants of the Turf*. Lexington, Ky.: The Blood-Horse, 1960.

Bradley, Hugh. *Such Was Saratoga*. New York: Doubleday, Doran, 1940.

Bray, Robert C., and Paul E. Bushnell, eds. *Diary of a Common Soldier in the American Revolution 1775–1783*. DeKalb: Northern Illinois Univ. Press, 1978.

Breslin, Jimmy. *Sunny Jim*. Garden City, N.Y.: Doubleday, 1962.

Britten, Evelyn Barrett. *Chronicles of Saratoga*. Saratoga Springs, N.Y.: Evelyn Barrett Britten, 1959.

Bucciferro, Maria. "Those Gambling Days." *Saratogian*, Sept. 13–15, 1989.

Carola, Chris; Beverley Mastrianni; and Michael L. Noonan, *George Bolster's Saratoga Springs*. Saratoga Springs: The Donning Company, 1990.

Carson, Gerald. *A Good Day at Saratoga*. New York: American Bar Association, 1978.

Chambers, Whiteclay, II. *To Raise an Army*. New York: Free Press, 1987.

Coates, Robert M. "A Reporter At Large." *The New Yorker* 20, no. 35 (Oct. 14, 1944): 47–51.

Cook, Adrian. *Armies of the Streets*. Lexington: Univ. Press of Kentucky, 1974.

Cook, Fred J. *The Pinkertons*. Garden City, N.Y.: Doubleday, 1974.

Cooke, Jacob E. *Tench Coxe and the Early Republic*. Chapel Hill: Univ. of North Carolina Press, 1978.

Crickmore, H. G., ed. *Racing Calendars*. 3 vols. New York: Printed by W. C. Whitney, 1901.

Crowther, Samuel, and Arthur Ruhl. *Rowing and Track Athletics*. New York: Macmillan, 1905.

Cunningham, Florence R. *Saratoga's First Hundred Years*. Fresno, Calif.: Valley, 1967.

Dal Verme, Francesco. *Seeing America and Its Great Men, The Journal and Letters of Count Francesco dal Verme 1783–1784*. Translated and edited by Elizabeth Cometti. Charlottesville: Univ. Press of Virginia, 1969.

Dempsey, Jack, with Barbara Piatelli Dempsey. *Dempsey*. New York: Harper and Row, 1977.

Dinnerstein, Leonard. *Anti-Semitism in America*. New York: Oxford, 1994.

Dowd, Charles N., M.D. *Charles F. Dowd, A.M., Ph.D.* New York: Knickerbocker, 1930.

Eakin, Sue, and Joseph Logsdon, eds. *Twelve Years a Slave, by Solomon Northup*. Baton Rouge: Louisiana State Univ. Press, 1968.

Eisenberg, Dennis; Uri Dan; and Eli Landau. *Meyer Lansky: Mogul of the Mob*. New York: Paddington, 1979.

Farley, Walter. *Man o' War*. New York: Random House, 1962.

Fashionable Tour: A Guide to Travelers Touring the Northern and Middle States. 4th ed. Saratoga Springs: G. M. Davison, 1830.

The Fireside Book of Horse Racing. New York: Simon and Schuster, 1963.

Fiske, Stephen. *Off-Hand Portraits of Prominent New Yorkers*. 1884. Reprint, New York: Arno, 1975.

Fitzpatrick, John C., ed. *Writings of George Washington*. Washington, D.C.: GPO, 1938.

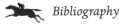 *Bibliography*

Fox, William F. *Regimental Losses in the American Civil War, 1861–1865*. Dayton, Oh.: Morningside Bookshop, 1985.

Freeman, Douglas Southall. *George Washington*. New York: Scribner's, 1952.

"From the American Traveller." *Troy Whig*, July 18, 1836.

Goodrich, S. G. *Recollections of a Lifetime*. Vol. 2. New York: Miller, Orton and Mulligan, 1857.

Grose, Edward F. *Centennial History of the Village of Ballston Spa*. Ballston Spa, N.Y.: Ballston Journal, 1907.

Harte, Bret. "That Ebrew Jew." *American Jewish Archives*, June 1954, 148.

Hatch, Alden, and Keene, Foxhall. *Full Tilt, the Sporting Memoirs of Foxhall Keene*. New York: Derrydale, 1938.

Heimer, Mel. *Fabulous Bawd, The Story of Saratoga*. New York: Holt, 1952.

Hervey, John. *Lady Suffolk, the Old Grey Mare of Long Island*. New York: Derrydale, 1936.

———. *Racing in America 1665–1865*. New York: Scribner Press, 1944.

———. *Racing in America 1922–1936*. New York: Scribner Press, 1937.

———. "The Turf Career of Man o' War," *Horse*, Aug. 1959–Dec. 1960, and *Chronicle of the Horse*, Jan.–Mar. 1961.

Hildreth, Samuel C., and James R. Crowell, *The Spell of the Turf*. Philadelphia: Lippincott, 1925.

Hirsch, Mark D. *William C. Whitney, Modern Warwick*. 1948. Reprint, Hamden, Conn.: Archon, 1969.

Hislop, Codman. *Eliphalet Nott*. Middletown, Conn.: Wesleyan Univ. Press, 1971.

A History of Temperance in Saratoga County, N.Y. Saratoga Springs: G. M. Davison, 1855.

Hotaling, Edward. "Views of Sport, The Thunder of Hooves, the Ring of Commentary" *New York Times*, Aug. 5, 1990.

———. "What's Doing in Saratoga." *New York Times*, June 16, 1991.

———. "What's Doing in Saratoga." *New York Times*, June 13, 1993.

Hoyt, John A., and Thomas H. Meeker, "Face-Off: Run for the Roses," *USA Today*, May 3, 1991.

Humphreys, Mary Gay. *Catherine Schuyler*. New York: Scribner's, 1897.

In a Pleasant Situation. Ballston Spa, N.Y.: Saratoga County Historical Society, 1986.

James, Henry. *Portraits of Places*. Boston: Houghton Mifflin, 1883.

Josephson, Matthew. *The Robber Barons*. New York: Harcourt, Brace, 1934.

Kelley, Robert F. *Racing in America 1937–1959*. New York: Scribner Press, 1960.

Kelly, Joe, ed. "The Horse Gave His Name to a Classic." *114th Preakness*. Baltimore: Maryland Jockey Club, 1989.

Kettlewell, James K. *Saratoga Springs: An Architectural History*. Saratoga Springs: Lyrical Ballad Book Store, 1991.

Koch, Lew. "Incredible Kelso." *SPUR*, Sept.–Oct. 1990.

Kofoed, Jack. *Brandy for Heroes*. New York: Dutton, 1938.

Lacey, Robert. *Little Man: Meyer Lansky and the Gangster Life*. Boston: Little, Brown, 1991.

Landon, Melville [Eli Perkins, pseud.]. *Saratoga in 1901*. New York: Sheldon, 1872.

Lane, Wheaton J. *Commodore Vanderbilt: An Epic of the Steam Age*. New York: Knopf, 1942.

Laurel and Pimlico '94 Media Guide. Baltimore: Maryland Jockey Club, 1994.

Leach, Brownie. *The Kentucky Derby Diamond Jubilee*. New York: Dial, 1949.

Leach, Margaret. *Reveille in Washington*. New York: Harper, 1941.

Lehr, Elizabeth Drexel. *'King Lehr' and the Gilded Age*. Philadelphia: Lippincott, 1935.

Livermore, Thomas L. *Numbers and Losses in the Civil War in America, 1861–1865*. Boston: Houghton Mifflin, 1901.

Livingston, Bernard. *Their Turf: America's Horsey Set and Its Princely Dynasties*. New York, Arbor House, 1973.

Lloyd, Alan. *The Great Prize Fight*. New York: Coward, McCann and Geoghegan, 1977.

Longrigg, Roger. *The History of Horse Racing*. New York: Stein and Day, 1972.

Look, Margaret K. *Courtney: Master Oarsman—Champion Coach*. Interlaken, N.Y.: Empire State Books, 1989.

Manning, Landon. *The Noble Animals, Tales of the Saratoga Turf*. Saratoga Springs, N.Y.: Landon Manning, 1973.

———. "Saratoga Racing History." In *Saratoga County Heritage*, 151–71. Ballston Spa, N.Y.: Saratoga County, 1974.

Martin, Ralph G. *Jennie: The Life of Lady Randolph Churchill*. Englewood Cliffs, N.J.: New American Library, 1969.

McPherson, James M. *Battle Cry of Freedom*. New York: Ballantine, 1988.

Mead, Chris. *Champion: Joe Louis, Black Hero in White America*. New York: Scribner's, 1985.

Mearns, Dan. "Bert Mulholland." *Members in the National Museum of Racing Hall of Fame*. Saratoga Springs, N.Y.: National Museum of Racing.

Mellon, Paul, with John Baskett. *Reflections in a Silver Spoon*. New York: Morrow, 1992.

Mendenhall, Thomas C. "The Isms of Rowing: Amateur and Professional," *The Oarsman* 7, no. 4 (Sept.–Oct. 1975): 27–28.

Menke, Frank G. *Down the Stretch: The Story of Colonel Matt Winn, As Told to Frank G. Menke*. New York: Smith and Durrell, 1945.

Morse, Jedidiah. *An Abridgment of the American Gazeteer*. Boston: Thomas and Andrews, 1798.

Nelson, Neil E. "Grand in Manner, Grand in History." *The Blood-Horse* 115, no. 16 (Apr. 22, 1989): 2204–6.

Nott, Eliphalet. *A Discourse Delivered in the Presbyterian Church, in the City of Albany, Before the Ladies' Society for the Relief of Distressed Women and Children, March 18, 1804*. Albany: Webster, 1804.

O'Connor, Eugene. *The Casino*. Saratoga Springs, N.Y.: Historical Society of Saratoga Springs, 1979.

O'Connor, Richard. *Courtroom Warrior: The Combative Career of William Travers Jerome*. Boston: Little, Brown, 1963.

Paine, Albert Bigelow. *Th. Nast, His Period and His Pictures*. 1904. Reprint, Princeton: Pyne, 1974.

Palmer, Joe H. *This Was Racing*. Edited by Red Smith. New York: Barnes, 1953.

Parmer, Charles B. *For Gold and Glory*. New York: Carrick and Evans, 1939.

Peterson, Virgil W. *The Mob*. Ottawa, Ill.: Green Hill, 1983.

Popik, Barry. "The Green 'Big Apple.'" *Irish America Magazine*, Jan.–Feb. 1994.

Pound, Arthur. *Johnson of the Mohawks*. New York: Macmillan, 1930.

Power, Tyrone. *Impressions of America*. Philadelphia: Carey, Lea Blanchard, 1836.

Reniers, Perceval. *The Springs of Virginia*. Chapel Hill: Univ. of North Carolina Press, 1955.

Resseguie, Harry E. "Merchant Prince: The Life and Times of Alexander Turner Stewart, with Something About Henry Hilton," 1963. Unpublished manuscript in the Skidmore College library.

Richman, Michael. *Daniel Chester French*. New York: Metropolitan Museum of Art, 1977.

Ritter, Halsted L. *Washington As a Businessman*. New York: Sears Publishing Co., 1931.

Robb, Alex M. *The Sanfords of Amsterdam*. New York: William-Frederick, 1969.

Robertson, William H. P. *The History of Thoroughbred Racing in America*. New York: Bonanza, 1964.

Rollins, Alfred B., Jr. *Roosevelt and Howe*. New York: Knopf, 1962.

Ross, Donna M. "Changing the Spa." *The Blood-Horse*, July 13, 1985.

———. "Preservation, Art and the Charm of Old Saratoga," *The Blood-Horse*, Aug. 6, 1983.

Rothstein, Carolyn. *Now I'll Tell*. New York: Vanguard, 1934.

Rudy, William II. *Racing in America 1960–1979*. New York: Scribner Press, 1980.

Rules and Regulations of Racing, Trotting and Betting, as Adopted by the Principal Turf Associations throughout the United States and Canada. New York: Brown, 1866.

Runyon, Damon. "Jim Dandy, 100–1, Beats Gallant Fox." *New York American*, Aug. 17, 1930, Sports section.

Sante, Luc. *Low Life, Lures and Snares of Old New York*. New York: Vintage, 1992.

"Saratoga and Schenectady Railroad." *American Railroad Journal*, July 21, 1832.

Saratoga County Communities. Clifton Park, N.Y.: Saratoga County Planning Board, 1980.

"Saratoga, the American Baden-Baden." *Every Saturday*, New York, Sept. 9, 1871.

"The Saratoga Racetrack Has Been Extensively Improved for the Racing Season, Which Opens Tomorrow." *New York Daily Tribune*, Aug. 3, 1902.

"Saratoga Track is Ready for Racing," *The Thoroughbred Record*, July 26, 1902.

Saxe, John Godfrey. *Poetical Works of John Godfrey Saxe*. Boston: Houghton Mifflin, 1892.

Schwartz, Jane. *Ruffian: Burning from the Start*. New York: Ballantine, 1991.

———. "Views of Sport: In Horses, We Glimpse Our Lost Nobility," *New York Times*, Sports section.

Sheldon, James L., and Reynolds, Jock. *Motion and Document—Sequence and Time: Eadweard Muybridge and Contemporary American Photography*. Andover, Mass.: Addison Gallery of American Art, 1991.

Simon, John Y., ed. *The Personal Memoirs of Julia Dent Grant*. New York: Putnam, 1975.

Sloan, Tod. *Tod Sloan by HIMSELF*. London: Grant Richards, 1915.

Smith, Carol Chandler. "Splendid Survivors: Horse Racing Stable Construction." Master's thesis, Cornell Univ., 1987.

Smith, Joseph. *Reminiscences of Saratoga*. New York: Knickerbocker, 1897.

Smith, Matthew Hale. *Sunshine and Shadow in New York*. Hartford: Burr, 1869.

Smith, Sally Bedell. *In All His Glory: The Life of William S. Paley*. New York: Simon and Schuster, 1990.

Snyder, Jimmy. *Jimmy the Greek, by Himself*. Chicago: Playboy Press, 1975.

Somers, Dale A. *The Rise of Sports in New Orleans*. Baton Rouge: Louisiana State Univ. Press, 1972.

Sorin, Gretchen Sullivan, and Jane W. Rehl. *Honorable Work: African Americans in the Resort Community of Saratoga Springs, 1870–1970*. Saratoga Springs, N.Y.: Historical Society of Saratoga Springs, 1992.

Spiegal, Ted. *Saratoga: The Place and Its People*. With essays by Peter Andrews, Jennifer Dunning, and Whitney Tower. New York: H. N. Abrams, 1988.

Steel, John H. *An Analysis of the Mineral Waters of Saratoga and Ballston*. Albany: Hosford, 1817.

———. *An Analysis of the Mineral Waters of Saratoga and Ballston*. 2nd ed. Saratoga Springs, N.Y.: G. M. Davison, 1838.

Stern, Madeleine B. *Purple Passage: The Life of Mrs. Frank Leslie*. Norman: Univ. of Oklahoma Press, 1953.

Stevens, Frank Walker. *Beginnings of the New York Central Railroad*. New York: Putnam, 1926.

Stiles, Lela. *The Man Behind Roosevelt*. Cleveland, Oh.: World Publishing Co., 1954.

Stout, Nancy. *Great American Thoroughbred Racetracks*. New York: Rizzoli, 1991.

Swanberg, W. A. *Whitney Father, Whitney Heiress*. New York: Scribner's, 1980.

Swanner, Grace Maguire. *Saratoga Queen of Spas*. Utica, N.Y.: North Country Books, 1988.

Sweeney, Beatrice. *The Grand Union Hotel: A Memorial and a Lament*. Saratoga Springs, N.Y.: Saratoga Springs Historical Society, 1982.

———. "Saratoga Springs." In *Saratoga County Heritage*, 539–65. Ballston Spa, N.Y.: Saratoga County, 1974.

Taub, Marion, and Sweeney, Beatrice. *Bibliography of Research Materials on Saratoga Springs, New York*. Saratoga Springs, N.Y.: Saratoga Springs Public Library, 1977.

"The Transformation of Saratoga—the New Race Course," *Turf, Field and Farm*, July 26, 1902.

Tuckerman, Bayard, ed. *Diary of Philip Hone*. New York: Dodd, Mead, 1889.

"The Turfman's Referee." *Rules and Regulations for the Government of Racing, Trotting and Betting*. New York: Brown, 1867.

Turner, G. "Description of the Chalybeate Springs, near Saratoga." *Columbian Magazine*, Mar. 1787.

Vosburgh, W. S. *Racing in America 1866–1921*. New York: Scribner Press, 1922.

Wall, E. Berry. *Neither Pest Nor Puritan*. New York: Dial, 1940.

Waller, George. *Saratoga, Saga of an Impious Era*. Englewood Cliffs, N.J.: Prentice-Hall, 1966.

Walworth, Mansfield. *Hotspur*. New York: Carleton, 1864.

W——H, W. D. "Editorial Correspondence of the Star." *The Weekly Star*, Aug. 13, 1859.

Watson, Winslow C., ed. *Men and Times of the Revolution, or Memoirs of Elkanah Watson*. New York: Dana, 1856.

Weeks, Lyman Horace, ed. *The American Turf*. New York: Historical Co., 1898.

Whitney, C. V. *High Peaks*. Lexington: Univ. Press of Kentucky, 1977.

Wickham, Robert S. *A Saratoga Boyhood*. Syracuse: Orange Publishing Co., 1948.

Woodruff, Hiram. *Trotting Horse of America*. 18th ed. Philadelphia: Porter and Coates, 1876.

Young, C. V. P. *Courtney and Cornell Rowing*. Ithaca, N.Y.: Cornell Publications, 1923.

INDEX

Page numbers in italics denote illustrations.

Abbey Hotel (Lansingburg), 35
Accountant, 180
Ace Admiral, 260
Acrobat, 106
Adams, John Quincy, 15, 101
Ada Nay, 179
Adelphi Hotel, xi; construction of, 119; help at, 135; Morrissey at, 121, 266; piazza of, 9; Schultz at, 243
Adirondack Railroad, 58
Adonis, Joe, 245, 246, 247, 260–61, 262
Affirmed, xii, 179, 287–91
Africa, 223
African-American athletes, 23, 192
African American jockeys: antebellum, 9, 23, 164; Civil War era, 44, 32in. 6; postbellum, 66–67, 73, 108, 119–20; in 1880s, 128; in 1890s, 141–43, 144; in early 1900s, 189–91; in 1920s, 226–27; in 1930s, 249; in 1970s, 284
African-American Louisianans, 62
African-American stable owners, 72, 302–3
African-American slaves, 21–22, 44
African-American tourists, 135–36, 156
African-American trainers, 91, 143
Agricultural fairs, 11, 27
Aiken (S.C.), 162, 292
Air conditioning, 178
Air travel, 223
Aknahthon, 241
Alabama Stakes, 99, 143, 148, 299
Alameda, 31
Alan-a-Dale, 189
Alarm, 99
Albany (N.Y.), 17, 18, 172, 224, 311n. 11
Albany Presbyterian Church, 10
Albert (jockey), 73, 74, 94
Alcoholic beverages, 30, 242. *See also* "Antifogmatics"; Bootlegging; Bourbon whiskey; Prohibition; Temperance movement
Aldebaran, 47, 57, 58, 59, 83
Aldridges boarding house (Ballston), 312n. 8

Alexander, Robert A., 73, 74, 75, 157
Alexandre, J. H., 182
Alexandria (Va.), 4
All-Aged Sweepstakes, 126
Allaire, Charley, 33
Allen, Dudley, 141, 143
Aloma's Ruler, 293
Alsab, 251
Altamont (jockey), 9
Alydar, xii, 287–91, 298, 301
Alysheba, 297, 324n. 3a
Ambrose, Eddy, 208
Ambrose, James, 25, 32–33, 61
Amendola, C. J., 255
American Association (baseball), 124, 157
American Bankers Association, 110
American Bar Association, 124
American Derby, 128, 180, 208
American Eclipse, 10, 48, 97
American Economic Association, 129
American Gazetteer (J. Morse), 6–7
American Gothic (G. Wood), 17
American Historical Association, 129
American Hotel (Rip Van Dam Hotel), 9, 48, 135, 326n. 23a
American Jockey Club, 74, 80, 85, 128, 158
American League (baseball), 157, 169, 179
American Locomotive Co., 257
American Museum of Natural History, 187
American Racing Manual, 322n. 9a, 323n. 14
American Revolution, 3, 6, 9
American Stud Book, 158
American Temperance Union, 101
American Tobacco Company, 182, 184
American Turf, The, 138
Americus Club, 30–31, 33
Amherst College, 110
Amsterdam (N.Y.), 165
Anastasia, Albert, 239
Ancient Title, 286
Anderson, George ("Spider"), 143

Anderson, Pete, 278
Andrew M., 199
Andrews, Wayne, 82
Angle Light, 279, 282
Annapolis Races, 4, 9
Annenberg, Moses, 227
Annieswood Stable, 80
Annihilate 'Em, 282, 283
Anthony, Susan B., 177
"Antifogmatics," 1, 2
Anti-Semitism, 117–18, 134, 135, 224
Antley, Chris, 300
A Phenomenon Stakes, 298
Applegate, H. C., 198
Appleton, John, 90
Appleton's Handbook, 37
Appomattox Courthouse, 61, 130
Aqueduct: capacity of, 275; declining attendance at, 298, 302; Kelso at, 272; opening of, 140, 269; simulcasts at, 295, 304
Arcade Building, 129
Arcaro, Eddie, 249; Battlefield and, 260; Citation and, 260; Hoop, Jr. and, 257; Jaipur and, 270; McLaughlin and, 128; Nashua and, 267; retirement of, 273; Whirlaway and, 252, 253, 255
Archer, Fred, 190
Architecture: Greek Revival, 19, 20; Victorian, 136–37, 171, 265–66, 276
Arden, Elizabeth, 260
Aristides, 106, 107, 108, 111, 121
"Arlington Million" (purse), 292, 293, 294
Arlington Park, 229, 292
Armistice, 207, 208
Army of the Potomac, 63
Around the World in Eighty Days (Verne), 150
Arrowhead Inn: in 1920s, 220, 221; in 1930s, 230, 246, 247; in 1940s, 261, 262
Artful, 182, 183, 185
Arthur, Chester A., 79, 129, 130
Arthur Froelich and Associates, 269, 275
Arts and Letters, 277
Asbury, Herbert: on Canfield, 150, 183; on Canfield's Club House, 175, 177, 183; on J. Gates, 178; on C. Mitchell, 169
Ascot Heath (Brooklyn), 4, 303
Ascot Heath (England), 48, 59, 60, 94
Ashe, Arthur, Jr., 191, 192
Ashland Farm, 157
A. S. Rowe's Hoop Skirt Store, 51
Assault, 244, 257, 258
Astaire, Fred, 268
Asteroid, 50, 56, 73, 108
Astor, John Jacob (1763–1848), 52, 116
Astor, John Jacob (1864–1912), 160

Astor, Mrs. Vincent, 230
Astor, William B., 65, 110; death of, 116; U. S. Grant and, 66; C. Vanderbilt and, 230; wealth of, 52
Astor, William W., 119
Astor family, 193
Astor House (N.Y.C.), 37
Athlene, 120
Athlete of the Year award, 287
Athletic Association of American Colleges, 115
Atkinson, Ted, 258, 266, 267
Atlantic Cable, 65
Atlantic City (N.J.), 227
Atlantics (baseball team), 70, 71, 94, 315n. 14
Attila, 106
Auerbach, Ann Hagedorn, 301
Aulisi, J. E., 316n. 8a
Austin, Gene, 239
Australian Totalisators, 237
Automobiles, 165, 175
Away from Holme, 278
Azoturia, 236
Azra, 142
Azucar, 243

Babcock, W. R., 83, 86
Bacon, Henry, 195
Bacon, T. G., 79
Baden-Baden (Germany), 84, 85, 89
Baden Baden, 119
Badgett, Billy, 298, 300
Baeza, Braulio, 276, 277, 278, 285
Bailey, Jerry, 306
Baird, Abingdon, 128
Baker, Frankie, 233
Baker, Hamilton, 89
Baldwin, Elias J. ("Lucky"), 133; estate of, 243; Hildreth and, 227; Los Angeles and, 148; Mollie McCarty and, 121; Volante and, 128
Ball, Evender Berry, 133–34
Ballarat, 154
Ballot, 184
Ballston Spa (N.Y.): boarding house in, 312n. 8; bridge construction in, 18; early history of, 7, 8, 11, 15; Lansky jailed at, 262–63; S. Nott at, 10; vacationers at, 129; H. & E. Williams at, 12, 13
Ballyhoo Bey, 162, 164, 181, 184
Baltimore, 68
Baltimore (Md.), 9
Baltimore and Ohio Railroad, 17
Bancroft, Mrs. Thomas, 276
Banigan, Harry, 156
Bankers, 110
Bank Mills (Calif.), 132–33

Bank of New York, 84

Banshee, 79

Barbarity, 76

Barbee, George, 106, 266, 318n. 23

Barber, C. H., 110

Barhyte, Ann, 27

Barhyte, Jacobus, 12, 15

Barhyte, James, 27

Barhyte, John, 27

Barhyte estate. *See* Yaddo (estate)

Barnes, 128

Barnes, Shelby ("Pike"), 143, 144

Barnum, P. T., 27, 37

Barrera, Laz, 285, 289

Barretto, W. H., 171

Barrie, Paddy, 241, 326n. 23a

Bartlett, Joseph Jackson, 63, 69

Baruch, Bernard, 245, 275

Baseball: accident potential in, 301; in Civil War era, 41, 54, 315n. 4a; collegiate, 102, 110; in early 1900s, 169, 179, 188; in 1880s, 124; in 1840s, 25; in 1890s, 157; English predecessors of, 48; gambling and, 46; New Jersey origins of, 146; in postbellum era, 70–71, 94, 114; press coverage of, 34; *Sporting World* on, 145. *See also* World Series

Basketball, 157

Batcheller, Catharine, 106

Batcheller, George, 106

Bateau, 225

Bath (Va.), 3, 4

Bathing, 245

Battlefield, 260

Bayakoa, 300

Bayard, Thomas, 53

Bayonet, 84

Bayswater, 75

Beacon Course (Hoboken), 25, 31, 146

Beard, Louie, 248

Beau Prince, 274

Beauregard, Gustave T., 39

Beaut (clubhouse worker), 191, 194, 224

Bejshak, Johnny, 244

Belair Stud, 228, 238, 267, 276

Beldame, 185

Bell, Alexander Graham, 115

Belle Meade (Tenn.), 157

Belle of Runnymede, 143

Bellesoeur, 260

Belmont, August: death of, 140; equipage of, 74; Glenelg and, 83, 86; Harry Bassett–Longfellow race and, 97; Kingfisher and, 88, 90; Landon and, 91–92; Lorillards and, 125; Morrissey club house and, 85; at Pimlico, 100;

posthumous sale of, 182, 222; Ronalds and, 75; rumored syndicate and, 137; stable of, 77, 96, 97; Sultana and, 116; track named for, 181; W. C. Whitney and, 159, 161; Woodbine and, 99

Belmont, August, II, 140; Beldame and, 185; Canfield and, 179; death of, 222; Fair Play and, 188, 197; Hildreth and, 198, 227; Jockey Club and, 158, 167, 172, 199; joint land purchase of, 180, 181; polo and, 196–97; Powers-Hunter Co. and, 206; private training park of, 172–73; J. T. Sloan and, 163–64; J. Widener and, 223

Belmont, August, III, 222

Belmont, August, IV, 298

Belmont, Eleanor Robson, 205

Belmont, George, 222

Belmont, Perry, 172, 182, 194

Belmont family, 174, 222–23

Belmont Park racetrack: attendance at, 286, 298, 302; Breeders' Cup at, 300; cash value of, 297; fires at, 222; modernization of, 223, 277; opening of, 181; reopening of, 197; Ruffian buried at, 285; Secretariat at, 279–81; Shilling dead at, 194–95; Travers Stakes at, 55; in World War II era, 255, 256, 257

Belmont Stakes: cash value of, 204; Dwyer victories in, 128; first, 76, 83; Kentucky Derby and, 107; McDaniel victories in, 113; at Morris Park, 139, 146

Ben Ali, 132

Ben Brush, 142, 197

"Benicia Boy." *See* Heenan, John Camel

Bennett, James Gordon, Jr., 196

Bennett, James Gordon, Sr., 26, 35; on hospitality, 313n. 22; sports journalism and, 25, 313n. 2b; at United States Hotel, 21

Benning (D.C.), 187

Benton, James, 103

Beppo, 25

Berghaus, Albert, 105, 112

Bergman, Ingrid, 257

Berkshire County (Mass.), 11

Bernie, Ben, 246

Best Blush, 297

Best Friend of Charleston (locomotive), 17

Betsey Baker, 15

Better Self, 259

Betting. *See* Gambling

Betts, Toney (Anthony Zito), 324n. 7c; on crooked practices, 218–19, 236; on Depression, 234, 237; on T. E. Dewey, 268; on Masseria, 227; on pari mutuel betting, 251; on Racing Commission, 241; on Rothstein, 217; F. Sullivan and, 242; on Tobin, 216; on women, 240; on World War II, 250

Bet Twice, 297
Bewitch, 260
Beyer, Andrew, 289, 295
"Bicycle Bob" (B. Pastor), 250
Bicycling, 159
Big A. *See* Aqueduct
Biglin brothers, 93
Big Red. *See* Man o' War; Secretariat
Big Red Spring, 78
Billings, C. K. G., 203
Billy Kelly, 203
Bird, Bill, 44, 47, 127, 128, 143
Birmingham, Stephen, 118, 135
Bitter Root Stock Farm (Mont.), 157, 167
Black Bess, 29
"Black Demon" (J. Lee), 190
Black Hawk, 29
Black jockeys. *See* African-American jockeys
Black Maria, 23, 225
Black Slave, 94
"Black Sox" (baseball team), 216
Black Stallion series (Farley), 259, 269
Blair, Frank, 63, 69
Blair, Gist, 313n. 12
Blanc, François, 85, 86
Blenheim II, 253–54
"Block men," 239
Blue Girl, 165, 168
Blue Goose Stable, 296
Blues, 165, 189
Bly, Nellie, 150, 151–56, 158, 239; C. Mitchell and, 151–52, 169
Boardman, 124
Board of Control, 146, 147, 157
Boat-racing. *See* Rowing
Bohemia Stable, 272
Bold Forbes, 278
Bold Ruler, 278, 279, 284
Bold Venture, 244, 257
Bonaparte, Joseph (King of Spain), 15
"Bookmaker's Wheel" (game), 151
Bookmaking: in 1870s, 94–95, 97, 118–19; in 1890s, 144–45, 146–47, 148, 154–55; in early 1900s, 165–66, 193, 275; in World War I era, 199; in 1920s, 218, 219, 220; in 1930s, 238–39, 250, 251
Booth, John, 311n. 11
Booth, John Wilkes, 62, 63
Bootlegging, 216, 223
Borrow, 201
Boston, 10, 23, 24, 46, 83
Bostwick, George (Pete), 234
Bourbon whiskey, 44
Bowdoin College, 116
Bowen, Edward, 291

Bowie, Oden, 53, 82, 97, 100
Bowie Public Library (Md.), 228
Bowling, 26
Bowmar, Dan, 180, 181, 196
Boxing. *See* Prizefighting
Brackett, Edgar Truman, 158, 169, 195
Braddock, James Joseph, 250
Bradford, J. A., 182
Bradley, Edward R., 247
Bradley, Hugh, 324n. 6c; on betting, 192; on "Dutch Book," 147; on Grannon, 166; on racism, 317n. 18; on Rothstein, 218; on sales, 247; on J. T. Sloan, 164; at United States Hotel, 242; on E. B. Wall, 134
Brady, James Cox, 278
Brady, Jim ("Diamond Jim"), 139, 158, 175; Accountant and, 180; Oiseau and, 185–86; J. T. Sloan and, 163
Brady, Matthew, 55, 63–64, 67
Brady, Nicholas, 284
Bramble, 126, 197
Brazil, 223
Breakers (Newport), 132, 161
Breakfasts, 247
Breakfast Stakes, 87
Breeders' Cup, 293, 294, 300, 301
Breeders' Cup Distaff Race, 300
Breslin, James, 82, 90, 118, 318n. 6
Bridgeland, J. A., 90
Brigand, 113
Brighton Beach, 187, 195
British racing. *See* English racing
Broad Street, 7
Broadview Lodge (Surrey), 224, 238
Bronx, 74, 160
Brook (nightclub), 219, 220; establishment of, 216; fire in, 246; in 1920s, 217; in 1930s, 234
Brookdale Farm (N.J.), 197, 200, 235
Brooklyn, 4, 70, 94, 303
Brooklyn Dodgers, 280
Brooklyn Jockey Club, 140
Brookmeade Farm, 238, 274
Brooks, C., 249
Brookside (Saratoga County History Center), 312n. 8
Broomstick, 157; Burns and, 189; Regret and, 199; Sysonby vs., 185, 186–87; Whisk Broom II and, 197
Brown, Ed, 119, 120
Brown, Sam, 186, 197
Brown Bud, 225
Brown University, 108, 109
Brush, Ben, 193
Bryan, Alexander, 6

Bryan, David, 26, 28, 29
Bryan, John, 6
Bryan, William Jennings, 160
Buchanan, 128
Buchanan, James, 101
Buckpasser, 179, 276
Buford, Abe, 90, 107
"Builders" (gamblers), 240
Bull, George H., 227; bathing by, 245; death of,
    256; dinner given by, 234; grounds improved by,
    212–13, 220; F. Roosevelt and, 230, 231; stall
    gate installed by, 228
Bull Lea, 253, 258, 259
Burch, Elliott, 274, 277
Burch, Preston, 274
Burgomaster, 180, 183
Burgoyne, Billy, 83; in Congress Spring Purse, 58;
    defeats of, 45, 46, 47; in Saratoga Cup, 68; in
    Travers, 56
Burgoyne, John, 6, 7, 45, 47
Burlew, Fred, 194, 321n. 6
Burns, Tommy, 189, 191
Burnt Hills Handicap, 236
Burr, Aaron, 14
Burrell, Lewis, Sr., 302–3
Burrell, Louis, 303
Burrell, Stanley, 302, 303
Busiris, 10
"Bute" (phenylbutazone), 301
Butler, Benjamin ("Beast"), 42, 63
Butler, James, 199, 201, 203, 225
Byrnes, Matt, 202
Byron, George Gordon, 99
Byzantine, 241

Cady, Steve, 280
Caesar, Julius, 130
Café Lena, 276
Cafés-tabacs, 95
Cairngorm, 180
Calhoun, John, 63
California, 31, 35; breeding in, 174; Muybridge re-
    search in, 113; purse distribution in, 253; racing
    associations in, 72; racing in, 23, 77, 237, 255;
    visitors from, 132–33
California Stakes, 133
Callahan, Johnny, 219
Call the Witness, 273
Calumet Farm, 258, 274, 277, 324n. 3a; Alydar and,
    287, 301; Citation and, 259, 260; Twilight Tear
    and, 256; Whirlaway and, 253
Cambridge University, 103
Camden (N.J.), 24

Cameron, A. S., 119
Cameron, Mary, 241
Cammack, Addison, 113
Campbell (owner), 144
Campfire, 203
Canada Southern Railroad, 131
Canadian horses, 42
Canadian owners, 174
Canadian racing, 169, 192, 195
Canadian steeplechasing, 97
Canfield (card game), 178
Canfield, Richard Albert, 175–79, 220, 251, 263;
    J. Gates and, 175, 176, 177–78; memorials to,
    183–84; C. Mitchell and, 169; Oiseau and, 186;
    Rothstein and, 217
Canfield's Club House, 188, 195; Bly and, 151; ex-
    pansion of, 178; garden of, 179; Historical So-
    ciety in, 183–84; A. P. Knapp and, 159; redec-
    oration of, 177; J. T. Sloan and, 164; success
    of, 150, 175
Canonero II, 279, 281
Cantor, Eddie, 221, 230
Cap and Bells, 162
Capitoline Ball Ground, 70
Capone, Al, 227, 237
Capote, Truman, 266
Captain Alcock, 207
Captain Moore, 44, 45–46, 59, 68
Carbine, 244
Carfano, Anthony ("Little Augie Pisano"), 227
Carmencita, 31
Carnegie, Andrew, 159
Carpenter, Rachel, 304
"Carpet joints," 246–47
Carroll, Virginia, 145
Carry Back, 274
Caruso, Enrico, 175
Casino (Newport), 129, 161
Casino (Saratoga). See Canfield's Club House
Casinos. See Gambling
Cassidy, George, 220, 227, 232, 324n. 11
Cassidy, Mars, 186, 202–3, 208, 212, 227
Cassidy, Marshall, 227
Cassidy, Wendell, 227
Castleton Farm (Ky.), 157, 184, 196
Cathcart, Robert, Jr., 119, 156
Catholic Church, 152
Catholic High School, 7, 60
Catholic immigrants, 30
Caughnawaga, 165
Cauthen, Steve ("Kid"), 287, 289
Cavalcade, 238, 243–44
Cavanagh, John G., 165, 167, 238, 239
"Cavanagh Special" (train), 165, 167, 216, 238

Caveat, 298
Celt, 196, 325n. 1
Central Catholic High School, 7, 60
Central New York Railroad. *See* New York Central Railroad
Central Park (N.Y.C.), 19, 25, 42
Centreville (N.Y.), 15
Chamberlin, Johnny, 84, 100, 111, 116
Chance Shot, 225
Change poles, 240
Charade, 143
Charles Fleischmann's Sons' (firm), 165, 166
Charleston (S.C.), 10, 13, 39
Charleston (steamer), 121
Charles Town (W. Va.), 240
Charley Riley, 59
Charlie Potatoes (dog), 273
Charon, 299
Checkmate, 126, 128
Chenery, Christopher, 279
Chenery, Helen (Penny), 279, *280*, 327n. 1b
Chesapeake, 107
"Chestnuts" (calluses), 241
Chicago, 184, 224
Chicago Black Sox (baseball team), 216
Chicago Club, 150, 216, 243, 261
Chief's Crown, 179, 294
Children: in 1890s, 153–54, 156, 159; in early 1900s, 173–74; in 1920s, 226; in 1980s, 293
Chilton, B. A., 159
Chinn, Herbert, 255
Chloral hydrate, 236
Chocolate Soldier. *See* Equipoise
Chompion, 277
Christiana Farm, 298
Christmas Handicap, 243
Chuckle, 235
Churchill, Henry, 107
Churchill, Jennie, 75, 107, 116, 161
Churchill, John, 107
Churchill, John Winston Spencer, 107, 161
Churchill, Randolph, 107, 116
Churchill, Winston, 107, 140, 268
Churchill Downs. *See* Kentucky Derby
Chutes, 77–78, 124, 171
Cincinnati Reds (baseball team), 157
Citation, 259–60, 274, 278
City and Suburban Handicap, 125
City College of New York, 115–16, 118
City Hall (Saratoga), 20, 110, 124, 169
City of Troy (steamer), 30
Civil War, 41, 60, 84; conclusion of, 61–62, 63, 69; Doubleday in, 188; explosives in, 51; inception of, 39; Jersey Derby and, 180; outlaws

in, 193; thoroughbred scarcity in, 56; turf records and, 83; veterans of, 130
Claiborne Farm (Ky.), 196, 228, 267, 279
Clair, Henry, 134
Clare, Tom, 232
Clarendon Hall, 51, 60, 117, 118, 135
Clark, Billy J., 11
Clark, Mrs. F. Ambrose, 227
Clark, M. Lewis, 107
Clark, Samuel Adams, 226
Clarke, John, 19, 20
Clarks Corners (N.Y.), 11
Clay, Henry, 21, 61, 157
Clay, John, 44, 56, 79, 107
Clayton, Alonzo, 142, *143*
Clergy, 15, 26, 90, 263
Cleveland, Grover, 129, 130, 160, 181
Clinton, George, 2, 3, 4
Clodian [Clodion?], 248, 326n. 12
Clover Bottom track, 10
Club houses. *See* Gambling
Club sandwiches, 178
Cobb, Ty, 207, 211
Cochrane, John, 79
Coe, S. W., 90
Coe, W. R., 212
Coldstream, 249
Cole, James M., 27
Colfax, Schuyler, 51
Colin, 187–88; Fair Play vs., 197, 205; M. Lilly and, *189*; McKinney and, 196; Man o' War and, 209; Regret and, 199
College of the City of New York, 115–16, 118
College sports, 102–6, 108–10, 115–16
Colonial Affair, 307
Colston, 190
Colston, Raleigh, 143, 190
Colt (judge), 53
Columbian Hotel, 71
Columbian Spring, 7
Columbia University, 105, 109, 115, 116
Columbin, Jean, 178
Combs, Leslie, II, 267, 296
Comiskey, Charlie, 157
Commanche Trail, 306
Commando, 187, 219, 325n. 1
Communist Manifesto, 33
Community Theater, 266
Comstock, Anthony, 136, 158
Concern, *306*
Coney Island Jockey Club, 128, 139, 140
Confederate Army, 193; generals, 130; officers, 195; troops, 41, 51
Congress. *See* United States Congress

Congress Hall: Breslin at, 82; Canfield land adjoining, 179; in Civil War era, 43, 53; construction of, 7, 312n. 16b; demolition of, 195; fire in, 71; Grant at, 66; Jews and, 118; Milbert drawing of, 8; piazzas of, 9, 20, 78; postbellum party at, 63; railroad magnates at, 106; reconstruction of, 78, 82; Sykes at, 16; C. Vanderbilt at, 84; Western Union office of, 53, 65; wing added to, 60
Congress Hall stakes race, 143, 162
Congress Park, 19–20; casino proposed in, 179; expansion of, 195; memorial gate in, 184; music at, 175; in postbellum era, 64
Congress Spring, 8, 19; discovery of, 6; Hathorn No. 1 and, 78; Kentuckians and, 44, purgative qualities of, 133; Sickles at, 48; tubing of, 7
Congress Spring Purse, 58
Congress Theater, 230
Congress Water, 18–19, 63, 129
Conley, Jess, 190
Conn, Billy, 250
Conquistador Cielo, 293, 294
Continental Congress, 312n. 4
Convention Hall, 150, 245
Conventions, 110
Cook, Fred J., 241
Cook, Mary, 194
Cooper, Albert, 143
Cooper, Gary, 257
Cooper, James Fenimore, 101
Cooperstown Hall of Fame, 188
Copeland, E., 106, 110
Cordero, Angel, Jr.: Chief's Crown and, 294; Cryptoclearance and, 298; Krone and, 303; Shake Shake Shake and, 289; M. Smith vs., 302; Velasquez and, 290
Cornelius (jockey), 23, 46
Cornell University, 293, 319nn. 4, 18; in track and field, 106, 110; in regattas, 103, 108, 109, 115, 124
Corning, Erastus, 49
Corning, Mrs. Parker, 249
Corrigan, Ed, 133, 140, 195
Corticosteroids, 301
Costello, Frank, 217, 246, 255, 262
"Cottages," 136–37, 265–66, 276
Cottrill, William, 79, 80, 99, 107
Council Bluffs (Iowa), 247
Counterfeit money, 240
Count Fleet, 228–29, 272
County fairs, 11, 27
Court Dress, 184
Courtney, Charles, 102, 106, 114, 124, 319n. 4
Cowan, Bill, 166
Coxe, Rebecca, 10–11

Coxe, Tench, 11
Crash of 1929, 228
Crawford, Frank, 84, 117
Crewman, 271
Cricket (game), 48, 70, 179, 188
Crickmore, H. G., 84, 127, 168–69, 315n. 7a, 317n. 21
Crickmore, 127, 128
Crime, 218–19. See also Fraud; Racketeering
Crimean War, 33
Criminal Type, 298, 300
Crist, Steve, 298–99, 300
Croll, Jimmy, 304, 306–7
Crosby, Bing, 221, 230, 243, 268
Cross and Dunn (comedy duo), 261
Crowninshield, Frank, 316n. 8a
Crowther, Samuel, Jr., 105, 108, 109
Cruguet, Jean, 277
Cryptoclearance, 298
Cubans, 53, 64
Cunningham, Dad, 31
Curiosity, 195
Currency question, 160
Currier and Ives prints: of Longfellow–Harry Bassett race, xii, 96, 99; of Morrissey, 32; of Saratoga, 90; of Sweeney, 242
Cushman, C. V. B., 224
Custer, George Armstrong, 115
C. V. Whitney Farm (Ky.), 157

Daily Double, 253
Daily Racing Form, 271, 322n. 9
Daingerfield, Algernon, 171
Dake, Bill, 276
Dalmatian, 194
Dalton, Joe, 276
Dal Verme, Francesco, 1
Daly, Marcus, 157, 167, 168, 184
Daly, Mike, 205, 206
Damascus, 276
Dance King, 296
Dance Spell, 286
Dandelion, 186, 189
Dangerous, 76, 227
Daniel, William, 220
Dark Secret, 238
Dark Star, 264
D'Artagnan, 112
Dartmouth College, 115, 116
Daughters of the American Revolution, 101
David Harum, 212
Davidson, John, 49, 61
Davies, Tommy, 211
Davis, Theodore R., 104

Day, Pat, 297, 298
"Days of the Slates," 238–41
Dead heats, 253
Death on the Pale Horse (B. West), 12
Defender, 97
De Fichy, Lou, 273
Dehere, 303
De Kwiatkowski, Henryk, 294, 301
Delahoussaye, Eddie, 190
Delano family, 53
Delaware Park, 253, 255, 295
Delhi, 180, 196
Del Mar track, 253, 292
Delmonico's restaurant, 177
Delmonico's (club). *See* Piping Rock (Saratoga);
    Riley's Lake House
Democratic Party: A. Belmont and, 74; A. Bel-
    mont II and, 172; Kefauver and, 262; McKinley
    election and, 161; in New York City, 34, 74, 79,
    114; New York governorship and, 234; in Sar-
    atoga, 159; W. C. Whitney and, 172, 181
Democratic State Committee, 160
Demorest's Dress Making Establishment, 51
Dempsey, Jack, 221–22, 245
Derby (Epsom Downs), 9, 168, 304
DeSpirito, Tony, 189, 266
Devil His Due, 307
Dewey, Melville, 135
Dewey, Thomas E., 246, 261, 262, 268
Dexter, 65
Diamond, Jack ("Legs"), 217, 243
Diana Handicap, *303*
Dick (jockey), 10, 73, 74
Diets, 302
Dinnen, John, 51
Dinner Party Stakes, 82, 87
Diomed, 9–10, 23
Discovery, 243–44
Discrimination. *See* Anti-Semitism; Racial
    discrimination
Diseases, 1, 245
Disowned, 29
Display, 220
District of Columbia, 9, 14, 21, 37
Diuretics, 301
Dr. Bedortha's Water Cure, 51
Dr. Fager, 276
Dodgers (baseball team), 280
Dominant, 196, 201
Domino: Colin and, 188; Commando and, 187;
    A. Cooper and, 143; earnings of, 144, 184;
    Henry of Navarre vs., 145–46; Man o' War
    and, 215; Zev and, 219
Donaldson, Walter, 219

Donerail, 201
Don Juan, 55
Donnacona, 207, 208, 212, 213, 220
Dos Passos, John, 240
Doswell, Thomas W., *77*, 96, 97, 113
Doto, Giuseppe. *See* Adonis, Joe
Doubleday, Abner, 25, 94, 179, 188; birth of, 13; at
    Fort Sumter, 39
Doubleday, Ulysses, 13
Dowd, Charles, 129, 195
Dowling, Francis, 36
Downs, W. H., 106, 115, 116
Draft riots (1863), 41, 74
Drake, John, 175
Dreicer's jewelry store, 134
Dreiser, Theodore, 240
Drew, Daniel, 52, 58–59, 61
Drexel, Elizabeth, 130, 135
Drexel, Joseph W., 129, 160
Drug use, 47, 218, 236, 301
"Dublin" (Third Ward), 30, 245
Ducat, 156
"Duck-shooers," 240
Dugan, Eddie, 194
Duke, James Buchanan, 182, 184
Duke of Magenta, *125*
Duller, George, 226
Duncan, Sam, 79–80
Dunham, A. C., 28
Dunne, Finley Peter, 181
Dunnigan, John, 251
DuPont, Allaire, 272
DuPont, Mrs. Allaire, 273
DuPont, William O., 224
DuPont family, 245
Durnell, Charles E., *173*
Durso, Joseph, 221, 292, 305, 306
Duryea, Herman, 169–70, 182, 274
"Dutch Book," 147
Dutchess County, 23
Dwyer, Mike, 126–28, 180, 271; betting "commis-
    sioners" of, 145; Brooklyn Jockey Club and, 140;
    at California Stakes, 133
Dwyer, Phil, 126–28, 180, 271; Brooklyn Jockey
    Club and, 140; Saratoga Association and, 172,
    182; at Saratoga Club (N.Y.C.), 175
Dyes, 241
Dylan, Bob, 276

Eakins, Thomas, 93
Earl, Chaffee, 228
Earley, Matthew, 143, *144*
Early, 190

Eastern Echo, 300

Eastland Farms, 224

East-West Stable, 286

Easy Goer, 298, 300

Ebbets, Charles, 188

Eckford baseball team, 41

Eclipse (eighteenth century), 4, 9

Eclipse (nineteenth century), 56, 76, 99, 180, 227

Eclipse Award, 271, 307; Eclipse Grass Horse award, 292–93

Edison, Thomas, 134

Eider, 226, 227

Eight-Thirty, 249

Eisenhower, Dwight D., 66

Electric lighting, 134, 178

Elevated railways. *See* Street railways

Elias, 29

Elizabeth II, Queen of England, 268

Elmendorf Farm (Ky.), 157, 223

Elysian Fields (N.Y.C.), 25, 41

Emancipation Proclamation, 41

Emerson, Ralph Waldo, 70

Emperor of Norfolk, 128

Empire City track, 188, 199

Endurance by Right, 168

Engineer II, 28

English gambling, 94, 118

English horses, 4, 9, 40, 195

English polo, 196

English racing: birthday rule in, 72; cruelty avoided in, 14; Mellon and, 274; Omaha and, 244; prizefighting and, 36; riding posture in, 164; Sanford and, 114; tracks for, 77; H. P. Whitney and, 197; W. C. Whitney and, 162, 168, 181

English rowing, 103

English sports, 48

English steeplechasing, 97

English stock farms, 157

English troops, 2, 3, 4, 6

Enquirer, 88

Entertainment market, 293

Epsom Downs (Derby), 9, 168, 304

Equipoise, 234, 237; in Santa Anita Handicap, 243; Shut Out and, 255; sire of, 196; Twenty Grand vs., 235, 236, 253

Erdenheim (Pa.), 223

Erie Railroad Company, 82

Espino, 225

Eustis, J. B., 106

Evans, Nat, 216

Excelsior Spring, 78

Exchange Hotel (Richmond), 94

Exclusive Native, 287

Exterminator, 203; Fourstardave and, 307; Kelso and, 272; in Saratoga Cup, 219; Sir Barton vs., 213, 215; sire of, 195

Fair Grounds (New Orleans), 248

Fair Play: Display and, 220; Golden Broom and, 207; Man o' War and, 188, 205; retirement of, 197; Sporting Blood and, 218; Stromboli and, 203

Fairview Stud (Tenn.), 174

Falsetto, 125

Fanny Holton, 121

Faraway Farm (Ky.), 249

Farish, Libby Rice, 285

Farley, Walter, 259, 269

Faro (game), 177–78

Farrell, Frank, 194

Fashion, 24

Fashion Course (Newton), 40, 42

Fasig Tipton Company: Bitter Root Farm and, 167; Cushman and, 224; Keeneland sales and, 256; outdoor auctions of, 206; Reed and, 174; Sabath and, 251; Tranter and, 201; visits to, 219; in World War II era, 255

Fator, Laverne, 225

Fellowcraft, 106

Female impersonators, 242

Fenelon, 251, 273

Fenway Park (Boston), 147

Ferber, Edna, 257

Ferguson, Andy, 211

Fernandez, Lolita, 31

Feustel, Louis, 205

Field athletics, 105–6, 110, 115–16

Fillmore, Millard, 28

Filly Triple Crown winners, 285

Financial crises. *See* Panics

Financiers. *See* Bankers

Fink, Jules, 268

Finn, 219

Fires, 51, 64, 71, 244, 246

Firestone, Bertram, 286, 291

Firestone, Mrs. Russell, 267

Firpo, Luis Angel, 221

"First Call," 72

Fisher, H. C. ("Bud"), 219

Fisk, Jim, 82, 84

Fit to Fight, 294

Fitzgerald, C. J., 171

FitzGerald, John J., 223

Fitzgerald, Thomas, 284

Fitzsimmons, James ("Sunny Jim"): earnings of, 234; Gallant Fox and, 228; Nashua and, 267;

Fitzsimmons, James (*continued*)
    Omaha and, 244; retirement of, 273; watch
    of, 268; Wheatley Stable and, 238
Flash Stakes, 180
Flatbush, 188
Flat Rock Spring, 7
Fleetwing, 57, 58, 69
Flegenheim, Arthur (Dutch Schultz), 217, 243
Fleischmann, J., 174
Fleischmann's Sons' (firm), 165, 166
Floral Fetes, 150
Floral Park (L.I.), 181
Flora Temple, 38
Florentine statuary, 179
Food and Drug Administration (FDA), 301
Foolish Pleasure, 179, *284*, 285, 286
Football, 94, 103
Ford, Henry, 222, 223
Ford's Theater (D.C.), 62
Forego, 273, 285–87, 328n. 5a
Forli, 285
Forrest, Nathan Bedford, 90
Forsyth, John, 21
Fort Saratoga, 2
Fort Sumter, 39
Fort Wagner, 44
Forty-Niner, 298
Forward Pass, 276–77
Foster, Stephen, 25, 28, 38
Fourstardave, 307
Fox, Della, 134
Fox, Norm, 276, 314n. 10b, 320n. 41
France: horse exports to, 195; horse imports from,
    197; musicians from, 178; pari-mutuel betting
    in, 95, 111; racing in, 168, 190, 195, 196, 223; in
    Revolutionary War, 3; stock farms in, 157;
    waiters from, 151; water exports of, 18–19
Francis, Tommy, 239
Franklin Square, 20
Fraud, 70, 128
French, Daniel Chester, 195
Froelich, Arthur, 269, 275
Fryer (police officer), 136
Furosemide, 301
Futurity (race), 139, 144, 193, 198

Gallahadion, 253
Gallant Fox, 228–*29*, 230, 248, 325n. 3; Assault
    and, 258; earnings of, 234; Granville and, 248;
    Jim Dandy vs., xii, 232–33; Nashua and, 267;
    Omaha and, 244, 273; Runyon and, 231; Sec-
    retariat and, 282
Gallant Sir, 237

Gallavant, 187
Gambling: antebellum, 26; Civil War era, 42,
    46–47; postbellum, 64, 70, 72–73, 84, 88–90,
    113; in 1880s, 127–28, 136, 137; in 1890s, 139, 145,
    150, 151–56, 158, 159; in early 1900s, 175, 176,
    179, 183, 192; World War I era, 199; in 1920s,
    216, 221, 223–24; in 1930s, 230–31, 234, 238–39,
    243, 246–47, 249–50; in 1940s, 258, 261–62. *See
    also* Bookmaking; Faro (game); Offtrack bet-
    ting; Pari-mutuel betting; Pool sales; Women
    bettors
Ganderluch, Dr., 16
Garden State Track, 255
Garfield, James A., 76, 129
Garrison, Edward ("Snapper"), 133, 140–41, *164*
Garryowen, 59
Gartland's Tenth Regiment Band, 175
Gas lighting, 58
Gate Dancer, 294
Gates, Horatio, 6
Gates, John ("Bet-a-Million"), 150, 248, 275; Can-
    field and, 175, 176, 177–78, 179; Durnell and,
    173; High Chancellor and, 172
Gato Del Sol, 293
Gaver, John, 266
Gay, George, 223
Geisha, 263
General Assembly, 291, 299
General Butler, 42
General Electric Company, 257, 326n. 25
General Harney, 112, 130
Genuine Risk, 201, 292, 298
George Mayer's Lager Beer Saloon, 51
German Americans, 58, 135
Germany: Haggin horses in, 195; immigrants
    from, 30; mercenaries from, 3; spas in, 245; in
    World War I, 199; in World War II, 250, 255,
    257
Gerry, Martha, 285
Getty, J. Paul, 221
Gettysburg, Battle of, 41, 48, 63
Geyelin, H. Laussat, 110
Giants (baseball team), 217
Gideon Putnam Hotel, 8, 245, 266
Gilcoyne, Thomas, *283*, 317n. 21, 32n. 6, 323n.
    23b
Gillie, 248
Gilman, John, 312n. 4
Gilman, Nicholas, 6
Gilpatrick (G. W. Patrick), 23, 83, 84; in Beppo–
    Lady Suffolk race, 25; black opponents of, 74;
    in Boston-Fashion race, 24; in Civil War
    races, 46, 47; in Harry Bassett–Longfellow
    race, 98; in Match Day race, 83; on post-Civil

War double bill, 68, 69; J. Rowe and, 187; San Francisco race and, 114; in Saratoga Cup, 68; in Sequel Stakes, 58, 76; Swim and, 91; in Travers, 56, 73; Ycaza and, 274–75

Gilpin, John, 97

Glencoe (imported), 23

Glencoe (J. Morgan), 40

Glenelg, 83, 86, 87

Glen Mitchell, 105–6, 110, 115, 137

Glen Riddle Farm (Md.), 206

Go for Gin, 305

Go for Wand, 298, 299–300, 302

Goldberg, Henry, 227

Golden Broom: Jeffords purchase of, 206; Man o' War vs., 208, 210, 211; at Riddle farm, 324n. 6b; trial of, 207

Golden Gloves (boxing), 250

Gold market, 84

Gold rush, 31

Goldsborough, Jack, 202

Goldsmith, 165

Gold standard, 160

Goldstein, Sophie, 320n. 41

Golf, 159, 196, 245

Gone with the Wind (film), 248

Gooch, Vivian, 323n. 3

Goodwin's Official Annual Turf Guide, 164

Gordon, Waxey (I. Wexler), 217

Gorgeous, 300

Gotham Book Mart, 240

Gould, Jay, 110; gold market and, 84; J. R. Keene and, 184; at Monmouth Park, 94; C. Vanderbilt and, 82; W. C. Whitney and, 160

Graf, Steffi, xii

Graham, Elizabeth Arden, 260

Graham, Frank, 264

Grand Union Handicap, 126, 143

Grand Union Hotel, 7, 91; anti-Semitism at, 117, 118, 134, 135; college ribbons at, 103; Courtney at, 102; Harrison at, 135, 321n. 24; Hyams at, 239, 250; McGrath at, 100; Morrissey and, 320n. 41; in 1930s, 242; in 1920s, 219; piazza of, 265; Pittsburgh Symphony at, 175; J. T. Sloan at, 163–64; Stewart purchase of, 90; S. Trask at, 136; E. B. Wall at, 133, 134; women at, 151. *See also* Union Hall; Union Hotel

Grand Union Hotel Stakes, 165, 211

Grannon, Riley, 145, 156, 166

Grant, Julia Dent, 66, 130

Grant, Ulysses S.: at Appomattox Courthouse, 61, 63, 130; at "College Games," 106; at Congress Hall, 66; death of, 130, 132; General Harney and, 112, 130; inauguration of, 79; at Jerome Park, 75; at Mount McGregor, 129–

30, 131; at RAAC regatta, 104; at Union Hotel, 82; at Vicksburg, 41

Grant's Cottage, 129–30, 131

Granville, 244, 248, 273

Gravesend Bay: in 1880s, 140; in 1890s, 144, 145, 163; in early 1900s, 146, 169, 174, 195

Gray Ghost. *See* Native Dancer

Great Depression, 230, 232, 237, 240, 253

Greater New York Association. *See* New York Racing Association

Great Metropolitan Handicap, 125

Great Republic Stakes, 185–87

Great Trial (race), 170

Greek Money, 270

Greek Revival architecture, 19, 20

Greeley, Horace, 33, 58, 63, 67, 70; candidacy of, 69; draft riots and, 41; moralism of, 122

Green Cave (club), 246

Greene, Caroline, 216

Greene, R. A., 115

Greentree Stable, 238, 274; Byzantine and, 241; Elmendorf Farm and, 157; formation of, 222; Shut Out and, 255; Tom Fool and, 266; in World War II era, 257

Grenada, 127

Greyhound, 10

Grey Lag, 218

Gridley, Robert, 26

Griffiths, Judge, 175

Grinstead, James A., 56, 107, 112

Grisette, 143

Guerin, Eric, 260, 266, 318n. 23

Guttenberg Race Track, 138, 146, 147, 193

Guys and Dolls (musical), 17, 42

Haggin, James Ben Ali, 132; horses sold by, 195; Mackay sale and, 174; Salvator and, 140; stock farms of, 157, 201, 223; Water Color and, 165; W. C. Whitney and, 167

Hagley, 278

Hail to Reason, 274, 276

Hall, A. Oakey, 91

Hall, J. L., 171

Hallandale (Fla.), 247

Hall of Fame (Cooperstown), 188

Hall of Fame (Saratoga). *See* National Museum of Racing and Hall of Fame

Hall of Springs, 245

Halma, 142

Ham, Elizabeth, 327n. 1b

Hamburg, 159, 162, 167–68; Burgomaster and, 180, 183; Jersey Lightning and, 199; H. P. Whitney purchase of, 182

Hamburg Place, 324n. 3a
Hamill, Jim, 41
Hamilton, Alexander, 7
Hamilton, Anthony, 144
Hamilton, James, 115
Hamilton Spring, 7
Hammer, M. C. *See* Burrell, Stanley
Hancock, A. B., 196, 228, 253
Hancock, Seth, 279
"Handbooks" (bookmakers), 218
Handicapping. *See* Gambling
Handicap Triple Crown winners, 266, 272, 294
Hanford, Carl, 272
Hanover, 157, 187
Harbor View Farm, 287
Harbut, Will, 249, 259
Harhill, Alex, 285
Hark (trainer), 22–23
Harlan, James, 52
Harlem Club, 246
Harlem Railroad, 43, 58–59, 117
Harness racing. *See* Trotting races
Harney, J. M., 112
Harper, Frank, 120
Harper, John: J. Hunter and, 90–91; jockey of, 95,
    99; on Longfellow, 93, 99; Nantura Stud and,
    157; photograph of, *92;* sign displayed by, 94
Harriman, Marie, 237
Harriman, W. Averell, 223, 224, 237, 268
Harrison, Benjamin, 118, 135, 32In. 24
Harry Bassett: Longfellow vs., xii, 88–100, 227,
    287; Preakness-Springbok race and, 113;
    Preakness vs., 102; Regret and, 199; sire of,
    93, 108, 157; at Supper Stakes, 87; Sysonby
    and, 187; Upset and, 209
Harry Clay, 65
Harry Scott, 236
Hartack, Bill, 189, 266, 267
Harte, Bret, 97, 117–18, 320n. 41
Harvard University: in football, 103; RAAC
    abandoned by, 109–10, 115; in regattas, 102,
    103, 104–5, 109; in track athletics, 116
Hastings, 197, 205
Hathorn, Frank, 137
Hathorn, H. H., 78, 82
Hathorn No. 1 (spring), 78
Hatton, Charles, 229, 325n. 3
Hatton, Gail, 325n. 3
Haughton, Edward, Jr., 255
Havana (Cuba), 247
Havemeyer, William, 184
Havre de Grace track, 194, 215
Hawkins, Abe, 74, 83; in Congress Spring Purse,
    58; on postbellum double bill, 67, 68, 69;

J. Rowe and, 187; in Sequel Stakes, 58; in slav-
    ery, 23; in Travers, 56, 57, 73
Hawksworth Farm, 291
Hawley, Sandy, *283*
Hawley, Warren, 255
Hawthorne Race Track, 237
Hayes, Rutherford B., 130
Haynie's Maria, 10
Hayward, Billy, 82, 106
Headley, Hal Price, 248
Healey, Tom, 237
Healy, Mrs., 29
Hebert, P. C., 79
Hechscher, J. G., 182
He Did, 244
Heenan, John Camel, 35, 69, 87, 93; Morrissey
    vs., 34, 36, 114; Sayers vs., 65, 119
Heenan, Tim, 35
Helmbold, 83, 86, 87, 88, 93
Helmbold, H. T., 86
Helmet, 184, 196
Helprin, Charlotte, 320n. 41
Hempstead (L.I.), 4
Heno, 166
Henry, 14, 97
Henry of Navarre, 144, 145, 146, 187
Herbert, Victor, 175
Herkimer (N.Y.), 4
Hertz, John D., 226
Hertz, Mrs. John D., 255
Hervey, John: on Beacon Course trotting
    race, 25; on big business, 251; on Discovery,
    244; on Equipoise, 234, 237; on Gallant Fox,
    228, 230; on Jim Dandy, 233; on Lexington,
    40; on Man o' War, 206, 210; on Rowe,
    212
Hialeah Park, 223, 237, 255, 273
Hi-de-Ho (nightclub), 246
High Chancellor, 172
High Echelon, 278
High Glee, 243
High Rock Spring, *3,* 7, 15
Hilarious, 193
Hildegarde (entertainer), 261
Hildreth, Mary, 194
Hildreth, Sam, 193–94, 195; death of, 227; Fitz-
    simmons and, 228; Grey Lag and, 218;
    Hurley Burley and, 180; W. Pinkerton and,
    241; Rothstein and, 216; Saratoga return of,
    198; Sinclair and, 219, 227; Stromboli and, 203;
    Walbaum and, 147, 193; W. C. Whitney and,
    162, 227
Hill, Jim, 286
Hill, Sally, 286

Hilton, Henry: anti-Semitism of, 117–18; estate of, 220, 266, 276; German employees of, 135; tennis facilities of, 157
Hilton, Jimmy, 134
Hindoo, 127–28, 187, 236
Hirsch, Mark, 161
Hirsch, Mary, 249
Hirsch, Max, 249
His Eminence, 157, 189
His Highness, 143–44
Historical Society of Saratoga Springs, 183–84
Historic preservation movement, 276
Hitchcock, Francis R., 167, 172, 193
Hitchcock, Thomas: death of, 255; joint land purchase of, 180; polo and, 196–97; Saratoga Association and, 172, 182; W. C. Whitney and, 162
Hobeau Farm, 281
Hoboken, 25, 31, 97, 146, 188
Hollywood Park, 253, 269
Holy Bull, 304, 305, 306, 307
Homer, Charles, 69
Homer, Winslow, 68–69, 86
Hone, Philip, 21
Honest Pleasure, 286, 299
Hoodwink, 215
Hooker, Joe, 63
Hoop, Jr., 257
Hop (dance), 21
Hopeful, 29
Hopeful (race), 179, 180, 211, 224–25, 278
Hopkins, Gwladys Crosby, 237
Horne, Field, 325–26n. 14b
Horse Haven: in antebellum era, 27; in postbellum era, 124–25; in 1890s, 140, 153; in early 1900s, 167, 174; in World War I era, 206; in 1930s, 238, 247. See also Saratoga Trotting Course
Horse of the Year award, 271; 1960–64 (Kelso), 272; 1968 (Dr. Fager), 276; 1969 (Arts and Letters), 277; 1972 (Secretariat), 279; 1977 (Seattle Slew), 286, 287; 1981 (John Henry), 293; 1982 (Conquistador Cielo), 293; 1984 (John Henry), 293
"Horse rooms," 224
Hosford, Marie Louise Schroeder. See Whitney, Marylou
Hotaling, Charles A., Sr., 270, 296, 326n. 25
Hotaling, Elizabeth, 326n. 21a, 327n. 15
Hotaling, Marthe Vincent, 296
Hotaling, Pete ("Monkey"), 124
Hotel Russell, 135, 224
Hotels: in antebellum era, 7–8, 20; in Civil War era, 48; Jews and, 118, 135; piazzas of (See Piazzas); in postbellum era, 103; schedules of, 148, 172
Hot Springs (Ark.), 174
Housebuster, 298, 300
House with the Bronze Door (N.Y.C.), 176
Howard, Charles, 249
Howard, E. Phocian, 242, 251
Howard, Thomas. See James, Jesse
Howe, Louis, 230, 266
Hoyt, John, 301
Hudson Bay Mining and Smelting Co., 235, 236
Hudson River, 6, 42
Hudson River Railroad, 43, 59, 116, 117
Huggins, John, 168
Hughes, Charles Evans, 192, 230, 326n. 16b
Humane Society, 301
Hunter, John: Alarm and, 99; Annieswood Stable and, 80; farm of, 74; J. Harper and, 90–91; Jerome Park Inaugural Stake and, 75; Jockey Club and, 158; judging by, 48; Saratoga Association and, 48, 61; Saratoga Cup and, 68; stable of, 96; Travers and, 56
Hurdle races, 38, 59, 80, 93, 97. See also Steeplechasing
Hurley Burley, 180
Hurricana Farm (N.Y.), 165
Husman, Harry, 260
Hyams, Maurice ("the Dancer"), 239, 250

Ida Hope, 133
Ignite, 142
Inaugural Stake (Jerome Park), 75
Independence, 25
"Indian Camp," 64, 179
Indian Joe (half-breed), 2
Ingleside (Calif.), 163
Inlander, 238
Inn at Saratoga, 2
Inspector B., 128
Intercollegiate Association of Amateur Athletes of America (IC4A), 115
Intercollegiate Rowing Association, 115, 124, 157, 322n. 5a. See also Rowing Association of American Colleges (RAAC)
Intercollegiate sports, 102–6, 108–10, 115–16
Interlaken (villa), 103, 261
"International Boat Race," 93
"Introductory Scramble," 116
Iodine Spring, 7
Irish Americans, 41, 58, 74
Irish Castle, 278
Irish immigrants, 30
Irish Lad, 169–70

Iron Horse. *See* Display
Iron Mask, 193, 194
Iroquois, 168
Irving, Washington, 101
Isolater, 251
Italian immigrants, 30
Italian restaurants, 245
Izard sisters, 13

Jack's (nightclub), 246
Jackson, Andrew, 10, 14, 15, 101
Jackson, Robert, 63
Jacobs, Hirsch, 258
Jacobs, Mike, 250
Jacobs, Patrice, 274
Jaipur: in Hopeful, 179; in Travers, xi, 270–71,
    277, 285, 291
Jake, 91
Jamaica (N.Y.), 180–81, 255, 257, 269
James, Basil, 259
James, Frank, 139, 150, 193, 241
James, Henry, 65, 86, 87, 97, 135
James, Jesse, 139, 150, 193
Jamestown, 236, 303
Janney, Stuart, Jr., 285
Japanese Americans, 255
Japanese owners, 286, 294, 295
Jardine, Edward, 41
Java Gold, 297
Jean Beraud, 162
Jeff Davis, 79
Jefferson, Thomas, 2, 4, 9
Jeffords, Walter, 205, 268, 271
Jeffords, Mrs. Walter, 205, 206, 207, 258
Jeffries, Jim, 192
Jerkens, Allen, 282, 307
Jerome, Clara, 75, 107
Jerome, Jennie. *See* Churchill, Jennie
Jerome, Larry, 75, 176–77
Jerome, Leonard, 74, 139–40; Coney Island
    Jockey Club and, 128, 139; draft riots and, 41;
    Harry Bassett–Longfellow race and, 97; in-
    laws of, 107, 116; Morrissey and, 122, 135; Panic
    of '73 and, 100; pari-mutuel system and, 95;
    polo and, 196; Saratoga Association and, 48,
    74, 139; at United States Hotel, 45; Wheatly
    and, 138
Jerome, William Travers, 176–77, 179, 183
Jerome Edgar, 44, 46
Jerome Park, 80, 122; founding of, 74–75, 84; Harry
    Bassett vs. Preakness at, 102; Hawkins at, 83;
    Kentucky at, 77; Monmouth Park and, 86,
    96; New York City purchase of, 139, 146; Pa-

role vs. Tom Ochiltree at, 120; pool-sale ban
    and, 118–19; schedule at, 76; Wheatly and, 138
Jerome Park Reservoir, 74
Jersey Derby, 50, 180
Jersey Lightning, 199
Jesse (clubhouse worker), 224
Jet Pilot, 258, 259
Jim Dandy, xii, 228, 232–33
Jimmy the Greek (J. Snyder), 248
Jim Riley, 114
Jockey Club: A. Belmont II and, 158, 167, 172, 199;
    A. Belmont IV and, 298; N. Brady and, 284;
    formation of, 157–58; Hildreth and, 198; J. R.
    Keene and, 184; O. M. Phipps and, 298; rac-
    ing commissions and, 229, 268; H. Sinclair and,
    236; Sturgis and, 223; Vosburgh and, 206; W. C.
    Whitney and, 162, 167; Woodward and, 234
Jockey Club Gold Cup winners: Affirmed, 291;
    Easy Goer, 298; John Henry, 293; Kelso, 272;
    Phalanx, 259; War Admiral, 249
Jockey clubs, 9, 10, 49–50, 72
Jockeys: costume of, 72; in early 1900s, 189–91;
    eighteenth-century concept of, 4; at Jerome
    Park, 74–75; Latin American, 269; million-
    dollar purses and, 294; racial integration of,
    68; riding posture of, 23, 133, 140, 142, 164;
    track facilities for, 172; unfair practices of, 70;
    World War II casualties among, 254–55. *See
    also* African-American jockeys
Jockey Y (building), 226, 227, 245, 275, 327n. 8b
Joe Daniels, 100
John B. Davidson, 44, 46
John B. Grier, 212, 214
John Henry, 292–93
John Knickerbocker's Livery, 51
John Morgan, 44, 46, 47
John P. Grier, 211, 230, 306
Johnson, Andrew, 78–79, 317n. 6
Johnson, Davy, 176
Johnson, Frank, 20
Johnson, Fred, 203
Johnson, Jack, 191–92
Johnson, William, 2, 165, 311n. 11
Johnson and Cox (firm), 35
Johnson Hall, 2
Johnston, Jimmy, 250
Jolley, LeRoy, 270
Jolley, Mrs. Moody, 270
Jones, Ben A., 252
Jones, Jimmy, 258
Jones, Paul, 212
Jones, Pearson, 255
Joyner, A. Jack, 197, 228
Juanita, 126

Judge Himes, 190
Jumel, Eliza, 15, 16–17
Jumel, Stephen, 17

Kalik, Max ("Kid Rags"), 239
Kane, Elizabeth, 205
Kapurthala, King of India, 149
Kaufman, George S., 257
Kayaderosseras Trail, 1–2
Kearney, Edward, 159
Keene, Foxhall: as athlete, 196, 197; in cast, 186;
    Domino and, 145; on father, 191; on Grand
    Union Hotel Stakes, 188; Mackay sale and,
    174; Sysonby and, 184, 185, 187; Taral and, 144;
    W. C. Whitney and, 168
Keene, James R.: on anti-betting bill, 192; Can-
    field and, 179; Castleton Farm and, 157; Colin
    and, 188; Commando and, 187; death of, 196;
    Delhi and, 180; Domino and, 145; Hildreth
    and, 194; Jockey Club and, 157–58, 184; racism
    of, 191; Saratoga Association and, 193; H. Sin-
    clair and, 219; J. T. Sloan and, 163; Spendthrift
    and, 125; Sysonby and, 182, 184–85; Taral and,
    144; Westchester Racing Association and, 140,
    181; W. C. Whitney and, 162, 164, 168; H. P.
    Whitney and, 183; mentioned, 126, 201
Keene, John Oliver, 248
Keeneland Association, 248
Keeneland Race Course, 292; opening of, 248;
    sales at, 256, 286, 294, 295
Kefauver, Estes, 262
Kelley, James, 95
Kelly, "Honest John," 145
Kelso, 272–73, 278, 285–86, 293
Kennedy, John F., 270
Kenner, Duncan, 23
Kenner Stakes, 113, 114, 125, 126–27. See also Miller
    Stakes
Kentucky: breeding in, 40, 157, 174; in Civil War,
    195; pari-mutuel betting in, 223; racing in, 10,
    23, 192; visitors from, 43–44; yearling sales in,
    256
Kentucky: Bold Ruler and, 278; Boston and, 23;
    death of, 108; Diomed and, 10; on double bill,
    65; Gilpatrick and, 83, 98; J. Hunter and, 90;
    at Jerome Park, 75, 77; in Jersey Derby, 50,
    180; Lady Suffolk and, 69; Longfellow and,
    99; Quadrangle and, 274–75; in Saratoga Cup,
    68, 73, 219; in Sequel Stakes, 58; sire of, 157;
    Sysonby and, 187; in Travers, 56, 57
Kentucky Association, 48
Kentucky Derby, 292; black jockeys in, 141, 142,
    190; breakfasts served at, 128; cash value of,

204, 253; first, 107–8, 112, 121; Jersey Derby and,
    180; opening of, 107; pari-mutuel machines at,
    199; Winn renewal of, 200–201; Woodburn win-
    ners at, 157
Kentucky Jockey Club Stakes, 235
Kentucky Stakes, 112
Kessler, George, 178
Ketchum, Edward, 71
Kettlewell, James K., 20, 171, 265
Key to the Mint, 279, 283, 297
Khrushchev, Nikita S., 270
Kilmer, Willis Sharpe, 202, 203, 226, 232
King, George, 255
Kingfisher, 86, 87; Longfellow vs., 88, 90–93;
    sire of, 108, 157; Sysonby and, 187; in Travers,
    143
King Hanover, 165
King Kelly. See Kelso
Kingman, 141
King Ranch (Tex.), 244, 257, 258
Kinnoul, 324n. 6b
Kleberg, Robert, 244
Knapp, A. P., 159
Knapp, Bill, 208, 211
Knapp, Clarence, 242
Knapp, H. K., 172, 182
Knickerbockers (baseball club), 25
Knickerbocker's Livery, 51
Knight Errant, 201
Koch, Lew, 273
Kofoed, Jack, 33
Kohler, Charles, 195
Krause, Robert, 275
Krik's Guide to the Turf, 77, 125, 318n. 17a
Krone, Julie, 302, 303-4
Krumpe, Jack, 281, 284
Ku Klux Klan, 191
Kummer, Clarence, 211, 212, 213, 214
Kurtsinger, Charlie, 238, 244, 248–49
Kwiatkowski, Henryk de, 294, 301

La Belle Farm (Ky.), 162, 180
Lacey, Robert, 216, 217, 246–47, 262–63
Ladana, 236
Lady Digby, 29, 46
Lady Golconda, 285
Lady Relief, 23
Lady Rotha, 201, 316n. 11b
Lady Suffolk, 24, 25–29, 38, 46; fame of, 69, 87,
    93; record set by, 119; trotting tradition and,
    254, 295
Lafayette, Marquis de, 15
Lake Avenue, 90

Lake George, 17

Lake houses, 220–21, 246–47, 261–62

Lake Lonely, 71, 220

Lake Placid Club, 135

Lake Shore Railroad, 83, 84, 131

Lambton, George, 162

Lancaster, 80

Landon, Melville, 90–91, 97, 203, 316nn. 2, 8a, 10b, 318n. 1

Landry, John, 283

Lane, Wheaton, 59, 117

Langtry, Lillie, 128

Lansky, Buddy, 247, 263

Lansky, Jake, 246

Lansky, Meyer, 227, 251; carpet joints of, 247; T. E. Dewey and, 261–62; imprisonment of, 262–63; navy and, 255; Piping Rock and, 246; Rothstein and, 217, 221

Lansky, Paul, 263

Lasix, 301

Lathrop, Daniel S., 137

Latin American jockeys, 269

Laughing Bridge, 285

Laurin, Lucien, 279, 280, 282

Lawrin, 249

Laxative waters, 133, 245

Lazy F Ranch Stable, 285

League of American Wheelmen, 159

Leamington, 108, 121, 168

Leavitt, Charles, 169, 170, 171

Leconte, 287

Lee, Bob, 298

Lee, Gypsy Rose, 261

Lee, Harry ("Light Horse"), 63

Lee, James, 190

Lee, Robert E., 41, 61, 63, 130

Leech, Edward, 137

Leggett, William, 101

Lehman, Herbert H., 241

Lehndorff, Ernst, 180, 205

Lehr, Mrs. Harry, 130, 135

Leland, Warren W., 60, 71, 82, 90

Leslie, Frank, 103, 104, 108, 112

Lewis, Isaac, 142, 143

Lewis, Joe E., 257, 262

Lewis, Morgan, 21

Lewis, Oliver, 107, 108

Lewisohn, Jesse, 176

Lexington: Bold Ruler and, 278; death of, 108; Diomed and, 10, 23; Duke of Magenta and, 125; Fellowcraft and, 106; four-mile record of, 77; Gilpatrick and, 46, 83; Harry Bassett and, 93; Jersey Derby contenders and, 50; Kentucky breeding and, 40, 157; Leconte vs., 287;

Phaeton and, 121; Preakness and, 87; rest for, 38; Saratoga Cup contenders and, 73; Sultana and, 116; Tom Bowling and, 102; Travis contenders and, 56

LiButti, Edith and Ralph, 307

Lido Venice (nightclub), 220, 224. See also Piping Rock (Saratoga)

Lighting, 58, 134, 178

Lightning, 202, 203

Lillian's (restaurant), 298

Lilly, Marshall, 189

Lincoln, Abraham: assassination of, 62, 63, 66; Emancipation Proclamation, 41; fast day proclaimed by, 58; Gettysburg Address, 47; Morrissey and, 37, 40, 60, 123; telegraph dispatches of, 51, 53; thanksgiving proclaimed by, 47

Lincoln, Mary Todd, 52

Lincoln, Robert Todd, 52

Lincoln Bath House, 245

Lincoln Memorial (D.C.), 195

Lind, Jenny, 75

Linda's Chief, 279

Lindsey's Arabian, 4

Lindy's restaurant (N.Y.C.), 217

Ling, Johnny, 34

Lite Light, 302–3

Littell, Mark, 106

Little Bighorn, Battle of, 115

Little Chief, 225

Little Club, 242

Littlefield, Charles, 55, 73, 74

Livingston, Bernard, 223

Liza, 148

Lizzie W., 44, 45–46, 47, 83, 127

Locust Hill Farm (Md.), 285

Loft, George W., 212, 220, 247

Loftus, John, 206, 209–11, 268, 324n. 6b

Log Cabin Stable, 223, 268

London bookmakers, 94

London Prize Ring Rules, 31, 32–33

Long Branch (N.J.), 59, 84, 118, 129

Long Dance, 143

Longden, Johnny, 248, 251, 256, 257

Longfellow, 264; Bold Ruler and, 278; Harry Bassett vs., xii, 88–100, 227, 287; at Nantura Stud, 157; plates of, 268; stride of, 215; Sysonby and, 187

Long Island Point (Canada), 34

Long Island Railroad, 118

Lord, Frank H., 90

Lord Rebeau, 286

Lorillard, George: death of, 127; Duke of Magenta and, 125; Dwyer brothers and, 126; Grenada and, 127; Monitor and, 125; Monmouth Park and, 140; Tom Ochiltree and, 116, 120

Lorillard, Griswold, 133, 134

Lorillard, Pierre, 52, 137; Attila and, 106; Boardman and, 124; Board of Control and, 146, 157; Dwyer brothers and, 126; Harry Bassett–Longfellow race and, 97; Iroquois and, 168; Liza and, 148; pari-mutuel system and, 95; Parole and, 112, 116, 120, 125; Simms and, 144; stables of, 77, 96, 140, 219; Tuxedo Park estate of, 120, 133

Lorillard family, 184

Lorillard Stakes, 125

Los Angeles, 142, 143, 148

Lost Cause, 79

Louis, Joe, 250

Louisiana Jockey Club, 23

Louisville and Nashville Railroad, 176

Louisville Jockey Club and Driving Park. *See* Kentucky Derby

Luce, Clarence, 178, 179

Luciano, Charles ("Lucky"), 227; Chicago Club under, 243; Costello and, 255; deportation of, 261; T. E. Dewey and, 245–46; Rothstein and, 217, 221

Lukas, D. Wayne, 294, 298, 305, 306

Lukas, Jeff, 304–5, 306

Luke Blackburn, 126–27

Lumley, Arthur, 316n. 2

Lunger, Jane duPont, 298

Lusitania (ship), 199–200, 244

Lustig, Victor, 240

Luther, Tom, 221, 222, 245

Lynchings, 191

Lyne, Lucien, 188

McAnally, Ron, 292, 293

McCall, S., 115

McCann, Tom, 31

McCarren, Patrick, 176

McCarron, Chris, 294

McCarthy, Clem, 212

McCartysville (Calif.), 132–33

McClelland, Byron, 145

McCoy, Lee, 264

McDaniel, David, 79, 80; Albert and, 73; Harry Bassett and, 93–94; Lorillards and, 125; Morrissey and, 83; Springbok and, 102, 106, 112–13; stable of, 77, 96, 100

McDaniel, Henry, 203

Macdonough, William, 140

McDowell, C., 171

McGaughey, Shug, 300

McGee, 195

McGee's store, 71

McGill University, 103

McGrath, Henry Price: Aristides and, 106; Chamberlin and, 111; in Civil War era, 47; death of, 157; at Kentucky Derby, 107; as "timing judge," 53; Tom Bowling and, 100, 101, 102

McGrath, Mike, 264

McGrathiana Stud, 100, 157, 195

Mackay, Clarence, 174, 179, 182

McKinley, William, 161

McKinney, Price, 196

McKinney, Rigan, 234

Mack (owner), 29

McLaughlin, Jimmy, 126, 127, 128, 260

McMahon, Carl, 224

McMenomy, John, 121–22

Macomber, John, 225

McPherson, James, 62, 130

McTaggart, T., 211

Madden, John: Capt. Alcock and, 207; death of, 227; Hamburg and, 162, 168; Irish Lad and, 170; Old Rosebud and, 198; Sir Barton and, 323n. 3b; Sir Madden and, 203; H. P. Whitney and, 183, 222; W. C. Whitney and, 166; Winkfield and, 190; Zev and, 219

Madden, Preston, 324n. 3a

Mlle. Demorest's Dress Making Establishment, 51

Mad Hatter, 219

Madison Square Club, 150

Madison Square Garden (N.Y.C.), 167, 182, 250, 273

Mad Play, 225

Maetall, 248

Magnolia, 4

Mahubah, 205

Maiden, 68, 121

Maid of Flight, 272

Maine Chance Farm, 260

Majestic Prince, 294

Maktoum bin Rashid al Maktoum, 295

Mamona, 44, 276

Mangona, John, 326n. 21a

Manhattan Club, 150, 183

Mann, J. M., 115

Manning, Landon, 29, 156, 202, 256

Man o' War, 205–15, 219, 221, 222; Ace Admiral and, 260; Bold Ruler and, 278; Count Fleet and, 256; death of, 259; Dehere and, 303; Harry Bassett and, 93; in Hopeful, 179; Jaipur–Ridan race and, 270, 271; John P. Grier and, 306; Loft and, 220; at Riddle farm, 324n. 6b; Ruffian and, 285; saddle of, 268; sale of, xi, 275, 294; Seabiscuit and, 249; Secretariat and, 206, 279, 281, 282, 283; sire of, 188; spring

Man o' War (*continued*)
  named for, 78; War Hero and, 237, 248; War
  Relic and, 253; Zev and, 219
Man o' War Cup, 249, 269
Maple, Eddie, 287, 299
Mara, Tim, 239
Marble House (Newport), 132
Marcus T. Reynolds and Associates, 251
Marguerite, 225, 228, 325n. 1
Marineland (Fla.), 236
Markey, Gene, 274
Marlboro Cup, 283
Marlborough, Duke of, 107, 161
Mars, Ethel V., 247
Martha, 164
Marvin, James: bowling and, 26; Defender and,
  98; home of, 20; Saratoga Association and,
  49, 61, 119, 137–38, 146; trotting course and, 27;
  C. Vanderbilt and, 82
Marvin, Thomas, 20
Marvin House, 64
Marx, Karl, 33, 314n. 7b
Marye's Heights, Battle of, 61
Maryland, 9, 192, 199, 223, 247
Maryland Jockey Club, 82, 146
Maryland Racing Commission, 225
Maskette, 184, 193, 196
Mason, Jack, 242
Massachusetts Handicap, 255
Masseria, Giuseppi ("Joe the Boss"), 227, 243
Master Car Builders' convention, 158
Master Charlie, 219–20
Match Days, 83, 106
Match races, 15–16, 31, 50, 194, 285
Maude S., 131
Mauney-House Tavern, 11
Maxwell (Yale athlete), 106
Mayer's Lager Beer Saloon, 51
Mead, Chris, 250
Meadow Brook (nightclub), 246
Meadow Brook (L.I.), 256
Meadow Stable (Va.), 279, 327n. 1b
Meany (jockey), 124
Mechanicville (N.Y.), 257
Mechanicville (race), 273
Medications. *See* Drug use
Meeker, Thomas, 301–2
Melanie, 145
Mellon, Paul, 274, 275, 277, 297, 304
Mellon Turf Course, 304
Melton, 184
Menken, Adah Isaacs, 35
Merciless, 76
Merrie Lassie, 248, 326n. 12

Merrill, 73, 83, 143
Messenger, 28
Metairie Jockey Club, 39, 50, 72, 77, 79
Metropolitan Handicap, 143
Metropolitan Jockey Club, 180
Metropolitan Opera, 160
Metropolitan Street Railway Company, 160, 161, 184
Meux, Lady, 168
Migliore, Richard, 305
Milam, Cal, 203
Milbert, Jacques, 8
Milky Way Farm (Tenn.), 247, 253
Miller, Andrew: death of, 203, 212; Lady Roth
  and, 201; Roamer and, 202; Saratoga Associa-
  tion and, 167, 172, 182, 193
Miller, Mrs. Andrew, 213
Miller, Charley, 83, 86, 318n. 23
Miller, Mackenzie ("Mack"), 294, 297, 304
Miller, Walter, 187, 188, 189
Miller Stakes, 213. *See also* Kenner Stakes
Mills, A. G., 179
Mills, Ogden, 224, 238
Mills Commission, 188
Milner, 113, 114
Ministers, 15, 26, 90, 263
Mississippi, 41
Miss Woodford, 128, 143
Mr. Nickerson, 298, 300, 301
Mitchell, Caleb, 137, 151–52, 158, 159, 169
Mitchell, Charley, 128
Moccasin, 15
Modesty, 128
Mohawk and Hudson Railroad, 17–18
Mohawk Indians, 1–2, 64
Mohawk II, 165
Mollie McCarty, 121
Molly Brant, 165
Monaco, 85, 86, 111
Monahan, Tom, 194
Monitor, 125
"Monkey-on-a-Stick" posture, 23, 164
Monmouth Cup, 88, 94
Monmouth Eclipse, 29
Monmouth Park, 93, 122, 180; expansion of, 140;
  fans at, 94; founding of, 86; Jerome Park and,
  86, 96; New York competition with, 258;
  pari-mutuel betting at, 95, 111; Salvator at, 141
Monroe, James, 14
Monte Carlo (Monaco), 85, 175
Montrose, 142
Montura, Duke, 264
Moon, Cary, 79–80, 86–87, 102
Moon's Lake House, 38, 148, 221; Courtney at,
  102; Duncan and, 79–80; H. James at, 86; in

postbellum era, 71; potato chips invented at, 37
Moore, Charles W., 196
Moore, T. G., 44, 68, 84
Moran, Frank, 192
Morgan, E. D., Jr., 172, 180
Morgan, Edwin D., 51
Morgan, Helen, 246
Morgan, Mrs. Henry Hayes, 238
Morgan, John, 40, 46, 56
Morgan, John Pierpont, 160, 176, 180
Morning (A. Thorwaldsen), 19
"Morning line," 239
Morningside, 165
Morning Telegraph (newspaper), 227
Morosini, Giulia, 163
Morris, Francis: farm of, 74; great-grandson of, 227; Hopeful and, 180; horses of, 56, 76, 99
Morris, Green, 165
Morris, John A., 139, 227
Morris Park, 139, 140, 146, 169, 181
Morrissey, 82–83
Morrissey, John: at Adelphi, 121, 266; advertisements of, 42, 43, 46; announcements of, 264; Arthur and, 79, 129; boat racing and, 93; Canfield and, 150, 184, 220; congressional career of, 76, 78–79, 83, 138, 317n. 1; Courtney and, 102, death of, xi, 121–22, 132, 136; Defender and, 97–98; draft riots and, 41; early career of, 30–40; editor and, 68; first thoroughbred race sponsored by, 45–48; Grand Union and, 320n. 41; Harry Bassett and, 94, 95; L. Jerome and, 74, 135; at Jerome Park, 75; John B. Davidson and, 44, 46; A. Lincoln and, 37, 40, 60, 123; Lizzie W. and, 127; McGrath and, 100, 107, 157; C. Mitchell and, 152; New York Senate race of, 114; Panic of '69 and, 84, 85; parimutuel system and, 97, 112, 250; Poole vs., 33, 34, 314n. 7b; pool-sale ban and, 119, 128, 192; C. Reed and, 120, 136, 174; Rothstein and, 217; safe of, 177; Saratoga Association and, 50, 110; spectators and, 67; A. Spencer and, 137; *Spirit of the Times* on, 113; sports complex concept of, 105; *Tribune* and, 70; C. Vanderbilt and, 61, 64–65, 74, 122; C. Vanderbilt II and, 131; W. H. Vanderbilt and, 82; Walbaum and, 146, 147; E. B. Wall and, 133; Wheatly and, 73, 138; W. C. Whitney and, 159; Wilkes on, 111–12; mentioned, 251, 263
Morrissey, John, Jr., 114, 116, 122
Morrissey, Susie Smith, 30, 122; aboard *Charleston*, 121; marriage of, 32, 34; in New York City, 31; personal appearance of, 65
Morrissey, Tim, 35

Morrissey's Club House: facilities of, 88–90; Harry Bassett and, 99; Henry James on, 86; museum in, 265; opening of, 84–85; regattas and, 103, 108
Morse, Charles, 220
Morse, Jedidiah, 6–7
Moscow, 28
Mose (trainer), 99
Mountain Boy, 82
Mount McGregor, 129–30, 131
Mount Vernon, 65
Mount Vernon (Va.), 4, 9, 312nn. 5, 8
Mulholland, Bert, 271
Murder in the second degree, 101
Murphy, Isaac: Ashe on, 191; Baldwin and, 133; Checkmate and, 128; Falsetto and, 125; photograph of, 126; J. Rowe and, 187; Salvator and, 140–41; Sande and, 228, 260; Vera Cruz and, 120; Winkfield and, 189; mentioned, 142
Murray, "Red Coat," 232
Music, 175, 221, 230, 275, 276
"Mutt and Jeff" (comic strip), 219
Mutual of New York (baseball team), 41, 70, 71, 94, 315n. 14
Muybridge, Eadweard, 113
"My Best Girl" (Donaldson), 219
Myers, Billy, 202
My Gallant, 281
My Request, 259
Myrtle Charm, 260
My Son, 227
"My Wild Irish Rose" (Olcott), 175

Naismith, James, 157
Nantura Stud, 157
Nashua, 179, 267
Nast, Thomas, 35, 85, 93, 114
Natchez, 258
National Association of Amateur Oarsmen, 102, 157
National Association of Professional Base Ball Players, 34, 70, 94
National Baseball Hall of Fame, 188
National Course (D.C.), 7, 10
National Horse Show, 60
National League (baseball), 124, 179
National Museum of Dance, 276, 296
National Museum of Racing and Hall of Fame, 28, 188, 265, 268, 296; Affirmed and, 291; Alydar and, 291, 301; Belmont pole at, 280; Board of Control minutes and, 321n. 21; Currier and Ives print in, 99; John Henry and, 293; movie shown in, 304; Mulholland and, 271; Murphy

National Museum of Racing (*continued*) and, 141; renovation of, 304; Rosoff mansion and, 233; S. Ross paintings at, 325–26n. 14b
National Steeplechase and Hunt Association, 273
National Steeplechase Day, 273
National Turf Writers Association, 271
Nation Wide News Service, 227
Native Americans, 1–2, 6, 64
Native Americans (political party), 30, 34
Native Dancer, 263–64; Alydar and, 287; Dehere and, 303; in Hopeful, 179; Ruffian and, 284, 285; Tom Fool and, 266
Nativism, 30
Naushon, 194
Nearly On Time, 287
Nerud, John, 276
Nevins, A. B., 106
"Newark Ike" (I. Steloff), 240
New Broom, 224
Newburgh (N.Y.), 2
New Deal, 228, 245
New Jersey, 23, 140, 146, 255
Newman's Lake House, 220, 261, 262
Newmarket (England), 36, 197
Newmarket Handicap, 125
New Orleans (La.), 21
New Orleans Fair Grounds, 248
New Orleans track. *See* Metairie Jockey Club
Newport (R.I.): in Civil War era, 42; equipage in, 74, 148; pleasure craft in, 55; politics in, 129; polo in, 196; rivalry with, 65–66, 137; Vanderbilt residences in, 132
Newport Jazz Festival–Saratoga, 275
Newspaper coverage: facilities for, 60; of U. S. Grant, 129–30; in 1920s, 223–24; of postbellum double bill, 65, 66, 316n. 1; of prizefighting, 34, 191–92; specialized, 145
New York Athletic Club, 124
New York Bar Association, 118
New York Base-Ball Club, 25
New York Cable Rail Company, 160
New York Central Railroad, 49, 65, 84, 116–17
New York Chamber of Commerce, 116
New York City: American Eclipse–Henry race and, 14; baseball in, 70, 188; British occupation of, 2; draft riots in, 41; federal patronage for, 79; Grant funeral in, 130; Harry Bassett–Longfellow race and, 94; Kefauver investigation in, 262; Lincoln in, 37; municipal taxes of, 258; nativism in, 30–31; newspapers of, 316n. 1; politics in, 34, 74, 79, 114; prostitution in, 246; racketeering in, 227; railroad service to, 18; street railways of, 159, 160, 161; trotting

in, 15, 82; in World War II, 255. *See also* Central Park (N.Y.C.)
New York City Ballet, 275
New York City gambling: antebellum era, 31, 37; postbellum era, 64, 108–9; early 1900s, 175–76, 183, 192
New York City Opera, 275
New York City racing: in 1890s, 138, 139–41; in early 1900s, 172, 192, 195, 197; in 1920s, 223; in 1930s, 228
New York Giants (baseball team), 217
New York Mets, 280
New York Mutuals (baseball team), 41, 70, 71, 94, 315n. 14
New York Racing Association, 268–69; attendance figures of, 298; Devil His Due and, 307; facilities improved by, 275; Mellon and, 304; million-dollar purses of, 296–97; officers of, 284; OTB and, 280; simulcasts of, 295; space shortage of, 292; timing by, 299. *See also* Jockey Club
New York Society for the Suppression of Vice, 136
New York State: anti-Semitism in, 118; boxing ban in, 32; counterfeit bills in, 240; Daily Double in, 253; early touring in, 12–13; gubernatorial election in, 234; horse-breeding associations in, 38; Lasix ban in, 301; pari-mutuel betting in, 250–51, 255; pool sales ban in, 118; purse distribution in, 253; racing ban in, 9, 14, 238; racing revenues of, 240, 275; railroad service in, 17–18, 43; Saratoga Spa opened by, 245; tennis championships in, 157
New York State Capitol, 311n. 11
New York State Court of Chancery, 101
New York State Fair, 27
New York State Legislature, 118; Assembly, 15, 24; Senate, 114, 122
New York State Racing and Wagering Board, 284
New York State Racing Commission, 172, 241, 243, 267
New York Times building, 41
New York Tribune building, 41
New York Yankees, 194
Niagara Falls, 13
Niblo's Garden Café, 14
Nichols, Joe, 270
Nichols and Halcott (firm), 106
Nick the Greek (N. A. Dandolos), 243
Nicol, Dave, 186–87
"Nighteyes" (calluses), 241
Night (A. Thorwaldsen), 19
Noble, T. A., 115
Nolan, Blanche, 224
Norfolk, 50, 56, 73, 108, 180

Normandy Farm (Ky.), 157
Northern Dancer, 294
Northern states: black migration to, 191; at Civil
    War close, 62; racing in, 23–24, 39, 40, 49–50,
    84
North-South races, 14, 15, 23–24, 60
Northup, Anne, 21
Northup, Henry, 22
Northup, Solomon, 21–22
Norton, Marie, 235, 237
Nott, Eliphalet and Sally, 10, 312n. 14b
Notter, Joe, 188, 189, 199
Novelty, 194
Nursery Stud (Ky.), 205, 206
Nursery Stud (L.I.), 140, 197, 222
Nussbaum, Abe ("Sparky"), 250

Oaklawn Park (Ark.), 174, 255, 292
Ocean House course, 77
O'Connor, Eugene, 178, 184
O'Donnell, John, 113
O'Donnell, Mary K., 325n. 20
O'Fallon, J., 79, 80
Offtrack betting: , xi, 95; in 1920s, 224; in 1970s,
    279–80, 281, 283–84; in 1980s, 295; in 1990s, 304
O'Grady, Jerry, 260–61
Oiseau, 185–86, 187
"Oklahoma" (training track), 174, 295
Olcott, Chauncey, 175, 234
Old Bones. See Exterminator
Olde Bryan Inn (restaurant), 6
Old Gray Mare. See Lady Suffolk
"Old Gray Mare, The" (S. Foster), 25
Old Rosebud, 198, 201
Old Westbury, 162
Oller, Pierre, 95, 111
Olmsted, Frederick Law, 136
Olympian, 162
Olympic Games, 105, 296
Omaha, 244, 273
Omar Khayyam, 203
O. M. Linthicum & Co., 18
Onaretto, 142
One Count, 266
O'Neill, Eugene, 240
Onion, 281–82, 283, 307
Optime, 184
"Oral betting," 199
Orange County (N.Y.), 120
Organized crime, 216–17, 227, 245–46
Ormonde, 140
Osgood, George A., 49, 56, 75
"Outlaw" horses, 158

Overton, William ("Monk"), 190
Owen (gambler), 152
Oxford University, 103
Ozark, 111, 113, 114

Paget, Gerald, 162
Paget, Sydney, 162, 180
Paley, William S., 135
Palmer, Jake, 92
Palmer, Joe, 240, 251, 253, 264, 265
Pan American Airways, 235
Panics: of 1857, 100; of 1869, 84, 85; of 1873, 100,
    102, 110; of 1893, 150. See also Crash of 1929
Pari-mutuel betting: abuses of, 110–11; "builders"
    and, 240; early, 95, 97, 100, 250; in former
    paddock, 275; at Hialeah Park, 237; at Ken-
    tucky Derby, 200–201; New Jersey ban on,
    140; in New York State, 250–51, 255; OTB
    and, 280; racing commissions and, 229–30;
    strike against, 286; J. Widener and, 223
Park Central Hotel (N.Y.C.), 219
Parmer, Charles, 189
Parole: debut of, 112; in England, 125; Extermina-
    tor and, 219; Tom Ochiltree vs., 116, 120, 121;
    Vera Cruz vs., 119
Passaic County Agricultural Association, 50
Pastor, Albie, 326n. 15b
Pastor, Bob, 250
Paterson (N.J.), 97
Paterson Derby, 83
Patrick, Gilbert Watson. See Gilpatrick (G. W.
    Patrick)
Patten, Alfonso, 27
Patti, Adelina, 75
Patti, 56, 57, 59
Paul Whiteman's Orchestra, 221, 230
Pavot, 256, 303
Payne, Flora. See Whitney, Flora
Payne, Oliver Hazard, 159, 181; death of, 222; dis-
    inherited kin of, 161; heirs of, 182; J. R. Keene
    and, 184
Payson, Edward, 11, 12
Payson, Joan, 222, 257
Payson, Virginia, 292
Peabody, George Foster, 220
Peabody Awards, 220
Pearl Harbor attack, 254
Pebbles, 199, 201
Pendergast, Tom, 224, 261
Pennant, 196, 198
Pennsylvania Institute of Fine Arts, 313n. 21a
Perkins, Eli. See Landon, Melville
Perkins, James ("Soup"), 142, 143

Perret, Craig, 299
Perrier, Louis, 18–19
Petee-Wrack, 225, 226, 233
Peter Pan, 184, 196
Petersburg (Va.), 51, 58
Petrie, John, 31, 34
Pettingill, Charles, 171, 208, 209
Peytona, 24
Phaeton, 121
Phalanx, 258–59
Phenylbutazone, 301
Phi Beta Kappa, 182, 193
Philadelphia, 12
Philadelphia Orchestra, 275
Philadelphia Races, 4
Philip Morris Company, 283
Phillips, H., 190
Phipps, Mrs. Henry Carnegie, 238, 278
Phipps, Ogden, 276, 284, 298
Phipps, Ogden Mills, 298
Photography, 113, 141, 243, 253
Piatt, Thomas, 251
Piazzas, 8–9, 20, 265; of Aldridges, 312n. 8;
     of Congress Hall, 9, 20, 78; of Union Hotel,
     82, 87
Pimlico: congressmen at, 121; founding of, 82;
     opening of, 87; riot at, 194; suspension of,
     146; War Admiral at, 249
Pincay, Lafitte, Jr., 283, 289–90, 294
Pinkerton detective agency, 198, 241, 260
Pinkerton family, 241
Pink Star, 227
Piping Rock (Locust Valley), 234
Piping Rock (Saratoga): in 1930s, 234, 246, 247; in
     1940s, 255; in postwar era, 261, 262. See also
     Lido Venice (nightclub)
"Pittsburgh Phil" (G. Smith), 145, 166, 172, 248
Pittsburgh Steelers (football team), 248
Pittsburgh Symphony, 175
Plattsburgh, 250
Plaudit, 142, 162
Playboy Revue, 242
Pleasant Colony, 293
Plumb, Mike, 273
PMU (Pari Mutuel-Urbain), 95
Poe, Edgar Allan, 27, 101, 266, 313n. 6
Poetess, 159
Poinsett, Joel Roberts, 21
Politics: immigrants and, 31; in New York City,
     34, 74, 79, 114; in Saratoga, 129
Polo, 196–97, 237
Polo Grounds (N.Y.C.), 196
Polynesian, 263
Pompey, 225

Pontifex, 278
Poole, "Butcher Bill," 30–31, 33, 34, 314n. 7b
Poole Association, 34
Pool sales: Civil War era, 44–45, 56; postbellum,
     67–68, 87, 95, 118, 119
Potato Chip Farm, 260
Potato chips, 80, 178; consumption of, 71; inven-
     tion of, 37, 314n. 22; production of, 86–87
Potato Products Company, 260
Potomac, 140, 144
Poughkeepskie, 23, 41
Povich, Shirley, 250
Power, Tyrone, 17, 23, 68, 164
Powers, Vince, 189
Powers-Hunter Co., 206
Preakness, 100, 102; Longfellow vs., 88; sale of,
     114–15; in Saratoga Cup, 112–13; sire of, 87, 108,
     157; Springbok vs., 106
Preakness Stakes, 115; cash value of, 204; first,
     111; Kentucky Derby and, 107; Pimlico and,
     87; starting gates at, 228; suspension of,
     146
Presidents, 10, 15, 28, 130
President Spring, 7
Press coverage. See Newspaper coverage
Price, Jack, 274
Price, Katherine, 274
Pricefixing, 106
Prince Albert, 213
Prince Hamburg, 186
Princess Bowling, 140, 143
Princeton University, 94, 103, 115, 116
Prior, J. W., 116
Pvt. Smiles, 281
Prix de l'Arc de Triomphe, 304
Prizefighting: antebellum, 31, 32–36, 48; post-
     bellum, 70; in 1880s, 124; in early 1900s, 191–
     92; in 1920s, 221–22; in 1930s, 245, 250
Proctor Knott, 144
Prohibition, 216, 242
Promenade, 142
Prospector's Gamble, 298
Prostitution, 242, 246
Prove Out, 283
Prudery, 218, 225, 236
Public address system, 264–65
Public Stock Exchange, 129
Pugilism. See Prizefighting
Pulling (reining), 125
Pullman, George, 150
Pulsifer, D. T., 140
Punch, 47
Purdy, John, 48, 61
Purdy, Samuel, 14, 48

Putnam, Gideon, 7, 8, 9, 71, 82
Putnam, Phila, 7
Pyrenees, 267

Quadrangle, 274–75
Queens County (N.Y.), 14, 181
Queens County Jockey Club, 140
Queen's Cup, 59
Queen's Plate, 55

Race America (film), 304
Race King, 185
Racial discrimination: postbellum, 72, 73–74,
    317n. 18; in early 1900s, 191; in 1920s, 226; in
    1960s, 275
Racing and Wagering Board (N.Y.S.), 284
Racing Calendars (Crickmore), 168–69, 317n. 21
Racing commissions, 223, 229
Racketeering, 216–17, 227, 245–46
"Railbirds," 53, 54
Railroads: early, 17–18; of New York State, 43;
    "Saratoga Compact" and, 106; time belts
    and, 129; United States Hotel and, 256–57;
    Vanderbilt holdings of, 116–17. See also Street
    railways; Subways; specific lines
Raise a Native, 287
Ramapo Farm, 195
Rancho Santa Anita, 121, 133
Rancocas Stud (N.J.), 120, 218, 219, 236
Randolph, Edith, 161
Randolph, John, 14
Ratings, 303
"Raven, The" (Poe), 27, 266
Rawle, Francis, 124
Rawlings, J. A., 63
Raymond, Henry, 51, 60
Ready, Dennis, 59
Reagan, Ronald, 37
Redemptorist Fathers, 261
Redfern, Arthur, 186
Red Knight, 172
Red Rain, 249
Red Spring, 7
Redstone Stable, 218
Reed, Charles, 122, 320n. 46; Athlene and, 120;
    St. Blaise and, 140; track management of, 124,
    136; yearlings sold by, 174
Reedy, Bill, 264
Reedy, Dennis, 44
Rees, Frank, 105
Regardless, 76
Regret, 179, 198–201, 209, 236

Reiff, Lester, 168
Reigh Count, 225, 226, 233, 255
Relentless, 76
Relic, 260
Remorseless, 76
Reno (Nev.), 190, 192
Rensselaer, 159
Rensselaer and Saratoga Railroad, 18
Reporters. See Newspaper coverage
Republican Party, 110, 160, 161
Resseguie, Harry, 118
Reviewer, 284
Revolutionary War, 3, 6, 9
Reynolds, David, 304
Reynolds, Marcus T., 251
Reynolds, Mrs., 42
Rhinelander, William, 160
Rhythm, 298
Rhythm Boys (musical group), 221, 230
Richmond, 83
Richmond (Va.), 9
Ridan, xi, 270–71, 277, 285, 291
Riddle, Samuel D.: Man o' War and, 205–6, 212,
    214, 215; property of, 249, 326n. 14; Saranac
    Handicap and, 253; War Admiral and, 248
Riddle, Mrs. Samuel D., 234
Ridgely, Kate, 31
Riding posture, 23, 133, 140, 142, 164
Riley, 140
Riley, Jim, 114
Riley's Lake House, 124, 148, 220, 261, 262
"Ringers," 241
Ringmaster, 56, 57
Rip Van Dam Hotel (American Hotel), 9, 48,
    135, 326n. 23a
Riva Ridge, 279, 283
Riverside Park (N.Y.C.), 130
Roach, Hal, 243
Roamer, 202–3, 214
Robertson, Alfred, 253
Robertson, William H. P.: on Citation, 260; on
    Garrison, 133; on Grannon, 145; on B. Knapp,
    211; on Ladana, 236; on Lexington, 40; on
    Nashua, 267; on "people's track," 180–81; on
    Roamer, 202; on Salvator–Tenny race, 141; on
    G. Smith, 145; on track construction, 253
Robinson, Jackie, 68
Rock City Falls, 114
Rockefeller, John D., Jr., 222
Rockefeller, John D., III, 275
Rockefeller, Laurance, 275
Rockefeller, Nelson, 275
Rockefeller, William, 160
Rockefeller family, 53

Rockne, Knute, 207
Rock Sand, 205
Rockton, 165
Rokeby Stable, 274, 279
Romero, Randy, 299
Ronalds, Fanny, 75
Rooney, Art, 248
Roosevelt, Eleanor, 230, 231
Roosevelt, Franklin D., 275; Bull and, 230, 231;
    Gallant Fox and, xii, 232; gambling sup-
    pressed by, 234; Prohibition and, 242;
    Saratoga Spa commission and, 245
Roosevelt, Kermit, 224
Roosevelt, Theodore, 181
Roosevelt family, 53
Root, Elihu, 181
Rosenthal, J. R., 136
Rose Tree II, 201
Rosoff, Sam, 268, 325n. 7; at Brook, 217; counter-
    feit bills and, 240; largess of, 233–34; mansion
    of, 265
Ross, J. K. L., 203, 204, 215
Ross, Sanford, 325–26n. 14b
Rothschild family, 74
Rothstein, Arnold, 216–18, 251, 263; cronies of,
    217, 221; death of, 219
Rounders (game), 48, 179, 188
Rowe, James, Jr., 227, 236
Rowe, Jimmy: on clubhouse opening, 224; Colin
    and, 187; death of, 227; Dwyer brothers and,
    126, 127; Fator and, 225; Fitzsimmons and,
    228; Harry Bassett and, 95, 96, 98–99; Hin-
    doo and, 236; horses purchased by, 196;
    injury to, 102; John P. Grier and, 306; D.
    McDaniel and, 94; Regret and, 199, 200; at
    Travers, 214; Upset and, 209, 212; Whisk
    Broom II and, 198; Wildair and, 215
Rowe's Hoop Skirt Store, 51
Rowing: amateur, 124, 157; collegiate, 103–5, 108–
    10, 114, 115, 157; in "International Boat Race,"
    93; at Poughkeepsie, 41; in Saratoga Rowing
    Association regatta, 102, 106
Rowing Association of American Colleges
    (RAAC), 103–5, 109–10, 114, 115
Royal Arch, 133
"Rube's Selections," 264
Rubin, Sam, 292, 293
Rudy, William H., 271, 278, 283–84, 285, 286
Ruffian, 284–85, 286, 287, 300, 302
Ruh, C. F., Jr., 164
Ruhl, Arthur, 105, 108, 109
Rules and Regulations for the Government of Rac-
    ing, Trotting, and Betting, 72, 317n. 16
Runaway Groom, 293

Running Water, 187
Runnymede (farm), 157
Runyon, Damon, 17, 230–31, 232, 233, 268
Russell, Lillian, 150, 158, 163, 175, 176
Rutgers University, 94
Ruth, Babe, 163, 221
Rutherford, 113
Ruthless, 76, 227
Rutledge, John and Julia, 13
Ryan, Paddy, 124
Ryan, Thomas Fortune, 160, 182, 184

Sabath, Albert, 251
St. Blaise, 140, 174
St. Clement's Church, 261, 327n. 9a
St. James, 223
St. James Hotel (N.Y.C.), 31, 134
St. Peter's Cemetery (Troy), 122
Salisbury Plain (L.I.), 4
Sallie McClelland, 143
Salt, 3, 4
Salvator, 140–41, 142, 202
Sample, John, 95, 96, 98–99
Sande, Earl, 225, 234; in Canada, 214; Gallant Fox
    and, 229, 232, 233; in Jamaica, 266; Man o'
    War and, 213; Murphy and, 228, 260; Notter
    and, 189; Zev and, 219
Sanford, John, 172, 207, 211, 226, 239
Sanford, Milton H.: in England, 114; party given
    by, 80, 82, 87; Preakness and, 106, 112–13
Sanford, Stephen, 165, 173, 198
Sanford Memorial Stakes, 198, 207–10
Sangster, Robert, 294, 295
Sans Souci (Ballston Spa hotel), 7, 11, 13
Santa Anita course, 243, 247, 255
Santos, José, 294, 298
Saranac Handicap, 253, 254
Saratoga (Calif.), 132–33
Saratoga (colt), 201
Saratoga (filly), 58
Saratoga and Schenectady Railroad, 17–18
Saratoga Association: double bill presented by,
    65; early 1900s officers of, 172, 182, 192–93; fa-
    cilities improved by, 169, 174, 251; first
    Travers and, 56, 58; founding of, 48–49, 139;
    grounds improved by, 213, 220; Horse Haven
    and, 125; incorporation of, 61; investments by,
    60; L. Jerome and, 48, 74, 139; land purchased
    by, 172; Metairie Jockey Club and, 50, 72;
    Morrissey and, 50, 110; resignations from,
    137–38; Rules and Regulations, 72, 317n. 16;
    safety measures of, 124; A. Spencer and, 136;

Von Stade and, 256; Walbaum and, 146, 147, 159; W. C. Whitney and, 164, 166, 167, 168
Saratoga Champion Stakes, 170
Saratoga Chips. *See* Potato chips
Saratoga Club (N.Y.C.), 175–76, 177
Saratoga Club. *See* Morrissey's Club House
"Saratoga Compact," 106
Saratoga County Agricultural Society, 73
Saratoga County History Center, 312n. 8
Saratoga Cup: first, 68, 83; Kentucky Derby and, 107; suspension of, 148, 159
Saratoga Derby, 180
Saratoga Flash Stakes, 180
Saratoga Golf Club, 159
Saratoga Handicap, 165
Saratoga Lake: amateur sculling on, 124, 157; collegiate sculling on, 104–5, 108–10, 115, 157; field sports on, 12; Native American lore about, 64; professional sculling on, 93; toll pike near, 71
Saratoga National Historical Park, 3
"Saratoga, or the Horse at Home" (Joe Palmer), 265
Saratoga Performing Arts Center (SPAC), 275–76, 296
Saratoga Raceway, 15, 73, 254
Saratoga Regiment, 61
Saratoga Rowing Association, 102, 106
Saratoga Spa, 245, 266
Saratoga Spa State Park, 7, 8
Saratoga Special, 165, 169, 170, 180
Saratoga Springs, An Architectural History (Kettlewell), 20
Saratoga Stakes, 58, 93, 106
Saratoga Test, 298, 299
Saratoga Trotting Course, 265; blacktopping of, 295; first thoroughbred race at, 45; Lexington at, 108; opening of, 27; origins of, 26; popularity of, 38. *See also* Horse Haven
Saratoga Trunk (Ferber), 257
Saratoga trunks, 37
Sayers, Tom, 36, 65, 119
Sayers, Tom, Jr., 119
Schenectady, 17, 18, 257
Schofield, John, 79
Schultz, Dutch, 217, 243
Schuttinger, Andy, 202, 214
Schuyler, Kitty, 6
Schuyler, Philip, 2, 3, 6, 7
Schuylerville, 2
Schwartz, Jane, 285, 302
Schwartz, Morton L., 244
Scott, A., 249
Scott, Winfield, 21

Scribner, Ben, 26, 89
Scribner, Lucy Skidmore, 195
Sculling. *See* Rowing
Scythian, 44
Seabiscuit, 228, 249, 324n. 11
Seagram, J. E., 174
Sea Hero, 304
Searle, Eleanor, 273
Sears, K. W., 106
Seattle Dancer, 295
Seattle Slew, 280, 288; Affirmed vs., 291; Forego vs., 286–87; Seattle Dancer and, 295; Slew o' Gold and, 293
Seattle Way, 304
Secretariat, 279–83, 286, 287, 301; General Assembly and, 291; in Hopeful, 179; Man o' War and, 206, 279, 281, 282, 283; naming of, 327n. 1b; Ruffian and, 285; successors of, 284
Segal, Harry, 227
Segregation. *See* Racial discrimination
Seligman, Joseph, 117, 135
Senior PGA Tour, xi
Sensitive Prince, 288
Sequel Stakes, 58, 76, 112
Seven Oaks, 47
Seventy-seventh New York Cavalry, 61
Sewell (jockey), 45–46, 47, 68, 83
Shaker Knit, 300
Shake Shake Shake, 289
Sham, 279, 280, 281
Shannon, Bob, 239
Shannon, George, 145
Sharkey, Jack, 222
Shaw, John, 119
Shaw, Tom, 239, 240
Shaw, Willie, 189
Shea Stadium, 280
Sheehan, Andy, 50
Sheepshead Bay: closing of, 195; in early 1900s, 169; Futurity at, 193; Hamburg at, 162; Hindoo at, 128; Salvator-Tenny race at, 140–41, 142; Sysonby at, 187; turf racing at, 139; Westerners and, 174; W. C. Whitney at, 162
Sheet writers, 239
Shelby, Dr., 91
Shem, 241
Shenanigans, 284
Sheridan, Philip Henry, 130
Sherman, William Tecumseh, 71, 130
Sherry's restaurant, 181
Shevlin, James, 175
Shillelah, 226
Shilling, Carroll, 194–95

Shoemaker, Willie, 189, 266–67; Damascus and, 276; Forego and, 286, 287; Jaipur and, 270–71; John Henry and, 293; Kelso and, 273
Short-stirrup crouch, 142
Shreiber, Barney, 166
Shut Out, 255, 304
Sickles, Daniel, 48, 63, 79
Sickle T., 251
Sidereal, 218
Siegel, Ben ("Bugsy"), 247, 261
Silver Cloud, 128
Silver coinage, 160
Silver Spoon, 273, 274
Simmons, Mrs. Elijah, 29
Simms, Willie, 142, 144, 162, 189
Simon, Monkey, 10
Simulcasts, 295, 304
Sinaloa II, 143
Sinclair, Harry, 217, 219, 227, 236, 253
Sir Barton, 203; at Kenilworth Park, 215; Loftus and, 206, 211; J. Madden and, 323n. 3; in Saratoga Handicap, 213
Sir Dixon, 128
Sir Gallahad III, 228, 230
Sir John, 128, 140
Siro's (restaurant), 298
Skedaddle, 56
"Skeleton wagons," 28
Skidmore College, 175; "cottages" and, 265; Hilton estate and, 134, 266, 276; predecessors of, 195; Surrey property and, 224
Skillful, 172
Slew o' Gold, 293, 294
Sloan, James ("Tod"), 23, 162–64, 180, 268
Sloan, John, 241
Sloane, Isabel Dodge, 238, 243, 245, 269, 274
Sly Fox, 142
Smith, Al, 224
Smith, Bob, 238
Smith, Carol Chandler, 323n. 21
Smith, George ("Pittsburgh Phil"), 145, 166, 172, 248
Smith, Joseph, 65
Smith, Mike, 302, 306
Smith, Susie. See Morrissey, Susie Smith
Smith's Interlaken (nightclub), 261, 262
Smoot, Charlie, 201, 226–27, 234
Smoot, George, 234, 235
Smoot, Tom, 234
Snyder, Jimmy, 248
Somethingroyal, 279
Sommer, Sigmund, 279
Sousa, John Philip, 175
South Carolina Railroad, 17

Southern racing, 22–23, 39, 77, 84. See also North-South races
Southern states, 62, 79, 191
Southern tourists, 317n. 7; antebellum, 13; at Lady Suffolk–Moscow race, 27; postbellum, 79; racism of, 317n. 18; on steamboats, 18; at Union course, 14
Spalding, Albert, 179
Spanish horses, 23
Spa Reservation, 195
Spat, 260
Specs (groom), 264
Spectacular Bid, 291
"Speed Boys" (syndicate), 268
Speedway, 175
Spell of the Turf, The (Hildreth), 193
Spencer, Albert, 122, 136, 137, 150, 177
Spencer, Jack, 156
Spencer Handicap, 136
Spendthrift, 125, 184, 205
Spendthrift Farm (Ky.), 157, 296
Spinaway, 148, 159, 180, 285
Spinner, W. E., 170
Spirit of Life (D. C. French), 195
Spokane, 139
Sporting Blood, 218, 219
Sports: in 1880s, 124; in 1890s, 157, 159; in early 1900s, 191; in 1920s, 221; in 1980s, 300
Spray, 273
Springbok, 100, 102, 106, 112–13, 219
Springs (water sources), 7, 245
Sprinter-of-the-Year award, 298
Spurt, 203, 225
Squires, Robert, 90
"Stable breakfasts," 247
Staeger, Sidney, 217
Stage Door Johnny, 276–77
Standard Oil Company, 159, 161
Standard Railway time, 129
Stanford, Leland, 113
Stanton, Edwin, 79
Star Bout, 259
Star Spring, 7
Starters, 208, 209, 219
Starting gates, 228, 239
State racing commissions, 223, 229
Steamboat travel, 18
Steeplechasing: early, 97; improved facilities for, 171; F. Keene in, 196; safety measures in, 124; C. Smoot in, 201, 226. See also Hurdle races
Steloff, Frances, 240
Steloff, Ike, 240
Stephens, Woody, 294
Stevens, Harry M., 231–32, 264

Index

Stevens, H. W., 115, 116

Stewart, A. T., 38, 110, 230; on ball committee, 65; death of, 116; legacy of, 117; Union Hall and, 90, 118, 315n. 5b; wealth of, 52

Stiles, Lela, 325n. 4

Stillwater (N.Y.), 6

Stimson, E. C., 116

Stoddard, Seneca Ray, 134

Stokes, Julie, 276

Stoneham, Charles, 217

Stonewall Jackson, 79

Storm Cat, 304

Stout, Nancy, 171

Stoval, John ("Kid"), 143

Stowe, Harriet Beecher, 21

Stratton, Charles (Tom Thumb), 27, 28

Street names, 7

Street railways, 159, 160, 161, 184. *See also* Subways

Stromboli, 201, 203

Stuart, Dan, 169

Stud Book (Jockey Club), 268

Stud farms, 40, 157, 174

Sturges, Charles, 158

Sturgis, Frank K., 223, 234

Stymie, 257, 258, 259

Suburban (race), 139

Subways, 161, 172. *See also* Street railways

Sugar market, 184

Sulky racing. *See* Trotting races

Sullivan, Frank, 173–74, 175, 242

Sullivan, John L., 124, 134, 144

Sullivan, Yankee (J. Ambrose), 25, 32–33, 61

Sultana, 116

Summer "cottages," 136–37, 265–66, 276

Summer Handicap, 126

Summer Squall, 179, 300

Summer Tan, 267

Sun Briar, 202, 203, 230

Sunday racing, 284

Sunday Silence, 298, 300

Sun Edwin, 225, 226

Sun Falcon, 232

Super Bowl, 65, 293

Supper Stakes, 87

Supreme Court, 326n. 16b

Surratt, Mary, 63

Surrey (Broadview Lodge), 224, 238

Survivor, 100, 111

Swamp Root (medicine), 203

Sweeney, Bea, 276

Sweeney, Edward C., 242

Sweep, 193, 196

Sweet Springs (Va.), 13

Sweet Tooth, 287

Swigert, Daniel, 86, 119, 127

Swim, Bob, 91, 92, 102

Swimmer, 207, 208

Swope, Herbert Bayard, 241, 251

Sword Dancer, 269, 276

Sykes, Zerubbabel, 16

Sympathy, 44, 45, 46, 47

Sysonby, 182, 184–87, 188, 199

Tabasco Cat, 304–5, 306

Talmadge (general), 21

Tammany politics, 34, 74, 79, 114

Tanya, 182, 183

Taral, Fred, 144, 145–46

Tarbel, Loran, 1, 2

Tattersall's Ring, 118

Taylor, E. P., 294

Taylor, Estelle, 222

Taylor, Karen, 286

Taylor, Mickey, 286, 293

Teapot Dome scandal, 236

Telephone, 115

Television broadcasts, 262, 279, 292, 294, 300. *See also* Simulcasts

Temperance movement, 11. *See also* Prohibition

Temperence Hill, 292

Temple Grove Seminary, 129, 195

Templeton Mills (Glasgow), 177

Ten Broeck, 120, 121

Ten Broeck, Richard, 114

Tennessee, 10, 23, 174

Tennis, 157

Tenny, 140–41, 142

Tentam, 283

Tenth Regiment Band, 175

Terwilliger's hardware store, 71

Textile, 194

Thankfuls (baseball team), 114

Thimble-rigging, 34

Third Avenue railway, 184

Third Ward (Saratoga), 30, 245

Thompson, George, 31

Thompson, Kay, 262

Thompson, L. S., 200, 201, 274

Thorndale, 226

Thoroughbred Racing Associations, 255, 271, 301

Thoroughbred Record, 271

Thorson, 248

Thorwaldsen, Albert, 19

Thracian, 226

Throg's Neck, Jr., 57

Thumb, Tom (C. Stratton), 27, 28

Thunder, 44, 46, 47, 236
Tiffany and Company, 120, 249
Tiger Stadium (Detroit), 147
Tilden, Bill, 221, 225
Timekeeping, 128–29, 195, 299
Tipperary, 56, 57, 58
Titanic (ship), 222
Tobin, Henry, 216
Tod Sloan by HIMSELF (J. T. Sloan), 164
Token Dance, 299
Tom Bowling: Buckpasser and, 276; in Flash
    Stakes, 100; injury to, 106; in Monmouth
    Hopeful, 180; sire of, 102, 108, 157; in Travers,
    101–2, 143
Tom Fool, 266, 267, 272, 274, 276
Tommy Atkins, 162
Tom Ochiltree: Chamberlin and, 111; Parole vs.,
    116; sire of, 108, 157; Ten Broeck vs., 121; Vera
    Cruz vs., 119, 120
Tompion, 273, 274, 277
Tompkins, Daniel, 14
Tomy Lee, 273
Top Flight, 236
Topgallant, 15
Toronto (Ont.), 55
Totalisators, 95, 237
Toto's (nightclub), 262
Tower, Whitney, 304
Town Hall, 20, 110, 124, 169
Track athletics, 105–6, 110, 115–16
Trainers, 91, 143
Tranter, E. J., 201, 247
Trask, Katrina, 136, 220
Trask, Spencer, 136, 137, 158, 195
Trattoria (restaurant), 298
Travers, William R.: Alarm and, 99; An-
    nieswood Stable and, 80; Harry Bassett–
    Longfellow race and, 97; humor of, 55–56,
    68, 315–16n. 8b, 316n. 10b; Jerome Park
    Inaugural Stake and, 75; Kentucky and, 56;
    J. Marvin and, 138, 146; Morrissey and, 122,
    135; New York Athletic Club and, 124; New
    York Chamber of Commerce and, 116; por-
    trait of, 49; prizes offered by, 102; Saratoga
    Association and, 48, 119; Morrissey's Club
    House and, 85; stable of, 96; E. B. Wall and,
    133
Travers Stakes, 55, 76, 77; Affirmed vs. Alydar
    in, *291;* black jockeys in, 143; cash value of,
    148, 297–98; Dwyer victories in, 128; first, 10,
    23, 56–58, 83; Jaipur vs. Ridan in, 270–71;
    Kentucky Derby and, 107, 112; McDaniel vic-
    tories in, 113; as Midsummer Derby, 225, 237,
    297; Man o' War Cup and, 269; Man o' War

vs. Upset in, *214;* Sporting Blood vs. Prudery
    in, *218;* suspension of, 277
Treaty of Paris, 2
Trial by Jury, 201
Triangle Publications, 271
Trifle, 23–24
"Triple" betting, 284
Triple Crown winners, xii, 272, 287–88, 325n. 3;
    Affirmed, 291; Assault, 258; Citation, 260;
    Count Fleet, 255; Gallant Fox, 229, 273;
    Omaha, 244, 273; precursors of, 107, 125, 206;
    Seattle Slew, 286; Secretariat, 280–81; Sir Bar-
    ton, 203–4, 323n. 3b; War Admiral, 248–49.
    See also Filly Triple Crown winners; Hand-
    icap Triple Crown winners
Trojan, 198
Tropical Park (Fla.), 237
Trotting Horses of America (Woodruff), 314n. 7a
Trotting races: at Beacon Course, 25; on double
    bill, 65, 67; early, 14–15; at Glen Mitchell, 110;
    Lady Suffolk in, 27–28; racial discrimination
    in, 73; at Saratoga Raceway, 254; W. H. Van-
    derbilt and, 82, 131; women in, 29
Troy (N.Y.): in Civil War era, 42; Morrissey fu-
    neral in, 122; Morrissey in, 30; regattas in, 106,
    114; tourists from, 172; travel connections in, 18
Truman, Harry S., 261
Truxton, 10
Tucker, Sophie, 246, 261
"Tuileries, Les" (Circular St.), 15
Tunney, Gene, 222, 231, 245
Turcotte, Ron: Krone and, 303; Secretariat and,
    279, 280, 281, 282; Winkfield and, 190
Turf and Sports Digest, 271
Turf racing, 139
Tuxedo jacket, 133
Tuxedo Park, 120, 133–34
Twain, Mark, 130, 133
Tweed, William ("Boss"), 75, 85, 117, 121
Tweedy, Helen (Penny), 279, 280, 327n. 1b
Twelve Years A Slave (S. Northup), 22
Twenty Grand, 228, 235, 236, 243, 253
Twice a Prince, 281
Twilight Tear, 256
Twombly, Florence, 131
Twombly, Hamilton, 131
Tyler, John, 28

Unaccounted For, 305
Unbridled, 301
Uncle, 188
Uncle Tom's Cabin (Stowe), 21
Underwood, Robert: Attila-Acrobat race and,

106; at Captain Moore–Lizzie W. race, 46; Cathcart and, 119; "French pools" and, 100; Harry Bassett–Longfellow race and, 97; at United States Hotel, 44–45; at White's Hotel, 67

Union Army: generals, 63, 130; troops, 41–42, 51, 64, 257. See also Army of the Potomac

Union Avenue, 60, 71–72

Union Club (N.Y.C.), 56, 316n. 8a

Union College, 10, 108, 115

Union Course (L.I.), 14, 15, 23, 24

Union Hall: in Civil War era, 43, 53, 58–59; construction of, 7; drawings of, 8, 52; fire at, 51; opera house of, 60; piazza of, 9, 20. See also Grand Union Hotel; Union Hotel

Union Hotel, 78; expansion of, 82; fire near, 71; piazza of, 82, 87; postbellum party at, 63. See also Grand Union Hotel; Union Hall

"United Americans," 34

United States Army Ordnance Training Center (Santa Anita), 255

United States Club, 150, 183

United States Congress: Kefauver investigation and, 262; J. Marvin in, 49; Morrissey in, 76, 78–79, 83, 123, 138, 317n. 1; Tom Ochiltree–Parole–Ten Broeck race and, 120–21. See also Continental Congress

United States Golf Association, 157

United States Hotel: in Civil War era, 42–43, 44–45, 52, 117; dancing at, 21; early visitors to, 15; in fiction, 231; fire at, 64, 71, 257; gambling adjacent to, 26; Jews and, 118, 135; Lady Suffolk–Moscow race and, 28; Marvin management of, 20, 82, 138; in 1940s, 256–57; in 1930s, 242; in 1920s, 219; piazza of, 265; pool sales at, 44–45; railroad magnates at, 106; reconstruction of, 103, 105; H. Segal at, 227; W. H. Vanderbilt at, 42–43, 130, 132; C. Vanderbilt at, 52, 117; C. Vanderbilt II and, 161; E. B. Wall at, 133; W. C. Whitney at, 172

United States Hotel Stakes, 126, 157

United States Open Championship, 196

United States presidents, 10, 15, 28, 130

United States Supreme Court, 326n. 16b

University Club (N.Y.C.), 316n. 8a

University of Notre Dame, 221

University of Pennsylvania, 93, 110, 115, 124, 157

Upset: at Kentucky Derby, 212; offspring of, 230; Onion and, 281; Man o' War vs., 206, 207–11, 210, 214

Ussery, Bob, 274

Vacations, 129

Vagrant, 119

Valentino, Rudolf, 234

Valenzuela, Ismael, 273

Valenzuela, Milo, 273

Vallera, 143, 148

Van Buren, Martin, 10, 15, 21, 28, 101

Vandal, 47

Vanderbilt, Alfred Gwynne, 161, 199–200

Vanderbilt, Alfred Gwynne, II, 244, 255, 264

Vanderbilt, Alice Gwynne, 237

Vanderbilt, Alva, 131

Vanderbilt, Consuelo, 161

Vanderbilt, Cornelius, 37–38; W. B. Astor and, 230; on ball committee, 65; bankers and, 110; boating experience of, 314n. 25; fortune of, 116 17, 131; Harlem Railroad and, 58–59, 61; Lake Shore Railroad and, 83; Morrissey and, 61, 64–65, 74, 122; New York Central Railroad and, 49, 65; Panic of '69 and, 84; portrait of, 39; railroad profits of, 43; reverses of, 82; Saratoga Association and, 48; Morrissey's Club House and, 85; "Saratoga Compact" and, 106; at United States Hotel, 52, 117; W. C. Whitney and, 159; mentioned, 45, 132, 184

Vanderbilt, Cornelius Jeremiah, 45, 52, 59, 117

Vanderbilt, Cornelius, II, 117, 131–32, 161

Vanderbilt, Florence, 131

Vanderbilt, Frank, 84, 117

Vanderbilt, Frederick, 117

Vanderbilt, George, 59, 82, 117

Vanderbilt, Gertrude. See Whitney, Gertrude Vanderbilt

Vanderbilt, Gloria, 237–38

Vanderbilt, Gloria Morgan, 237–38

Vanderbilt, Mrs. Graham Fair, 224, 230, 234

Vanderbilt, Reggie, 176

Vanderbilt, Sophia, 82

Vanderbilt, William H., 52, 82; death of, 131, 132; Drew and, 59; inheritance of, 117; S. Morrissey and, 65; at United States Hotel, 42–43, 130, 132; W. C. Whitney and, 159

Vanderbilt, William Kissam, 117, 131–32, 196

Vanderbilt family, 135, 156; in 1930s, 242, 245; W. C. Whitney and, 159, 160

Varner, Jimmy, 264

Varsity sports, 102–6, 108–10, 115–16

Vasquez, Jacinto, 282, 285

Vecsey, George, 293

Veitch, John, 287, 288, 289

Veitch, Michael, 287

Veitch, Silas, 287

Veitch, Syl, 259, 270, 278, 287

Velasquez, Jorge, xii, 288, 289, 290

Vera Cruz, 119, 120

Verme, Francesco Dal, 1

Verne, Jules, 150
Veterinarians, 302
Viator, 112
Vicksburg (Miss.), 41, 66
Victoria, Queen of England, 55
Victorian, 225, 226, 233
Victorian architecture: domestic, 136–37, 265–66, 276; public, 171
Vienna, 256
Vincent, Marthe, 296
Virginia: breeding in, 10; in Civil War, 61; early jockeys of, 9; springs of, 11, 129; yearling prices in, 247
Vititoe, Harry, 206
Volante, 128, 133
Volodyovski, 168
Volturno, 124, 126
Von Borries, Philip, 191
Von Stade, F. Skiddy, 256
Vosburgh, Walter S., 169, 171, 322n. 7b; on Civil War, 84; on Colin, 188; on Man o' War, 206, 212, 215; on Omar Khayyam, 203; on Sysonby, 184–85, 187; on W. C. Whitney, 168

Wait, Charles, 276
Wait, Newman, Jr. ("Pete"), 276
Wajima, 286
Wakeman, W. J., 115
Walbaum, Gottfried ("Dutch Fred," "Gus"), 138, 146–49, 156; facilities built by, 147, 170, 171; Hildreth and, 193; Kearney and, 159; New York club of, 176; schedule established by, 148, 172; Travers suspended by, 277; W. C. Whitney and, 164, 165, 166; R. T. Wilson, Jr. and, 167; women gamblers and, 154–55
Walcott (owner), 144
Walker, G. Herbert, 223
Walker, Jimmy, 223
Walker, Mrs. Jimmy, 224
Walker, Will, 119
Walker's, 278
Wall, Charles, 90, 133
Wall, Evender Berry, 133–34, 150, 158
Waller, George, 133, 268
Walters, Johnny, 165, 226
Walworth, Ellen Hardin, 101
Walworth, Frank, 101
Walworth, Mansfield, 101
Walworth, Reuben Hyde, 101, 311n. 3
Walworth v. People, 101
War Admiral, 228, 248–49, 324n. 11
Ward, Ellis, 93
Ward, Josh, 41, 93, 102

Ward, Zeb, 56, 96
War Hero, 237
War Relic, 253, 254
Washington, George, 11, 15, 49–50, 242; Altamont and, 9; American Gazetteer and, 6–7; architectural influence of, 8, 9; attempted purchase of Saratoga Springs by, 2–5; modesty of, 66; visit by, 1; O. Williams and, 12
Washington Bath House, 245
Washington (D.C.), 9, 14, 21, 37
Washington Park (Chicago), 128, 260
Washington Spring, 7
Water Color, 165
Watercure, 165
Watson, Elkanah, 11, 13, 27, 312n. 16b
Watson, James, 44, 47, 56
Watson, Thomas, 115
Watson, Winslow C., 312n. 16
Watson, W. M., 115–16
Watts, William, 240
Webster, Daniel, 28, 63, 101
Weldon, J. W., 44, 83, 91
Wellswood Plantation, 22–23
Wences, Señor (ventriloquist), 261
Wesleyan University, 106, 115
West, Benjamin, 12
West, Ed, 143
Westbrook Stable (Islip), 120
Westchester Racing Association, 140, 181, 222
Western Union Telegraph Company, 53, 222
West Point Academy, 263
Wexler, Irving, 217
Wheatley Stable, 238, 248, 249
Wheatly, Charles: Attila-Acrobat race and, 106; Kentucky Association and, 48; at Morrissey funeral, 122–23; notoriety of, 73; Saratoga Association and, 49, 50, 138, 147; Spirit of the Times on, 113; starting by, 72; track improvements of, 54–55
Wheat market, 184
Whelpley, James, 28
Whichone, 232, 233
Whirlaway: Arcaro and, 260; Gallant Fox and, 228; in Hopeful, 179, 253; Longden and, 251; in Massachusetts Handicap, 255; poster of, 252; in Saranac Handicap, 253, 254
Whisk Broom II: Forego and, 285; Kelso and, 272; New Broom and, 224; record weight on, 198, 244; sire of, 197; Whiskery and, 236
Whiskery, 236
Whist Bridge Club, 183
Whistler, James, 179
White, John H., 49
Whitehead, Samuel, 147, 159

Whitely, Frank, 284

Whiteman, Paul, 221, 230, 246

White's Hotel, 56, 67

White Sulphur Spring Hotel, 221

Whitman, Walt, 37

Whitney, Barbara, 235

Whitney, Cornelius Vanderbilt ("Sonny"), 132, 235–36, 325n. 9; in army air corps, 255; birth of, 161; cousin of, 244; death of, 295; earnings of, 274; Equipoise and, 236, 237, 243; *Gone with the Wind* and, 248; High Glee and, 243; on ladies, 296; National Museum of Dance and, 276; National Museum of Racing and, 265; Phalanx and, 258–59; third Travers of, 277

Whitney, Dorothy, 161, 181, 182, 222

Whitney, Edith, 161

Whitney, Eleanor, 273

Whitney, Flora, 159, 160, 161, 235

Whitney, Gertrude Vanderbilt, 161, 235, 237

Whitney, Gwladys, 237

Whitney, Harry Payne, 161, 181; death of, 235; horses purchased by, 196, 201; Irish Lad and, 169–70; Prudery and, 218; racing career of, 182–83, 197, 198, 222; Regret and, 199, *200*; Reiff and, 168; Riddle and, 212, 214; Saratoga Association and, 182, 193; E. P. Taylor and, 294; L. S. Thompson and, 200, 201, 274; Upset and, 206; Victorian and, 225, 233; Whichone and, 232

Whitney, Helen Hay, 222, 238, 243, 255, 257

Whitney, Joan. *See* Payson, Joan

Whitney, John Hay ("Jock"), 135, 222; German capture of, 255; *Gone with the Wind* and, 248; Greentree and, 257; Racing Commission and, 241

Whitney, Marie, 235

Whitney, Marylou, 273, 276, 295–96, 297

Whitney, Pauline, 161, 162, 181, 182, 222

Whitney, William Collins, 159–62, 165–81; Fasig Tipton and, 201; Hildreth and, 162, 227; J. R. Keene and, 162, 164, 168, 184; legacy of, 182; J. Widener and, 237; R. T. Wilson and, 167, 227; mentioned, 184, 205, 238, 269

Whitney, William Payne, 181; event named for, 225; Peter Pan and, 196; uncle of, 161, 182; wealth of, 222

Whitney family, 274, 295–96; Keeneland Association and, 248; MacKay sale and, 174; in 1930s, 237–38, 242; racing rivalry within, 234; Saratoga Performing Arts Center and, 275

Whitney Farm (Ky.), 157, 235

Whitney Museum of American Art (N.Y.C.), 235, 237

Whitney Park, 235

Whitney Stud Book, 180

Whittaker, Albert, 190

Whitten Brothers, 145

Whittingham, Charlie, 294

Wichita Oil, 283

Wickham, Bob, 153, 154, 155, 156, 163

Widener, George D., Jr.: Battlefield and, 260; Crewman and, 271; Jaipur and, 270; Jamestown and, 236; "Man o' War Cup" for, 249; Mellon and, 304; St. James and, 223

Widener, Joseph, 174, 222–23, 237

Widener, Peter A. B., 160, 223

Widener, Peter A. B., II, 223

Widener family, 242

Wilcox, Ella Wheeler, 141

Wild Again, 294

Wildair, 212, 215

Wild Idle, 113

Wild Ride (Auerbach), 301

Wilkes, George: on horse naming, 318n. 1; on Morrissey, 111–12; on pari mutuel system, 110–11; *Rules and Regulations* and, 317n. 16; self-advertisement of, 315n. 7a, 317n. 8

Willard, Jess, 221

Willard's Hotel (D.C.), 37

Williams, Ansel, 101, 143

Williams, Edward, 12–13

Williams, Henry, 12–13

Williams, Otho, 4, 9, 12, 13

Williams, Roy ("Tiny"), 143

Williams Brothers (entertainers), 262

Williamsburg Jockey Club, 4

Williams College, 108, 115

Willoughby, H., 115

Willow Hour, 293

Wilson, Edmund, 130

Wilson, Richard T., Jr.: Campfire and, 203; Canfield and, 179; at clubhouse opening, 224; death of, 227; Gallavant and, 187; Naushon and, 194; J. Rowe and, 227; Saratoga Association and, 172, 182, 192, 193; W. C. Whitney and, 167, 227; Yellow Hand and, 212

Windsor Hotel, 134, 135

Windsor Hotel Stakes, 127

Winkfield, Jimmy, 189–90, 284

Winn, Matt, 200–201, 204

Winner's circle, 264

Winning Colors, 298

Winslow, Albert, 133

Winter racing, 146

Wishing Well (restaurant), 298

Wolcott, Edward, 175

Wolfson, Lou, 287

Women: antebellum, 10, 26, 27, 29, 303; Civil

Women: (*continued*)
   War era, 45, 46, 53, 58, 59; postbellum, 64, 67,
      68–69, 80, 85, 86, 108; in 1880s, 127, 133; in
      1890s, 151, 153–56; in early 1900s, 171, 177, 195;
      in 1920s, 224, 238; in 1930s, 238, 239–40, 251; in
      1940s, 253. *See also* Prostitution
Women bettors: in Civil War era, 46; in post-
      bellum era, 64; in 1880s, 127; in 1890s, 151, 153–
      56; in 1930s, 239–40, 251; in 1940s, 253
Won't Tell You, 287
Wood, Fernando, 31, 34, 90
Wood, Grant, 17
Woodbine (track), 55
Woodbine, 99
Woodburn Farm (Ky.), 40, 73, 157
Woodington, Earl C., 223
Woodlawn estate, 134
Woodlawn Oval, 72, 157, 159
Woodruff, Hiram, 24, 65, 73, 314n. 7a
Woodward, Milton, 264
Woodward, William: daughter of, 276; death of,
      267; Gallant Fox and, 228; Jockey Club and,
      234; mansion of, 265; Marguerite and, 225
Woodward, William, Jr., 267
Woodward, Mrs. William, Jr., 267
Woolley, Monty, 175
Worden, W. W., 172, 182
Worden Hotel, 242
Workman, Ray ("Sonny"), 232
World Series, 65, 179, 216, 293
World War I, 195, 198, 199–200, 205, 222
World War II, 274; casualties of, 254–55; conclu-

sion of, 257, 258; inception of, 250; indiffer-
      ence to, 253; Travers Stakes in, 55
Wright, Lucille, 274
Wright, Silas, 28
Wright, Warren, 242, 252, 253, 258, 324n. 3a
Wright, William, 253

Yaddo (estate), 276; artists at, 220, 266, 277; early
      owner of, 12; S. Trask and, 136
Yale University: in baseball, 102; in field and
      track, 106, 115; RAAC abandoned by, 109–10;
      in regattas, 103, 104–5, 109
Yankee, 168
Yankee Sullivan (J. Ambrose), 25, 32–33, 61
Ycaza, Manuel, 269, 270, 275
Yellow Cab company, 226
Yellow Hand, 212
YMCA. *See* Jockey Y (building)
Yonkers Raceway, 188
Young, Milton, 157, 182, 195
Young, William, 304
Young Democracy (organization), 85
Young Morrill, 65
Young Peter, 258
Young Women's Industrial Club. *See* Skidmore
      College
Your Host, 272

Zev, 219
Zigzag, 59
Zito, Anthony. *See* Betts, Toney